AF745430

MICROECONOMICS

Microeconomics is concerned with the production, consumption and distribution of goods by the micro units of individuals, firms and markets within the economy. It can also be considered a study of scarcity and the choices to be made for the attainment of goals within constraints. These goals are those set by consumers, producers and policy makers in the market.

This book provides a brand new approach to the teaching and study of microeconomics – an elementary guide to the fundamental principles of the subject. It gives students from all parts of the world the opportunity to understand and appreciate the value of microeconomic tools and concepts for analysing market processes in their economic environment, as well as maintaining a perspective on issues of trade and competitiveness, thus drawing attention to the relevance of microeconomic theory beyond the domestic scene to issues of trade and competitiveness on the international arena.

The book contains a wealth of international application insights and covers topics such as:

- elasticity
- Cobb–Douglas production functions
- dynamic stability of market equilibrium
- monopolies and monopolistic competition
- project analysis.

The perfect introduction to the building blocks of contemporary microeconomic theory, this book will be of interest to undergraduate students in international economics, industrial economics, managerial economics and agricultural economics. It will also be a useful reference guide for graduates requiring a break down of difficult microeconomic principles.

Judy Whitehead is Senior Lecturer in Economics at the University of the West Indies, Cave Hill, Barbados.

MICROECONOMICS

A global text

Judy A. Whitehead

Routledge
Taylor & Francis Group
LONDON AND NEW YORK

First published 2010 by Routledge

Published 2014 by Routledge
2 Park Square, Milton Park, Abingdon, Oxon, OX14 4RN

Simultaneously published in the USA and Canada
by Routledge
711 Third Avenue, New York, NY 10017 USA

Routledge is an imprint of the Taylor & Francis Group, an informa business

© 2010 Judy A. Whitehead

Typeset in Times New Roman by Keyword Group Ltd.

All rights reserved. No part of this book may be reprinted or reproduced or utilized in any form or by any electronic, mechanical, or other means, now known or hereafter invented, including photocopying and recording, or in any information storage or retrieval system, without permission in writing from the publishers.

British Library Cataloguing in Publication Data
A catalogue record for this book is available from the British Library

Library of Congress Cataloging in Publication Data
Whitehead, Judy A.
Microeconomics: a global text/Judy Whitehead.
p. cm.
includes bibliographical references and index
1. Microeconomics.
I. Title.
HB172.W45 2009
338.5—dc22 2009010868

ISBN 13: 978-0-415-45452-0 (hbk)
ISBN 13: 978-0-415-45453-7 (pbk)
ISBN 13: 978-0-203-87061-7 (ebk)

Contents

Preface

The writing of this book was motivated primarily by the clamour for such a text from my students, to whom I have listened over the many years of teaching the course of Microeconomics at university level. The prevailing sentiment expressed was that, while the course seemed to come alive and have clarity and relevance in the classroom, a text book was needed that would treat the subject in a similar way. Moreover, in my interactions with students and colleagues from other institutions in North America, Europe and elsewhere, the recurring opinion was the Microeconomics course is difficult to understand, abstract and, in many cases, not relevant to the situations with which they are familiar. This book is intended to fill the void with its triad of objectives, namely: to improve understanding, reduce abstraction and increase global relevance of the subject.

According to the students, the perception of difficulty derives from the way in which mathematics is incorporated (or not incorporated) within the subject matter. They see two extremes: in one case the mathematics is so reduced, the resulting outcomes seem unintelligible (what exactly is $MC = MR$ anyway?); in the opposite case, the mathematics seems to be for the specialized mathematician and appears to be on a track separate from the economics. This book takes a middle road, where mathematics is incorporated in a simplified and consistent way, to encourage the students to see mathematics as a language that lends greater precision and concision to microeconomics. Mathematics must be seen to elucidate rather than to obfuscate. Derivations are handled in a pedestrian way with explanations embedded in order to ensure that students can understand why and how the resulting conclusions are reached even without advanced knowledge of calculus and trigonometry.

The perception of microeconomics as abstract is said to derive from the way in which the concepts, tools and the theories appear to be taught as ends in themselves. Astonishingly, some teaching colleagues also share this view of the subject they teach. One lecturer in microeconomics spoke of the difficulty in getting across abstract concepts that led nowhere ('you teach the concept of elasticity and then, what?'). The approach is to remove the abstraction by showing that these concepts have highly important practical applications such as the significance of price elasticity of demand for the way in which price changes affect the total revenue of the seller (any seller, anywhere!) and its relationship to the mark-up suppliers apply to cost.

In order to enhance the perception of relevance of the subject matter of microeconomics, the applications are made in a generic way. Some students erroneously conclude that microeconomics is only for the large corporations. By presenting the material with broad statements on applicability, the aim is to dispel this myth. Certain topics such as X-efficiency, Linear and Dynamic Programming and Project Analysis (investment criteria) are included because of their practical usefulness within a wide range of economic spheres. Moreover, the book seeks to enhance the relevance of the subject by maintaining a perspective on the use of microeconomics within a macro policy framework by casting certain microeconomic outcomes in the light of trade and competitiveness policy and that of general economic growth and development. This is seen in topics such as the Cobb–Douglas production function, income elasticities and in the tools of general equilibrium analysis.

The book is intended primarily as a text for university students in the second or third year of their undergraduate studies in economics. The material covers the typical intermediate course, which is normally compulsory for students of economics, and related areas such a business and management studies. The comprehensive yet in-depth nature of the material and the generic, global context within which it is cast renders the book suitable for students across a wide range of economic environments.

Acknowledgements

This book has benefited directly and indirectly from the comments and or actions of many who have come into contact with the material at various stages of completion. The comments and queries from students who had access to earlier drafts allowed timely changes and corrections to be made. The requests for some of the material by colleagues and others teaching similar courses and from others using the material despite the availability of other texts, showed that the book fills a void and provided the encouragement that was needed as an impetus to complete the writing of the text. Special thanks are due to Kerry-Ann Alleyne, who served briefly as a Research Assistant and undertook the initially daunting task of converting all the illustrations into a graphics format with which we were totally unfamiliar. Along with Kerry-Ann, thanks must also be extended to Crystol Thomas and Annette Greene, who assisted with the arduous task of reading portions of the final versions to check for errors. I, however, take full responsibility for any remaining errors or omissions. Finally, I must give special thanks to my husband and sons for stoically enduring the neglect and for their support as I toiled through the night to meet deadlines. Special thanks to my younger son Jean-Paul, who so nobly granted me unlimited access to his computer when I had the dubious distinction of having three computers (including my laptop) crash fatally within the space of two weeks.

To my sons James and Jean-Paul

List of Figures

List of Tables

List of Boxed Examples

1 Introduction to Microeconomics

Scenario; Definition of Microeconomics; Analytical Tools; Graphs and Geometry; The Calculus of Variations; The Methodology of Microeconomics; The Methodological Controversy – Scientific Validity

1.1 SCENARIO

The increasing globalization of production and consumption provides a new impetus to the study of microeconomics. The seemingly unending compulsion to increase production and improve competitiveness in domestic and international markets elevates the study of consumption, production and markets to the level of a critical component within the discipline of economics. This is the focus of microeconomics.

An understanding of the behaviour of these micro units in an economy is central to the formulation of industrial and trade policy which must complement each other and form an integral part of an overall growth strategy. It must be acknowledged that it is not nations per se that consume, produce and trade, rather that trade takes place between individual consuming and producing units in the respective trading nations. Consequently, a grasp of microeconomic principles is essential to the formulation of an inclusive policy for trade, economic growth and development, whether in a planned economy, a newly emerging market economy or a fully industrialized market economy.

The sub-prime mortgage market crisis in the United States of America that precipitated the global financial crisis of 2008 with its negative ramifications for the productive sectors, adds to the relevance of a sub-discipline that closely examines the behaviour of the micro decision-making units in an economy.

The purpose of this book is to present microeconomic fundamentals in a simple yet sufficiently comprehensive way to allow for a complete understanding of the subject by students of economics and other practitioners globally. The intention is to alter the perception among students that microeconomics is abstract, difficult and has little or no relevance within their sphere of economic activity. The approach is to take the study of microeconomics through from first principles to application in a straightforward, meaningful and generic manner so that its universal relevance may be easily understood and appreciated. Topics such as elasticity, Cobb–Douglas production functions and dynamic stability of market equilibrium are treated in ways to make the student or practitioner more comfortable with their significance and applicability.

Superimposed on this is the infusing of mathematical or quantitative techniques in an uncomplicated yet pervasive and detailed way so as to allow the student to appreciate the use of mathematics as a language that lends greater precision and rigour, rather than abstraction or distraction, to the sub-discipline of microeconomics. Derivations are worked through, often in pedestrian fashion, in order to facilitate comprehension and absorption and to inculcate a sense of their purpose and the significance of the results.

1.2 DEFINITION OF MICROECONOMICS

Microeconomics, as a central core area of the discipline of economics, must be defined within the overall definition of economics. A typical definition of economics is that it is the study of the production, consumption and distribution of goods and services. Economics is sometimes also described as the study of the allocation of scarce resources among competing ends. Both these definitions aptly fit the sub-discipline of microeconomics.

Economics has been dichotomized into microeconomics and macroeconomics. This division separates the analysis into two levels. Macroeconomics is concerned with aggregates such as the Gross National Product, the money supply and employment or unemployment rates, while microeconomics is concerned with the behaviour of individuals, firms and small groups up to the level of the industry or market. It can therefore be said to be concerned with the production, consumption and distribution of goods by the micro units of individuals, firms and markets within the economy. It can also be considered a study of scarcity and the choices to be made for the attainment of goals within constraints. These goals are those set by consumers, producers and policy makers in the market.

Microeconomics uses a structured or scientific approach to the investigation of the behaviour of these individual units of consumers and producers within a market in order to explain and predict how they respond to various signals in the market and how they are affected by the market structure. The study of these micro units is done within a theoretical framework that goes back to first principles to establish behavioural laws that may then be applied to the market. Indeed, some economists are bold enough to claim that microeconomics is to business or management studies what physics is to engineering.

It is recognized, however, that modern microeconomics goes beyond the role of the establishment of laws and deals with the use and application of these laws as well. This makes the study of microeconomics indispensable to the players in the market if they want to have an even chance of success in the market or to those who may want to re-engineer the market.

1.3 TOOLS, GADGETS AND GIZMOS

Microeconomics, like the rest of economics, is replete with various analytical tools, gadgets and gizmos, many of which are borrowed from the discipline of mathematics. Since microeconomic theory and analysis is done within the context of scarcity, where the behaviour of the individual units is conditioned by the need to achieve goals by making choices that require them to allocate scarce resources among competing ends, it is essentially a problem of constrained optimization or one of allocation within bounds. This type of problem is one for which the discipline of mathematics already has accepted procedures to provide the required solutions. In addition, the need to illustrate and demonstrate relationships and derive outcomes that are largely quantitative in nature makes the discipline of microeconomics particularly amenable to the use of mathematical techniques and tools.

In order to avoid getting lost in the rigours of mathematics, the student or practitioner of economics must view the use of mathematics as a means of adding precision while simplifying the discipline of economics. Mathematical tools must be seen as helping to elucidate or facilitate rather than to obfuscate or complicate microeconomic analysis and should be used in limited amounts only for this purpose. Mathematics may be considered a language which allows the economist to speak more precisely and concisely.

From the mathematical tool bag, some of the most useful for this purpose at hand include the ubiquitous graph and other techniques of geometry, the calculus of variations and myriad other techniques related to matrix algebra, difference equations and special techniques for constrained optimization which is the centrepiece of microeconomics. These include, *inter alia*, the technique of the Lagrangian Multiplier method for constrained optimization and the techniques of Linear and Dynamic Programming.

1.3.1 The geometry of microeconomics

In microeconomics, graphs are used extensively for the purpose of illustration and explanation.

Economic analysis is carried out under the *ceteris paribus* assumption by which everything else is held constant while changes are made to only one variable and its impact upon another is assessed. One example is the assessment of the impact of changes in price on the quantity demanded of a product or service, while income, the prices of other goods, taste and all other variables that may affect the quantity demanded, are held constant. In this way, much of microeconomic analysis is done by showing how one variable reacts against another. This type of relationship between two variables is easily captured in a two-dimensional graph.

1.3.1.1 GRAPHING A FUNCTION – NEGATIVE AND POSITIVE RELATIONSHIPS

Mathematically, a function with just two variables may be written as:

$$y = f(x)$$

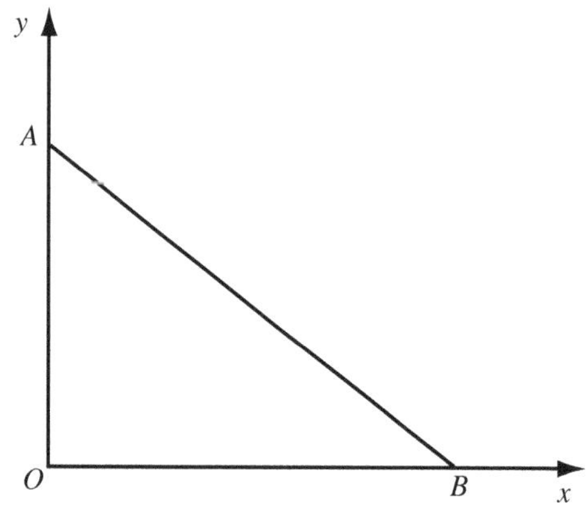

Figure 1.1
Graphing a negative relationship $y = f(x)$

What this says is that there is a relationship between the variables y *and* x. In addition, it reveals that y depends on x or that the movement in the value of y depends on the movement in the value of x and not the other way around. This is because the variable y is on the vertical axis. The implication is that this variable (y) is the dependent variable, the movement of which is dependent on the movement of the variable (x) on the horizontal axis.

Figure 1.1 illustrates the case where the relationship between the two variables (x and y) is a negative one. This gives the information that, as the variable x increases in value, the value of the variable y decreases. Where the relationship is functional ($y = f(x)$), it says that a positive movement in variable x causes a negative movement in variable y.

It is useful to note that, while the demand curve displays this negative relationship, it typically is drawn with the dependent variable on the horizontal rather than the vertical axis based on the way the standard demand equation is written ($Q = f(P)$). Hence, whereas the demand equation as written says that the quantity demanded depends on the price of the good, the illustration of the demand curve is inverted and shows that the price depends on the quantity. This happens because the demand equation written is based on that attributed to the economist Leon Walras (1834–1910), whereas the illustration used is that attributed to the economist Alfred Marshall (1842–1924).

It may be noted further that, in illustrating a negative relationship, it is not necessary for the relationship to be causal or for the direction of causality to have been determined. It is just necessary for the values of the two variables to move in opposite directions when they impact on each other.

Figure 1.2 illustrates a positive functional relationship for $y = f(x)$. This says that as the value of variable x increases, it causes variable y to increase. An example of this positive relationship is a normal supply curve, which shows an increase in price causing an increase in the quantity demanded. It should again be noted that, like the demand function discussed above and for the same reason, the supply function is also written with quantity as a function of price whereas it is typically drawn in the inverse, with price as a function of quantity.

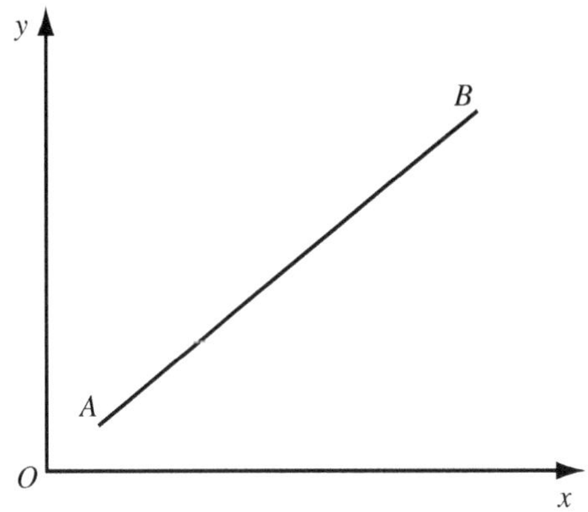

Figure 1.2
Graphing a positive relationship $y = f(x)$

Horizontal and vertical summation in a graph

A troubling aspect of graphing relationships is the summation of curves whether horizontal or vertical. Where the summation is horizontal, the total curve at every point along its vertical length is the added horizontal width at each vertical point of all the curves being summed. As an example consider the limiting case of two curves being added horizontally.

Figure 1.3 shows the horizontal summation of two curves L_1 and L_2 to give L_T. All three curves are in the same scale. This could represent, for example, the summation of demand curves in separate sub-markets to give an overall demand curve ($L_1 + L_2 = L_T$). Along the y-axis are the points a, b, c and d. At point a, there is only the distance from the y-axis to the L_1 curve that must be included in the total curve L_T. The curve L_2 starts at the point b and must therefore be added to L_1 from this point. This creates a kink on the total curve L_T. At point c, the horizontal distance from the y-axis to the L_1 curve is added to the horizontal distance from the y-axis to the L_2 curve to give the total horizontal distance from the y-axis for the total curve L_T (as measured by the dashed lines at c). The same effect can be observed at the point d on the y-axis. Measuring along

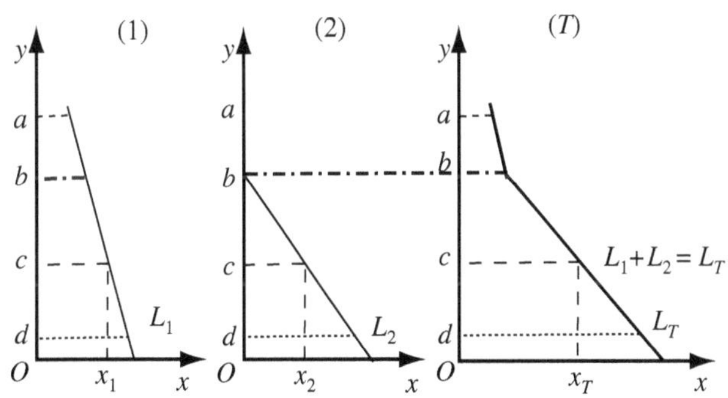

Figure 1.3
Horizontal summation of linear curves

the x-axis, the summation also gives $x_1 + x_2 = x_T$ based on the distances at the level c on the y-axis.

For vertical summation of curves, the dashed lines would go vertically upwards from the x-axis to give a total curve. This is illustrated in Figure 1.4, in the section below on non-linear curves.

1.3.1.2 NON-LINEAR CURVES

In many cases, the relationship between two variables may take on a non-linear form. Total variable cost curves, for example, are specified as a cubic polynomial relationship between variable costs (C) and output (Q) with alternating signs and could be written as follows:

$$C = b_1Q - b_2Q^2 + b_3Q^3$$

This type of specification gives a curve that increases first at a decreasing rate and later at an increasing rate.

Curves which change their rates of change over the length of the curve are common in economics and are central to the discipline of microeconomics. This type of curve is shown in Figure 1.4 along with an example of vertical summation of curves.

Using Figure 1.4, consider the line C_1 to represent fixed cost whereas the non-linear curve C_2 represents the variable cost curve. This variable cost curve can be observed to increase at a decreasing rate at first and then to increase at an increasing rate. The point at which the change in rates of increase occurs (point of inflexion) is of great importance in microeconomics because of its impact on the related marginal curve important for determining equilibrium.

From Figure 1.4, the procedure for vertical summation can be seen. Here, the C_1 curve is added to the C_2 curve. In this case, the C_1 curve is a straight line and so the same vertical distance is added to the C_2 curve at every point along its extent. This is shown

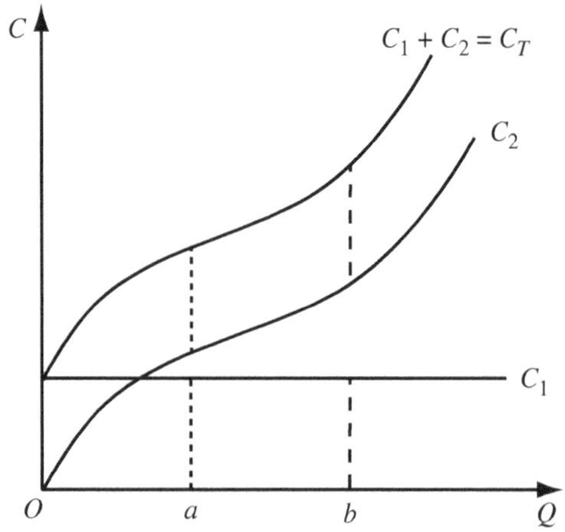

Figure 1.4
Vertical summation of curves – non-linear curves

by the dashed vertical lines that push the C_2 curve upward by the height of the C_1 curve to give the C_T curve. This represents a parallel upward shift in the curve. Where the C_1 line is curved, the same procedure is applied except that the distance added to the C_2 curve would differ at every point as the height of the C_1 curve differs.

1.3.1.3 GRAPHING TOTAL, AVERAGE AND MARGINAL RELATIONSHIPS

Other techniques in geometry help to derive average and marginal curves from total curves. As an example, consider another curve that increases at varying rate such as the total product curve. The related marginal curve can be found by drawing tangents to the total product curve at points along the curve. It is then possible to measure the relevant marginal product at every point by measuring the slope of the tangent at the point. Moreover, the point of inflexion can be found when the slopes of the tangents change from getting steeper to getting flatter (or vice-versa for other curves).

The average curve can be derived from the total curve by recognizing that the tangent of the angle made by a ray from the origin to a point on the curve is the average. Recall that the tangent (tan) of an angle (θ) is:

$$\tan\theta = \frac{\text{Opposite}}{\text{Adjacent}}$$

Consequently, for a curve such as a total product or total cost curve, the ray from the origin to a point on the curve creates an angle (θ) at the origin. If the ray is extended to the total product (or similar) curve and a perpendicular is dropped to the x-axis, then a triangle is created. With reference to the angle made at the origin, the opposite side of the triangle measures total product (or revenue or cost or whatever variable is on the y-axis), whereas the adjacent side measures the variable on the x-axis up to the point where the ray intersects with the total product (or other) curve.

Figure 1.5 illustrates a total product of labour curve. The tangent to a point gives the marginal product of labour and so the tangent at point T has a slope of zero which says the marginal product of labour is zero at this point (total product is a maximum). Consequently, adding another unit of labour at this point adds nothing more to the total output of labour. If these tangent lines were drawn all along the TP_L curve moving from the origin, they would be seen to get increasingly steeper at the beginning and then start to get increasingly flatter after the point of inflexion (R), until the tangent becomes horizontal (TP_L = maximum) at the point T.

With regard to the average product of labour, this can be found by measuring the tan of the angle θ made by the ray from the origin to any point on the TP_L curve such as the point A. The average product of labour at the point A may therefore be given as:

$$AP_L^{(A)} = \tan\,\theta = \frac{AB}{OB}$$

This technique is useful since it illustrates how the average product of labour changes from one point to another along the total product of the labour curve by drawing rays from the origin to the total product curve at different points and examining how the size of the angle θ changes. The larger the angle θ, the larger the value $\tan\theta$ and, by extension, the larger the average product of labour (AP_L).

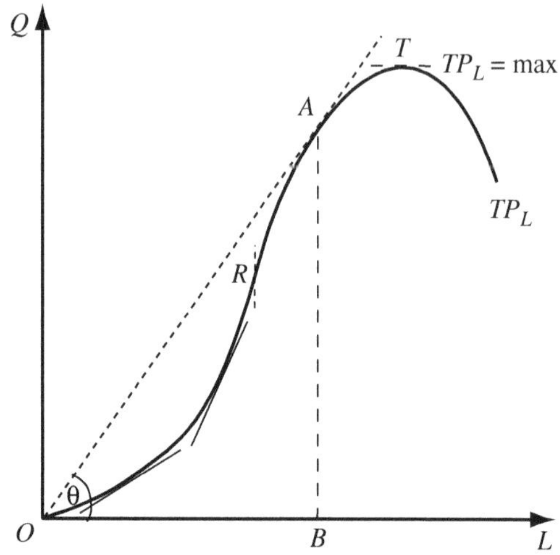

Figure 1.5
Techniques for deriving average and marginal curves from total curves

This technique can be applied when illustrating the relationship between the total of any variable and its average.

1.3.2 The Calculus of Variations

At the centre of microeconomics is marginal analysis (e.g. $MC = MR$). Marginal refers to incremental changes. Consuming and producing units are theorized to operate at the margin. This is because, central to microeconomics theory, the units of consumers and producers are assumed to be rational in that they seek to optimize. The consumer seeks to maximize satisfaction from consuming and the producer aims to maximize profits or, with certain constraints, to maximize output or minimize production costs. Mathematically, maxima and minima are found at the margin. Operationally, optimizing or finding solutions at the margin is easily handled by the use of the technique of the Calculus of Variations.

The aim here is not to teach the Calculus of Variations but to show how and why it is used to facilitate microeconomic analysis. In microeconomics it is simply a tool used to derive the necessary and sufficient conditions for a maximum or a minimum of a function. Once a functional relationship is correctly specified by economists, the application of the technique allows for the correct and precise answers to be found.

1.3.2.1 OPTIMIZING WITH A SINGLE FUNCTION

The Calculus of Variations uses necessary and sufficient conditions, also known as first- and second-order conditions respectively, to determine the maximum or minimum value of a function. These conditions use the first and second derivatives of a function.

The necessary condition

The first-order or necessary condition uses the first derivative of a function. What is of particular importance to economic analysis is that the first derivative of a function (e.g. $y = f(x)$) is actually the slope or gradient of the function. Put another way, the first derivative of the function $y = f(x)$, expressed as:

$$\frac{dy}{dx}$$

is actually the rate of change of one variable against the other. This complements the use of the graphs since each line drawn has a gradient or slope that tells a story of how one variable changes in response to changes by the other.

Using the first derivative of the function under consideration, the first-order condition for an optimum (whether maximum or minimum) requires that the first derivative of the function be equal to zero. This requires the slope of the curve to be zero in order for there to be a maximum or a minimum position. The reason for this is easy to visualize on the typical two-dimensional graph. Consider a total product curve as depicted earlier in Figure 1.5 that relates total product (output (Q)) to the quantity of labour (L) used, all other factors being fixed (captured as $\overline{K}$). This gives the function: $Q = f(L)_{\overline{K}}$. As there are multiple variables (L, K) with only one being considered (L) and the other held constant, the partial derivative is used. Hence, the requirement for a maximum or minimum is where the first partial derivative of the function is zero:

$$\frac{\partial Q}{\partial L} = 0$$

This is the first-order condition and is fulfilled at the point T.

In this case, point T is a maximum. However, if the curve had fallen first and then risen, there would have been a point fulfilling the first-order condition (with a slope of zero) which would have been a minimum rather than a maximum. Because the first-order condition can only tell that the point is a maximum or minimum but cannot tell which it is, it is said to be necessary but not sufficient.

The sufficient condition

The sufficient or second-order condition indicates whether the point at which the slope is zero is a maximum or a minimum point. This is done using the second derivative of the function. Formally, a function written as $y = f(x)$ requires the use of the second derivative, written as:

$$\frac{d^2y}{dx^2}$$

Consider that, at a practical level, whereas the first derivative of a function gives the slope of the function or the rate of change of the variables against one another, the second derivative gives the slope of the slope of the function or the rate of change of the rate of change of the variables against one another. Identifying a maximum or a minimum therefore depends on whether the slope is changing to negative or positive at the momentary zero point. If it changes to the negative, then it means the curve falls from the zero slope point. This identifies that point as a maximum. A slope that is changing to positive or rising from the zero slope point identifies that point as a minimum.

Formally then, for the function $y = f(x)$, the second-order condition for a maximum becomes:

$$\frac{d^2y}{dx^2} < 0$$

For a minimum, the condition becomes:

$$\frac{d^2y}{dx^2} > 0$$

Referring again to the functional relationship in Figure 1.5, the curve in the relationship $Q = f(L)_{\overline{K}}$ can be observed to have a negative change from the point T which fulfils the second-order condition for a maximum. The second-order partial derivative becomes:

$$\frac{\partial^2 Q}{\partial L^2} < 0$$

The benefits of using the Calculus of Variations derive largely from the way in which it readily handles more complicated functions than the one in the example above. A major advantage is that it obviates the need to graph the function in order to visually identify the maximum or minimum points. This is particularly useful where there are several variables in the function which would prevent it from being graphed in a two-dimensional space or where the functional relationship is more complicated (polynomial, logarithmic, etc.).

The Calculus of Variations is therefore a tool or gadget which facilitates economic analysis and lends greater precision and concision to the task of optimizing.

1.3.2.2 OPTIMIZING WITH TWO FUNCTIONS

In some cases in microeconomics, the optimization process, rather than seeking the maximum or minimum of a single function, is trying to identify the greatest gap between the two functional relationships. Once again, the Calculus of Variations provides the tools necessary to facilitate the analysis.

An example of this is the firm seeking to maximize profits. These profits are the difference between revenues and costs. Total revenue (TR) and total cost (TC) have their own respective functional relationship and in this case the aim is not to maximize or minimize either one of the individual functions but to maximize the difference between the two curves. Hence the aim is no longer to identify the point at which the slope of either of the functions is zero. Hence a slightly different gadget is used to fit this analytical requirement.

The necessary condition

The fact is that the greatest difference between two curves is where their slopes are equal. Since the slope measured at each point along a curve gives the marginal curves, this occurs where their marginal curves are equal. Hence, where it is necessary to find the maximum profits then, since profits are defined as the difference between revenue and costs, it is necessary to identify the point at which there is the greatest difference between the total revenue and total cost curves. This occurs where their slopes are equal rather than where either one (or both) is zero (except by co-incidence).

The functional relationship for total cost (C) and total revenue (R) respectively as they relate to output (Q) may be expressed formally as:

$$C = f(Q) \quad \text{and} \quad R = f(Q)$$

Hence the first-order condition may be expressed as:

$$\frac{\partial C}{\partial Q} = \frac{\partial R}{\partial Q}$$

This indicates that the slope of the Total Cost curve must be equal to the slope of the total revenue curve as a necessary condition for a minimum or a maximum. Since the slope of a curve is the marginal value of that curve, it means that the marginal cost must be equal to the marginal revenue, giving the famous equilibrium (profit maximizing) condition ($MC = MR$). In layman's terms, it simply means that the addition to total cost must be equal to the addition to total revenue.

An understanding of this should take away some of the mystery of marginal analysis, often viewed as some strange creature invented by economists to confuse the uninitiated.

The sufficient condition

The condition given above is just the necessary or first-order condition for a maximum of profits because, as shown in Figure 1.6, where both curves are varying in slope along their lengths, it is possible to identify multiple points at which their slopes are equal. Hence, the above condition ($MC = MR$) is necessary but not sufficient for optimization.

Figure 1.6 shows a typical diagram of total cost and total revenue curves in a perfectly competitive market. It should be noted that the two slopes are equal both in an area representing losses (where TC is greater than TR) and in another area representing profits (where TR is greater than TC). Interestingly, the line ab represents the maximum loss whereas the line cd represents the maximum profits. It is clear that applying the first-order condition alone would not guarantee identifying the position of maximum profits. Furthermore, if the wrong point is chosen, then, rather than maximizing profits, the firm would actually be maximizing losses.

Consequently, the second-order or sufficient condition must then be applied to determine which one represents the maximum profits. In this case, the second-order condition for a maximum would use the second derivative of the two functions. Now, since the second derivative is the slope of the slope, and since the second derivative

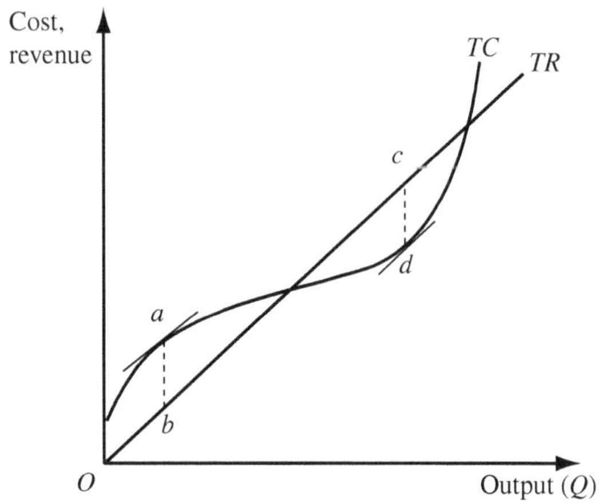

Figure 1.6
Optimizing with two functions

must be negative for a maximum, the second-order condition for a maximum of profits may be written as:

$$\frac{\partial^2 C}{\partial Q^2} - \frac{\partial^2 R}{\partial Q^2} < 0 \qquad \text{or} \qquad \frac{\partial^2 C}{\partial Q^2} > \frac{\partial^2 R}{\partial Q^2}$$

Translating, it simply says that the slope of the marginal cost curve must be greater than the slope of the marginal revenue curve for there to be maximum profits. It means that the slope of the total cost curve must be increasing faster than the slope of the total revenue curve at the point where the slopes are equal. That derives from mathematics rather than economics and has already been proven and established in that discipline.

For microeconomics, the use of this technique facilitates the economic analysis by obviating the need for meticulous and time-consuming graphing and measurement of the relationships and the differences between them. Here, once again, the use of mathematics allows the economist to speak more concisely and with greater precision thereby improving analytical efficiency. Once the functions are specified, all that is needed is to differentiate twice and the answer to the optimization problem emerges, saving long attempts at arguments to explain and justify the results.

1.3.3 Constrained optimization

The focus of microeconomics on the 'allocation of scarce resources among competing ends' suggests that a central problem is that of constrained optimization (the consumer seeking to maximize utility subject to a given income; the producer constrained by cost and seeking to maximize output in order to maximize profits). Another mathematical gadget is readily available to facilitate this analysis by economists. This is the technique of the Lagrangian Multiplier method for constrained optimization, a technique already established and proven to give the correct and precise answer to how to optimize within bounds.

The typical constrained optimization problem consists of:

- An objective function
- A constraint function

The objective is to maximize (or minimize) the objective function subject to the restriction of the constraint function. An example of this is the case of the utility maximizing consumer. In this case, the objective is to maximize utility (U) which is a function of (depends on) the quantities (Q) of the goods consumed (say goods x and y). The constraint is the consumer's income (Y) which is given. In this example, the objective function and constraint function respectively are set up as:

$$\text{Max: } U = f(Q_x, Q_y) \quad \text{(objective function)}$$

subject to:

$$\overline{Y} = P_x Q_x + P_y Q_y \quad \text{(constraint function)}$$

The technique then proceeds as follows:

- Set the constraint function equal to zero:

$$(\overline{Y} - P_x Q_x - P_y Q_y = 0)$$

- Multiply by (λ) the Lagrangian multiplier:

$$\lambda(\overline{Y} - P_x Q_x - P_y Q_y)$$

- Add the Lagrangian to the objective function to form (ϕ), the composite function:

$$\phi = U + \lambda(\overline{Y} - P_x Q_x - P_y Q_y)$$

- Differentiate the composite function once with respect to each variable (Q_x, Q_y) and λ and set it equal to zero to satisfy the first-order condition for a maximum (or minimum).
- Differentiate the first derivative to get the second derivative of the composite function and set it to less than or greater than zero depending on whether the aim is to maximize or to minimize.

In using this established technique, the optimization of the composite function is proven to be equivalent to optimizing the objective function subject to the constraint. Once the functions have been correctly specified and the procedure has been followed, there is no need to expound on why the result is a valid one thereby saving much time and effort, particularly where the relationships are complex.

Optimizing within bounds is also done using the technique of linear programming. This is explained and illustrated in Chapter 7.

1.4 THE METHODOLOGY OF MICROECONOMIC THEORY

The methodology of microeconomics is bound up in the use of a particular approach to the explanation and prediction of the behaviour of individual economic units as they consume and produce economic goods and services. The key issue revolves around whether the approach used by micro-economists can be considered scientific.

1.4.1 Microeconomics as a science

The issue of whether microeconomic theory is a scientific theory has long been debated. It must be emphasized that the use of mathematics in itself does not make microeconomic theory a scientific theory. Labelling a discipline a science has more to do with the nature or structure of inquiry and the testability of the outcomes than with the fact that mathematical techniques are used. Many consider that, in a formal sense, microeconomic theory is a scientific theory. This is examined further.

A scientific theory may be described as a structured attempt to examine the behaviour of certain phenomena in order to explain and predict this behaviour in a consistent and logical manner that accords with reality. The procedure is to identify and select the critical variables and examine the way in which they interact to achieve particular outcomes. In carrying out this exercise, a whole set of models may be used to build the theory. At the end of the modelling, the results, a set of predictions about the behaviour of the variables under study, must be testable or verifiable and must be subjected to such testing.

With regard to microeconomic theory then, the objective of theorizing is to explain and predict the behaviour of individual units within the economy with regard to consumption, production and distribution of goods and services. The objective, therefore, is to derive testable propositions concerning the behaviour of economic units within a society using a structured approach to the investigation. Once these propositions are tested and verified, the theory generates a law (such as the law of demand).

1.4.2 The structure of a scientific theory

The scientific method of investigation requires that the investigation of the economic phenomena under consideration must proceed in a structured way. As a mnemonic, this structure may be viewed using the alphabetical format set out below as *A*, *B*, *C*.

Theory may be considered to consist of:

- Assumptions (*A*)
- Logical deductions or body of the theory (*B*)
- Conclusions or theorems that are testable propositions (*C*)

At the lowest level are the empirical observations. These establish the characteristics of the variables under study as well as consider any specific consistencies in the behaviour of the variables. These are the assumptions or axioms (*A*). They are supposed to be basic truths. As an example, utility theory uses as an axiom that the consumer is rational in a particular way. That is, the consumer seeks to maximize the utility derived from consumption, given the consumer's income and the price of the good(s). The scientific approach does not require every single consumer to have this objective, but that the occurrence be sufficiently regular to consider it is the rule rather than the exception.

At the next level are the logical deductions which form the body of the theory (*B*). These are the interrelationships among the variables and may reflect a body of models of the way in which the variables behave and the conditions under which they do so. Using the same example of utility theory, the body of the ordinal theory models the behaviour of the consumer using the indifference curves (derived from the axiom of diminishing marginal utility) and the budget line based on the restricted income of the consumer.

Finally, there are the conclusions or theorems which derive from the theory (*C*). These conclusions or theorems must be verifiable or testable. In order to accept these conclusions as 'laws' the conclusions or theorems must be *tested and validated* in some way. Out of utility theory comes the conclusion or prediction that as price falls consumers buy more units of the good, all things being equal (*ceteris paribus*). Once tested and verified, it can be called a law, and, in this case, the result is called the Law of Demand.

1.4.3 Apriorism vs Empiricism

The foregoing section describes the scientific approach in a manner that may be described as the deductive or a priori approach to theory. Many theorists consider that theory, by nature, is deductive. This means that, starting from certain basic plausible assumptions, definite conclusions (theorems) are derived. This, however, is not the only approach used.

It is possible to use two different approaches to theories:

- The deductive or a priori approach
- The inductive or empirical approach

The deductive approach follows the structure set out above from the lowest to the highest, starting with the assumptions (*A*) and proceeding through the body of models (*B*) to the conclusions (*C*). Once the conclusions have been tested and found acceptable, the theory is considered to have been validated.

On the other hand, the inductive or empirical approach uses statistical information which is collected and tested for trends and relationships. Once these statistical trends and relationships have been identified these findings are then used to infer the theory.

The two alternative approaches may also be labelled apriorism and empiricism.

Apriorism

A priori (not prior) reasoning goes from cause to effect and represents the belief there are concepts that can be formulated with no prior evidence of the result. It is the doctrine, generally attributed to the eighteenth-century philosopher Immanuel Kant, that there are concepts (axioms) which do not come from experience (no prior experience required) but that it is through the application of these concepts that experience is gained. The view is that there are concepts that are innate to the mind without any prior experience of the outcome of their application (i.e. that the mind itself makes a contribution to knowledge).

This allows the theoretical process to be deductive, starting with the axioms (assumptions) as basic truths revealed by the mind even without experience of the result of their application. From these axioms, logical deductions can be made that lead to conclusions or hypotheses that can be tested to ascertain whether they accord with or correctly predict the reality of the experience.

Empiricism

Empiricism, on the other hand, is the doctrine that all knowledge comes from experience and, in its more radical form, is associated with William James, a nineteenth-century philosopher. This favours the inductive approach where knowledge starts from the experience through the collection of data or information and the observation or study of this information is used to infer a theory.

In microeconomics, as in economics as a whole, this empiricist or inductive approach relies on the use of statistical data and the application of various techniques of statistical inference. This has tended to increase in prevalence with the advent of high-speed computers and the advancement of techniques of Econometrics and Applied Statistics.

Much of standard microeconomic theory, however, uses the deductive or a priori approach, beginning with assumptions that are supposed to be of the nature of axioms or basic truths innate to the mind and following through to conclusions or predictions. The standard fare still predominantly tends to rely on axioms of the utility maximizing consumer and the profit maximizing producer. However, in many cases, the assumptions are more in the nature of observances of experience. For example, under the market structure of monopoly, the assumption of a single seller is more of an observation than an innate formulation of the mind.

Increasingly, micro-economists are resorting to empiricism to infer a theory. In particular, the ready availability of time-series or cross-section data in this information age, along with the facility of computer software to specify and re-specify formulations and to test and re-test the fit of the results, all serve to make the empirical approach highly attractive to economists. Increasingly available data sources on the internet provide a constant temptation to use the information in an econometrics package and see what fits, while the developments in econometrics allow for increasingly sophisticated techniques of testing such as the Granger causality test and tests for unit roots, all of which serve to give the empiricist the somewhat guarded assurance that the data by itself can provide a reliable theory.

It is often easy to forget that correlation does not imply causation or that a good fit can be purely accidental. Nevertheless, a lot more attention is being paid to the empirical

BOX 1.1 A CAUTION ON EMPIRICISM

Consider the following statements given hypothetically as a research finding:

Americans are heavy beer drinkers and eat a high fat diet and have a high rate of heart disease. Germans are heavy beer drinkers and eat a high fat diet but have a low rate of heart disease.

The British are heavy wine drinkers and eat a high fat diet and have a high rate of heart disease. The French are heavy wine drinkers and eat a high fat diet but have a low rate of heart disease.

Question: Assuming that these are facts that are empirically valid, what may be reasonably inferred from this as a theory of the cause of heart disease?

Possible Answer: Speaking English is a cause of heart disease.

Source: Anonymous

approach as witnessed by the fascination with the specification of empirical demand functions and empirical production functions, among others.

It is useful to view the two approaches as complementary. Statistical or empirical studies may indicate a certain relationship, but the direction of a causal relationship or whether a causal relationship exists at all can only be explained by the theory. The goal of scientific inquiry is usually both to explain and to predict. The use of theory is not only to give accurate predictions but also to help provide an understanding of how and why the predictions work.

It is generally agreed that good theory is based on realistic assumptions and a sound logical structure.

1.4.4 Is microeconomics really a science?

Despite the use of the scientific method of investigation, the question persists of whether microeconomics or indeed economics as a whole is a science. Much of this argument relates to the ability to test the conclusions or predictions in order to determine whether they accord with reality. Proper verification requires that the experiment be repeatable and the test results must be consistent. This typically requires a controlled environment where extraneous matter and exogenous variables can be excluded from influence on the test results.

As a social science, achieving this level of control is highly impracticable. In economics, it is far more difficult to control the variables which are not being subject to testing but which also impact on the test results. That is, there is very little opportunity to create a true laboratory environment for testing the results of a theory to determine its validity and to match the 'all other things being equal' (*ceteris paribus*) conditions under which the theory is formed. Moreover, it may not be possible in microeconomics to repeat the tests, under the exact same conditions, a sufficient number of times to claim laws that can be certified as irrefutable.

Clearly then, economics as a social science, is not an 'exact' science. It is not exact to the extent of some of the physical sciences. Nevertheless, it should be recognized that, in microeconomics:

- Every effort is made to carry out testing of conclusions as required for scientific inquiry.
- While it is difficult to control all the variables, economic testing resorts to the law of large numbers (i.e. if enough observations are made, the true trend may be identified).
- Efforts are made through econometric techniques to identify and eliminate the effects of extraneous matter or 'noise'.

It should also be noted that, even in the physical sciences, findings on the behaviour of physical phenomena are not as irrefutable as is often claimed. This is so in several areas of the physical sciences, in particular, those of biology, medical sciences and even physics.

Nevertheless, economics is based on the development of theories which may be tested and the formulation of laws. As such there is a difference between economics and Business Studies. Business or Management Studies is the application of such laws or theories. As noted earlier, the connection between economics and business studies is often compared to that of physics and engineering.

A dismal science?

Nineteenth-century economist Thomas Carlyle (1795–1881) described economics as a dismal science. This description fits economics as a science because of the continued concern with the scarce resources which have to be allocated to competing ends (constrained optimization). For economics, scarcity is not a temporary phase affecting only a part of the economy. It is omni-present and ever present.

However, some economists believe Carlyle was making a reference to the work of the eighteenth-century Thomas Malthus, who predicted that population growth would outstrip the world ability to increase the production of food. This was an extremely dismal prediction on the central concern of economics – scarcity. His actual target, however, was economist John Stuart Mill (1806–1873) who tended to favour the free market and defended limited government participation in and regulation of the free market.

Carlyle's use of the phrase 'dismal science' is first noted in a pamphlet written by him in 1849 bearing the title 'Occasional Discourse on the Negro Question'. In it he used adjectives such as dreary, desolate, abject and distressing to describe economics as a science. This comes some years after the abolition of slavery in the British West Indies and, in this discourse, his rant was actually against the liberalization of slaves and the promotion of the free market and supply and demand economics (as promoted by Mill). His was a Mathusian line with a twist, for he saw economists and their market liberalization philosophy as being responsible for the dismal economic prospects.

BOX 1.2 SPENDING OUT OF A RECESSION: A PERSPECTIVE ON PRODUCTION AND CONSUMPTION CHOICES FOR THE USA UNDER GLOBALIZATION

A stimulus package for the USA to spend its way out of recession?

If we spend that money at Wal-Mart, the money will go to China.
If we spend it on gasoline it will go to the Arabs.
If we purchase a computer it will go to India.
If we purchase fruit and vegetables it will go to Mexico, Honduras, and Guatemala.
If we purchase a good car it will go to Japan.
If we purchase knick knacks it will go to Taiwan ... And none of it will help the American economy.

The only way to keep that money here at home is to buy prostitutes, weed, beer, cigarettes, whiskey, lottery tickets and tattoos, since these are the only products still produced in the USA. Thank you for your help and please support the USA.

Source: Adapted from various internet sites including: http://www.ksl.com/?nid=148&sid=3208855

He chided his fellow economists for their failure to recognize the value of controlling the labour market through slavery. Indeed, he even argued that slavery was of benefit to the slaves themselves. His call therefore, was for the re-introduction of slavery, without which the problem of economic scarcity would continue to become more acute.

Despite the growth in world output to unprecedented levels since these dire predictions were made and the general failure of the eighteenth- and nineteenth-century predictions of global starvation to come to pass (the 'great depression' notwithstanding), the dismal predictions on scarcity and the focus of economics on 'the allocation of scarce resource among competing ends' remains.

At the heart of this problem of scarcity then is the need for choices to be made. These choices are those of the allocation of these scarce resources. Hence, there is the use of the budget line, isocost line and other forms of constraints in the process of optimization (maximization) of satisfaction, profits and other variables.

The issues of economic choices and their impact of economic growth and development become even more stark in the current environment of global economic liberalization and the expansion of global trade.

1.4.5 Why economists disagree

Disagreement among economists is often the subject of much humour. It has been said that, if there are three economists in a room, there are at least four different opinions on any single matter. However, the extent of disagreement if often overstated. Furthermore, there are certain reasons for the disagreements that do exist.

Much of this apparent disagreement rests on the distinction between Normative and Positive economics.

Normative vs. positive economics

Positive economics refers to the laws of economics (i.e. what is), whereas normative economics refers to what ought to be.

There is general agreement among economists on the laws, or positive economics of what is. The disagreement usually pertains to the normative side (what ought to be). This is mainly because the normative side requires value judgements or subjective evaluations. These value judgements may refer to the effect of policies on the various competing social groups, their response to the policies and the effect of this response on the outcome of the implementation of policies.

But there are other reasons why economists disagree. These relate to the fact that economics, as a social science, cannot stand entirely on its own. Other factors impact on economic outcomes. In particular, social, cultural, political, legal, administrative and other consequences (i.e. their costs and benefits) must be taken into account. This makes economic judgements even more sensitive to contrasting personal views and preferences and hence more prone to subjectivity.

In addition, in economics, the circular nature of events or feedback actions must also be taken into account. For example, if a trading country (Country 1) bans imports of a good (wheat) from its trading partner (Country 2), Country 2 now receives less income and foreign currency from Country 1 and is therefore unable to purchase as much from Country 1 (and perhaps from many other countries) as it did before.

In another example, consider that whereas a single firm may benefit from laying off a large portion of its staff, if all firms do the same then all firms will suffer because of reduced purchasing power as the level of unemployment rises.

1.5 THE METHODOLOGICAL CONTROVERSY – SCIENTIFIC VALIDITY

The methodological controversy in microeconomics pertains to the issue of establishing the scientific validity of a theory. In this regard, the seemingly contrasting views of Friedman and Samuelson are examined with an attempt at reconciliation.

Although it is accepted that theories should be able to explain and to predict, there has been some controversy on how to determine whether a theory has 'scientific validity'. On this score, there have in the past been two major schools of thought. One of these is associated with Milton Friedman and the other with Paul Samuelson and is sometimes referred to as the Friedman–Samuelson controversy. Many economists consider that the controversy is over with Friedman having lost. However, it is not as clear-cut as that and it is important for students of economics to examine the controversy and be informed by it in their interactions with microeconomic theory.

At the heart of this controversy is the question of how to judge a theory. The controversy is often labelled 'Instrumentalism vs. Descriptivism' or 'Positivism vs. Realism'. Instrumentalism or Positivism is associated with Milton Friedman. Descriptivism or

Realism is associated with Paul Samuelson. One asserts that scientific validity derives from the predictive ability of a theory whereas the other asserts that it derives from the extent to which the assumptions are founded in reality.

1.5.1 Instrumentalism or positivism

Instrumentalism is the thesis that a theory in science is merely an instrument for the prediction of observable reality. The view is held that assumptions or axioms are merely tools or instruments which are selected for their ease or convenience in use. The axioms cannot be called true or false. The theory is then validated by the conformity of its predictions with observable reality. This view is associated with economist Milton Friedman.

According to Friedman (1958: 8–9): 'A theory is not to be judged by the 'realism' of its assumptions but by examining the concordance of the theory's logical consequences with the phenomena the theory is designed to explain'.

For Friedman, therefore, a theory is evaluated by its predictive power. For him, the test of the validity of a hypothesis is the comparison of its predictions with experience. According to him, realism would render the theory useless, devoid of predictive power.

Friedman goes further to say that a new hypothesis can only be accepted if it brings better predictions for a wide range of phenomena.

Consequently, his contention is that it is the predictive power of a theory that matters and determines its validity in a scientific sense. But he goes further to say that the truth or falsity of the assumptions is irrelevant. Indeed, he went as far as to say (Friedman 1958: 20): '... truly important and significant hypotheses will be found to have assumptions that are wildly inaccurate descriptive representations of reality and, in general, the more significant the theory, the more unrealistic the assumptions (in this sense)'.

This appears to confirm that Friedman has taken an extreme position where he suggests that assumptions are not only unimportant or irrelevant to determining the scientific validity of a theory but that there can be a negative relationship between validity of assumptions and the scientific validity of the theory.

1.5.2 Descriptivism or realism

Descriptivism or realism, on the other hand, is the doctrine that the assumptions or axioms of a theory must be realistic or must describe reality. This is associated with the views of economist Paul Samuelson.

Samuelson (1963) describes Friedman's position on the apparent negative relationship between the validity of assumptions and the scientific validity of a theory as the **F-Twist** (the Friedman Twist) – praising the shortcomings of a theory as its virtues. According to Samuelson (1963: 233): 'A theory is just a description of observable experience, a convenient and mnemonic representation of empirical reality'.

The implication is that the assumptions or axioms must be realistic or describe reality. The question is whether he means that it must fully describe every facet of the reality it sets out to deal with. This extended meaning seems unlikely as the phrase 'convenient and mnemonic representation' suggests it is necessary to find a short-hand

and easy to remember (mnemonic) way to describe a larger more complex and intractable reality.

Samuelson goes on to describe a theory as:

> A set of axioms, postulates or hypotheses that stipulate something about observable reality. The set is either refutable or confirmable in principle by observation. The theory has a set of consequences which are logically implied by the theory and a set of assumptions which logically imply the theory.
>
> (Samuelson 1963: 233)

Consequently, Samuelson asks how the consequences of a theory can be valid and the theory and assumptions not valid. As a mathematician, he is concerned with logic and considers that a logical deduction from assumptions that are not valid cannot be valid. Further, as a corollary to this, he contends that it is absurd to maintain, in the case where only some of the consequences are valid, that the theory and the assumptions are important though invalid.

Samuelson sets out the structure of a scientific theory in the standard manner mentioned earlier, viz.:

A – The assumptions
B – The body of the theory
C – The consequences

He then states his theorem in the following way:

> If C is the complete or full set of consequences of the theory, B, then C is identical or logically equivalent to B and shares the same degree of realism with B. C implies B as well as being implied by it. It is nonsense to think that C could be realistic and B unrealistic, and nonsense to think that the unrealism of B could then arise and be irrelevant.
>
> (Samuelson 1963: 234)

Samuelson goes on to say:

> Suppose the weak axiom C- is valid and the strong axiom is definitely not. (Friedman's) F-Twist says 'never mind that B is unrealistic, its consequence C- is realistic and that is all that counts'. ... But since B is unrealistic, the fact that C-, one of its implications is valid, does not in any way atone for the fact that C – (C-) is definitely false. Only that part of B which is in C- has been vindicated by the validity of C-. That other part B – (B-) has been refuted.
>
> (Samuelson 1963: 234)

The battle lines appeared to have been rigidly drawn between the two schools of thought. However, as others sought to critique the work of the two protagonists, a resolution of the two apparently starkly contrasting positions seemed to emerge. Nagel (1963) and Wong (1973) are among the most notable.

1.5.3 Nagel's critique

Nagel tries to find a compromise. He tends to provide support to Friedman more than to Samuelson.

Nagel argues that the goals of a theory are explanation *and* prediction. The theory simplifies and sacrifices descriptive realism to gain understanding. He considers the important feature to be that a theory gives a sufficiently good approximation for the purposes at hand.

Nagel sets out to show that Friedman's argument is sound although it lacks cogency. He says in his defence of Friedman: 'Sound conclusions are sometimes supported by erroneous arguments, and the error is compounded when a sound conclusion is declared to be mistaken on the grounds that the argument for it is mistaken' (Nagel, 1963: 211).

He refers to Friedman's reference to Galileo's law for freely falling bodies (i.e. 'if a body falls toward earth in a vacuum, its instantaneous acceleration is constant') where Friedman asks whether this law does in fact 'assume' that bodies actually fall through a vacuum. Friedman contends that since a vacuum does not exist, this shows that the result can be accepted and applied although the assumption is unrealistic. The term 'vacuum' he thinks can be omitted and the theory still gives good predictions.

Nagel thinks Friedman made an error by supposing that theoretical terms can, in general, be replaced by non-theoretical ones, without altering the meaning and function of the statements containing them. This, Nagel thinks is dubious.

Nagel examines Friedman's defence of unrealistic assumptions by reference to the 'maximization of returns' hypothesis. He says firms behave 'as if' they were seeking rationally to maximize their expected returns and had full knowledge of the data needed to succeed in this attempt. Friedman then claims that these admitted facts do not affect the validity of the hypothesis. It is important only that the facts are in good agreement with the various implications of the hypothesis and firms whose actions are markedly inconsistent with it do not survive for long.

Friedman's error

According to Nagel, most matters mentioned in Friedman's 'as if' formulation are irrelevant to the substantive content of the hypothesis. The hypothesis must not then be understood as either asserting or implying that firms conduct their affairs in order to achieve some objective. Thus, in this case, he contends that the hypothesis is a somewhat loosely expressed empirical generalization about the returns firms actually receive as the outcome of their overt behaviour, and it specifies no determinants in explanation of that behaviour.

Nagel contends that the hypothesis must be understood as dealing with Pure Cases requiring the use of theoretical terms which cannot be replaced by non-theoretical ones. Thus the facts Friedman freely admits but thinks are irrelevant may, in this case, be quite pertinent in assessing the merits of the hypothesis.

In essence, these axioms require the use of theoretical statements which may appear unrealistic but which cannot be replaced by non-theoretical statements. Thus these are not simply there for convenience but because they serve a special purpose needed for any theoretical formulation.

1.5.4 Wong's critique

Wong, writing on the matter, concludes that Samuelson's misinterpretation of Friedman's methodology has led to the failure of his critique. Wong criticizes Samuelson.

Wong's view may be summarized as: Logical equivalency (description) as required by Samuelson, denies a theory of any explained content while instrumentalism (Friedman) disregards the explanatory content of a theory. Theory must be explanatory and informative.

Friedman had focused on positive economics. The study 'what is' rather than 'what should be'. In positive economics the aim is to use generalizations in order to make correct predictions about consequent changes. Theory must therefore be evaluated by its predictive power and by testing the validity of the resulting hypothesis by comparison of its predictions with experience.

For Friedman, realism, as required by Samuelson, would render the theory useless, devoid of predictive power.

Wong criticizes Samuelson. He contends that Samuelson's misinterpretation of Friedman's methodology has led to the failure of his (Samuelson's) critique. Wong critiques Samuelson's theorem that says, if *C* is the complete or full set of consequences of the theory, *B*, then *C* is identical or logically equivalent to *B* and shares the same degree of realism with *B*.

Wong argues that it is not clear how completeness of *C* is shown. A theory is considered complete with respect to a set of statement if their set is logically deductible from the axiom set of the theory using the given rule of inference. Thus the complete set must be enumerated before showing whether the set is deductible from the axiom set. He argues further that, even if complete, it does not mean that the derived propositions or theorems are logically equivalent to the axiom set. He argues further still, that even if the set of axioms is logically equivalent to the set of consequences, Samuelson's position is still untenable.

According to Wong, the *explanans* (explanative statements) must logically entail the set of statements which describe what is to be explained (the *explanandum*). To be testable *explanans* must have testable consequences in addition to the *explanandum*. But a statement of logical equivalence has no express empirical content. The *explanans* (axiom set) is just a restatement of the *explanandum* (consequence set).

Assumption or predictions?

The methodological controversy is presented in some detail so that micro-economists may appreciate how economists have agonized over the way in which theory is presented and accepted. It is important to find a resolution and learn from the controversy.

What is significant here is to realize that both assumptions and predictions are important in theorizing. Both Friedman and Samuelson realize that assumptions are abstractions from reality, which means that they cannot fully describe reality in all of its facets. Friedman tends to call them unrealistic for this purpose. This may be an unfortunate term and, as Nagel points out, Friedman's argument for his sound conclusion on the importance of predictions may be discarded because of his weak arguments. Indeed, because of the weak arguments of Friedman in this and other matters (e.g. the theory of money), following Friedman's doctrines has sometimes been described as Friedmania. This, however, does not invalidate his emphasis on the need for a theory to have good predictive power.

It is clear that the assumptions cannot describe all of the reality but are abstractions from reality and must therefore represent that reality in some way. Take, for example, the series of numbers 2, 4, 8, 10. The mean of these numbers is the number 6. This number is not contained in the reality of the set of numbers given (2, 4, 8, 10), nevertheless, since the mean is considered to be a representative descriptive statistic, the number 6 can be considered as representative of that reality even though it is not contained in that reality. The fact that the number 6 is not in the reality does not invalidate it as descriptive of that reality.

The lesson from this is that a theory must explain and predict. In order for a theory to explain, there must be some acceptable logical connection between assumptions, body and conclusions. However, in the final analysis, the predictions must be on target, if a theory is to be accepted. Additional sources on the methodology of Economics include Blaug (1986) and Hausman (1989).

REVIEW QUESTIONS FOR CHAPTER 1

1 Explain:

(a) What is the difference between microeconomics and macroeconomics.
(b) Why mathematics may be useful in microeconomic theory.

2 With respect to the use of illustrations in microeconomics:

(a) Using a total product of labour curve, show how geometry is used to find the relevant average and marginal product curves.
(b) Show how horizontal summation may be done using two curves to make a total curve.
(c) Show vertical summation using a fixed and a variable cost curve to give the total cost.

3 Explain carefully the role of the Calculus of Variations as a tool in microeconomic theory.

4 Examine why and how the Lagrangian multiplier method is employed to assist with the problem of constrained optimization in microeconomic theory.

5 Discuss:

(a) Apriorism and empiricism in the methodology of microeconomics.
(b) Inductive vs. deductive reasoning.
(c) Normative vs. positive economics.
(d) Why economists differ.

6 With regard to the methodology of microeconomic theory discuss:

(a) The term 'scientific method' and comment on its relevance to microeconomic theory.
(b) Whether or to what extent microeconomics can be called a science.

7 With respect to the methodology of Microeconomic theory carefully examine the role of assumptions and predictions in determining the 'scientific validity' of a theory and attempt a resolution of the Friedman–Samuelson controversy.

RECOMMENDED READING FOR CHAPTER 1

Blaug, M. (1986) 'Economic Methodology in One Easy Lesson', in M. Blaug (ed.) (1986) *Economic History and the History of Economics*, New York: New York University Press, Ch. 14.
Friedman, M. (1958) 'The Methodology of Positive Economics', in M. Friedman (1958) *Essays in Positive Economics*, Chicago: University of Chicago Press: 3–43.
Hausman, D. M. (1989) 'Economic Methodology in a Nutshell', *Journal of Political Economy*, 3(2): 115–27.
Nagel, E. (1963) 'Assumptions in Economic Theory', *American Economic Review*, Papers and Proceedings, 53(2): 211–19.
Samuelson, P. A. (1963) 'Problems of Methodology – Discussion', *American Economic Review*, Papers and Proceedings, 54: 232–6.
Wong, S. (1973) 'The F-Twist and the Methodology of Paul Samuelson', *American Economic Review*, 63(3): 312–25.

2 Theory of the Consumer

Cardinal Utility Theory; Ordinal Utility Theory and Revealed Preference Theory; Utility and the Demand Function; The Demand Curve and The Law of Demand; The Engel Curve.

The study of the economic behaviour of the individual consumer is a prequel to the study of demand for goods and services in the product (commodities) market. This is utility theory which goes back to first principles. The theories provide the foundation for the law of demand, indicating how and why consumers respond in particular ways to the structure of incentives and various other factors (prices, income, tastes) in the market. An understanding of consumer behaviour and how consumers optimize within budget constraints is useful, particularly to sellers in their quest for market advantage and greater competitiveness.

2.1 THE INDIVIDUAL CONSUMER AND UTILITY MAXIMIZATION

Consumer theory has its genesis in the theory of utility maximization. The concept of utility or satisfaction is central to the study of the consumer behaviour in the market. This refers to the satisfaction individuals derive from the consumption of goods and services.

The standard theory of the consumer follows the traditional deductive approach using the scientific method of inquiry. This approach proceeds in a structured way from assumptions, through the body of the theory to its testable conclusions. The traditional analysis of the consumer is done under certainty. The consumer is always assumed to be rational and to optimize with respect to the given values for income and market price. Consumers are assumed to have full knowledge of the available commodities and their prices in the market, and to know their income limit. Consumers plan to spend their income to attain the highest possible satisfaction (utility) within these parameters.

In general, there are considered to be two major approaches to the theory of utility maximization: The Cardinal theory and the Ordinal theory. A third approach, the Revealed Preference theory, is usually viewed as an addendum or upgrade to the

Ordinal theory but may be considered a theory in its own right. The Ordinal theory is buoyed by the Revealed Preference theory.

The study of the consumer traces the utility theories from the Classical utility theory, through the Ordinal utility theory to the modification brought to the Ordinal utility theory by the Revealed Preference theory.

As the study proceeds, it may be observed that all three approaches lead to the same conclusion or testable hypothesis: that, normally, as the price of a good falls, the quantity demanded increases. This becomes known as the Law of Demand and is applied throughout economics and Business/Management Studies. It may also be observed that the revisions of utility theory over time are due to concerns with the assumptions of the theory, as discussed under the methodology of microeconomic theory (see Chapter 1), even though the predictions have already been found acceptable.

The study of utility maximization begins with the Cardinal utility theory.

2.2 THE CARDINAL UTILITY THEORY

The Cardinal utility theory is considered to be the oldest version of utility theory. Central to the Cardinal theory is the concept of measurable utility. The assumption is that utility or satisfaction is measurable on a cardinal scale (i.e. a scale with zero as the origin). It was believed that this measurement could be done in money, or in the older vintages, in subjective units called Utils. The concept of measurable utility is attributed mainly to the nineteenth-century economists, including Gossen (1854), Jevons (1871) and Walras (1874). Another economist, Marshall (1890), is often included with this group because of his assumption of additive and independent utilities which would imply measurability of utility.

2.2.1 Assumptions of the Cardinal utility theory

The principal assumptions of the Cardinal theory may be set out as follows:

- The consumer is rational. This implies that the consumer aims at the maximization of utility given income and prices.
- Utility is measured by the monetary units the consumer is willing to pay for another unit of a commodity.
- The marginal utility of money is constant. This assumption is necessary if money is to be used as a measuring rod, in order to prevent money from becoming an 'elastic' ruler. It means that a unit of money (e.g. one dollar) has the same utility to the holder no matter how much money the holder possesses.
- There is diminishing marginal utility for a commodity.
- The total utility of a basket of goods depends on the quantities of the individual commodities. For a basket comprising two goods x and y, the total utility (U) for the consumer is the sum of the utilities gained from the two goods. This may be expressed as:

$$U = U_x + U_y$$

2.2.2 Consumer equilibrium under the Cardinal theory

Consider a single commodity (x), the price of which is given. The consumer seeks to maximize the utility from consuming the commodity.

The maximation of utility – consumer equilibrium

According to the Cardinal theory, the equilibrium of the consumer is derived as set out below.

Utility for the individual consumer depends on the quantity consumed of commodity x. Thus the utility function for the consumer is expressed as:

$$U = fQ_x$$

On buying Q_x the consumer has an expenditure on good x (E_x) such that:

$$E_x = Q_x\overline{P}_x$$

The consumer's objective is to maximize the difference between utility received and the expenditure made on the good. This objective function may be expressed as:

$$\text{Max: } U - \overline{P}_x Q_x$$

The calculus of variations is used in order to precisely identify an optimum position. For this, the partial derivative of the objective function with respect to Q_x must be set equal to zero. This may be expressed as:

$$\frac{\partial U}{\partial Q_x} - \frac{\partial(\overline{P}_x Q_x)}{\partial Q_x} = 0$$

Or:

$$\frac{\partial U}{\partial Q_x} - \overline{P}_x = 0$$

Rearranging, this gives:

$$\frac{\partial U}{\partial Q_x} = \overline{P}_x$$

Since:

$$\frac{\partial U}{\partial Q_x} = MU_x$$

this gives:

$$MU_x = \overline{P}_x$$

Hence, the consumer achieves equilibrium (maximum satisfaction) when the incremental utility (utility from the last unit) derived from a commodity is just equal to the given price of that commodity.

The corollary is that, where the incremental utility is greater than the price the rational consumer buys more units of the commodity as the satisfaction from that extra unit of the commodity is greater than the cost of the unit. Correspondingly, when the satisfaction derived from that extra unit of the commodity is less than the price for that unit, the consumer would not be willing to pay for that unit. This works well as long as it is considered that utility can be measured in money units (i.e. the money paid for a unit of the commodity).

Multiple commodities

The equilibrium condition for good x can be done similarly for any other good. Hence for good y, the equilibrium condition would be:

$$MU_y = \overline{P}_y$$

Since the marginal utility of a good is equal to the price of the good, then:

$$\frac{MU_x}{\overline{P}_x} = 1 \quad and \quad \frac{MU_y}{\overline{P}_y} = 1$$

Hence:

$$\frac{MU_x}{\overline{P}_x} = \frac{MU_y}{\overline{P}_y}$$

Extending to any number (N) of goods, the equilibrium condition requires the equality of the ratios of the marginal utilities of the individual commodities to their price. This is expressed as:

$$\frac{MU_x}{\overline{P}_x} = \frac{MU_y}{\overline{P}_y} = \cdots = \frac{MU_N}{\overline{P}_N} = MU \ of \ money$$

Consequently, for any two goods, say, x and y, the equilibrium position can also be written as:

$$\frac{MU_x}{MU_y} = \frac{\overline{P}_x}{\overline{P}_y}$$

The implication is that the utility derived from spending an additional unit of money must be the same for all commodities or customers can increase welfare by spending more on some and less on others until equilibrium is achieved.

2.2.3 Derivation of the demand curve – Cardinal theory

Consider the total utility curve of the consumer as depicted in Figure 2.1. This is based on the axiom of diminishing marginal utility. As more of good x is consumed, the total utility derived from x increases but at a decreasing rate. This is because the additional utility from every extra unit is less than that from the previous unit. Eventually, there is an additional unit consumed that adds nothing (zero) to the consumer's total utility. This occurs at the quantity Q_T. This is the point of satiation. After this, the addition to the total utility from an extra unit becomes negative (<0). As a result, the total revenue curve begins to decline.

The marginal utility of good x (MU_X) is the slope of the total utility function:

$$U_X = f(Q_X)$$

Hence, if tangents are drawn to the total utility curve, these tangents would continue to decrease in slope (i.e. get flatter) until the top of the total utility curve (T) is reached, when the tangent would be horizontal, having a slope of zero. This occurs at the quantity Q_T of commodity x. Beyond this point, the slope of the tangents would become negative.

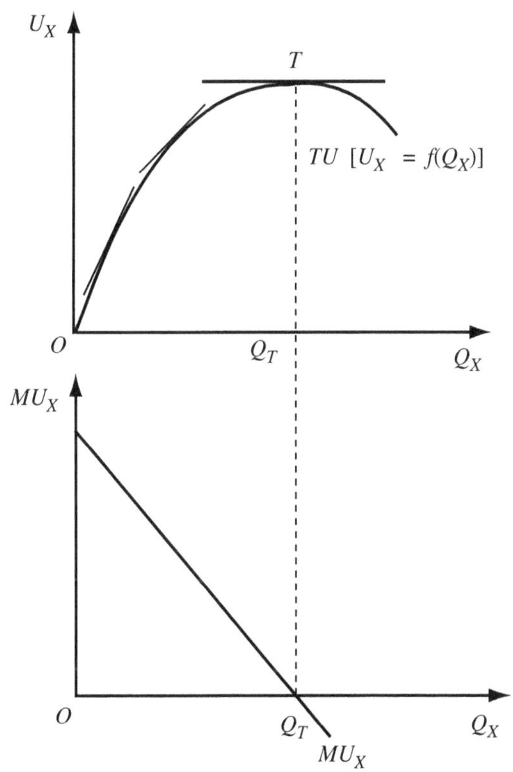

Figure 2.1
The total utility curve and its related marginal utility curve

Consequently, in Figure 2.1, the relevant marginal utility (MU) curve, as measured by the slope of the total utility curve of good x, keeps declining until it reaches zero at the quantity Q_T and then becomes negative.

The demand curve

The equilibrium condition was previously derived as:

$$MU_x = P_x$$

It can be seen that, along the marginal utility of x curve, for every level of marginal utility, there is a corresponding equilibrium price of good x. Hence:

$$MU_{x1} = P_{x1}$$
$$MU_{x2} = P_{x2}$$
$$\vdots$$
$$MU_{xN} = P_{xN}$$

As a result of this corresponding relationship between the marginal utility of good x and its price, it means that the marginal utility can be replaced by price and so the marginal utility curve can be replaced by a curve relating price to the quantity of commodity x. This curve (AB) in Figure 2.2 is the demand curve. It is shown to be derived directly from the marginal utility curve (upper diagram). For each quantity, the relevant price is that at which $MU = P$. This price-quantity combination represents a point on the individual's demand curve.

It should be recognized that, since negative prices are not meaningful in economics, the demand curve (AB) does not fall below zero price. Consequently, the demand curve represents only the positive portion of the commodity's marginal utility curve.

2.2.4 Critique of the Cardinal theory

The Cardinal theory led to a conclusion that generated the standard demand curve that is known to give good predictions with the law of demand. Nevertheless, the theory was not considered satisfactory particularly because of some of its assumptions. Three basic weaknesses of the Cardinal theory were identified:

1 The assumption of cardinal measurement of utility was deemed unsatisfactory. The absolute measurement of satisfaction in an objective way, either in Utils or in money, was considered to be unacceptable.
2 The assumption of constant marginal utility of money was judged to be unrealistic. The view was held that, as income increases, the marginal utility of money (utility of one dollar) falls.
3 The assumption of diminishing marginal utility for a good was challenged. It could not be accepted that the 'axiom' was indeed a basic truth. It could only be considered

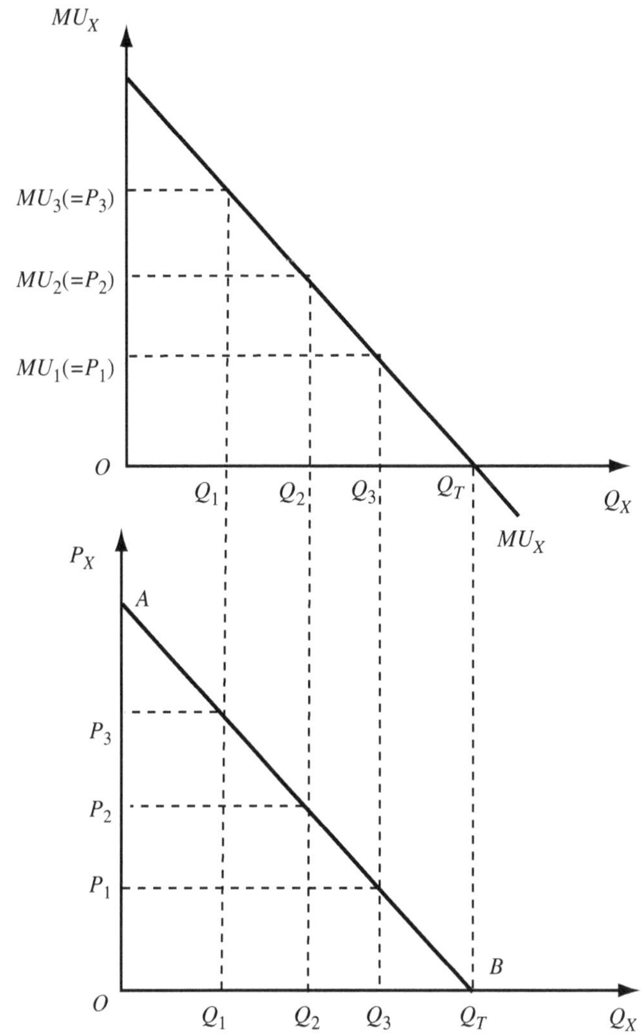

Figure 2.2
Derivation of the demand curve under the Cardinal theory

a psychological law, established by introspection, which must be taken for granted.

2.3 THE ORDINAL UTILITY THEORY (INDIFFERENCE CURVES)

The Ordinal utility theory of the consumer was considered to represent an advance over the Cardinal theory as it sought to avoid the major weakness identified above. In doing so, the Ordinal theory introduced new tools of consumer analysis, in particular, the indifference curve and the budget line, that have held a central and lasting place in the tool bag of economic analysis.

2.3.1 Assumptions of the Ordinal utility theory

The major assumptions of the Ordinal utility theory are:

- The consumer is rational. This signifies that the consumer seeks to maximize utility (satisfaction) from consuming commodities, within the parameters of given income and the prices of the commodities.
- Utility is ordinal. This indicates that the consumer can rank preferences only. This ranking does not require cardinality as in the cardinal theory. An ordinal ranking says only that a higher number means a greater preference but does not say that there is absolute measurement (e.g. it does not say that the rank of 4 means twice the utility as a rank of 2 – just that 4 is preferred to 2). This obviates the need for measurement of utility in money (or Utils).
- There is consistency and transitivity of choice. This may be expressed as:

$$\text{If } A > B \text{ then } B < A \text{ (consistency)}$$

$$\text{If } A > B \text{ and } B > C, \text{ then } C < A \text{ (transitivity)}$$

- There is a diminishing marginal rate of substitution between commodities. This replaces the axiom of diminishing marginal utility in the Cardinal theory which has been criticized for being largely unfounded. The diminishing marginal rate of substitution (implied in the shape of the indifference curve), means that, as the consumer has increasingly more of one of the commodities (say, commodity x), the consumer is less and less willing to give up the other commodity (say, commodity y), to get more of that first commodity (commodity x). This requires preferences for goods to change only relative to each other rather than absolutely.
- Total utility depends on quantities of the commodities consumed. This may be expressed, for N commodities, as:

$$U = f(Q_1, Q_2, Q_3, \ldots, Q_N)$$

Once the need to measure utility is obviated by the assumption of ordinality (ranking only) of choices, two of the criticisms levelled against the Cardinal theory were removed: the need to use money as a measuring rod for utility and the need to assume that there is a constant marginal utility of money. The other criticism of the Cardinal theory, the assumption of diminishing marginal utility of goods, was removed by the Ordinal theory's assumption of a diminishing marginal rate of substitution between any two goods.

2.3.2 Consumer equilibrium under the Ordinal theory

The maximization of utility or satisfaction by the consumer, given prices and the consumer's income (budget), is derived under the Ordinal theory with the use of several analytical tools. These include the indifference curves, the budget line and the mathematical technique of the Lagrangian multiplier method for constrained optimization.

2.3.2.1 INDIFFERENCE CURVES

Indifference curves are consistent with the assumption of a ranking of consumer preferences (rather than measurement). Their shape implies the diminishing marginal rate of substitution that replaces the disputed diminishing marginal utility in the Cardinal theory. The major features of these curves are as follows:

- The curve is negatively sloped.
- The points along the curve represent the same level of utility from different combination of the two commodities.
- The further the curve is from the origin, the higher the level of utility (satisfaction).
- The curve is convex to the origin, implying diminishing marginal rate of substitution of the commodities.
- The slope of indifference curve, measured by the tangent to a point on the curve, is called the marginal rate of substitution and is expressed as:

$$-\frac{\mathrm{d}Q_y}{\mathrm{d}Q_x} = MRS_{x,y}$$

It may be noted that the concept of marginal rate of substitution (*MRS*) is intended to replace the concept of marginal utilities. However, as will become clearer later, the marginal rate of substitution is simply the ratio of the marginal utilities of commodities.

Derivation of the indifference curve – finding the slope

Figure 2.3 illustrates the indifference curve and its properties. The curve is shown sloping downwards (i.e. negatively sloped) and with a reducing slope as it falls (i.e. it flattens out). The quantity of good y being given up (Δy) to get an extra unit of good x (Δx) is shown to fall as the consumer has more of good x.

To find the slope of the indifference curve first consider the utility function:

$$U = f(Q_x, Q_y)$$

The indifference curve is the locus of points where utility (satisfaction) is constant, that is where there is zero difference in utility. Hence, it is necessary to find the total differential of the utility function and set it equal to zero.

Using the Calculus of Variations, the total differential of the utility function (U) may be expressed as:

$$\mathrm{d}U = \frac{\partial U}{\partial Q_x}\,\mathrm{d}Q_x + \frac{\partial U}{\partial Q_y}\,\mathrm{d}Q_y$$

This total differential is set equal to zero to represent points along the indifference curve and is set out as:

$$\mathrm{d}U = \frac{\partial U}{\partial Q_x}\,\mathrm{d}Q_x + \frac{\partial U}{\partial Q_y}\,\mathrm{d}Q_y = 0$$

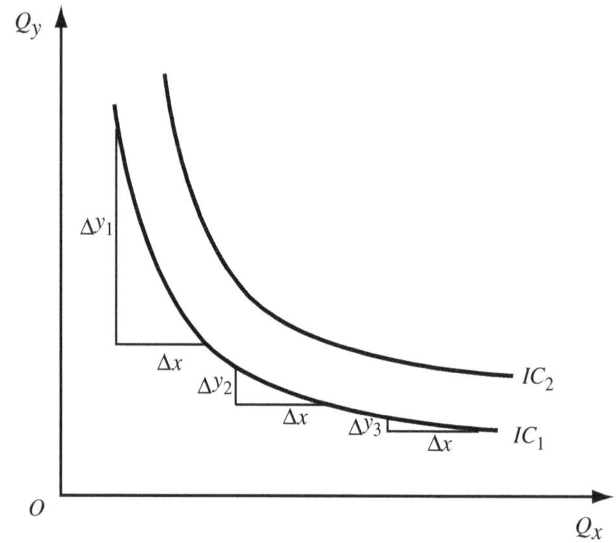

Figure 2.3
The indifference curve and the axiom of diminishing marginal rate of substitution

Given that the change in utility as a result of a change in the quantity of a good is called the marginal utility (MU) of the good, the following may be noted:

$$\frac{\partial U}{\partial Q_x} = MU_x \quad and \quad \frac{\partial U}{\partial Q_y} = MU_y$$

Consequently, the total differential of the utility function may be written as:

$$\mathrm{d}U = MU_x\, \mathrm{d}Q_x + MU_y\, \mathrm{d}Q_y = 0$$

This implies that:

$$MU_x\, \mathrm{d}Q_x = -MU_y\, \mathrm{d}Q_y$$

Cross multiplying gives:

$$\frac{MU_x}{MU_y} = -\frac{\mathrm{d}Q_y}{\mathrm{d}Q_x}$$

This says that the slope of the indifference curve is the marginal rate of substitution of one good for the other. This is so since the slope of the indifference curve is expressed as:

$$-\frac{\mathrm{d}Q_y}{\mathrm{d}Q_x}$$

Moreover, the ratio of marginal utilities of the goods is called the marginal rate of substitution (*MRS*) and may be expressed as:

$$\frac{MU_x}{MU_y} = -\frac{\mathrm{d}Q_y}{\mathrm{d}Q_x} = MRS_{x,y}$$

It is useful to note that, at any point along an indifference curve the following relationship holds:

$$MRS_{x,y} = MRS_{y,x}$$

It may also be noted that the marginal rate of substitution (*MRS*) included in the Ordinal theory is simply the ratio of the marginal utilities of the two goods.

Diminishing marginal rate of substitution

An integral assumption of the Ordinal theory is that there is a diminishing marginal rate of substitution between any two goods. This means, for example, that the number of units of commodity y a consumer is willing to give up in order to get an additional unit of commodity x decreases as the amount of commodity x the consumer has increases relative to the amount of commodity y. Hence the indifference curve represents a decreasing marginal rate of substitution.

Figure 2.3 shows that, initially the consumer gives up Δy_1 to get the extra unit (Δx) of good x. However, as the consumer has more of good x and less of good y, the consumer is only willing to give up the smaller quantity (Δy_2) of good y to get another similar extra unit (Δx) of good x. Further, as the consumer has even more of good x and less of good y, the amount of good y the consumer is willing to give up to get a similar additional unit of good x diminishes further to the quantity Δy_3.

This is responsible for the indifference curve, not only being negatively sloped, but being convex to the origin. The curve decreases at a decreasing rate (i.e. it flattens out as it falls).

Figure 2.3 also shows that there is a series of such curves, the further from the origin, the higher the utility the curve represents. Thus IC_2 represents a higher utility for the consumer than IC_1.

2.3.2.2 THE BUDGET CONSTRAINT

The consumer has a limited income. This limit is used to construct the budget line as another analytical tool in the study of consumer behaviour. The total budget (Y) is the sum of the total funds that can be expended on all the commodities. For N commodities, this would be:

$$(P_1Q_1 + P_2Q_2 + P_3Q_3 + \cdots + P_NQ_N)$$

In considering the two commodity case (goods x and y), the budget equation may be expressed as:

$$Y = P_xQ_x + P_yQ_y$$

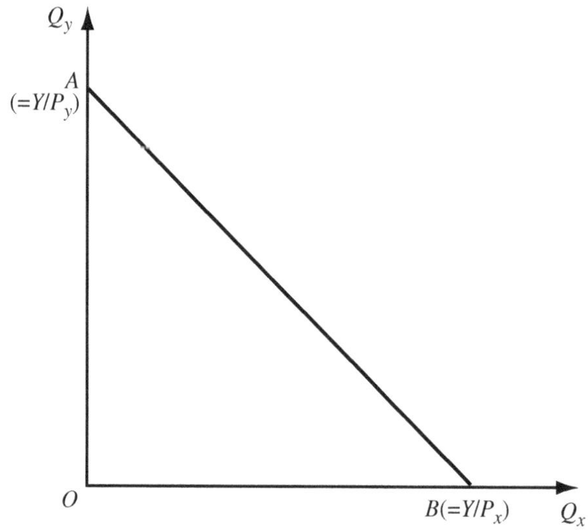

Figure 2.4
The consumer's budget constraint

This budget line is illustrated in Figure 2.4. As shown in the diagram, the consumer's budget is such that if the whole budget is spent on good x, then OB of good x can be purchased. If the whole budget is spent on good y, then OA of good y can be purchased. Alternatively, the consumer can purchase any combination of goods x and y given by the budget line (AB).

Using the budget equation and the illustration in Figure 2.4, if all the consumer's budget is all spent on good y ($Q_x = 0$), the amount of good y that can be purchased is found as follows:

$$Y = P_x Q_x + P_y Q_y$$

If:

$$Q_x = 0$$

then:

$$Y = P_y Q_y$$

Therefore:

$$Q_y = \frac{Y}{P_y}$$

Hence, in Figure 2.4, the distance OA which represents the quantity of good y is:

$$OA = \frac{Y}{P_y}$$

Similarly, for good x, if none of good y is purchased, then:

$$Q_y = 0$$

Hence:

$$Y = P_x Q_x$$

and:

$$Q_x = \frac{Y}{P_x}$$

Consequently, the distance OB is:

$$OB = \frac{Y}{P_x}$$

Slope of the budget line

The slope of the budget line is useful for finding the equilibrium of the consumer. In this case, the slope of the line AB in Figure 2.4 may be identified as:

$$-\frac{\mathrm{d}Q_y}{\mathrm{d}Q_x} = \frac{OA}{OB}$$

Hence, the slope of the budget line is:

$$\frac{OA}{OB} = \frac{Y/P_y}{Y/P_x} = \frac{P_x}{P_y}$$

This is the ratio of the price of good x to the price of good y.

Alternatively, the slope of the budget line could be found directly by identifying the slope of the budget equation as follows.

Take the budget equation:

$$Y = P_x Q_x + P_y Q_y$$

Make good y (Q_y) the subject of the equation by rearranging the budget equation and dividing throughout by the price of y as follows:

$$P_y Q_y = Y - P_x Q_x$$

$$Q_y = \frac{Y}{P_y} - \frac{P_x}{P_y} Q_x$$

This gives the relationship between the quantity of good y and the quantity of good x as shown in Figure 2.4. From this relationship, it may be observed that the intercept of the budget line is:

$$\frac{Y}{P_y}$$

and the slope of the budget line is:

$$\frac{P_x}{P_y}$$

2.3.2.3 EQUILIBRIUM WITH CONSTRAINED OPTIMIZATION

Using the indifference curve and the budget line as tools of analysis, the equilibrium of the consumer means reaching the highest utility given the available budget. Diagrammatically, this can be represented as a fixed budget line and a set of indifference curves for which the consumer seeks to reach the highest utility without exceeding the budget constraint. This is illustrated in Figure 2.5.

Indifference curve IC_1 in Figure 2.5 cuts the consumer's budget line at the point R. However, the utility maximizing consumer can do better by moving to a higher indifference curve such as IC_2. This is the highest utility the consumer can obtain

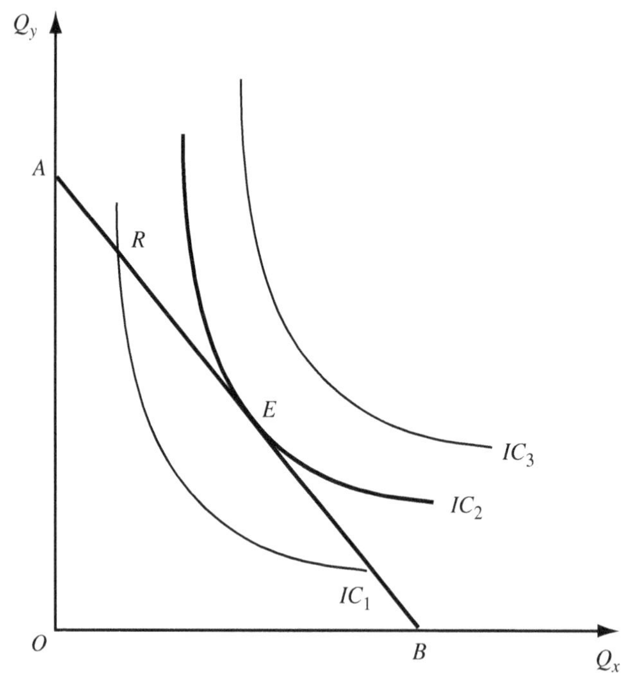

Figure 2.5
Consumer equilibrium

given the consumer's budget being the budget line *AB*. The highest indifference curve available to the consumer is the one that is just tangent to the budget line. The consumer is therefore in equilibrium at the point *E*. The consumer is indifferent between point *E* and any other point on IC_2, but every other point on IC_2 is unavailable to the consumer because it is beyond the consumer's budget. The consumer would prefer to be on IC_3 but this is unattainable.

Knowing from above that the slope of the indifference curve is:

$$\frac{MU_x}{MU_y}$$

and that the slope of the budget line is:

$$\frac{P_x}{P_y}$$

the equilibrium of the consumer can be stated as:

$$\frac{MU_x}{MU_y} = \frac{P_x}{P_y}$$

It may also be restated as:

$$\frac{MU_x}{P_x} = \frac{MU_y}{P_y}$$

In other words, the consumer will get the most satisfaction from spending the given budget amount by ensuring that the satisfaction from the last unit purchased of each of the two goods is in exact proportion to the prices of the two goods. Or, that the ratio of the satisfaction from the last unit purchased of a good to its price is the same for both (all) goods.

The corollary to this is that, if the last unit purchased of one good (say, good y) gives relatively more utility to its price than the other good (say, good x), that is:

$$\frac{MU_x}{P_x} < \frac{MU_y}{P_y}$$

the rational consumer would seek to purchase more of good y and less of good x. In doing so, by the axiom of diminishing marginal utility, the marginal (incremental) utility of good y would decrease relative to that of good x. It is only when the relative incremental utilities come into equilibrium with the relative prices of the goods that there would be no further incentive to increase consumption of good y relative to good x. This holds for any number of goods. Hence for N goods, the equilibrium condition could be written as:

$$\frac{MU_1}{P_1} = \frac{MU_2}{P_2} = \cdots = \frac{MU_N}{P_N}$$

The Lagrangian multiplier method for constrained optimization

An alternative and more precise method of identifying the consumer's equilibrium is to derive it directly using the Lagrangian multiplier method for constrained optimization. For the simplified two-commodity case, this may be done as follows.

Set up the objective function (maximize utility):

$$\text{Max: } U = f(Q_x,\ Q_y)$$

Subject to constraint function (income constraint):

$$Y = Q_x P_x + Q_y P_y$$

Set the constraint equal to zero:

$$Y - Q_x P_x + Q_y P_y = 0$$

Multiply the constraint by the Lagrangian Multiplier (λ):

$$\lambda(Y - Q_x P_x - Q_y P_y)$$

Form the composite function (ϕ) by adding the Lagrangian to the objective function:

$$\phi = U + \lambda(Y - P_x Q_x - P_y Q_y)$$

To find the conditions for a maximization of utility subject to the income constraint, the optimization procedure is performed on the composite function. The optimization of the composite function is equivalent to the optimization of the objective function subject to the constraint. The optimization procedure requires finding the first- and second-order conditions for a maximum (or minimum).

First-order condition

The first-order condition is found by taking the partial first derivatives of the composite function and setting each of them equal to zero.

Using the composite function:

$$\phi = U + \lambda(Y - P_x Q_x - P_y Q_y)$$

Differentiate partially, with respect to Q_x, Q_y, λ and set equal to zero.

Differentiating partially, with respect to Q_x, gives:

$$\frac{\partial U}{\partial Q_x} - \lambda P_x = 0 \qquad (1)$$

Differentiating partially, with respect to Q_y, gives:

$$\frac{\partial U}{\partial Q_Y} - \lambda P_Y = 0 \qquad (2)$$

Differentiating partially, with respect to λ, gives:

$$Y - Q_x P_x - Q_y P_y = 0 \qquad (3)$$

From (1) above:

$$\frac{\partial U}{\partial Q_x} = \lambda P_x$$

From (2) above:

$$\frac{\partial U}{\partial Q_Y} = \lambda P_Y$$

Equation (3) above verifies the effect of a one-unit change in the constraint function on the objective function.

Given that:

$$\frac{\partial U}{\partial Q_x} = MU_x \quad and \quad \frac{\partial U}{\partial Q_y} = MU_y$$

the following results are implied by (1) and (2) above:

$$MU_x = \lambda P_x$$

and:

$$MU_y = \lambda P_y$$

Consequently, from (1) and (2) above, the first-order condition for the equilibrium of the consumer under the Ordinal theory can be written as:

$$\frac{MU_x}{P_x} = \lambda \quad and \quad \frac{MU_y}{P_y} = \lambda$$

But, since the ratio of the marginal utility of each commodity to its price is equal to λ, they are both equal to each other. Hence, the following result is implied:

$$\frac{MU_x}{P_x} = \frac{MU_y}{P_y}$$

This condition may also be re-written as:

$$\frac{MU_x}{MU_y} = \frac{P_x}{P_y}$$

This says that the ratio of the marginal utilities of the two goods (x and y) must be equal to the ratio of their prices. Recall that the ratio of the marginal utilities (the marginal rate of substitution) of the two goods is the slope of the indifference curve and the ratio of the prices of the two goods is the slope of the budget line (*AB* in Figure 2.5). Thus, equilibrium requires equality of the slopes of the indifference curve and the (fixed) budget line and may be expressed as:

$$\frac{MU_x}{MU_y} = \frac{P_x}{P_y} = MRS_{x,y}$$

This takes place at the point E in Figure 2.5.

Although cardinality of utility is not required, the $MRS_{x,y}$ requires knowledge of the ratio of the marginal utilities. Hence, the concept of marginal utility is contained in the shape of the curve, although no cardinal measurement is required. All that is needed is a diminishing marginal rate of substitution which does not require diminishing marginal utilities of the individual commodities in the utility function. This is considered an improvement over the Cardinal theory.

It may be noted, however, that the equilibrium condition under the Ordinal theory is the same as under the Cardinal theory for multiple goods. For two goods, both theories give the condition:

$$\frac{MU_x}{MU_y} = \frac{P_x}{P_y}$$

The difference, however, is that in the Cardinal, the numerators on both sides of the equation are equal to each other and the denominators on each side are equal to each other giving:

$$MU_x = P_x \quad and \quad MU_y = P_y$$

In the Ordinal, only the ratios are equal. Marginal utility and price are not equal and are separated by the factor λ such that:

$$MU_x = \lambda P_x \quad and \quad MU_y = \lambda P_y$$

Hence the Cardinal result implies the Ordinal but the Ordinal does not imply the Cardinal. The separation of this equality between marginal utility of price also contributes to the view that the Ordinal is superior to the Cardinal theory.

The second-order condition

The second-order condition for a maximum requires that the second derivative of the composite function (ϕ) must be negative. Formally, the solution requires the construction of the Hessian matrix of partial second derivatives. The principal minors of the bordered Hessian determinant must alternate in sign.

However, there is a simpler way to ensure that the second-order condition is fulfilled in relation to the consumer. The assumption of diminishing marginal rate of substitution ensures that this second-order or sufficient condition for a maximum is fulfilled. The curve is not only negatively sloped but decreases at a decreasing rate (slope of the slope is negative). The second-order condition for a maximum is therefore satisfied by the convexity of the indifference curve.

2.3.3 Derivation of the demand curve – Ordinal theory

The Ordinal theory has a different way and a new set of tools for deriving the demand curve than under the Cardinal theory. Although the testable conclusion is the same demand law, the path to this conclusion is substantially different. The indifference curves and budget line tools are used to derive the demand curve through the construction of the Price Consumption Curve (*PCC*) and the use of income and substitution effects.

2.3.3.1 INCOME AND SUBSTITUTION EFFECTS: PRICE CONSUMPTION CURVE

The Price Consumption Curve is illustrated in Figure 2.6. Consider a budget line *AB* with a consumer equilibrium point at *R*. Consider, then, that the price of good *x* falls while the price of good *y* and all other influences on the demand for good *x* remain constant. This allows an examination of how the quantity demanded of good *x* changes as the price of good *x* changes *ceteris paribus*.

The compensating variation

The fall in the price of good *x* means that, with the same income, more of good *x* can be bought. This is shown by a pivoting of the budget line from *B* to *B′* along the *x*-axis.

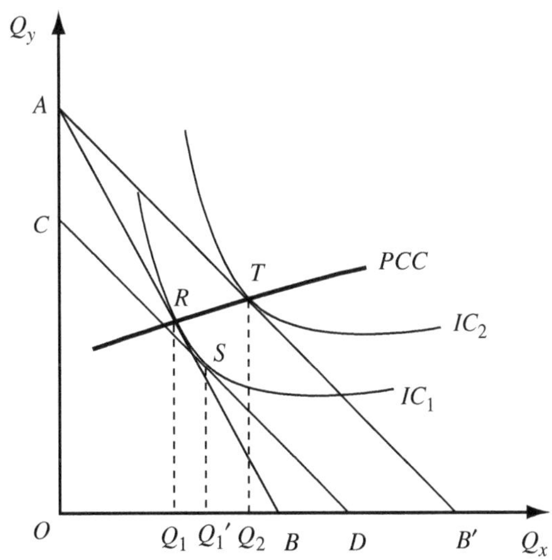

Figure 2.6
Income and substitution effects and the price consumption curve (*PCC*)

The budget line remains anchored at the point A on the y-axis as the price of good y has not changed.

The fall in the price of good x has a similar effect to that of giving the consumer more income. The new budget line CD is the representative price ratio at the income level which would exist if the income gain from the fall in price of x were completely taxed away and the consumer were held to the same utility level (indifference curve) as before the fall in the price of good x. It represents the utility from the initial level of income before the price fall and is referred to as the ***Compensating Variation***.

Substitution and income effect

As a result of the fall in the price of good x, two effects are distinguished. One is the substitution effect and the other is the income effect.

The substitution effect is reflected in the movement from point R to S. It is the movement along the original indifference curve due to the relative change (fall) in the price of the good (x) when the effect of the windfall (income) benefit due to the fall in the price of good x is not taken into consideration. According to the Slutsky theorem, the substitution effect of a price change is always negative. This indicates that a fall in price of a good always causes an increase in consumption of the good along the same indifference curve. Similarly, an increase in the price leads to a fall in consumption along the same indifference curve (IC_1).

In Figure 2.6, the substitution effect of the fall in the price of good x leads to an increase in the consumption of good x from Q_1 to Q_1'.

The income effect, on the other hand, is reflected in the movement from S to T in Figure 2.6. It takes into consideration the windfall gain in income to the consumer from the fall in the price of good x. This effect shows a movement from a lower indifference curve IC_1 to a higher indifference curve IC_2. For a normal good, the income effect is positive. This signifies that the increase in income leads to an increase in the consumption of the good that has caused the effective increase.

The positive income effect enhances the negative price effect since they both move the quantity of good x consumed in the same direction. In Figure 2.6, the income effect moves consumption of good x from Q_1' to Q_2. The total effect of the fall in the price of good x is to move the consumer equilibrium from point R to point T, thereby moving quantity demanded of good x from Q_1 to Q_2.

It may be noted that if good x were an inferior good, the income effect would take away from, rather than add to, the substitution effect. As a result, the new Q_2 would lie somewhere between Q_1 and Q_1'. Further, if good x were a Giffen good, the income effect would completely overwhelm the substitution effect and the demand for good x after the fall in its price would be less than before (i.e. Q_2 would be less than Q_1).

The Price Consumption Curve (PCC)

The total or overall effect of the change in the price of good x is the movement from point R to point T and goes from one final equilibrium position to another. The Price Consumption Curve (PCC) is the locus of points of final consumer equilibrium as the price of a commodity changes. R and T are therefore points on the PCC for good x.

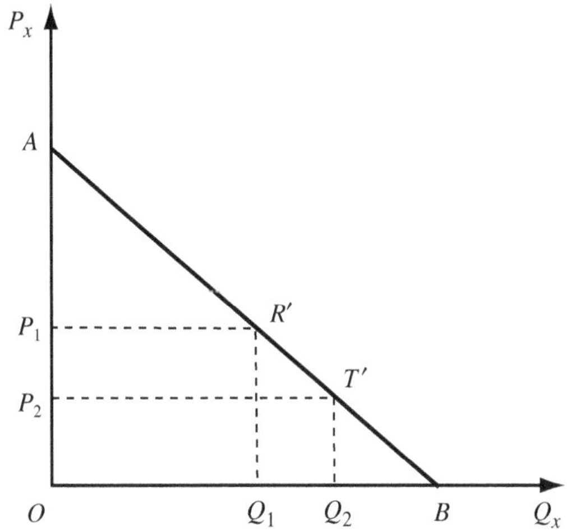

Figure 2.7
Derivation of the demand curve under the Ordinal theory

Continuing to lower the price of good x would lead to new final equilibrium points with each new fall in the price of the good. Tracing through these equilibrium points would give the *PCC* for good x.

2.3.3.2 DERIVATION OF THE DEMAND CURVE

As the price of commodity x falls, causing the budget line to pivot from AB to AB', the quantity of commodity x consumed rises from Q_1 to Q_2 after the income and substitution effects are worked out. This information can be transposed to a new diagram with price and quantity of good x on the y-axis and x-axis respectively. This is illustrated in Figure 2.7.

Consider P_1 as the initial price of commodity x given relatively by the slope of the budget line AB. The consumer demands quantity Q_1 of commodity x. As the price of commodity x falls to that given by the slope of the pivoted budget line AB' the quantity the consumer demands of commodity x increases to Q_2. This new price may be labelled P_2. These price-quantity combinations can be plotted in the product-demand space as shown in Figure 2.7. The locus of such points derived from the *PCC* gives the demand curve.

The points R' and T' on the demand curve reflect the points R and T on the *PCC*. This gives the testable conclusion that as the price of a commodity falls, the quantity demanded of that commodity increases ***ceteris paribus*** (except for a Giffen good). More generally, it says that the quantity demand of a good varies inversely with changes in the price of the good. When tested this establishes the ***Law of Demand*** and gives a downward sloping demand curve.

2.3.4 Income changes – the Engel curve

The tools of indifference curves and budget lines may also be used to examine the effect on the quantity demanded of changes in income *ceteris paribus*. In this case prices are

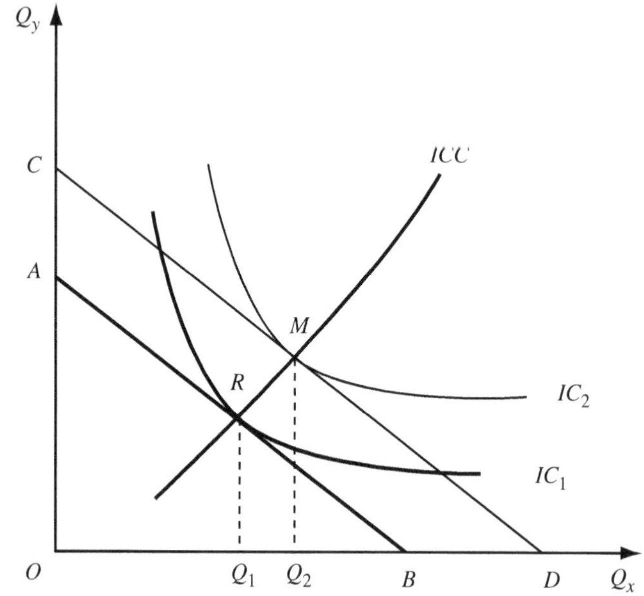

Figure 2.8
The income-consumption curve

held constant and income alone is allowed to vary. From this is derived the Income Consumption Curve (*ICC*) from which the Engel curve is derived.

2.3.4.1 THE INCOME CONSUMPTION CURVE (*ICC*)

Figure 2.8 illustrates the Income Consumption Curve (*ICC*). The ratio of prices of goods x and y are held constant as the effect of changes in income on the quantity demanded is examined. The original budget line is *AB* and the consumer is initially in equilibrium at point *R* on indifference curve IC_1.

Consider that there is an increase in real income that shifts the budget line *AB* outwards to the new budget line *CD*. This is a parallel outward shift of the budget line. The consumer can now move to a higher indifference curve such as IC_2 and have a new equilibrium point *M*. The locus of shifting equilibrium points as the budget line shifts outwards gives the Income Consumption Curve (*ICC*). Hence *R* and *M* are two points on the *ICC*.

At the initial level of income given by the budget line *AB*, the consumer demands quantity Q_1 of good x. When income increases to give the consumer the new budget line *CD*, the consumer's demand for good x increases to Q_2.

This positive relationship between income and the quantity demanded of a commodity is standard for a normal good. For an inferior good, the increase in real income leads to a reduction in the demand of the good while a fall in real income leads to an increase in the demand for the good. Giffen goods, as described earlier, are a more extreme form of inferior goods sufficient to cause the demand curve for the good to be positively (rather than negatively) sloped. Sales of inferior or Giffen goods therefore tend to be countercyclical, decreasing in times of economic boom and increasing in times of recession.

Sir Robert Giffen considered bread and wheat to have the extreme characteristics of inferior goods in Britain in the late nineteenth century. Similarly, potatoes in Ireland were considered Giffen goods during the Irish potato famine although this is disputed in more recent studies (Rosen, 1999). More recently, a study by David McKenzie (2002) on the Mexican tortilla industry, used the 1995 fall in real income in Mexico due to the Mexican currency (Peso) crisis and the subsequent rise in the price of the tortilla due to the removal of government subsidies on the product in 1999, to examine whether the tortilla was a Giffen good in Mexico. The authors concluded that the tortilla is an inferior good but not as extreme as a Giffen good. A study by Jensen and Miller (2007) found that, in China, rice and noodles were Giffen goods among the poor.

This classification of commodities as inferior or Giffen typically fits the basic staples in foodstuffs consumed by the poorer sections of the society. As real income rises and consumers become more affluent, they tend to shift away from the more traditional food staples and towards commodities that were previously priced out of their reach. Because of the countercyclical nature of inferior or Giffen goods, countries marketing such goods may tend to languish during times of economic boom, but may suffer less during (or take advantage of) times of economic recession.

2.3.4.2 DERIVATION OF THE ENGEL CURVE

The Income Consumption Curve may be transposed to the Engel curve. The Engel curve relates the changes in the quantity demanded of a commodity to changes in the (real) income of the consumer (constant prices). This is useful for illustrating and measuring the income elasticity of demand.

The increase in (real) income that was measured by an outward shift of the budget line is now measured on the Y-axis. This income is labelled as Y (distinguish from good y) and actually represents real income, which may be considered as nominal income deflated by an appropriate price index so that it represents the consumer's real command over goods and services. The budget lines AB and CD can be considered as representing levels of income Y_1 and Y_2 respectively. Hence the points R and M on the Income Consumption Curve can now be plotted on another curve as R' and M' showing that, as real income increases from Y_1 to Y_2, the quantity of commodity x consumed increases from Q_1 to Q_2. The line joining these and similar equilibrium points for combinations of good x and income levels Y is the ***Engel*** curve.

The Engel curve is usually drawn backward bending. This reflects ***Engel's Law*** and is dealt with under the income elasticity of demand. This suggests that for commodities such as food, at first, as real income increases, the demand for such a commodity increases faster than the increase in real income. However, as real income continues to increase, the demand for such a commodity increases at a decreasing rate until there is zero increase, after which the demand actually decreases with further increases in real income.

Figure 2.9 shows the Engel curve increasing at a decreasing rate relative to the x-axis, reaching a turning point and then bending back on itself. After the real income

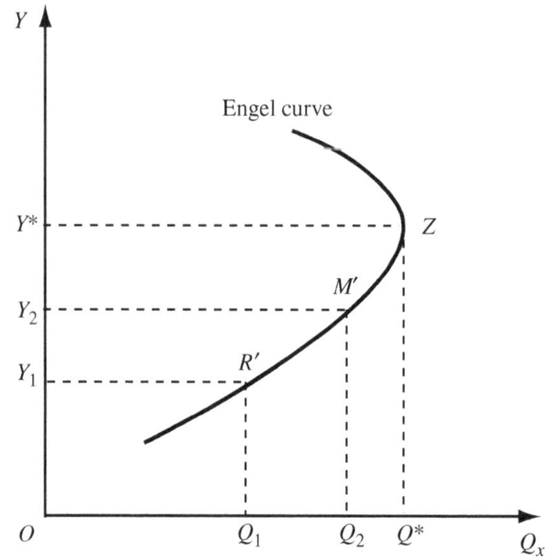

Figure 2.9
The Engel curve

level of Y^* is reached the demand for good x declines, rather than increases, with further increases in real income. Consequently, for a market Engel curve, it is useful for the seller of good x to be aware that the demand for good x cannot exceed the quantity Q^* and, furthermore, would begin to decline as real income in the market exceeds Y^*.

The significance of the Engel curve is discussed further under the topic of income elasticity of demand in Chapter 3.

2.3.5 Critique of the Ordinal theory

Despite the introduction of new analytical tools, the elimination of the doubtful assumption of the Cardinal theory and the acceptable conclusion of the Law of Demand, there were still some concerns with the Ordinal theory. As with the criticisms of the Cardinal theory, the concerns revolved around the realism or acceptability of the assumptions. The following is a list of the major concerns:

- *Ordinality of Utility*. The assumption that consumers are able to order preferences as precisely and rationally as required by the theory was considered doubtful.
- *Existence and convexity of indifference curves*. There was concern that the theory did not establish either the existence or the convexity of the indifference curves.
- *Time period of the analysis*. It was felt that the theory could only apply in the short-run as consumer preferences would change over time.
- *Rationality*. There was a view that the theory did not consider other factors that could make the consumer appear to be irrational (such as external effects on consumption).

The Revealed Preference Theory attempts to remedy some of these perceived faults with the Ordinal Utility theory.

2.4 THE REVEALED PREFERENCE (*RP*) THEORY

The Revealed Preference (*RP*) theory was introduced by economist Paul Samuelson (1938). It is based on the Revealed Preference axiom and does not require the use of indifference curves or their restrictive assumptions. The Revealed Preference theory is considered to have made two major contributions to utility theory and, in particular, to the Ordinal utility theory:

1 It establishes the existence of the demand curve directly without the need for an elaborate version of utility theory.
2 It establishes the existence and convexity of indifference curves and does not simply accept them as assumptions (axioms), thereby eliminating a major concern of the standard Ordinal Utility theory.

It is therefore considered to be useful in shoring up or adding buoyancy to the standard Ordinal theory.

2.4.1 Assumptions of the Revealed Preference Theory

The Revealed Preference Theory rests on very simplified assumptions. These are:

1 *Rationality*. The consumer's behaviour is based on rationality. This means simply that the consumer prefers more to less.
2 *The axiom of Revealed Preference*. The consumer's choice of a bundle of goods when other bundles are available and not chosen reveals the consumer's preference for that bundle over any other bundle available given the budget situation (constraint).
3 *Consistency*. The consumer is consistent. If $A > B$ then $B < A$. This is the standard consistency axiom but is now called the ***Weak Axiom of Revealed Preference***.
4 *Transitivity*. The consumer's preference is transitive. If $A > B$ and $B > C$ then $C < A$. This is called the ***Strong Axiom of Revealed Preference***.

'Revealing' preferences

Consider a consumer with budget line *AB*. All combinations of the goods on or within the budget line are available to the consumer given the consumer's income. The consumer chooses bundle *Z* on the line *AB*. Let *R* be any other bundle that lies on or within the budget line *AB*. Then *Z* is said to be revealed preferred to *R*. The choice of *Z* when *R* was available ***reveals*** that the consumer prefers *Z* to *R*. These bundles are shown in Figure 2.10.

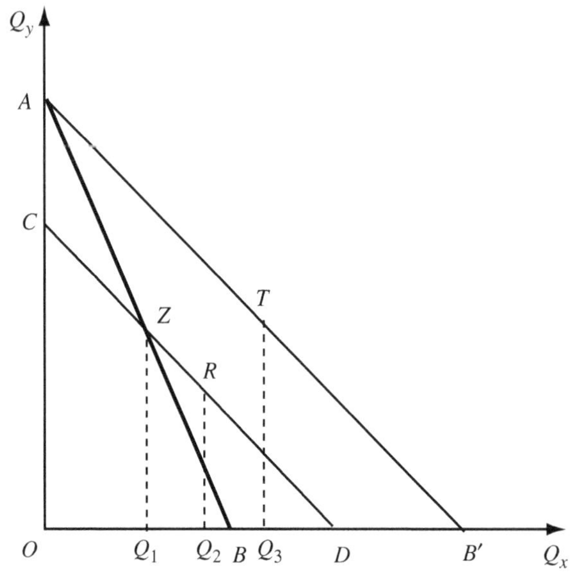

Figure 2.10
Derivation of the demand curve under the Revealed Preference theory

The weak axiom of Revealed Preference

The weak axiom of Revealed Preference is the usual consistency condition on choices and is attributed to economist Paul Samuelson (1938) based on earlier work by Abraham Wald (1902–1950). It says that, assuming Z and R are different bundles of commodities, if bundle Z is revealed preferred to R when they are both available in the same budget set (on or below the same budget line), then it is never the case that R is revealed preferred to Z when they are both available.

As a corollary, if bundle Z is chosen when bundle R is available, then the only price income situation is which R could be chosen is one in which Z is not in the budget set.

It is possible to relate this to the standard utility theory by considering that when the consumer chooses bundle Z with the given budget set, there is an indifference curve tangent to the budget line at Z. However, for R to be available along with Z, then R must also be in that budget set and hence must be on a lower indifference curve, thereby giving R a lower utility than Z.

The strong axiom of Revealed Preference

The strong axiom of Revealed Preference is required to ensure that consumer choices are transitive in the case of a large number of bundles of commodities. This strong axiom of Revealed Preference is attributed to economist H. Houthakker (1950).

Using Figure 2.10 and having established that Z is revealed preferred to R, then, if R is preferred to another bundle, say M, in the same budget set, Z must also be preferred to M. Put differently, bundle M must not be revealed preferred to bundle Z once they are in the same budget set. Thus the weak axiom may be seen as a special case of the strong axiom, when the number of commodity bundles being compared is reduced to two.

A more elaborate exposition of Revealed Preference theory may be found in Henderson and Quandt (1984).

2.4.2 Derivation of the demand curve under *RP* theory

The Revealed Preference theory establishes the demand curve without using assumptions of the utility theory.

Using Figure 2.10, consider the case of two goods x and y. The consumer faces the budget line AB and, by purchasing the basket of goods labelled Z, the consumer's preference for the bundle Z is revealed. This suggests that every other available combination of the two goods to the left, right and below Z is revealed inferior to Z since they were in the same budget set as Z but were not chosen. At Z the consumer is demanding the quantity Q_1 of good x.

Now, consider a fall in the price of good x. The budget line pivots to AB'. The question to be answered is whether the consumer would now buy more of good x.

To examine this, a compensating variation of income is made by passing a budget line parallel to AB' through the point Z so that Z is also within the new budget set. This new budget line CD is an attempt to take away the income effect of the fall in the price of good x.

The substitution effect and the law of demand

With the introduction of the compensation variation line CD, the direction in which the consumer will move from the point Z can be established by contrary. Based on the assumptions of the theory, the consumer will not move from the point Z to anywhere on the line segment AZ since choices on this segment were available previously but were not chosen (weak axiom). Similarly, the consumer will not now choose any bundle on the line segment CZ since this was also available previously and was not chosen. Hence, in order for the consumer to choose anything other than the bundle Z, the consumer must choose a bundle somewhere along the line segment ZD as points on this line segment were not available previously, when the consumer chose bundle Z.

By choosing a point on the line segment ZD such as R, as shown in Figure 2.10, the consumer chooses to have more of x than previously and moves from consuming Q_1 to Q_2 of good x. This is the substitution effect. The Revealed Preference approach shows (proves) that the substitution effect is negative (i.e. a fall in the price of x reduces the quantity demanded of x). This effect proves the law of demand.

The income effect

With the extra income due to the fall in the price of good x, the consumer would move to a new point such as T consuming Q_3 of good x. This is the income effect and so long as good x is a normal good the income effect is positive and an increase in income leads to an increase in the consumption of good x. This income effect adds to the substitution effect.

The Law of Demand

Consequently, as the price of good x falls from the relative price of AB to that of AB', the consumer must choose more of x and, in this example, moves from consuming Q_1 of good x to Q_3 of good x. This establishes the Law of Demand.

The Revealed Preference theory was able to derive the demand curve and establish the law of demand using what is considered to be a simpler and more acceptable set of assumptions than the standard Ordinal theory. Moreover, it was not necessary to venture into the territory of utility theory in order to derive the demand curve.

The Revealed Preference theory is not without its share of criticisms and, in particular, concern has been expressed for the way the theory seeks to use an empirical result, the revealed choice of the consumer, to derive a theory. Nevertheless, the *RP* theory makes a special contribution to the standard Ordinal theory as it provides the elements for proving the existence and convexity of the indifference curve employed by that theory.

2.4.3 Establishing the existence and convexity of indifference curves using the *RP* theory

The Ordinal utility theory was criticized for its assumption of Diminishing Marginal Rate of Substitution. This assumption is central to the Ordinal theory since it gives the tool of the indifference curve and provides the indifference map for the consumer. Yet it was not considered to be completely accepted as it was derived from introspection.

One important by-product of the Revealed Preference theory is its ability to assist in establishing the existence and convexity of indifference curves. It can be proven that a consumer who always conforms to the simple set of axioms of the *RP* theory must possess an indifference map.

Figure 2.11 illustrates how the existence and convexity of the indifference curve may be established. On the budget constraint AB the consumer chooses bundle Z. This is the consumer's revealed preference. Hence, all other bundles on the budget line AB and all others below the budget line are inferior to Z.

Figure 2.11 shows that, from the revealed preference point (Z) two perpendiculars can be constructed, one moving horizontally from Z and the other vertically. Together they form a right angle at the point Z. The significance of these lines is that they demarcate areas where a Pareto type improvement can be achieved. That is, the consumer can have more of one good without having less of the other. The line from Z in the direction of R indicates the limit of the area where the consumer can have more of good x while holding the quantity of good y constant. Similarly, the line from Z in the direction of S indicates the limit of the area where the consumer can have more of good y while holding the quantity of good x constant. Inside the area bounded by these two lines ZR and ZT the consumer can have more of both goods.

Based on the assumption of the *RP* model, that consumers prefer more to less, all bundles of goods x and y in the area TZR are preferred bundles representing Pareto improvement since they contain more of one good with at least as much of the other.

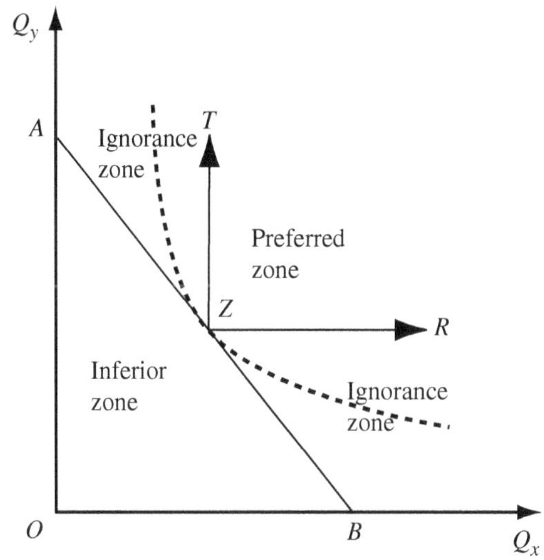

Figure 2.11
Establishing the existence and convexity of indifference curves using the Revealed Preference theory

So far, the following is known:

- The rest of the budget line *AB* and all the area under the line are inferior to the point *Z*. Consider that this can be represented by a negative sign relative to *Z*. This is labelled the 'inferior zone'.
- The region bounded by *TZR* is preferred to the point *Z* and therefore is considered superior to *Z*. This superiority may be represented by a positive sign relative to *Z*.

Nothing, however, is known about the two zones *BZR* and *AZT* that lie between the inferior zone and the preferred zone. These are called the ignorance zones. It is not known exactly which of the bundles of goods in these areas are preferred, indifferent or inferior to *Z*. What is known, however, is that if the preferred zone is positive relative to *Z* and the inferior zone is negative relative to *Z*, then somewhere between positive and negative there must be zero.

The indifference curve through *Z* is the line where the consumer is indifferent (i.e. has zero difference in preference) to the bundle at *Z*. Hence this line of zero difference in preference must lie somewhere between the confirmed preferred area and the confirmed inferior area. This indicates that:

- Moving from the point *Z*, the indifference curve (IC) through *Z* must move off the rest of the budget line *AB* on both sides of the point *Z* as these points are negative to *Z* and so cannot be indifferent to *Z*. Hence the IC cannot be the straight diagonal line *AB*.
- The indifference curve through *Z* cannot incorporate the lines *ZR* and *ZT* as these lines mark the zone with bundles that are positive to *Z* and so cannot be indifferent to *Z*. Hence IC cannot coincide with *TZR*.

- The indifference curve must therefore pass from Z through the 'ignorance zones' on either side of Z and therefore its locus must describe a line convex to the origin.
- Moreover, since in order to get from negative (−) to Z in the inferior zone to positive (+) to Z in the preferred zone, it is necessary to have a range in which there is zero to Z. Consequently, the locus of points of zero difference (indifference) to Z must exist.

In this way, the Revealed Preference theory can be used to establish the existence and convexity of the indifference curve. This renders the troublesome assumption of diminishing marginal rate of substitution unnecessary and, in this way, bolsters the standard Ordinal Utility theory of the consumer.

What is of significance is that the three approaches, Cardinal, Ordinal and Revealed Preference, all come to the same conclusion or prediction, namely, that as price falls (*ceteris paribus*) the consumer demands more of a good. The evolution of utility theories has been based more on the concern with assumptions and analytical tools than with any doubts about the conclusions or predictions of the model. This 'Law of Demand', with its downward sloping demand curve, is one of the most recognized or recognizable laws coming out of microeconomic theory. It is employed throughout economics, business and management studies and has widespread practical applications.

REVIEW QUESTIONS FOR CHAPTER 2

1 Within the context of demand analysis:

(a) Set out the assumptions of the Cardinal theory.
(b) Derive and illustrate how equilibrium of the consumer is achieved under the Cardinal theory.

2 With regard to the Cardinal utility theory:

(a) Explain and illustrate how the consumer's demand curve is derived.
(b) Outline the criticisms made against this theory and explain how the Ordinal theory sought to overcome them.

3 With regard to the Ordinal utility theory and using two goods only:

(a) Explain and illustrate the properties of the indifference curves and show why and how the slope of the curve is the marginal rate of substitution.
(b) Show why the slope of the budget line is the ratio of the prices of the two goods.

4 Consider a typical consumer, Seanette, who has a total budget (B) for spending on two goods, food and clothes. Explain:

(a) How, according to the Ordinal theory about Seanette's optimizing behaviour may be derived.

(b) How the income consumption curve may be used to derive the demand curve from Seanette's equilibrium position.

5 Shakira is a consumer purchasing two goods, x and y with a given (fixed) budget:

(a) Explain what the Revealed Preference axioms say about Shakira's behaviour.
(b) Illustrate and explain how the 'Revealed Preference' (*RP*) theory may be used to derive the Shakira's demand curve.

6 Examine how the Revealed Preference theory is used to prove the existence and convexity of the indifference curve and why it is said to shore up the Ordinal theory.
7 Attempt an explanation about why there have been changes and revisions to utility theory when, from the Cardinal to the Revealed Preference theory, the conclusion or prediction is the same Law of Demand.

RECOMMENDED READING FOR CHAPTER 2

Henderson, J. M. and Quandt, R. E. (1984) *Microeconomic Theory: A Mathematical Approach*, New York: McGraw Hill, Ch. 2.

Houthakker, H. S. (1950) 'Revealed Preference and the Utility Function', *Economica* (New Series) 17: 159–74.

Jensen, R. and Miller, N. (2007) 'Giffen Behavior: Theory and Evidence', Harvard University: John F. Kennedy School of Government, *KGS Faculty Research Working Paper Series*, Working Paper Number: RWP07-030. Online Posting. Available at: <http://ksgnotes1.harvard.edu/Research/wpaper.nsf/rwp/RWP07-030>.

McKenzie, D. (2002) 'Are Tortillas a Giffen Good in Mexico', *Economics Bulletin*, 15(1): 1–7. Online Posting. Available at: <http://www.economicsbulletin.com/2002/volume15/EB-01O10003A.pdf>.

Rosen, S. (1999) 'Potato Paradoxes', *Journal of Political Economy*, 107(6): 294–313.

Samuelson, P. (1938) 'A Note on the Pure Theory of Consumers' Behaviour', *Economica*, 5: 61–71.

3 Market Demand and Elasticity

From Individual to Market Demand; Own-Price Elasticity of Demand; Income Elasticity of Demand; Cross-Price Elasticity of Demand.

The demand curve for the individual consumer, derived from utility theory, was shown in Chapter 2 to be downward sloping for a normal good. The demands of individual consumers are now aggregated to arrive at the market demand, following which the concept of elasticity of demand is introduced.

The elasticity concept is central to economic analysis and wide-ranging in its application, from the village shoe-repairer to the largest conglomerate and extending to trade policy at the national level. However, since elasticity is not highly intuitive in its construction and use, it often tends to be misunderstood and under-appreciated. This chapter examines price, income and cross elasticity of demand and their application to show their significance for economic analysis.

3.1 FROM INDIVIDUAL DEMAND TO MARKET DEMAND

Using different approaches, the Cardinal, the Ordinal and the Revealed Preference theories, the conclusion is the same, namely, that the individual's demand curve is downward sloping (negatively sloped) for a normal good. The downward sloping demand curve for the individual consumer is based on the ***ceteris paribus*** assumption, thereby holding constant all factors that affect demand other than the price of the product being demanded. These other factors being held constant are referred to as ***shift factors***.

Changes in price are reflected in movements along the demand curve. Changes in the other factors which affect demand, such as income, taste or preferences and the price of other goods, are reflected in a shift in the demand curve. These shift factors affect the position of the demand curve.

Demand is also affected *inter alia* by:

- The availability of credit
- The nature of the distribution of income
- Market size

- Accumulated wealth or affluence of the population
- Cultural habits and behaviour
- External influences from foreign media such as television and the internet (demonstration effect)
- The consumption behaviour of others in the market (see Bandwagon, Snob and Veblen effects in Chapter 4).

3.1.1 Derivation of market demand

The market demand for a given commodity is simply the horizontal summation of the demands of the individual consumers.

Consider a market with n consumers. The market demand is the ***horizontal*** summation of the demand curves of all n consumers. This is illustrated for two consumers (A and B) in Figure 3.1.

It should be recognized that, although for one consumer a good may be a Giffen good (i.e. with a positively sloped demand curve), the market demand will still have the normal negative slope unless it is a Giffen good for a large enough number of consumers in that market.

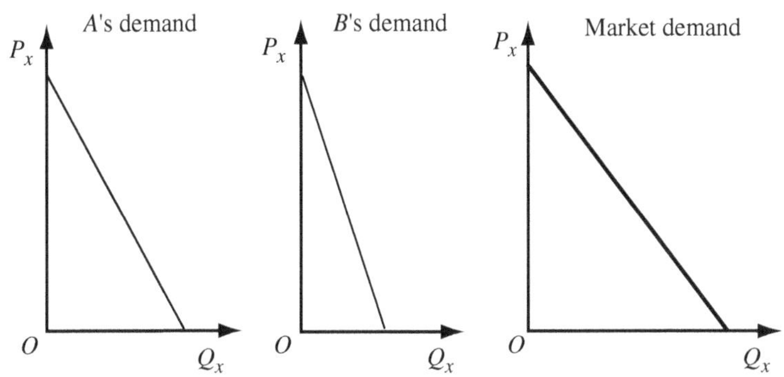

Figure 3.1
Horizontal summation of individual demands to give market demand

3.1.2 Shape of the demand curve

The demand curve is usually drawn as a straight line (linear demand curve). However, it may also take the form of a curve, usually one that is convex to the origin.

The linear demand curve

The linear demand function, expressing the relationship between the quantity demanded (Q) and the price (P) of a commodity may be written as:

$$Q = b_0 - b_1 P$$

where,

$$b_0 = \text{intercept}$$

$$b_1 = \text{slope (or gradient) of the function}$$

It is important to understand that, while the demand function is written with quantity (Q) as a function of price (P), it is drawn with price (P) as a function of quantity (Q). Therefore quantity is placed on the X-axis. The expression is Walrasian in nature whereas the drawing is based on Marshallian principles. These terms refer to economists Walras and Marshall and are explained further in Chapter 8.

This linear negatively sloped demand curve describes a constant slope but a changing elasticity at different prices. This is explained in the next section.

The non-linear demand curve

Most common form of the non-linear curve is the 'constant-elasticity-of-demand curve' which implies constant-elasticity at all prices. This is written as:

$$Q = b_0 P^{b_1}$$

where b_1 is the constant price elasticity of demand. This curve describes a rectangular hyperbola.

3.2 THE PRICE ELASTICITY OF DEMAND

3.2.1 Definition

The price elasticity of demand (η_P) is sometimes referred to as the own-price elasticity of demand. This is to distinguish the responsiveness of the quantity demanded of a good to its own price rather than to the price of another good (cross price elasticity). It may be defined as:

$$\eta_P = \frac{\text{proportionate change in } Q_x}{\text{proportionate change in } P_x}$$

Using this formula the price elasticity of demand for good x can be written as:

$$\eta_P = \frac{\mathrm{d}Q_x/Q_x}{\mathrm{d}P_x/P_x}$$

Re-writing:

$$\eta_P = \frac{\mathrm{d}Q_x}{\mathrm{d}P_x} \cdot \frac{P_x}{Q_x}$$

Price elasticity of demand may be identified as elastic, inelastic or unitary elastic depending on the value of η_P as follows:

- If $\eta_P > 1$ in absolute terms, demand is said to be price elastic.
- If $\eta_P < 1$ in absolute terms, demand is said to be price inelastic.
- If $\eta_P = 1$ in absolute terms, demand is said to be unitary elastic.

It should be noted that price elasticity of demand for normal goods carries a negative value. That is because of the negative relationship between price and quantity (i.e. as price goes up, quantity goes down). However, typically, the value for price elasticity (η_P) is written without the negative sign as the negative sign is understood. Where computation is involved the negative sign must be used.

Consequences of the value of price elasticity

Where the demand for a commodity is price elastic ($\eta_P > 1$ in absolute terms), the percentage change in the quantity demanded is greater than the percentage change in price and in the opposite direction. The significance is that if price is reduced by a certain proportion (say 10 per cent), the quantity demanded is increased by a greater proportion (say 15 per cent). Thus a price reduction leads to increased consumer expenditure on the good and consequently increased revenue for the seller of the good. A price increase, on the other hand, leads to a reduction in revenue for the seller of the good.

Conversely, where the demand for a commodity is price inelastic ($\eta_P < 1$ in absolute terms) the percentage change in the quantity demanded is smaller than the percentage change in price again in the opposite direction. As a result, if price is reduced by a certain proportion (say 10 per cent), the quantity demanded is increased by a smaller proportion (say 5 per cent). Thus a price reduction leads to decreased consumer expenditure on the good and consequently reduced revenue for the seller of the good. Conversely, a price increase leads to increased revenue for the seller of the good.

With unit price elasticity of demand ($\eta_P = 1$ in absolute terms), the percentage change in the quantity demanded is exactly equal to the percentage change in price but in the opposite direction. Consequently, if price is reduced by a certain proportion (say 10 per cent), the quantity demanded is increased by the same proportion (10 per cent) and similarly for a price decrease. Consequently, neither a price increase nor a price decrease would affect the total expenditure on the product and so the seller's revenue from the sale of the product remains unchanged with a change in price.

The value of the price elasticity of demand depends on:

- *The availability of substitutes.* Demand for a commodity is more price elastic where there are close substitutes.
- *The extent to which the commodities may be characterized as luxuries or necessities.* Luxury goods are more price elastic whereas necessities are more inelastic.
- *Time period.* Demand is more price elastic in the long-run than in the short-run.
- *Alternative uses.* The more alternative uses a commodity has, the greater the price elasticity of demand.

- *The proportion of total income spent on the product.* The greater the proportion the higher the elasticity.

Arc elasticity of demand

The above measures of price elasticity of demand refer to what may be called the point elasticity of demand. This is appropriate for small changes in price. For larger changes in price, the formula for arc price elasticity of demand is used. This may be expressed (with the subscript x omitted) as:

$$\eta_P = \frac{\Delta Q}{\Delta P} \cdot \frac{(P_1 + P_2)/2}{(Q_1 + Q_2)/2}$$

3.2.2 The *PCC* and the price elasticity of demand

Price elasticity of demand may be determined from the shape of the price consumption curve (*PCC*). As explained in Chapter 2, the price consumption curve is the line joining successive equilibrium points as the price of good x falls. The price elasticity of demand can be derived from the price consumption curve using money and one good (x).

The relationship is as follows:

- Where $\eta_P = 1$ in absolute terms (unitary elastic demand), the *PCC* is a horizontal line.
- Where $\eta_P < 1$ in absolute terms (inelastic demand), the *PCC* is an upward sloping line.
- Where $\eta_P > 1$ in absolute terms (elastic demand), the *PCC* is a downward sloping line.

Unitary elastic demand

Figure 3.2 describes a consumer's budget line *AB* and an equilibrium point *R* on indifference curve IC_1. Focusing on good x, define good y as the money the consumer can spend on all other goods (except x). Since good y is money, the price is always *one* (e.g. it takes a dollar to buy a dollar). At *R*, the consumer purchases OX_1 of good x and has to spend on other goods (i.e. *AU* of money is spent on good x).

As explained earlier, the slope of the budget line *AB* is:

$$\text{Slope } AB = \frac{P_x}{P_y}$$

With the price of good y equal to one, this makes the slope of *AB* equal to the price of good x (P_x).

With a fall in the price of good x, the budget line pivots from *AB* to *AB*′. When the price of good x is reduced, the quantity of good x increases from Ox_1 to Ox_2 but the money retained for other purchases remains at *OU*. This means money spent on good x remains constant. Thus the additional amount of x demanded just offsets the price decrease and,

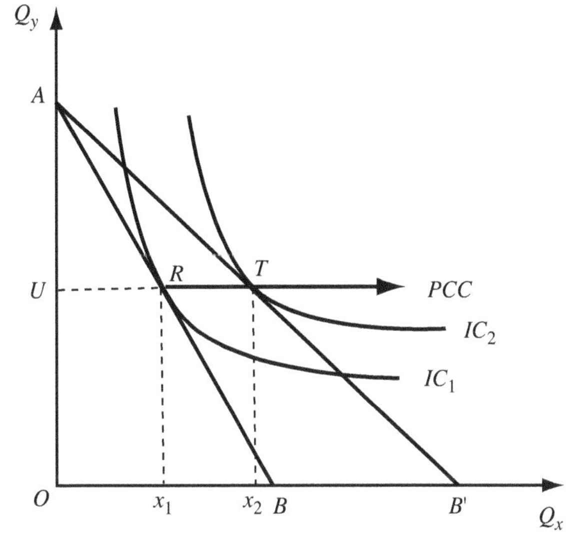

Figure 3.2
A horizontal price consumption curve (*PCC*): unit elasticity

consequently, the proportionate increase in the quantity of good x purchased is equal to the proportionate decrease in price, thereby making the *PCC* a horizontal line (zero slope) and meeting the definition of unit price elasticity of demand ($\eta_P = 1$).

Inelastic demand

Figure 3.3 shows a price-consumption-curve that is upward sloping. This represents inelastic demand ($\eta_P < 1$). As the price of good x decreases from slope AB to AB', more of good x is purchased. But there is an increase from OU to OC of the money spent on other goods. As a consequence, the consumer's expenditure on good x reduces from AU to AC.

The fall in the price of good x has caused the consumer's total expenditure on good x to decrease. Thus the proportionate increase in the quantity of x purchased is less than the proportionate decrease in the price of x and hence the price elasticity of demand for good x is less than one, meaning that the consumer's demand is price inelastic.

Figure 3.4 shows a price-consumption-curve that is downward sloping. This represents elastic demand ($\eta_P > 1$). As before, with a decrease in the price of good x from slope AB to AB', more of good x is purchased. However, there is a decrease from OU to OV of the money spent on other goods. As a consequence, the consumer's expenditure on good x increases from AU to AV, signifying that the demand for x is price elastic. As price of x falls so much more of x is purchased that the amount of money left over to spend on other goods is reduced by the amount UV.

The decrease in the price of good x has caused an increase in the consumer's total expenditure on good x. This indicates that the proportionate increase in the quantity

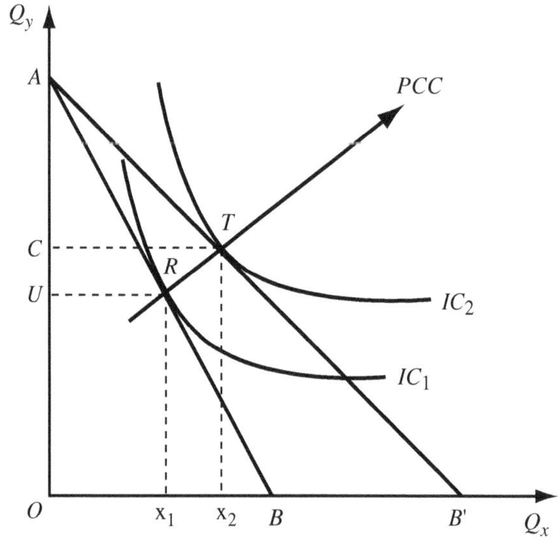

Figure 3.3
An upward sloping price consumption curve (*PCC*): inelastic demand

of x demanded is greater than proportionate decrease in price of x and hence the price elasticity of demand of good x is greater than one ($\eta_P > 1$).

In general, it is the total effect of a price change that is considered. The analysis focuses on how the equilibrium position changes with variations in the price of a commodity (x).

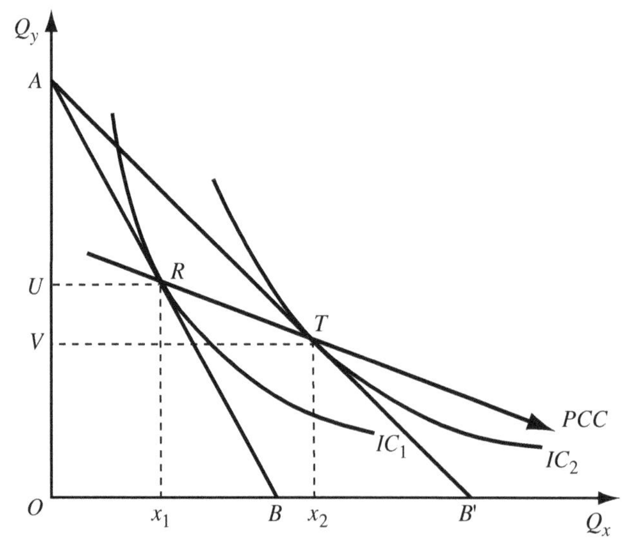

Figure 3.4
A downward sloping price consumption curve (*PCC*): elastic demand

3.2.3 Variation of price elasticity along demand curve

The price elasticity of demand varies everywhere along a linear, negatively-sloped demand curve. Using the formula for point elasticity:

$$\eta_P = \frac{dQ_x}{dP_x} \cdot \frac{P_x}{Q_x}$$

Figure 3.5 may be used to illustrate the derivation of the price elasticity of demand (η_P) at the point, R.

The elasticity formula may be applied at the point R ($\eta_P(R)$) as follows:

$$\eta_P(R) = \frac{dQ_x}{dP_x} \cdot \frac{P_x}{Q_x}$$

In the formula:

$$\frac{dQ_x}{dP_x}$$

is the inverse of the slope of the demand curve at R. The actual slope at R is:

$$\frac{dP_x}{dQ_x} = \frac{RS}{SB}$$

Hence the inverse of the slope at R is:

$$\frac{dQ_x}{dP_x} = \frac{SB}{RS}$$

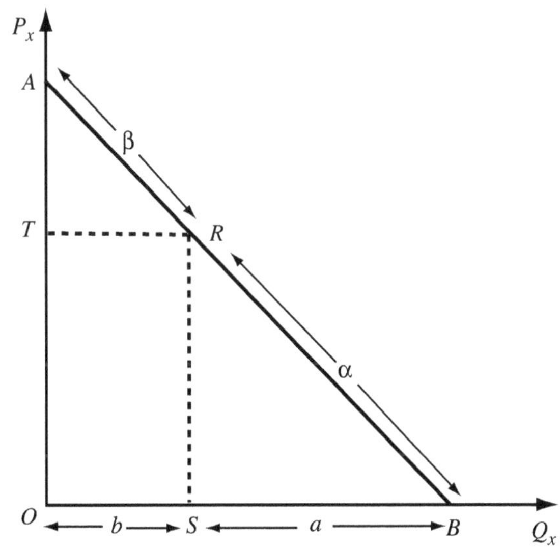

Figure 3.5
Derivation of price elasticity along a linear, negatively sloped demand curve

The other component of the elasticity formula applied to the point R is:

$$\frac{P_x}{Q_x} = \frac{OT}{OS} = \frac{RS}{OS}$$

Putting the components of the formula together gives:

$$\eta_P(R) = \frac{SB}{RS} \cdot \frac{RS}{OS}$$

or:

$$\eta_P(R) = \frac{SB}{OS}$$

Using Figure 3.5, this may be written as:

$$\eta_P(R) = \frac{a}{b}$$

A useful mnemonic is that the price elasticity of demand at a point on the demand curve is ***the distance between the perpendicular and the tangent divided by the distance between the perpendicular and the origin***. This relates to the perpendicular dropped from that point to the X-axis and the tangent to that point is the demand curve which reaches the X-axis.

Using the rule that says that a perpendicular from the hypotenuse to an adjacent side cuts the adjacent side in the same proportion as it cuts the hypotenuse, the short cut formula may be transferred from the X-axis to the length of the demand curve. The following holds:

$$\eta_P(R) = \frac{a}{b} = \frac{\alpha}{\beta}$$

This is convenient in that it allows the easy visual determination of the elasticity at any point along the demand curve by observing the relative lengths of the distance of the areas below and above the point under consideration. It also facilitates the observation that the price elasticity of demand varies at every point along the demand curve when that curve is a linear, negatively sloped curve.

In general, it may be observed that the price elasticity of demand varies from zero to infinity along the linear negatively sloped demand curve. More specifically, the following results should be noted using Figure 3.6:

- As the point R is moved downwards, α gets smaller while β gets larger. Hence:

$$\eta_P = \frac{\alpha}{\beta} \text{ gets smaller}$$

- As the point R is moved upwards along the demand curve, α gets larger while β gets smaller. Hence:

$$\eta_P = \frac{\alpha}{\beta} \text{ gets larger}$$

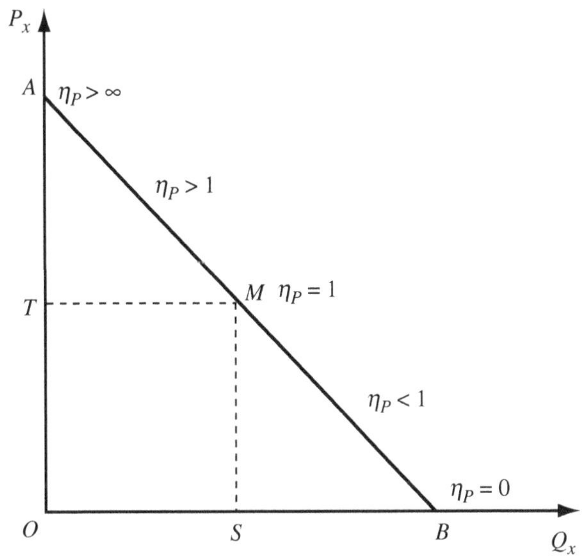

Figure 3.6
Variation of price elasticity along a linear, negatively sloped demand curve

- At the mid-point of the demand curve (M), $\alpha = \beta$, hence:

$$\eta_P(M) = \frac{\alpha}{\beta} = 1$$

- At point B on the demand curve $\alpha = 0$, hence:

$$\eta_P(B) = \frac{0}{\beta} = 0$$

- At point A on the demand curve $\beta = 0$, hence:

$$\eta_P(A) = \frac{\alpha}{0} = \infty$$

Knowledge of the way in which price elasticity of demand varies along the typical straight line negatively sloped demand curve is extremely useful in the decision-making process of the seller. This is because of the relationship between price elasticity and total and marginal revenue of the seller. This is examined further.

3.2.4 Market demand, total and marginal revenue

The application of the demand curve along with the concept of elasticity has its greatest analytical value in the understanding of the relationship between demand, price, elasticity and total and marginal revenue. This important relationship is illustrated graphically in Figure 3.7.

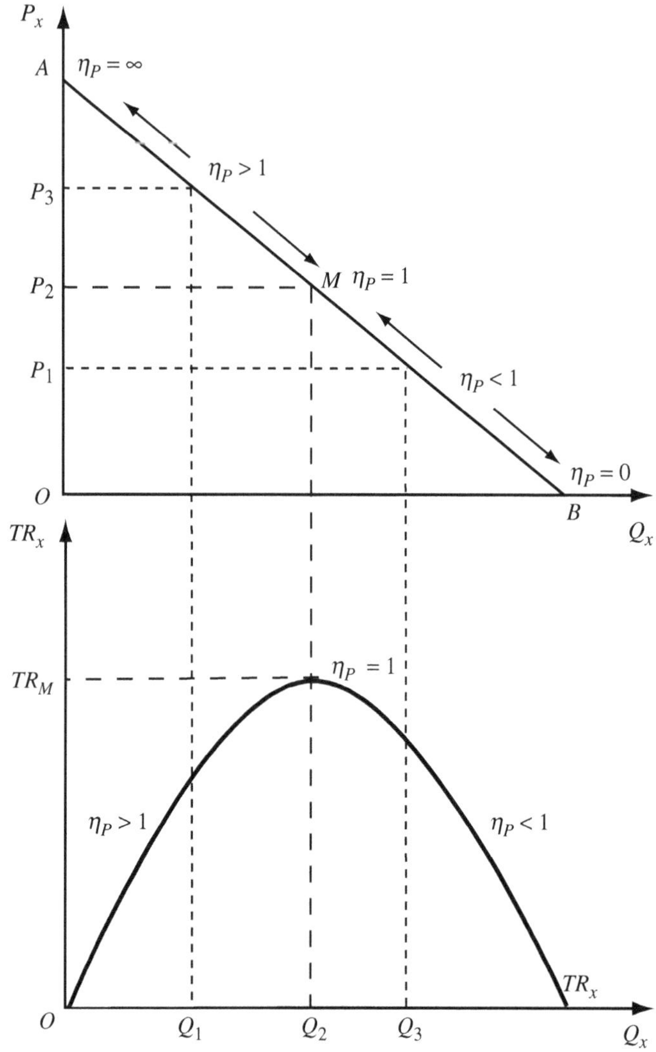

Figure 3.7
Changes in price, elasticity and total revenue of a firm

In the top part of the illustration in Figure 3.7, *AB* is the market demand curve for good *x*. At price P_2, the quantity Q_2 of good *x* is demanded and sold. Total revenue for the seller is *PQ*, which may be identified as OP_2 multiplied by OQ_2. *M* is the mid-point of the demand curve. This is the point at which total revenue is at a maximum. Consequently, P_2 is the price at which the seller's revenue is maximized. It must be noted that this is ***not*** the point at which profits are maximized ($MC = MR$) unless marginal costs are zero. Total revenue is represented in the bottom portion of Figure 3.7.

Total revenue curve

Diagrammatically, total revenue is the area under the demand curve at a given price and quantity. Total revenue at any point on the demand curve is derived by drawing perpendiculars from that point on the demand curve to the price and quantity axes and multiplying the relevant price by quantity. Figure 3.7 shows that at the mid-point (M) of the demand curve AB, total revenue is at its maximum. This is also the point where the price elasticity is equal to one (unitary elasticity). The maximum total revenue available is TR_M and is achieved by selling the quantity Q_2 which corresponds to the mid-point of the demand curve where the price is at P_2.

It should be noted from Figure 3.7 that, should the price be lowered from P_2, then the revenue to the seller is reduced even though a larger quantity is sold. Lowering the price to P_1 causes sales to increase to Q_2 but revenue to fall from its peak. Similarly, raising the price from P_2 to P_3 also causes total revenue to fall from its peak.

Marginal revenue

Marginal revenue is the change in the total revenue resulting from selling an additional unit of the commodity. If the demand curve is linear, then it is obvious that, in order to sell an additional unit of good x, its price must fall. Since the whole quantity will be sold at the new lower price, the marginal revenue will be equal to the price of the extra unit sold minus the loss from selling all previous units at the new lower price:

$$MR = P_2 - (P_1 - P_2)Q_x$$

where:

Q_x = quantity sold before fall in price

P_1 = old price

P_2 = new price

Thus MR is always less than price for any output Q_x given that $(P_1 - P_2) = \Delta P$ is positive (i.e. price is falling) and Q_x is positive. The marginal revenue curve measures the slope of the total revenue curve. This is illustrated in Figure 3.8.

Derivation of the MR curve

The marginal revenue curve measures the ***slope of the total revenue curve***.

Since the marginal revenue is the value of the slope of the total revenue curve at each point, then tangents drawn at successive points along the total revenue curve would show a continuously declining slope (TR curve increasing at a decreasing rate) until the TR curve is at its maximum. At the maximum point of the TR curve the slope (marginal revenue) is zero. Hence, the marginal revenue (MR) curve falls and reaches zero where the TR is at its maximum (at quantity of Q_2). After quantity Q_2, the marginal revenue curve goes negative (i.e. slope of TR is negative beyond quantity Q_2).

The demand equation

A linear demand curve can be represented by an equation such as:

$$P = a_0 - a_1 Q$$

where a_0 is the intercept and a_1 the slope.

As indicated earlier, the demand curve as drawn (Marshallian) is the inverse of the demand function as written (Walrasian). The conversion may be made as follows.

Take the demand equation written as:

$$Q = b_0 - b_1 P$$

Solving for P gives:

$$P = \frac{b_0}{b_1} - \frac{1}{b_1}Q$$

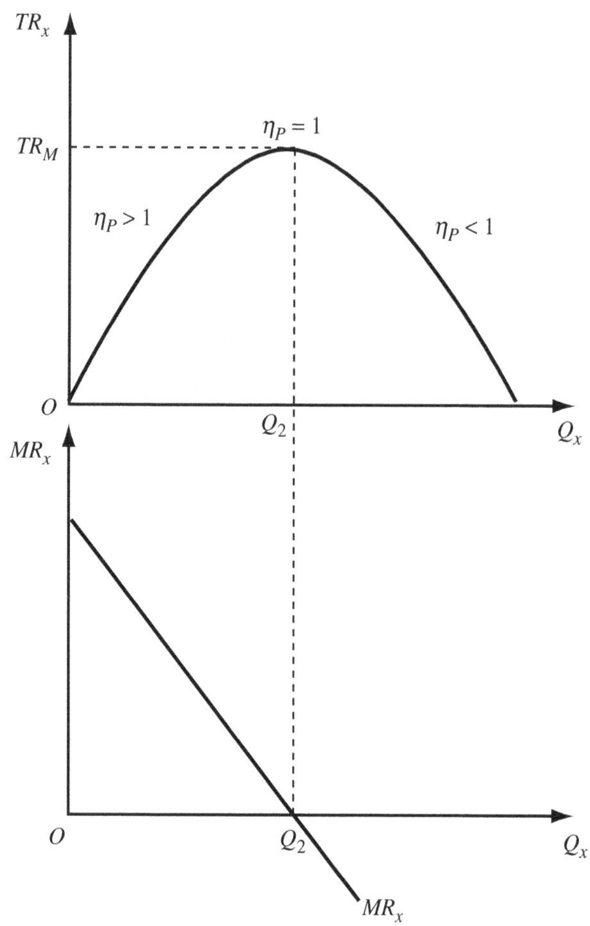

Figure 3.8
Relationship between total and marginal revenue

Renaming coefficients, let:

$$\frac{b_0}{b_1} = a_0 \qquad \text{and} \qquad \frac{1}{b_1} = a_1$$

Hence, the demand curve as drawn may be written as:

$$P = a_0 - a_1 Q$$

3.2.5 Relationship of marginal revenue to demand curve

Total revenue is:

$$TR = PQ$$

Substitute, using the expression for price in the demand curve as drawn:

$$P = a_0 - a_1 Q$$

This gives an expression for total revenue as:

$$TR = PQ = (a_0 - a_1 Q)Q$$

or:

$$TR = a_0 Q - a_1 Q^2$$

Since *MR* is the slope of the *TR* curve, it can be written as:

$$MR = \frac{\mathrm{d}(TR)}{\mathrm{d}Q} = a_0 - 2a_1 Q$$

When the *MR* curve is compared to the linear demand curve, it may be noted that the *MR* curve has the same intercept a_0 as the demand curve on the *Y*-axis ***but it has a slope that is twice as steep***.

Graphical derivation of MR curve

Consider a linear negatively sloped demand curve. The marginal revenue (*MR*) can be found at any given quantity *Q*. It is already known that the *MR* will be smaller than the current price.

It is known that, given the demand curve, for the quantity *OS* to be purchased, price must be at *OT*. At price *OT* the total revenue is the area under the demand curve, *OTGS*. Figure 3.9 illustrates that the marginal revenue curve has the same intercept but twice the slope as the demand curve (i.e. it falls twice as fast as the demand curve). Graphically, since the *MR* curve falls twice as fast as the demand curve, it must lie halfway between the demand curve and the *Y*-axis. To identify the location of the *MR* curve, find the mid-point (*M*) on the perpendicular *TG* from the demand curve to the *Y*-axis (price axis).

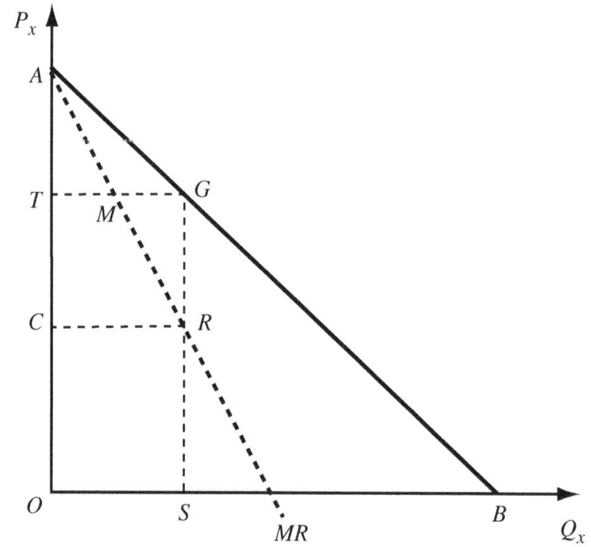

Figure 3.9
Relationship between demand and marginal revenue curves

The *MR* curve must pass through this point *M* which is halfway between the demand curve at *G* and the *Y*-axis at *T*. Draw a straight line from the point *A* (same intercept as the demand curve) passing through the point *M* and project to the *X*-axis. This line is the *MR* curve.

It is important to note that the *MR* line will also cut the quantity axis (*X*-axis) half way between the origin (*O*) and the demand curve (*B*). It therefore bisects the market quantity at any price.

From this, it can be observed that, if a perpendicular is dropped from the point *G* on the demand curve the marginal revenue curve cuts the perpendicular *GS* at the point *R*. This shows that the marginal revenue at quantity *S* is less than the price of quantity *S* ($OC < OT$ or $SR < SG$). It should be observed that the gap between price and marginal revenue widens and that, at the mid-point of the demand curve, the difference between price and *MR* is exactly equal to the price (since *MR* is zero). After the mid-point of the demand curve *MR* become negative.

Derivation of the MR curve from a non-linear demand curve

Figure 3.10 describes a non-linear demand curve. The curved line is the demand curve. In order to find the marginal revenue (*MR*) curve:

- Take (at least) two points on the demand curve (D_1 and D_2).
- Drop perpendiculars from these points on the demand curve to the *X*-axis at Q_1 and Q_2 respectively.
- Draw perpendiculars from D_1 and D_2 to the *Y*-axis at the points *T* and *C* respectively.
- Draw tangents to the points D_1 and D_2 and extend the tangents to the *Y*-axis.

- Draw *MR*-type curves from the points where these tangents start on the *Y*-axis (the intercept) letting each one cut the respective horizontal perpendicular line in half (i.e. the *MR*-type line for the tangent at D_1 must cut the perpendicular line TD_1 at its mid-point and the *MR*-type line for the tangent at D_2 must cut the line CD_2 at its mid-point).
- Project the *MR*-type lines until they cut the vertical perpendiculars from D_1 and D_2 (D_1Q_1 and D_2Q_2). They cut at R_1 and R_2.
- Join the points R_1 and R_2. These are points on the marginal revenue curve for the non-linear demand curve.

The locus of R_1, R_2 and similar points is the relevant marginal revenue curve for the non-linear demand curve.

3.2.6 Relationship between marginal revenue and price elasticity of demand (η_P)

The relationship between marginal revenue (*MR*) and price elasticity of demand (η_P) is critical for the theory of pricing.

As previously established, the total revenue is highest where $MR = 0$ and this is where price elasticity of demand (η_P) is: $\eta_P = 1$. Before this point, *MR* is positive and elasticity is: $\eta_P > 1$. After this point MR is negative and price elasticity is $\eta_P < 1$.

To establish the relationship, consider the demand function as drawn:

$$P = f(Q)$$

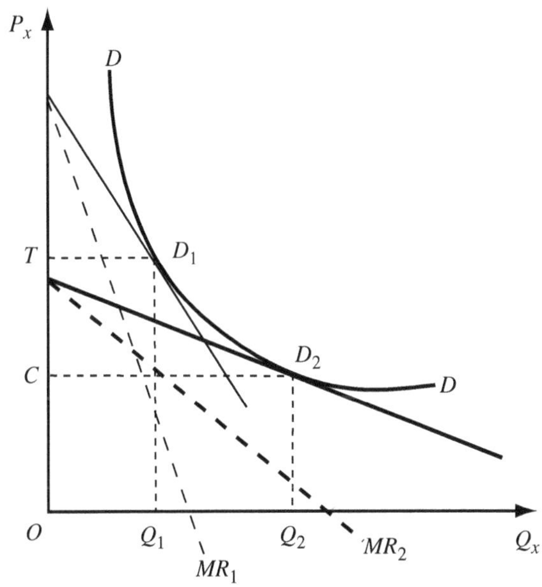

Figure 3.10
Deriving the marginal revenue from a non-linear demand curve

Consider the total revenue:

$$TR = PQ = [f(Q)]Q$$

Hence:

$$MR = \frac{\mathrm{d}(PQ)}{\mathrm{d}Q} = P\frac{\mathrm{d}Q}{\mathrm{d}Q} + Q\frac{\mathrm{d}P}{\mathrm{d}Q}$$

Thus:

$$MR = P + Q\frac{\mathrm{d}P}{\mathrm{d}Q}$$

Recall that price elasticity of demand may be written as follows:

$$\eta_P = -\frac{\mathrm{d}Q}{\mathrm{d}P} \cdot \frac{P}{Q}$$

The negative sign for price elasticity of demand is included here, as is required for computational purposes because of the negative relationship between change in price and change in quantity.

In order to establish the relationship between *MR* and price elasticity, one must be substituted into the other. In order to substitute price elasticity into the *MR* equation, it is necessary to re-arrange the price elasticity equation in order to find an element in common with *MR*. This is:

$$\frac{\mathrm{d}P}{\mathrm{d}Q}$$

Re-arranging the elasticity equation gives:

$$\frac{\mathrm{d}Q}{\mathrm{d}P} = -\frac{Q}{P}\eta_P$$

or:

$$\frac{\mathrm{d}P}{\mathrm{d}Q} = -\frac{P}{Q\eta_P}$$

Thus given that:

$$MR = P + Q\frac{\mathrm{d}P}{\mathrm{d}Q}$$

the following substitution should be made:

$$-\frac{P}{Q\eta_P} \quad \text{for} \quad \frac{\mathrm{d}P}{\mathrm{d}Q}$$

This gives:

$$MR = P - Q\frac{P}{Q\eta_P}$$

This implies that:

$$MR = P - \frac{P}{\eta_P}$$

or:

$$MR = P\left(1 - \frac{1}{\eta_P}\right)$$

This is a critically important result for microeconomic analysis. From this result it follows that:

When $\eta_P = 1$, $MR = 0$ (*TR* is a maximum and demand curve is at mid-point).

When $\eta_P > 1$, $MR > 0$ (*TR* is rising and demand curve is in upper half).

When $\eta_P < 1$, $MR < 0$ (*TR* is falling and demand curve is in lower half).

3.2.7 Applications of price elasticity of demand to pricing decisions

As a consequence of the above relationship, a change in price has a different (and opposite) effect on total revenue, depending on whether the price changes are taking place in the upper (elastic) or lower (inelastic) portion of the demand curve.

- When price is in the elastic (upper) half of the demand curve, an increase in price reduces the total revenue of the seller and a reduction in price increases the total revenue of the seller.
- When price is in the in-elastic (lower) half of the demand curve, an increase in price increases the total revenue of the seller and a reduction in price reduces the total revenue of the seller.

This is an important result that is not generally recognized. Intuitively, sellers usually accept that an increase in price always increases total revenue. However, since firms should ***always*** operate in the upper half of their demand curve (needed for profit maximization), then raising the price must mean a reduction in their total revenue.

Total revenue and profits

It is of great importance to recognize that, while raising price while operating in the upper half of the demand curve will ***always*** reduce total revenue, it will not always reduce total profit. The profit maximization point is somewhere in the upper half of the demand curve. Profits are maximized where $MC = MR$ and since MC is greater than zero, MR must also be greater than zero. MR is only greater than zero in the upper half of the demand curve since *MR* goes to zero at the point related to the mid-point of the demand curve and then becomes negative thereafter. Hence:

- When price is increased in the upper (elastic) portion of the demand curve from the mid-point of the demand curve towards the profit-maximization point, the seller experiences a reduction in total revenue ***but an increase in profits***.
- When price is increased from the profit-maximization point, the seller experiences a reduction in both total revenue and profits.
- When price is reduced in the upper portion of the demand curve the seller always experiences an increase in revenue so long as the reduction does not go below the mid-point of the demand curve. However, if the reduction goes below the profit maximization point (which is above the mid-point), there is an increase in revenue but a decrease in profit.
- When price is increased in the lower half of the demand curve, both total revenue and profits increase.
- When price is decreased in the lower half of the demand curve, both total revenue and profits decrease.

A more detailed exposition on the effects of price elasticity of demand on revenue and profits is provided in Chapter 10.

International trade, price elasticity of demand and devaluation

The significance of price elasticity of demand for the revenue of a firm is similar to that for a trading country on the demand side. If a country is exporting a commodity that is price inelastic in the foreign market to which the country is exporting, then raising the price of that commodity raises total revenue (foreign exchange receipts) for that country. On the contrary, if the commodity is price elastic in the export market, then raising the price of the commodity results in a fall in total revenue and a fall in foreign exchange receipts. However, profitability for the country depends on whether the rise in price takes the price above the profit maximization point for that particular commodity.

Very often, price changes in exports are effected through movements in the exchange rates. A currency devaluation by an exporting country is essentially an attempt to lower the price of the country's exports (and raise the price of its imports). However, in some cases, unsophisticated governments sometimes believe or are led to believe that a drop in the price of their exports through devaluation of their currency would allow more of their goods to be sold abroad and that selling more goods abroad must necessarily mean taking more revenue (foreign exchange) from exports and be more profitable for the exporting country. This would happen only where the export goods are highly price elastic in the export market.

Moreover, the devaluing country must also consider the domestic price elasticity of demand for the imported goods into the country. The price of these imports will rise but if domestic demand for them is inelastic, then reduction in domestic consumption will be smaller than the increase in price, leading to an increase in revenues for the foreign suppliers to the detriment of the domestic economy.

Countries aiming to benefit from a currency devaluation must pay special attention to price elasticities of demand for both their imports and for their exports. This is the foundation of the Marshall–Lerner condition, which states that in order for a fall in a country's exchange rate (devaluation) to reduce the country's Balance of Payments deficit (i.e. increase the country's foreign reserves), the sum of the price elasticity of demand coefficients for exports and imports must be greater than one.

3.3 THE INCOME ELASTICITY OF DEMAND

In addition to the price elasticity of demand, the income elasticity of demand provides a useful tool for the analysis of consumer behaviour and for planning by the firm or the state.

3.3.1 Definition of income elasticity of demand

The income elasticity (η_Y) for commodity x may be defined as:

$$\eta_Y = \frac{\text{proportionate change in quantity of good } x\,(Q_x)}{\text{proportionate change in income } (Y)}$$

This may be written as:

$$\eta_Y = \frac{\mathrm{d}Q_x/Q_x}{\mathrm{d}Y/Y}$$

or:

$$\eta_Y = \frac{\mathrm{d}Q_x}{\mathrm{d}Y} \cdot \frac{Y}{Q_x}$$

where the Y used for income in the above equations is really the $\bar{Y}$ used to symbolize real (as opposed to nominal) income.

As explained in Chapter 2, the income-consumption curve (*ICC*) is used to derive the Engel curve. The Engel curve is then used for illustration of the income elasticity of demand. The Engel curve shows the relationship between real income ($\bar{Y}$) and the quantity of commodity x demanded (Q_x).

Using Figure 3.11, the income elasticity of demand η_Y for good x may be computed using the formula for income elasticity. The income elasticity at the point R ($\eta_Y(R)$) on the Engel curve is found diagrammatically as follows:

- Drop a perpendicular from the point R to the X-axis at S.
- Take a perpendicular from the point R across to the Y-axis at A.
- Identify from the diagram, the components of the income elasticity formula:

$$\eta_Y = \frac{\mathrm{d}Q_x}{\mathrm{d}Y} \cdot \frac{Y}{Q_x}$$

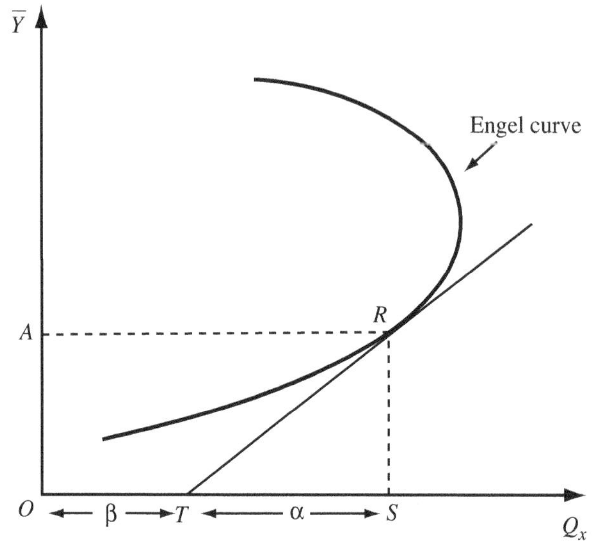

Figure 3.11
The Engel curve and income elasticity of demand

In the income elasticity formula given above, it is the ***inverse*** of the slope of the Engel curve that is represented by the expression:

$$\frac{dQ_x}{dY}$$

In Figure 3.11, the slope of the Engel curve at the point R may be expressed as:

$$\frac{dY}{dQ_x} = \frac{RS}{TS}$$

- Hence, inverting the slope at the point R gives:

$$\frac{dQ_x}{dY} = \frac{TS}{SR}$$

- Also from the elasticity formula, the following may be identified at the point R: $Y = OA$ and $Q_x = OS$. Hence:

$$\frac{Y}{Q_x} = \frac{OA}{OS}$$

- Since OA is equal to SR, the above expression may be written as:

$$\frac{Y}{Q_x} = \frac{SR}{OS}$$

- Hence, the income elasticity at the point R on the Engel curve is:

$$\eta_Y(R) = \frac{dQ_x}{dY} \cdot \frac{Y}{Q_x} = \frac{TS}{SR} \cdot \frac{SR}{OS} = \frac{TS}{OS}$$

Graphically, then, the income elasticity at the point R may be identified as:

$$\eta_Y(R) = \frac{TS}{OS}$$

It is useful to note that, as a mnemonic, this formula may be translated as follows.

Income elasticity of demand at any point (R) along an Engel curve may be measured along the X-axis, as ***the distance between the perpendicular and the tangent (TS) divided by the distance between the perpendicular and the origin (OS)***. In the example in Figure 3.11, the perpendicular from the point R meets the X-axis at the point S, whereas the tangent from the point R meets the X-axis at the point T. The origin is the point O.

Thus graphically, using Figure 3.11, income elasticity at the point R may be described as:

$$\eta_Y(R) = \frac{TS}{OS} = \frac{\alpha}{\beta}$$

3.3.2 Variation in income elasticity along an Engel curve

Consider other points in addition to point R on the Engel curve.

At the point N in Figure 3.12, the income elasticity is:

$$\eta_Y(N) = \frac{GL}{LN} \cdot \frac{LN}{OL} = \frac{GL}{OL}$$

This income elasticity at N may be measured using the short-hand diagrammatic formula of the distance between the perpendicular and the tangent (GL) divided by the distance between the perpendicular and the origin (OL) along the X-axis. In the example in Figure 3.12, the perpendicular from the point N meets the X-axis at the point L, whereas the tangent from the point M meets the X-axis at the point G. The origin is the point O. This gives:

$$\eta_Y(N) = \frac{GL}{OL} = \frac{\alpha}{\beta}$$

Now, since $GL > OL$, the result is:

$$\eta_Y(N) = \frac{GL}{OL} > 1$$

The following should also be noted:

- Where the tangent at any point extends to the left of the origin on the X-axis, the income elasticity of demand at that point is greater than 1 or:

$$\eta_Y > 1$$

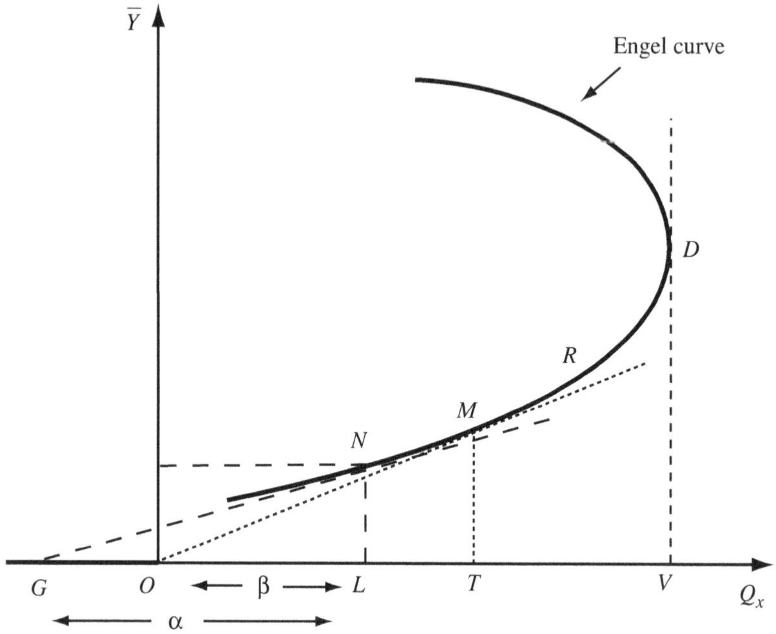

Figure 3.12
Variation in income elasticity along the Engel curve

- The tangent at the point M on the Engel curve in Figure 3.12 extends through the origin (O) and the perpendicular reaches the X-axis at the point T. This indicates that the distance between the perpendicular and the tangent (OT) is the same as the distance between the perpendicular and the origin (OT). Hence at the point M (or at any point where the tangent to the point is a ray from the origin), the income elasticity of demand is:

$$\eta_Y(M) = \frac{OT}{OT} = 1$$

- Where the tangent at any point on the Engel curve does not extend as far as the origin (such as at the point R) then the income elasticity of demand at that point is less than one, or:

$$\eta_Y < 1$$

- At the turning point D, the income elasticity of demand is ***zero***. This is because the numerator (difference between the perpendicular and the tangent) is zero, since the perpendicular DV is also the tangent to the point D. Hence:

$$\eta_Y(D) = \frac{0}{OV} = 0$$

- For points beyond the turning point D, where the tangent intersects the X-axis to the right of the perpendicular from the turning point (DV), then the income elasticity is negative. That is:

$$\eta_Y < 0.$$

In general, the income elasticity of demand decreases as real income increases. Furthermore:

- For a superior good: $\eta_Y > 1$
- For a normal good: $1 < \eta_Y > 0$
- For an inferior good: $\eta_Y < 0$

3.3.3 Application of income elasticity of demand

The following are features of the income elasticity of demand:

- Income elasticity of demand may be used to classify goods into luxuries or necessities. It may also be used to give an indication of the state of development of a country.
- A high value for income elasticity of demand (greater than one) implies that the commodity is a luxury. The importance of this is that, as real income increases, the demand for the commodity increases more than proportionately. This causes the demand curve for the commodity to shift outwards.
- A low but positive value for income elasticity of demand (greater than zero but less than one) implies that the commodity is a necessity (i.e. quantity demanded not particularly responsive to income levels). Hence as real income increases, the demand for the commodity increases less than proportionately. The demand curve for the commodity still shifts outwards but only moderately so.
- A value for income elasticity of demand that is less than zero implies that the commodity is an inferior good. An increase in income is met with a decreased demand for this type of commodity. Consequently, when real income increases, the demand curve shifts inwards. Conversely, when real income decreases, the demand curve for an inferior good shifts outwards.
- The value of the income elasticity of demand is affected by time. Consumption adjusts with a time lag.

Inferior goods

Inferior goods are not necessarily intrinsically inferior in nature but are commodities which, in a particular economic environment, are considered commonplace, cheap and readily available to low income earners. As real income improves consumers tend to reject such commodities in favour of commodities they could not previously afford, hence their income elasticity of demand is less than zero (i.e. negative).

However, in recessionary times, with decreases in real income, the demand for inferior goods (and services) increases. There have been many examples of this phenomenon over time. In the 2008 financial crisis that spread across the world industrial countries, it was immediately noticeable that demand was increasing for certain goods and services that, in better financial times, were the domain of the lower income consumers only. Prof. Greg Mankiw of Harvard University (Mankiw, 2008) reported that during this time, even as consumers were cutting back on purchases of many items, sales of Spam (a name of a brand of canned luncheon meat now more familiarly known as a common noun representing undesirable material received via the internet) were holding steady.

Mankiw (2008) also reported the comments of a spokesperson for a major supermarket chain who indicated the demand for rice and beans (described as 'belly fillers') had recorded a double digit increase under the adverse growth prospects for the American economy. These are obviously commodities that had been abandoned by many as real income was increasing but were being reverted to as real income started to fall. As inferior goods they are on the backward bending portion of the Engel curve which shows a negative relationship between income and consumption of the commodity.

It is useful to note that a commodity that is an inferior good in one country may be a normal or even a superior good in another country. One example is that of (Irish) potatoes. In countries where they are widely grown and are plentiful and cheap, such as in Ireland, other parts of Europe and South America in the Andean region, may be seen as a symbol of low income consumption and fit the description of an inferior good. However, in parts of Asia, Africa and the Caribbean where these potatoes must be imported and are relatively expensive, their increased consumption (particularly as potato chips or French fries) may reflect growing real income representing a normal or even a superior good. Hence, the term 'inferior good' is not used in a globally pejorative sense as an intrinsic unfavourable characteristic of the good, but is simply contextual.

Engel's law

Engel's law says: The percentage of income spent on food declines as real income increases or more precisely, the incremental spending on food out of incremental income declines as real income increases.

This law is used to measure welfare and the stage of development of an economy. In a poor country, a large percentage of income is spent on food. Initially, as the people in a country gain more wealth (higher per capita ***real*** income), the proportion of the additional income spent on food increases. However, as real income continues to increase, the proportion of the additional income spent on food declines. Consequently, the changes in the incremental spending on food out of increasing income may be used as an indicator of the extent to which a society is becoming affluent.

Engel's law, however, may be applied not only to food, but to almost any other product depending on the position at which it is situated in its product cycle. Almost any product (food or service) that has been on the market in the same form over a long enough period tends to have the desire for it wane. As a consequence, it will eventually face this broader version of Engel's law. Suppliers of goods and services often find it necessary to continue to re-invent or re-engineer their products in order to enhance the market preference for that product and delay the onset of the backward bending portion of the Engel curve.

Importance of income elasticity for demand and revenue

As explained above, income elasticity of demand affects the demand curve. It is a shift factor. With an increase in real income, an income elasticity greater than zero for a commodity shifts the demand curve outwards, whereas an income elasticity of less than zero shifts the demand curve inwards.

An outward shift in the demand curve means that the firm can increase its total revenue either by selling the same quantity at a higher price, or a greater quantity at the same price. The firm may do some of both as it moves to a new $MC = MR$ profit maximization position in response to the outward shift in the demand curve and, consequently, in the marginal revenue curve.

The higher the income elasticity of demand for a good, the greater is the outward shift in the demand curve for that good and the greater the increase in profitability of the firm supplying the good when income increases in the market.

An income elasticity of demand of say, three ($\eta_Y = 3$), for a commodity means that as income increases in that market by any percentage, then the demand for that commodity increases by three times as much. For example, if income in the market for the commodity should increase by 10 per cent, the demand for that commodity would increase by 30 per cent. This allows the firm or organization selling the commodity to have an increase in gross income three times the growth rate of income in the market to which it is selling. The firm selling the product with that level of income elasticity is enabled to grow faster than the growth in the market to which it is selling.

Application to the firm – Expansion plans

A firm considering whether to expand should seek to ascertain the relevant value and trends in the income elasticity of demand for its goods. It also needs to obtain forecasting information on whether the economy in which it is selling is approaching boom or bust. If the market situation experiences a boom that is likely to continue for the medium term, then a high (and increasing) income elasticity means that the firm can increase both output and price over time and hence improve its revenue and its profitability (assuming constant or near constant costs). The firm should therefore consider expanding in order to take advantage of the market conditions.

On the contrary, where the commodity being sold by the firm has a negative income elasticity of demand, then boom conditions and increasing wealth lead to a reduced demand (inward shift of the demand curve) for the commodity. This would see the firm's revenue and profits reducing when income in its target market is increasing. A firm selling a commodity that is an inferior good should shelve any expansion plans during a period of economic boom and rising real incomes.

The reverse would hold true in times of recession or falling real incomes. During the 2008 financial crisis in the major industrialized countries, several observations were made about increases in demand for inferior goods and services. As an example, lengthening lines at hot-dog stands and single-window take-out snackettes were observed as middle and lower level executives abandoned the expensive restaurants where they previously had lunch during the boom times. Where the recession is expected to be prolonged, the clue to the providers of such 'inferior' goods and services would be to expand.

Application to a country – Trade policy

All that is said above in relation to income elasticity and revenue for a firm can be applied to a country trading in the international arena. A country that is exporting to the international market should consider the income elasticity of demand and the economic climate in its target market. The same analysis applies to a country as to a firm and so the conditions which must be considered are similar to those of a firm as set out above.

Many developing countries sell commodities that may fit the description of 'inferior' goods, which, as said before, is not a pejorative term but simply means that as income increases, the demand decreases. As a consequence, countries depending on export of these inferior goods must find that, as incomes in their international markets increase, the demand curve for their export commodities shifts inwards. The inward shift means that these developing countries must either drop their prices to sell the same output or be forced to sell less if they want to retain the same market price (or some of both).

Nevertheless, any country that persists in concentrating on exporting a commodity(s) with negative income elasticity of demand would find that, as world income grows, the demand for their exports would fall, thereby causing the exporting country's total revenue from abroad (and foreign exchange reserves) to fall. To the extent that export growth is being used to fuel domestic growth, domestic growth would be retarded and the income gap between this exporting country and the rest of the world (its export market) would continue to widen. The country would tend to see a secular deterioration in its terms of trade.

The condition would be exacerbated where the developing country is importing normal or luxury goods from the same international market to which it is selling its 'inferior' goods. Every attempt to grow domestic income would be met by an increase in the demand for these imports almost equal to or greater than the increase in domestic income.

The reverse would be true in times of recession where the demand for the inferior goods would tend to increase or to fall less than the fall in real income. However, recessions tend to be generally of shorter duration than periods of growth.

The trade policy implications of income elasticity of demand suggest that for growth through trade to take place, the exports should be concentrated on high income elasticity goods or services. Some evidence of this is seen in the rapid growth of the Japanese economy through the export of high income elasticity of demand goods to western markets. In particular, the export of automobiles proved to be a major boost to export receipts of that country. Many studies, including those done by Chow (1957, 1960), examined the income elasticity for automobiles and found it to be greater than two. Studies generally showed an income elasticity of demand for automobiles (A) in the region of three ($\eta_Y(A) = 3$). This meant that an average increase in income in the Western markets of 10 per cent would have resulted in an increase in the demand for automobiles by 30 per cent. This would have allowed Japanese automobile exports to grow faster than the growth in the markets to which they were exporting. With automobiles as the major export, the export growth multiplier would then have allowed that economy to grow at a rate faster than the growth rate in its export markets.

This experience is similar to the rapid growth that took place in the East Asian Newly Industrializing Countries (NICs) after 1970, where their growth in export value exceeded the growth in the countries to which they were exporting through the export of high income elasticity of demand goods and services.

In general, studies have found that basic foodstuffs have the lowest (and often negative) income elasticity of demand, while manufactured goods tend to have income elasticity values between zero and one. Service industries tend to have the highest values for income elasticity of demand. However, within these broad categories there are many variations. In developing country markets, sugar, tea and margarine are among commodities found to have the lowest (and mostly negative) income elasticity values.

Azzam (2003) found negative or close to zero income elasticity values for a number of foodstuffs of the types exported by developing countries. These included cane sugar (−0.412), soybean oil (0.186) and roasted coffee (0.397). It should be noted, however, that, in many developing countries, the income elasticity of demand for these same products may be much higher than in the export markets in the developed world. For example, Ramasubban (1983) found the income elasticity of demand for sugar in Tanzania to be 1.2 compared with the zero or negative rates found in developed country markets.

These findings on income elasticity of demand suggest that trade policy for growth must focus on exporting goods and services with high income elasticity of demand. Services such as tourism, international business and the financial sector are often highly recommended where trading is with highly developed countries. However, it is possible to find niches in many other areas of dynamic demand.

3.4 CROSS PRICE ELASTICITY OF DEMAND

3.4.1 Definition

The cross price elasticity of demand, η_{xy}, measures the responsiveness of quantity demanded of one commodity (x) to a change in the price of another commodity (y). It is used to identify substitutes and complements and to determine the extent of an industry or product group.

For cross price elasticity with regard to two goods only, the quantity of good x demanded depends not only on the price of good x but on the price of good y as well. The function may therefore be written as:

$$Q_x = f(P_x, P_y)$$

As established earlier, the price elasticity of demand for commodity x is:

$$\eta_x = \frac{\mathrm{d}Q_x}{Q_x} \div \frac{\mathrm{d}P_x}{P_x}$$

The cross price elasticity of demand becomes:

$$\eta_{xy} = \frac{\mathrm{d}Q_x}{Q_x} \div \frac{\mathrm{d}P_y}{P_y}$$

Formally then, the cross price elasticity (cross elasticity) between goods x and y (η_{xy}) may be expressed as:

$$\eta_{xy} = \frac{\text{proportionate change in quantity of good } x(Q_x)}{\text{proportionate change in price of good } y(P_y)}$$

This may be further set out as:

$$\eta_{xy} = \frac{\mathrm{d}Q_x/Q_x}{\mathrm{d}P_y/P_y} = \frac{\mathrm{d}Q_x}{Q_x} \cdot \frac{P_y}{\mathrm{d}P_y} = \frac{\mathrm{d}Q_x}{\mathrm{d}P_y} \cdot \frac{P_y}{Q_x}$$

3.4.2 Application of cross price elasticity

Classification of goods into substitutes or complements

Goods are classified as substitutes or complements depending on whether $\eta_{xy} > 0$ or $\eta_{xy} < 0$ as follows:

- If $\eta_{xy} < 0$ (negative), then the goods x and y are complementary goods.
- If $\eta_{xy} > 0$ (positive), then the goods x and y are substitute goods.

Identification of industry or product group

Cross price elasticity is also used to assist with the definition of firms which form an industry. The main determinant of the cross price elasticity is the nature of the commodities relative to their uses. If two goods can satisfy the same need the cross price elasticity is high and vice versa. A high value for cross price elasticity therefore tends to suggest that the commodities belong to the same industry.

The value and sign for cross price elasticity can, in some cases, be misleading for defining an industry. Some items may appear to be strong substitutes but be quite unrelated as common goods. With the steep increase in the price of oil in the mid 2000s, some unusual substitutes have been observed other than the usual substitution of small cars for larger, gas-guzzling ones. Moneyterms, UK (2008) noted that the increase in oil prices led to an increase in the demand for camels in Rajasthan. These two cannot be even remotely construed as belonging to the same industry or product group. Similarly where, in the past, smokers wanting to be rid of their addiction to cigarettes would sometimes turn to chewing gum, the two (cigarettes and gum), although appearing to be substitutes in the smoker's mind, could not reasonably be considered as industrial substitutes.

Public sector policies must also consider cross price elasticities. Any tax imposed on an industry that leads to a fall in demand for the goods of that industry will also impose a similar burden on any industry producing complementary goods. On the other hand, it will have a positive impact on an industry producing substitute goods. Similarly, where government preferences in procurement favour a particular industry, the favour extends to any industry producing a complementary product.

The outcomes of the effects of price, income and cross elasticities on consumption, revenues and profits are, in the main, not intuitive. Consequently, it is imperative that all types of elasticities of demand be understood at all levels within the private and public sectors as they can have tremendous effects on revenues and profitability of enterprises, on the consuming public and on a country success or failure in the international trading arena.

REVIEW QUESTIONS FOR CHAPTER 3

1 Explain carefully the concept of elasticity and:

(a) Show why and how price elasticity varies along a straight line negatively sloped demand curve.
(b) Graph the relationship between the demand curve and the marginal and total revenue curves.
(c) Hence or otherwise show how a change in price by a firm affects the revenue of the firm.
(d) Illustrate how income elasticity varies along an Engel curve and the information it provides for managerial decision making within the firm.

2 Show and explain the derivation of the Engel curve from the income–consumption curve, explaining the significance of income elasticity for management decisions.

3 With regard to the concept of elasticity of demand:

(a) Showing how and why price elasticity of demand (η_P) varies along a negatively sloped linear demand curve ***carefully*** explain and ***illustrate*** why a firm operating where $\eta_P > 1$ may not achieve an increase in revenue or profits when it increases its price. Compare this result with that for a firm operating where $\eta_P < 1$.
(b) Show how income elasticity (η_Y) is measured and, using the Engel curve, explain how it might be used to assist a country deciding whether to expand an export industry.
(c) Briefly explain cross price elasticity of demand and discuss its economic significance.

4 Assume you are a consultant to a firm PlumpChick, a producer of chicken for the domestic market. Explain convincingly to the management of PlumpChick:

(a) The concept of price elasticity of demand (η_P) illustrating how the value of elasticity depends on where PlumpChick is selling on its downward sloping demand curve.
(b) How price elasticity of demand (η_P) and total revenue are related to help PlumpChick understand why every time it raises its price its revenue declines further and what is the connection to the firm's profitability.
(c) The concept of income elasticity of demand (η_Y) using the Engel curve to show what factors might cause you to advise PlumpChick not to consider expanding their plant capacity at this time.

(d) Why an increase in the price of chicken results in an increase in the demand for fish using the concept of cross price elasticity of demand (η_{xy}).

5 HardBench is a hypothetical manufacturer of wooden furniture. Attempt to explain to this firm:

(a) Why its price elasticity (η_P) is less than one because of its position on the demand curve.
(b) Why, given the relationship between demand, marginal revenue and total revenue, HardBench should increase its price if it wants to increase revenue and profits.
(c) Why income elasticity (η_Y) findings along the Engel curve for the product might suggest that HardBench should seriously consider plans for expansion.
(d) Why a government tax on plastic furniture should be helpful to HardBench because of the sign and value of cross price elasticity (η_{XY}).

6 Country *A* is exporting sugar to and importing high-tech manufactures and services from country *B*. Explain how and why:

(a) Country *A* is seeing a fall in its income relative to country *B*.
(b) A devaluation of the currency of country *A* relative to that of country *B* makes country *A* relatively worse off.

RECOMMENDED READING FOR CHAPTER 3

Azzam, A. (2003) 'Estimates and Interpretation of Income Elasticities of Demand for Food Products', *Cornhusker Economics*, Lincoln: University of Nebraska. Online posting. Available at: <http://digitalcommons.unl.edu/agecon_cornhusker/103> (Accessed November 30, 2008).

Chow, G. (1957) *Demand for Automobiles in the United States*, Amsterdam: North Holland.

Chow, G. (1960) 'Statistical Demand Functions for Automobiles and Their Use for Forecasting', in Harberger, A. (ed.) *The Demand for Durable Goods*, Chicago: University of Chicago Press: 149–78.

Mankiw, G. (2008) 'Inferior Goods', *Greg Mankiw's Blog: Random Observations for Students of Economics*. Online posting. Available at: <http://gregmankiw.blogspot.com/2008/11/inferior-goods.html> (Accessed November 30, 2008).

Ramasubban, T. A. (1983) 'An econometric Analysis of Consumer Demand for Sugar in Tanzania', *The Developing Economies* 21(2): 160–83. Online posting. Available at: http://www.ide.go.jp/English/Publish/De/pdf/83_02_04.pdf (Accessed November 28, 2008).

Schultz, H. (1966) *The Theory and Measurement of Demand*, Chicago: University of Chicago Press.

Wold, H. and Juréen, L. (1952) *Demand Analysis: A Study in Econometrics*, NY: Wiley (new edition (1982), Greenwood Press).

4 Topics in Demand Analysis

Consumer and Producer Surplus; Price Index (Laspèyres, Paasche); The "Characteristics" Approach; Price/Rent Controls; External Effects on Consumption; The Neumann-Morgenstern Utility Index; Empirical Demand Functions.

There are several additional topics within the theory of the consumer that enhance the understanding of consumer behaviour and have valuable real-world applications. As with many areas of microeconomics, these applications tend to be universal in nature, having relevance within many types of economies. This chapter introduces additional concepts and furnishes new analytical tools and approaches that are useful to sellers, buyers and policy makers in any environment.

The topics examined in this chapter are:

1 Consumer and Producer surplus
2 Laspeyrès and Paasche price indices and the income index
3 The characteristics approach to demand analysis
4 Price and rent controls
5 External effects on consumption
6 The Neumann–Morgenstern utility index
7 Empirical demand models

4.1 CONSUMER AND PRODUCER SURPLUS

The consumer surplus and producer surplus concepts are used extensively in economic analysis. The uses range from the application to price controls, to price discrimination, to government taxation and extend into centre of the analysis of international trade. These concepts are an integral part of the analysis of welfare gains and losses.

4.1.1 Measuring consumer and producer surplus

The concept of consumer surplus is credited to economist Alfred Marshall (1890). The surplus was measured in monetary units and defined as: 'the difference between the amount of money that a consumer actually pays to buy a certain quantity of a commodity x, and what he would be willing to pay for this quantity rather than do without it'.

The concept of the producer surplus may also be introduced. It may be defined loosely as the difference between what a producer actually receives for the sale of goods and what the producer would have been willing to receive rather than go without selling.

The basic concepts of consumer surplus and producer surplus are illustrated graphically in Figure 4.1. Graphically, at price P_1 the consumer buys quantity Q_3. However, the consumer would have been willing to pay P_2 to acquire quantity Q_2 and P_3 to acquire Q_1. This shows that when market price is in equilibrium at P_1, the customer buys Q_3 but would have been willing to pay higher prices for the earlier units of the commodity. This implies that the consumer has gained from acquiring those earlier units at a price below what he/she was willing to pay for them. This difference is the consumer's surplus represented by the darker shaded area.

The consumer surplus may therefore be recognized as the area above the equilibrium price line and below the demand curve.

On the other hand, the ***producer surplus*** is recognized as the area below the equilibrium price and above the supply curve. The producer was willing to supply smaller quantities of the commodity x at lower prices than P_1 as shown by the market supply curve LT. Every unit sold at the equilibrium price P_1 that the producer would have been willing to sell at a lower price, benefits the producer. This gain on every unit

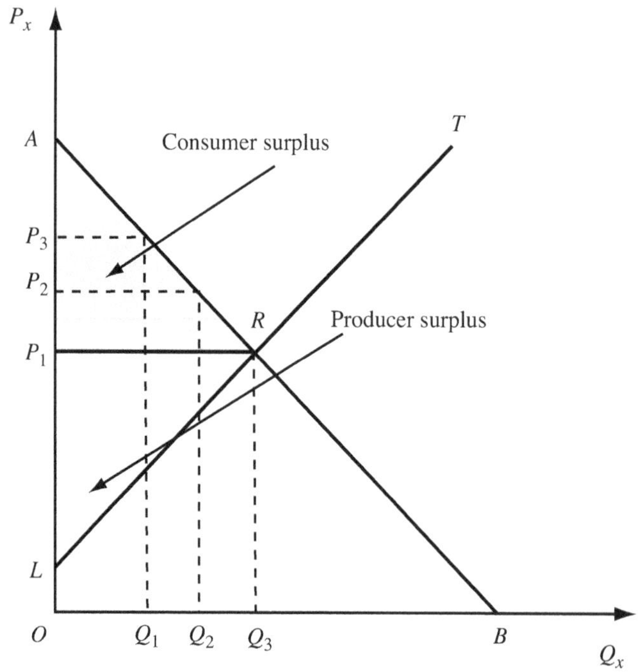

Figure 4.1
Consumer and producer surplus

up to Q_3 is summed to become the producer surplus and may be identified as the area LRP_1 or the more lightly shaded area.

Although both consumer surplus and producer surplus concepts are central to the analysis of welfare and the gains from trade, much more attention is paid to the measurement of the consumer surplus. The Marshallian and the modern approaches are considered.

4.1.2 The Marshallian approach consumer surplus

The tools of the indifference curve and budget lines may also be used to explain Marshallian consumer surplus. Marshall uses money with a marginal utility that is constant. Hence one unit of money can be valued at one.

The Marshallian measurement of consumer surplus is illustrated in Figure 4.2. Representing one unit of money as one (1), the consumer's income is OA. If the entire consumer's income is spent on good x, the consumer can obtain OB of good x.

With the budget line AB, the consumer is in equilibrium at point E on indifference curve IC_3. The consumer buys OQ_1 of good x and retains OM_3 of money. In other words, the consumer spends AM_3 on good x.

To graphically measure the consumer surplus using Marshall's assumption of constant marginal utility (MU) of money, draw an indifference curve through A (the total consumer's income). Since MU of money is constant, the new curve, IC_1, must be vertically parallel to first curve, IC_3, having the same slope at quantity OQ_1. This shows that for the consumer to have the same satisfaction as retaining all his/her income (at A on IC_1), the consumer can buy OQ_1 of good x and retain OM_1 of income. This indicates

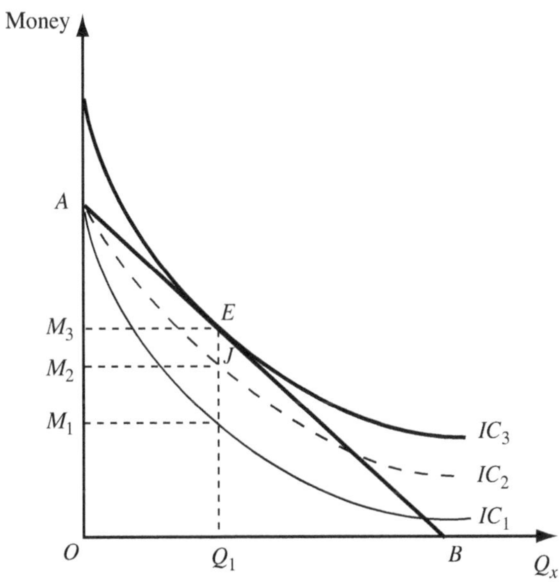

Figure 4.2
Marshallian consumer surplus

that the consumer is willing to pay M_1A for OQ_1 rather than go without it. Thus the consumer surplus is M_1M_3.

Alternative measure

If it is assumed that the MU of money is not constant, the slope of the lower indifference curve is less steep implying that when the consumer has less money the consumer is less willing to trade money for good x. This gives an indifference curve IC_2 that is flatter than Marshall's curve IC_1. This says that the consumer is willing to take OQ_1 of good x and retain OM_2 of income instead of the OM_1 under constant marginal utility of money. Thus, instead of being willing to pay M_1A for OQ_1, the consumer is only willing to pay M_2A compared to the M_3A that is required to be paid. The consumer surplus is therefore measured as the distance M_2M_3, which is less than the distance M_1M_3.

At quantity OQ_1:

$$\left[\frac{\text{slope of } IC_2}{\text{at } J}\right] < \left[\frac{\text{slope of } IC_3}{\text{at } E}\right]$$

or:

$$\frac{MU_X^{(J)}}{MU_M} < \frac{MU_X^{(E)}}{MU_M}$$

4.1.3 Modern measurement of consumer surplus

In the modern approach, the use of money as a measuring rod is removed, and so too is the need for the restrictive assumption of constant marginal utility of money. The modern solution measures consumer surplus in terms of quantity of goods exchanged for each other. The consumer surplus for good x is measured in terms of the quantity of good y times the price of good y.

This approach, measuring the consumer surplus for good x, is illustrated in Figure 4.3. The consumer has a budget constraint y_2B and is in initial equilibrium at point E on IC_2. The consumer can spend the entire budget on good y and purchase y_2 or all on good x and purchase OB. IC_2 reaches the axis for good y at y_3. This shows that the consumer is indifferent between spending the entire budget on good y only (buying y_3) and spending on both x and y at the combination given by the coordinates of the point E, thereby having Q_2 of good x.

In the modern version, the consumer surplus may be measured in either one of two ways:

- The compensation effect
- The equivalence effect

4.1.3.1 THE COMPENSATION EFFECT

This measurement shows how much money the consumer would have to be compensated with in order to be at least as well off as at the equilibrium point E, if the consumer

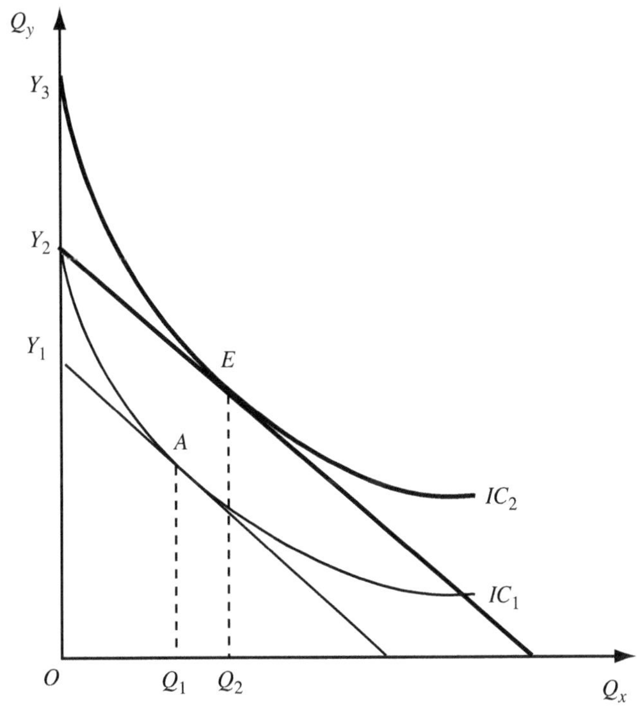

Figure 4.3
Modern measurement of consumer surplus

is forced to go without good x. If the consumer has to do without good x (consume only good y), then for the consumer to be equally well off the consumer must be able to stay on IC_2. Consuming only good y on IC_2 means that the consumer must be compensated with enough income to permit consuming y_3 of good y. Now the consumer's budget only allows consumption of y_2 if the entire budget is spent on good y. Hence, in order to keep the consumer as well off as at E, it would be necessary to increase the consumer's income to a level such that the consumer can increase consumption of good y from y_2 to y_3. The distance y_2y_3 therefore represents the compensation effect.

This however is only measured in quantities of good y. In order to get a value measurement, it is necessary to multiply the quantity of good y by its price. The compensation effect may therefore be measured as $(y_2y_3)P_y$.

4.1.3.2 THE EQUIVALENCE EFFECT

Alternatively, the measurement may be done from a completely different perspective. The question now is, if the consumer is forced to consume only good y (i.e. go without good x) on the current budget (i.e. stay on budget line y_2B) then what is it equivalent to as an income reduction?

Clearly, if the consumer spends all the current income on good y, thereby consuming y_2 (going without x), then the consumer cannot stay on indifference curve IC_2 and must go onto a lower indifference curve. This is equivalent to a reduction in income for the consumer.

To measure this equivalence, an indifference curve is drawn through the point y_2 where the consumer must now operate. This is IC_1 meaning that the consumer is now less well off but by how much is still to be determined. The technique is to shift the budget line inwards until it is tangent to this lower indifference curve. This happens at the point A. This means the consumer is indifferent between consuming only good y and consuming at A with both x (Q_1) and y. This loss may therefore be measured by the reduction in the intercept of the budget line from y_2 to y_1. Hence the distance on the Y-axis, y_2y_1 is used to measure the equivalence effect.

In order to convert this to a value, the distance y_2y_1 is multiplied by the price of y. Thus the equivalence effect is $(y_2y_1)P_y$.

It may be noted that although the compensation effect and the equivalence effect may both be used to measure the consumer surplus, they are not identical and cannot be expected to give identical values. One or the other may be used.

4.2 PRICE INDICES

The ordinal utility theory proves useful in the construction of index numbers of the cost of living. These indices are associated with the measurement of inflation and other concerns about the cost of living (e.g. whether wages are keeping pace with the cost of living) and changes in welfare. Price indices are a highly practical tool used by governments, the unions, the business community and producers.

Two main price indices are used – The Laspèyres Price Index and the Paasche Price Index. These are usually compared to an Income index to assess welfare improvements of the working population.

The economic problem is often of this type: If a worker earned \$10,000 in 1980 and \$12,000 in 2008, a 20 per cent increase in income, was that worker really better off in 2008, or were prices so much higher in 2008 that the worker was actually worse off?

With the index, the worker's real income can be determined by dividing the worker's money income by a price index. Thus, if prices went up by less than 20 per cent between 1980 and 2008, the worker is better off in 2008 than in 1980, otherwise the worker is not better off. But price indices are not ideal.

4.2.1 The Laspèyres Price Index

The subscript zero (0) is used to denote base year quantities and prices and the subscript one (1) to denote current year prices and quantities.

The Laspèyres Index measures the change in the cost of the market basket purchased by the consumer in the original or base year (1980) between the base year and the current year (2008).

4.2.1.1 CONSTRUCTION OF THE LASPÈYRES INDEX

The approach is to take the base year goods and compare them in base year prices and in current prices. The Laspèyres index measures the change in the cost of the market basket purchased by the consumer in the original year. From this it can be assessed whether the consumer is better off in terms of command over goods and services.

Using the subscripts zero and one to represent the base year and the current year respectively, then, for a consumer with a basket consisting of n goods, the Laspèyres price index (L) may be written as:

$$L = \frac{\sum_{i=1}^{n} Q_{i0}P_{i1}}{\sum_{i=1}^{n} Q_{i0}P_{i0}} \cdot 100$$

4.2.1.2 USE OF THE LASPÈYRES INDEX

In 2008, the cost of the same (current) market basket that was bought in 1980 is:

$$\sum_{i=1}^{n} Q_{i0}P_{i1}$$

Now if the change in the family's income between 1980 and 2008 exceeds this amount, the family will be better off in 2008, since they can buy the same market basket as in 1980 and more. The family's income in 2008 is:

$$\sum_{i=1}^{n} Q_{i1}P_{i1}$$

The family's income in 2008 will exceed the current year cost of the base year basket of goods if:

$$\frac{\sum_{i=1}^{n} Q_{i0}P_{i1}}{\sum_{i=1}^{n} Q_{i0}P_{i0}} < \frac{\sum_{i=1}^{n} Q_{i1}P_{i1}}{\sum_{i=1}^{n} Q_{i0}P_{i0}}$$

Divide both sides of the inequality by $\sum_{i=1}^{n} Q_{i0}P_{i0}$ [income in the base year] then the family must be better off in 2008 than in 1980 if the Laspèyres Index is less than the ratio of 2008 to 1980 income – 1.20 in this case.

4.2.2 The Paasche Price Index

The Paasche Price Index, on the other hand, measures the change in the cost of the market basket purchased in the current year between the current year and the base year.

Thus the Paasche Index (P) may be written as:

$$P - \frac{\sum_{i=1}^{n} Q_{i1}P_{i1}}{\sum_{i=1}^{n} Q_{i1}P_{i0}} \cdot 100$$

To determine what may be inferred from this index, consider that the family's income went up by 20 per cent between 1980 and 2008. The family must have been better off in 1980 if they could have bought the 2008 market basket in 1980 but did not do so. Thus they must have been better off in 1980 (i.e. worse off now) if:

$$\sum_{i=1}^{n} Q_{io}P_{i0} > \sum_{i=1}^{n} Q_{i1}P_{i0}$$

This suggests that the 2008 basket could have been purchased in base year (1980) but was not. Behind this analysis is the assumption that tastes have remained constant from the base year to the present year.

4.2.3 The income index

The Paasche and Laspèyres' price indices must be compared with the income index to be of relevance. This index compares the base year income with the current year income. It considers the increase in the current year's income over the base year income.

The income index may be written as:

$$I = \frac{\sum_{i=1}^{n} Q_{i1}P_{i1}}{\sum_{i=1}^{n} Q_{i0}P_{i0}} \cdot 100$$

where:

$$\sum_{i=1}^{n} Q_{i0}P_{i0}, \text{ is the base year income}$$

and:

$$\sum_{i=1}^{n} Q_{i1}P_{i1} \text{ is the current year income}$$

Then if $L < I$ it may be concluded that the consumer is better off in the current year (i.e. was worse off in the base year). This comparison may be set out as:

$$\frac{\sum_{i=1}^{n} Q_{i0}P_{i1}}{\sum_{i=1}^{n} Q_{i0}P_{i0}} < \frac{\sum_{i=1}^{n} Q_{i1}P_{i1}}{\sum_{i=1}^{n} Q_{i0}P_{i0}}$$

However, if $I < P$, the consumer was better off in the base year (i.e. worse off now). This may be expressed as:

$$\frac{\sum_{i=1}^{n} Q_{i1}P_{i1}}{\sum_{i=1}^{n} Q_{i0}P_{i0}} < \frac{\sum_{i=1}^{n} Q_{i1}P_{i1}}{\sum_{i=1}^{n} Q_{i1}P_{i0}}$$

In summary, the Laspèyres condition tells if the consumer's welfare has improved from the base year to the present whereas the Paasche's condition tells if welfare was greater in the base year than in the present year. It can be inferred that welfare has increased for the consumer whose ratio of present money income to earlier income is greater than the Laspèyres Index. It can also be inferred that welfare has decreased for the consumer whose earlier money income is less than the Paasche Index. Where neither condition holds, it is not possible to conclude whether welfare has increased, decreased or remained constant. The results are of no value.

These results are based on the assumption that the consumer's tastes and the quality of goods remain constant during the relevant time interval. Otherwise the problem is completely intractable if not meaningless.

4.2.4 Application of price indices

The standard analytical tools of indifference curves and budget lines may be used in applying price indices to the study of the consumer.

The Laspèyres case

Figure 4.4 shows the family's indifference curves, IC_1, IC_2, the budget line of 1980 (AB) and the family's 1980 market basket E_1. Computing the cost of the family's 1980 market basket at 2008 prices show how well off the family is in 2008 with enough money income to purchase the 1980 basket, E_1. Thus the 2008 budget line is CD showing that relative prices for goods x and y have changed over the years.

From Figure 4.4, the family, in 2008, can attain the same bundle of goods E_1 and be on the same indifference curve as in 1980, but, more importantly, the family can now reach a higher indifference curve IC_2. The family is therefore better off in the current year than in the base year (1980).

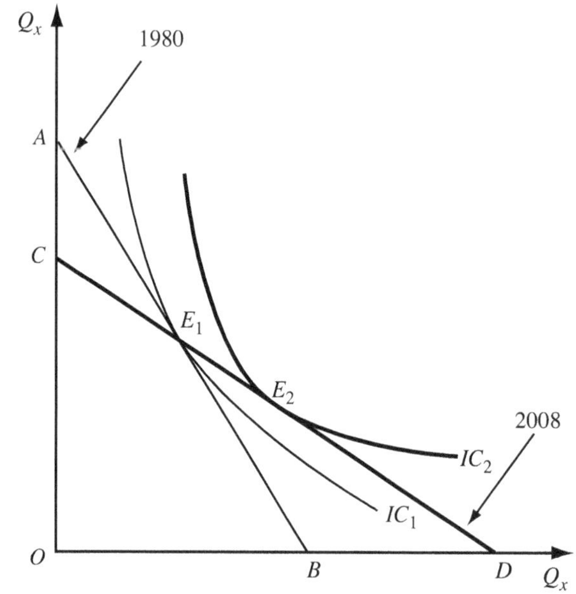

Figure 4.4
The Laspèyres price index

The Paasche case

For the Paasche price index, Figure 4.5 shows the budget line in 2008 (*AB*), the current year, and the family's market basket at E_1 on IC_1. Computing how much the 2008 basket would have cost in the base year, 1980 shows how well off the family would have been in 1980 with the same amount of money income. The 1980 budget line (*CD*) is therefore drawn through the point E_1 and shows a different price ratio (slope) than in 2008. It can be seen that, in 1980 the family could have consumed E_1 and could have been just as well off as in 2008, but more importantly, the family could have attained a higher indifference curve IC_2 by consuming at E_2. Thus it is possible to conclude that the consumer was better off in the base year, 1980.

The ability to measure whether and to what extent the consumer is better off now or was better off previously is highly significant to many groups concerned with the well being of the members of a society. Updated price indices are typically published on a monthly basis and used as an indication of inflation. Comparisons of price indices (usually Laspèyres) with the income index are often part of the negotiations on wages contracts between trade unions and employers.

4.3 THE CHARACTERISTICS APPROACH TO DEMAND THEORY

The characteristics approach to demand theory is attributed to Kelvin Lancaster (1971). This approach views commodities as bundles of attributes or characteristics

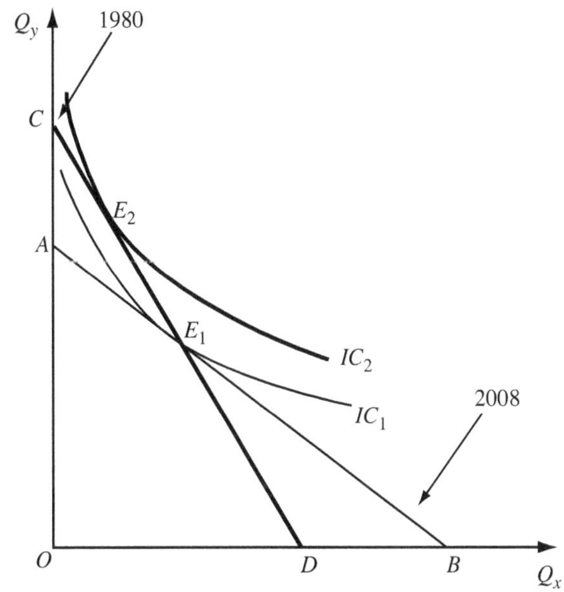

Figure 4.5
The Paasche price index

and, in so doing, is considered to enrich the theory of consumer choice. It considers that it is the individual characteristics of a commodity that give utility to the consumer. Several different commodities may yield the same attribute in different mixtures with other attributes. Some examples are the characteristics of food such as flavour, texture, colour, calories, carbohydrates, fats, protein, vitamins and minerals.

It is assumed that, where the number of goods exceeds the number of characteristics, consumers can easily make a trade off among characteristics by varying the combination of goods that they buy.

4.3.1 Concepts and tools

Consumption technology

Lancaster uses the concept of a 'consumption' technology. Each good represents a technology for producing the characteristics desired 'consumption'. These are the characteristics or attributes desired by the consumer.

The tools

The usual tools of indifference curves and budget lines are used but these are constructed in 'characteristics' space (where the characteristics are represented on the axes). They are drawn to indicate the characteristics rather than the goods themselves.

Table 4.1 Hypothetical characteristics or attributes of fruit used as an example

	Characteristics (attributes)	
Goods	Vitamin A (units)	Vitamin C (units)
Oranges	2	10
Apples	10	2
Mangoes	8	8

4.3.2 Optimization with the 'characteristics' approach

A practical example is used to illustrate how the consumer optimizes with respect to the characteristics of goods.

Consider three goods, oranges, apples and mangoes, each possessing two characteristics (attributes) desired by the consumers: vitamin A and vitamin C. Table 4.1 shows hypothetically the respective quantities of the attributes in each good.

4.3.2.1 BUDGET LINES AND INDIFFERENCE CURVES IN CHARACTERISTICS SPACE

Using the hypothetical information in Table 4.1, it is possible to construct budget lines and indifference curves in characteristics space. This permits an equilibrium position to be found for the consumer. To achieve this, the following assumptions may be made:

- Each good costs $1.00 (for simplicity).
- The consumer has $10.00 to spend.

The budget constraint may be defined as the quantities of vitamins A and C that $10.00 can yield to the consumer.

Consider $10.00 spent on oranges. At a cost of $1.00 per orange, this will give the consumer 10 oranges. Since each orange contains two units of vitamin A and 10 units of vitamin C, the consumer spending all $10.00 on oranges will get 20 units of vitamin A and 100 units of vitamin C. This combination of characteristics gives one of the extreme points on the characteristics budget line. The full set of points is shown in Table 4.2.

Figure 4.6 illustrates how the budget lines and indifference curves are handled in characteristics space in order that consumer equilibrium can be achieved. The lines *ac* and *cb* are characteristics budget lines. If the consumer spends all $10.00 on oranges, then the consumer is at point *a*, whereas, if all $10.00 is spent on apples, the consumer is at point *b*. Spending all $10.00 on mangoes puts the consumer at point *c*. When the consumer is on *ac* or *cb*, the consumer is buying combinations of oranges and mangoes and combinations of mangoes and apples respectively. The line *ab* represents combinations of oranges and apples. These are all budget lines in characteristics space.

Now indifference curves are added in the characteristics space. These show how the consumer is indifferent between combinations of vitamins A and C. The consumer tries to reach the highest indifference curve given the constraint of the characteristics-based budget lines.

Table 4.2 Quantities of characteristics available from given budget

	Characteristics for \$10.00 spent	
Goods	**Vitamin A (units)**	**Vitamin C (units)**
Oranges	20	100
Apples	100	20
Mangoes	80	80

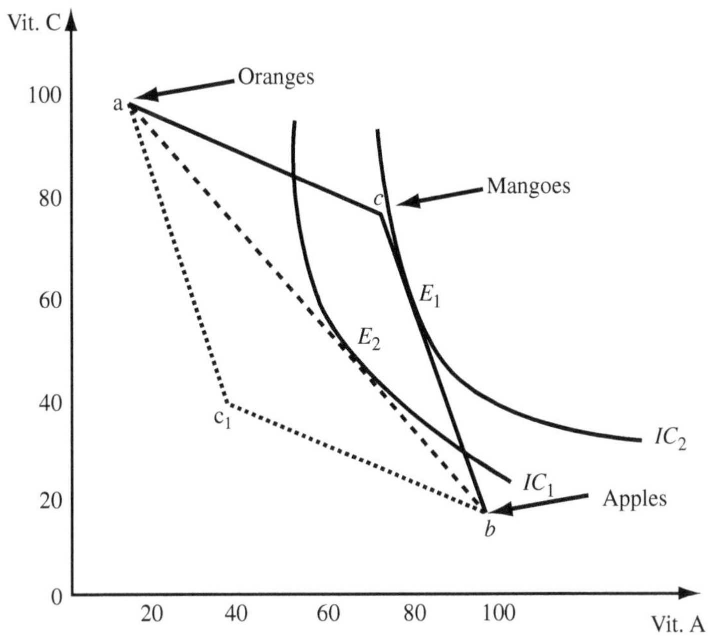

Figure 4.6
The characteristics approach

4.3.2.2 ACHIEVING EQUILIBRIUM

Equilibrium is at point E_1 in Figure 4.6 where the consumer is on the highest attainable indifference curve IC_2.

The following should be noted about the consumer equilibrium:

- At E_1 the consumer buys a combination of mangoes and apples. The closer the equilibrium point is to the mangoes point (*c*) the more mangoes in the consumer's basket, and similarly for apples if the equilibrium point is closer to the apples point (*b*).
- The consumer, in equilibrium, does not consume any oranges (no combination of oranges and mangoes).

- The line *ab* is available but inferior. The consumer would not choose a combination of oranges and apples as a higher level of welfare (utility) is available elsewhere off this line.
- The co-ordinates of the point E_1 show the optimal combination of vitamin C and vitamin A chosen by the consumer.

4.3.3 The characteristics approach and price increases

One of the beneficial aspects of the 'characteristics' approach is that it allows consideration of a change in the price of a good on the demand for the good through its characteristics. As an example, consider an increase in the price of mangoes. This would cause the budget constraints to shift inwards to the origin because a smaller quantity of mangoes and consequently the associated vitamins can now be bought.

One example is to assume that the price of mangoes doubles to $2.00 per unit. If the entire $10.00 is spent on mangoes, then the consumer can now buy only five mangoes instead of 10. This also means that the consumer consumes only 40 units of vitamin A and 40 units of vitamin C from spending all $10.00 on mangoes rather than the 80 units of each vitamin that were obtainable before.

The mangoes point in the diagram therefore shifts from point *c* to point c_1 (representing 40 units of vitamin A and 40 units of vitamin C). As a result, the new equilibrium position is at E_2 on IC_2.

The effects of the price rise in mangoes are as follows:

- The budget lines *ac* and *cb* are no longer relevant.
- Equilibrium takes place along budget line *ab*, a line that was previously not relevant.
- The highest indifference curve attainable by the consumer is now IC_2.
- There is a nutrition substitution effect. The customer substitutes vitamin A for vitamin C.
- There is an efficiency effect. This is a change in the optimal mix of oranges and apples. At the higher price, mangoes are now excluded from the optimal mix.

It is useful for a producer to consider the characteristics approach where the product being supplied is known to be demanded for its properties or attributes only (e.g. some herbal products, health and wellness goods and services). This is not a new theory of the consumer but a modification that allows a new thinking on consumer behaviour and the consideration of a characteristics demand curve.

4.4 PRICE AND RENT CONTROLS

Price and rent controls are manifested in the imposition of price ceilings and price floors. These are attempts to make sure that the equilibrium price in the market is not reached. They are mainly efforts to transfer consumer and/or producer surplus from one group to the other in order to achieve some social objective.

In principle, economists have difficulty recommending this type of interference in the market, largely because of the negative unintended effects. Alternative measures are usually proposed in order to achieve the same or similar objectives. These alternatives are typically found under the heading of the theory of optimal intervention.

For this topic, it is useful to recall that:

- ***Consumer surplus*** is the area above the equilibrium price line and below the demand curve.
- ***Producer surplus*** is the area below the equilibrium price line and above the supply curve.

Price and rent controls are usually captured under two headings:

- Price ceilings
- Price floors.

4.4.1 Price ceilings

4.4.1.1 THE OBJECTIVE OF A PRICE CEILING

A price ceiling is a form of price control where the market price is set below the normal equilibrium price and prevents the equilibrium price from being achieved.

The objective of the price ceiling is to lower the price for consumers. This may be done in the case of certain goods (usually necessities) and sometimes in the case of rental rates for houses. The aim is to keep costs down for low-income earners.

The achievement of these aims is effected through the intended transfer of some of the producer surplus to the consumer. The aim then is to increase the consumer surplus at the expense of the producer.

Figure 4.7 shows the market demand and supply curves. The normal market equilibrium would give price P^* at quantity Q^*.

A price ceiling is imposed at a price ***below*** the equilibrium price P^* at price P_C. The objective is to prevent market price from rising to P^*. The market price is held down to P_C in order to effect the transfer of a part of the producer surplus to the consumer.

Using the definitions of consumer and producer surplus, Figure 4.7 shows that, at the original equilibrium market price P^*, the consumer surplus comprises the areas a and b, while the producer surplus is comprised of the areas c, d and e. A price ceiling at P_C is now imposed.

4.4.1.2 EFFECTS OF A PRICE CEILING

From Figure 4.7 it can be seen that with the imposition of the price ceiling at P_C the following effects are realized:

- There is ***excess demand*** at price P_C. This indicates that the quantity consumers demand (Q_2) at P_C is greater than the quantity (Q_1) that suppliers are willing to bring to the market at that price. Hence there is a shortage of the commodity in the market. This results from the increase in consumers willing to buy at

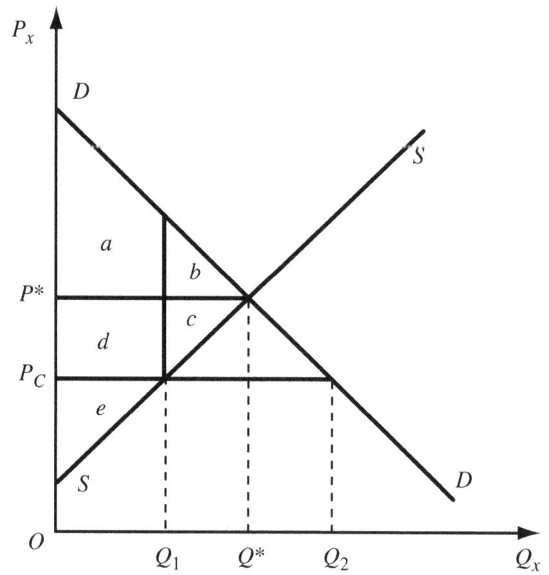

Figure 4.7
Effects of a price ceiling

the new lower price and the reduction in suppliers willing to supply at the new lower price.

- The producer surplus at price P_C is reduced from the areas *d*, *e* and *c* to just the area *e*.
- The consumer surplus at price P_C is increased from the areas *a* and *b* to the areas *a* and *d*.

4.4.1.3 UNINTENDED EFFECTS OF A PRICE CEILING

There are certain undesirable and largely unintended effects of price ceilings that lead economists to avoid recommending them. These include the development of an informal market (black market) and the deadweight loss. In addition, there are several other undesirable effects particularly related to rent controls.

Development of the informal market (blackmarket)

The excess of demand over supply at the ceiling price leads to intrusion into the market by brokers who are able to obtain the good now in relatively short supply (with respect to demand) and who seek to re-sell them at a higher price in the informal market. From the demand curve, it can be seen that there are persons who are willing to pay a price higher than the controlled price, P_C (persons are willing to pay up to the demand curve). These persons are often targeted by the re-sellers or 'blackmarketeers' who are able to acquire the product at the low controlled price and can re-sell at the higher prices some consumers are willing to pay for this limited quantity rather than go without.

These resellers are able to capture much of the consumer surplus above P_C (the areas *d* and *a*) and defeat the purpose of the price ceiling.

Generation of a deadweight loss

For this purpose, a deadweight loss may be defined as a loss to one group in society that is not gained by another group. With the implementation of the price ceiling, trading in the market stops at quantity Q_1. That is the total amount suppliers are willing to supply at that low price. It does not matter that consumers are willing to purchase the higher quantity Q_2 as there is no supply in this area. Consequently, the market activity is curtailed at Q_1 and, as a result of this, the attempt to put into effect the transfer of producer surplus to the consumer results in two areas of welfare loss, as follows:

1 The producer loses areas *c* and *d* but the consumer gains only *d*. Thus area *c* may be considered an area of producer surplus lost to the producer but not gained by the consumer.
2 The consumer, who had areas *a* and *b*, now gains area *d* but loses area *b*. Hence area *b* represents the area of consumer surplus lost to the consumer and not gained by anyone.

These two areas *b* and *c* constitute the deadweight (welfare) loss to the society (consumers and producers) from the imposition of a price ceiling.

In addition to the above, the shortage in supply at the controlled price means that a number of the buyers for whom the price ceiling was designed will be unable to acquire the goods. Previously, consumers up to Q^* were able to obtain the good. Now the good is available to consumers only up to Q_1. Consumers between Q_1 and Q^* are now unable to get the product. Moreover, consumers between Q^* and Q_2 represent new entrants into the market (new demand) that now must also go unfulfilled. The market tends to become creative in finding ways to ration the short supply and the persons for whom the low price is intended may not be beneficiaries.

Where the price control is a control on the price of housing (rent control), the longer-term effects must also be considered. These relate mainly to greater long-term shortage as the incentive to construct new buildings for rental is reduced and building maintenance is limited with the lower rents. Availability of rental units shrinks with the passage of time, exacerbating the excess demand situation. This situation was seen in New York and in many European cities (Stockholm, etc.) after World War II when rent controls were imposed.

In addition, to assist with rationing in the face of excess demand, landlords tend to impose other forms of non-rent payment such as large down-payments, payments for services or appurtenances attached to the house (utilities, drapes, keys) to boost income and select among tenants, often eliminating the poorer potential tenants the rent control was intended to serve. There is also the tendency to practice discrimination in the selection of tenants, often overlooking those with low income (payment risk), children (damage risk) and dogs or other pets. Baird (1980) examines further.

Economists tend to prefer alternative ways of assisting low income earners to have access to the basic necessities. This is part of the ***theory of optimal intervention***.

The recommendation is for a combination of taxes and subsidies to achieve the welfare transfer without a welfare reduction.

4.4.2 Price floors

The price floor works on the opposite side of the equilibrium price. A price floor is set above the normal equilibrium price in the market. The aim is to benefit the producer by preventing the price of the goods in question from falling to the normal market price. This is often done as price support for farmers in order to raise their income through higher prices for their produce. The intention is to transfer some of the consumer surplus to the producer. A minimum wage is also a price floor.

4.4.2.1 THE EFFECTS OF A PRICE FLOOR

From Figure 4.8 it can be seen that prior to the imposition of the price floor, the equilibrium price is P^* and the quantity Q^*, the consumer surplus is the combination of the areas *a*, *b* and *c*, while the producer surplus is the areas *d* and *e*.

With the imposition of the price floor at P_F, the following effects are manifested:

- There is excess supply at price P_F, that is, the quantity consumers demand (Q_1) at that price is smaller than the quantity (Q_2) producers are willing to supply on the market. Hence there is a surplus of the commodity in the market. This results from the increase in suppliers willing to supply at the new higher price and the reduction in consumers willing to buy at the new higher price. The same applies to a minimum wage.

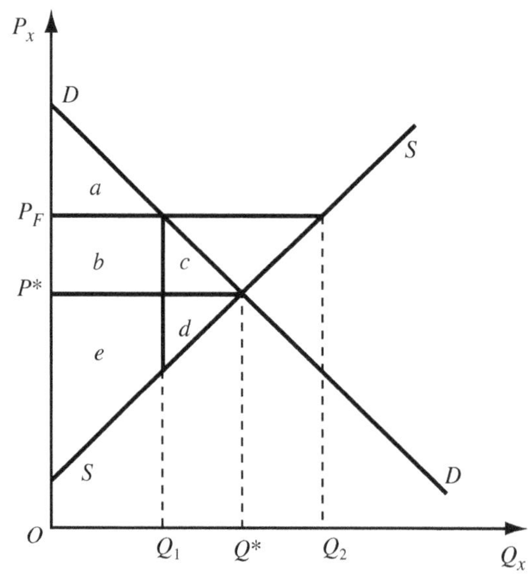

Figure 4.8
Effects of a price floor

- The consumer surplus at price P_F is reduced from the areas *a*, *b* and *c* to just the area *a*.
- The producer surplus at price P_F is increased from the areas *e* and *b* to the areas *e* and *b*.

4.4.2.2 UNINTENDED EFFECTS OF A PRICE FLOOR

As with the price ceiling there are unintended effects. In this case economic activity in the market ends where demand ends. The excess supply cannot be transacted in the market as there is no demand beyond Q_1. This causes certain undesirable effects. In particular, the following unintended effects should be noted.

The deadweight loss

As with the price ceilings, the price floor results in two areas of deadweight loss in welfare to the society. These are as follows.

- In attempting to transfer consumer surplus to the producer areas *b* and *c* are taken from the consumer but only *b* is transferred to the producer (there is no economic activity in the area *c*). Thus area *c* becomes an area of deadweight (welfare) loss to the society.
- The producer gains area *b*. However, the producer also now loses area *d* as there is no economic activity in area *d*. This is not gained by the consumer.

The surplus problem

In attempting to help the producer with high prices for the products, the problem of glut management now has to be introduced. With the higher price, producers now want to supply more than consumers want to buy at the set price. Where this surplus is generated, there is the question of storage or disposal of the surplus at the guaranteed price. This policy is often applied to farmers in order to ensure adequate farming income. If the excess supply is disposed of in the domestic market, it will affect the price the farmers can get for the regular supply in the market and the price floor (higher price) will not hold as farmers seek to sell in an informal market to offload excess supplies. Governments imposing such a policy will then have to find storage for products (costly where the products are perishable) and seek to dispose in overseas markets. In Europe price supports for farmers led to meat 'mountains', milk 'lakes' and other such storage features in an effort to prevent the surplus products from affecting the domestic market price. This is a welfare cost.

The unemployment problem

Where the price floor is a minimum wage (i.e. set above the equilibrium wage), the difference between Q_1 and Q_2 in Figure 4.8 is unemployment. Of this, the difference between Q^* and Q_2 represents new entrants into the labour market seeking employment at the new higher wage but unable to find it. Furthermore, the difference between

Q_1 and Q^* represents the loss of employment by some of those who were previously employed. This issue is further explored in Brown (1988).

The implications of price controls are largely counterintuitive. Groups clamouring for price controls often consider only the intended effects but are unaware of the types of effects that may hurt members of the same group for which the controls are intended. Because of these negative unintended effects, economists tend to prefer the recommendation of corrective taxes and subsidies to lower the level of welfare losses due to price distortions in the market. The recommended policy requires the taxing of one group to absorb some of their consumer or producer surplus (as the case may be) and the delivery of subsidies to the group needing the assistance in the market.

4.5 EXTERNAL EFFECTS ON DEMAND

The introduction of the role of external effects on demand is attributed to Harvey Leibenstein (1950). In particular, three external effects were identified, namely, the Bandwagon, Snob and Veblen effects.

These effects are called 'external' since they refer to effects on demand outside of the intrinsic value (or the characteristics) of the good to the consumers. According to Leibenstein, consumers may purchase goods because others are buying them (bandwagon effect), because of the desire to be exclusive (snob effect) or because of the high showroom or conspicuous price (Veblen effect). Because they affect the elasticity of the demand curve and even the sign (Veblen effect), it is useful for suppliers to be aware of these effects in the market. These effects are considered *seriatim.*

4.5.1 The Bandwagon effect

The case where a consumer's desire for a good is positively influenced by the purchases of others represents the Bandwagon effect. In this case, as consumers buy more of the good, other consumers' taste or preference for the good is increased. This is due to the consumers' desire to 'jump on the bandwagon' and be 'in fashion' to fit in with their peers. The more consumers buy these goods, the more other consumers want to buy them as well. Some examples observed over time have been the wearing of blue jeans, brand name shoes and clothes and the toting around of various electronic gadgets including cellular phones and music players.

The Bandwagon effect therefore manifests itself as a shift factor in the demand for the good. Moreover, it feeds on itself since, as more persons acquire the good, this further influences others and keeps shifting the demand curve outwards. Leibenstein recognized that increased demand (shifts) based on increased purchases by others cannot continue indefinitely, and identified a ***diminishing marginal external effect***, due to income limitations.

In examining the practical nature of the process, Leibenstein refers to a *gadanken-experiment* which is a kind of iterative process whereby consumers are asked to plot their demand curve based on how much they believe others are buying of the good. Once the quantity is known, it causes a further outward shift in demand, which itself causes a

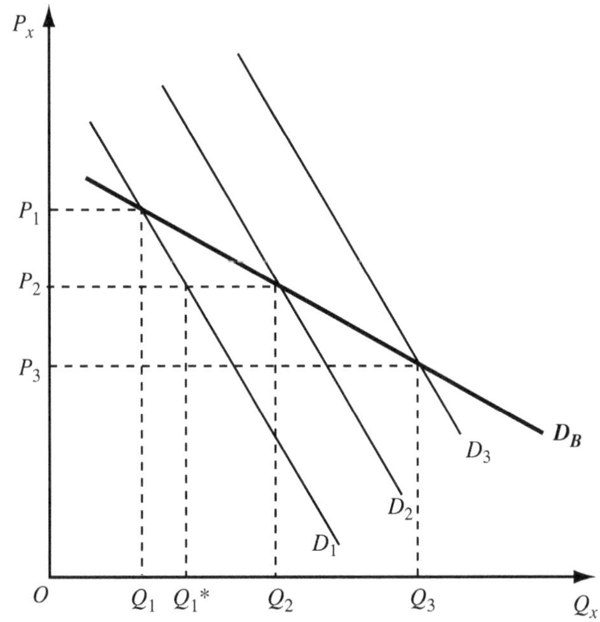

Figure 4.9
Identifying the Bandwagon Demand Curve

further outward shift. This results in the construction of a series of demand curves based on the consumption levels in the market.

The Bandwagon effect may be illustrated as in Figure 4.9. The demand curve D_1 is based on the collective knowledge or belief that the level of demand in the market is Q_1 and similarly for other demand curves. With perfect knowledge, if the demand is actually at this level (Q_1) then there is only one price (P_1) on this demand curve (D_1) that is an equilibrium price in the market. Similarly, if the actual demand is at D_2 then the equilibrium price is P_2, and this continues with the other curves. Hence, the demand curve keeps shifting due to the positive marginal external effect on consumption as prices change.

Consequently, the effect of a price fall may be analysed. Assume price falls from P_1 to P_2. It would be expected that demand would move along the original demand curve D_1 to the quantity Q_1^*. This would be the normal price effect. However the external (bandwagon) effect takes over as the increase in quantity demanded leads others to increase their preference for the good and shifts the demand curve out to D_2. As a result, the fall in price leads to a further expansion in demand all the way out to Q_2 on the demand curve D_2.

A similar occurrence takes place when price is dropped to P_3 and equilibrium shift over to the D_3 curve giving an equilibrium quantity of Q_3.

Tracing the locus of these equilibrium points on outward shifting demand curves as price falls, the resulting curve is the ***Bandwagon Demand Curve (D_B)*** shown in Figure 4.9. The bandwagon demand curve is more elastic than the individual demand curves. The seller of a bandwagon type good should be aware of this increased responsiveness to price change.

Price, bandwagon and total effects

It is possible to classify the effects of the price changes on the quantity demanded. When price is lowered from P_1 to P_2, the movement along the original demand curve D_1 is referred to as the price effect, whereas the movement across the new demand curve D_2 is classified as the bandwagon effect. Along the quantity axis, the distance $Q_1Q_1^*$ may be labelled the price effect while the distance $Q_1^*Q_2$ may be labelled the bandwagon effect. The two distances together (Q_1Q_2) is called the total effect of the price change.

4.5.2 The Snob effect

The Snob effect is the desire for exclusivity by the consumer. It is a negative shift effect in response to quantity bought by others and is opposite to the bandwagon effect. As the price of a snob good falls and others come into the market (movement along the demand curve), the preference (taste) for the good by the 'snobs' in the market diminishes. This leads to an inward shift in the demand curve in response to the belief or actual knowledge of quantity being demanded in the market. The Snob effect is illustrated in Figure 4.10.

With the Snob effect, as price falls from P_1 to P_2 quantity is expected to increase to Q_1^* along the demand curve D_1. However, as the increase in quantity demanded as a result of the price fall takes place, the 'snobs' lose their taste or preference for the good, thereby causing the demand curve to shift inwards to D_2. This leads to the final

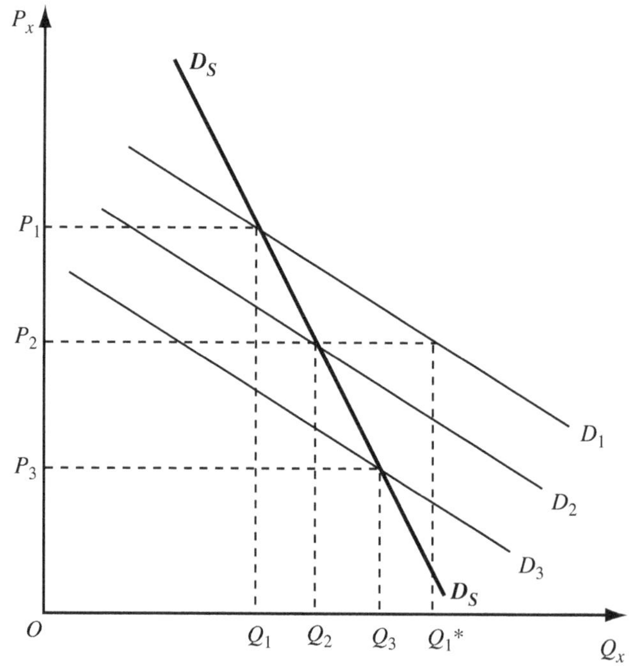

Figure 4.10
Identifying the Snob Demand Curve

equilibrium at P_2 with the quantity supplied at Q_2. Similarly, a fall in price to P_3 would result in the quantity Q_3 along the inwardly shifted demand curve D_3. The locus of these equilibrium points on inward-shifting demand curves as price falls is the ***Snob Demand Curve (*D_S*).***

Similarly to the case of the bandwagon effect, it is possible to separate the effect of the price change into price and snob effects. Here, when price falls from P_1 to P_2, the distance represented by the movement along the original demand curve D_1 is identified as the price effect. This is the distance from Q_1 to Q_1^*. The movement back to the inwardly shifted demand curve, D_2, is identified as the snob effect.

The snob effect therefore takes away from the price effect. However, it covers only a part of the price effect and does not completely overwhelm it.

This snob demand curve is less elastic than the individual demand curves. It is therefore important for the supplier of a 'snob' good to be aware of the reduced responsiveness to changes in the price of the good as the snob effect takes hold. Making the good more readily available through the reduction in price would make it less appealing to the 'snobs' in the market. These goods may include rare antiques and paintings, unique crystal and porcelain items and high fashion clothing and accessories. Snob items are often expensive and there is a thin line between the snob effect and the Veblen effect described below.

4.5.3 The Veblen effect

The Veblen effect, unlike the other two effects, is a response by consumers to the ostentatious price of the good rather than to the quantity others are buying. It is the effect generally known as conspicuous consumption. An example may be a Ferrari car which may be purchased by many in the market, not specifically for its performance record on the car racing circuit but because it carries a higher rather than a lower price.

In this case the demand curves are drawn with respect to consumers' demands in response to the 'showroom' price of the good. A lower showroom price leads to an inward shift in the demand curve for the good. In this case the Veblen effect completely overwhelms the price effect leading to a positively sloped Veblen demand curve. This is illustrated in Figure 4.11.

In the case of the Veblen effect as price falls from P_1 to P_2 quantity is expected to increase to Q_1^* along the demand curve D_1. However, as a result of the price fall itself, those consumers who are buying the good for the purpose of 'conspicuous consumption' (due to the visibly high price of the good) become less interested in the good thereby causing the demand curve to shift inwards to D_2. The price fall causes the final equilibrium to reside on D_2 instead of D_1. Hence at P_2 the quantity supplied is Q_2. Similarly, a fall in price to P_3 would result in the quantity Q_3 along the inwardly shifted demand curve D_3. The locus of these equilibrium points on inward-shifting demand curves as price falls is the *Veblen Demand Curve* D_V.

Similarly to the case of the bandwagon effect, it is possible to separate the effect of the price change into price and snob effects. Here, when price falls from P_1 to P_2, the distance represented by the movement along the original demand curve D_1 is identified as the price effect. This is the distance from Q_1 to Q_1^*. The movement back to the demand curve D_2 is identified as the Veblen effect.

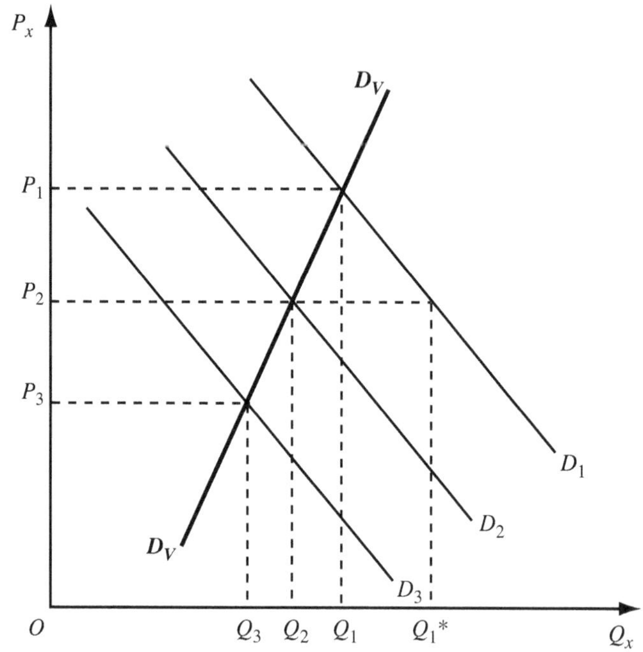

Figure 4.11
Identifying the Veblen Demand Curve

It is useful to note that the Veblen effect does not just take away from the price effect. The Veblen effect completely overwhelms the price effect and leads to a positively-sloped demand curve. Hence, with a prominent Veblen effect in the market, as price falls the quantity of the good demanded in the market falls as well.

It is important for a supplier of a Veblen effect good to be aware of the nature of this effect, since the lowering of price has a perverse effect on sales of the good as the 'Veblen' consumers lose interest in the good.

4.6 THE NEÜMANN–MORGENSTERN (NM) UTILITY INDEX

The classical Cardinal utility theory was partly discredited because of the central concept of measurable utility. The cardinality (measurability) of utility required some type of objective measuring tool and money was considered unsuitable because it required the (unrealistic) assumption of a constant marginal utility of money.

Neümann and Morgenstern (1944), however, returned to the measurability of utility although not strictly in a cardinal sense and were able to use measures to rank utilities that were more than the mere ranking of the Ordinal utility theory and constituted measurability in a restricted sense. This concept of measurability is explored in Alchian (1953).

This form of 'measurement' allowed them to be able to construct a Utility Index that possessed measures of cardinality where the numbers, though not cardinal on a scale beginning at zero, had meaningful intervals and so allowed any scale of numbers to be converted into another scale (as with temperature – from Fahrenheit to Centigrade).

Neümann–Morgenstern dealt with expected utility (not utility of expected value). They worked on the theory of demand under risk. Hence, they were concerned with the probability of utility rather than utility with certainty. In their work they developed the utility index, which also applied under conditions of certainty and allowed the 'measurability' of utility though in a restricted sense.

4.6.1 Assumptions (axioms)

The construction of the index is based on the following five axioms:

The axiom of complete ordering (consistency and transitivity)

This states that, where A, B and C are bundles of commodities for the consumer, then:

- If $A > B, B \not> A$ (consistency).
- If $A > B \, and \, B > C,\ then\ C \not> A$ (transitivity).

The axiom of continuity

This states that for three outcomes A, B and C such that: $A > B$ and $B > C$, then there exists a probability P_A such that:

$$U_B = P_A[U_A] + [1 - P_A]U_C$$

where U_A is the utility of outcome A, U_B is the utility of outcome B and U_C is the utility of outcome C.

The axiom of independence

This states that if there are two sets of chance outcomes (say, lotteries) L_1 and L_2, then if:

$$L_1 = A + C$$

and:

$$L_2 = B + C$$

then, if:

$$A = B$$

and:

$$P_A = P_B$$

it means that:

$$L_1 = L_2$$

This says that outcome C has its own independent unique value (utility) to the consumer that is unaffected by being connected with outcome B as opposed to outcome A. It implies that if A and B are of the same value to the consumer, then (A with C) and (B with C) are also the same to the consumer so long as A and B have the same probability of occurring.

The axiom of unequal probability

This states that if, for the consumer $A > B$, and:

$$L_1 = A + B$$

$$L_2 = A + B$$

then:

$$L_1 > L_2 \quad \text{if } P_A(L_1) > P_A(L_2)$$

This states that since the two chance occurrences (say, lotteries L_1 and L_2) have the identical outcomes, the only difference they can make to the consumer taking a chance on them is the differences in the probability of winning (P_A). The lottery with the higher probability of winning is the preferred lottery.

The axiom of complexity

Consider that there are two chance opportunities (say lotteries) L_1 and L_2 such that:

$$L_1: \quad A + B \text{ (simple)}$$

$$L_2: \quad A + B \text{ (complex)}$$

If:

$$P_A(L_1) = P_A(L_2)$$

Then:

$$L_1 = L_2$$

This says if one lottery (L_1) is a simple game (e.g. the game has only one stage), whereas the other lottery (L_2) is a complex game (multiple stages before the final outcome), then, so long as they both have the same final outcomes and the same probablity of winning, then the consumer is indifferent between the two lotteries.

This requires that the consumer be fully rational and play the game (lottery) solely for the chance of winning rather than for the nature of the game itself. This axiom eliminates the 'born gambler' type who gets utility from the game itself.

The axioms require a rational consumer who is only interested in the chance of winning, ruling out the 'born gambler' who would take the change no matter how small the probability of winning and the completely risk averse person who would not take a chance no matter how great the possibility of winning.

4.6.2 Construction of the Neümann–Morgenstern Utility Index

The construction of the Neümann–Morgenstern Utility Index is done around the use of the axiom of continuity:

$$U_B = P_A[U_A] + [1 - P_A]\, U_C$$

The procedure is as follows:

- Assume arbitrary values for the upper and lower outcomes (A and C), say:

$$U_A = 100$$
$$U_C = 10$$

- Ascertain ***from the consumer*** the probability that makes the consumer indifferent between outcome B with certainty and a chance to win with outcomes A and C, say:

$$P_A = 0.1$$

  Hence:

$$P_C = 0.9$$

- Substitute the above values into the equation for the axiom of continuity:

$$\begin{aligned} U_B &= 0.1[100] + 0.9[10] \\ &= 10 + 9 \\ U_B &= 19 \end{aligned}$$

  The utility index (X) may therefore be written as:

$$U_A = 100$$
$$U_B = 19$$
$$U_C = 10$$

Hence the utility values are monotonically decreasing from A to C or monotonically increasing from C to A.

In order to find out the significance of this index, it is useful to use the same given values of the probabilities ***provided by the consumer***. The arbitrarily assigned utility values attached to the highest and lowest valued outcomes (A and C) are now changed.

Hence, the same probabilities, P_A and consequently P_C are now used with different U_A and U_C values.

Assume the new arbitrarily given values are:

$$U_A = 500$$
$$U_C = 20$$

Again, substituting these new values into the axiom of continuity gives:

$$\begin{aligned} U_B &= 0.1[500] + 0.9[20] \\ &= 50 + 18 \\ U_B &= 68 \end{aligned}$$

Hence, the second Utility Index (Y) reads:

$$U_A = 500$$
$$U_B = 68$$
$$U_C = 20$$

Now consider the relationship between the first index (X) and the second index (Y). This is shown in Table 4.3.

To understand the implication of this, consider the ***row intervals***. For each index the interval between U_A and U_B is ***nine*** times the interval between U_B and U_C ($9 \times 9 = 81$ and $9 \times 48 = 432$).

Because the intervals are related, then the relationship among the utility values is more than a simple monotonic ranking (ordinal). This describes a ***Linear Monotonic*** relationship among the utility values when constructed according to the method used by Neümann–Morgenstern.

A Linear Monotonic relationship takes the form:

$$X = a + bY$$

The significance of the linear monotonic relationship is that this relationship represents measurement in a restricted sense. For, although the utility numbers are not measurable on a scale starting at zero (i.e. are not cardinal in a strict sense), the fact that the intervals between the numbers are systematically related allows a measurement of the relative differences in utility and so constitute measurability ***in a restricted sense***.

Table 4.3 Relationship between index X and index Y

Utility	Index X	Index Y	Row intervals X	Row intervals Y
U_A	100	500		
U_B	19	68	$U_A - U_B = 81$	$U_A - U_B = 432$
U_C	10	20	$U_B - U_C = 9$	$U_B - U_C = 48$

This form of measurement is similar to that found in the measurement of temperature, for example, where the relationship between degrees Fahrenheit and Centigrade (Celsius) may be expressed as:

$$F = 32 + \tfrac{9}{5}C$$

This is a linear monotonic relationship used to convert temperature values from degrees Centigrade (Celsius) into degrees Fahrenheit. The intervals in these two scales are systematically related even though the extreme values are completely different. For Fahrenheit, 32 to 212 is equivalent to Centigrade's 0 to 100 (freezing to boiling). The fact that these are both relative values but yet are considered measurements (of temperature) suggests that having a linear monotonic relationship between two variables can be accepted as having measurability in a restricted sense. It may be noted that absolute measurement of temperature can now be done using degrees Kelvin.

This approach led to a re-birth of the notion of measurable utility without the cardinal restrictions. Although it was developed in relation to risk situations, it can also be applied under conditions of certainty. It allows a complete ranking of utility required by the Ordinal utility theory but goes further and enhances the Cardinal utility theory by providing values for measurable utility. Its major drawback, however, is that this approach still does not permit interpersonal comparisons of utility.

4.7 EMPIRICAL DEMAND FUNCTIONS

Rather than go the route of the deductive utility theory an alternative approach is to go the route of empiricism. This is sometimes referred to as the pragmatic approach to demand analysis and used empirical data to formulate demand functions directly.

Typically, firms seeking to make decisions about their market participation do not go through utility theory. It is often more practical to use empirical time-series or cross-section data to determine the demand function with the help of tools supplied by the economics sub-discipline of econometrics.

In this approach, the demand function for good X may be expressed as:

$$Q_X^D = f(P_X, P_O, Y, e)$$

where:

P_X = Price of good X
P_O = Price of other goods
Y = Income
e = Error term

4.7.1 The constant elasticity of demand function

The most popular form is that of the constant elasticity of demand function. This function may be expressed as:

$$Q_X = b_0 P_X^{b_1} P_0^{b_2} Y^{b_3} e^{b_4 \Delta t}$$

This functional form is popular for many reasons, including the following:

- It is log-linear and so is easier to work with as the multiplicative relationship becomes linear in the logs giving an additive relationship.
- The co-efficients b_1, b_2, b_3 are the elasticities of demand, namely: price, cross and income elasticity respectively.

To explain further, this function in its log-linear form (linear in the logs of the variables) can be expressed as:

$$\log Q_X = \log b_0 + b_1 \log P_X + b_2 \log P_O + b_3 Y$$

Hence the multiplicative relationship becomes additive when logs are taken. Moreover, the coefficients are elasticities. To show this, consider the price elasticity as an example:

$$b_1 = \text{price elasticity}$$

Differentiate the demand function (above) with respect to Q_x. This gives:

$$\frac{\partial \log Q_X}{\partial \log P_X} = b_1$$

It has been established in mathematics that the change in the log of a variable is proportionate to the change in the variable, then:

$$\partial \log Q_X = \frac{\partial Q_X}{Q_X}$$

and:

$$\partial \log P_X = \frac{\partial P_X}{P_X}$$

In addition:

$$\frac{\partial Q_X}{Q_X} \Big/ \frac{\partial P_X}{P_X} = \frac{\partial Q_X}{\partial P_X}\frac{P_X}{Q_X} = \eta_p$$

where η_p is the price elasticity of demand for good x.

The same holds for cross and income elasticities. b_2 is the cross elasticity of demand and b_3 is the income elasticity of demand.

Demand models may also use real income (i.e. use a deflator) and relative prices. For example, the demand function may be expressed as:

$$Q_X^D = b_0 \left(\frac{P_X}{P}\right)^{b_1} \left(\frac{P_0}{P}\right)^{b_2} \left(\frac{Y}{P}\right)^{b_3}$$

where P is a general price index.

This assumes:

- No money illusion
- Zero homogeneity

The significance is that the coefficients of prices and incomes must add to zero. Hence the formulation makes use of real income and of relative prices.

Through the use of data and econometric techniques, the demand function can be specified and the producer has immediate information on the nature of the demand curve and consequent marginal and average curves on which to plan production. This is of special use where the producer is entering a new market for the producer whether at the national, regional or global level.

One caveat, however, is that some caution must be exercised in relation to empiricism as the data may show relationships that are purely statistical rather than real and hence may be providing false information. This may happen in the absence of any recourse made to theory, as indicated in Box 1.1 of Chapter 1. However, in many cases, the empirical demand function relates to accepted demand theory both in choice of variables and specification of the relationship.

4.7.2 Other specifications of demand functions

The specifications of empirical demand functions may take several forms, these forms include:

- Linear
- Semi-logarithmic
- Double-logarithmic
- Inverse semi-logarithmic

In addition, some models introduce time lags and leads in a dynamic approach. Typically these are distributed lag models. These include models based on the stock adjustment principle, where demand depends on the stocks possessed by the consumer and those based on the habit creation principle, where the more the consumer uses the greater the demand (addiction principle).

In summary, using econometric techniques, and based on trial and error, the mathematical specification giving the best fit for the empirical production function is retained.

REVIEW QUESTIONS FOR CHAPTER 4

1 Explain the concept of the consumer surplus showing how it may be measured using:

   (a) The Marshallian approach.
   (b) The modern approach.

2 With regard to price indices:

(a) Distinguish between the Laspèyres and Paasche price indices.
(b) Construct an Income index and show how it is used in conjunction with the Laspèyres and Paasche price indices to assess changes in welfare.

3 Explain and illustrate the 'characteristics' approach to demand analysis showing the similarities and differences between this and the standard ordinal approach.

4 With regard to price controls:

(a) Illustrate the use of a price ceiling and clearly set out the intended effects and the unintended effects on welfare.
(b) Show and explain the difference between price ceilings and price floors in terms of the target group of beneficiaries and the nature of the welfare loss due to unintended effects.

5 Examine how bandwagon, snob and Veblen effects, respectively, alter the demand curve for a product and assess the significance for sellers.

6 With regard to the Neümann–Morgenstern utility index:

(a) Set out the five axioms for the index to be constructed.
(b) Using the axiom of continuity, construct a Neümann–Morgenstern utility index using arbitrary end values.
(c) Construct a second index using the same probabilities but different end values and explain why the index is said to be measure utility (in a restricted sense).

7 Consider the use of empirical demand functions with regard to:

(a) The specification options available and the ability to by-pass utility theory.
(b) The way in which the log-linear formulation allows the elasticities of demand to be derived directly.

Multiple choice questions

Indicate the single correct answer to each of the following questions:

1 Consider the Laspèyres (L) and Paasche (P) price indices and the income index (I). Using the subscripts 0 and 1 for the base and current years respectively, and with i goods, it is fair to say:

(a) The Laspèyres price index (L) may be written as $L = \frac{\sum_{i=1}^{t} Q_{i0}P_{i1}}{\sum_{i=1}^{t} Q_{i0}P_{i0}}$. ☐
(b) The income index is written as $I = \frac{\sum_{i=1}^{t} Q_{i0}P_{i1}}{\sum_{i=1}^{t} Q_{i1}P_{i1}}$. ☐
(c) If $L > I$ the consumer is better off in the current time period. ☐
(d) If $P > L$ the consumer was better off in the base year. ☐

2 With regard to Leibenstein's analysis of external effects on consumption, it is fair to say:

(a) The snob effect makes the demand curve more elastic. ☐
(b) The bandwagon effect adds to the price effect and makes the slope of the demand curve flatter. ☐
(c) The bandwagon effect causes the demand curve to become positively sloped. ☐
(d) The Veblen effect makes the demand curve less elastic. ☐

3 With reference to the Neümann–Morgenstern (N–M) utility index and its revival of measurable utility, consider that there are three outcomes A, B and C with utilities to the consumer $U(A)$, $U(B)$ and $U(C)$ respectively, where $A > B$ and $B > C$. Now if (P_A) is the probability of outcome A, which one of the following is **FALSE**?

(a) The axiom on continuity may be set out as

$$U(B) = P_A[U(A)] + (1 - P_A)[U(C)].$$ ☐

(b) When P_A, given by a consumer, is used to construct a utility index (a ranking of $U(A)$, $U(B)$ and $U(C)$), then any other utility index constructed with that P_A is a linear monotonic transformation of the first. ☐
(c) For each N–M utility index constructed, the intervals between the utility numbers in the ranking remain proportionally constant. ☐
(d) The consumer must be either a born gambler or a completely risk averse person. ☐

4 In the empirical approach to demand analysis, a demand equation for good x (Q_X^D) is formulated and econometric methods are used. A popular formulation is the multiplicative form: $Q_X^D = a_0 P_X^{a_1} P_O^{a_2} Y^{a_3} e^{a_4 \Delta t}$, where $P_X =$ the price of good x, $P_O =$ the price of other goods and $Y =$ income. With regard to this function which of the following is **FALSE**?

(a) This demand function is log-linear. ☐
(b) a_0 is the slope of the demand curve. ☐
(c) The function may be used in time-series or cross-section empirical studies. ☐
(d) The co-efficients are the elasticities of demand. ☐

RECOMMENDED READING FOR CHAPTER 4

Alchian, A. A. (1953) 'The Meaning of Utility Measurement', *American Economic Review* (March).

Baird, C. W. (1980) *Rent Control: The Perennial Folly*, Washington, DC: The Cato Institute, 60–61.

Brown, C. (1988) 'Minimum Wage Laws: Are They Overrated?', *Journal of Economic Perspectives* 2(3).

Henderson, J. M. and Quandt, R. E. (1984) *Microeconomic Theory: A Mathematical Approach*, McGraw Hill, Ch. 3.
Lancaster, K. J. (1971) *Consumer Demand: A New Approach*, New York: Columbia University Press.
Leibenstein, H. (1950) 'Bandwagon, Snob and Veblen Effects in the Theory of Consumers' Demand', *Quarterly Journal of Economics*, 64: 183–207.
Marshall, A. (1890) *Principles of Economics* (8th Edn, 1920), London: Macmillan.
Neumann, V. and Morgenstern, O. (1944) *Theory of Games and Economic Behaviour* (1953 edition), Princeton, NJ: Princeton University Press.

5 The Producer and Optimal Production Choices

Technology and the Production Function; Short-run Equilibrium; Long-run Equilibrium; The Multi-product Firm

The theory of the producer deals with the production function (relationship between inputs and outputs) and the way in which it is used by a producer to maximize profits. The production function, unlike the consumption function, is not strictly a construct of economics. It is supposed to specify a real (physical) relationship expressed in quantities of inputs and outputs and is determined by technology. It is therefore considered to be 'given' to the firm. Production theory shows how the producer must use the knowledge of the production relationships in the most profitable way, both in the short- and the long-run. The producer must choose a level of output and the quantities of inputs consistent with meeting the goal of profit maximization. An understanding of the optimization process is essential therefore to any producer whether operating at the local, regional or global level.

5.1 TECHNOLOGY AND THE PRODUCTION FUNCTION

The production function, specifying the way in which inputs are translated into outputs by a producer or firm, constitutes only the foundation or necessary condition for the producer to maximize profits. Since this is a 'real' or technical relationship 'given' to the firm by the engineers and technical persons who design and implement production processes and plants, the economic considerations must be superimposed on the technical. The production theory that follows shows how producers may use knowledge of this relationship for their purpose.

5.1.1 Basic assumptions

The basic assumptions that relate to the producer and to production optimization are:

- The producer is rational. This indicates that the producer aims to maximize profits given technology and prices.
- The price of output is given. In essence, the basic study of the producer assumes that the producer is selling in a market which may be described as perfectly competitive, that is, one in which the producer has no control over the price received for the product. This is done for simplicity.
- The prices of inputs are given. This assumption also helps to simplify the analysis and is similar to the one above in that it is based on the assumption of perfect competition in the market.
- The producer has access to as many units of inputs as are needed for production.
- The producer has full knowledge of the technology. This allows the producer to construct and use a production function.

5.1.2 The production function

The production function expresses the physical relationships between inputs and outputs and may be written as:

$$Q = f(K, L, D, E)$$

where:

Q = Output quantified and measured in real terms
K = Capital, including knowledge in the form of books, manuals, databases and intellectual property such as patents
L = Labour specifically referring to hourly, daily or weekly paid workers
D = Land including natural resources
E = Entrepreneurial input including organizational and managerial techniques

Any other input vital to the production process may be included. Typically, however, only two inputs are used for ease of analysis and the production function is written as:

$$Q = f(K, L)$$

The factor input K usually is taken to encapsulate all the fixed factors of production (overheads). The labour (L) factor input is typically considered to be the variable factor and may be taken to cover operating factors of production.

It is assumed that the specification of the functional form of this relationship is known to the producer.

5.1.3 Concepts and tools

5.1.3.1 CONCEPT OF SHORT- AND LONG-RUN

Production theory distinguishes between the short- and the long-run. In the short-run only the variable (operating) factors are considered while the other factors are held constant. However, in the long-run all factor inputs are variable.

The short-run or variable factor inputs include all those that depend on the quantity of output and that vary as the quantity of output varies. Typically, these would include labour as human (or kinetic) energy, electrical or fossil fuel energy and any other inputs that vary directly with output quantity.

The long-run or fixed factor inputs are those overhead costs that are incurred irrespective of the how output may vary from day to day.

5.1.3.2 ANALYTICAL TECHNIQUES AND TOOLS

The analytical techniques and tools used are similar to those used for consumer analysis.

At the centre is marginal analysis. This is because the basic objective is that of optimization. Using mathematics to lend precision to the analysis, the technique of the calculus of variations is applied in order to determine the conditions for optimization (profit maximization). Since this technique works in terms of slopes and slopes of slopes (first- and second-order conditions), the results are expressed in terms of marginal (rates of change) variables.

The basic tools include:

- The short-run tools of the total, average and marginal product curves which are similar in concept to the total and marginal utility curves of the consumer and the total, average and marginal revenue curves used in demand analysis.
- The long-run tools of the isoquant and isocost which are similar to the indifference curve and the budget line respectively of consumer analysis.

In addition, there are tools such as the isocline and expenditure elasticity curves which are similar to the income–consumption curve and the Engel curve of consumer analysis.

New tools introduced for production analysis include the Edgeworth box and the production possibility curve (product transformation curve) used in the analysis of the multi-product firm.

5.2 OPTIMIZING BEHAVIOUR IN THE SHORT-RUN

As established earlier, in the short-run not all factors are variable. Usually capital (K), representing all overhead factors, is taken as fixed. Typically, labour (L), representing the operational inputs, is considered the only variable factor in the short-run.

5.2.1 The short-run production function

The short-run production function is usually written as:

$$Q = f(L)_{\overline{K}}$$

This expresses output as a function of the variable input labour for a given level of the fixed factors represented by capital.

5.2.1.1 THE LAW OF VARIABLE PROPORTIONS

The short-run production function is characterized by the operation of the ***law of variable proportions*** or the ***law of eventually diminishing returns to a variable factor.*** This must not be confused with the law of returns to scale which belongs to the long-run production function.

With capital fixed ($\overline{K}$) and labour (L) variable, additional increments of labour to the fixed capital cause the total product (output) to increase, first at an increasing rate, then at a decreasing rate, to stop increasing (zero increase) and finally to decrease. This is captured in the shape of the total product curve and reflects the ***Law of Variable Proportions***. This is shown in Figure 5.1.

In Figure 5.1, the total product increases at an increasing rate up to the point R, then increases at a decreasing rate up to a maximum total product of OD at the point T where there is no further increase. Thereafter it decreases. Point R then, represents a point of inflexion. It suggests that when the quantity of labour added to

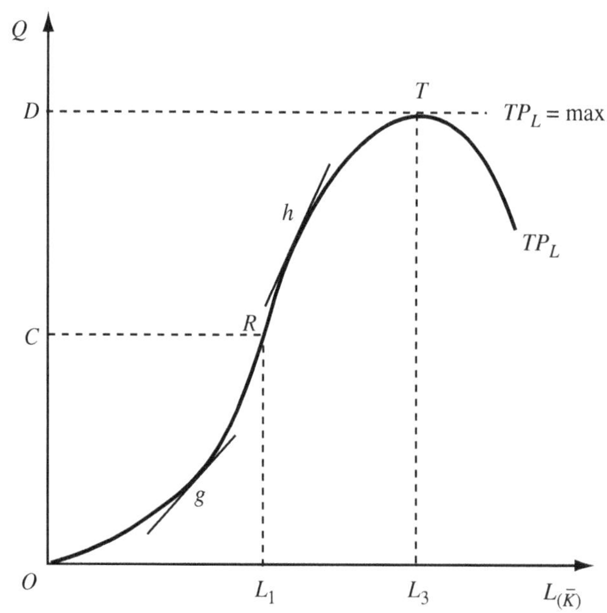

Figure 5.1
The total product of labour curve

the fixed quantity of capital in the production plant reaches the level OL_1, the returns to labour (or the amount of the product gained from adding each additional unit of labour) begin to diminish. Hence, from this point, every additional unit of labour added beyond OL_1 contributes less to the total output than the one before. Before point R was reached, every unit of labour added to the fixed capital in the plant was adding more to the total output than the one before. Point R then can be considered the point where the eventually diminishing returns to the variable factor set in. Output or total product still increases but at a decreasing rate. This continues up to the point T on the total product curve, which represents the quantity of labour OL_3 being used in the plant.

The point T is a stationary point. At this point, coincident with the quantity of labour OL_3 being employed in production, an additional unit of labour in the plant adds nothing to the total output of the plant. This is the point where the total product from the use of labour with a fixed amount of capital is at a maximum. This is similar to the point of satiation on the consumer's total utility curve.

Beyond T, the returns to the variable factor (labour) actually decrease. As a result, every unit of labour added beyond the quantity OL_3 not only adds less to total output than the one before but ***actually causes the total output of the plant to decrease***. Producers must therefore be acutely aware that, in their quest for more output from a fixed investment in plant equipment (capital), they do not find themselves hiring labour beyond the point where marginal product is zero as the additional labour will now cause the plant to actually produce less than before the extra labour was hired. The plant is now overcrowded, workers get into each other's way and there are literally too many hands in the plant.

5.2.1.2 THE AVERAGE AND MARGINAL PRODUCT OF LABOUR

The average and marginal products of labour are essential in finding the optimum position for the producer. Diagrammatically, these values can be identified using tangents and rays (from the origin) to points on the total product curve.

Average product of labour

The average product (AP) of a factor is the total product divided by the quantity of the factor.

Consider the short-run production function:

$$Q = f(L)_{\overline{K}}$$

Then the average product of labour at the point R is:

$$AP_L^{(R)} = \frac{Q}{L} = \frac{OC}{OL_1} = \frac{RL_1}{OL_1}$$

This indicates that the average product may be measured geometrically as the tangent (tan = opposite/adjacent) of the angle made by a ray from the origin to the point R.

Using Figure 5.2, it may be observed that as rays are drawn from the origin to points on the total product curve moving up the curve from the origin to the point R, the angle made at the origin widens and hence the tan of the angle increases, causing AP_L to increase until it reaches a maximum at the point S. Beyond the point S the rays from the origin make smaller and smaller angles and hence smaller and smaller values for the tan of the angles. This indicates that beyond S the average product is falling.

Average product is therefore at a maximum at the point S on the total product curve. This corresponds with a quantity of labour in the plant of OL_1.

Marginal product of labour

The marginal product (MP) of a factor is the partial derivative of the production function with respect to that factor. It is therefore the slope of the total product curve taken at successive points on the curve. Consequently, at the point R:

$$MP_L^{(R)} = \frac{\partial Q}{\partial L} = \text{slope of total product curve at the point } R$$

If successive small tangent lines are drawn to the total product curve, the slope of these tangent lines will at first increase, reach a point of inflexion (in the region of the point R) and then decrease. It may be noted that the tangent drawn at the point g is on the underside of the total product curve but beyond the point R, a tangent to the curve, such as the point h in Figure 5.1, would have to be drawn on the outer side of the curve. This suggests that, whereas prior to reaching the point R, the slopes of the tangents are

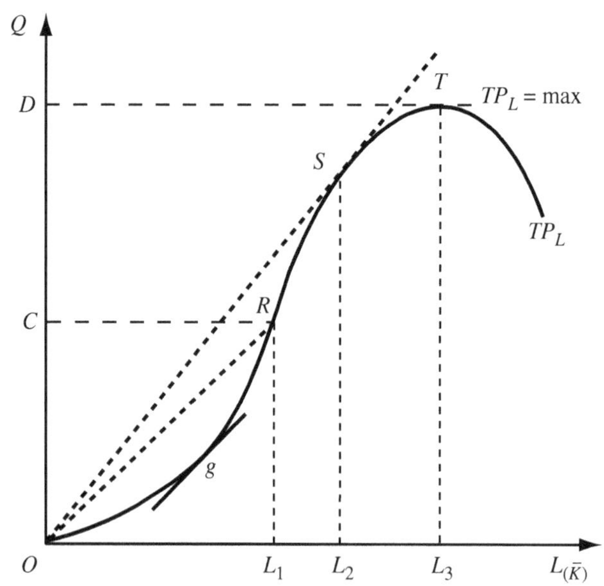

Figure 5.2
Total product curve with rays and tangents

increasing, after R, they are flattening out. This identifies R as the point of inflexion. At the point T, the slope of the total product curve is zero and, hence, so is the marginal product of labour.

Relationship between average and marginal product of labour

It may be noted that when the average product is a maximum (at the point S), the ray from the origin becomes a tangent to the total product curve. It signifies that ***the average product and the marginal product are equal at this point*** (since the marginal product is measured by the tangent to the curve). Hence, the average product and the marginal product of labour are equal where the average product is at its maximum. This occurs when the quantity OL_2 of labour is being used. These relationships are illustrated further in Figure 5.3.

From Figure 5.3, it may be observed that initially MP_L is above AP_L. The tangents at points A and B (measuring the marginal products) are steeper than rays (measuring the average product) at these points. Where the marginal is above the average, it pulls the average up. Hence the higher MP_L pulls up the AP_L until $MP_L = AP_L$ (where AP_L is a maximum). Then MP_L falls below AP_L and begins to pull AP_L down. At T, MP_L goes to zero, then becomes negative and continues to further pull down the AP_L.

5.2.2 Optimization of the producer in the short-run

In the short-run the producer maximizes profits in the region referred to as stage II of the production function (see region labeled II in Figure 5.3). This starts where the average product of labour AP_L is at its highest and ends where the marginal product of labour MP_L becomes zero. In terms of labour use this is identified as the range of labour use from L_2 to L_3.

This is the optimal region because, for any given wage rate, the producer should not stop adding labour to the fixed capital where the average product of labour (or output per person) is still increasing as labour is added. On the other hand, the producer should not continue to add labour where each unit of labour causes the total output of the plant to decrease (beyond where $MP_L = 0$). The actual equilibrium may be derived more precisely with the use of mathematics.

Mathematical derivation of short-run equilibrium

Since the producer aims to maximize profits, the formal derivation of equilibrium may be done using the calculus of variations.

The first-order condition

The objective function of the producer is:

$$\text{Max: } \Pi = R - C$$

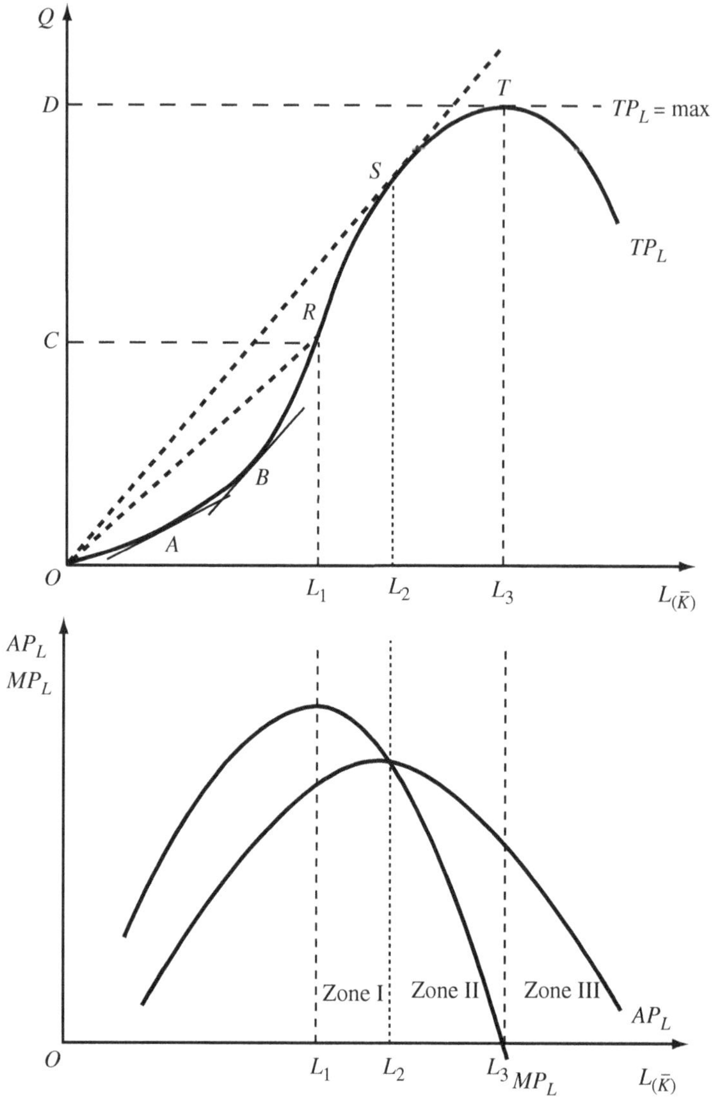

Figure 5.3
Total, average and marginal product of labour curves

where:

$$R = \overline{P}Q \qquad \text{and} \qquad Q = f(L)_{\overline{K}}$$

With capital (K) fixed, the cost equation (constraint) becomes:

$$C = \overline{w}L + \overline{rK}$$

or:

$$C = \overline{w}L + \overline{F}$$

Hence, the objective function becomes:

$$\text{Max: } \Pi = \overline{P}Q - \overline{w}L - \overline{F}$$

Differentiating with respect to labour only (since all other factors are fixed) gives:

$$\frac{\partial \Pi}{\partial L} = \overline{P}\frac{dQ}{dL} - \overline{w} = 0$$

It has already been established that:

$$\frac{dQ}{dL} = MP_L$$

The result shows that profit maximization requires the condition:

$$\overline{P}MP_L - \overline{w} = 0$$

or:

$$\overline{P}MP_L = \overline{w}$$

This implies that the value of the marginal product of labour must be equal to the wage rate in order for the firm to maximize its profits. In layman's terms it means that the incremental contribution of an extra unit of labour to the value of output must be equal to the cost of that extra unit of labour. It says that, for a single variable factor input, the producer must keep increasing the use of that factor up to the point where the value of the additional output generated by the last unit of the factor is exactly equal to the given factor's price. Prior to that point, the contribution of a unit of the factor to the revenue of the producer exceeds the cost of a unit of the factor so the producer adds more to profit and can continue to do so until the equilibrium point is reached.

Subsequent to reaching the equilibrium point, the contribution of a unit of the factor to the revenue of the producer is less than the cost of a unit of the factor so the producer loses money with each additional unit of labour employed. In essence then, the producer can increase profit as long as the addition to total revenue (value of incremental output) from the employment of an additional unit of an input (K or L), exceeds the cost of the additional unit.

Clearly, then, the producer should continue hiring additional units of labour until the profit maximization (equilibrium) point is reached and discontinues hiring once this point is reached. The producer must be aware of this and try to identify the point in order to be competitive or to remain in business in the face of competitive pricing of the product in the market.

The equilibrium position may be expressed as:

$$MP_L = \frac{\overline{w}}{\overline{P}}$$

For completeness, the second-order condition for a maximum should be applied. It may be noted that the second-order condition for a maximum would give the requirement that the slope of the marginal product of labour be negative ($slope\, MP_L < 0$). This puts the equilibrium position in stage II of the production function as described earlier. Moreover, since the wage is the average cost of labour, it cannot exceed the value of the average product of labour. This means the equilibrium wage cannot be above the maximum point of the average product curve and confirms the range given in stage II.

Once a producer in the short-run knows the firm's MP_L curve, then multiplying the MP_L by the price of the product and employing labour until this is equated to the going wage rate would give the firm its optimal (profit maximizing) quantity of labour to hire. It only remains for the producer to check that production is in the range where the MP_L is declining as labour units are added.

This is of great significance to firms, particularly where they are now forced to compete in a global market from a previously protected domestic market. Many unsophisticated firms are apprehensive about engaging in global competition. However, being armed with the knowledge of how to optimize allows the producer to have greater competence and more confidence when facing international competition.

5.3 OPTIMIZING BEHAVIOUR OF THE PRODUCER IN THE LONG-RUN

In the long-run all factor inputs are variable. Removing the restriction of fixed factors of production, the optimization problem for the producer may now be written as:

$$\text{Max: } \Pi = R - C$$

where the following holds:

$$R = \overline{P}Q$$

$$Q = f(L, K)$$

$$C = \overline{w}L + \bar{r}K$$

The optimizing problem may be written as:

$$\text{Max: } \Pi = \overline{P}Q - \overline{w}L - \bar{r}K$$

The producer is assumed to take prices as given. Hence:

$\overline{P} =$ the given price of the good being produced

$\overline{w} =$ the going wage rate

$\bar{r} =$ the going price of capital (rental rate)

5.3.1 Assumptions and tools of analysis

5.3.1.1 BASIC ASSUMPTIONS

The basic assumptions concerning the producer in the long-run are as follows:

- The producer is rational. That is the producer is in operation to maximize profits (Π).
- The producer knows the technology and can choose the optimal combination of factors.
- All the factors needed by the producer to maximize profits are available.
- The prices of factors are given.
- The price of the commodity is given.

The firm has the goal of profit maximization (Π max) and, because $\Pi = R - C$, the firm must do so by maximizing the difference between total revenue (R) and total cost (C).

Further, in order to deal with at least two variable factors, the tools of isoquant and isocost curves are introduced. The isoquant, which is similar to the consumer's indifference curve, defines the rate of technical substitution, while the isocost line, similar to the consumer's budget line, defines the price ratio of the factor inputs.

5.3.1.2 THE ISOQUANT

The isoquant is the locus of points of combinations of factors along which the total difference in output quantity (Q) is zero (i.e. where output remains the same). This is similar to the indifference curve in consumer analysis and possesses similar properties. They are convex to the origin, do not cross each other and the further from the origin, the higher the quantity of output represented by the isoquant (Q_1, Q_2, Q_3).

The slope of the isoquant has a particular significance for the equilibrium process and may be derived with reference to Figure 5.4. The curve reflects the diminishing marginal rate of technical substitution (substitution of capital for labour or vice versa) in production.

The slope of the isoquant may be derived formally with a mathematical approach using, once again, the calculus of variations.

Take the production function:

$$Q = f(K, L)$$

Since the isoquant is the line along which there is no difference in output, then it is necessary to differentiate the production function (Q) totally and set that total difference equal to zero.

Hence:

$$\frac{\partial Q}{\partial K}\mathrm{d}K + \frac{\partial Q}{\partial L}\mathrm{d}L = 0$$

This implies that:

$$\frac{\partial Q}{\partial K}\mathrm{d}K = -\frac{\partial Q}{\partial L}\mathrm{d}L$$

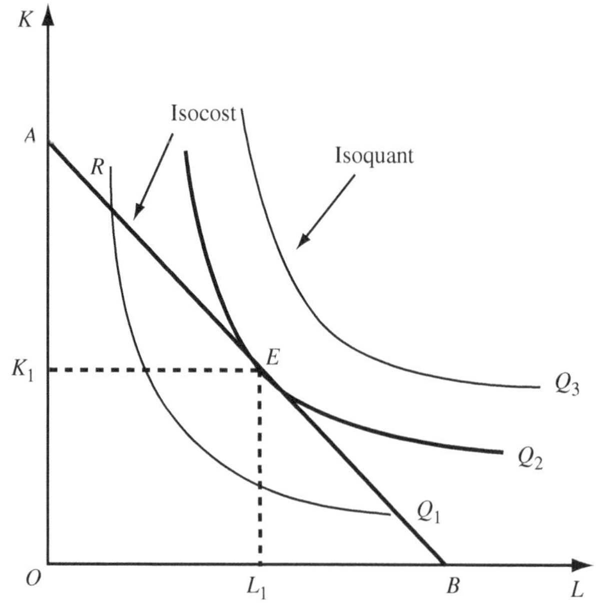

Figure 5.4
Isoquant and isocost lines

But since:

$$\frac{\partial Q}{\partial K} = MP_K \qquad and \qquad \frac{\partial Q}{\partial L} = MP_L$$

consequently:

$$MP_K \mathrm{d}K = -MP_L \mathrm{d}L$$

Re-arranging gives:

$$-\frac{\mathrm{d}K}{\mathrm{d}L} = \frac{MP_L}{MP_K}$$

Using Figure 5.4, it can be seen that the slope of the isoquant is:

$$-\frac{\mathrm{d}K}{\mathrm{d}L}$$

It follows therefore that the slope of the isoquant happens to be a measurement of the ratio of marginal product of labour to the marginal product of capital expressed as:

$$\frac{MP_L}{MP_K}$$

This ratio is called the marginal rate of technical substitution of labour for capital and is written as $MRTS_{L,K}$.

Formally, then, the slope of the isoquant is such that:

$$-\frac{\mathrm{d}K}{\mathrm{d}L}=\frac{MP_L}{MP_K}=MRTS_{L,K}$$

This result is used later in the optimization process.

5.3.1.3 THE ISOCOST LINE

The isocost line, as illustrated in Figure 5.4, is derived from the firm's budget equation:

$$C=\overline{w}L+\bar{r}K$$

The line *AB* shows that the firm (producer) could spend all of its budgeted funds on capital and purchase *OA* units of capital or spend all on labour and purchase *OB* units of labour.

The slope of the isocost or budget line gives the price ratio of labour to capital and may be found as follows.

Take the cost function:

$$C=\overline{w}L+\bar{r}K$$

Then:

$$\bar{r}K=C-\overline{w}L$$

This may be re-written as:

$$K=\frac{C}{\bar{r}}-\frac{\overline{w}}{\bar{r}}L$$

where:

$$\frac{C}{\bar{r}}=\text{Intercept}$$

and:

$$\frac{\overline{w}}{\bar{r}}=\text{Slope of isocost line}$$

In layman's terms, the slope of the isocost line is the ratio of the unit cost of labour (w) to the unit cost of capital (r), also known as the wage–rental ratio.

5.3.2 Optimizing behaviour of the firm in the long-run

In order to maximize profits, the producer must choose the optimal combination of factors. The typical producer may be expected to face given prices of the good in the market and of the factor inputs labour and capital. This may not be so where the producer is a very large supplier in a very small market. However, with increasing trade liberalization, each individual producer is more likely to be taking these prices as given and seeking to maximize profits within these parameters.

The equilibrium (profit maximizing behaviour) of the producer in considered under three scenarios as follows:

Case I – The producer is unconstrained.

Case II – The producer is constrained by cost and must therefore seek to maximize output for the given cost.

Case III – The producer is constrained by output and must therefore seek to minimize cost for the given output.

Using the mathematical techniques for optimization and, in particular, for constrained optimization, the equilibrium conditions for the producer may be formally derived. In particular, for the solution to the problem of constrained optimization, the Lagrangian multiplier method is applied.

It is useful to note that there is some dissimilarity between the optimization process for the consumer and that for the producer. In the case of the consumer, there is a utility function $U = f(x, y)$ where the consumer seeks to maximize utility (U). For the producer, however, with a production function: $Q = f(K, L)$, ***the specific objective is not to maximize output* (*Q*) per se, *but to maximize profits* (Π).** The maximization of output only becomes an objective when the producer is constrained by cost (Case II).

The cases are now examined in detail.

5.3.2.1 CASE I – EQUILIBRIUM FOR THE UNCONSTRAINED PRODUCER

In this case, the producer is neither constrained by cost (budget) nor by output (market restriction). This is unlike the case of the consumer where it is assumed that there is always a budget constraint consistent with the scarcity theme of economics (allocation of scarce resources among competing ends). In this case the objective for the producer is straightforward and may be set out as:

$$\text{Max: } \Pi = R - C$$

where the following holds:

$$R = \overline{P}Q$$
$$C = \overline{w}L + \bar{r}K$$

It may be noted that, in this case, it is only the prices that are fixed for the firm. These prices are: the price of the product and the prices of the factors of production.

Consequently, the objective function may be set out as:

$$\text{Max: } \Pi = \overline{P}Q - (\overline{w}L + \bar{r}K)$$

First-order condition

The first-order condition requires finding the first derivative of the function and setting it equal to zero (to identify the turning point). Since L and K are separable, only partial differentiation is required. The function is differentiated partially with respect to L and K respectively.

Differentiating partially with respect to labour gives:

$$\frac{\partial \Pi}{\partial L} = \overline{P}\frac{\mathrm{d}Q}{\mathrm{d}L} - \overline{w} = 0$$

This may be re-written as:

$$\overline{P}MP_L = \overline{w}$$

It signifies that the value of the marginal product (MP) of labour must be equal to the price of labour (wage rate). In layman's terms, the incremental contribution of an extra unit of labour to the value of output must be equal to the cost of that extra unit of labour. This would be the case for a single variable factor in production. However, two factors are operating together and must be considered simultaneously.

Continuing from above, the condition for labour may be put in real terms as:

$$MP_L = \frac{\overline{w}}{\overline{P}}$$

This implies that:

$$\overline{P} = \frac{\overline{w}}{MP_L} \tag{1}$$

Turning to the other factor, capital, and differentiating partially with respect to this factor gives:

$$\frac{\partial \Pi}{\partial K} = \overline{P}\frac{\mathrm{d}Q}{\mathrm{d}K} - \bar{r} = 0$$

This may be re-stated as:

$$\overline{P}MP_K = \bar{r}$$

As in the case of labour, this says that, if capital were the only factor (variable), the value of MP of capital must be equal to price of capital (rental rate).

The result can be put in real terms as:

$$MP_K = \frac{\bar{r}}{\overline{P}}$$

This gives:

$$P = \frac{\bar{r}}{MP_K} \tag{2}$$

Optimizing for both factors simultaneously, using (1) and (2) above, the equilibrium position becomes:

$$\overline{P} = \frac{\overline{w}}{MP_L} = \frac{\bar{r}}{MP_K}$$

This implies that:

$$\frac{\overline{w}}{MP_L} = \frac{\bar{r}}{MP_K}$$

This may be re-written as:

$$\frac{\overline{w}}{\bar{r}} = \frac{MP_L}{MP_K}$$

Diagrammatically, it requires that the slope of the isocost (w/r) must be equal to the slope of the isoquant (MP_L/MP_K). For the producer, it means that, in a practical sense, the money the producer pays for a unit of labour relative to that paid for a unit of capital must be in the same proportion as the unit of labour and unit of capital each adds to the output of the producer.

Moreover, it requires the producer to employ all factors until the contribution of the last unit employed of each is in the same ratio as the relative prices of the factors. This occurs at the point E in Figure 5.4.

As a corollary, if the value of the added output from the last unit employed of, say, factor L compared to factor K is greater than the relative price of labour to capital, then the producer can gain by utilizing more of labour relative to capital. The increasing use of labour relative to capital will reduce the productivity of labour relative to capital and eventually the ratios to prices will come into equilibrium. In the meantime, the producer would have gained.

This can be seen by considering the point R in Figure 5.4. At R, the isoquant is cutting the isocost rather than being tangent to it, signifying that their slopes are not equal. As a consequence, if the producer chooses point R, the level of output is lower at Q_1 (rather than Q_2) for the same expenditure on production (budget line AB). The producer can gain output (move to Q_2) for the same expenditure on production (given by budget line AB) by moving to the point E, where the slope of the budget line is equal to the slope of the isoquant.

Second-order condition

So far, only the first-order condition for profit maximization has been derived. The second-order condition requires that the second derivative of the objective function be less than zero. Formally, this condition requires that the Hessian matrix of second derivatives is negative definite at the solution point. For this to happen, the diagonal elements of the Hessian determinant must all be negative and the principal minors must alternate in sign. This requires all three of the following:

$$\frac{\partial^2 \Pi}{\partial K^2} < 0$$

$$\frac{\partial^2 \Pi}{\partial L^2} < 0$$

and:

$$\begin{vmatrix} f_{11} & f_{12} \\ f_{21} & f_{22} \end{vmatrix} > 0$$

It may be noted that this condition is fulfilled by the shape of the isoquant. This is achieved through the isoquant's convexity to the origin which must exist because of the assumption of diminishing marginal rate of technical substitution in production. This diminishing marginal rate of technical substitution holds true so long as the production process is continuous and there is adequate substitutability between the two factors (K, L).

In a practical sense, the equilibrium condition implies that profit must be decreasing with respect to further application of either K or L. In reality, an equilibrium (profit maximizing) position cannot make sense if the addition of more factors of production is going to further increase profit.

5.3.2.2 CASE II – EQUILIBRIUM FOR PRODUCER CONSTRAINED BY COST

This is the case where the producer has a restricted budget. This case may represent a small producer with limited access to funds. The producer still needs to maximize profits given the limited availability of funds. In this case, the maximization of profit resolves into the maximization of output subject to a cost constraint. It is useful to note that this is the only occasion when a producer should have the maximization of output as the aim since it is only when there is a cost constraint that the maximization of output coincides with the maximization of profit.

Once again, the overall objective to maximize profits is expressed as:

$$\text{Max: } \Pi = R - C$$

The cost constraint means that, graphically, the isocost line is given. A bar is placed on the cost (C) to represent cost being fixed as set out below:

$$\text{Max: } \Pi = R - \overline{C}$$

This may be expanded to:

$$\text{Max: } \Pi = \overline{P}Q - (\overline{wL} + \overline{rK})$$

Consequently, with cost and price fixed, the only way to maximize profit is through the maximization of output (Q). The problem therefore resolves into that of maximizing output subject to the cost constraint. This makes it a constrained optimization problem.

The constrained optimization procedure

The problem of constrained optimization may be solved using the Lagrangian Multiplier method. The procedure is described below.

The aim is to maximize profits by maximizing output subject to a cost constraint. Hence, the objective function becomes:

$$\text{Max: } Q = f(K, L)$$

Subject to the cost constraint function:

$$C = \overline{w}L + \overline{r}K$$

Using the Lagrangian multiplier method, the constraint is set equal to zero and multiplied by the Lagrangian multiplier (λ). Setting the constraint to zero gives:

$$C - \overline{w}L - \overline{r}K = 0$$

This is then multiplied by the Lagrangian multiplier (λ) to give:

$$\lambda(C - \overline{w}L - \overline{r}K)$$

Adding the Lagrangian $\lambda(C - \overline{w}L - \overline{r}K)$ to the objective function gives the ***composite function***:

$$\phi = Q + \lambda(C - \overline{w}L - \overline{r}K)$$

The maximization of the composite function ϕ is equivalent to the maximization of the objective function subject to the cost constraint.

First-order condition

For the first-order condition to be met, the partial derivatives with respect to L, K and λ must be equal to zero. This gives:

$$\frac{\partial \phi}{\partial L} = \frac{\partial Q}{\partial L} + \lambda(-\overline{w}) = 0 \quad (1)$$

$$\frac{\partial \phi}{\partial K} = \frac{\partial Q}{\partial K} + \lambda(-\overline{r}) = 0 \quad (2)$$

$$\frac{\partial \phi}{\partial \lambda} = C - \overline{w}L - \overline{r}K = 0 \quad (3)$$

Equation (3) verifies the impact of a one-unit increase in the constraint function on the objective function. Finding a solution directly involves the first two equations.

Using Equation (1) and solving for λ with respect to labour gives:

$$\lambda(-\overline{w}) = -\frac{\partial Q}{\partial L}$$

This implies that:

$$\lambda = \frac{\partial Q/\partial L}{\overline{w}}$$

This may be re-written as:

$$\lambda = \frac{MP_L}{\overline{w}}$$

By definition:

$$\frac{\partial Q}{\partial L} = MP_L$$

Similarly, using Equation (2) and solving for λ with respect to capital gives:

$$\lambda = \frac{MP_K}{\bar{r}}$$

Consequently:

$$\lambda = \frac{MP_L}{\overline{w}} = \frac{MP_K}{r}$$

This implies that:

$$\frac{MP_L}{MP_K} = \frac{\overline{w}}{\bar{r}}$$

Once again, the solution is achieved where the slope of the isoquant is equal to the slope of the isocost. Only in this case the ***isocost is fixed***.

Second-order condition

The second-order condition requires finding the second-order direct and cross-partial derivatives for x, y and λ. These are:

$$f_{xx}, f_{xy}, f_{x\lambda}, f_{yx}, f_{yy}, f_{y\lambda}, f_{\gamma x}, f_{\lambda y}, f_{\lambda\lambda}$$

Formally, this condition requires that the Hessian matrix of second derivatives is negative definite at the solution point. For this to happen, the diagonal elements of the Hessian determinant must all be negative and the principal minors must alternate in sign. This second-order condition, similarly to Case I (above), is fulfilled by the convexity to the origin of the isoquant (diminishing marginal rate of technical substitution).

However, unlike the unconstrained case, it is no longer a situation where, for each factor input, the producer must keep increasing the use of that factor up to the point where the value of the additional output generated by the last unit of the factor is exactly equal to the given factor's price. In the constrained case, the result can be interpreted only in terms of ratios.

In a practical way, the result requires the producer to employ all factors until the contribution to total revenue of the last unit employed of each factor is in the same ratio as the prices of the factors. This result can be extended to any number of factor inputs.

There is also the same implication that, as a corollary, if the value of the added output from the last unit employed of, say, factor L compared to, say, factor K is greater than the relative price of labour to capital, then the producer can gain by utilizing more of labour relative to capital. As this happens, the productivity of labour falls and eventually the two ratios come into equilibrium. There are no further gains for the producer hence profits are maximized. This is shown in the movement from the point R to the point E in Figure 5.4, as explained for the unconstrained case (Case I) above.

Diagrammatically, with the isocost fixed, the point of equilibrium tells the producer not only how much output to produce but also gives the actual quantities of capital and labour the producer must use in order to maximize profits. That is, the solution gives the point on the producer's fixed budget line (E) where production should take place. The co-ordinates of this point give the corresponding amounts of capital (K_1) and labour (L_1).

5.3.2.3 CASE III – EQUILIBRIUM FOR PRODUCER CONSTRAINED BY OUTPUT

For completeness, the third case of the producer constrained by output may be examined. This case may be viewed as the small market case. Here the producer may be supplying a protected small home market or a small protected segment of a larger market.

Once again, the aim of the producer is to maximize profits, set out as:

$$\text{Max: } \Pi = R - C$$

However, given the output constraint (fixed isoquant), the optimization problem becomes:

$$\text{Max: } \Pi = \overline{P}\,\overline{Q} - (\overline{w}L + \bar{r}K)$$

In this case, the maximization of profit (Π) (for a given level of output) can only be achieved through the minimization of cost. With output (Q) constrained, and with prices of output and factors fixed for the producer, the only option for the producer to maximize profits is to minimize costs through the optimal use and combination of capital (K) and labour (L).

The conditions for equilibrium are formally the same as in Cases I and II above (i.e. there must be tangency of isoquant and isocost and the isoquant must be convex to the origin).

Diagrammatically, in this case, however, there is one given (fixed) isoquant and several isocost lines, all parallel to each other since the relative prices of factors are assumed constant. The producer has therefore to seek to reach the lowest isocost. This is the one that is just tangent to the given isoquant.

Mathematical derivation of equilibrium becomes that of the minimize cost subject to a fixed output and may be set out as:

$$\text{Min: } C = (\overline{w}L + \bar{r}K)$$

subject to:

$$\overline{Q} = f(K, L)$$

To apply the Lagrangian method for constrained optimization, the constraint is rewritten as:

$$\overline{Q} - f(K, L) = 0$$

Multiplying by the Lagrangian multiplier and adding to the objective function, the composite function becomes:

$$\phi = C + \lambda[\overline{Q} - f(L, K)]$$

or:

$$\phi = \overline{w}L + \bar{r}K + \lambda[\overline{Q} - f(L, K)]$$

Taking partial derivatives of ϕ with respect to L, K and λ and equating to zero gives the first-order conditions:

$$\frac{\partial \phi}{\partial L} = \overline{w} - \lambda \frac{\partial (L, K)}{\partial L} = 0$$

This is continued to give the following three equations:

$$\frac{\partial \phi}{\partial L} = \overline{w} - \lambda \frac{\partial Q}{\partial L} = 0 \quad (1)$$

$$\frac{\partial \phi}{\partial K} = \bar{r} - \lambda \frac{\partial Q}{\partial K} = 0 \quad (2)$$

$$\frac{\partial \phi}{\partial \lambda} = [(Q - f(L, K)] = 0 \quad (3)$$

From (1) and (2) above respectively:

$$\overline{w} = \lambda \frac{\partial Q}{\partial L}$$

and:

$$\bar{r} = \lambda \frac{\partial Q}{\partial K}$$

But, since:

$$\frac{\partial Q}{\partial L} = MP_L \quad \textit{and} \quad \frac{\partial Q}{\partial K} = MP_K$$

the above results give:

$$\lambda = \frac{\overline{w}}{MP_L}$$

and:

$$\lambda = \frac{\bar{r}}{MP_K}$$

It indicates that:

$$\frac{\overline{w}}{MP_L} = \frac{\bar{r}}{MP_K}$$

This implies that:

$$\frac{\overline{w}}{\bar{r}} = \frac{MP_L}{MP_K} = MRTS_{L,K}$$

The second-order condition is again fulfilled by the convexity to the origin of the isoquant. Where the bordered Hessian determinant is used for the second-order condition, Equation (3) above is used in finding the second-order cross partial derivatives.

Thus the result is essentially the same as in the other two cases. Only here, the isoquant is fixed. With the isoquant fixed, the point of equilibrium position tells the producer what is the minimum cost of production and what are the actual and relative quantities of capital and labour that must be used in order to maximize profits. That is, the solution gives the point on the producer's fixed isoquant where production should take place. If the isoquant is fixed at Q_2 in Figure 5.4, then the lowest available cost of production would be that given by the isocost line AB. K_1 and L_1 would be identified as the appropriate cost-minimizing quantities of the factor inputs capital and labour that the producer should employ.

This result also tells the producer that the factors should be hired until their relative incremental contributions to output are proportionately equal to their relative costs. This can be extended to any number of inputs.

5.3.3 Effect of relative factor price changes

5.3.3.1 OUTPUT AND SUBSTITUTION EFFECTS

The output and substitution effects in production are similar to the income and substitution effects in consumption.

Using Figure 5.5, the initial equilibrium is at R on isoquant AB. Consider a fall in price of labour (L). This causes AB to pivot along the x-axis to AB'. Using the compensating variation line (CD), the substitution effect is from R to S, the output effect from S to T and the profit-maximization effect from T to V.

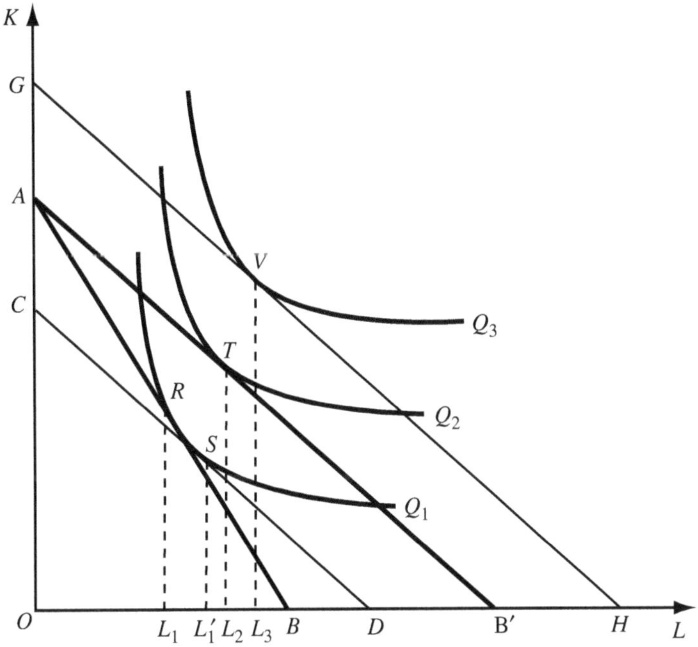

Figure 5.5
Output and substitution effects

Substitution effect

A price fall in labour leads to increased use of labour with the substitution effect. This is the change in labour usage attributed solely to the change in relative prices and is always negative (i.e. price of the factor falls, use of the factor increases along the same isoquant). To illustrate this, a compensating variation line is drawn to take away the budget increase effect of the fall in the price of labour. This line is *CD* in Figure 5.5 and is tangent to the same isoquant as the initial isocost line *AB*. The producer is therefore held to the same output level as before the fall in the price of labour but the new slope of the isocost reflects the changes in relative prices consequent upon the fall in the price of labour.

The movement from *R* to *S* shows the negative relationship between the price and quantity of labour employed *ceteris paribus*. The fall in the price of labour results in an increase in the quantity of labour employed when the impact of the fall in wages on the producer's expenditure is removed. This is the substitution effect.

Output effect

The output effect is similar to the income effect of the consumer. The outcome depends on whether the factor is normal, superior or inferior. For a normal factor the shift is to a point on the higher isoquant such that there is a further increase in labour usage. This usually involves an increase in capital usage as well. If the factor is a superior factor then relatively more of the factor is used in combination with the other factor. If the factor is inferior, relatively less is used in combination with the other factor.

The output effect is shown in the movement from *S* to *T* in Figure 5.5. In this illustration, if a ray were to be drawn from the origin to point *S* and to point *T*, it would be found to be steeper when drawn to point *T*. The steeper the angle of the ray the higher the capital/labour ratio. Hence, while the substitution leads to greater labour intensity in production, the output effect takes away some of that labour intensity.

The profit maximization effect

In addition, there is a profit maximization effect. This has no parallel in the theory of the consumer. In order to maximize profits when the price of an input falls, the producer must shift to another level of output in order to equate marginal cost (*MC*) and marginal revenue (*MR*). This effect moves production from point *T* to point *V* in Figure 5.5. The final equilibrium from the fall in the price of labour is therefore at the point *V* and the total effect of the fall in the price of labour is the movement from point *R* to point *V*.

5.3.3.2 INFERIOR FACTOR INPUTS

If labour is an inferior factor, then a ray from the origin drawn to the point *V* would show a steeper slope than at the original point *R*. This would suggest that, as the price of labour falls, the production process becomes relatively more capital intensive, contrary to the normal expectation. This is consistent with the general tendency for labour to become an inferior factor as plant output is expanded.

Similar effects could also occur where there is a fall in the price of capital. With increased global investment under increased trade liberalization, countries witnessing a net inflow of capital could experience a relative fall in the price of capital as it becomes less scarce (or more plentiful). Typically, though, capital is often a normal or superior factor as production is expanded. Consequently, with the fall in the price of capital, the production process becomes more capital intensive.

While inferior goods in consumption are associated with a negative income effect, inferior inputs in production are associated with negative output and profit maximization effects. The new equilibrium represents an increased ratio of capital to labour when the price of labour falls. Thus labour is considered an inferior factor input.

Typically, as a production plant expands, the process is expected to become more capital intensive. Thus if labour is an inferior input, the saving from the reduction in the price of labour would be used primarily to purchase more capital relative to labour and increase the capital intensity of the plant.

Diagrammatically, the ray from the origin to the final equilibrium point would be steeper than the ray to the initial equilibrium point in the case where labour is an inferior factor and the price of labour falls relative to the price of capital.

5.3.4 Optimal expansion and returns to scale

In the long-run, since all factors of production are variable, the firm can expand its output to the extent that is necessary to achieve the maximization of profits.

With given factor prices ($\overline{w}, \bar{r}$) and a given production function, the optional expansion path is the locus of the points of tangency of successive isocost lines and isoquants. The expansion path is an isocline (same gradient) along which output will expand ***when factor prices remain constant***.

Homogeneous vs. non-homogeneous production function

Figure 5.6 shows a homogeneous production function. In a homogeneous production function, the factor inputs can be increased in the same proportion in order to expand production (output). The line *OR* describes the expansion path (isocline). Where a production function is homogeneous, the expansion path (isocline) is a straight line out of the origin. The slope of the isocline describes the capital–labour (K/L) ratio in the production plant and, in the homogeneous production function, this K/L ratio remains constant as production is expanded (*ceteris paribus*). This ratio (the slope of the isocline) depends on the ratio of factor prices (w/r).

Consequently, as the isocost line is shifted outward in parallel fashion from *AB* to *CD* and to *GH*, the successive equilibrium points with the isoquants move in a straight line ray from the origin through the points E_1, E_2, and E_3, as shown in Figure 5.6.

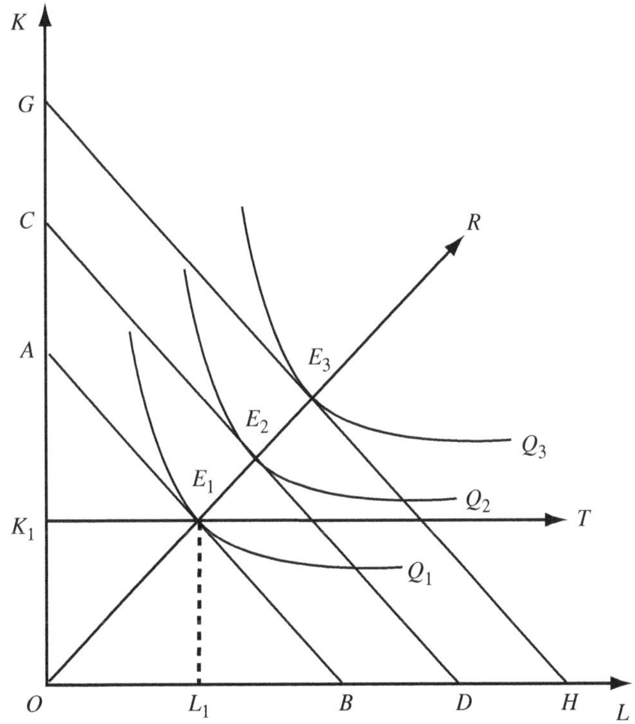

Figure 5.6
Expansion path of production (isocline)

Where a production function is non-homogenous, the expansion line is not a straight line even where the ratio of factor prices remains constant. The isocline, in this case, is a curve that bends and turns on its outward path. The expansion path thus shows how factor proportions change when output or expenditure changes (factor price ratios remaining constant).

Returns to scale

The returns to scale of a production function describe the extent to which an increase in inputs leads to an increase in output. In a homogeneous production function such as the one depicted in Figure 5.6, the returns to scale are measured by the distance between successive isoquants.

The typical production function first exhibits increasing, then constant and then decreasing returns to scale, in that order. Similar to the Law of Variable Proportions, which characterizes the short-run production function, the Laws of Returns to Scale characterizes the long-run production function.

With increasing returns to scale, the isoquants along the expansion path (isocline) get increasingly closer together. This is because an increase of output by a certain proportion requires less than a proportionate increase in the factor inputs. So, for example, consider that, initially, the production of one unit of output (Q) requires three unit of capital and two units of labour. With increasing returns to scale, the production of two units of output would require proportionately less of these inputs (i.e. less than twice the amount of these inputs). So, instead of requiring six units of capital and four units of labour, the production of two units of output would require, say, four units of capital and three units of labour.

For decreasing returns to scale the converse would hold as the isoquants get further apart from each other. Continuing with the example from above, the production of two units of production would require more than twice the amount of the inputs required for one unit of production. Hence, instead of requiring six units of capital and four units of labour, the production of two units of output would require, say, eight units of capital and five units of labour.

The case of constant returns to scale is that where a proportionate increase in output requires the same proportionate increase in inputs. Successive isoquants are equidistant from each other. This is similar to the case of the strict Cobb–Douglas production function. However, with the standard production function, constant returns to scale do not represent a full production function but only a point on a regular production function, a point which lies between increasing and decreasing returns to scale.

Expansion in the short-run

Figure 5.6 also shows the short-run expansion path. In the short-run all factors are fixed except one. The expansion path is a straight line parallel to the variable factor. The line $K_F T$ describes a short-run expansion path for labour (L) with capital fixed at K_F.

Expenditure elasticity

Expenditure elasticity (η_L, η_K) may be used to classify inputs into normal, inferior and superior. This is similar to the concept of income elasticity for the consumer that is derived from the income consumption curve (*ICC*) and allows a commodity to be classified as superior, normal and inferior.

For the producer, the expenditure elasticity of a factor of production is derived from the expansion path. For a factor labour (*L*), the expenditure elasticity may be classified as:

$$\eta_L > 1 - \text{Superior factor}$$

$$\eta_L < 1 - \text{Inferior factor}$$

$$\eta_L = 1 - \text{Normal factor}$$

The expenditure elasticity of labour (*L*) may be defined as the relative responsiveness of the employment of labour to changes in the total expenditure on inputs:

$$\eta_L = \frac{\%\ \text{change in usage of labour}(L)}{\%\ \text{change in total expenditure}(E)}$$

This may be expressed as:

$$\eta_L = \frac{\partial L/L}{\partial E/E} = \frac{\partial L}{\partial E} \cdot \frac{E}{L}$$

The expenditure elasticity curve for a factor is therefore similar to the Engel curve for the commodity.

Consider a commodity with a production function such that the factor input labour has an expenditure elasticity (η_L) such that:

$$\eta_L < 1$$

The significance of this is that the expansion of output in the industry that produces that commodity would result in a less than proportionate increase in the employment of labour. Concomitantly, it would mean a greater than proportionate increase in the use of capital. In a labour-surplus economy the effects of output expansion of use of the surplus labour may be disappointing. However, the higher capital intensity from the expanded output means an increase in the productivity of labour and an improved income to labour.

5.4 THE MULTI-PRODUCT FIRM

The previous analysis considered that any producer (firm) produced a single commodity. However, in reality, producers may be producing multiple commodities at the same time and in the same production plant.

The analysis of the multi-product firm adds a whole new dimension to the study of the producer. It provides a new set of analytical tools and concepts which are useful, not only in the analysis of the producer, but for other more advanced areas of economics. In particular, the technique and concepts used, such as the Edgeworth Box and the Product Transformation Curve, are of special relevance to the analysis of international trade.

5.4.1 The production function of a multi-product firm

Now, consider, for simplicity, a firm that produces only two commodities, x and y. This can later be extended to any number of commodities. Each product is produced by two factors, capital (K) and labour (L).

The assumptions of the model may be summarized as follows:

- Each product has its own production function.
- The aim of the producer is to maximize profits.
- The production technology is known to the producer.
- The prices of the products are given.
- The prices of the factors are given.

Consider that there is a single producer of two goods x and y with respective production functions as follows:

$$x = f_1(L, K)$$
$$y = f_2(L, K)$$

The production function for each commodity has a set of isoquants with the usual properties. The production functions of the two goods are not identical. That is, one is more capital intensive than the other.

The producer seeks the maximum profits. In order to achieve this, the producer has to find the optimal combination of the two commodities to produce with the given resources in the plant and must determine the optimal allocation of resources to the production of each of these two goods.

5.4.2 Tools, techniques and behavioural relationships

The analysis requires the use of the Edgeworth Box, the contract curve and the production possibility curve along with the iso-revenue curve. Central to the analysis is the concept of Pareto optimality (efficiency).

5.4.2.1 THE EDGEWORTH BOX

The Edgeworth Box is used extensively in the analysis of International Trade and in other areas of economic analysis particularly in the study of general equilibrium. It represents a case where the total resources are fixed and there is the need for the most efficient allocation of these resources in order to maximize the gains from their use. It is therefore an essential in the study of what may be described as 'the economic problem', that is, 'the allocation of scarce resources among competing ends'.

In the analysis of the multi-product firm, the Edgeworth Box represents the total quantities of the factors (K, L) available to the firm for the production of goods x and y. At issue is the allocation of these given (scarce) factor resources to the competing ends of goods x and y in production.

Figure 5.7 shows the isoquant maps for goods x and y respectively. The production functions for goods x and y are such that good x is the more labour intensive good in production while good y is the relatively more capital intensive good in production.

The isoquant maps for these two goods are combined to form the Edgeworth Box, a tool that is used in the determination of the optimal quantity of the two goods and the allocation of the factors inputs to the production of the two goods.

In the construction of the Edgeworth Box, the isoquant map for good y is rotated 180° and placed over the isoquant map for good x to form a box, the dimensions of which are the total amount of capital (K) and labour (L) available to the firm. This is illustrated in Figure 5.8.

Inside the box, the isoquants for goods x and y are convex to opposite origins and become tangent to each other in a regular pattern depending on the differences in the relative shapes of the respective isoquants. The points at which these isoquants for the respective goods are tangent to each other form an efficiency locus characterized by Pareto Optimality and the contracted path is given the name the Contract curve.

Pareto optimality

The concept central to the use of the Edgeworth Box is that of ***Pareto Optimality*** or ***Pareto Efficiency*** which defines a state where there can be no further benefit from a re-allocation of resources. This state of Pareto Optimality means that, in order to produce

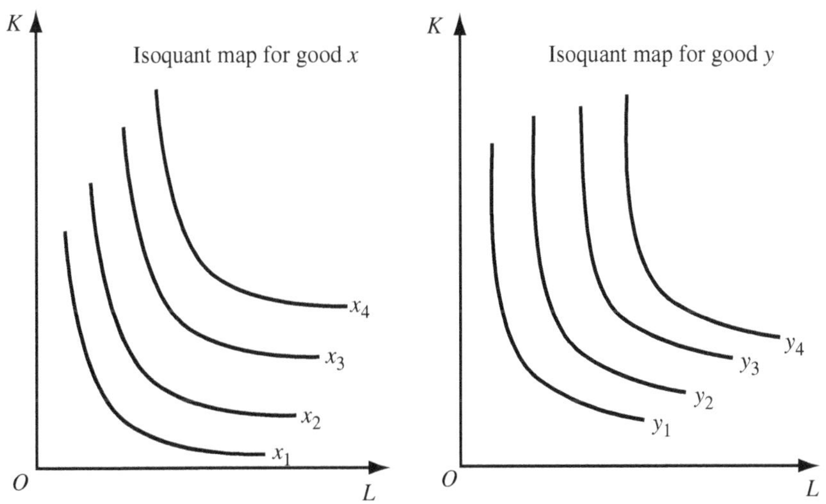

Figure 5.7
Isoquant maps for good x (left) and good y (right) respectively

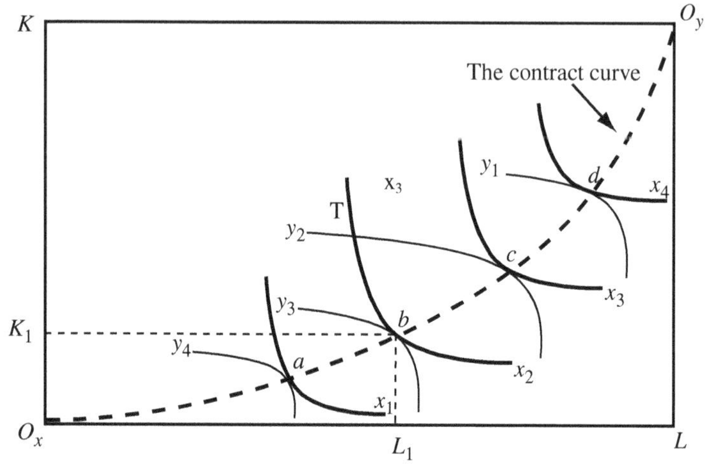

Figure 5.8
The Edgeworth box of production

more of one good, the production of the other ***must*** be reduced. If it is not possible to gain from a further reallocation of resources, then the existing condition must be that of the highest efficiency or optimality. The locus of such efficiency points constitute an efficiency frontier along which combinations of outputs may be varied but the production of one good can only be increased at the expense of the other good. This occurs along the Contract curve as illustrated in Figure 5.8.

Pareto optimality should be distinguished from ***Pareto Improvement***. A Pareto improvement refers to the situation where more of one good can be produced without a reduction in the other. This occurs in a movement from off the contract curve (e.g. point T) to a point on the curve (e.g. point a or point b).

The contract curve

As the line joining the points of tangency of the isoquants, the contract curve is the locus of points at which the marginal rate of technical substitution of the two factors, capital (K) and labour (L) is the same for both commodities x and y. Hence this is the locus of points where:

$$MRTS^x_{L,K} = MRTS^y_{L,K}$$

It also means that at each point along the curve the isoquants are tangent to the factor price ratio such that:

$$MRTS^x_{L,K} = MRTS^y_{L,K} = \frac{w}{r}$$

Only points on the contact curve are technically efficient (achieving Pareto efficiency or optimality). Any point off the contract curve means a lower output of ***at least one*** good. Along the curve the production of more of one good can only be achieved by a reduction in the production of the other. All points in the box, whether on or off the contract curve, represent the use of all the resources.

The points off the contract curve are all less efficient than those on the curve. As an example, consider production at a point off the contract curve such as at point T in Figure 5.8. Then compare this with production at point b or c on the contract curve. With all resources being used the firm can produce as follows.

At point T, which is off the contract curve, the firm produces the combination y_2 and x_2. This may be compared to points on the curve. Consider the movement to either point b or point c on the contract curve. These points are chosen because one or other of the goods can be held constant while the other is changed. This allows for easier and less ambiguous comparisons of gains.

Movement from point T *to point* b

At point b on the contract curve the firm produces the combination y_3 and x_2. This represents an increase in the production of good y without a reduction in the production of good x. This is a Pareto improvement gained by moving from a point off the contract curve to a point on the curve.

Movement from point T *to point* c

At point c on the contract curve the firm produces the combination y_2 and x_3. This represents an increase in the production of good x without a reduction in the production of good y. This again represents a Pareto improvement gained from a point off the contract curve to a point on the curve.

It can be seen, therefore, that by moving on to the contract curve at b or at c from the point T off the contract curve, the firm can increase the production of one good while holding the quantity of the other good constant. Furthermore, movement on to the contract curve between b and c allows more of ***both*** goods to be produced.

Hence the movement from points off the curve to points on the curve constitute a ***Pareto improvement***. To take advantage of this improvement the firm must stay on the contract curve. At any point on the contract curve the optimal allocation of resources to the production of each good is determined. For example, at the point b, the optimal allocation is O_xL_1 of labour and O_xK_1 of capital to the production of good x and the remainder (reading from the origin (O_y) for good y) to the production of good y.

Movements along the curve, say from point a to point b or from point b to point c, will increase the output of good x but reduce the output of good y and vice versa. The actual choice of a point on the contract curve depends on the ratio of prices of the two factor inputs or, when taken into production space on the Product Transformation Curve, the relative prices of the two goods define the optimal point.

5.4.2.2 THE PRODUCTION POSSIBILITY FRONTIER

The Production Possibility Frontier (PPF) is also known as the Product Transformation Curve and these terms will be used interchangeably. The curve represents the translation into product space of the locus of points of combinations of x and y which use up all the available resources of the firm and are on the Pareto efficiency locus (i.e. points on the contract curve).

This curve is therefore derived from and reflects the contract curve. Each point on the contract curve defines a point on the production possibility frontier. This curve is illustrated in Figure 5.9. Along the product transformation curve, the information from the Edgeworth Box is mapped into production space with the products good x and good y on the axes. The points a, b, c and d on the contract curve in Figure 5.8 are represented on the product transformation curve in Figure 5.9 as a', b', c' and d'.

As noted previously, inside the Edgeworth Box the points of tangency occur where the slope of an isoquant for good x is equal to the slope of an isoquant for good y, expressed as:

$$MRTS^{x}_{L,K} = MRTS^{y}_{L,K}$$

Consequently, it must be remembered that this condition is represented at all points along the production possibility frontier (PPF) or product transformation curve. The Pareto optimality condition from inside the Edgeworth Box is therefore transferred to the PPF which now also represents the locus of efficiency in resource allocation.

Points off the contract curve are represented by points inside the production possibility frontier. All points inside the frontier are inefficient. Point T in the Edgeworth Box is represented as point T' inside the production possibility frontier, representing inefficiency in the allocation of resources. Greater output of at least one good can be achieved while the other is held constant by moving to a point such as a' or b' on the product transformation curve.

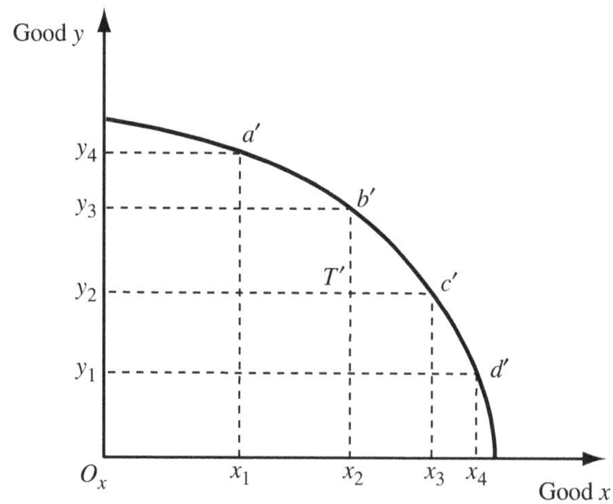

Figure 5.9
The production possibility frontier (*PPF*)

Slope of the production possibility curve

The slope of the Production Possibility curve (frontier) is called the Marginal Rate of Product Transformation (*MRPT*). It reflects the opportunity cost of transferring the fixed resources from the production of one good into the production of the other.

The *MRPT* may be written as:

$$-\frac{\mathrm{d}Y}{\mathrm{d}X} = MRPT_{XY} = \text{ Marginal Rate of Product Transformation}$$

A reduction in level of good y releases factors of production:

$$\partial L_y(MP_{L,y}) + \partial K_y(MP_{K,y})$$

An increase in level of good x requires additional factors:

$$\partial L_x(MP_{L,x}) + \partial K_x\left(MP_{K,y}\right)$$

For factors to remain fully employed the factors released from the decrease in good y must be equal to the factors absorbed in the increase of good x. Thus:

$$-\partial L_y = +\partial L_x$$
$$-\partial K_y = +\partial K_x$$

For efficient production the firm must stay on the curve, not inside it. Consequently, the slope of the isoquant of good x must be equal to the slope of isoquant of good y. This gives:

$$\frac{MP_{L,x}}{MP_{K,x}} = \frac{MP_{L,y}}{MP_{K,y}}$$

The slope of the production possibility curve then becomes:

$$-\frac{\mathrm{d}y}{\mathrm{d}x} = \frac{MP_{K,y}}{MP_{K,x}}$$

or:

$$-\frac{\mathrm{d}y}{\mathrm{d}x} = \frac{MP_{L,y}}{MP_{L,x}}$$

Hence:

$$-\frac{\mathrm{d}y}{\mathrm{d}x} = \frac{MP_{K,y}}{MP_{K,x}} = \frac{MP_{L,y}}{MP_{L,x}}$$

It must be noted that the curve represents ***opportunity cost***. It represents the cost of giving up one good in order to get an extra unit of the other. As such it can be taken to represent the ratio of the marginal costs of the two goods and may be expressed as:

$$\frac{MC_X}{MC_Y}$$

Under perfect competition, as assumed for the producer, the marginal cost is equal to price and, hence, the slope of the Production Possibility Frontier may be represented by the relative prices of the two goods as:

$$\frac{P_X}{P_Y}$$

With regards to opportunity cost, it must be noted that the *PPF* reflects ***increasing opportunity cost*** giving the curve a concavity to the origin shape. This is because, as stated earlier, the two goods have different factor intensities – one good is relatively labour intensive while the other is relatively capital intensive. This difference in relative factor intensity causes the contract curve to bend off of the diagonal in the Edgeworth Box. The greater the difference in relative factor intensities of the goods, the more the contract departs from the diagonal and consequently, the more bowed out (concave to the origin) is the *PPF* derived from it.

Consequently, moving down along the curve, increasingly more of good y has to be given up to obtain the same incremental increase of good x. This is the increasing opportunity cost. It occurs because the factors released in the production of good y are not in the same proportion as those required for the production of good x. Where y is the relatively capital intensive good and x the relatively labour intensive good, then giving up y to expand production of x means that more capital to labour is being released than can be absorbed in the production of good x. This is the increasing opportunity cost.

5.4.3 Optimization of the multi-product firm

The optimal combination of products is the output pair of goods x and y that yields the highest revenue to the producer. Since the inputs are fixed, the cost to the producer is fixed. Profit maximization therefore becomes the quest to find the combination of goods x and y that yield the highest revenue to the firm.

This introduces the tool of the iso-revenue curve for the producer.

5.4.3.1 THE ISO-REVENUE CURVE

The revenue equation for the multi-product producer is:

$$\overline{R} = P_X Q_X + P_Y Q_Y$$

In order to get the particular level of revenue represented by the revenue line *AB*, in Figure 5.10, the firm must sell either *OA* of good y or *OB* of good x or any combination of goods x and y along the fixed revenue line *AB*. Along the line *AB* there is the same level of revenue, hence it is referred to as the ***iso-revenue*** line.

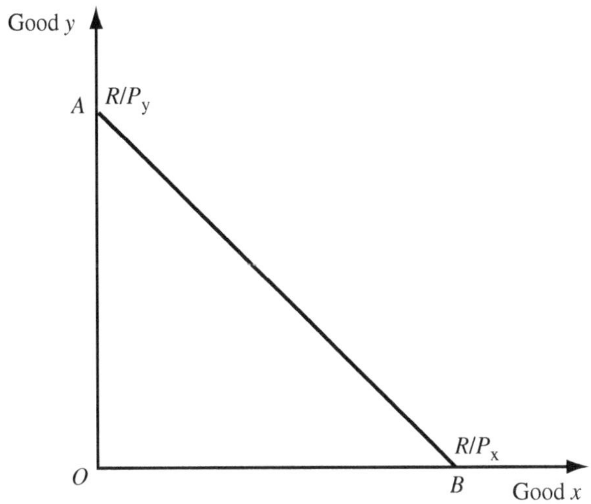

Figure 5.10
The iso-revenue curve

At the end points of the iso-revenue line (A, B), the firm sells only one of the two goods. Hence, at point A, the total revenue from selling only commodity y is:

$$\overline{R} = P_y Q_y$$

As a result, the quantity of good y (Q_y) that must be sold to reach the given level of total revenue is:

$$Q_y = \frac{\overline{R}}{P_y} = OA$$

At point B, the total revenue from selling only commodity x is:

$$\overline{R} = P_x Q_x$$

Hence, the quantity of good x (Q_x) that must be sold to reach the given level of total revenue is:

$$OB = \frac{\overline{R}}{P_x}$$

Consequently, the slope of iso-revenue curve (OA/OB), as shown in Figure 5.10, is:

$$\frac{OA}{OB} = \frac{\overline{R}/P_y}{\overline{R}/P_x} = \frac{\overline{R}}{P_y} \cdot \frac{P_x}{\overline{R}} = \frac{P_x}{P_y}$$

Alternatively, using the equation for the iso-revenue curve, the slope may be found directly as follows:

$$\overline{R} = P_x Q_x + P_y Q_y$$

Making Q_y the subject gives:

$$Q_y = \frac{\overline{R}}{P_y} - \frac{P_x}{P_y}Q_x$$

This identifies the intercept as:

$$\frac{\overline{R}}{P_y}$$

The slope or gradient is shown to be:

$$\frac{P_x}{P_y}$$

The slope of the iso-revenue line is therefore the ratio of the prices of the two goods under production:

$$\frac{OA}{OB} = \frac{P_x}{P_y}$$

The further the iso-revenue curve is from the origin, the higher the level of revenue it represents. The aim of the multi-product firm is to reach the highest revenue attainable given the production possibilities available.

5.4.3.2 EQUILIBRIUM OF THE MULTI-PRODUCT FIRM

The equilibrium for the multi-product producer brings together the Production Possibility Frontier (*PPF*) and the iso-revenue curve. The *PPF* gives the ***technical*** efficiency of the producer, given the available resources in the production plant. But any point on the frontier represents optimal efficiency as in Pareto Optimality. The determination of the ***economically optimal point*** for the producer requires reaching the highest iso-revenue curve. The highest iso-revenue curve attainable is the one that is just tangent to the *PPF*.

Figure 5.11 illustrates this equilibrium for the multi-product firm. The iso-revenue curves are superimposed on the production possibility frontier. The equilibrium point is at *E* (representing the point c') where the producer firm reaches the highest attainable iso-revenue curve. This is the one (R_3) that is tangent to the production possibility frontier. This gives the maximum revenue of R_3 and this indicates that the firm should produce Oy_2 of good *y* and Ox_3 of good *x* in order to maximize its profits. The iso-revenue line of R_4 is more desirable but not attainable since it is outside of the production possibility frontier.

It may be noted that iso-revenue line R_2 cuts the *PPF* but does not represent an equilibrium because the producer can achieve a higher revenue from that same *PPF* by moving to one that is tangent to the *PPF*.

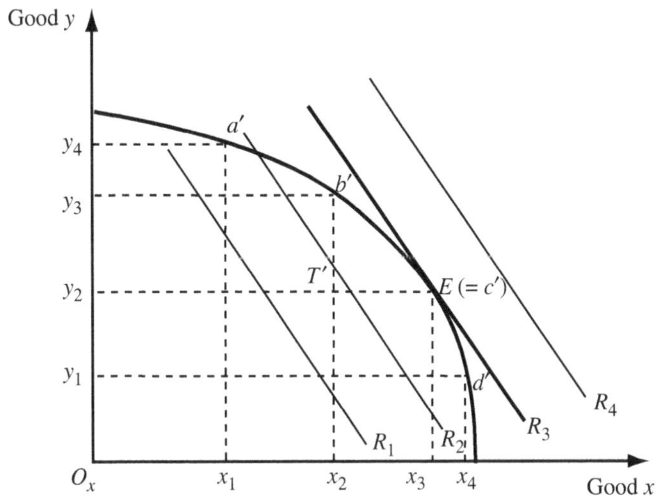

Figure 5.11
Equilibrium of the multi-product firm

Maximization of profit

Assuming that the quantities of factor inputs available to a firm are given and prices of these factor inputs are given (i.e. the firm has given costs), then the firm will maximize profits by maximizing revenue (R) at point E, the point of tangency between product possibility curve and highest iso-revenue curve. The PPF is determined by the technology and provides the necessary condition for the producer to achieve full technical efficiency. The sufficient condition for maximization of profit is provided by the iso-revenue curve which determines at which technically efficient point the greatest revenue (and hence the greatest profit) accrues to the producer.

Consequently, at equilibrium:

$$-\frac{\partial y}{\partial x} = \frac{MP_{L,y}}{MP_{L,x}} = \frac{MP_{K,y}}{MP_{K,x}} = \frac{P_x}{P_y}$$

Alternatively:

$$\frac{MP_{L,y}}{MP_{K,y}} = \frac{MP_{L,x}}{MP_{K,x}}$$

In other words, the producer of multiple products with given resources should reallocate resources until the addition to total output from the last unit added (marginal product) of each factor input is in the same ratio for all products.

It has previously been established that, along the product transformation curve (also the PPF), the slope represents the opportunity cost of one good in terms of the other. The slope therefore gives the ratio of the marginal cost of the two goods. Hence, in practical terms, the equilibrium condition indicates that the producer should ensure that the incremental cost (marginal cost) of producing each of the goods is proportional to the price of the goods or that:

$$\frac{MC_x}{MC_y} = \frac{P_x}{P_y}$$

This extends to any number of goods and is vital to the producer being able to produce efficiently and attain the level of competitiveness required in an internationally competitive market.

REVIEW QUESTIONS FOR CHAPTER 5

1 Explain in detail how profit maximization can be achieved for a firm in the ***Short-run*** showing why the producer must operate in 'zone 2' of the production function.

2 Derive the ***Long-run*** profit maximizing condition for a firm that is:

(a) ***Not constrained*** (by output or cost)
(b) Constrained by cost
(c) Constrained by output

3 With regard to a multi-product firm producing two products, and using two factors of production:

(a) Show how the technique of the Edgeworth Box may be used to identify the most technically efficient combination of outputs.
(b) Derive the production possibilities curve from the contract curve in the Edgeworth Box.
(c) Show how iso-revenue curves may be constructed.
(d) Carefully illustrate how the product transformation curve and the iso-revenue curves may be used in determining the profit maximization combination of outputs for the firm.

Multiple choice questions

Indicate the single correct answer for each of the following questions.

1 In the short-run a producer has a production function $Q = f(L)_K$ where output (Q) is a function of the labour input (L) with all other factors (represented by capital (K)) held constant. It is fair to say that the producer can maximize profits only:

(a) In the stage of the production function where the marginal product of labour curve is falling and is below the average product of labour curve but above zero. ☐
(b) In the stage of the production function where the marginal product of labour is rising and is above the average product of labour. ☐

(c) Where the average product of labour is at its maximum. ☐
(d) In the declining region of the Total Product of labour curve. ☐

2 In the long-run, the optimization problem (Max: $\Pi = R - C$) for the producer producing a single product, x, using two factors, labour (L) and capital (K) may be set out as follows:

(a) Max : $Q = f(K, L)$, subject to $C = \overline{w}L + \bar{r}K$ where the producer is constrained by cost. ☐
(b) Max : $Q = f(K, L)$, where the producer is constrained by output. ☐
(c) Min : $C = \overline{w}L + \bar{r}K$, where the producer is unconstrained. ☐
(d) Max : $\Pi = Q - \lambda(\overline{w}L + \bar{r}K)$, where the producer is constrained by cost. ☐

3 A multi-product firm is producing two goods (x and y) with different factor intensities such that it may be depicted in an Edgeworth Box. The firm has fixed amounts of the factors given by the dimensions of the box. Based on this, it is fair to say that:

(a) Pareto Optimality (efficiency) for this firm is achieved at a point off the contract curve. ☐
(b) The contract curve is used to construct the product transformation (production possibilities) curve. ☐
(c) A Pareto improvement is achieved as production shifts from left to right along the contract curve. ☐
(d) At all points in the box, the two factors capital (K) and labour (L) are used efficiently. ☐

RECOMMENDED READING FOR CHAPTER 5

Henderson, J. M. and Quandt, R. E. (1984) *Microeconomic Theory: A Mathematical Approach*, McGraw Hill, Ch. 4.
Koutsoyiannis, A. (1979) *Modern Microeconomics* (2nd Edn), London: MacMillan.
Robinson, J. (1953–54) 'The Production Function and the Theory of Capital', *Review of Economic Studies*, 21(54): 81–106.
Solow, R. M. (1955–56) 'The Production Function and the Theory of Capital', *Review of Economic Studies*, 23(61): 101–8.

6 Costs and Scale

Traditional Cost Theory: Short-run, Long-run; Modern Cost Theory: Short-run, Long-run; Economies of Scale. Returns to Scale and the Homogeneous Production Function: The Cobb–Douglas Production Function.

Cost functions are derived from production functions and show the relationship between the quantity produced and the cost of production. This cost of production is the cost of the factor inputs used in the production process. As a result, there is a direct relationship between the production function and the cost function. In an era with an emphasis on cost competitiveness, it is essential to have an understanding of the nature of cost functions, differences between short- and long-run costs and the significance of scale for unit costs.

Cost theory is examined with regard to the traditional theory and the modern theory. Each of these is divided into the short-run and the long-run. The short-run considers the relationships among total, average and marginal costs. This provides a backdrop for the study of the nature of long-run costs and the significance of scale for the producer.

The special case of the Cobb–Douglas production function is examined in order to understand its special properties and the significance for scale and cost competitiveness.

6.1 TRADITIONAL COST THEORY – THE SHORT-RUN

The laws of production are given to economists by engineers and others who design production plants. These are the ones who determine the real relationships between inputs and outputs. The laws describe the technically possible ways of increasing the level of production.

In the short-run, the cost function (C) may be written simplistically as a function of the quantity of output (Q) as:

$$C = f(Q)$$

where output is a function of labour (L) for all other factors (subsumed under capital (K)) being fixed, expressed as the short-run production function:

$$Q = f(L)_{\overline{K}}$$

Thus the cost function is dependent on the production function. This gives the cost curve its shape while other factors shift the cost curve.

6.1.1 Short-run total costs

The short-run total costs (TC) are the sum of the total fixed costs (TFC) and the total variable costs (TVC). This is expressed as:

$$TC = TFC + TVC$$

The fixed costs are usually those that do not vary directly on a day-to-day basis with the daily output of the production plant. These are the overhead expenses that are incurred whether or not production takes place on any given day. The typical fixed costs, often subsumed under capital (K), include:

- Building depreciation and repair costs and land maintenance costs
- Costs for depreciation (wear and tear) of machinery and equipment
- Remuneration of salaried employees and senior administrative staff (those with annual salaries)
- Lump-sum to cover normal profit (opportunity cost), risk and any lump-sum taxes.

The variable costs are the day-to-day operation expenses and vary with the quantity produced. These costs include:

- Wages of labour (weekly, daily, hourly payments)
- Operational expenses directly related to levels of output (energy costs, utilities, ongoing maintenance)
- Raw material and intermediate goods inputs

Short-run total fixed cost (TFC)

Since the total fixed cost (TFC) is a constant, it is graphed as a straight line parallel to the X-axis. Its level is not affected by the quantity of output in the given time period. This is illustrated in Figure 6.1.

Short-run total variable cost (TVC)

Since the cost function is derived from the production function, the total variable cost (TVC) is derived from the short-run production function. As a result the TVC curve reflects the ***Law of Variable Proportions*** (law of eventually diminishing returns to a variable factor) that characterizes the shape of the short-run total product (TP) curve.

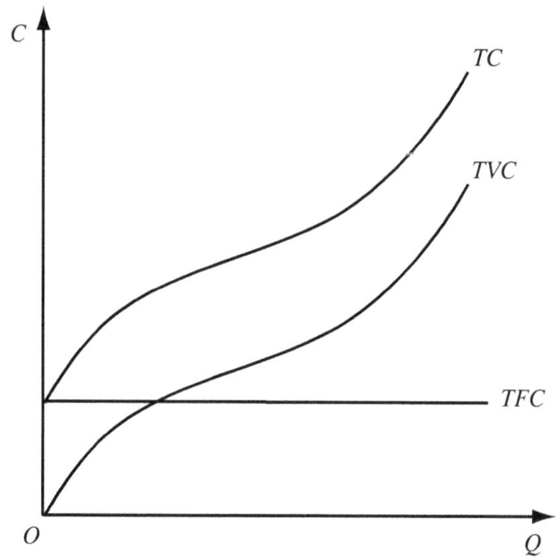

Figure 6.1
Short-run fixed, variable and total costs

According to this law, in the initial stages of production, as more of the variable factor is employed and added to the fixed factor(s) the productivity of the variable factor increases causing output to increase at an increasing rate. This continues until the optimal combination of the fixed and variable factors is reached. Beyond this point as more of the variable factor is added to the fixed factors the productivity of the variable factors declines causing output to increase at a decreasing rate.

Since the short-run variable cost is simply the quantity of the variable factor times its price (given the fixed factor), then when the output of the factor is increasing at an increasing rate, the cost is increasing at a decreasing rate. Conversely, when the output of the factor is increasing at a decreasing rate, the cost attributed to the factor is increasing at an increasing rate.

Consequently, the short-run total variable cost curve increases at a decreasing rate and then increases at an increasing rate as shown in Figure 6.1.

Short-run total cost

The short-run total cost curve is the sum of the total variable cost and the total fixed cost for every output quantity. Diagrammatically, it is the vertical summation of the *TFC* and the *TVC* curves. It has the same shape as the *TVC* curve as it represents a vertically upward displacement of the *TVC* by a distance equal to the height of the *TFC* curve.

The short-run total cost (*TC*) function in the traditional cost theory may be represented mathematically as:

$$TC = b_0 + b_1 Q - b_2 Q^2 + b_3 Q^3$$

In this expression, the total fixed cost (TFC) may be represented by:

$$TFC = b_0$$

The total variable cost may be represented by the cubic polynomial form:

$$TVC = b_1Q - b_2Q^2 + b_3Q^3$$

6.1.2 Short-run average and marginal costs

Average fixed cost

The short-run average fixed cost (AFC) may be expressed as:

$$AFC = \frac{TFC}{Q} = \frac{b_0}{Q}$$

Since the total fixed cost (TFC) is a constant (b_0) (a horizontal straight line), then as output (Q) expands the value of the average fixed cost (AFC) gets increasingly smaller. It does not go to zero but approaches the axes asymptotically.

Consequently, the short-run total fixed cost curve has the shape that is described mathematically as a rectangular hyperbola as depicted in Figure 6.2.

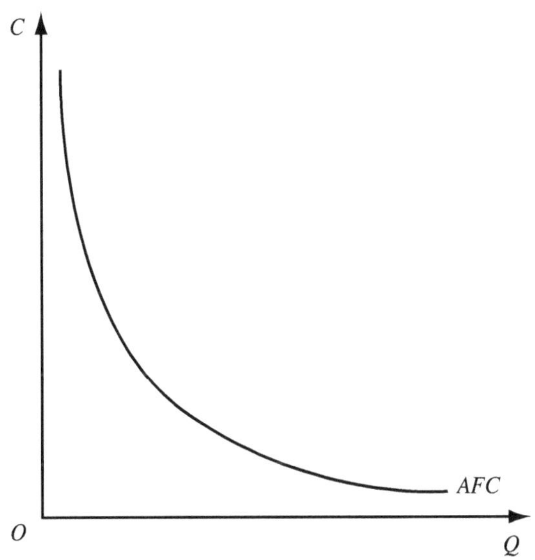

Figure 6.2
Short-run average fixed cost curve

Short-run average variable cost

The short-run average variable cost (AVC) is the variable cost per unit of output and is measured as:

$$AVC = \frac{TVC}{Q}$$

From above, the TVC was expressed as the cubic polynomial:

$$TVC = b_1Q - b_2Q^2 + b_3Q^3$$

From this, the AVC derives its U-shape as it becomes:

$$AVC = b_1 - b_2Q + b_3Q^2$$

Diagrammatically, the AVC at any output (Q) is derived from the ATC by dropping a perpendicular from the ATC to the x-axis (the quantity axis). The AVC at that output (Q) is the vertical distance (TVC) divided by the distance along the x-axis (Q). The geometry of this is that the AVC at any output level (Q) is the tan (opposite/adjacent) of the angle θ formed by a ray from the origin to the point on the TVC curve directly above that output level (Q).

Using Figure 6.3, it may be observed that as a ray is drawn from the origin to different points on the TVC curve the angle (θ) first decreases and then increases. In the same manner, the tan of the angle first decreases and then increases and so does the AVC. The angle made by the ray decreases as it is drawn to points going from point a to point b on the TVC curve. This indicates that the AVC curve is declining. It continues to decrease up to the point d at which the ray from the origin becomes a tangent to the TVC curve. This gives the lowest point on the AVC. After the point d, the angle made by the ray increases, thus the AVC curve turns up again.

Short-run marginal cost

The marginal cost (MC) is defined as the change in total costs resulting from a unit change in output. This may be expressed as:

$$MC = \frac{\mathrm{d}(TVC)}{\mathrm{d}Q}$$

Again the functional form of the total variable cost curve may be used:

$$TVC = b_1Q - b_2Q^2 + b_3Q^3$$

This gives the marginal cost as:

$$MC = b_1 - 2b_2Q + 3b_3Q^2$$

This gives it a similar slope to the average cost curve but the same intercept b_1 but with twice the negative pull in response to Q and three times the positive pull in response

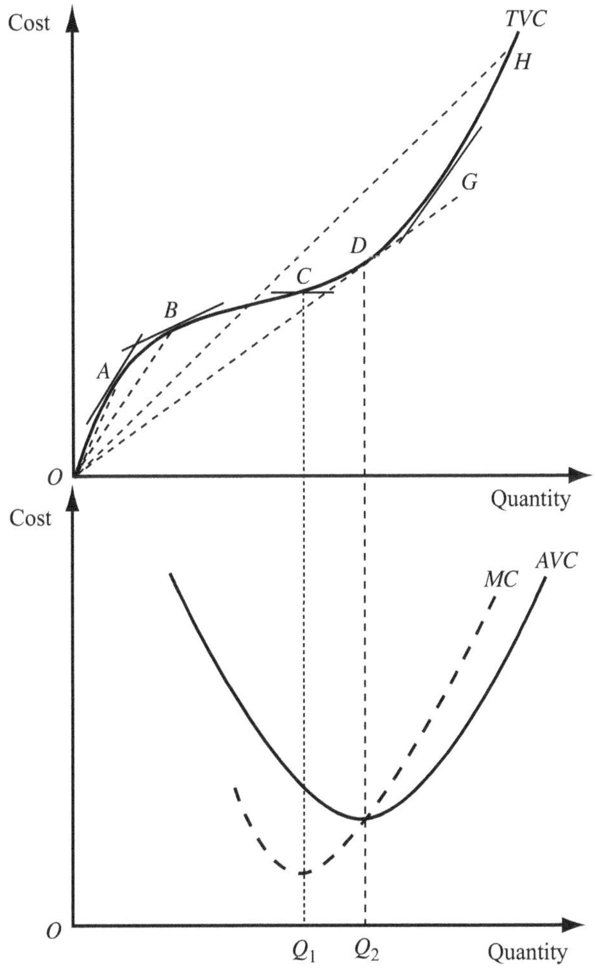

Figure 6.3
Deriving average variable and marginal cost curves from the total variable cost curve

to *Q*-squared. The upshot of this is to give the *MC* curve a much tighter U-shape than the *AVC* curve.

Diagrammatically, the *MC* curve is the slope of the *TVC* curve. Hence it may be measured by the tangents drawn to points on the *TVC* curve.

Using Figure 6.3, it may be observed that successive tangents drawn to the *TVC* curve decline in slope from point *a* to point *b*. As a result, the relevant marginal cost curve is falling. Point *c* is a point of inflexion. At point *c* the slopes of successive tangents stop declining and start to increase. This signifies that point *c* marks the minimum point of the marginal cost curve after which the curve rises.

From the point *c* on the *TVC* curve, the slopes of the tangents (and hence the marginal cost curve) continue to rise until, at the point *d* on the *TVC*, the tangent to the curve (*MC*) and the ray from the origin to the curve (*AVC*) are the same. At this point the average variable cost and the marginal cost are one and the same.

It is useful to note that the point d is at the output (Q) where the AVC curve is at its minimum point. Hence, ***the MC is equal to the AVC where the AVC is at its minimum point***.

6.1.3 Short-run cost interrelationships

The short-run average total cost (ATC) curve is the vertical summation of the average variable cost (AVC) curve and the average fixed cost (AFC) curve. This is illustrated in Figure 6.4.

Both ATC and AVC are U-shaped but the minimum point on ATC occurs to the right of the minimum point on the AVC curve. This is because the ATC includes the AFC with the AVC and, since the AFC falls continuously with output the rise in AVC is partially offset by the continued fall in AFC. Moreover, because the AFC approaches the x-axis asymptotically, the AVC and ATC also come closer together asymptotically, as shown in Figure 6.4.

Representing the short-run total cost (TC) function as the traditional cost theory in its mathematical form, the average total cost may similarly be set out. These are:

$$TC = b_0 + b_1Q - b_2Q^2 + b_3Q^3$$
$$ATC = \frac{b_0}{Q} + b_1 - b_2Q + b_3Q^2$$

This shows the effect of the asymptotically decreasing average fixed cost on the U-shaped average variable cost.

Relationship between MC *and* ATC

The marginal cost (MC) curve cuts both the AVC and the ATC at their lowest points. When the marginal cost is below the average cost, it pulls the average cost down.

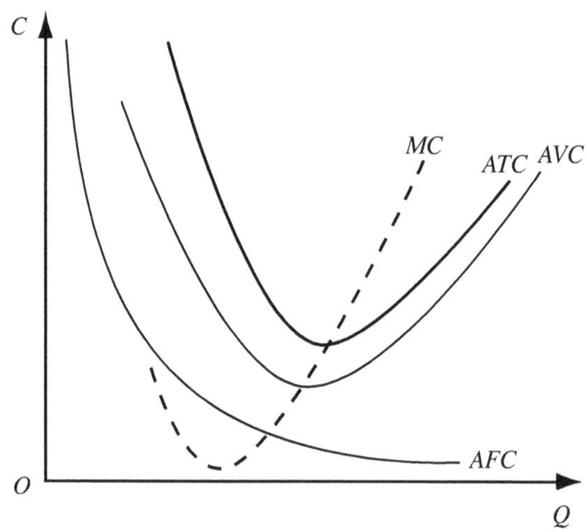

Figure 6.4
Relationship among short-run average and marginal cost curves

When the marginal cost is above the average cost, it pulls the average cost up. Hence, the average and marginal can only be equal when the average is at a minimum and, at that point, the marginal cost must be rising (in order to pull the average up).

To create this effect, the falling marginal cost curve that is pulling down the average must reach its minimum point before the average cost reaches its minimum point. When the marginal cost curve begins to rise, it first moderates the falling average cost and then, after they are equated, it pulls up the average cost. This goes for both the average variable cost and the average total cost.

Significance for the producer

The minimum point of the short-run average variable cost curve (AVC) is the point of the ***optimal combination of inputs*** for a given plant size. It is also referred to as the ***designed capacity*** of the plant. It provides the lowest unit cost of operation once a plant is established (i.e. once the fixed cost is given) and hence provides the greatest opportunity for the producer to become cost competitive in the short-run with the existing plant.

Consequently, it is important for a producer to understand these relationships. A producer, operating with a given plant (i.e. in the short-run), must be able to realize that where the incremental cost of expanding output is less than the average cost of production, then the optimal combination of inputs has not yet been reached and the plant is being under-utilized. Unit costs are higher than they could be for that plant size.

Conversely, where the incremental cost of additional output is greater than the average cost, the producer should realize that the plant is being over-utilized and the average cost of production is greater than the minimum cost that is attainable from that size plant. Where the market conditions are leading the producer to remain uncompetitive, it may be necessary for the producer to move to a larger (or smaller) scale plant. This movement to a different scale plant must take place in the long-run.

6.2 LONG-RUN COSTS IN THE TRADITIONAL THEORY

In the long-run all factors are variable. The long-run cost curve is a planning or *ex-ante* cost curve. The producer is able to consider the alternative scales of plant and select the appropriate scale in advance of producing with it. Once the plant scale has been selected and established, the producer is then in the short-run time period.

6.2.1 The long-run average cost curve

The basin-shaped curve

The long-run cost curve is derived from the expansion path (isocline) of the long-run production function:

$$Q = f(L, K)$$

The specification of the production function describes the law of returns to scale as explained in Chapter 5. The traditional function features increasing, constant then decreasing returns to scale. The shape of the long-run average cost curve therefore reflects the law of returns to scale. Initially, the increasing returns to scale cause the long-run total product curve to increase at an increasing rate. At later outputs, the decreasing returns to scale cause the total product curve to increase at a decreasing rate. In between the two is the momentary point of constant returns to scale. This gives a long-run total product curve that has a shape not too dissimilar from that of the short-run total product curve.

This shape for the long-run total product curve is reflected in the long-run average cost curve in much the same way that the short-run total product curve is reflected in the short-run average variable cost curve. This gives a long-run average cost curve that has a basic U-shape but is wider since the long-run curve extends over a larger range of output than the short-run curve. This makes the long-run average cost curve more aptly described as basin-shaped as shown in Figure 6.5.

The envelope curve

The long-run traditional cost curve described above as a basin-shaped curve is also described as an envelope curve. This is because of the way it envelopes the short-run cost curves.

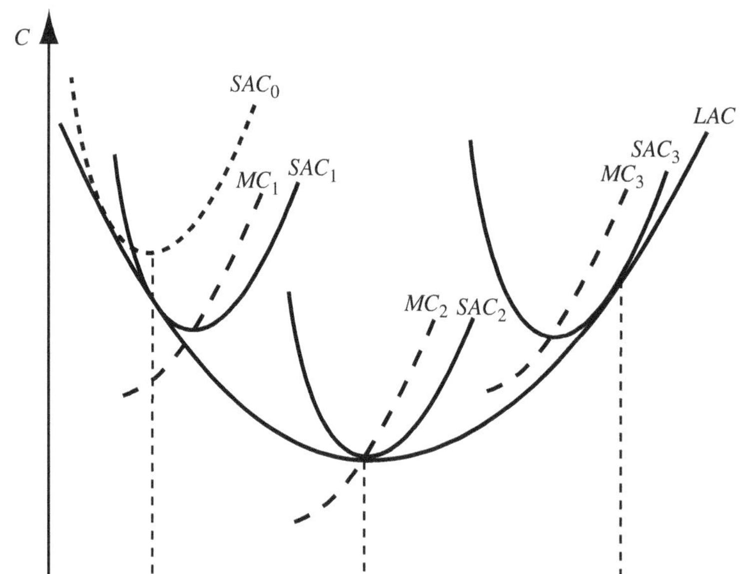

Figure 6.5
Relationship between long-run and short-run average cost curves

Each point on the long-run average cost (LAC) curve corresponds to a point on the particular short-run average cost (SAC) curve which is tangent to the LAC at that point. To understand this, consider, for simplicity, that there are three technologies (out of an infinite number) available to the firm each representing a different plant size (e.g. small, medium and large scale plants). These plant sizes are identified by their respective short-run average cost (SAC) curves SAC_1, SAC_2 and SAC_3, as shown in Figure 6.5.

If the producer is desirous of producing at Q_1 the lowest cost plant size is that represented by the small scale plant SAC_1. For an output of Q_2 the producer's lowest cost is that plant size represented by SAC_2. For a larger output of Q_3 the lowest cost option is the plant size represented by SAC_3.

It should be recognized that, at output Q_1, the producer will be under-utilizing the plant given by SAC_1. However, as shown in Figure 6.5, under-utilizing SAC_1 to produce the quantity Q_1 is less costly than using a smaller scale plant, such as SAC_0, having a designed capacity (minimum point of the SAC) that coincides with output Q_1. It can be seen that the minimum point of the SAC_0 curve lies above the SAC_1 curve at output Q_1, indicating higher average costs in the optimally used SAC_0 plant than in the under-utilized larger SAC_1 plant.

On the other hand, at output Q_3 the producer will be over-utilizing the plant given by SAC_3. However, this is less costly than using a larger scale plant with a designed capacity (minimum point of the SAC) that coincides with Q_3, since again the costs would be higher in the optimally-used plant than in the over-utilized SAC_3 plant.

It is only on SAC_2 that the designed capacity of the plant (min. SAC) coincides with the lowest average cost of production of any plant at the particular scale of output (Q_2). This is because the plant represented by SAC_2 has its minimum point (designed or optimal capacity) at the minimum point of the long-run average cost (LAC) curve.

The assumption of an infinite number of plants, each represented by its respective SAC, gives rise to a continuous long-run curve. This curve is the locus of points denoting the least cost of producing each level of output. It should be observed that, on the falling portion of the LAC, the SACs are tangent to the LAC at less than their optimal or designed capacity (min. SAC) and so the plants are under utilized. On the rising portion of the LAC, the SACs are tangent at greater than optimal or designed capacity thereby having over-utilized plants. When the plant size selected is that of the optimal scale (min. LAC), that plant is used at its optimal or designed capacity.

The long-run average cost curve ($LRAC$) is therefore called the envelope curve because of the way it envelopes the short-run average cost ($SRAC$) curves as it identifies the lowest cost plant to be used for producing each output level.

Practical significance

As an *ex-ante* or planning curve for the long-run, knowledge of the shape of the LAC allows the producer to select the short-run plant size which can produce the output for the targeted market size at the least possible cost. This is extremely important for cost competitiveness for many reasons.

First, it is important to know where the optimal scale lies. This is the output at which the minimum average cost (unit cost) of production exists (min. LAC). If the producer cannot reach the minimum point of the *LAC* and has to compete with others who can, then this producer will have a higher unit cost of production and suffer a cost disadvantage when competing with other producers. A producer may need to look beyond a traditional small domestic or regional market in order to reach the optimal scale and become cost competitive.

Second, the producer needs to know the relationship between short- and long-run unit costs in order to choose the least-cost level of plant utilization. This relationship is somewhat counter-intuitive since, where the producer cannot produce with the optimal scale plant (i.e. at min. *LAC*) then the appropriate under-utilization of plant at small scales or over-utilization at large scales become more cost effective than utilization of the plant at its designed capacity. This is not likely to be known by a less sophisticated producer.

Third, although conceptually there may be an infinite number of plant sizes possible according to the technology, engineers who design the production plants tend to limit their designs to a few discrete sizes. These are typically the more popular sizes close to the optimal scale. Purchasing an 'off the shelf' production plant in order to produce in a small market situation could mean inordinately high unit costs. If the plant at SAC_2 in Figure 6.5 is used to produce the output Q_1, the unit costs would be much higher and the producer much less cost competitive, than if the plant at SAC_1 were used.

From a policy perspective, where a domestic producer supplying a small internal market is operating less than optimal scale and hence has a higher cost than an international producer selling in the same domestic market, any amount of protection (through tariffs or quotas) would not allow this firm to eventually become competitive. The solution would be to get output up to the optimal scale in order to get unit costs down to a competitive level. For this, the firm might have to target a larger market (regional or international).

6.2.2 The long-run marginal cost curve

The long-run marginal cost curve (*LMC*) is derived from short-run *MC* curves but does not envelope them. The *LMC* curve is formed by the points of intersection of the *SMC* curves with vertical lines (to the x-axis) down from the points of tangency of the corresponding *SAC* curves and the long-run average cost (*LAC*) curve.

Consequently, the long-run marginal cost curve is the locus of points on the respective *MC* curves pertaining to each output level on the *LAC*. This is illustrated in Figure 6.6.

The long-run marginal cost must be equal to the short-run marginal cost at the output where the long-run average cost curve is tangent to the short-run average cost curve. Hence, using Figure 6.6, the relevant long-run marginal cost (*LMC*) at Q_1 is the short-run marginal cost (*SMC*) pertaining to SAC_1 at that quantity (Q_1). This is similar for Q_2 and Q_3.

It should be observed that the *LMC* intersects the *LAC* at the *LAC*'s minimum point. To the left of the *LAC*'s minimum point the relevant points on the *SMC* lie below the *LAC* curve, whereas to the right of the *LAC*'s minimum point the relevant points on the *SMC* lie above the *LAC*.

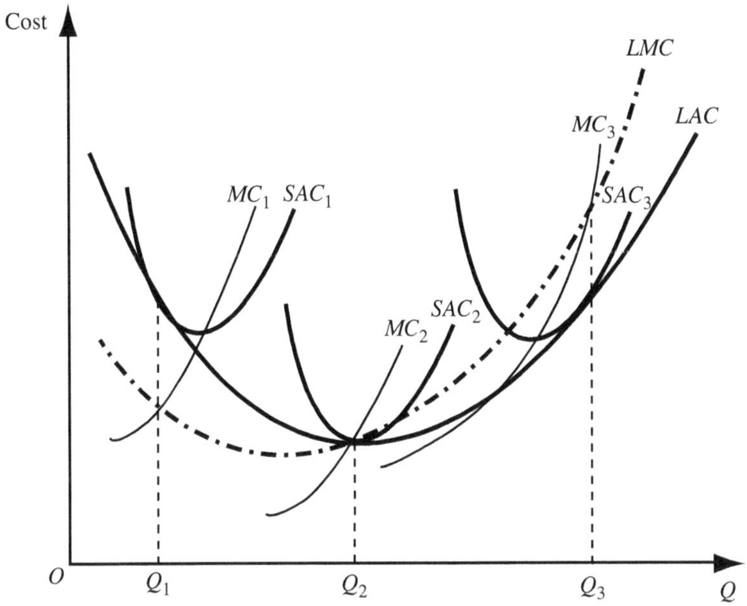

Figure 6.6
The long-run marginal cost curve

At the minimum point of the *LAC* the following condition obtains:

$$\text{Min. } SAC = \text{ Min. } LAC = LMC$$

6.2.3 Social costs vs. private costs

Before examining the modern theory of cost, it is useful to consider differences in types of costs that are used in an economic sense. The main distinction is between social and private cost. It is also useful to distinguish between explicit and implicit cost.

Private cost

Typically, the cost being considered under cost analysis is private cost. This is the price the producer pays in the market to obtain the resources to produce a given output. The term is also used to refer to the opportunity cost of production since the producer could have invested the financial resources in another economic activity. Overall, the term private refers to the use of values in the regular market pertaining to the private sector rather than the government (public) sector or where social values may be used.

Social cost

Social cost in production represents a type of shadow or implicit valuation of factors used in terms of their cost to society as a whole. In this case, certain externalities may have to be taken into account that are not represented in the private or market cost of the resources used in production.

The concept of opportunity cost may also be used in the computation of social cost but this represents the social opportunity cost. This could be measured as the amount of resources a society must give up in order to produce good x rather than good y.

Explicit vs. implicit cost

Explicit cost is the standard accountable production cost such as that for rent, wages and raw materials. Explicit cost includes the standard fixed and variable costs of production that require payment out of the producer's budget. These costs are regular expenses to the firm.

Implicit cost is usually considered to be equivalent to opportunity cost in the sense that it would refer to the return the producer could obtain from investing in the next best alternative use of the producer's time and money. This is sometimes called the 'normal' return on investment. As such implicit cost, identified as normal profit in economics, is included in the fixed cost of production and is considered part of the overhead costs of the firm.

In economics, the fixed cost curve includes both explicit fixed costs and implicit costs referred to as normal profit.

Pure economic profit

The concept in economics of pure economic profit is different from the concept of profit in normal accounting. Since 'normal profit' or investment opportunity cost is included as a fixed cost, then a ***pure economic profit*** is earned from producing good x, if and only if the producer's total receipts exceed the sum of explicit and implicit costs.

Since normal profit is included in economic cost, the pure economic profit must be less than accounting profit. It could therefore be defined as accounting profit minus the producer's opportunity cost. Hence, from accounting profit, the economist subtracts the return the producer could earn in the next best alternative use of the producer's time and money.

This pure economic profit is sometimes known as excess profit. It is sometimes referred to as the profit over and above that which is necessary to keep the producer (firm) in that particular productive activity.

6.3 THE MODERN THEORY OF COST

Modern theories of short-run and long-run cost functions emerged from around the late 1930s. The U-shaped short-run and basin-shaped long-run average cost curves were challenged both empirically and theoretically. For short-run costs the area of reserve capacity was introduced, leading to a 'saucer-shaped' average cost curve, while, for long-run costs, the L-shaped average cost curve was introduced.

6.3.1 The modern short-run theory of cost

The modern short-run average fixed cost curve

Since fixed costs are, by definition, those that do not vary with the level of output, the fixed cost curve under the modern theory must be the same horizontal line as under the traditional cost theory. Hence, total fixed cost (*TFC*) is a constant and may be expressed as:

$$TFC = b_0$$

Consequently, the average fixed cost curve, defined as the total fixed cost divided by output quantity, may be expressed as:

$$AFC = \frac{TFC}{Q} = \frac{b_o}{Q}$$

Hence, as quantity (Q) increases the average fixed cost must be declining continuously and approaching zero asymptotically in the same way as the average fixed cost in the traditional theory. The AFC curve in the modern theory therefore has the standard shape of the rectangular hyperbola. This is illustrated in Figure 6.7.

The modern short-run average variable cost curve

The modern short-run average variable cost curve varies substantially from that of the traditional theory. The theory is based on findings that producers tend to favour a production plant which offers great flexibility of output levels for similar unit costs rather than one with a single optimal output level. Moreover, design engineers tend to build some reserve capacity into their modern plant design. This reserve capacity is considered to extend across some types of small machinery that can easily be added

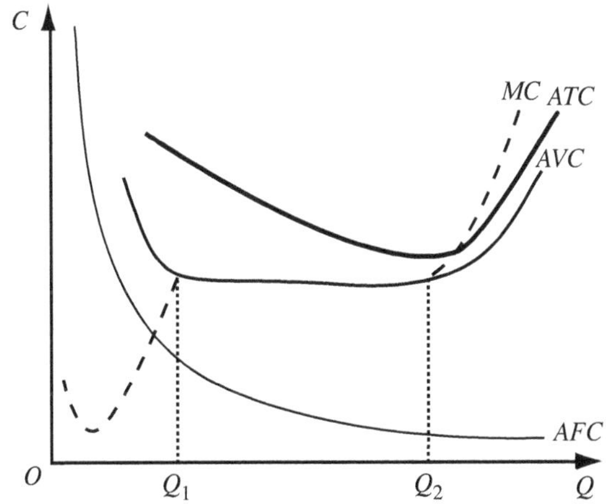

Figure 6.7
The modern short-run cost curves

or removed. Administrative areas of the productive activity are also deemed to possess this type of flexibility (possibly through out-sourcing, contracting of professionals or use of consultants).

As a result of the modern designs, the total cost (TVC) curve, over the range of reserve capacity, would be described by a positively sloped straight line of the form:

$$TVC = b_1 Q$$

This positively sloped straight line total variable cost curve over the range of reserve capacity gives rise to an average variable cost (AVC) curve that is a horizontal line in that region. This AVC curve is of the form:

$$AVC = \frac{TVC}{Q} = \frac{b_1 Q}{Q} = b_1$$

The average variable cost is therefore at a fixed level in the area of reserve capacity. Outside of this range, the normal attributes of the standard cost curve apply.

As a consequence, the short-run average variable cost ($SAVC$) of the modern theory may be described as saucer-shaped. It is a modification of the standard U-shaped curve, having a flat stretch over a broad range in the centre to reflect the built-in reserve capacity. This is illustrated in Figure 6.7. The area of reserve capacity lies between Q_1 and Q_2. This range is not due to excess capacity or under-utilized capacity and should not be confused with these concepts.

The modern short-run marginal cost curve

Over the area of reserve capacity, the marginal cost is equal to the average variable cost. This is because the marginal cost (MC) curve, as the slope of the total variable cost curve, is the same as the average of that curve when the curve is a straight positively-sloped line. The marginal cost curve may therefore be expressed as:

$$MC = \frac{\partial(TVC)}{\partial Q} = \frac{\partial(b_1 Q)}{\partial Q} = b_1$$

This is the same result as for the average variable cost curve, showing that the average and marginal cost curves coincide along the area of reserve capacity. Once again, outside of this region of reserve capacity, the standard relationships hold as shown in Figure 6.7.

The modern short-run average total cost curve

The average total cost curve is simply the vertical summation of the average variable cost (AVC) curve. Over the area of reserve capacity the total cost (TC) may be written as:

$$TC = b_0 + b_1 Q$$

This indicates that total cost is the summation of the fixed (TFC) and variable costs (TVC):

$$TC = TFC + TVC$$

The average total cost (ATC) along the area of reserved capacity in the modern theory may therefore be expressed as:

$$ATC = \frac{TC}{Q} = \frac{TFC + TVC}{Q} = \frac{b_0 + b_1 Q}{Q}$$

This gives the following result:

$$ATC = \frac{b_0}{Q} + b_1$$

The average total cost is therefore the vertical addition of the continuously falling average fixed cost to the constant average variable cost along the area of reserve capacity. Outside of this range, the standard cost relationships apply. ATC is falling over the range of reserve capacity as shown in Figure 6.7.

The practical significance of the use of a technology so designed with a built-in flexibility is that the producer is more readily responsive to fluctuations in the market demand over the short-run. This would reduce or, in some cases, obviate the need for long-run type adjustments to plant size and scale except in cases of major shifts in the level of demand. This would apply not only to manufacturing type operations but to service industries in the modern service economy where the plant under consideration could be a hotel, a financial institution or other such enterprise.

6.3.2 The modern long-run theory of cost

The modern theory contends that the long-run average cost (LAC) curve is L-shaped or inverse-J-shaped rather than basin-shaped as in the standard theory. The contention is that the factors such as managerial, organizational or administrative inefficiencies at large scales, which previously caused the LAC to turn upwards, no longer have such an effect in the modern firm. Improved management and organizational techniques and automation stave off or minimize the inefficiencies that would otherwise characterize very large scales of output.

The contention is that average production costs would continuously fall with increases in output due to the technical (productive) economies achieved at large scale (increasing returns to scale). This fall would more than offset any minimal rise in unit costs due to the organizational type of inefficiencies.

Overall then, the LAC would fall fairly steeply at first then, instead of rising, it would simply fall less steeply and level off. Where it levels off sharply to flatten out, this gives the L-shape and where it does not flatten completely but still falls gently, the inverted-J-shape is the one used to describe it.

Additionally, the modern theory of long-run costs assumes a different behaviour by producers. It is considered that producers never fully utilize (or over-utilize) a production plant intentionally and in using the planning or ex-ante long run information, they select a plant size which they can use at somewhere between two-thirds and three-quarters of its designed capacity.

Diagrammatics of the modern long-run cost curve

Consider out of an infinite number of plant sizes, a selection of four individual sizes. These give the short-run average cost (*SAC*) curves. Average costs continue to fall as the plant scale increases and producers plan to operate any plant at a typical load factor of between two-thirds and three-quarters of the plant's designed capacity.

For each of the four individual plant sizes selected for this analysis, the illustration used the short-run average cost (*SAC*) curve which represents the short-run average total cost and includes production costs, managerial or administration costs, other overhead costs and allowance for normal profit (opportunity cost).

The long-run average cost (*LAC*) curve is the locus of points on the individual *SAC* curves that represent between two-thirds and three-quarters of the designed capacity of each plant size. Considering that there are potentially an infinite number of plant sizes that could be designed, the *LAC* can be assumed to be a continuous curve made up of such points. This is illustrated in Figure 6.8.

In the modern theory, the *LAC* curve no longer envelopes the *SAC* curves, rather it intersects them. Moreover, because of continuing managerial and production efficiencies at larger scales, the *LAC* continues to fall, even though it tends to level off. This levelling off of the *LAC* occurs in the region around the output level Q^* in Figure 6.8.

The minimum optimal scale

The concept of a minimum optimal scale replaces that of the single optimal scale in the traditional theory. This is the point at which all possible scale economies have been reaped or largely so. Beyond this, the *LAC* tends to flatten out. Point Q^* in Figure 6.8 may therefore be considered to represent the minimum optimal scale.

With the modern shape of the *LAC*, the *LMC* now lies below *LAC* until minimum optimum scale is reached and coincides with the *LAC* beyond that level of output where

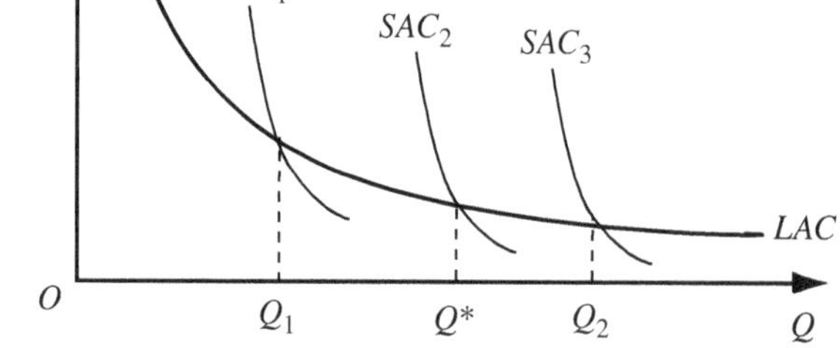

Figure 6.8
The modern long-run cost curve

the *LAC* becomes completely horizontal. In the case in which the *LAC* continues to fall, albeit slowly, the *LMC* must remain below the *LAC* since it is the marginal that pulls the average down when the marginal value is below the average value.

Significance of the modern LAC curve

The modern *LAC* curve indicates that producers who want to be price competitive must seek to attain at least the level of production represented by the minimum optimal scale (Q^*). Producers who are limited either by the size of their market or by the availability of funds and can only reach, say, level Q_1, will find that they remain uncompetitive on price with other larger producers who produce at or above the quantity Q^* and are selling in the same market.

As a corollary, it also suggests, however, that once a producer can attain the minimum optimum scale, producers operating at much larger scales would have little if any cost advantage. The signal to producers fearing competition in a newly opened market, for example, is to seek to identify the minimum optimal scale for their industry and attempt to reach this level of output in order to meet any competitive challenges. This assumes that the firms are all using the same technology (managerial, production, etc.) meaning that they are essentially using the same production function.

6.4 ECONOMIES OF SCALE

The concept of economies of scale is a long-run phenomenon. These economies of scale are internal to the firm and may arise from increasing the number of plants (plant replication) as well as from increasing plant size. They may also derive from expanding the plant with the same product or by diversifying into other products. Diseconomies of scale must be considered as well.

Internal economies and diseconomies of scale should be distinguished from external economies and diseconomies. Whereas internal economies determine the ***shape*** of the long-run average cost curve, external economies cause shifts in the ***position*** of the long-run average cost curve. External economies and diseconomies are exogenous factors generally outside of the producer's control, such as the cost of inputs.

Economies and diseconomies of scale should also be distinguished from economies and diseconomies of scope although there are some interrelationships. Typically, economies of scale are considered to be related to the supply or production side while economies of scope are related to the demand or marketing side and particularly to the bundling of goods for sale. However, in some cases, the promotional or marketing activities are included in the consideration of economies of scale in production. These can be seen as part of the administrative or managerial techniques which are part of the production function.

Typically, the economies or diseconomies of scale mirror the returns to scale of the production function, increasing, constant and decreasing in the traditional cost theory or constantly decreasing in the modern theory. Returns to scale are considered to be only the technical part of economies of scale.

It should be noted, in passing, that the minimum point of the *LAC* at which the production function is often considered to switch from increasing to decreasing returns to scale is not strictly technically correct. It can be contended that the point of inflexion that signals the turning point is at the minimum of the *LMC* curve and this is to the left of the minimum point of the *LAC*.

6.4.1 Classification of economies of scale

Economies of scale may be separated into those related to production per se and those that come from the effect of the scale of production on the factors external to the firm that affect internal costs. This second type is sometimes not considered internal economies of scale as internal economies are expected to take place *ceteris paribus*.

The two categories considered may be identified as:

- Real internal economies and diseconomies
- Internal effects on external economies and diseconomies

6.4.1.1 REAL INTERNAL ECONOMIES AND DISECONOMIES OF SCALE

Real internal economies and diseconomies of scale are those largely built into the production function and are associated with the nature of the returns to scale of the production function. These include:

- Technical
- Managerial, organizational or administrative
- Promotional or marketing
- Inventory (storage) and transportation

Technical economies and diseconomies

The technical economies are usually technology driven and relate to the extent to which the technology allows for labour and machinery specialization, automation of processes, relationships between equipment capacity and equipment costs, the nature of set-up and running costs and certain indivisibilities of equipment.

Typically, assembly line automated processes lend themselves to greater economies of scale or reduction of unit costs as production is expanded. These benefits may tend to peter out after certain production levels are reached. Batch or labour intensive processes tend to have more limited opportunities for the realization of technical scale economies or for increasing returns to scale.

Managerial, organizational or administrative economies and diseconomies

Managerial economies are associated with both production and selling. The economies relate to the ability for management processes to be more highly mechanized and automated and to become more specialized with the scale of the plant.

Beyond a certain size and scope these efficiency gains tend to be reduced or even to be eliminated or reversed. This may be due to the complexities of managing a large organization, which could result in a lack of focus on the primary goal of profit maximization through the diffusion of management goals and the unwieldiness of the management process.

Promotional or marketing economies and diseconomies

These economies and diseconomies are associated with market research, advertising and other forms of promotion, selling or distribution expenses. The larger the output, the smaller the promotional or marketing cost per unit. The more products bundled together the greater the economies of marketing scope. With larger quantities of output, the lower the per-unit costs of market research and internal research and development (R and D) for the introduction of new variants of products.

Beyond a very large scale these economies are expected to dissipate and lead to diseconomies. Excessive bundling of products (scope) and extra promotional activities tend to have diminishing returns to scale beyond a certain level.

Inventory (storage) and transportation economies

As output increases, there are gains from the greater predictability of the need for inventories to meet fluctuations in market demand and production. These are sometimes referred to as stochastic economies.

The actual unit costs of storage of product also tend to reduce with large quantities mainly due to the engineering relationship between surface area and carrying capacity of storage areas. In addition, transportation costs, both on the side of delivery of inputs and distribution of outputs, tend to become more economical with larger volume.

6.4.1.2 INTERNAL EFFECTS ON EXTERNAL ECONOMIES

Often as a firm gets larger, it can influence factors outside the firm. In a strict sense, these factors affect the position of the *LAC* rather than its shape and so should be considered external economies rather than internal economies of scale. However, where these effects are directly attributed to the size or scale of the plant, they can reasonably be incorporated into the shape of the cost curve. These factors include:

- The ability to obtain discounts on raw materials and other productive inputs on large volumes of purchases. Firms purchasing inputs by container load often pay substantially lower unit costs than for less-than-container load (*LCL*) purchases.
- The ability to obtain finance at lower interest rates. Banks and other finance houses typically offer premium (lower) interest rates on loans to large enterprises. As enterprises become larger, it becomes easier to issue equity paper (shares) and reduce their debt to equity ratio. This reduces the burden of fixed interest payments to the banks. Dividends paid on shares depend on profits and profitability of the enterprise.

- The ability to move goods at lower costs through the use of large warehouses for direct sales to the consumers of the products or through collusion with the distributive sector.
- Ability to negotiate lower prices for other services to the firm because of the large size of the firm (e.g. with brokers, freight forwarders, etc.)
- Large size combined with monopsonistic (sole buyer) power in the labour market may allow firms to pay lower wages. This may be referred to a monopsonistic exploitation (see Chapter 14).

6.4.2 Empirical evidence on costs

Empirical cost studies may take many forms. These include:

- Statistical cost studies
- Questionnaires
- Engineering cost studies
- Studies based on the survivor technique

6.4.2.1 STATISTICAL COST STUDIES

Statistical cost studies designed to measure costs and scale have proliferated particularly since the 1930s. They generally use the application of regression analysis to time series or cross-section data. In time series analysis, the researcher gathers data on cost, inputs and outputs of firms over time. Alternatively, in cross-section analysis, the researcher acquires such data across different size firms at a single point in time.

Several specifications of functions may be tried to ascertain the best fit. These include:

- Linear functions
- Quadratic functions
- Cubic functions

Linear cost functions

A linear cost function is typically of the form:

$$C = b_0 + b_1 Q_1$$

This implies that b_0 is the fixed cost and $b_1 Q_1$ the variable cost. From this function the average variable cost (AVC) and marginal cost (MC) are:

$$AVC = \frac{C}{Q} = b_1$$

$$MC = \frac{\partial C}{\partial Q} = b_1$$

For a linear cost function or for a linear segment of any cost function, the average and marginal costs are identical along the linear path. In the modern theory of cost this type of cost function is found in the short-run.

Quadratic cost functions

A quadratic cost function takes the form:

$$C = b_0 + b_1Q + b_2Q^2$$

This form of the function implies that *AVC* and *MC* are constantly increasing. In this case, since the marginal pulls the average up when the marginal is above the average, the marginal cost in this form is always greater than the average cost ($MC > AVC$) for all output levels. The forms of the *AVC* and the *MC* curves are given below:

$$AVC = \frac{C}{Q} = b_1 + b_2Q$$

$$MC = \frac{\mathrm{d}C}{\mathrm{d}Q} = b_1 + 2b_2Q$$

The *MC* has twice the positive slope of the *AVC* and draws the *AVC* upward.

Cubic cost functions

The cubic cost function is the more typical one and takes the form:

$$C = b_0 + b_1Q - b_2Q^2 + b_3Q^3$$

This gives the more typical U-shaped average and marginal cost curves as set out earlier in this chapter. The forms of the *AVC* and the *MC* curves are given below:

$$AVC = \frac{C}{Q} = b_1 - b_2Q + b_3Q^2$$

$$MC = \frac{\mathrm{d}C}{\mathrm{d}Q} = b_1 + 2b_2Q + 3b_3Q^2$$

Although popular because of their ease of construction, there are several problems associated with the generation of time-series and cross-section statistical cost functions from empirical studies. These include the following:

- Cost curves are constructed under the *ceteris paribus* assumption. This requires that factor and other input prices are held constant. In the real world this is not practicable and so, particularly in time-series studies, the resulting cost curve is a mixture of true production relationships as well as changes in input costs.
- All of the requisite data may not be available. This is particularly so with firm level studies. Aggregate data may be more readily available. Data deficiencies may be due to data not being collected on a regular basis, firms not responding to requests because of privacy issues and overall data insufficiency.

- Empirical cost studies rely on accounting data which is ex-post in nature. This differs from the theoretical cost function which describes an *ex-ante* relationship between costs and output. Accounting figures show what turned out rather than what was intended
- Cost function may be mis-specified. Several specifications may be tried when using statistical cost analysis, including additive, multiplicative, log linear, double log and inverse log. The one giving the best fit may be considered the most suitable but this could vary with the data.
- Technology is not static. In time series studies technology may be changing over time. Hence the cost curve derived may be a composite of many curves each resulting from a different technology. Also, firms in the sample will actually be using different technologies.
- Factor prices may change over time. In time series statistical studies it may be difficult to separate real movements from monetary movements. This may dull the differences between shifts in the cost curve (due to factor price changes) and the shape of the curve (due to factor usage).
- Difficulty in measuring inflation. Time series statistical cost studies are particularly affected by inflation over the study period. It may be difficult to find the appropriate deflator for the particular industry.

Many of the findings do not support the theoretical U-shaped or basin-shaped costs of the traditional cost theory. They show results that are more consistent with the modern theory of costs. They find that, in the short-run, the total variable cost may be described as a positively sloped straight line. This would mean that the average variable cost and the marginal cost is constant over a fairly wide range of output. They also show the long-run average cost curves approximating the L-shape.

The earlier statistical cost studies are summarized by Smith (1955) and Johnson (1960).

6.4.2.2 QUESTIONNAIRE STUDIES

Questionnaires may be used to survey managers in order to get their opinion on what is their view on the optimum scale of plant and how costs vary with scale.

Questionnaires may be distributed to managers seeking their answers to the relevant questions on costs. The questionnaires need to be sufficiently simple, non-time consuming and well targeted in order to both get a good response rate and acquire the appropriate information. Typically, because firms are usually concerned with privacy issues, firms need to be assured of confidentiality.

The technique of canvassing managers in order to identify the nature of costs and scale was popularized by Bain (1956).

6.4.2.3 ENGINEERING COST STUDIES

The technical relationship between input and output levels that define the production function are discovered using the available engineering information from design and industrial engineers. This provides the 'real' production function. The economics researcher adds prices and costs to identify the cost function.

This is closest to the actual textbook cost function which is derived from a real production function. The engineering production function describes a real or technical relationship between inputs and outputs. These real inputs are then multiplied by their respective prices to give the cost function.

In an engineering production function study using the dynamic programming technique for a multi-stage process, Whitehead (1990) found that, for a highly automated process (production of pasteurized milk), the long-run average cost-curve was L-shaped. This shape was due largely to unexploited economies of scale.

The implication of this finding is that, although technically it is possible for engineers to design systems to benefit from further economies of scale using larger capacity equipment, engineers tend, after a certain output capacity is reached, to replicate the equipment instead. This replication may be done for safety reasons and to prevent the disruptions that could be caused by the catastrophic breakdown of ultra large-scale production equipment.

Since the production function as seen by an economist is largely the result of decisions by design engineers, the modern L-shaped long-run cost curve may represent the exercise of caution by engineers when designing large, modern production plants.

6.4.2.4 THE SURVIVOR TECHNIQUE

The survivor technique was popularized by Stigler (1958). The basic postulate of the survivor technique is that competition by different sizes of firms sifts out the most efficient enterprises by size. It is based on the Darwinian doctrine of survival of the fittest. The firm that has the most efficient size (i.e. lowest average costs) will have the greatest ability to survive through time.

Survival fitness is measured by the ability of the firm to increase its market share. The objective is to find the size plant that is gaining more and more of the total industry output. The conclusion is that the size plant that is gaining market share is most likely the one that lies within the range of optimum scale. The method traces out the long-run curve by examining the development over time of firms operating at different scales of output. The methodology used is that of classifying plants in an industry according to size and determining the change in the share of industry output for each size class over time. The conclusion is that the plant size that is experiencing growth relative to the others must be within the optimum size range.

Much of the early empirical work was done by Saving (1961) using data from 1947 to 1954. Saving initially chose a sample of 200 industries but 68 of them had to be eliminated to prevent unreliability of data.

Methodology

The methodology used was as follows:

- Grouping of firms by size class.
- Computation of the percentage of industry value-added accounted for by each size class for the two years 1947 and 1954.

- Computation of an index of growth in size class. This was done by dividing the 1954 value-added percentage by the 1947 percentage in each size class.
- Identification of the size classes with increasing percentage.

Main findings

The main findings could be summarized as follows:

- Increasing size classes should be expected to lie in a continuous group but some industries had two or more distinct groups of size classes with increasing relative shares. The solution was to discard these industries.
- The industries show a wide variation in both mean and minimum optimum size.
- The magnitudes of these optimum sizes are quite small relative to the size of the industries. For 71.9 per cent of the industries the optimum size is less than 1 per cent of the respective industry's total value added. This indicates that both the mean and the minimum optimum sizes are usually small when compared with their respective industry sizes.
- The range of optimum size is usually large relative to its respective mean optimum size.
- In those industries in which the plants compete in national markets, optimum size is rarely so large as to necessitate non-competitive industry behaviour.
- The primary determinants of optimum size are the industry size and capital intensiveness.
- The elasticity of optimum size (both mean and minimum with respect to industry size) is approximately 0.5, hence large industries are likely to have relatively small optimum sizes (optimum size measured as a percentage of total industry value added).
- The range of optimum size is primarily statistically determined by the mean optimum size.

Many economists disregard the technique as being fatally flawed and unreliable for identifying the optimal scale. However, the survivor technique still attracts attention. In a recent study Giordano (2008) found that the technique is still credible as an empirical method of identifying economies of scale.

6.5 COBB–DOUGLAS PRODUCTION AND COST FUNCTIONS

The Cobb–Douglas production function was popularized by Charles Cobb and Paul Douglas (1928) in their famous article where they tested the function using aggregate data. The origin of this famous production function specification is not attributed to Cobb and Douglas but goes much further back in time to nineteenth-century economist Knut Wicksell (1851–1926). It is in the class of the Constant Elasticity of Substitution (CES) production functions. These functions are discussed by Arrow *et al.* (1961).

One of the significant features of the function for producers is the relationship between scale and costs. The strict Cobb–Douglas production function is one that reflects constant returns to scale, a feature that may be described as a case where 'scale does not matter' as there are no increasing or decreasing returns to scale.

6.5.1 CES production functions

A Constant Elasticity of Substitution (CES) production function has two major characteristics:

- It is homogeneous of degree one (linearly homogeneous).
- It has a constant elasticity of substitution.

A homogeneous of degree one production function can be written as:

$$Q = AK^{\alpha}L^{1-\alpha} + K$$

This requires the conditions: $A > 0$ and $0 < \alpha < 1$.

As a general class of production functions the CES production function may be written as:

$$Q = A[\alpha K^{-P} + (1-\alpha)L^{-P}]^{-1/P}$$

This function is homogeneous of degree one such that any increase in the factors (K, L) by a given proportion increases output by that same proportion. This is written as:

$$A[\alpha(\lambda K)^{-P} + (1-\alpha)(\lambda L)^{-P}]^{-1/P} = \lambda A[\alpha K^{-P} + (1-\alpha)L^{-P}]^{-1/P}$$

The marginal productivities of the factor inputs are:

$$\frac{\partial Q}{\partial K} = \frac{\alpha}{A^P}\left(\frac{Q}{K}\right)^{P+1}$$

$$\frac{\partial Q}{\partial L} = \frac{1-\alpha}{A^P}\left(\frac{Q}{L}\right)^{P+1}$$

The marginal rate of technical substitution is:

$$MRTS = \frac{\alpha}{1-\alpha}\left(\frac{L}{K}\right)^{P+1}$$

The CES production function is more general than the Cobb–Douglas type. The elasticity of substitution (σ) measures the relative change in the input ratio in response to a relative change in the marginal rate of technical substitution (*MRTS*). For the CES the elasticity of substitution is:

$$\sigma = \left(\frac{1}{1+p}\right)$$

If $\sigma = 1$, the CES production function reduces to the Cobb–Douglas production function as a special case.

6.5.2 The Cobb–Douglas production function – properties

As noted above, the Cobb–Douglas production function is a special case of the Constant Elasticity of Substitution (CES) production function where the elasticity of substitution is equal to one. The function is of special interest because of the properties which have implications for unit costs and scale.

The principal properties of the strict Cobb–Douglas production function may be summarized as follows:

- The function is homogeneous of degree one. This means that if inputs are all expanded in the same proportion then output expands in that same proportion.
- The Average Products of the factors are homogeneous of degree zero. This signifies that the average productivities of the factors depend only on the ratio in which the inputs are combined and are independent of the absolute amounts of the inputs employed.
- The Marginal Products of the factors are homogeneous of degree zero. This means that the marginal productivities of the factors depend only on the ratio in which the inputs are combined and are independent of the absolute amounts of the inputs employed.
- The expansion path (isocline) is a straight line out of the origin.
- The elasticity of substitution is equal to one.

These properties are examined seriatim below.

6.5.2.1 HOMOGENEITY OF DEGREE ONE

Consider a production function:

$$Q = f(L, K)$$

When both factors are increased by the same proportion λ, the new function for the larger scale plant becomes:

$$Q^* = f(\lambda L, \lambda K)$$

If λ can be factored out of the new equation, then the new level of output Q^* can be expressed as function of λ raised to any power υ and the initial level of output, such as:

$$Q^* = \lambda^{\upsilon}(L, K)$$

Then the new function for the scaled-up plant can be written as:

$$Q^* = \lambda^{\upsilon} Q$$

Here the production function is called homogeneous. If λ cannot be factored out, the production function is called non-homogeneous.

The power v to which λ is raised is called the degree of homogeneity of the function and is a measure of the returns to scale as follows:

$v = 1$ Constant returns to scale (linear homogeneity)

$v < 1$ Decreasing returns to scale

$v > 1$ Increasing returns to scale

Returns to scale describes the output response to a proportionate increase in all inputs. A constant-returns-to-scale production function is variously referred to as linearly homogenous or homogenous of degree one.

The general Cobb–Douglas production function is written as:

$$Q = Ak^{\alpha}L^{\beta}$$

More specifically, the strict Cobb–Douglas production function is written as:

$$Q = Ak^{\alpha}L^{1-\alpha}$$

The strict Cobb–Douglas production is homogenous of degree one. That is, it is linearly homogenous exhibiting constant returns to scale and is a constant elasticity function.

Returns to scale are measured by the sum of the exponents:

$$\alpha + (1 - \alpha) = v$$

For the Cobb–Douglas function, $v = 1$.

This can be shown by considering the scaled-up plant showing L and K are increased by λ. The new level of output is:

$$Q^* = A(\lambda K)^{\alpha}(\lambda L)^{1-\alpha}$$

Expanding gives:

$$Q^* = A\lambda^{\alpha}K^{\alpha}\lambda^{1-\alpha}L^{1-\alpha}$$

Factoring out gives:

$$Q^* = (AK^{\alpha}L^{1-\alpha})(\lambda)^{\alpha+(1-\alpha)}$$

Using the original production function:

$$Q = AK^{\alpha}L^{1-\alpha}$$

Q* can be re-written as:

$$Q^* = (\lambda)^{\alpha+(1-\alpha)}Q$$

and since:

$$\alpha - (1 - \alpha) = v = 1$$

then the expanded output can be written as:

$$Q^* = (\lambda)^1 Q$$

or:

$$Q^* = \lambda Q$$

Hence the factor increase λ can be factored out and the degree to which the factor is raised is one. This is therefore a function homogeneous of degree one.

This simply says that whatever factor of increase is done to the inputs the same factor of increase is done to the output. A doubling of all factor inputs will double the output while a quadrupling of the input factors will quadruple the output, and so on.

6.5.2.2 AVERAGE PRODUCTS – HOMOGENEOUS OF DEGREE ZERO

For the average products of the factors of homogeneous of degree zero, consider two scales of plant, original scale and large scale.

Average product of capital – original scale plant

For the function:

$$Q = AK^{\alpha}L^{1-\alpha}$$

where:

$$0 < \alpha < 1$$

consider the average product of capital (K):

$$AP_K = \frac{Q}{K}$$

Hence:

$$AP_K = \frac{AK^{\alpha}L^{1-\alpha}}{K}$$

Working with indices and recalling that $1/K = K^{-1}$ gives:

$$AP_K = AK^{\alpha-1}L^{1-\alpha}$$

Re-writing gives:

$$AP_K = A\frac{K^{\alpha-1}}{L^{1-\alpha}} = A\left(\frac{K}{L}\right)^{\alpha-1}$$

or:

$$AP_K = A\left(\frac{K}{L}\right)^{\alpha-1}$$

Average product of capital – larger scale plant

For the expanded plant with capital and labour increased by a factor of λ:

$$Q^* = A(\lambda K)^{\alpha}(\lambda L)^{1-\alpha}$$

The average product of capital at the new level (λK) is:

$$AP_{\lambda K} = \frac{Q}{\lambda K}$$

Hence:

$$AP_{\lambda K} = \frac{A(\lambda K)^{\alpha}(\lambda L)^{1-\alpha}}{(\lambda K)} = A(\lambda K)^{\alpha-1}(\lambda L)^{1-\alpha}$$

Factoring out λ and adding indices, the result is:

$$AP_{\lambda K} = \lambda^{(\alpha-1)+(1-\alpha)}A(K)^{\alpha-1}(L)^{1-\alpha}$$

The average product becomes:

$$AP_{\lambda K} = \lambda^0 A(K)^{\alpha-1}(L)^{1-\alpha} = \lambda^0 A\frac{K^{\alpha-1}}{L^{1-\alpha}}$$

This shows that the average product of capital is homogeneous of degree zero (the power to which λ is raised).

Since $\lambda^0 = 1$, then:

$$AP_{\lambda K} = A\frac{K^{\alpha-1}}{L^{1-\alpha}} = A\left(\frac{K}{L}\right)^{\alpha-1}$$

Hence:

$$AP_{\lambda K} = AP_K$$

This result indicates that the average product of capital is the same whether the plant is the original (small) scale or the expanded (large) scale. It may be concluded then that, with regard to average capital productivity, scale does not matter when the production is of the strict Cobb–Douglas type.

The same may be said for labour productivity. This may be examined briefly.

Average product of labour – original scale plant

By the same process as above, the average product of labour (AP_L) can be found for the original scale plant using the original relationship:

$$Q = AK^{\alpha}L^{1-\alpha}$$

This gives an average product of labour:

$$AP_L = \frac{Q}{L} = AK^{\alpha}L^{1-\alpha-1}$$

This may be re-written as:

$$AP_L = A\left(\frac{K}{L}\right)^{\alpha}$$

Average product of labour – larger scale plant

For the expanded plant, the average product of the labour employed ($AP_{\lambda L}$) can be found using the function for the expanded plant:

$$Q^* = A(\lambda K)^{\alpha}(\lambda L)^{1-\alpha}$$

The average product of the expanded labour becomes:

$$AP_{\lambda L} = \frac{Q}{\lambda L} = A(\lambda K)^{\alpha}(\lambda L)^{1-\alpha-1}$$

This may be re-written as:

$$AP_{\lambda L} = \lambda^{\alpha+(1-\alpha-1)}A(K)^{\alpha}(L)^{1-\alpha-1} = \lambda^0\left[A\left(\frac{K}{L}\right)^{\alpha}\right]$$

Hence:

$$AP_{\lambda L} = \lambda^0 AP_L = AP_L$$

The homogeneity of degree zero says that the average productivity of labour does not vary with the scale of plant.

6.5.2.3 MARGINAL PRODUCTS HOMOGENEOUS OF DEGREE ZERO

The marginal products of the factors of production are also homogeneous of degree zero for the strict Cobb–Douglas production function. This is because the partial derivatives of a function homogeneous of degree v are homogeneous of degree $v - 1$. Thus, where $v = 1$, the partial derivatives are of degree zero, indicating that the marginal productivities of the factors are constant with scale and depend only on the ratio in which the factors are combined. This is given by the technology and usually refers to a batch or manually based process.

Marginal product of capital – original scale plant

For the function:

$$Q = AK^{\alpha}L^{1-\alpha}$$

The marginal product of capital (K) may be written as:

$$MP_K = \frac{\partial Q}{\partial K} = \alpha AK^{\alpha-1}L^{1-\alpha}$$

This may be re-written as:

$$MP_K = \alpha A\left(\frac{K}{L}\right)^{\alpha-1}$$

Marginal product of capital – larger scale plant

Where the factor inputs K and L are both increased by the same proportion λ then for the production function:

$$Q^* = A(\lambda K)^{\alpha}(\lambda L)^{1-\alpha}$$

The marginal product of the increased capital, λK, is:

$$MP_{\lambda K} = \alpha A(\lambda K)^{\alpha-1}(\lambda L)^{1-\alpha}$$

Factoring out λ and adding indices:

$$MP_{\lambda K} = \lambda^{(\alpha-1)+(1-\alpha)}\alpha A(K)^{\alpha-1}(L)^{1-\alpha}$$

This implies that:

$$MP_{\lambda K} = \lambda^{0}\alpha A(K)^{\alpha-1}(L)^{1-\alpha} = \lambda^{0}\alpha A\left(\frac{K}{L}\right)^{\alpha-1}$$

This can be re-written as:

$$MP_{\lambda K} = \lambda^{0}MP_K = MP_K$$

Hence the MP_K is homogeneous of degree zero.

This is a significant result because it says that the marginal product of the factor does not change as the factor is increased when all factors are increased in the same proportion. Scaling up of the plant therefore does not affect the marginal productivity of factors in a Cobb–Douglas production function (homogeneous of degree one).

Marginal product of labour – original scale plant

The same applies to the marginal product of labour. For the original scale plant:

$$Q = AK^{\alpha}L^{1-\alpha}$$

The marginal product of labour is:

$$MP_L = (1-\alpha)\,AK^{\alpha}L^{-\alpha}$$

This may be re-written as:

$$MP_L = (1-\alpha)\,A\left(\frac{K}{L}\right)^{\alpha}$$

Marginal product of labour – larger scale plant

For the larger scale plant:

$$Q^* = A(\lambda K)^{\alpha}(\lambda L)^{1-\alpha}$$

The marginal product of labour (λL) is:

$$MP_{\lambda L} = \lambda^{\alpha-\alpha}(1-\alpha)A\left(\frac{K}{L}\right)^{\alpha}$$

or:

$$MP_{\lambda L} = \lambda^0 MP_L = MP_L$$

Consequently, the marginal products of the factors are independent of the quantities of the factors used in a homogeneous production function of degree one. Marginal productivity of the factors is dependent only on the capital labour ratio (K/L) in production.

6.5.2.4 STRAIGHT LINE EXPANSION PATH (ISOCLINE)

The expansion path of Cobb–Douglas production function is a straight line out of the origin.

From the above it is known that the marginal productivities of the factors depend only on the proportion in which the factors (K and L) are used. The isocline (expansion path) is the locus of points at which the marginal rate of technical substitution (*MRTS*) is equal to the fixed input price ratio of the factors of production. Hence:

$$MRTS_{L,K} = \frac{MP_L}{MP_K} = \frac{w}{r}$$

This ratio remains constant as output expands. Thus successive points of equilibrium at constant input prices remain in a straight line.

To demonstrate this, recall that the first-order condition for a constrained optimum requires that:

$$\frac{MP_L}{MP_K} = \frac{w}{r}$$

and, from above:

$$\frac{MP_L}{MP_K} = \frac{(1-\alpha)AK^{\alpha}L^{-\alpha}}{\alpha AK^{\alpha-1}L^{1-\alpha}}$$

But K and L are in both the numerator and the denominator and so is A. Cancelling gives:

$$\frac{MP_L}{MP_K} = \left(\frac{1-\alpha}{\alpha}\right)\frac{K}{L}$$

Hence in equilibrium the expansion path may be described as the path along which:

$$\left(\frac{1-\alpha}{\alpha}\right)\frac{K}{L} = \frac{w}{r}$$

Cross multiplying gives:

$$(1-\alpha)rK = \alpha wL$$

or:

$$(1-\alpha)rK - \alpha wL = 0$$

This describes a straight line out of the origin in the isoquant plane.

Considering that α, $(1-\alpha)$, w and r are all constants, the above equation may be rewritten as:

$$\beta_0 K = \beta_1 L$$

or:

$$K = \frac{\beta_1}{\beta_0}L$$

or:

$$K = bL$$

where:

$$b = \frac{\beta_1}{\beta_0}$$

There is therefore a direct linear relationship between K and L with no intercept.

6.5.2.5 ELASTICITY OF SUBSTITUTION EQUAL TO ONE

As a member of the class of Constant Elasticity of Substitution (CES) production functions, the elasticity of substitution (σ) of a Cobb–Douglas production function is not just constant but is equal to one.

The elasticity of substitution (σ) measures the responsiveness of the capital–labour ratio to changes in the marginal rate of technical substitution. But since the marginal rate of technical substitution is equal to the wage–rental ratio (w/r), the elasticity of substitution actually measures the responsiveness of the capital–labour ratio to the changes in the wage–rental ratio. It poses a question such as how much more capital intensive production would become if wages rise relative to the cost of capital.

Where the elasticity of substitution is equal to one, it says that a rise in the wage–rental ratio by any proportion will be met by a rise in the capital–labour ratio in production by the same proportion and vice-versa. Consequently, the change in capital–labour ratio would completely offset any change in the wage–rental ratio, thereby leaving the wages share (and capital share) in output constant even with changing wage–rental ratios. Hence the presence of an aggregate Cobb–Douglas production was used to explain the empirical phenomenon of the relative constancy of relative factor shares over time. Although this finding of relative constancy has been challenged, it still holds some interest but is beyond the scope of this book.

To show that $\sigma = 1$ for the Cobb–Douglas production function, consider the following:

$$\sigma = \frac{\dfrac{\partial(K/L)}{(K/L)}}{\dfrac{\partial(MRTS_{L,K})}{(MRTS_{L,K})}}$$

It has already been established that the marginal rate of technical substitution is:

$$MRTS_{L,K} = \frac{MP_L}{MP_K} = \left(\frac{1-\alpha}{\alpha}\right)\frac{K}{L}$$

Hence:

$$\sigma = \frac{\dfrac{\partial(K/L)}{(K/L)}}{\dfrac{\partial[(1-\alpha)/\alpha][K/L]}{[(1-\alpha)/\alpha][K/L]}}$$

However, because the following is a constant:

$$\left(\frac{1-\alpha}{\alpha}\right)$$

It can be taken outside the differential sign as follows:

$$\partial\left(\frac{1-\alpha}{\alpha}\right)\frac{K}{L} = \left(\frac{1-\alpha}{\alpha}\right)\partial\frac{K}{L}$$

Therefore the equation for σ may be re-written as:

$$\sigma = \frac{\dfrac{\partial(K/L)}{(K/L)}}{\dfrac{[(1-\alpha)/\alpha]\partial[K/L]}{[(1-\alpha)/\alpha][K/L]}}$$

Cancelling $(1-\alpha)/\alpha$ in the denominator gives:

$$\sigma = \frac{\dfrac{\partial(K/L)}{(K/L)}}{\dfrac{\partial(K/L)}{(K/L)}} = 1$$

6.5.3 Cobb–Douglas production function and cost competitiveness

The above properties show that with the (strict) Cobb–Douglas production function, scale does not matter as far as technical efficiencies are concerned. It is a linear homogeneous production function (homogeneous of degree one). The significance of this is that, when inputs are increased together by any factor (λ), output increases by the same factor. Consequently, scaling up of the production plant is done by replication and there are constant returns to scale. Put differently, there are no scale economies on the technical side of production.

6.5.3.1 THE ISOCLINE

Consider a production process using two factor inputs only, capital (K) and labour (L) and a production function described by the Cobb–Douglas type. If it takes two units of labour together with one unit of capital to produce one unit of output, then, for the production of ten units of output ($\lambda = 10$), it would take twenty (10×2) units of labour in conjunction with ten units of capital. For this reason, not only is the expansion path (isocline) a straight line, as shown in property 4 (above) but, in addition, the isoquants along the isocline are equidistant from each other. This is illustrated in Figure 6.9.

In the top illustration of Figure 6.9, the production process is of the Cobb–Douglas constant-returns-to-scale type. The production of an initial quantity (Q_1) of the commodity under consideration requires the combination of factor inputs shown as L_1 of labour and K_1 of capital. In order to produce twice the amount of that commodity ($2Q_1$), twice the amount of both inputs must be used. Hence the coordinates of the point ($2Q_1$) on the isocline must be the points on the axes representing twice the initial amount of labour ($2L_1$) and twice the initial amount of capital ($2K_1$). Similarly, the production of three times the initial amount of the commodity requires three times the initial quantities of the factor inputs.

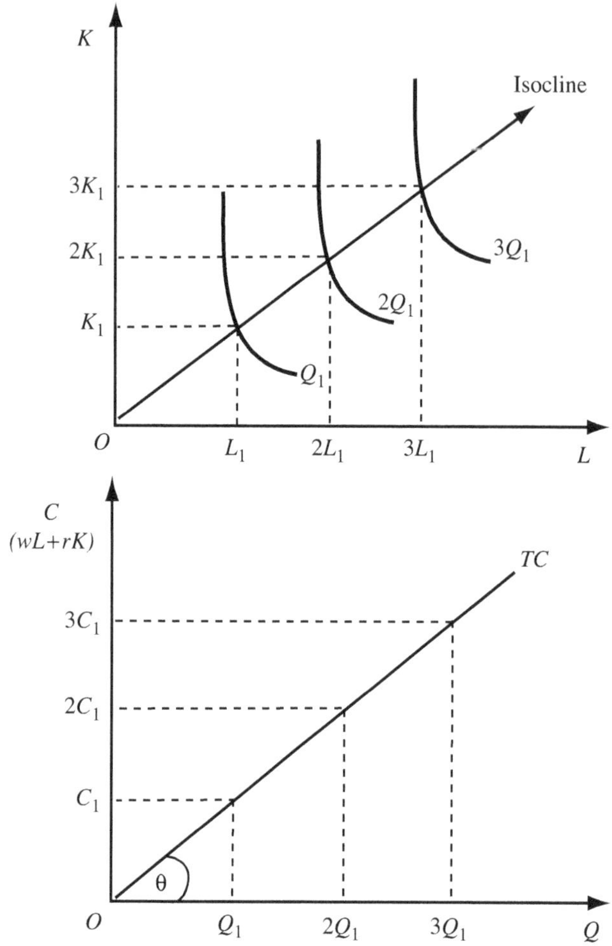

Figure 6.9
The Cobb–Douglas *CRTS* production function and its total cost curve

6.5.3.2 THE TOTAL COST CURVE

This has the impact on the total cost curve such that the curve is represented by a ray from the origin, a straight line increasing at a constant rate, as described in the lower part of Figure 6.9. This is done *ceteris paribus* assuming that the wage rate of labour (w) and the rental rate of capital (r) do not change. For the initial quantity (Q_1) of the commodity, the cost would be:

$$C_1 = \overline{w}L_1 + \bar{r}K_1$$

Hence, the cost for twice the initial quantity ($2Q_1$)would be($2C_1$), where:

$$2C_1 = \overline{w}(2L_1) + \bar{r}(2K_1)$$

This could also be stated as:

$$2C_1 = 2(\overline{w}L_1 + \bar{r}K_1)$$

This pattern continues for higher multiples of the initial quantity such that the cost of $3Q_1$ would be $3C_1$, as shown in Figure 6.9. By the same token, the cost for N times the output (NQ_1) would be NC_1.

As a consequence of this relationship, the total cost (TC) curve derived from the Cobb–Douglas production is a straight line out of the origin, as shown in Figure 6.9. It is useful to note that this curve is drawn *ceteris paribus* and therefore the consideration is that unit input prices and all other influences on costs are held constant.

6.5.3.3 THE LONG-RUN AVERAGE COST CURVE

The significance of this long-run total cost curve being a ray from the origin is that the resulting long-run average cost ($LRAC$) curve must be a horizontal straight line. The average cost curve, as shown earlier, is derived from the total cost and is measured at its various points as the tangent (opposite/adjacent) of the angle (ϕ) made by a ray from the origin to the points on the total cost curve. Since the total cost curve is itself a ray from the origin, then the average cost remains the same over the whole length of the total cost curve and is equal to the tan of the angle (ϕ) made by that ray. This gives a constant long-run average cost curve (*LRAC-CD*), as illustrated in Figure 6.10.

6.5.3.4 SCALE AND COST COMPETITIVENESS

A constant long-run average cost curve means that the unit cost (average cost) of producing the commodity does not vary with the scale of the operations. The significance of this is that it allows a small scale producer to be as cost competitive on production as a large scale producer. Properties 2 and 3 (above) of the Cobb–Douglas production function show that average and marginal productivities of the factor inputs are homogeneous of degree zero. The implication is, that for this production function, capital and labour productivity remain the same regardless of the scale of output. Their levels are dependent only on the capital/labour ratio of the production process and this ratio does not change with scale under a constant-returns-to-scale production function.

Using Figure 6.10, it may be seen that a small scale producer limited, for example, by the small scale of a domestic market, may be producing the quantity Q_S at a unit cost given as C_C on the Cobb–Douglas long-run average cost curve (*LRAC-CD*). Meanwhile, a large scale producer, supplying a much larger regional or global market for the same product and producing the quantity Q^*, has the identical unit cost (C_C) on the *LRAC-CD*. Consequently, there is no production cost advantage to large scale production as would be obtained under the typical production function described in the previous chapter. This is based on the technical characteristics of production alone.

Figure 6.10 also provides a comparison between the Cobb–Douglas production function and the typical production function which provides the more familiar U-shaped

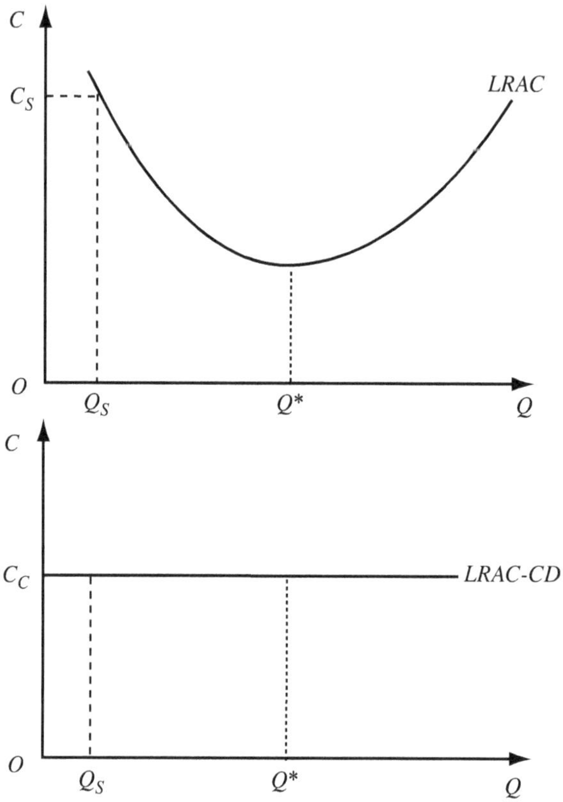

Figure 6.10
The *LRAC* of the Cobb–Douglas *CRTS* production function and the standard *LRAC*

(or basin-shaped) long-run average cost curve (*LRAC*). Here, for example, the producer for the small local market producing the quantity Q_S would have the high unit cost of C_S, whereas the larger scale producer for the regional or global market that can reach the optimal scale at Q^* would have the much lower unit cost of C_S.

The significance of the Cobb–Douglas production function at the micro (industry) level is that small domestic producers in an industry characterized by such a function stand a better chance of facing the competition from larger firms external to their market when an economy or region opens up to a more global level of trade. Unit costs of the larger producers should be comparable to those of the smaller producers. With the typical production and cost functions, a small scale domestic firm would be uncompetitive in the face of a larger foreign firm that can reach the optimal scale of production.

The corollary to this is that where small domestic firms are willing only to supply their small domestic market while the economy is open to global competition, they are more likely to be cost competitive if they are producing a commodity characterized by a production function of the Cobb–Douglas type. If the production function is of the typical one that gives rise to the basin-shaped cost curve, then, in order to be cost competitive in the face of competition from larger regional or global firms, the small domestic producer would have to seek to expand output to reach the minimal optimal scale and may have to do so by exporting.

As a postscript, it must be noted that much of the work on the Cobb–Douglas production function has been done at the aggregate level and there is no clear link between the function at the micro level and the macro level. However, this does not diminish the significance of the function at the firm or industry level. The function characterizes processes that typically are batch or largely manual. Several industries for the manufacture of small craft type items such as handbags, hats and umbrellas are considered to be of the Cobb–Douglas type. Garment manufacture is often considered to fit into this category.

It should also be noted that, despite the similarity in costs across scale or the absence of internal production economies of scale, there may be differences in the unit costs from one economic environment to the other because of shift factors such as the actual costs of the factor inputs. In addition, the parameter A in the functional specification of the Cobb–Douglas production function is the efficiency parameter. This is also a shift factor which can be taken to represent differences in total factor productivity. A higher efficiency means lower unit costs right across the range of output. This could also affect cost competitiveness when firms are from different economic environments.

REVIEW QUESTIONS FOR CHAPTER 6

1 With reference to short-run costs:

   (a) Graph the short-run cost total fixed and variable cost curves in the traditional theory.
   (b) Show how average and marginal cost curves are derived from the total cost curves.
   (c) Derive the short-run equilibrium of the producer.

2 Explain and illustrate:

   (a) The relationship between the short-run and the long-run average-cost curves explaining why the *LAC* is considered a planning or *ex-ante* curve.
   (b) The construction of the long-run marginal cost curve

3 Explain:

   (a) The theory that underpins the modern short-run average variable cost curve.
   (b) The relationship between the short-run average and marginal cost curves in the modern theory of costs.

4 Examine:

   (a) The reasons for the L-shaped long-run average cost curve in the modern theory of costs.

(b) The various methods used to empirically confirm the shape of the long-run average cost curve addressing their findings.

5 With regard to the Cobb–Douglas constant-returns-to-scale production function:

(a) Set out the five major properties of this function.
(b) Clearly illustrate and set out the significance of these properties for scale and cost competitiveness in small scale versus large scale production plants.
(c) Comment on the implication for cost and scale in the standard and in the Cobb–Douglas functions for cost competitiveness between a small domestic firm and a large international firm in the same industry under trade liberalization.

RECOMMENDED READING FOR CHAPTER 6

Arrow, K., Chenery, H. B., Minhas, B. and Solow, R. (1961) 'Capital Labour Substitution and Economic efficiency', *The Review of Economics and Statistics*, 43(3): 228–32.

Bain, J. S. (1956) *Barriers to New Competition*, Harvard University Press.

Cobb, C. W. and Douglas, P. H. (1928) 'A Theory of Production', *American Economic Review*, 18(Supplement): 139–65.

Downes, A. (1987) 'Production Function Analysis in the Manufacturing Sector of Barbados', *Journal of Economic Development*, 12(2): 161–82.

Giordano, J. N. (2008) 'Economies of Scale after Deregulation in LTL Trucking: A Test Case for the Survivor Technique', *Managerial and Decision Economics*, NY: Wiley, 29(4): 357–70.

Johnson, J. (1960) *Statistical Cost Analysis*, NY: McGraw-Hill.

Saving, T. R. (1961) 'Estimation of Optimum Size of Plant by the Survivor Technique', *Quarterly Journal of Economics*, 75(4): 569–607.

Smith, C. A. (1955) 'Survey of the Empirical Evidence on Economies of Scale', in G. J. Stigler (ed.) *Business Concentration and Price Policy*, National Bureau of Economic Research, Princeton University Press.

Stigler, G. J. (1958) 'The Economies of Scale', *Journal of Law and Economics*, 1: 54–71.

Weiss, L. W. (1964) 'The Survival Technique and the Extent of Sub-Optimal Capacity', *Journal of Political Economy*, 72: 246–61.

Whitehead, J. (1990) *Empirical Production Function Analysis and Optimal Technological Choice for Economists*, London: Gower, Chs. 3, 4, and 7.

Zech, C. (1981) 'An Empirical Estimation of a Production Function: The Case of Major League Baseball', *The American Economist*, 25: 19–23.

7 Linear and Dynamic Programming and X-efficiency

Linear Programming: The Primal Problem and Resource Allocation, The Dual Problem and Resource Valuation; Dynamic Programming: The Direct Method for Directed Stages; X-efficiency

The typical optimization problem in production is generally assumed to be one that can be solved using the calculus of variations. This requires the standard production function that is continuous in factor substitutability and is twice differentiable. In reality, there are many production processes that do not conform to this traditional mould. This chapter considers some alternatives that assist with optimization in a more practical scenario where the traditional does not fit. The Linear Programming approach is shown as a practical alternative where there are few process alternatives or, in the limiting case, only one and where the plant is a multi-product, one with fixed resources. The Dynamic Programming technique is shown as it applies to the case of discrete multi-stage production processes and their optimization. Leibenstein's concept of X-efficiency is introduced to assist with understanding how firms may move on to their true production possibilities frontier and reduce costs in order to optimize and to become more cost competitive. This is particularly useful to firms facing increased pressures to lower prices whether they operate domestically or in the global market.

7.1 LINEAR PROGRAMMING

The Linear Programming technique is appropriate for optimization pertaining to production processes in which relationships between inputs and outputs are linear. It provides a method of optimization for a class of production problems that cannot be handled by the standard techniques of the calculus of variations and the Lagrangian multiplier method for constrained optimization. In this case, there are few (or in the limiting case, one) production processes, which rules out the use of the smooth isoquant and with it the use of differentiation as a tool for optimization.

7.1.1 The setting of the problem

Many processes are characterized by limited substitutability or, in extreme cases, by a single process technology (combination of inputs) for producing a particular commodity. The principal prerequisites for the application of the Linear Programming technique are:

- The production function must be homogeneous. This indicates that the producer must be able to expand production using the inputs in the same proportion.
- The production function must be characterized by constant returns to scale. The implication here is that a proportionate increase in inputs must result in the same proportionate increase in output (e.g. a doubling of inputs must result in a doubling of output).

A Linear Programming problem consists of two parts:

- The Primal
- The Dual

The Primal

This is the original Linear Programming problem. The Primal is a problem of resource allocation. The producer must decide how to allocate the scarce (given) resources in the plant among competing ends (the multiple products). It is therefore the classic economic problem.

The Dual

Every primal problem has a corresponding problem called the Dual, in which the direction of optimization is reversed. For example, a primal problem of maximization has a corresponding dual problem of minimization and vice-versa. The dual is a problem of resource valuation. In the dual, the producer seeks to identify and ascribe a value to the bottleneck resources that are constraining production. The values found are implicit valuations or shadow prices of meaning and significance only within that particular production environment.

The Linear Programming technique is best demonstrated by application to a typical problem. In this case a simple problem will be used as an example, one that consists of three input resources and has only one production technology option. The problem is solved graphically. Since the focus here is not on the computational skill but on the meaning and interpretation of the results, the simpler graphical approach is used to give a visual perspective of the solution. For more complex problems, the use of the simplex algorithm, an iterative technique, is required. This is facilitated in this modern era by the use of the appropriate computer software.

The linear programming solution is particularly useful in the short-run when all the resources of the firm may be considered fixed and the problem is simply that of finding the optimal allocation of these fixed resources and determining where the bottlenecks are so decisions may be made on whether to purchase more resources. It is also particularly useful for the multi-product firm with given resources and replaces the smooth production possibility frontier (PPF) curve (transformation curve) in the traditional analysis. That smooth PPF curve is replaced by a set of line segments.

Consider a typical Linear Programming production problem for a hypothetical production plant set out as follows.

A vehicle manufacturer produces two types of vehicles: sedan cars (C) and Sport Utility Vehicles or SUVs (S) using the same production resources that are limited within the firm in the current time frame. The inputs used in the production of SUVs and sedan cars are Machinery and Equipment (M), Trained Technician Services (T) and Building Floor Space (B). There is a single production technology that is homogeneous and displays constant returns to scale.

The production technology:
The production of one SUV requires 2 units of trained technician services, 5 units of machinery and equipment and 8 units of building space.

The production of one sedan car requires 6 units of trained technician services, 3 units of machinery and equipment and 2 units of building space.

The resource limits:
The firm has available to it 36 units of trained technician services (T), 30 units of machinery and equipment (M) and 40 units of building space (B).

Contribution of output to profits:
The objective of the firm is to maximize profits (Π). The firm knows that from selling one SUV it makes $4,000 in profit and from selling one sedan car it makes $5,000 in profits.

The Primal problem

The firm needs to determine:

- The correct mix on sedan cars and SUVs to produce in order to maximize profits within the resource input constraints.
- The maximum profits that can be generated by the production plant.
- How to allocate the available units of equipment (M), units of trained technicians services (T) and building space (B) to production of sedan cars (C) and SUVs (S) in order to maximize profits within the constraints given by the limited amounts of these resource inputs in the existing production plant.

The Dual problem

The firm needs to identify:

- Which of the three resource inputs are fully utilized (the bottleneck resources) and provide the constraints to production.
- Which (if any) of the resources remain underutilized (the slack resource(s)).

- The value to the firm (implicit valuation) of the bottleneck resources in terms of their contribution to the profits of the firm.
- How the implicit valuation of the bottleneck resources compare to the market price of these resources.

7.1.2 The linear programming primal solution

7.1.2.1 THE STRUCTURE OF THE SOLUTION

The Linear Programming technique for solution of the primal problem consists of three parts:

- The objective function
- The technical constraints
- The non-negativity constraints

The objective function

The objective is to maximize profits given the information of the quantum of profit generated for the firm by selling individual units of output. It is assumed that the firm can sell all it wants for the same profit per unit. Since the firm gains $4,000.00 from the sale of one SUV and $5,000.00 from the sale of one sedan car, the objective function may be expressed as:

$$\text{Max}: \Pi = 4{,}000S + 5{,}000C$$

The technical constraints

The technical constraints are given by the production function. This is a combination of the technical relationships in production (input requirements per unit of output) and the limit of the amount of the resources available. It is set up as limits for each resource input constraint. The inputs may be considered separately based on the information given in the problem as set out above.

Trained technician services (T)
The production of one SUV requires two units of trained technician services while the production of one sedan car requires six units of trained technician services. There are only thirty-six units of trained technician services available. Hence two units of these services, multiplied by the number of SUVs produced, plus six units of these services, multiplied by the number of sedan cars produced, cannot exceed the total of thirty-six units available to the firm in a given time period.

Machinery and equipment (M)
The production of one SUV requires five units of machinery and equipment while the production of one sedan car requires three units of machinery and equipment. There are only thirty units of machinery and equipment available. Hence five units of these services,

multiplied by the number of SUVs produced, plus three units of these services, multiplied by the number of sedan cars produced, cannot exceed the total of thirty units available to the firm in a given time period.

Building Floor Space (B)
The production of one SUV requires eight units of machinery and equipment while the production of one sedan car requires two units of machinery and equipment. There are only forty units of machinery and equipment available. Hence eight units of these services, multiplied by the number of SUVs produced, plus two units of these services, multiplied by the number of sedan cars produced, cannot exceed the total of forty units available to the firm in a given time period.

These technical constraints may therefore be expressed as follows:

$$2S + 6C \leq 36 \quad (T) \quad \text{Trained technician services constraint} \tag{1}$$

$$5S + 3C \leq 30 \quad (M) \quad \text{Machinery and equipment constraint} \tag{2}$$

$$8S + 2C \leq 40 \quad (B) \quad \text{Building floor space constraint} \tag{3}$$

The non-negativity constraints

The non-negativity constraints are there to ensure that the solution does not involve negative quantities of output. These are expressed as:

$$S \geq 0; \quad C \geq 0$$

7.1.2.2 THE GRAPHICAL SOLUTION TO THE PRIMAL PROBLEM

The solution to the primal problem is done in five stages, as follows:

- Identify the boundaries of the technically feasible area. This area may be described as that where none of the constraints is exceeded. Graphically, it is necessary to draw in the constraint lines and identify the area that is within all of the constraints. This is equivalent to identifying the production possibility frontier in the standard theory of the multi-product firm.
- Identify the slope of the iso-profit line. This is equivalent to finding the slope of the iso-revenue line in the standard theory of the multi-product firm.
- Graphically shift the iso-profit line until it is at the greatest distance it can be from the origin without exceeding the boundary of the technically feasible area. In this case, it will most likely fall at the juncture of two lines (constraints).
- Read off the co-ordinates of this optimal point to identify the quantities of the two commodities being produced that maximize the objective function (profits in this case). More accurately, solve simultaneously the two constraint equations that cross at the identified optimal point.
- Put this information into the constraint equations in order to determine the allocation of input resources to each of the two products.

Identifing the boundaries of the technically feasible area

Using Figure 7.1, each constraint is graphed individually as follows:

Trained technician services constraint:
If no SUVs are produced then the firm can produce: $\frac{36}{6} = 6$ *Sedan cars*
If no sedan cars are produced then the firm can produce: $\frac{36}{2} = 18$ *SUVs*

Machinery and equipment constraint:
If no SUVs are produced then the firm can produce: $\frac{30}{3} = 10$ *Sedan cars*
If no sedan cars are produced then the firm can produce: $\frac{30}{5} = 6$ *SUVs*

Building constraint:
If no SUVs are produced then the firm can produce: $\frac{40}{2} = 20$ *Sedan cars*
If no sedan cars are produced then the firm can produce: $\frac{40}{8} = 5$ *SUVs*

These extreme points are plotted for each constraint.

From Figure 7.1 it can be observed that the technically feasible region is the area from the origin bounded by the constraints. It is the area in which no constraint is exceeded and is represented by the shaded area bounded by the constraint lines connecting at the points *d*, *a*, *b* and *g*. Consequently, the solution may be found at any of these points or along any of the lines connecting the points. If the solution were to be found at

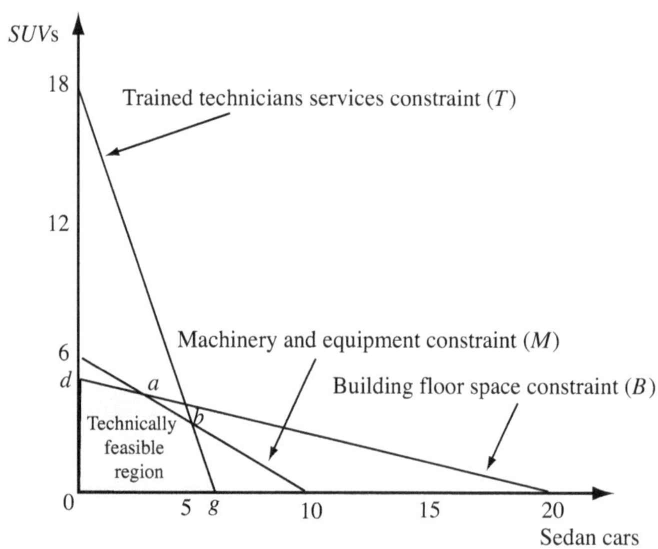

Figure 7.1
The linear programming technical constraints and the technically feasible region

point d or g, this would constitute a corner solution. It would mean that only one type of vehicle would be produced.

This feasible area is similar to the production possibility frontier in the case of the multi-product firm in the standard theory. The firm seeks to produce on the frontier. While all points on the boundary of the feasible region are technically efficient, the firm must find the economically optimum solution. This involves use of the isoprofit lines, similar to the iso-revenue lines of the standard theory. In this way the firm tries to reach the highest isoprofit line that does not exceed the boundaries of the technically feasible region.

The slope of the isoprofit line must be found. The line is then shifted in parallel fashion to the extremity of the technically feasible region to find the highest profit attainable by the firm from its existing resources. This is illustrated in Figure 7.2. The isoprofit line is the dashed line.

Finding slope of the isoprofit line

The slope of the isoprofit line is found from the objective function:

$$\Pi = 4{,}000S + 5{,}000C$$

Making S the subject (since S is on the Y-axis) gives:

$$4{,}000S = \Pi - 5{,}000C$$

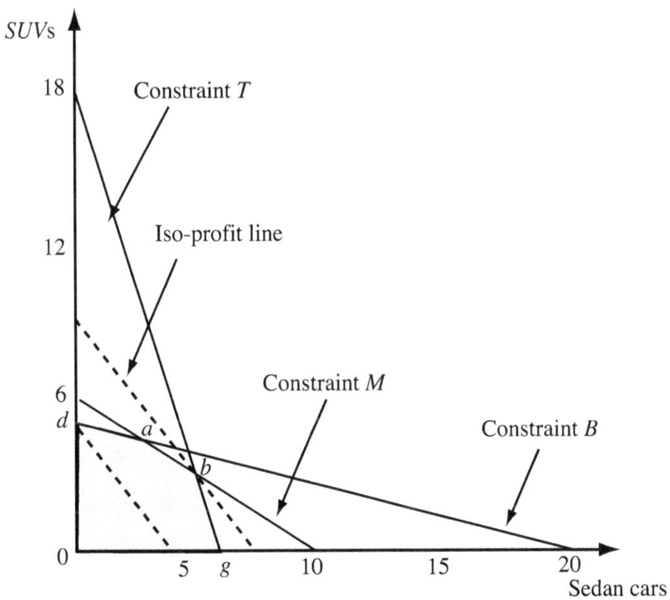

Figure 7.2
The iso-profit curve and the optimal solution to the primal problem

This gives:

$$S = \frac{\Pi}{4{,}000} - \frac{5{,}000}{4{,}000}C$$

Hence, the intercept of the isoprofit line is:

$$\frac{\Pi}{4{,}000}$$

and the ***slope*** of the isoprofit line is:

$$-\frac{5{,}000}{4{,}000} = \frac{-5}{4}$$

Shifting of isoprofit line to outer boundary

Placing a line with a negative 5/4 slope on to the diagram in Figure 7.2 (the dashed line) and sliding it out to the edge of the feasible region, it can be seen that the optimum is at the intersection of the machinery and equipment and the trained technician services constraints (point *b*).

Solving for optimal quantities of the two types of automobiles

Reading off the co-ordinates of the point *b* gives the optimal number of SUVs (3) and sedan cars (5) that the firm should make for profit maximization. However, for greater precision, it is useful to solve simultaneously for *S* and *C* using the equations of the two intersecting constraints at the optimal point (trained technician services, machinery and equipment). Solving simultaneously gives the following result.
Trained technician services constraint:

$$2S + 6C = 36 \tag{1}$$

Machinery and equipment constraint:

$$5S + 3C = 30 \tag{2}$$

Multiplying equation (2) × 2 gives:

$$10S + 6C = 60 \tag{3}$$

Subtracting (1) from (3) gives:

$$8S = 24 \tag{4}$$

$$S = 3$$

Hence the optimal number of SUVs to be produced is three. To find the corresponding optimal number of sedan cars:

substitute for S in (1). This gives:

$$2(3) + 6C = 36$$
$$6 + 6C = 36$$
$$6C = 30$$
$$C = 5$$

Hence, the optimum production level for profit maximization, given the resource constraints, is:

3 SUVs and 5 sedan cars

Computing maximum profit and resource allocation

The optimal values for the two products SUVs (3) and sedan cars (5) may be entered into the objective (profit) function to identify the maximum profit the firm can make from its given resources.

Thus for the objective function:

$$\text{Max} : \Pi = 4{,}000S + 5{,}000C$$

The optimal value is:

$$\Pi = 4{,}000(3) + 5{,}000(5)$$
$$\Pi = 12{,}000 + 25{,}000$$
$$\Pi = \$37{,}000$$

The maximum profit that can be made from the existing resources in this hypothetical production plant is \$37,000.00. This is achieved by producing three SUVs and five sedan cars per time period.

Identifying the optimal resource allocation is dealt with in detail below.

7.1.2.3 IDENTIFYING THE OPTIMAL RESOURCE ALLOCATION

The objective is to find out how to allocate the resources of trained technician services, machinery and equipment and building floor space to the production of SUVs and sedan cars so that profit is maximized.

The solution is to insert the optimal values found for SUVs ($S = 3$) and for sedan cars ($C = 5$) into the respective constraint equations to determine this allocation.

Using the constraints:

$$2S + 6C \leq 36 \quad (T) \quad \text{Trained technician services constraint} \qquad (1)$$
$$5S + 3C \leq 30 \quad (M) \quad \text{Machinery and equipment constraint} \qquad (2)$$
$$8S + 2C \leq 40 \quad (B) \quad \text{Building floor space constraint} \qquad (3)$$

The allocations become as follows.

Allocation of trained technician services (T)

Based on the trained technician services constraint:

$$2S + 6C \leq 36$$

$$2(3) + 6(5) \leq 36$$

Allocate [2(3) =] 6 units of trained technician services to the production of SUVs and [6(5) =] 30 units of trained technicians services to sedan cars, for a total of [30+6 =] 36 units of trained technicians services used. This indicates that the trained technician services are fully utilized.

Allocation of machinery and equipment (M)

Based on the machinery and equipment constraint:

$$5S + 3C \leq 30$$

$$5(3) + 3(5) \leq 30$$

Allocate [5(3) =] 15 machinery and equipment units to the production of SUVs and [3(5) =] 15 machinery and equipment units to the production of sedan cars, for a total of [15+15 =] 30 machinery and equipment units used. This indicates that the machinery and equipment input resources are fully utilized.

Allocation of building floor space (B)

Based on the building floor space constraint:

$$8S + 2C \leq 40$$

$$8(3) + 2(5) \leq 40$$

Allocate [8(3) =] 24 building floor space units to the production of SUVs and [2(5) =] 10 building space units to the production of sedan cars, for a total of [24+10 =] 34 building space units. The building floor space resource in the plant is under-utilized (34<40).

From this result it is known that building space remains under-utilized and is therefore the ***slack*** resource. The other fully utilized resources of trained technician services and machinery and equipment are known as bottleneck resources.

Any expansion of the firm would require purchasing more of the bottleneck variables in order to better utilize the slack resource. Whether these inputs should be purchased or not depends on how valuable they are to the firm compared to how much they cost to acquire. How valuable these resources are to the firm (their shadow value) is determined by the results of the solution to the dual problem (resource valuation). In the computation of the dual, the slack resource carries a value of zero.

7.1.3 The linear programming dual

The linear programming dual problem is one of resource valuation. The values determined here are the shadow values or implicit valuation of the resources in the firm. These values have meaning only within the context of the firm under study. The values of the resources to the firm are then compared with the market price of the resources.

In the computation of the dual, the bottleneck resources come out with positive values. The values are in terms of a unit of the objective function (i.e. profits). If the market value of the resource is lower than its implicit value to the firm then the firm may buy in additional units. Buying additional units of the bottleneck resources helps the firm to make more use of its slack resource(s) and leads to greater profits.

7.1.3.1 RELATIONSHIP BETWEEN PRIMAL AND DUAL PROBLEMS

If a solution exists for the primal problem, then a solution also exists for the dual problem. Furthermore the solution value to both problems is identical, that is, the maximum value of the primal objective function is exactly equal to the minimum value of the dual function.

Formulation of the dual problem

In matrix terminology, the dual is essentially the transpose of the primal. The following are the principal features of the dual as compared to the primal:

- In the dual the row vector of coefficients in the objective function in the primal is transposed into the column vector of constants for the dual constraints.
- The column vector of constraints from the primal problem is transposed into the row vector of coefficients for the objective function in the dual.
- The rows of the coefficient matrix of the constraints in the primal are transposed into columns for the coefficient matrix of constraints in the dual.
- The inequality signs of the technical constraints are reversed, but the non-negativity constraints on decision variables are always retained.
- Primal decision variables are replaced by dual decision variables.

Formally, the relationship between the primal and dual problems may be set out as follows.

If the primal is:

$$\text{Max} : \Pi = \lambda_1 x_1 + \lambda_2 x_2 + \lambda_3 x_3$$

subject to:

$$\alpha_{11}x_1 + \alpha_{12}x_2 + \alpha_{13}x_3 \leq \beta_1$$

$$\alpha_{21}x_1 + \alpha_{22}x_2 + \alpha_{23}x_3 \leq \beta_2$$

$$\alpha_{31}x_1 + \alpha_{32}x_2 + \alpha_{33}x_3 \leq \beta_3$$

Non-negativity constraints:

$$x_1, x_2, x_3 \geq 0$$

Then the dual is:

$$\text{Min : Cost} = \beta_1 V_1 + \beta_2 V_2 + \beta_3 V_3$$

subject to:

$$\alpha_{11} V_1 + \alpha_{21} V_2 + \alpha_{31} V_3 \geq \lambda_1$$
$$\alpha_{12} V_1 + \alpha_{22} V_2 + \alpha_{32} V_3 \geq \lambda_2$$
$$\alpha_{13} V_1 + \alpha_{23} V_2 + \alpha_{33} V_3 \geq \lambda_3$$

Non-negativity constraints:

$$V_1, V_2, V_3 \geq 0$$

The principal interest in the dual here is the economic interpretation that can be placed on the Linear Programming (*LP*) problems and their duals. The computational aspects are secondary.

Solution to the dual

Using the same problem as the primal (above), and taking into account the information on the formulation of the dual, the dual to that primal problem is set out as follows.

Objective function:

$$\text{Min : Cost} = 36V_T + 30V_M + 40V_B$$

where:

V_T is the dual valuation variable for the trained technicians services resource
V_M is the dual valuation variable for the machinery and equipment resource
V_B is the dual valuation variable for the building floor space resource

The technical constraints:

$$2V_T + 5V_M + 8V_B \geq 4{,}000 \quad \text{(SUVs)}$$
$$6V_T + 3V_M + 2V_B \geq 5{,}000 \quad \text{(sedan cars)}$$

The non-negativity constraints:

$$V_T, V_K, V_B \geq 0$$

This dual problem as set out above has three variables and only two equations. Hence it cannot be solved simultaneously. A work around may be done by ascribing the value of zero to the building floor space variable since it has already been determined that it is a slack (under-utilized) variable and hence additional units have no value to the firm. The solution may be found where the problem is solved using the simplex method instead of the graphical method.

7.1.3.2 INTERPRETATION OF THE DUAL

The solution value of the objective function

The solution value of the dual objective function is the same as that of the primal. That is:

$$\text{If Max}\Pi = \$37{,}000,$$

$$\text{then Min Cost} = \$37{,}000.$$

Significance of the shadow values of the dual variables

The values obtained for V_T, V_M and V_B are called the ***shadow prices or implicit valuation*** of the resources. These values in the dual problem are interpreted as the implicit valuations to the firm of a unit of trained technician services, a unit of machinery and equipment services and a unit of building space. The valuations are in terms of units of profit.

Thus, without attempting to compute the values of the dual variables, consider the following ***hypothetical*** results:

V_T has value of 5

V_M has value of 3

V_B has value of 0

This would mean that a unit of trained technician services has an implicit value to the firm of five units of profits, a unit of machinery and equipment has a value of three units of profits, while a unit of building floor space has a value of zero units of profit (is a slack resource). If a unit of profit is \$1.00, then these values are \$5.00, \$3.00 and \$0.00 respectively. The significance is that additional units of these bottleneck resources should be bought only if the market price of the resource is lower than the implicit value of the resource.

The dual is to be interpreted as the choosing of values to assign to the trained technician services, machinery and equipment and building floor space so as to minimize the value of the resource stocks, subject to the constraint that the trained technician services, machinery and equipment and building floor space used in production of SUVs to produce 1 SUV is assigned a value of at least 1 unit of profit on a SUV, and similarly for the production of sedan cars. Thus the basic theorem of Linear Programming asserts that the minimizing value of the resource stocks equals the maximum value of the profits from those stocks.

The importance of the dual to the firm manager or decision maker is that the values determined by the dual are the maximum amounts that the manager should be willing to spend in order to obtain additional units of the bottleneck resources.

7.2 DYNAMIC PROGRAMMING FOR MULTI-STAGE PROCESSES

In Chapter 6, reference was made to the use of engineering production functions to determine the shape of the long-run cost curve. Engineering functions are intended to represent the 'real' production relationships to which unit costs can be applied in order to identify the economic cost functions.

However, this is not an easy task. Many production processes are not the straightforward continuous textbook processes and so difficulties can arise in identifying the relationship between inputs and outputs. A special difficulty arises where the technology is multi-stage in nature. In the typical complex multi-stage manufacturing process, the analysis of technological relationships often necessitates the disaggregation of the production process into its component parts, such as the individual unit operations or 'tasks'. The difficulty arises in trying to optimize over the individual operations or stages to determine the optimum for the overall composite production process in the plant.

Where a multi-stage processing activity is disaggregated into its component sub-processes (stages), it would be necessary to consider all the separate technological alternatives for each sub-process at each stage and then combine them into composite plants and evaluate each combination. However, with just a few alternatives at each stage and with only a few stages, the number of composite plants that can be synthesized for evaluation could be quite considerable. This complicates the process of the determination of the optimal (lowest cost) combination of sub-process alternatives. The large number of variables and discontinuities in the relationships renders the calculus inappropriate, and the magnitude of the number of possible alternative combinations makes evaluation by complete enumeration highly impracticable. A study at the David Livingstone Institute estimated that there were approximately 1.5 million million (British billion, US trillion) alternatives for a production process disaggregated into eight sub-processes or stages (James, 1975).

In this regard, the crucial problem in finding the optimal technological choice for these discrete multi-stage production processes was identified as: '... that of evolving a methodology which would make feasible the appraisal of a very large number of (composite) technologies' (James, 1975: 96).

The Dynamic Programming technique is a technique that is readily amenable to deal with this type of process. The purpose of including this topic is to provide an opening into a very practical technique for solving the problem of cost minimization and identifying the optimal combination of techniques from each of the production stages.

7.2.1 The dynamic programming solution model

The Dynamic Programming technique overcomes many of the shortcomings of the calculus method when applied to discrete multi-stage processes. In particular, it eliminates the difficulty with calculus of finding a solution to the differential equations. Its special advantage lies in its computational efficiency.

The efficiency the Dynamic Programming optimization technique for handling discrete (staged) processes derives from the application of Bellman's (1957) 'principle of optimality' by which the determination of one variable leaves the problem with one less variable to solve at the next stage in the process. The technique systematizes the search for the optimum in a complex process, by decomposing the overall optimization problem with several variables into a series of simpler individual problems (sub-processes or stages) each possessing a few (or, in the extreme, one) of the total number of variables in the larger problem. The technique works in such a way that by optimizing the simple component sub-problems in a particular manner, it leads to the optimal solution of the larger, more complex problem.

In applying the Dynamic Programming technique to the problem of finding the lowest cost combination of sub-process alternatives for a disaggregated multi-stage manufacturing process, a specially customized version of the technique is required. This is permitted by the high degree of flexibility of the technique. A special interpretation is required both at the conceptual level and at the procedural level.

In applying the Dynamic Programming technique to a production process certain customizations must be done:

1 The 'stages' in Dynamic Programming nomenclature are considered here to be the points in the manufacturing process at which technological decisions are made.

2 The Dynamic Programming 'states' at any stage may be defined in terms of the characteristics which describe the nature of the processed or semi-processed product at that particular stage in the production process. These states must be the ones that are relevant to the performance of the process at subsequent stages in the production process.

   If there are r_n possible input states which can be identified for a process at a particular stage n, then, using the Dynamic Programming formulation, the states at that stage may be described by a state vector at stage n,

$$S_n = (S_{1n}, S_{2n}, ...S_{rn})$$

3 The dimensions of the state vector will be allowed to vary from one stage to the other. In addition, the 'state' descriptors employed need not be numerical values but may be alpha-numeric descriptors of the characteristics of the intermediate outputs in a processing plant. This special facility of Dynamic Programming is important for this problem because it allows the physical description of the technology to remain identifiable throughout the optimization procedure.

4 For a production process, the decisions set may be regarded as the set of available technological choices. The decisions are those pertaining to the type and/or vintage of the technology (e.g. batch, continuous, manual, mechanized, automatic, etc.) and, to other particulars such as capacity (e.g. through-put rate, volume) of the system. Formally, if there are m decisions to be taken, then this may be represented by a decision vector at any individual stage n as:

$$D_n = (d_{1n}, d_{2n}, \ldots d_{mn})$$

   where the decision rule is written as,

$$D_n = \tilde{D}_n(S_n)$$

5 For the typical multi-stage production process, it must be noted, for computational purposes, that the 'policy' is usually of the pure type (as opposed to mixed), where, at

any stage, the state uniquely determines the decisions that can be taken. In addition, the policy typically is non-stationary, whereby the decision rules vary depending on the particular stage reached.

6 The 'transformation function', which takes into account the inter-relationships between successive stages, is used here to describe the way in which a (technological) decision at a particular stage transforms the state (of the product) at that stage into a state at the subsequent stage. The transformation of states over decisions is expressed formally as:

$$S_{n+1} = T_{Dn}(S_n)$$

The Dynamic Programming procedure works in such a way that the state of the product at the final stage (N) can be deduced from the state of the product at the first stage by successive application of the respective transformation functions, to give:

$$S_{N+1} = T_{DN}(T_{DN-1}(T_{DN-2}(\ldots T_{D2}(T_{D1}(S_1))))).$$

Implicit in this transformation procedure is the notion of independence of the past. As a result, for a state at any stage $n(1(n < N))$, the transformation to a state at stage $n + 1$ depends only on the present state, n, and does not require any knowledge of the past history of the system, since the state descriptors include *all* the information from previous stages relevant to the future stages. Thus, the future is uniquely determined by the present.

This uniqueness theorem is a central part of the technique's optimizational efficiency, and derives from its operational 'Principle of Optimality' which allows the past stages, once optimized, to be 'forgotten' as the optimization procedure moves forward to the next stage.

7.2.2 The solution algorithm

In a discrete multi-stage production process with a finite number of stages, the process is often sequential and deterministic in the sense that the transformation function determines the outcome of the decisions made on the state of the product as it moves through a sequence of stages. The appropriate algorithm must therefore be one of those available for the solution of the discrete deterministic case. These include:

- Successive approximation in function space
- Successive approximation in policy space
- The direct method for directed stages

Selections (a) and (b) above would accommodate processes that are stationary and non-finite. However, the typical multi-stage production process would tend to be finite and directed. With this type of process, the individual stages are connected in a series where there is no recycle of matter, energy or information back from the output end to the input end. This system, described as acyclic, has information flowing in one direction only.

The direct method for directed stages

In this very prevalent case, solution of the problem requires the use of the algorithm commonly referred to as the Direct Method for Directed Stages ((c) above).

Procedurally, then, the return or objective function is specified, and the basic non-stationary recurrence relationship peculiar to the Dynamic Programming technique is formulated to be solved following the prescribed procedure.

Where the objective is to minimize cost, then a cost must be associated with each decision made at each stage. This cost may be described as a penalty attached to having the product in a particular state at a particular stage. In this cost function the stage costs are separable additively and piece-wise continuous.

In Dynamic Programming formulation, the objective function may be expressed formally, for a process with N stages, as:

$$f_N(S_N) = \max\,[h(S_N, D_N) + f_{N-1}(S_{N-1})]$$

Here $f_N(S_N)$ gives the value (cost) of the path from S_1 to S_N, as the optimization takes place in the contracted manner of this technique.

The recursive optimization procedure for the direct method therefore may be summarily described as:

$$f_N(S_N) = \max\,[h(S_N, D_N) + f_{N-1}(S_{N-1})]$$

$$f_{N-1}(S_{N-1}) = \max\,[h(S_{N-1}, D_{N-1}) + f_{N-2}(S_{N-2})]$$

$$\vdots$$

$$f_1(S_1) = \max\,[h(S_1, D_1)]$$

This is subject to the transformation relationship:

$$S_N = T_{DN}(S_{N-1})$$

Hence, by this procedure, successively larger portions of the staged production process are optimized. $f_1(S_1)$ is found first from the first stage cost function $h(S_1, D_1)$ (the first sub-optimization) and this result is substituted into $f_2(S_2)$ (the second sub-optimization), which is then substituted into $f_3(S_3)$, and so on up to $f_N(S_N)$, the final sub-optimization to be done. This gives the final optimal solution, $f_N^*(S_N)$.

It may be noted that with the optimization taking place in the contracted manner of this technique, the optimal technical decision at any stage is not necessarily that which is optimal (least cost) for that individual stage, but that which is on the optimal contracted path (the least cost path) which leads to the overall optimal value for the composite process in the plant.

7.2.3 Customizing dynamic programming

Discontinuities and indivisibilities

Procedurally, in handling discontinuities and indivisibilities in the production relationships at the level of individual stages, advantage may be taken of the technique's flexibility to work with discrete data. These data may be tabulated. Hence, at each of the $n = 1, 2, \ldots, N$ stages with m options at each stage, the respective engineering-based cost data may be represented by an $m \times r$ matrix.

Once the final-stage matrix has been computed and the column vector of optimal values has been found, the global optimal value, $f_N^*(S_N)$, can be determined from a search over these minimum values.

The computational efficiency of this technique leads to a situation such that once the currently optimal values have been found from among the C_{rm} cost values at each individual stage, the remaining values can then be 'forgotten'. Hence, in an $r \times m$ matrix of cost values, $((r \times m) - r)$ values can be discarded. Overall, in an optimization problem with n stages, with m state variables at each stage, and where each variable can assume ten values, then the number of overall considerations by complete enumeration of the alternatives for evaluation would require the consideration of 10^{nm}. With Dynamic Programming, this would be $n \times 10^m$.

The direction of recursion

The Dynamic Programming Technique allows the recursive procedure to be executed either in a forward or backward direction with respect to product or information flow. For the multi-stage production process, it is often more convenient to carry out the recursive procedure in a backward direction, that is, the direction opposite to that of the material flow. This allows the analytical structure to be more compatible with the flow of design information, which is usually the reverse of the material flow.

Identifying the composite optimum – the backtracking procedure

Special advantage may be taken of the Dynamic Programming backtracking procedure to permit the identification of the optimal set of technological decisions (optimal composite technology) for the complete multi-stage production process. This has a special significance in studies of technology choice.

The global optimum $f_N^*(S_N)$ identifies precisely the optimal input state and system technological decision at the final stage to be optimized, which is a unique optimal position with regard to the whole composite process. This node therefore denotes a point on the optimal contracted path.

This input state represents an output state from the previous stage. A reading of the output state vector from the previous stage allows the identification of the corresponding input state and technological decision that is on the optimal path. This back-tracking procedure is continued through to the first stage to have been optimized in the recursive procedure. As a result all the components of the optimal plant technology can be identified.

One drawback to the use of the Dynamic Programming technique is the problem of dimensionality. This occurs when the number of state variables becomes too large. As these variables increase the computational needs to increase exponentially. Nevertheless, the computational requirements are still enormously less than that which would be required for a complete enumeration.

7.2.4 Application and results

Whitehead (1990) applied this technique to the problem of cost minimization in order to determine the optimal technological choice for the production of pasteurized milk in the dairy processing industry, using engineering data collected in the United Kingdom. The intention here is only to outline the procedure as a viable method of handling a practical problem rather than provide a detailed solution which would be too extensive for this purpose.

The process for producing the pasteurised milk product was disaggregated into four sub-processes or stages, namely:

- Stage one – reception
- Stage two – pasteurization/homogenization
- Stage three – bottling
- Stage four – stacking and loading

Using engineering design information the range of engineering (or technological) alternatives and the relationships between input combinations and output levels were identified for each stage. These relationships were represented as discrete data points because of the indivisibilities and discontinuities found to exist in the engineering designs of many equipment systems and particularly so in the more manual systems and those requiring the use of vats (i.e. batch systems).

Instead of broad groupings of inputs classed as 'capital' and 'labour', this approach used physically identifiable variables. The fixed or 'investment' inputs were represented by individual equipment systems of certain capacities, and their concomitant floor-space requirements as determined by engineering norms, while the variable or 'operating' inputs were represented by labour units (man hours) and units of thermal and motor energy. Investment inputs costs were diurnalized for the analysis using the method of the joint approach to asset replacement and interest charges.

With the production relationships expressed in physical terms, the optimization of cost with respect to a given quantity can be done for any particular economic environment by the application to the physical quantities of prices relevant or appropriate to that particular environment.

In the example here, the optimization procedure was executed using a set of relative prices for labour, capital interest charges and energy tariffs, to represent an economy characterized by high-capital and energy costs combined with low wages. The optimization was done with respect to a plant with an output level of 1,000 gallons per day, with the results expressed in the currency of the United Kingdom (Stg.£).

It may be noted here that, for the pasteurized milk production process, the transformation function is of the non-stationary type since the (technological) decisions at any stage in the process are different from those at any other stage.

For stage one – reception:

- Two initial states of the incoming product were identified (tanker, can)
- Four alternative technologies with ten different capacities.
- Thus, in the decision vector D, there are in all $M = 10 \times 4 = 40$ elements for the $R = 1$ input state for each of the two separate initial input states.

- At the reception stage, therefore, the recursive cost matrix is a 40×1 matrix (vector).

For stage two – pasteurization:

- 5 batch capacities and 10 HTST capacities giving $M = 15$ components in the decision vector.
- Cost allowances must be made to cover storage needs due to the requirement for 'engineering around variations'.

For stage three – filling and casing:

- The 15 minimum values from the decision rows then become the costs attached to the $R = 15$ input states for the filling and casing stage.
- Six technological systems, ten filling rates have been identified. This gives a total of $(10 \times 6 =)$ 60 elements in the decision sector.
- These decisions are made with respect to the $(R =)$ 15 output states from the pasteurizing stage $(U_1, \ldots, U_{15})$, giving a recursive cost matrix of $(60 \times 15 =)$ 900 elements.

For stage four – stacking and loading:

- The 60×1 row minima optimal state value output vector $(U_1, \ldots, U_{60})$ which gives the minimum values for each decision made is the input state vector with $R = 60$ for the final stage – stacking and loading.
- At stage four, four technological system alternatives were found ranging from manual to fully automatic. Ten stacking and loading rates were identified for each. The decisions were made with respect to the sixty input states identified as the optimal output states from the filling and casing stage, giving an overall recursive cost matrix of $(4 \times 60 =)$ 240 elements.

The row minima give the final output values in a forward (in terms of product flow) recursive optimization procedure such as the one described so far. These 40 values would give the final set of optima as the product comes out of the final stage (N).

In the case of the technology choice problem, the use of the Dynamic Programming technique in this manner enhances the engineering approach to the extent that it allows not only the optimal value to be found for the multi-stage process but it has also allowed all the composite parts of the optimal plant technology to remain clearly identifiable when the backtracking procedure is performed. As a result, this development extends the practicability of the engineering approach to determining the 'real' production relationships. In particular, it overcomes the handicap associated with optimization by calculus in these circumstances and has a special beneficial side-effect of lending greater precision to the method of determining what, in a particular economic environment, is the optimal technology choice for a multi-stage manufacturing process.

Using the backward recursion to identify the optimal component sub-processes over the four stages, the fourth stage in the multi-stage process is handled first (at the one-stage

Table 7.1 Summary of dynamic programming 3-stage optimal costs (Stg.£)

Input states from stage 1	Stage 2 Technological decisions		
	D_1	D_2	Row minima
S_1	181.7	**154.2**	**154.2**
S_2	186.4	163.8	163.8
S_3	197.4	174.8	174.8
S_4	202.3	178.3	178.3
S_5	175.2	151.3	151.3
S_6	175.2	151.3	151.3
S_7	180.6	154.0	154.0
S_8	186.7	157.4	157.4
S_9	186.7	157.4	157.4
S_{10}	188.6	159.3	159.3

Source: Adapted from Whitehead (1990).

level), the third stage is handled second (at the two-stage level) and so on. Thus the second stage in the four-stage process is handled third (at the three-stage level) and, finally, the first stage in the process is handled fourth (at the four-stage level). Table 7.1 is used to illustrate how the results of the recursive procedure may be set out at the three-stage recursive level (stage 2 in the production process).

It should be observed that the cumulative optimal values on the contracted optimal path to this stage are indicated in bold print. This is used to show that the optimal value on the contracted path need not be the optimal value for that individual stage.

Table 7.2 shows the optimal values at the four-stage optimization process which represents stage 1 in the production process. Again, it shows that the optimal overall value for the entire multi-stage process, the value in bold, is not optimal (lowest cost) for that individual stage.

Further to this, the results show an L-shaped long-run cost curve. This was found to be due to what may be termed 'unexploited economies of scale'. It was found that engineers tend to make use of the efficiencies of larger scale up to a point, after which,

Table 7.2 Summary of dynamic programming 4-stage optimal costs (Stg.£)

Initial input state	Stage 1 Technological decisions				Global minimum value
	D_1	D_2	D_3	D_4	
Technology 1	**210.8**	217.7	263.6	275.1	**210.8**
Technology 2	161.0	182.6	176.0	184.9	161.0

Source: Adapted from Whitehead (1990).

for reasons which include preventing catastrophic breakdowns, the systems tend to be replicated.

Nevertheless, the dynamic programming technique allows a unique way to solve a practical problem that assists those planning industrial activity to more readily identify the lowest cost method of production and or to identify the minimum optimal scale.

This technique has been applied to other optimization problems in economics. Adda and Cooper (2003) have applied the technique of Dynamic Programming to many other areas, including macroeconomic problems such a stochastic growth models and investment and to handle issues related to employment and search in labour markets. They also extended the technique to other areas of microeconomics, including specification of utility and constraints and price setting.

Outside of economics, one of the more famous applications of the technique is in the Duckworth–Lewis system applied to shortened matches in the game of cricket.

7.3 THE CONCEPT OF X- EFFICIENCY

The concept of X-efficiency was introduced by Leibenstein (1966). Previously, the concept of efficiency in economics was associated with reallocation of resources. Perfect Competition was shown to be the market structure that made the most efficient use of economic resources (as explained in Chapter 9). Reallocation of economic resources away from monopoly and other forms of imperfect competition towards perfect competition was considered to be the way to achieve greater economic efficiency in an economy. Leibenstein focused directly on the individual production plant at what is sometimes described as the micro-micro level, examining the factors responsible for intra-plant efficiency gains. The concept, similar to the more recently developed total factor productivity (TFP) concept, has special relevance to industrial growth and development through productivity increases.

7.3.1 Definition of X-efficiency

7.3.1.1 THE 'X' FACTOR

A definition of X-efficiency is not clear cut. It is more readily defined in terms of its effects than on its identity. X-efficiency is the unknown factor (the '*X*' factor) in a production plant which allows output to be increased without an increase in inputs of factors of production. Indeed, it may also allow output to be increased while the total volume of inputs is actually reduced.

It may also be defined by contrary, again with regard to its effects rather than its identity. Blois (1972) offers a definition of ***X-inefficiency*** as: the degree to which actual output is less than maximum output (for given inputs).

Leibenstein (1966) distinguishes two types of efficiency:

- Allocative efficiency
- X-efficiency

Allocative efficiency refers to output gains from efforts to allocate resources towards the optimal market structure of perfect competition and to prevent price distortions such as tariffs and other interference in the market. Monopoly, it is argued, allows inefficient firms to exist. Tariffs and other interferences in the market such as price controls (see Chapter 4) are welfare reducing and lead to inefficiencies.

By contrast, X-efficiency represents this apparent but unknown factor of production that is within the firm and is neither bought nor traded. It occurs even where Monopoly is not present. Firms operating under market conditions of Perfect Competition may still suffer from X-inefficiency. The market is responsible for external pressure to force efficiency but there is also the need for internal pressure for full efficiency to be realized.

X-efficiency, therefore, is generated within the firm. It involves the consideration of motivation and incentives. However, Leibenstein (1966) hastens to point out that, while motivation is a major element of X-efficiency, it is not the only one. Consequently, he rejects the use of the labels 'motivation efficiency' or 'incentive efficiency'. Nevertheless, it is clear that this is an efficiency that derives from a managerial or organizational source.

However defined, an increase in X-efficiency is responsible for the effective reduction in the quantity of inputs required per unit of output and hence a reduction in unit costs of production. As such, it allows output to grow without a concomitant increase in the factors of production or to grow faster than the growth in the relevant factors of production. The effect of it is to push the production possibility frontier (*PPF*) outward despite the Edgeworth Box (see Chapters 5 and 15) retaining the same dimensions.

This is illustrated in Figure 7.3. Here, the X-inefficient firm operates on the *PPF* labelled *CD* which lies entirely within the X-efficient *PPF* of *AB*. The firm, producing

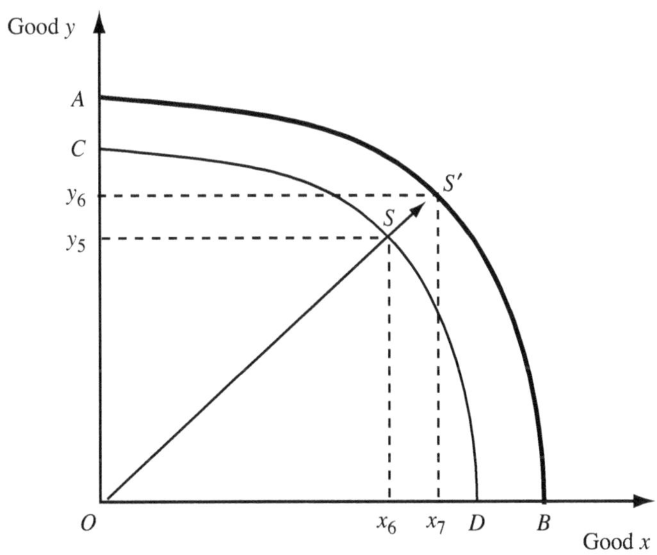

Figure 7.3
Outward shift in the production possibility frontier due to X-efficiency

at the point S, can move to the point S'. Hence, with the same resources, the firm can now produce Y_6 and X_7 rather than the lower, X-inefficient quantities of Y_5 and X_6.

This makes X-efficiency an important factor in economic growth and development. This interest was sparked by the 'unexplained residual' in the well known Harrod–Domar model of economic growth in which some 20 per cent of growth could not be explained by the growth of factor inputs. This residual was attributed to an increase in efficiency via technological change or productivity growth. X-efficiency relates to this residual.

7.3.1.2 TOTAL FACTOR PRODUCTIVITY

The fascination with the 'residual' factor that allows output to grow without increases in the purchased inputs or to grow faster than the increases in these inputs has continued. More recently, this factor has been studied under the heading of Total Factor Productivity (*TFP*). *TFP* is effectively that portion of output change that cannot be accounted for by changes in the quantity and quality of labour and capital. It is all part of the effort to discover what makes factors of production more productive in some environments at different times to others.

The concept of *TFP* is not new and dates back to early studies in 'growth accounting' that identified a large residual in economic growth not accounted for by growth in capital and labour. The early work in *TFP* is associated with Solow (1957) who found that between 1900 and 1940 some 88 per cent of growth in output could not be accounted for by growth in capital and was part of the residual attributed to growth in *TFP*.

Much attention has been devoted to refining the methods for measuring *TFP*. Solow (1957) used a growth accounting method which makes total factor productivity growth (*TFPG*) a residual, as follows:

$$Qtg = TFPG + SkKTG + SlLtg$$

where:

Qtg	= output growth rate
$TFPG$	= the growth in TFP
Sk	= the income share of capital
Ktg	= the capital growth rate
Sl	= the income share of labour
Ltg	= the growth rate of labour

The growth accounting method was refined and updated over time to improve its accuracy. In addition, another method, the econometric approach, attempted to measure productivity by estimating an explicitly specified aggregate production function in order to derive productive growth directly from the relationships. These methods have however failed to account for the rapid growth in fast growing developing countries, as witnessed in the East Asian Newly Industrializing Countries referred to as the 'tigers'. This appears to be due to the methods' failure to capture the way in which 'embedded' technology in capital can mask the productivity growth that leads to economic growth (Whitehead, 2006).

It is evident that, even though they seem to be both concerned with measuring the same residual factor in output growth, *TFP* is handled at the aggregate level as part of economic growth theory whereas X-efficiency is a micro-micro concept. As such, X-efficiency looks more closely at the factors within the individual plant that leads to this increase in output.

7.3.2 Characteristics of X-efficiency

X-efficiency, as a source of improved productivity within the work place, has to do with:

- Motivation (workers and management)
- Directed effort or intensity of effort
- Diminishing marginal utility of effort
- Inert areas where the extra effort is not worth the utility

This approach suggests that:

- The production function is not fully known or specified. There are inputs that are not included in the production function. Factors which contribute to output such as intensity of effort and care to avoid wastage are not easily measurable and are not included in the production function.
- Not all inputs are purchasable. This relates to the above. For example, workers are usually paid for their time but not for their effort or the quantity or quality of their output. Human capital cannot be purchased.
- Not all inputs are traded. Even where an input may be identifiable and purchasable it may not be traded. Typically, the level of a worker's qualification may be a criterion used for selection and can be traded. Their application of knowledge manifested in failure rates in accomplishing tasks or the extent of wastes created by the worker, even if quantifiable, may not be on the table to be considered or traded.
- Inputs are not always used in the same units as purchased. For example, inputs may be purchased at a monthly rate but not fully utilized for the entire time period. This could include workers and machinery or equipment.
- Workers need to be motivated to be fully productive. This motivation is largely a managerial or organizational function. Managers need to motivate the workers in order for them to increase the intensity of their efforts and other factors that would boost efficiency.

Utility of effort

Much attention therefore is paid to the allocation of effort and intensity of effort and the role of management in this regard. In particular, it is assumed that:

- Workers get some utility from the effort they put into a job.
- Initially, there is a positive relationship between the effort expended and the utility derived from making the effort.
- Beyond some level of effort, there is diminishing marginal utility of effort.

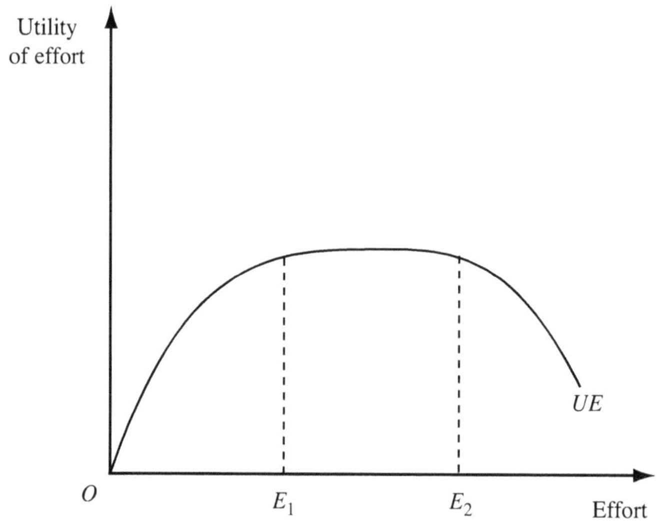

Figure 7.4
Utility of effort and inert areas

- Over some area of effort there is no increase in utility (zero utility of effort gain). This is called the ***inert area***.
- Beyond this inert area, additional effort causes the utility of effort to fall.
- There is interdependence of effort levels among workers as one worker's effort level depends on another's.
- Changing the effort level of workers requires effort by those in authority.

A graph of the relationship between the level of effort and the utility of effort takes the shape of a table or plateau. This is illustrated in Figure 7.4.

Leibenstein (1969) introduced the concept of inert areas. In Figure 7.4 the region between effort levels E_1 and E_2 may be described as an inert area. Initially, as the worker expends more effort, the utility derived from making the effort increases. However, once the beginning of the inert area (E_1) is reached, the worker derives no greater utility from making greater effort at work. This continues until the end of the inert area (E_2), following which any additional effort actually causes the utility derived from effort to fall.

Workers also derive utility from the money they receive. However, this bears no relationship to the effort they give as they are paid for time rather than for effort. The utility of the money (*UM*) received for their time at work is constant. The utility of money may be added to the utility of effort to give the total utility of money and effort (*TUME*). This curve would have the same shape and inert area as the utility of effort (*UE*) curve.

Role of management

Those in authority (the managers) play a very important role in the process of motivation of workers and other factors which lead to greater efficiency in the work place. Of great importance, then, is the allocation of managers, as managers determine not only their own productivity but the productivity of others in the organization. Hence, the misallocation of managers can be of great cost to the firm as it hinders the theorized optimal decision making of the firm. This is considered to be one type of distortion that cannot be handled by existing microeconomic theory.

This makes the achievement of X-efficiency dependent on the selection of managers who have to make the appropriate decisions and who have to motivate the workers at the lower levels within the organization. Part of the role of managers is to lift the utility of effort (*UE*) curve of the workers, extending the positive portion of the curve before the inert area sets in. But managers have their own *UE* curve. This has to rise higher than that of the workers if the managers are to raise that of the workers below them in the organization.

X-efficiency, then, is a managerial, motivational efficiency and more. It is also about appropriate decision making within the firm. In some cases the firm may need to make use of consulting services in order to achieve the theorized minimum costs or to move on to the true production possibility frontier.

7.3.3 Allocative vs. X-efficiency: Empirical evidence

Leibenstein explains that allocative efficiency involves only net marginal effects. The basic assumption is that every firm purchases and utilizes all of its inputs 'efficiently', thus what is left is simply the consequences of price and quantity distortions. Allocative efficiency refers to the gains derived from the removal of price distortions due to monopoly (imperfect competition) and other form of price distorting interferences in the market such as tariffs. Attention is therefore focused on the measurement of the welfare or efficiency loss that is due to such distortions or the efficiency gains that would result from the elimination of such allocative distortions. It is contended that the evidence suggests that gains from the removal of X-inefficiency are greater than those from the removal of allocative inefficiency.

Gains from allocative efficiency: The empirical evidence

Leibenstein (1966) presents empirical evidence on the efficiency gains from allocative efficiency. These are studies on the gains from the reallocation of resources. Two of the studies attempt to measure the social welfare cost of monopoly whereas four of the studies attempt to measure the benefits of reducing or eliminating restrictions to trade (tariffs).

The studies all reveal that the welfare loss as a percentage of Gross or Net National Product attributed to the misallocation of resources is minuscule.

These studies show welfare losses from misallocation of resources due to monopoly of 0.07 and 0.01 per cent. Losses from misallocation due to tariffs are measured at 0.18, 0.1, 1.0 and 0.0075 per cent, respectively. These results suggest that the efficiency loss due to monopoly is less than one-tenth of 1 per cent and even as low as one-hundredth of 1 per cent. Similarly, the efficiency losses from distortions due to tariffs are, at their highest, 1 per cent. From these results, it is concluded that the welfare or allocative efficiency gains from the removal of these misallocations (or distortions) are negligible.

In addition, Leibenstein noted that benefits to be derived from the superior allocation of resources due to the formation of the European common market (economic integration) are also negligible. Gains from increased specialization were found to be less than one-twentieth of 1 per cent of the gross social product of the countries involved. The available evidence renders allocative inefficiency of trivial significance.

Gains from X-efficiency: The empirical evidence

At issue is whether it is possible to generate X-efficiency gains greater than those from allocative efficiency. According to Blois (1972), evidence suggests that X-efficiency waste is larger than that of allocative efficiency. This implies that the magnitudes of gains from improved X-efficiency are much larger.

Leibenstein (1966) drew on the data derived from the results of various ILO Productivity Missions. These results showed substantial increases in labour productivity and concomitant reductions in unit costs due to labour and capital savings. These productivity gains did not require increases in capital and involved only changes to procedures and methods within the organization. The internal changes implemented to effect these efficiencies were identified in accordance with the following categories and utilized in Table 7.2:

- Machine utilization and flow (*MU*)
- Materials handling (*MH*)
- Payments by results (*PR*)
- Plant layout reorganization (*PL*)
- Simple technical alterations (*ST*)
- Training and supervision of workers (*TS*)
- Waste control (*WC*)
- Work methods (*WM*)

Table 7.3 summarizes the cases in which the increases in labour productivity are 50 per cent or over.

Many of the internal organizational changes shown in Table 7.3 result in labour productivity gains in the order of 5 to 500 per cent. The unit cost reductions due to savings in labour and capital are mostly in the region of 30 to 83 per cent. This is an astounding difference to the gains found to accrue to the economy from allocative efficiency of less than 1 per cent.

However, it must be noted that, whereas the gains from allocative efficiency are done on an aggregate basis and refers to an entire economy, the gains from X-efficiency pertain only to individual plants. Whether this can be extended to an entire economy or not is another matter. Nevertheless, the magnitudes of the gains at the level of individual plants are so large they suggest that some attention be paid to these results.

Even though the evidence relates only to individual plants (including an agricultural operation), the productivity gains and consequent cost savings are sufficient to suggest that firms concerned about cost competitiveness, particularly with regard to trade liberalization, may benefit from consideration of X-efficiency. The suggestion is that, with the appropriate selection of managers who can implement the requisite changes and

Table 7.3 Summary of productivity changes

Country	Production activity	Changes implemented	Labour productivity increase (%)	Labour savings (%)	Capital savings (%)
India	Engineering firm – One operation	*WM*	500	83	83
India	Engineering firm – One operation	*WM*	385	79	79
Pakistan	Textile plant – Weaving	*ST, WT, PR*	141	29	29
India	Engineering firm – One operation	*WM, MU*	102	50	50
India	Seven textile mills	n.a.	5–250	5–71	5–71
Burma	Moulding railroad brake shoes	*PL, WM, MU*	100	50	50
Burma	Chair assembly	*PL, MU*	100	50	50
Israel	Orange picking	*WM*	91	47	—
Israel	Refrigerator assembly	*WM, MU, PR*	75	43	43
Pakistan	Textile plants – bleaching	*ST, WT, PR*	59	37	37
Pakistan	Textile plants – weaving	*ST, WT, PR*	50	33	33
Thailand	Saucepan polishing	*WC, MH*	50	33	—

Source: Adapted from Leibenstein (1966).

generate a suitable degree of motivation, individual operations can substantially reduce unit costs.

In addition to the internal factors revealed by the study, other factors need to be taken into account. Three elements are considered significant in determining X-efficiency:

- Intra-plant motivational efficiency
- External motivational efficiency
- Non-market input efficiency.

Leibenstein (1966) presents other evidence to show the significance of productivity gains through factors other than capital differences. These include two refineries in Egypt, with labour productivity in one almost twice that of the other with a change in management leading to a change in productivity; similar plants in Britain and the USA had lower productivity in the British plant; variations between the output of best and poorest workers were as much as four to one. The results of empirical studies also highlighted the importance of using consultants.

7.3.4 Recent studies on X-efficiency

Interest in the concept and measurement of X-efficiency has continued to attract economists. Frantz (1988) provides a comprehensive picture of the theory and applications of X-efficiency to that time.

Much of the recent empirical work on X-efficiency has focused on the services sector and on the banking industry in particular. DeYoung (1997) used a 'thick cost frontier' methodology to estimate pre- and post-merger X-efficiency in 348 bank mergers in 1987/88 in the USA and found little evidence of improvements in X-efficiency post-merger. He considered that motivations other than cost were driving the mergers.

Management in the acquiring firm should be superior to that in the firm being acquired and this should lead to efficiency gains post merger. Efficiency gains were found to be concentrated in cases where the acquiring bank made frequent acquisitions which he ascribed to the 'experience effect'.

On the cost efficiency of commercial banks Kwan (2001), using a stochastic econometric cost frontier approach, found that the X-efficiency of Hong Kong banks on average was about 16–30 per cent of their observed total costs. This percentage was similar to findings for the USA's banking industry. Of significance is the finding that the average large bank is less efficient than the average small bank. This is particularly useful for small national banks and suggests that they have to seek to be more efficient to survive in the competitive market.

Potts (2006) adds X-efficacy as a companion concept to X-efficiency, defining efficacy as the ability to produce an intended result, whereas efficiency means getting things done well. The suggestion is that efficacy is being able to get things done at all which involves building a system of rules that works. Efficiency is viewed as a second stage process which relates to comparison of the outcome with other outcomes. Part of the problem is that the comparison is with best practice which itself may be subjective.

Not surprisingly, Xiaolan *et al.* (2007) found that firms with higher formality in management practices are more productive than those with informal management practices. This lends greater credence to the view that proper management practices are significant for achieving greater efficiency.

Button and Weyman-Jones (1994) point out that too many empirical studies have come up with substantial measures of inefficiency to ignore its importance for normative economics.

Leibenstein's work was couched in a framework of development (Leibenstein, 1978) and contained a dynamic element that did not fit well within the strict neoclassical framework in economics. It is sometimes seen as belonging to the realm of evolutionary economics.

It is suggested that the theory of X-efficiency may be used to explain why the absorption of capital can be limited in under-developed countries. Developing countries are often viewed as being deficient in persons with managerial skills. It could be used to recommend that these countries focus on the development of their managerial capabilities and focus on intra-plant efficiency and the use of consultants where appropriate.

REVIEW QUESTIONS FOR CHAPTER 7

1 Use a practical example to show the application of the Linear Programming technique to solve the problems of ***resource allocation*** and ***resource valuation*** in a firm producing two products with three resources which are in limited supply within the firm.

2 Consider the following Linear Programming problem.

A firm produces two related products, widget 1 (w_1) and widget 2 (w_2). Both products use inputs A, B and C. To produce a unit of widget 1 the firm must use 6 units of input A, 5 units of input B and 2 units of input C. To produce a unit of widget 2 the firm must use 2 units of input A, 5 units of input B and 4 units of input C. The total units of inputs A, B and C available to the firm are 36, 40 and 28, respectively. The objective of the firm is to maximize profits and the firm makes \$5.00 in profit from the sale of each unit of widget 1 and \$3.00 from the sale of each unit of widget 2.

Using the graphical approach, show how the Linear Programming technique may be used to determine:

(a) The maximum profits the firm may achieve.
(b) The optimal allocation of resources A, B and C to the two competing products, widget 1 and widget 2.
(c) How, hypothetically, can a firm identify its bottleneck resources and determine whether it should purchase more of these resources.

3 Briefly explain the advantages of employing the Dynamic Programming approach to identifying the lowest cost combination of production processes in a multi-staged production process.
4 Discuss the similarities and differences between the concepts of X-efficiency and Total Factor Productivity (*TFP*) and their relevance to increased competitiveness.
5 Distinguish between allocative efficiency and X-efficiency and comment on the empirical differences found in their significance for output growth.
6 Carefully explain Leibenstein's concept of X-efficiency within the context of evolutionary economics and discuss whether this may assist producers in improving their cost competitiveness in the global market.
7 Discuss the nature and significance (if any) of the findings of the ILO study on productivity gains from internal changes and comment on the recent studies that attempt to measure X-efficiency.

RECOMMENDED READING FOR CHAPTER 7

Adda, J. and Cooper, R. (2003) *Dynamic Economics: Dynamic Programming, Theory and Applications*, MIT Press.

Beckmann, J. (1968) *Dynamic Programming of Economic Decisions*, New York, Berlin, etc.: Springer-Verlag.

Bellman, R. (1957) *Dynamic Programming*, Princeton University Press (Dover Paperback Edition (2003)).

Blois, K. J. (1972) 'A note on X-Efficiency and Profit Maximization', *Quarterly Journal of Economics*, 86(2): 310–12.

Blois, K. J. (1974) 'Some Comments on the Theory of Inert Areas and the Definition of X-Efficiency', *Quarterly Journal of Economics*, 88(4): 681–6.

Button, K. J. and Weyman-Jones, T. G. (1994) 'X-Efficiency and Technical Efficiency', *Public Choice*, 80(1–2): 83–104.

DeYoung, R. (1997) 'Bank Mergers, X-Efficiency, and the Market for Corporate Control', *Managerial Finance*, 23(1): 32–47. Available online: http://www.emeraldinsight.com/10.1108/eb018600 (Accessed Nov. 15, 2008).

Dorfman, R. (1953) 'Mathematical or "Linear" Programming: A Non-Mathematical Exposition', *American Economic Review*, 43(5): 797–825.

Frantz, R. S. (1988) *X-Efficiency: Theory, Evidence and Applications*, Boston: Kluwer.

Frantz, R. S. (1990) 'X-Efficiency: Past, Present and Future,' in K. Weiermair and M. Perlman, *Studies in Economic Rationality*, University of Michigan, Ann Arbor.

James, J. (1975) 'A Report on a Pilot Investigation of the Choice of Technology in Developing Countries', University of Strathclyde: *David Livingstone Institute of Overseas Development Studies*.

Katz, H. C., Kochan, T. A. and Keefe, J. H. (1987) 'Industrial Relations and Productivity in the US Automobile Industry', *Brookings Papers on Economic Activity*, 3: 685–727.

Kurz, M. and Manne, A. S. (1963) 'Engineering Estimates of Capital-Labour Substitution in Metal Machining', *American Economic Review*, 53(4): 662–81.

Kwan, S. (2001) 'The X-Efficiency of Commercial Banks in Hong Kong', *Federal Reserve Bank of San Francisco*: FRB of San Francisco Working Paper No. 2002–14.

Liebenstein, H. (1966) 'Allocative Efficiency vs. X-efficiency', *American Economic Review*, 56(3): 392–415.

Leibenstein, H. (1969) 'Organisational or Frictional Equilibria, X-Efficiency and the Rate of Innovation', *Quarterly Journal of Economics*, 83: 600–23.

Leibenstein, H. (1978) *General X-Efficiency Theory and Economic Development*, Oxford University Press.

Potts, J. (2006) ' "X-Efficacy" vs X-Efficiency', in R. Frantz, *Renaissance in Behavioral Economics*, NY: Routledge.

Solow, R. M. (1957) 'Technical Change and the Aggregate Production Function', *Review of Economics and Statistics*, 39: 312–20.

Whitehead, J. (1990) *Empirical Production Analysis and Optimal Technology Choice for Economists*, UK: Gower (Avebury).

Whitehead, J. (2006) 'The Krugman Twist and the Lewis Model: East Asian Lessons for the Caribbean under Globalization', *Social and Economic Studies*, 54(3): 222–46.

Xiolan, F., Eisingerich, A. B. and De Hoyos, R. (2007) 'Clusters of Management Practices, Structural Embeddedness and Firm Productivity', *International Development, 008*, Oxford: University of Oxford: 1–38. Online posting. Available at: <http://www.qeh.ox.ac.uk/pdf/pdf-slptmd/SLPTMD%20WP%20008-Fu.pdf>.

8 Equilibrium in an Isolated Market

Existence of Market Equilibrium; Uniqueness of Market Equilibrium; Stability of Market Equilibrium: Static Stability (Walrasian, Marshallian); Dynamic Stability; Significance of Dynamic Stability.

In the earlier chapters, demand (consumer) and supply (producer) were treated separately. This chapter deals with the interaction between demand and supply in the market. The analysis is restricted to a single isolated market which means that there is no consideration of loops and feedbacks from one market to the other. The existence, uniqueness and stability of equilibrium are examined with stability being separated into its static and dynamic (time path) components. The aim is to identify the conditions under which markets clear (i.e. supply equals demand) and to use this information for policy, both for suppliers and consumers as well as for public policy makers.

8.1 EXISTENCE OF MARKET EQUILIBRIUM

Equilibrium will exist if demand and supply have at least one point in common in the positive quadrant. In general, equilibrium in a single isolated market exists where supply equals demand.

8.1.1 Commodity market equilibrium

In a perfectly competitive commodity market price can adjust to bring equilibrium where quantity demanded (Q_D) is equal to quantity supplied (Q_S) or where, at the equilibrium price, excess demand is zero:

$$Q_D - Q_S = 0$$

Typically, the demand slope is negative:

$$Q_D = a - bP$$

whereas the supply slope is positive:

$$Q_S = \alpha + \beta P$$

Typically, market equilibrium is considered in the Walrasian sense with quantity demanded being a function of price (as above). The Walrasian approach should be viewed as that of the auctioneer in which price bidding is used to clear the supply in the market. It should be remembered, however, that the demand and supply curves, as drawn, follow the Marshallian approach with price being a function of quantity (i.e. quantity is on the X-axis). The curves as drawn are therefore the inverse of the curves as written. This is of extreme importance when results derived are being applied to illustrations.

Buyers and sellers bid in the market. If the price is too low and consumers find that there is scarcity, the price is bid up. Demand is reduced at the higher prices whereas supply is increased. An equilibrium price is reached when neither consumers nor producers have any incentive to change the price (re-contract).

Demand and supply equations may be solved for the price at which equilibrium takes place. Assume demand and supply equations as set out below.

The demand equation (showing quantity demanded (Q_D) negatively related to price (P)):

$$Q_D = 300 - 35P$$

The supply equation (showing quantity supplied (Q_S) positively related to price):

$$Q_S = 50 + 15P$$

At equilibrium:

$$Q_D - Q_S = 0$$

Equating demand and supply gives the following value for the equilibrium price (P_e):

$$300 - 35P - 50 - 15P = 0$$

$$250 - 50P = 0$$

$$P = \frac{250}{50} \quad \text{or} \quad P_e = 5$$

Where the supply and demand curves have at least one intersection in the positive quadrant, equilibrium may be said to exist. There may, however, be cases in which this is violated and an equilibrium price or quantity cannot be found at any non-negative price. Some of these violations are examined below.

8.1.2 Non-existence of equilibrium

There are market situations which prevent the intersection of demand and supply schedules and thereby prevent equilibrium from occurring. Cases of non-existence of equilibrium are summarized as follows:

Non-existence case 1

In this case, the highest price consumers are willing to pay is lower than the lowest price suppliers are willing or able to supply any quantity to the market. This is illustrated in Figure 8.1. P_1 is the highest price at which any quantity of this commodity is demanded whereas P_2 is the lowest price at which any quantity can be supplied to the market.

This phenomenon may occur where a commodity is extremely expensive to produce and bring to market but is low in use-value to consumers. An example of this is the case where a new technology throws up a new near-substitute commodity that is both cheaper to produce and more desirable than the previous commodity. This could cause the demand for the older commodity to shift inwards to a position where it no longer intersects with the high-cost supply curve as it lies everywhere below it. The product with the older technology may then be rendered obsolete through insufficiency of demand.

This phenomenon is sometimes observed in the electronics industry and particularly in the area of computers and components. One example of this is the technological developments that lowered the cost and made widespread the use and availability of flat panel LCD (Liquid Crystal Display) computer monitors. The increasing preference for them shifted demand inward for the older, more bulky CRT (Cathode Ray Tube) monitors.

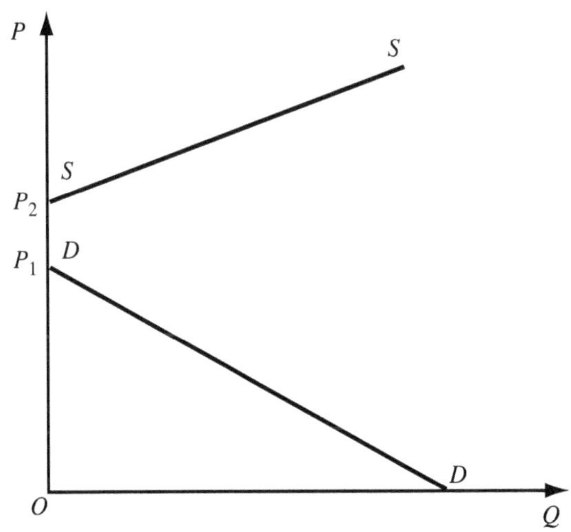

Figure 8.1
Non-existence of equilibrium: The highest demand price is lower than lowest supply price

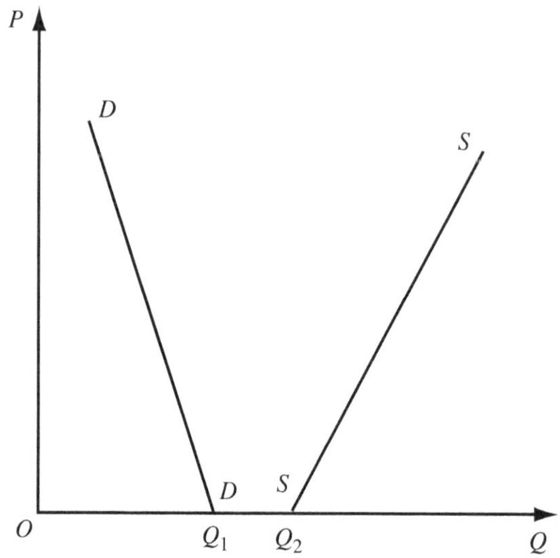

Figure 8.2
Non-existence of equilibrium: Supply exceeds demand at every non-negative price

Non-existence case 2

Another case is that where supply exceeds demand at every non-negative price. Here, the largest quantity the market would take at zero price (free) (Q_1) is less than the market would supply at zero price (Q_2). This is illustrated in Figure 8.2.

This represents the case of a persistent glut that continues to exist even if the commodity is given away. It could be a seasonal phenomenon for a crop that is widely grown in its natural habitat and is so abundant at harvest time that the supply cannot be cleared in the market even if given away. An equilibrium price therefore does not exist.

8.2 UNIQUENESS OF MARKET EQUILIBRIUM

8.2.1 A single equilibrium point

Even where equilibrium exists it may not be unique. Where supply equals demand at one price–quantity combination only, then the equilibrium is unique.

Where the demand and supply curves are both linear, the equilibrium, where it exists, will be unique. In the standard demand and supply functions, the demand curve is negatively sloped and the supply curve positively sloped throughout. In such a case there will be a single (unique) equilibrium point as they can only cross each other once.

Where the demand curves both slope in the same direction, whether this be in a negative or a positive direction, the curves can still intersect with each other only once so long as they are linear.

The analysis of markets typically assumes that there is a unique price–quantity equilibrium position in a single market. The standard demand and supply curves are typically depicted as linear and hence, where an equilibrium position exists, it must be unique. This is the case where demand is a single-valued function of price and so is supply.

However, this assumption of uniqueness may sometimes be violated. As long as one of the curves is non-linear, the potential exists for the uniqueness of equilibrium to be violated.

8.2.2 Non-uniqueness of equilibrium

The violation of uniqueness could occur under many situations including the following.

Non-uniqueness case 1

This is the case where quantity demanded is a single-valued function of price but quantity supplied is not a single valued function of price. Hence the supply curve is not linear. An example of this is the backward bending supply curve of labour. As illustrated in Figure 8.3, when price rises from an equilibrium position at P_1 with quantity Q_2 it moves towards another equilibrium position at a higher price, P_2, with a lower quantity Q_1.

An example of this type of non-uniqueness is the backward bending supply curve of labour where quantity of labour supplied is related to the real price of labour (real wages). As real wages increase the supply of labour increases initially only to fall later as real wages increase as society becomes more affluent, preferring more leisure to work.

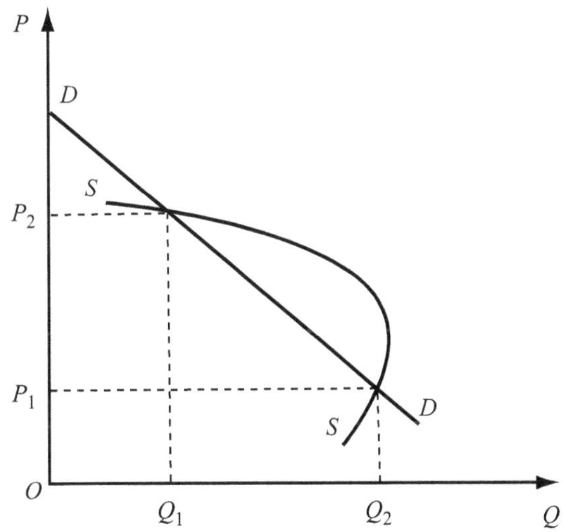

Figure 8.3
Non-uniqueness of equilibrium: The backward-bending supply curve

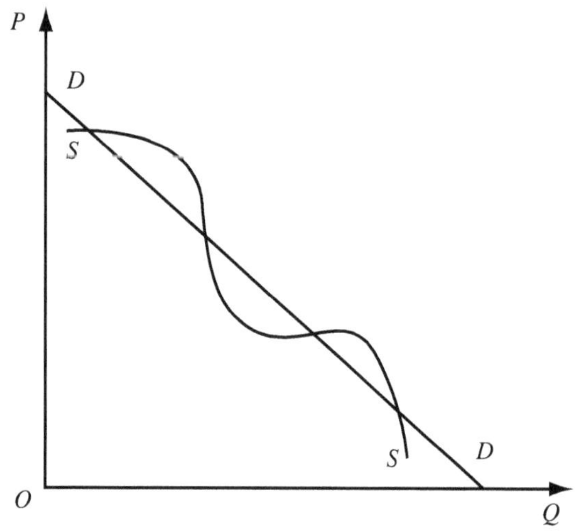

Figure 8.4
Non-uniqueness of equilibrium: Multiple equilibria

Non-uniqueness case 2

This represents an extension of the first case above. Here, the supply curve may bend backwards and then forwards again. Hence, there are more than two equilibrium points. The supply curve may be negatively sloped throughout but meander along the demand curve generating multiple equilibrium points. This is illustrated in Figure 8.4.

Non-uniqueness case 3

This is the case where there may be a range of equilibrium points where the demand and supply curves coincide. The two curves do not actually intersect or cross each other but run along the same path over a range. This is illustrated in Figure 8.5.

In Figure 8.5 supply and demand curves are not single valued functions. The demand curve is negative at higher price levels but becomes positive at lower price levels. Hence, as price falls, this commodity takes on the nature of a Giffin good. The supply curve rises negatively in response to price and later takes on the usual positive slope. As a result, the curves come towards each other, touch over a range (*AB*) and then turn away from each other. This gives an equilibrium range with a number of price–quantity combinations, each of which may be used to represent equilibrium.

8.3 THE STABILITY OF EQUILIBRIUM – STATIC STABILITY

Assuming that equilibrium exists and is unique, consideration must be given to whether it is stable. Stability of equilibrium requires that where an equilibrium is disturbed market conditions ensure that there is a return to equilibrium. This may be looked at in both the static sense and the dynamic sense. The issues of existence and uniqueness of

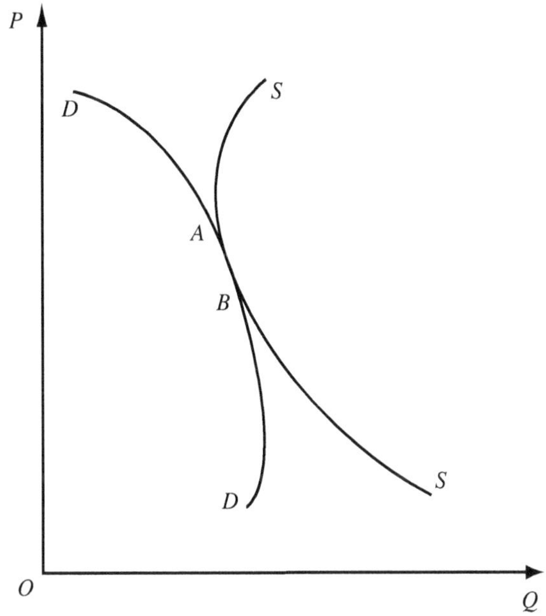

Figure 8.5
Non-uniqueness of equilibrium: An equilibrium range

equilibrium are relatively simple matters. It is the question of stability of equilibrium, with its sub-divisions into static stability and dynamic stability that adds complications.

8.3.1 Static vs. dynamic stability of equilibrium

It cannot be taken for granted that a market will always regain equilibrium once its equilibrium has been disturbed. At issue is whether a system, once it moves into disequilibrium, will naturally return to equilibrium. Not all equilibrium positions are stable such that, with any movement away from equilibrium, market forces would naturally be put in motion to induce a return to equilibrium. Thus, it can be said that an equilibrium is stable where, following a disturbance, there is a movement towards a return to equilibrium and unstable if there is not.

In summary, the following definitions may be used:

- *Stable equilibrium* – An equilibrium is stable if the conditions are such that there is a return to equilibrium following a disturbance of equilibrium or where the system has been in disequilibrium.
- *Unstable equilibrium* – An equilibrium is unstable if the conditions are such that the system does not return to equilibrium following a disturbance from equilibrium or where the system has been in disequilibrium.

The stability of equilibrium in a market may be examined from both static and dynamic perspectives. In static stability, only the direction of change is considered, whereas in dynamic stability, the ***time path*** of the adjustment is taken into account. This section is concerned only with static stability.

Since static stability does not take into account the time path of the adjustment process, it is understood to consider only the nature of the change, that is, whether it is towards or away from equilibrium. It is based on assumptions of market behaviour of buyers and sellers. The exercise being undertaken here is to identify the conditions required for there to be static stability in an isolated market.

For there to be static stability of equilibrium in an isolated market, two different conditions must be satisfied. These are identified as:

- The Walrasian stability condition
- The Marshallian stability condition

8.3.2 The Walrasian condition for static stability

The Walrasian demand equation is written with quantity as a function of price:

$$Q_D = f(P)$$

Consequently, the Walrasian stability condition is based on the assumption that buyers raise their bids when quantity demanded is in excess of quantity supplied and that sellers lower their prices when quantity supplied is in excess of quantity demanded.

Walras is likened to the auctioneer where excess demand for an item being auctioned causes the price to be bid upwards. Price is therefore the equilibrating factor in the market. Hence, a market would be Walrasian stable if ***a price rise diminishes excess demand quantity*** (E).

To illustrate this, consider that excess demand quantity at a given price P [$E(P)$] is the difference between the quantity demanded at this price $Q_D(P)$ and the quantity supplied at this price $Q_S(P)$:

$$E(P) = Q_D(P) - Q_S(P)$$

According to the Walrasian (auctioneer) behavioural assumption, when excess demand quantity is positive buyers tend to raise their bids and when excess demand is negative sellers tend to lower their prices. This gives the condition that a market is stable in a static sense ***when a price rise diminishes excess demand***. Consequently, the change in excess demand in relationship to a change in price must be negative. This condition can be written as:

$$\frac{\partial E}{\partial P} = \frac{\partial Q_D}{\partial P} - \frac{\partial Q_S}{\partial P} < 0 \quad (1)$$

The condition could be interpreted as saying that the supply slope of the function should be algebraically greater than the demand slope of the function. However, it must be remembered that the Walrasian demand equation is the inverse of the demand function as drawn. Hence, it is really saying that the inverse of the supply slope as drawn should be greater algebraically than the inverse of the demand slope as drawn. Nevertheless, where

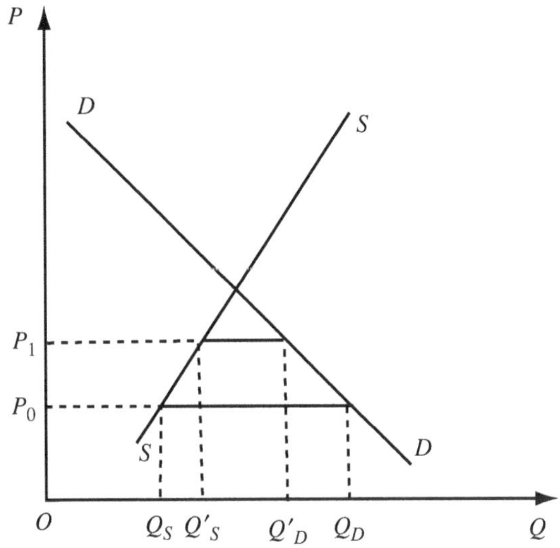

Figure 8.6
The Walrasian condition for static stability of equilibrium

the supply curve is positively sloped and the demand curve negatively sloped, the Walrasian condition is fulfilled. Figure 8.6 illustrates the Walrasian stability condition.

In Figure 8.6, P_0 is an initial disequilibrium position. Here, excess demand quantity is positive and equal to the distance Q_SQ_D. An increase in price to P_1 reduces excess demand quantity to the distance $Q'_SQ'_D$. This is a movement towards equilibrium and fulfils the static stability condition based on the Walrasian behavioural principle.

8.3.3 The Marshallian condition for static stability

The Marshallian stability condition states that producers will tend to raise their output when the excess demand price is positive and lower it when it is negative. In this case the equilibrating factor is ***quantity rather than price***. The Marshallian demand equation therefore represents price as a function of quantity demanded. It is therefore the inverse of the Walrasian function but represents the demand and supply curves as drawn. The aim here is to identify the conditions under which ***a rise in quantity reduces excess demand price***. Excess demand price may be defined as the extent to which the price consumers are willing to pay for a given quantity exceeds the price producers are willing to supply that quantity.

The Marshallian function can therefore be expressed showing price as an inverse function of demand and supply. This may be illustrated using the Walrasian demand function:

$$Q_D = f(P)$$

This functional relationship may be expressed as:

$$Q_D = a - bP$$

Converting to the Marshallian demand equation by making price (P) the subject, gives:

$$bP = a - Q_D$$

The Marshallian demand equation is therefore the inverse of the Walrasian and may be written as:

$$P = \frac{a}{b} - \frac{1}{b}Q$$

Re-writing gives:

$$P = \alpha - \beta Q$$

where:

$$\alpha = \frac{a}{b} \qquad \text{and} \qquad \beta = \frac{1}{b}$$

In expressing price as a function of quantity, the Marshallian equations express the demand and supply curves as drawn.

The excess demand price (F) may be expressed as the difference between the demand price P_D and the supply price P_S for a given quantity (Q):

$$F(P) = P_D(Q) - P_S(Q)$$

According to the Marshallian mechanism, if excess demand price is positive (demand price greater than supply price), the producer realizes that consumers are offering a higher price than the firm needs to supply that quantity and concludes that the firm can profitably increase the quantity supplied. A negative excess demand price (supply price greater than demand price for a given quantity) leads to the converse reasoning and the firm cuts back its supply.

Thus equilibrium is stable in the Marshallian sense if an increase in quantity (Q) reduces the excess demand price (F). This condition may be stated as:

$$\frac{\partial F}{\partial Q} = \frac{\partial P_D}{\partial Q} - \frac{\partial P_S}{\partial Q} < 0 \qquad (2)$$

This may be interpreted as saying that, in the Marshallian demand and supply functions, the supply slope should be algebraically greater than the demand slope. Since the Marshallian is the same as the drawn curves, this coincides with the demand and supply curves as seen in the diagram and as illustrated in Figure 8.7. Where the supply curve is positively sloped and the demand curve negatively sloped, the Marshallian condition for static stability of equilibrium is fulfilled.

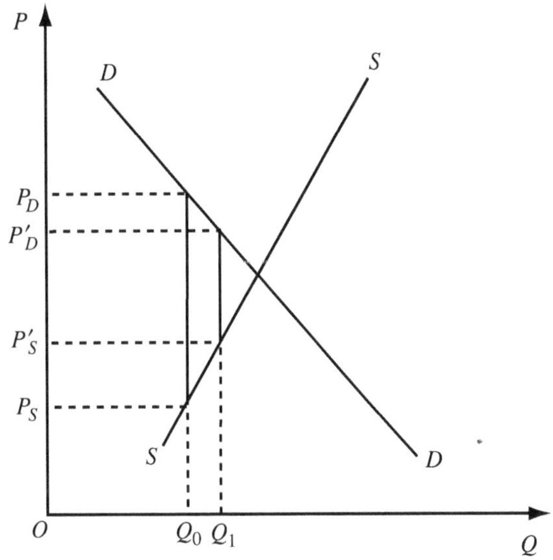

Figure 8.7
The Marshallian condition for static stability of equilibrium

At the quantity Q_0 in Figure 8.7 there is excess demand price equal to the vertical distance P_SP_D. This is positive excess demand price and, as a result, suppliers increase output quantity. Consider output is increased to Q_1. The increase in quantity supplied reduces the excess demand price to $P'_SP'_D$.

Both Walrasian and Marshallian rules are accepted as normal market behaviour. Hence, it is considered that for there to be static stability of equilibrium, both the Walrasian and Marshallian conditions must be met simultaneously. Where the demand curve has a negative slope and the supply curve has a positive slope both of these conditions, identified as (1) and (2) above, are satisfied. Thus the ordinary demand and supply curves are stable according to both Walrasian and Marshallian definitions.

8.3.4 Static instablity conditions

Where both demand and supply curves are negatively sloped or where they are both positively sloped the conditions for static stability of equilibrium break down as both the Walrasian and Marshallian conditions cannot be met simultaneously. This is because one condition is the inverse of the other (e.g. if $4 > 2$ then $\frac{1}{4} < \frac{1}{2}$). Hence equilibrium, when stable in the Walrasian sense, cannot also be stable in the Marshallian sense.

Instability case 1 – Both demand and supply curves are negatively sloped

In Figure 8.8 both curves are negatively sloped. However, the supply curve has a steeper negative slope which, algebraically, gives it a lower value than the demand slope as drawn. This violates the Marshallian condition but fulfils the Walrasian condition.

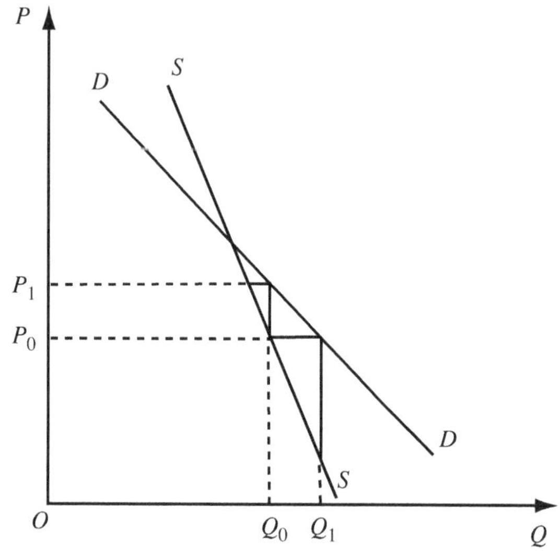

Figure 8.8
Walrasian stable, Marshallian unstable

With the Walrasian approach measuring excess demand quantity at a given price and the Marshallian measuring excess demand price at a given quantity, the incompatibility between the two may be observed in Figure 8.8. Here, an increase in price from P_0 to P_1 is seen to reduce excess demand quantity measured as the horizontal difference between the demand and supply curves (solid horizontal lines). Hence this configuration of demand and supply curves is Walrasian stable. However, an increase in quantity from Q_0 to Q_1 increases rather than reduces the excess demand price measured as the vertical gap between the demand and supply curves (solid vertical lines). Hence this configuration of demand and supply curves is Marshallian unstable.

Where, however, the demand curve is steeper than the supply curve while both curves are negatively sloped, the Marshallian condition holds and not the Walrasian. This is illustrated in Figure 8.9. In this case, the supply curve has the lower negative slope and therefore the algebraically greater slope as drawn (Marshallian).

Figure 8.9 shows that with an increase in price from P_0 to P_1 the excess demand quantity, as shown by the horizontal distances between the demand and supply curves (solid lines), increases rather than decreases, confirming that this configuration is Walrasian unstable. On the other hand, the increase in supply from Q_0 to Q_1 leads to a reduction is excess demand price as shown by the vertical distances between the demand and supply curves. Hence this case is Marshallian stable and Walrasian unstable.

Instability case 2 – Both demand and supply curves are positively sloped

Where both supply and demand schedules are positively sloped, the problem is the same. Both conditions cannot hold simultaneously. Consider the case where the supply curve is steeper (i.e. greater algebraically) than the demand curve as drawn. As is illustrated in Figure 8.10, this is Marshallian stable but Walrasian unstable.

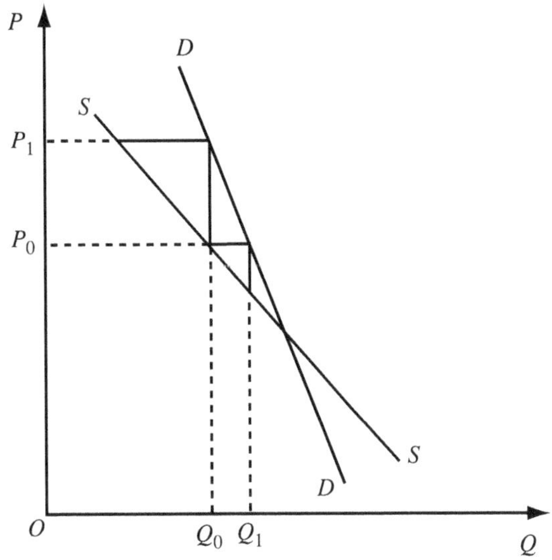

Figure 8.9
Walrasian unstable, Marshallian stable

In this case, once again, the solid horizontal lines are used to measure the excess demand quantity and the solid vertical lines to measure excess demand price. Figure 8.10 shows that, with positive excess demand quantity at price P_0 as price is bid up to P_1, the excess demand quantity increases rather than decreases. This is therefore unstable according to the Walrasian condition. But here the Marshallian condition holds. Consider the excess demand price at the quantity Q_0. If suppliers should increase quantity to Q_1 then the excess demand price is reduced and the movement is towards equilibrium.

Where, however, the two curves are positively sloped but their positions are reversed, then the market conditions become Walrasian stable and Marshallian unstable. This is illustrated in Figure 8.11.

With the steeper positively sloped demand curve, an increase in price from P_0 to P_1 reduces the excess demand quantity, making it Walrasian stable. However, with excess demand price at quantity Q_0, an increase in supply to quantity Q_1 exacerbates the situation, leading away from equilibrium and rendering it Marshallian unstable.

In summary, where the demand curve is negatively sloped and the supply curve is positively sloped, then both conditions are fulfilled. Note that the two conditions cannot simultaneously hold if both curves are negatively sloped or positively sloped, no matter which curve is steeper. This is because one condition is the inverse of the other. Static stability of market equilibrium requires that both conditions hold. Hence, it is only with the market demand and supply curves taking the normal signs that a market can be considered statically stable.

This has practical importance in any single isolated market whether in the commodity market, factor market or the financial market. Even where equilibrium is not achieved or even is not desirable, it is important to ensure that wild movements away from equilibrium are not the norm as it can lead to chaos in the market. Interference in

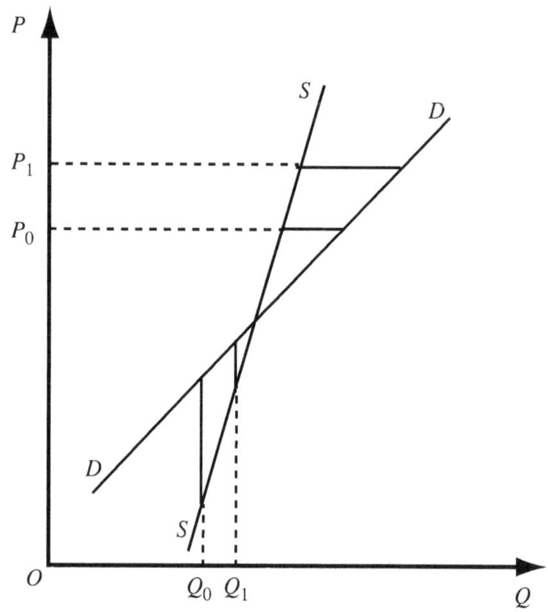

Figure 8.10
Marshallian stable, Walrasian unstable

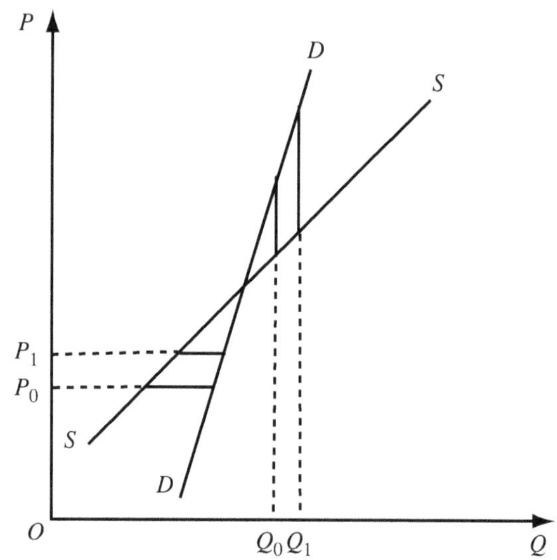

Figure 8.11
Marshallian unstable, Walrasian stable

the market to alter equilibrium prices or quantities can lead to instability. In addition speculative activity can sometimes lead to spectacular instability, as seen in the price of oil on the world market and in the collapse of mortgage markets, as evidenced by events in Thailand that led to the East Asian financial crisis of 1997 (Kaufman *et al.*, 1999) and in the United States in 2008 (Muolo and Padilla, 2008).

8.4 DYNAMIC STABILITY AND THE COBWEB MODEL

8.4.1 The nature of dynamic stability

Dynamic stability introduces the ***time path*** of the adjustment process. The static stability conditions looked at the rate of change of excess demand quantity with respect to price (Walrasian) and the rate of change of excess demand price, with respect to quantity (Marshallian). Now with dynamic stability the time path to equilibrium is important. The process involves re-contracting. Both static and dynamic stability depend upon the slopes of the demand and the supply curves but dynamic stability is also concerned with the magnitude of the adjustment from period to period. The two are fundamentally different approaches to stability. However, while dynamic stability implies static stability, the reverse need not hold true.

As with static stability, dynamic stability has two approaches:

- ***Walrasian*** – Equilibrium is stable in a dynamic sense if the price converges to (or approaches) the equilibrium price over time.
- ***Marshallian*** – Equilibrium is stable in a dynamic sense if the quantity supplied converges to the equilibrium quantity.

In this Walrasian approach (auctioneer model) the price is observed each time period and the analysis of dynamic stability investigates the course of price over time from one time period to the other and the effect on excess demand quantity. The equilibrium is dynamically stable if the actual price level approaches the equilibrium level as time tends towards infinity.

The analysis here focuses on the ***Cobweb*** model, a model so called because of the way in which prices and quantities oscillate around the equilibrium point. This is a model with lagged supply response to price which has special relevance to the agriculture sector. It is part of a wider model of dynamic stability, a subject dealt with in greater detail in Henderson and Quandt (1980).

8.4.2 Mechanics of the Cobweb model

In the Cobweb model demand and supply responses to prices are different. Demand prices respond immediately to clear the market supply quantity. Suppliers respond to market prices with a time lag. Supply adjustments are not instantaneous and are usually the result of a long gestational period for a product to come to market from the time the production decision is made. This is particularly relevant to the production of agricultural commodities.

The aim is to identify the conditions under which the fluctuations in prices and output would be dampened so that, over time, the price would settle to the equilibrium price. The significance is that this would bring greater certainty and stability to the producers' incomes and to the consumers' spending budgets for these commodities.

Following Henderson and Quandt (1980), the effort to find the solution conditions for dynamic stability to the lagged supply adjustment (Cobweb) problem proceeds by:

- Setting up the demand and lagged supply functions
- Applying the solution formula for a first-order difference equation
- Identifying the expression for the equilibrium price
- Identifying the conditions that lead a system over time to the equilibrium price

Setting up the demand and lagged supply functions

The demand and lagged supply equations may be set up as follows:

$$Q_t^D = a + bP_t$$

$$Q_t^S = \alpha + \beta P_{t-1}$$

Thus the quantity demanded in any time period (t), Q_t^D, depends on the price in the current time period (P_t) whereas the quantity supplied in the current time period, Q_t^S, depends on the price in the previous time period (P_{t-1}). The value of b in the demand equation would be expected to be negative.

But in any period price must adjust to bring about the equality such that:

$$Q_t^D = Q_t^S$$

Thus equality of the demand and supply equations gives:

$$a + bP_t = \alpha + \beta P_{t-1}$$

Solving for P_t:

$$bP_t = \alpha - a + \beta P_{t-1} \tag{1}$$

or:

$$P_t = \frac{\beta}{b} P_{t-1} + \frac{\alpha - a}{b}$$

This is a first-order difference equation. The explanatory or independent variable P_{t-1} is a lagged version of the dependent variable P_t. Where a variable is to be explained by a lagged version of itself, the solution requires an iterative process, beginning by initializing the variable to P_0 at time $t = 0$. The end result of this process is captured in a solution formula that may be applied. This is done here.

Applying the solution formula for a first-order difference equation

The solution to this first-order difference equation may be derived from the proven mathematical formula for the general solution to a first-order differential equation as set out below. This is simply borrowed from the discipline of mathematics and applied here.

The standard formula considers a first-order difference equation of the form:

$$y_t = ay_{t-1} + b$$

where a and b are constants.

Initializing the value of y_t as y_0 when $t = 0$, the solution equation is arrived at through a series of iterations and the solution of the first-order difference equation of the form above is given by the formula:

$$y_t = \left(y_0 - \frac{b}{1-a}\right)a^t + \frac{b}{1-a}$$

This applies to the case where $a \neq 1$ (as applies to this case). However, where $a = 1$, then the solution becomes:

$$y_t = y_0 + b_t$$

The above formula may then be applied to the purpose at hand. Initializing:

$$P_t = P_0 \qquad \text{when} \qquad t = 0$$

Substituting:

$$P_t \text{ and } P_{t-1} \qquad \text{for} \qquad y_t \text{ and } y_{t-1}$$

and:

$$\left(\frac{\beta}{b}\right) \text{ for } a \qquad \textit{and} \qquad \left(\frac{\alpha - a}{b}\right) \text{ for } b$$

The substitution gives:

$$P_t = \left(P_0 - \frac{(\alpha - a)/b}{(b-\beta)/b}\right)\left(\frac{\beta}{b}\right)^t + \left(\frac{(\alpha - a)/b}{(b-\beta)/b}\right)$$

This becomes:

$$P_t = \left(P_0 - \frac{\alpha - a}{b-\beta}\right)\left(\frac{\beta}{b}\right)^t + \left(\frac{\alpha - a}{b-\beta}\right) \tag{2}$$

But the expression for the equilibrium price (P_e) is:

$$\left(\frac{\alpha - a}{b-\beta}\right) = P_e$$

Identifying the expression for the equilibrium price

It is important to prove that, in the solution equation, the equilibrium price (P_e) is the expression:

$$\left(\frac{\alpha - a}{b - \beta}\right) = P_e$$

Following the time path to equilibrium, the equilibrium price is reached when price is the same in two consecutive time periods, signifying that equilibrium is dynamically stable. Consequently, the equilibrium price occurs when:

$$P_t = P_{t-1}$$

Re-writing the equilibrium equation (Equation (1) above) to make P_{t-1} equal to P_t, gives:

$$bP_t = \alpha - a + \beta P_t$$

Solving for P_t (= P_e):

$$bP_t - \beta P_t = \alpha - a$$

$$P_t(b - \beta) = \alpha - a$$

$$P_t = \frac{\alpha - a}{b - \beta} = P_e$$

Substituting P_e for $\dfrac{\alpha - a}{b - \beta}$ in the solution Equation (2) above gives:

$$P_t = (P_0 - P_e)\left(\frac{\beta}{b}\right)^t + P_e$$

Identifying the conditions that lead over time to the stable equilibrium price

Dynamic stability of equilibrium requires that the present price tends to the equilibrium price as time moves towards infinity and is expressed as:

$$P_t \rightarrow P_e \quad \text{as} \quad t \rightarrow \infty$$

In order for this to happen, the first part of the equation must go to zero as time moves towards infinity, expressed as:

$$(P_0 - P_e)\left(\frac{\beta}{b}\right)^t \rightarrow 0 \quad \text{as} \quad t \rightarrow \infty$$

Since the initial price (P_0) is not the equilibrium price (P_e) then, in the solution equation:

$$P_0 \neq P_e$$

This means that the first expression is not zero, or:

$$P_0 - P_e \neq 0$$

It follows then that the solution requires:

$$\left(\frac{\beta}{b}\right)^t \rightarrow 0 \qquad as \qquad t \rightarrow \infty$$

In order for the above fraction to approach zero as the exponent t increases, the denominator must be greater than the numerator. This condition, ***which is the condition for dynamic stability***, may be expressed as:

$$|b| > |\beta|$$

Now, $|b|$ is the gradient or slope of the demand equation as written and $|\beta|$ is the gradient or slope of the supply equation ***as written*** (Walrasian). The modulus is used for these values since the signs (positive or negative) do not matter (unlike the case of static stability). These values therefore are the absolute values of the slopes.

Recall, however, that the demand and supply equations are written as the inverse of the way in which they are drawn (Walrasian vs. Marshallian). This indicates that $|b|$ ***is the inverse of the demand slope and*** $|\beta|$ ***is the inverse of the supply slope as drawn***.

Hence, referring to the diagrams and using the slopes ***as drawn*** (Marshallian), the dynamic stability condition for a market with lagged supply adjustment must be re-written as:

$$\left|\frac{1}{b}\right| < \left|\frac{1}{\beta}\right|$$

This condition for dynamic stability says that the supply slope ***as drawn*** must be greater in absolute value than the demand slope ***as drawn***.

If the condition is violated then the equilibrium is dynamically unstable. Any disturbance to equilibrium will not cause a return to equilibrium over time.

8.4.3 The stability condition and the Cobweb pattern

The stability condition may be illustrated for the 'cobweb' model using the condition for dynamic stability:

$$\left|\frac{1}{b}\right| < \left|\frac{1}{\beta}\right|$$

Recalling that the absolute slope of the demand curve as drawn is:

$$\left|\frac{1}{b}\right|$$

and the absolute slope of the supply curve as drawn is:

$$\left|\frac{1}{\beta}\right|$$

then a market will be dynamically stable where the absolute slope of the supply curve as drawn is greater than the absolute slope of the demand curve as drawn. This can be illustrated showing the Cobweb pattern. It can be shown that, where this condition is not fulfilled, the market will be dynamically unstable.

The illustrations show:

- Stability. Convergence or damped oscillations (oscillations with decreasing amplitude)
- Instability. Divergence or explosive oscillations (oscillations with increasing amplitude)
- Instability. Constant disequilibrium (oscillations with constant amplitude).

8.4.3.1 CONVERGENCE TO EQUILIBRIUM – DAMPED OSCILLATIONS

In the case where the stability condition is met (i.e. where the absolute slope of the supply curve as drawn is greater than the absolute slope of the demand curve as drawn), the amplitude of oscillations around the equilibrium point will decrease. This means that, over time, the price in the market will tend to the equilibrium price.

Stability – Convergence or damped oscillations (oscillations with decreasing amplitude)

Figure 8.12 illustrates the case of a supply curve (*SS*) with a greater (steeper) absolute slope than the demand curve (*DD*).

Consider the case of a farmer producing a commodity, say potatoes, that takes some time between sowing and reaping to bring to the market. Initially the market is in disequilibrium. The potato supply of Q_0, brought to the market in time t_0, is cleared in the same time period at a price of P_0. This price is above the equilibrium price, as shown in Figure 8.12.

With a price of P_0, potato farmers respond by planting a larger crop of potatoes, viewing the high price as an incentive to supply a higher output. This higher output (S_1) comes in the next time period t_1 when farmers bring the harvested crop that was planted in t_0 to the market.

When this larger quantity of potatoes, Q_1, reaches the market, it can only clear at the market clearing price for that quantity of P_1. This is a lower than equilibrium price. Because of this lower price in time t_1, farmers contract their planting of potatoes. This lower quantity, Q_2 (S_2), comes forth to market in time period t_2. Once again, with the restricted output, consumers are willing to pay a higher price, P_2, that clears the quantity Q_2 from the market. It should be recognized that P_2, although higher than P_1, is still lower than P_0. This higher price evokes a larger quantity than Q_2 in the next time period, but not as much as Q_1. This continues until the equilibrium price is reached. This system is stable.

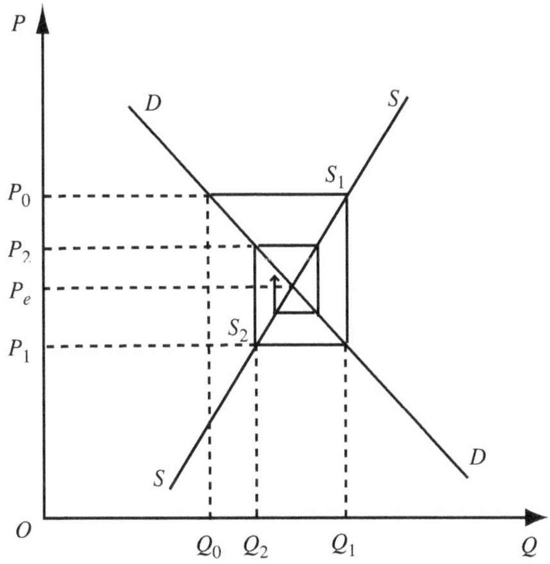

Figure 8.12
Cobweb model with dynamic stability: Convergence through damped oscillations (oscillations with decreasing amplitude)

In each time period, the glut and scarcity reduces as the swings around the equilibrium price decrease in width and the model moves over time towards equilibrium. This represents a convergence to equilibrium over time as these oscillations are damped or are said to have decreasing amplitude. Dynamic equilibrium is achieved when the price remains the same from one time period to the other.

Where the slope of the demand curve has a smaller absolute value than the slope of the supply curve the oscillations decrease in amplitude and the market is dynamically stable.

8.4.3.2 DIVERGENCE FROM EQUILIBRIUM – EXPLOSIVE OSCILLATIONS

Where the slope of the demand curve has greater absolute value than the slope of the supply curve, the oscillations will increase rather than decrease in amplitude, rendering the market dynamically unstable.

Instability – Divergence or explosive oscillations (oscillations with increasing amplitude)

As illustrated in Figure 8.13, the same process takes place but price fluctuations become larger and larger as the market is subject to explosive oscillations.

Figure 8.13 shows that, as farmers respond to the high (above equilibrium) price of P_0, the increased quantity (Q_1) comes to market in the next time period (t_1). The market responds immediately with a fall in price to P_1. In response to this low price, the farmers cut back planting of potatoes, resulting in a reduced quantity of the crop (Q_2) coming on

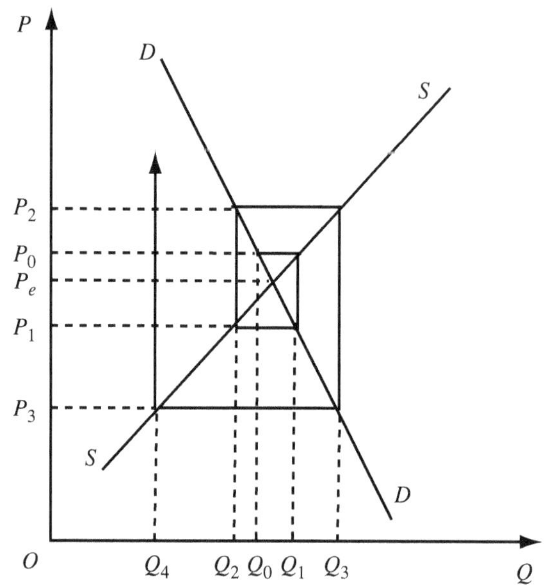

Figure 8.13
Cobweb model with dynamic instability: Divergence through explosive oscillations (oscillations with increasing amplitude)

the market in the following time period (t_2). Prices are bid up immediately to P_2 which brings forth a larger quantity (Q_3) in time period (t_3) and the process continues.

It may be observed that the sequence of prices over time leads to a movement increasingly further away from the equilibrium price P_e. Each price fall is greater than the one before and so is each price rise. The gluts and scarcities of potatoes are amplified with each incremental time period. With the demand curve steeper than the supply curve, the oscillations around the equilibrium point become explosive as they increase in amplitude. The market is unstable as it moves further away from equilibrium.

8.4.3.3 DIVERGENCE FROM EQUILIBRIUM – CONSTANT OSCILLATIONS

Where the demand and supply curves have the same slopes in absolute values, the market is dynamically unstable but the oscillations, instead of increasing, will have constant amplitude.

Instability – Non-convergence or continuous oscillations (oscillations with constant amplitude)

The oscillations around the equilibrium point neither widen nor narrow. Hence, although the system does not move further away from equilibrium, it still does not get any closer. This is illustrated in Figure 8.14.

As Figure 8.14 illustrates, the above-equilibrium price of P_0 draws a response from farmers to produce Q_1 which reaches the market in the next time period. Price then falls

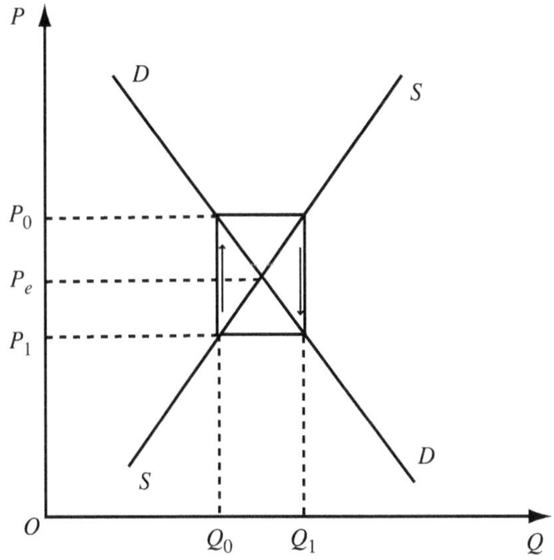

Figure 8.14
Cobweb model with dynamic instability: Oscillations with constant amplitude

immediately to P_1 which is below equilibrium. In response, farmers cut back planting to exactly what it was in the initial time period (Q_0), leading to a price that is the same as in the initial time period (P_0). The market price therefore continues to swing between P_0 and P_1 and the supply gluts and scarcities alternate at the same levels from one time period to the other. The oscillations around the equilibrium point have a constant amplitude and the system remains unstable.

8.4.4 Demand and supply with slopes in the same direction

It has been pointed out that the condition for dynamic stability of equilibrium uses the absolute values of the slopes of the demand and supply curves. Hence, the sign or direction of the slope (negative or positive) is irrelevant to the process.

Where the demand and supply slopes are in the same direction the price level will either increase or decrease continually. When the value of absolute value of the slope of the supply curve is greater than the absolute value of the slope of the demand curve, as drawn, then price will converge to the equilibrium price over time. Where the demand curve has the greater absolute slope, price will diverge in either an upward or downward direction.

Figure 8.15 illustrates the case of the supply curve with a greater absolute value (steeper) than the demand curve. This is shown for the two cases, first, where both demand and supply curves are positively sloped and, second, where both curves are negatively sloped. Following the mechanism described above, the movements over time lead to a stable equilibrium.

On the other hand Figure 8.16 illustrates the case of the demand curve with a greater absolute value (steeper) than the supply curve. This is also shown for the two cases,

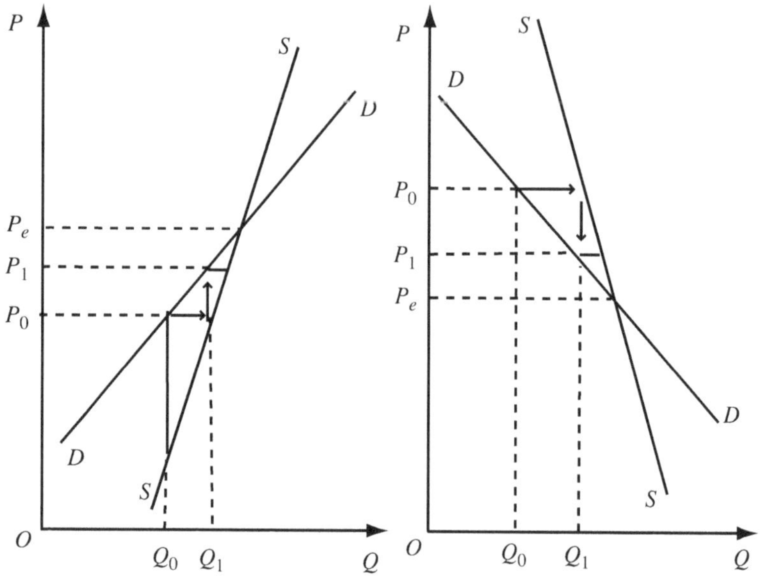

Figure 8.15
Cobweb model with dynamic stability where demand and supply curves both slope in the same direction

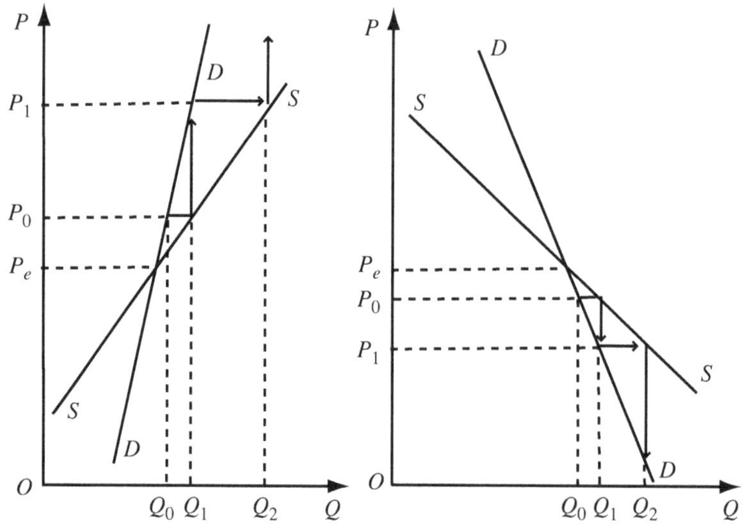

Figure 8.16
Cobweb model with dynamic instability where demand and supply curves both slope in the same direction

first, where both demand and supply curves are positively sloped and, second, where both curves are negatively sloped. Again, following the mechanism described above, the movements over time lead away from equilibrium, signifying instability.

8.5 APPLICATION OF DYNAMIC STABILITY CONDITIONS

The Cobweb model has particular significance for certain types of markets where supply quantity responds with a lag to market price. This may fit a number of industries but has special relevance to the agricultural sector. Knowledge of the condition for stability may be of use to this sector. Certain characteristics of agricultural products fit the Cobweb model. These include the following:

- Many agricultural products have a long gestation period (from planting to reaping) and are subject to the vagaries of the weather. Consequently the market supply in response to price materializes only after a time lag.
- Much of agricultural produce is highly perishable. As a result the quantity brought fresh to the market must be cleared immediately. Hence the market clearing price for that quantity must occur in the same time period in which the produce is brought to market.
- In many countries the farming community is made up of several small units (family farms, peasant farmers, etc.). Consequently, they often lack sophisticated information systems that would allow for proper supply planning. Moreover, the large number of small sellers may mean that, as a price taker, each supplier simply tries to catch a high price by expanding production or avoid a low price by contracting production without realizing that all the other competitors are doing the same. This may repeat in a somewhat naïve and myopic pattern, leading to a vicious cycle of gluts, scarcities, low and high prices.

This type of instability in the agricultural sector (or in any sector with a similar pattern) often wreaks havoc on the suppliers' incomes. It also affects the consumers, who may find it difficult to budget for these items, particularly where the items are a large part of their overall income. This has a special application to food products. In an effort to stabilize prices for consumers and income for farmers, it may be necessary for some type of intervention in the market in order to dampen the oscillations. Knowledge of the reasons for the explosive or constant oscillations can assist in any type of intervention that may be necessary to bring about stability.

Intervention must be predicated upon knowledge and understanding of the condition for achieving dynamic stability. It must be recognized that dynamic stability requires that the absolute slope of the supply curve be greater than the absolute slope of the demand curve. In a practical sense, it could be recognized that, given the demand function in the market, the cause of the instability is that supply is too elastic. That is, the supply is over-responsive to price.

Market interventions may be taken either to make the demand more elastic or to make the supply less elastic or both. Typically, it is more practicable to intervene directly in the supply market. Interventions must therefore seek to ensure that suppliers become less responsive to price in their production decisions. For farmers, these interventions make take several forms, including the following.

Advice to farmers

Farmers may need to be educated as to the reasons for the market swings – that they are overly responsive to price (given the market demand). Advice on the structure of the perfectly competitive market structure and on the futility of trying to 'catch' a high price by over producing and hoping the high price will remain until the harvest, since each supplier is doing the same, may help to mitigate the problem. Farmers could be advised on countercyclical planting (planting when price is low) and other techniques that involve hedging in order to dampen the oscillations in the market.

Production planning by suppliers

A more direct form of intervention is having suppliers form an association or co-operative to share information on production in order to reduce their over-responsiveness to price. Where producers are willing to provide information on planting decisions in a timely manner to a central body, the data gathered may be used to inform the members on how to avoid the market oscillations through more appropriate production planning.

State planning

At the highest level of intervention, the state may assign quotas to individual suppliers through full state planning of the sector in order to determine the quantities that come to the market in each time period. The state may also intervene on the demand side in a form of rationing or may fix prices in the market or implement a price floor (price control) as a support mechanism for suppliers. However, as demonstrated in Chapter 4, efforts at price control may be counter-productive and welfare reducing for the society as a whole.

Nevertheless, the realization that, for market equilibrium to be stable in a dynamic sense, where there is lagged supply response to price, the absolute supply elasticity must be less than the absolute demand elasticity (supply slope must be greater in absolute value than the demand slope) is useful information. It allows for suppliers or the government to take corrective measures to bring some measure of stability to a widely fluctuating market.

REVIEW QUESTIONS FOR CHAPTER 8

1 With regard to equilibrium in a single isolated market, explain and illustrate:

(a) The concept of existence of equilibrium.
(b) The concept of uniqueness of equilibrium.
(c) The concept of stability of equilibrium and differentiate between static and dynamic stability of equilibrium.

2 With regard to the stability of equilibrium in a single, isolated market:

(a) Derive the Walrasian condition for static stability of equilibrium.
(b) Derive the Marshallian condition for static stability of equilibrium.
(c) Illustrate and explain why both the Walrasian and Marshallian conditions cannot hold simultaneously when the demand and supply curves are sloped in the same direction.

3 With regard to the dynamic stability of equilibrium in a market with lagged supply response:

(a) Set up the demand and supply equations for the Cobweb model.
(b) Show how and why the solution to a first-order difference equation must be applied in the process of deriving the stability condition for the Cobweb model.
(c) Carefully derive the final stability condition for the Cobweb model explaining it in terms of slopes of demand and supply curves.

4 With regard to the condition for dynamic stability in the Cobweb model illustrate diagrammatically:

(a) The achievement of damped oscillations (convergence).
(b) The two cases of instability with explosive and constant oscillations.

5 Consider how the information on this model may be used to explain:

(a) Problems with instability in incomes and prices in the agricultural sector.
(b) How state intervention may be used to assist with the stabilization of incomes and prices for farmers.
(c) Briefly explain how information on static and dynamic stability may be used to provide corrective measures in any market affected by instability and comment on the role of the mortgage market in the Asian financial crisis of 1997 and the USA financial crisis of 2008.

RECOMMENDED READING FOR CHAPTER 8

Henderson, J. M. and Quandt, R. E. (1980) *Microeconomic Theory: A Mathematical Approach*, 3rd edn, New York: McGraw Hill, Ch. 6.

Kaufman, G. G., Krueger, T. H. and Hunter, W. C. (1999) *The Asian Financial Crisis: Origins, Implications and Solutions*, Springer.

Muolo, P. and Padilla, M. (2008) *Chain of Blame: How Wall Street Caused the Mortgage and Credit Crisis*, NJ: Wiley.

9 The Perfectly Competitive Market

Equilibrium of the Firm and Industry in Short-run and Long-run; Perfect Competition and Economic Efficiency; Industry Dynamics: Changes in Demand, Costs and Taxes.

The market structure of Perfect Competition is often considered a highly desirable one particularly from the point of view of economic efficiency in a static, distributive sense. This is in consonance with the view that trading in increasingly competitive markets is, in theory, beneficial to economic welfare because of the greater efficiency in the use of economic resources. While this may or may not hold true in reality, it is nevertheless of importance to understand the intricacies and mechanics of this model which has received so much attention.

Perfect Competition is the centrepiece of the traditional theory of the firm. It is one of the four basic models of market structure that make up the traditional theory of the firm. The others are Monopoly, Monopolistic Competition and Oligopoly. As a model of market structure, it is used to explain and predict the behaviour of firms which are part of this industry. Furthermore, as one of the so-called 'marginalist' models of the firm, the firm is theorized to maximize profits by following the 'marginalist' rule of equating marginal revenue with marginal cost.

These marginalist models are later contrasted with the more modern alternative models of the firm which are included in the study of market structure. Newer models have proliferated since the 1930 and particularly since the 1950s and include the Managerial, Behavioural, Average-cost/Mark-up Pricing and Entry-Prevention models.

9.1 ASSUMPTIONS AND FUNDAMENTALS OF THE MODEL

9.1.1 Basic assumptions

The basic assumptions of the model of Perfect Competition are as follows:

- There are many buyers and sellers (firms) in the industry. There are so many buyers and sellers that no single buyer or seller can influence price or output sufficiently to alter the equilibrium of the industry.

- The firms all produce a homogeneous product. The products of the different firms are indistinguishable from each other. Hence, no single firm has any market power on its own.
- The firm is rational, that is, it aims to maximize profits. There is a single goal in a single monolithic firm.
- There is free entry and exit of firms (long-run). Any existing or new firm is free to enter the industry and there is no capital, preference or any other barrier to entry.
- There is perfect knowledge of costs and demand. The production technology available to any one firm is available and known to all firms and individual firms know the demand in terms of the price at which they can sell their product.
- All factors required by the firm are freely available. The firm's output is not restricted by unavailability of factors and the prices of factors are given to the firm. This signifies that the firm is also a price taker on the input side.
- There is no government intervention in the industry. There are no official distortions that affect the ability of the industry to reach its 'natural' equilibrium.

9.1.2 Demand features

This market structure has peculiar demand features for the firm. The assumption of a large number of buyers and sellers means that the firm in a perfectly competitive industry cannot determine the market price on its own and is therefore deemed a ***price-taker***. The equilibrium price in the market is determined by the demand and supply in the market (industry). The firm can sell all it wishes to sell at the going market price.

The demand curve for the firm is therefore a horizontal straight line at the level of the equilibrium market price. It should be appreciated that, for this market structure, two diagrams, firm and industry, must be used simultaneously. It must be recognized that the two diagrams are on different scales.

In Figure 9.1 the diagram to the right shows the intersection of the supply and demand curves in the market giving an equilibrium price of P^* and an equilibrium quantity of Q^*. Once this equilibrium price is determined in the market, the individual firm can sell all its units at this price. This price line for the firm therefore becomes its demand curve, or average revenue (AR) curve. Moreover, since each additional unit can be sold at the same price, this demand or average revenue curve is also the firm's marginal revenue (MR) curve.

Hence the firm in a perfectly competitive market structure faces a horizontal (perfectly elastic) demand curve such that: $P = AR = MR$.

9.1.3 Supply (cost) features

The model of perfect competition, like all the traditional models of the firm, adopts the traditional U-shaped short-run cost curve and basin-shaped long-run cost curve.

The supply curve of the firm is its Marginal Cost (MC) curve above its intersection with the Average Variable Cost (AVC) curve (the closing down point). This becomes clearer once the short-run optimizing behaviour is understood.

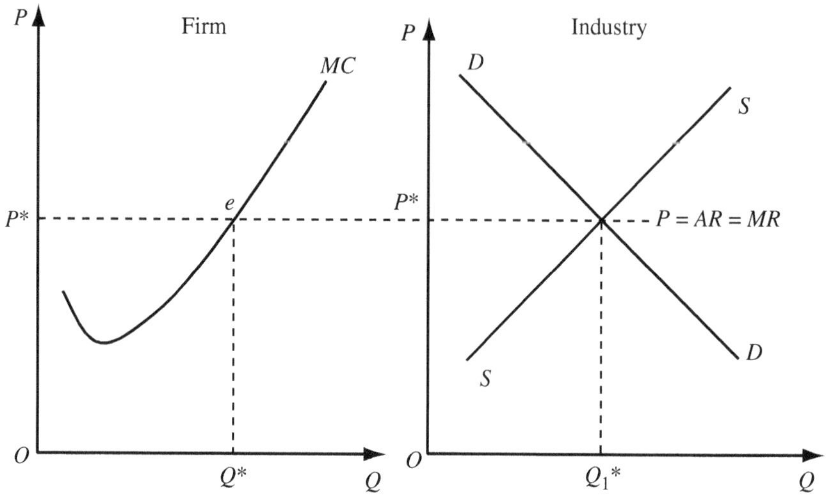

Figure 9.1
The price-taker firm's price is determined by industry equilibrium under Perfect Competition ($P = AR = MR$)

9.2 SHORT-RUN EQUILIBRIUM

The individual firm in a perfectly competitive industry is a price taker. Its equilibrium price depends on the industry price. Hence, it is necessary to consider the firm and industry (market) equilibrium simultaneously.

Since the aim of the firm is to maximize profits, the firm is considered to be in equilibrium when its profits are maximized. There are two basic approaches to equilibrium:

- The total revenue–total cost approach
- The marginal revenue–marginal cost approach

These will be dealt with separately.

The firm aims to maximize profit (Π) where profit is measured as the difference between total revenue (TR) and total cost (TC) expressed as:

$$\Pi = TR - TC$$

9.2.1 The total revenue–total cost approach

Profit is the difference between total revenue and total costs. Hence, in the diagrams in Figure 9.2 profits start at Q_1 and end at Q_2, the points where the total revenue (TR) and the total cost (TC) curves intersect. Diagrammatically, profit is maximized where there is the greatest (vertical) difference between the total revenue and total cost curves. Mathematically, using the calculus of variations, this incidentally is where the slopes of the TR and TC curves are the same. Since the slope of the TR curve is the marginal

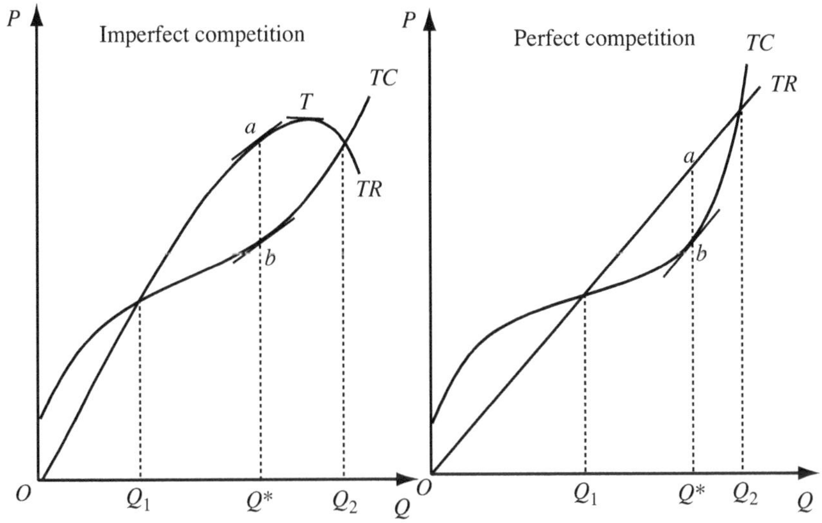

Figure 9.2
The total-revenue, total-cost approach to profit maximization with the special case of Perfect Competition on the right

revenue (*MR*) and the slope of the total cost curve is the marginal cost (*MC*) then this is where $MC = MR$.

The total revenue–total cost approach may be considered with respect to the general case (for all markets) and the specific case of Perfect Competition.

In general, for a firm facing a downward sloping demand curve, the total revenue (*TR*) curve assumes its typical shape, as in the left diagram of Figure 9.2. The total cost (*TC*) curve also assumes its usual shape as a result of the cubic polynomial cost function. The point *T* is where total revenue is at its highest. This is where the slope of the *TR* curve (*MR*) is zero ($MR = 0$). Since profit is maximized where the slope of the total cost curve (*MC*) is equal to the slope of the total revenue curve (*MR*), and since the slope of the marginal cost curve is not zero directly below the point *T* (or anywhere along its length), the point *T* cannot represent a profit maximization point. Furthermore, since the *TC* curve has a positive slope throughout, the two slopes can only be equal when the *TR* curve is rising (i.e. before the point *T*). Consequently, the profit maximizing point must lie to the left of the point *T* at the point represented by the quantity Q^*. The vertical distance *ab* is where there is the greatest vertical difference between the *TR* and the *TC* curves and hence where the maximum profit is obtained. Since the slopes of *TC* and *TR* are equal, it means that *MC* is equal to *MR*.

For the perfectly competitive firm, however, the *TR* curve is a straight line out of the origin (all additional units can be sold at the same price – i.e. the firm is a price taker) as shown in the diagram to the right in Figure 9.2. The profit maximization position is therefore the point where a line drawn tangent to the *TC* curve is parallel to the *TR* curve (i.e. the slope of the *TC* curve is equal to the slope of the *TR* curve). Maximum profit is represented by the distance *ab* and is found at the quantity Q^*.

The $TR - TC$ approach is awkward when firms are combined together in a study of the industry, hence the alternative $MC = MR$ approach is often used.

9.2.2 The marginal cost–marginal revenue ($MC = MR$) approach

It has been noted that the greatest distance between the TR and TC curves is where the slopes of these two curves are equal. Hence, the slope of the TR curve (i.e. MR) must be equal to the slope of TC curve (i.e. MC). This is the first-order condition and is necessary but not sufficient. This can be formally derived as follows.

The first-order (necessary) condition for profit maximization

The aim of the firm is to maximize profits hence the objective function may be written as:

$$\text{Max: } \Pi = R - C$$

Differentiating with respect to quantity:

$$\frac{\partial \Pi}{\partial Q} = \frac{\partial R}{\partial Q} - \frac{\partial C}{\partial Q} = 0$$

Hence:

$$\frac{\partial R}{\partial Q} = \frac{\partial C}{\partial Q}$$

or:

$$MR = MC$$

It should be noted that, since the first derivative of a function is the slope of the function, MC is the slope of the TC (now written simply as C) and MR is the slope of the revenue function (R). Hence:

$$\frac{\partial C}{\partial Q} = MC$$

$$\frac{\partial R}{\partial Q} = MR$$

The second-order (sufficient) condition for profit maximization

This first-order condition is necessary ***but not sufficient***. The second-order condition must therefore be found. In order to maximize a function the second derivative must be less than zero. Thus, the second order condition becomes:

$$\frac{\partial^2 \pi}{\partial Q^2} = \frac{\partial^2 R}{\partial Q^2} - \frac{\partial^2 C}{\partial Q^2} < 0$$

This may be re-written as:

$$\frac{\partial^2 R}{\partial Q^2} < \frac{\partial^2 C}{\partial Q^2}$$

Recalling that the second-derivative is the slope of the first derivative, then, the slope of the *MR* curve is:

$$\frac{\partial^2 R}{\partial Q^2}$$

and the slope of the *MC* curve is:

$$\frac{\partial^2 C}{\partial Q^2}$$

The second-order condition for profit maximization may therefore be stated as:

$$\text{Slope } MC > \text{Slope } MR$$

The conditions for equilibrium (profit maximization) may now be stated thus:

- first-order condition (necessary condition): $MC = MR$
- second-order condition (sufficient condition): Slope MC > slope MR

For the firm in a perfectly competitive industry, since the $MR = AR$ and the *AR* curve is horizontal, the *MR* curve is also horizontal. This means it has a slope of zero. Hence, in order for the *MC* curve to have a greater slope than the *MR* curve, the *MC* curve must have a positive slope. Consequently, the second-order condition is fulfilled ***only*** where the ***MC curve is rising*** (i.e. has a positive slope) at its point of intersection with the horizontal *MR* curve. This is extremely important for a firm in this market structure.

9.2.3 Importance of second-order condition for perfect competition

For a firm in a perfect competition industry, the second-order condition is of extreme importance. This is so for three principal reasons.

1 Since the *MR* curve for the firm under perfect competition is horizontal, it is highly likely for the *MC* curve to cut the *MR* curve twice. The first-order condition would then be met twice (at e_1 and e_2 in Figure 9.3). It is therefore essential that the second-order condition be checked for fulfilment.

2 When the perfectly competitive firm is operating where the first-order condition is fulfilled but the second-order is not, then the firm ***MUST be making a LOSS***. This is because the *MC* curve is falling at e_1 instead of rising and where *MC* is falling, then *AC* ***must*** be above *MC* (the falling *MC* brings down the *AC*, hence *AC* must

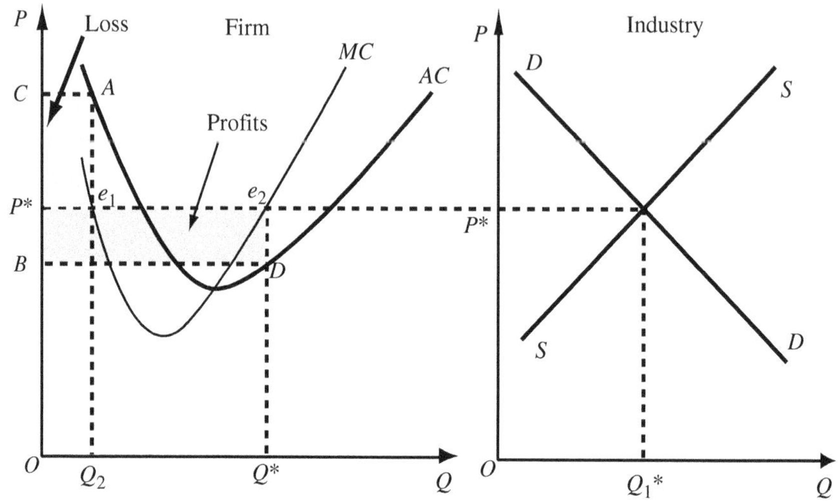

Figure 9.3
Firm in perfectly competitive industry makes a loss where the second-order condition for profit maximization is not fulfilled

be above *MC*). And since $MC = MR$ at this point, and $MR = AR$, then $MC = AR$. Thus, since *AC* is above *MC*, *AC* must also be above *AR*. The average cost of production ***must*** be above the average revenue from production, which means that the firm ***must*** be suffering a loss. This loss is shown in Figure 9.3 in the lightly shaded area CAe_1P^*. At e_2 the firm may be making a profit or a loss. At e_2, if the firm is making a profit, then it is maximizing profits and if it is making a loss then it is minimizing losses. Figure 9.3 shows the firm making a profit (excess profits) equivalent to the darker shaded area P^*e_2DB.

3 The perfectly competitive firm operating at e_1 is not only making a loss but is actually maximizing losses. Since $MC = MR$ where there is the greatest total difference between the *TR* and *TC* curves, this is also true in the area of losses (refer to Figure 9.2 to see area of losses). Hence the loss at e_1 is the greatest loss for the firm.

In the final short-run equilibrium, where both first- and second-order conditions are fulfilled, some firms may make excess profits while others make losses because of differences in cost conditions and should, in theory, only occur in the very short-run until all firms have the same information and can access the same resources. Figure 9.4 illustrates the case. Firm *A* is the high cost firm operating at a loss, represented by the lightly shaded area in the leftmost diagram, whereas firm *B* is a low cost firm making excess profits, as represented by the darker shaded area in the middle diagram of Figure 9.4.

9.2.4 The *MC* and supply curves

Under Perfect Competition, the supply curve for the firm is the *MC* curve to the right of (above) the ***closing down point***. The closing down point is at the minimum point of

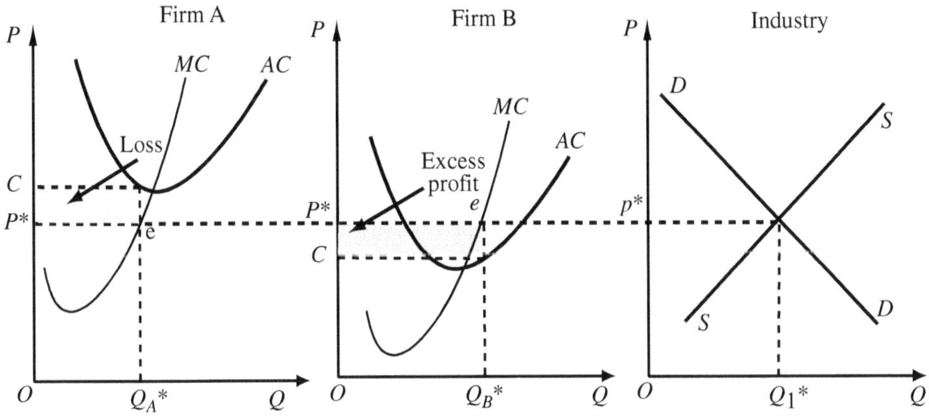

Figure 9.4
Loss-making and profit-making firms in a perfectly competitive industry

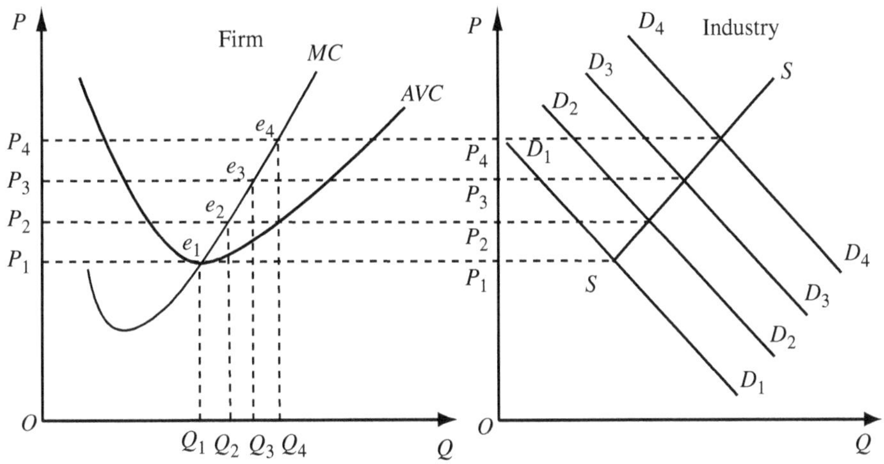

Figure 9.5
The supply curve of the firm in a perfectly competitive industry

the short-run average variable cost (*AVC*) curve. When price is at this point, the firm is just covering its day to day (operating) expenses. If price should go below Min. *AVC*, the firm cannot continue to operate and must close down.

This is illustrated by the two diagrams in Figure 9.5. The firm in the left diagram takes its equilibrium price from the market (industry) equilibrium between supply and demand in the diagram on the right. Since, for a perfectly competitive firm $P = MR$, the equilibrium point is where $P = MC$ (i.e. $MR = MC$). Hence, as demand in the market shifts giving new equilibrium prices from P_1 through P_4, the equilibrium points for the firm shift along the *MC* curve from e_1 through e_4.

The supply curve for the firm is described by the locus of points beginning at e_1 and going through e_4 and beyond. The industry or market supply curve is simply the horizontal sum of the supply curves of the individual firms in the industry.

9.3 LONG-RUN EQUILIBRIUM

The adjustment to long-run equilibrium in the industry is governed by the market mechanism and effected through the entry and exit of firms. In the long-run, all firms end up at the minimum point of the *LAC* curve, and the demand curve for the firm is tangent to the minimum point of the *LAC* curve.

9.3.1 The market mechanism

The existence of excess profits in the short-run encourages the entry of new firms and expansion of existing firms (building larger plants) in the long-run. The result of this is an expansion in supply, manifested as an outward shift in the industry supply curve, and a consequential fall in the equilibrium price. Entry continues until all excess profits are eroded and there is no further incentive for firms to enter or to expand. The process ceases when the expanded supply causes the equilibrium price to fall to the minimum point of the long-run average cost curve. This expanded supply is shown in the industry diagram in Figure 9.6 as an outward (downward) shift in the supply curve from S_1 to S_2. Consequently, the equilibrium price falls from P_1 to P_2. The rightward shift continues until the new equilibrium price coincides with the minimum point of the *LAC* curve.

The final long-run equilibrium position is:

$$P = MR = AR = \text{Min. } LAC = \text{Min. } SAC$$

Figure 9.6 shows the initial short-run equilibrium position for the firm at P_1Q_1 providing excess profits. Here, each firm is on its short-run SAC_1 curve. The excess profits encourage the entry of new firms and the expansion of existing firms. As a result of the expansion in supply in the industry, the supply curve shifts outwards from S_1S_1 to S_2S_2. The entry of firms ceases at this point as all excess profits are eroded. All existing and new firms are on SAC_2, producing at Q_2.

For the industry (market), long-run equilibrium is achieved when all firms are at minimum point of the *LAC* curve. In the long-run there are zero excess profits in the industry. No additional firms are attracted into the industry and there is no reason for firms to exit.

9.3.2 Perfect competition and economic efficiency

In this market structure, the industry is considered to achieve economic efficiency through the optimal allocation of resources in the long-run. This is because of the following features of the long-run equilibrium:

- All firms operate at the optimal scale which means that output is produced at minimum feasible cost using the lowest cost plant. The lowest cost or optimal scale plant is that which is found at the minimum point of the long-run average cost curve (Min. *LAC*).

- Since all firms are at minimum point of the *LAC*, they are at the point which coincides with the minimum point of their *SAC*. This indicates that the plant is used optimally (i.e. at full or designed capacity).
- All firms make just normal profits (zero excess profits) because price (or average revenue) is tangent to their long-run and short-run average cost of production.
- The consumer pays the lowest price possible. This is the price that just covers marginal cost or opportunity cost of production.

It should be recognized that the perfectly competitive market structure meets the conditions for economic efficiency only in a static sense. The outcome is desirable only where there are no further opportunities for economic growth. Since firms make only normal profits (opportunity cost of investment) it leaves no room for research and development to generate new products and processes. Consequently, the model does not allow for firms to generate what the classical economists called a 'wages fund' for expansion of industry and further employment. The expansion requires a surplus above normal profits out of which new productive activities are spawned to foster growth in output and employment.

9.4 PREDICTIONS OF THE MODEL

An understanding of the mechanics of the model allows predictions to be made about the outcome of changes to key variables such as demand, costs and taxes. This takes the analysis into the realm of dynamics or comparative statics.

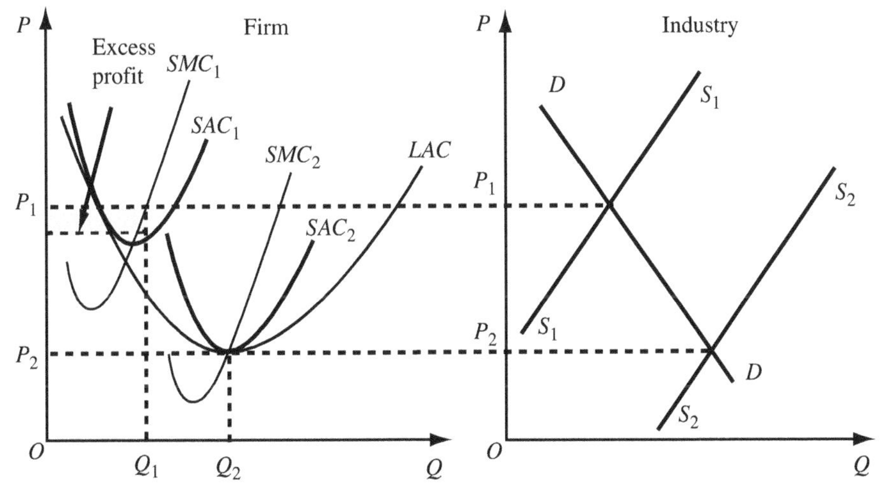

Figure 9.6
The movement from short-run to long-run equilibrium under Perfect Competition

9.4.1 Effect of changes in demand

Consider that the perfectly competitive firm is in its long-run equilibrium (at min. *LAC*) when there is an increase in demand manifested as an outward shift in the demand curve. This increase in demand may be caused by an increase in income, taste or preference for the product, or change in the price of another related product. The market mechanism operates in the following sequence:

- The increase in demand shifts the demand curve to the right.
- This results in a rise in equilibrium price.
- This leads to an increase in excess profits (Π) for all firms in the industry.
- The excess profits provide an incentive for the entry of new firms.
- The increased output from the new firms cause an outward (rightward) shift in the supply curve.
- The increased supply causes a fall in the equilibrium price in the industry.
- The entry of new firms, rightward shift in the supply curve and consequent fall in the equilibrium price continues until all excess profits are eliminated and firms are at the minimum point of the *LAC*. Note that there are now more firms in the industry.

Before the change in demand, price is at the minimum point of the *LAC* and after the process has worked itself out, price is again at the minimum point of the *LAC*. However, this final equilibrium price may or may not be the same as the initial equilibrium price before the increase in demand since the new position of the *LAC* may or may not be the same as before. This depends on whether the industry is a ***constant***, *increasing* or ***decreasing*** cost industry. This nomenclature refers to the conditions outside of the industry that affect the cost of inputs into the industry and are affected by the change in demand within the industry. This is of the nature of external economies and diseconomies.

Constant cost industry

Consider an increase in demand for the product of the perfectly competitive firm. With a constant cost industry, as the industry expands and demands more inputs, there is no change in the price of inputs and so the *LAC* remains in the same position as before the expansion in the industry. Hence the final equilibrium returns to the same as the original point.

The mechanism of adjustment may therefore be described in the following sequence, making reference to Figure 9.7:

- The firm is in long-run equilibrium at price P_0 when there is an increase in demand. This increase causes the demand curve to shift to the right from DD to D_1D_1.
- This leads an increase in equilibrium price from P_0 to P_1.
- This brings short-run excess profits, as shown by the shaded area in Figure 9.7.

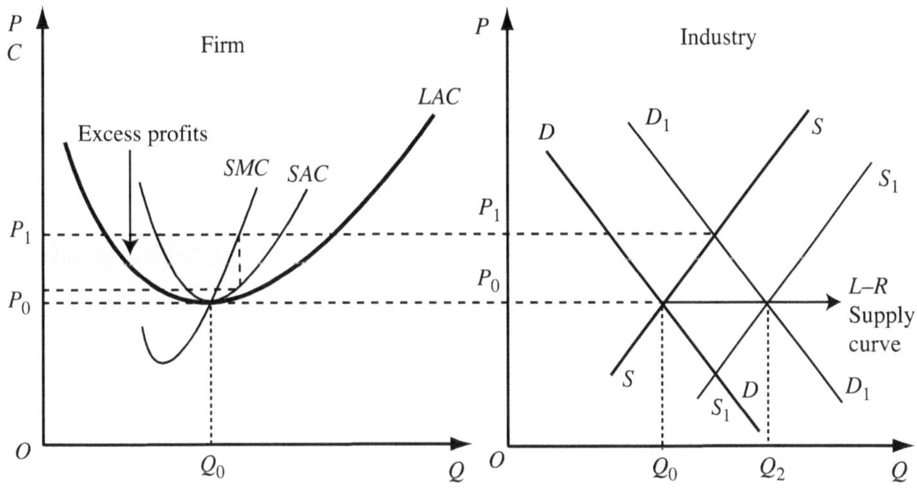

Figure 9.7
The long-run industry supply curve under Perfect Competition for a constant-cost industry

- The excess profits attract new firms which enter the industry. Existing and new firms are expected to all have the same costs.
- The new firms add to output causing an outward shift in the supply curve.
- The outward shift in the supply curve leads to a fall in the equilibrium price.
- The process of entry, increased supply and falling price continues until all excess profits are exhausted. This occurs when price is falls to min. *LAC*. There is no further incentive for firms to enter or to exit.

However, with this expansion in output in the industry, the *LAC* curve has remained in the same position as illustrated in Figure 9.7. Consequently, after entry, when supply shifts out sufficiently to cause price to fall to the minimum point of the *LAC*, the new final price is the same as the original price since Min. *LAC* is in the same position as before the increase in demand. Thus price returns to P_0 and the long-run supply curve for the industry is a horizontal line as shown by the arrowed line in Figure 9.7. All firms are now producing at Q_0, but the number of firms in the industry is now greater.

Increasing cost industry

For an increasing cost industry, the long-run supply curve has a positive slope. This results from the existence of certain ***external*** diseconomies, which force up the price of inputs as more of them are demanded because of the expansion of the industry due to the increase in demand. The increase in the price of inputs causes the *LAC* to shift upwards as industry supply increases.

Using the graphs in Figure 9.8, the market mechanism is similar to that described above.

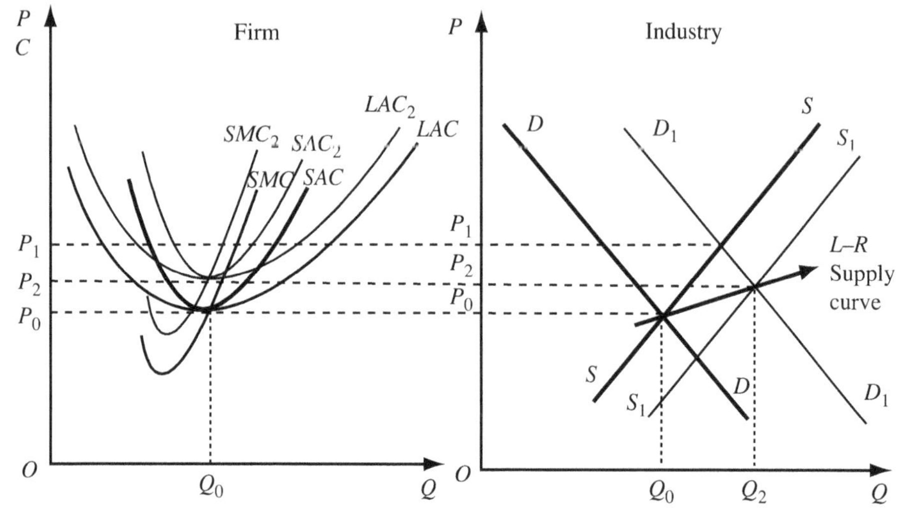

Figure 9.8
The long-run industry supply curve under Perfect Competition for an increasing-cost industry

The increase in demand causes the demand curve to shift to the right from *DD* to D_1D_1 causing the equilibrium price to rise from P_0 to P_1, thereby generating excess profits. These excess profits attract the entry of firms and the increased output shifts the supply curve to the right causing the equilibrium price to fall until it reaches min. *LAC*. The difference here is that min. *LAC* is now higher than it was before the increase in demand. Factors external to the firm have caused the cost of inputs to increase now that a larger quantity of inputs is demanded by the firm. This has shifted the *LAC* upwards and the *SMC* along with it, thereby squeezing out some of the excess profits and curbing the incentive to new firms to enter the industry and expand supply. Because the outward shift of the supply curve is curtailed, the equilibrium price does not fall as far as it would under a constant cost industry. Hence, in Figure 9.8, the new final equilibrium price level, P_2, is above the original equilibrium price level P_0 and industry supply moves from Q_0 to Q_2. Consequently, the long-run supply curve in the industry is upward sloping.

It is important to note, however, that each firm still supplies Q_0. The increased supply comes from the larger number of firms in the industry. This number is not as large as in the case of the constant cost industry.

Deceasing cost industry

For a decreasing-cost industry the long-run supply curve has a negative slope. In this case there are external economies which lead to a reduction in the price of inputs to the industry as industry demand for these inputs increases.

Using the diagrams in Figure 9.9, the mechanism once again follows the process described for the other two cases above. In this case, as before, in the final equilibrium after the increase in demand and expansion in supply, price falls back to the min. *LAC*.

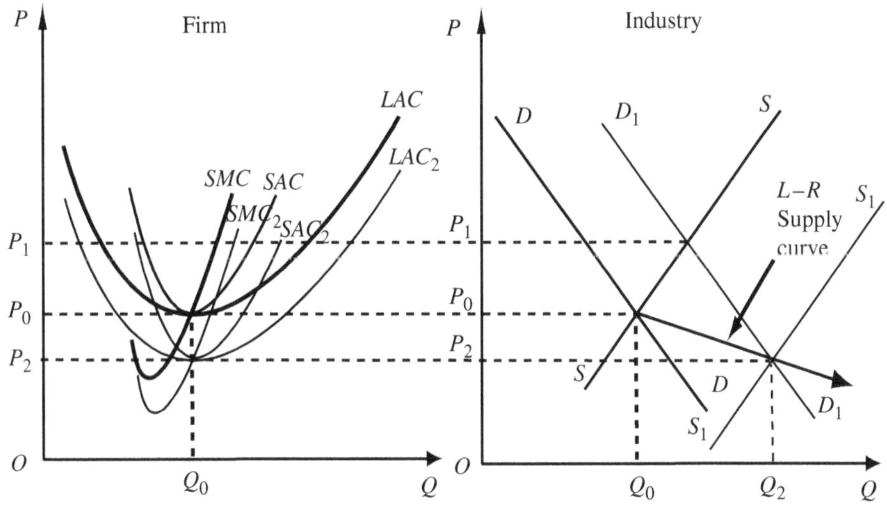

Figure 9.9
The long-run industry supply curve under Perfect Competition for a decreasing-cost industry

However, with the increased demand for inputs causing their price to fall, the *LAC* curve has shifted downwards (and the *SMC*). This adds to the excess profits remaining in the industry thereby further sustaining the incentive for firms to enter and causing a greater rightward shift in the supply curve. Hence, as price falls to the new min. *LAC* this is now below the original min. *LAC*. Hence, as shown in Figure 9.9, the new final equilibrium price level P_2 is ***below*** the original equilibrium price level P_0 and the quantity supplied in the market has moved from Q_0 to Q_2. Consequently the long-run supply curve is downward sloping as shown by the arrowed curve in Figure 9.9.

Each firm still supplies Q_0. The increased supply comes from the larger number of firms in the industry. In this case the number of firms is larger than either in the constant cost or increasing cost case.

Implication of the analysis

The implication of the foregoing analysis is that an expansion of demand for the output of a perfectly competitive industry, whether for the domestic market or for export, may or may not lead to a reduction in the price of that commodity in the long-run. In the first place, the initial price increase due to the increased demand and the consequential augmentation of profits will in the long-run be completely wiped out through the entry of new players within the industry. Additionally, the final effect of the increased demand on prices in the industry depends on factors outside of the industry and prices could be higher, lower or the same. Firms end up with just normal profits but the economic gain could be measured in the expansion of the number of firms in the industry and the increased demand for inputs.

9.4.2 Effect of changes in costs

Changes in fixed costs

Consider a perfectly competitive firm that is in the long-run equilibrium position when there is a change in fixed costs.

In the short-run if there is an increase in fixed costs in a perfectly competitive industry, that is in the long-run equilibrium, there is no change in the equilibrium quantity or price. The market mechanism works as follows:

- There is an increase in fixed costs while the firm is in its long-run equilibrium at min. *LAC*.
- This leads to an increase in the average fixed cost (*AFC*) and short-run average total cost (*SATC*) curves but ***there is no change in SMC or SAVC*** curves as illustrated in Figure 9.10 (fixed costs do not affect marginal costs).
- Hence the $MC = MR$ position remains unchanged and so do the equilibrium price and quantity (P_0, Q_0) as shown in Figure 9.10.
- However, the firms will not be covering their average total costs and will therefore be making losses.

In the longer term, because of the losses being incurred, some firms (the weakest or the smartest) will exit the industry. The industry supply curve will shift upwards to the left. This leads to a higher equilibrium price in the industry and a reduction in quantity supplied because of fewer firms in the industry. Thus output is lower and price higher in the long-run.

This analysis is of importance because the idea of leaving price and quantity unchanged in the face of rising fixed costs is highly counter intuitive. Yet, any other action would move each firm from the profit maximizing (or loss minimizing) position and be worse for the firm. In the final analysis, some firms will have to exit. This is significant from

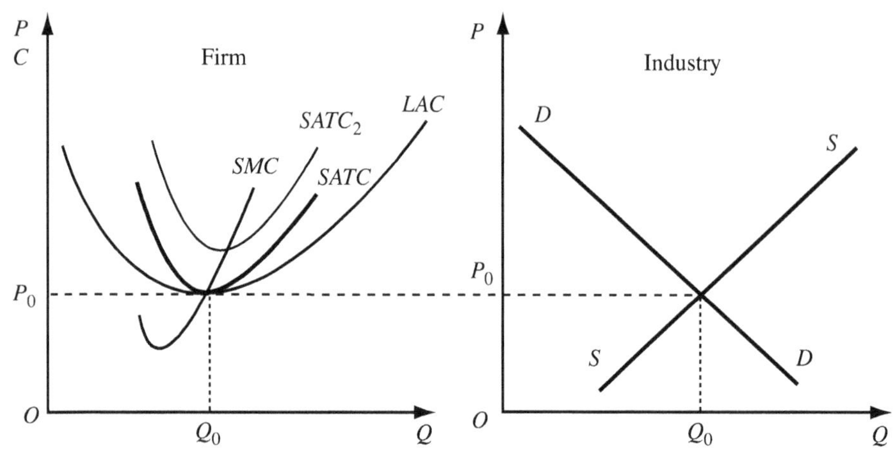

Figure 9.10
An increase in fixed cost has no short-run effect on equilibrium price or quantity for a firm in a perfectly competitive industry

a policy perspective as it suggests that, where fixed costs are increasing, the number of firms in a perfectly competitive industry will be reduced as some firms will be forced to go out of business.

Changes in variable costs

Consider again a perfectly competitive firm in the long-run equilibrium position when there is an increase in variable costs. In the case of variable costs the short-run marginal cost (*SMC*) curve is affected. The mechanism is as follows:

- The increase in variable costs shifts the *SMC* curve upwards and to the left. This is shown in Figure 9.11.
- This shift from *SMC* to SMC_2 in Figure 9.11 leads to an immediate short-run contraction in supply for each firm from Q_0 to Q_2.
- The contraction in supply by each firm causes the industry supply curve to contract as reflected in a shift upwards and to the left (inwards). The *AVC* and *ATC* curves all rise.
- The inward shift in the supply curve causes the equilibrium price to rise immediately in the short-run and the quantity supplied to fall. This is unlike the case of an increase in fixed costs.

Where prices have not caught up to the new higher *SATC* and min. *LAC* then, in the long-run, the losses suffered cause firms to exit, leading to further contraction in output and rise in price until price reaches the new higher min. *LAC*. In the long-run, therefore, prices are higher, quantity lower and there are fewer firms in the industry because of the increase in variable costs. It is significant that, unlike in the case of an increase in fixed costs where there is no change in price or quantity in the short-run, part of the

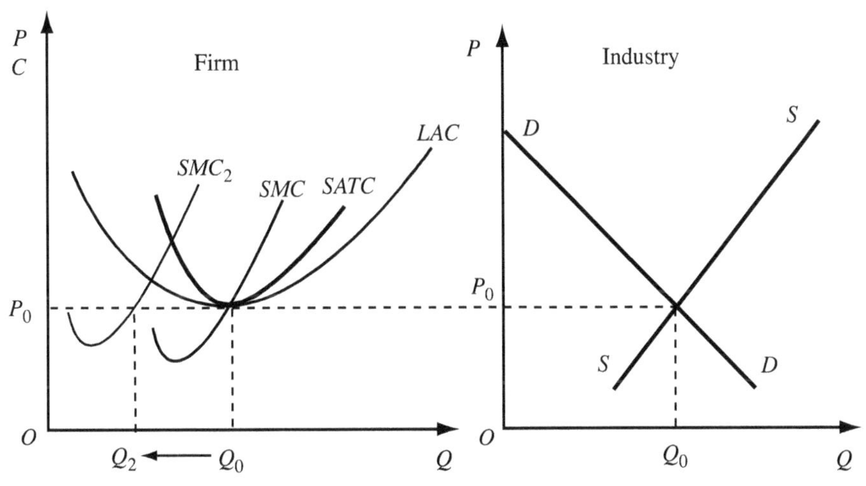

Figure 9.11
Short-run effect of an increase in variable cost on firm in a perfectly competitive industry

increase in variable costs is passed on immediately through higher prices and reduced supply.

9.4.3 Effect of imposition of a tax

Lump-sum tax or profits tax

The effects of a lump-sum tax are identical to those of an increase in fixed costs for a firm in the long-run equilibrium position under perfect competition. When a lump-sum tax is imposed, it has to be treated by the firm as a fixed cost. Consequently, a change in the lump-sum tax affects neither the *MC* nor *MR*. In the short-run therefore the equilibrium price and quantity should remain unchanged. Because of the higher fixed costs, the firm incurs losses which encourage the exit of firms in the long-run leading to a higher equilibrium price and lower output in the industry.

The effects of a profits tax are similar to those of a lump-sum tax. Profits are reduced or losses occur, but $MC = MR$ is not affected and so there is no change in the equilibrium price and quantity in the short-run. In the long-run, because of the losses, firms exit, the supply curve shifts upwards and to the left, leading to a reduced supply, higher prices and a reduced number of firms in the industry.

In a practical sense, public policy on taxes applied to firms in a perfectly competitive industry in its long-run equilibrium position must take into account such effects. A lump-sum or profits tax on such firms, even though not affecting price or output initially, would put the firms into a loss position. Furthermore, it would lead to higher prices, lower output and fewer firms in the long-run.

Per-unit or sales tax

A per unit or sales tax is one charged on every unit of output sold. As such it affects the *MC* of the firm (for all firms). The effect is therefore similar to that of an increase in variable costs. The *MC* curve shifts upwards and to the left for all firms causing the market supply curve to shift upwards and to the left, leading to a reduced supply and a higher price in the short-run.

This is exacerbated in the long-run as prices rise further and supply is also reduced further as firms exit the industry. This is the same pattern as explained under the effect of an increase in variable costs. This outcome must be taken into account in public policy when a per-unit tax such as a sales tax or a value-added tax (VAT) is levied on firms in a perfectly competitive industry. It should be noted, however, that the full extent of the tax may or may not be passed on to the consumer. This analysis falls under the heading of the incidence of the tax.

Incidence of the tax

At issue here is the question of 'who bears the tax' which is known as the 'incidence' of the tax. If the intention is to tax the consumer as in a consumption tax or a VAT, then all of the tax may not be borne by the consumer. Instead, the supplier may be forced to bear a portion of the tax. If, on the other hand, the intention is to tax the supplier, then the

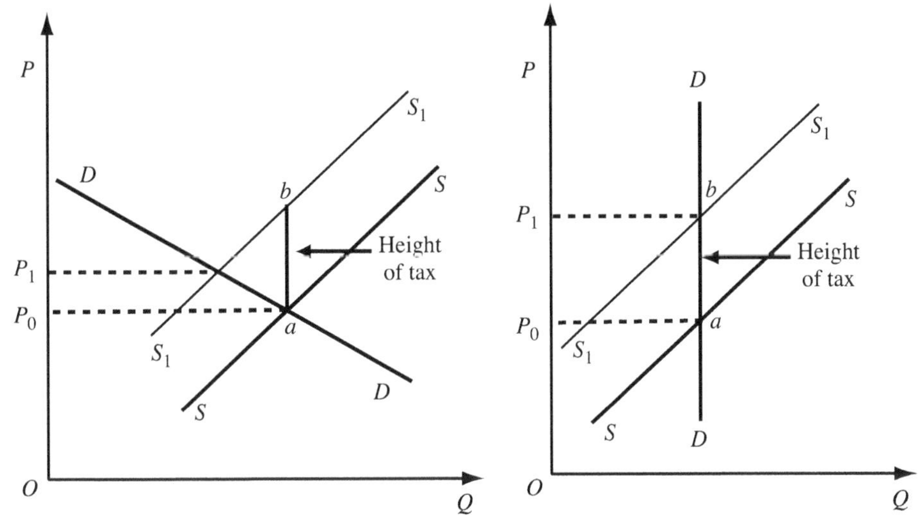

Figure 9.12
The role of the slopes of the demand and supply curves in determining the incidence of a tax on firms in a perfectly competitive industry

supplier may be able to pass a portion of the tax to the consumer. How much of the tax is borne by the consumer and how much is borne by the supplier (firm) depends not on the wishes of the tax administrator but on the relative slopes of the demand and supply curves. The more elastic the supply curve and the more inelastic the demand curve, the more of the tax is passed on to the consumer. This is shown in Figure 9.12.

In Figure 9.12, the left diagram shows a relatively elastic demand curve with relatively inelastic supply curves. The imposition of the tax shifts the supply curve upwards and to the left from *SS* to S_1S_1. The vertical distance between the two supply curves, *ab*, is the height of the tax. This causes the equilibrium price to increase from P_0 to P_1, a smaller price increase than the level of the tax imposed. This shows that all of the tax is not passed on to the consumer.

With infinite supply elasticity, or perfect inelasticity of demand, the whole of the tax burden is borne by the consumer. If the supply curve is negatively sloped the imposition of a specific sales tax leads to an increase in price which is greater than the tax imposed. The case of a perfectly inelastic demand curve is shown in the diagram on the right in Figure 9.12. The height of the tax, the vertical distance *ab* between the two supply curves, is the same as the increase in price from P_0 to P_1. This indicates that the entire tax placed on the supplier is passed on to (and paid by) the consumer.

As explained above, there are cases where the entire tax placed on the supplier can be passed on to the consumer. This is where the demand curve is perfectly inelastic (i.e. vertical) or where the supply curve is perfectly elastic (horizontal). In general, the more inelastic is demand, the more of a tax is passed on to the consumer. Likewise, the more elastic the supply, the more of a tax is passed on to the consumer.

On the contrary, the more elastic the demand, or the more inelastic the supply, the more of the tax is borne by the supplier. Hence, if the motivation for the tax is to collect from the consumer, then the tax may not fall totally on those for whom it was intended. Similarly, a tax intended to fall on the supplier may instead be paid largely by the consumer. Consequently, it is important that the incidence of the tax be clearly understood by the appropriate tax imposing authorities before a tax is implemented.

REVIEW QUESTIONS FOR CHAPTER 9

1 Carib Fishers is a hypothetical firm in a perfectly competitive industry.

(a) Carefully derive the first- and second-order conditions for Carib Fishers to achieve its goal of profit maximization in the market.
(b) Explain and illustrate why it is so important for Carib Fishers to ensure that its second-order condition for profit maximization is met.

2 Assume that Fruitier Enterprises is a representative firm in a perfectly competitive industry. Using diagrams explain:

(a) Why the demand curve for Fruitier Enterprises is a horizontal straight line.
(b) Why the marginal cost curve of Fruitier Enterprises is the firm's supply curve.

3 With regard to the perfectly competitive market, explain and illustrate:

(a) How the market mechanism operates to take the firm and industry from short-run to long-run equilibrium.
(b) How and why the perfectly competitive market is said to achieve 'economic efficiency' in the long-run equilibrium position.

4 A perfectly competitive industry is in its long-run equilibrium. Explain and illustrate how and why:

(a) An increase in demand affects the long-run equilibrium price, output and number of firms in the industry depending on whether it is in a constant, increasing or decreasing cost industry.
(b) An increase in fixed costs should not cause firms to sell at a higher price or reduce output in the short-run.
(c) An increase in variable costs affects industry price and output in the short- and the long-run.

5 With regard to a perfectly competitive industry:

(a) Explain and illustrate the theorized effect of a lump-sum or profits tax on equilibrium price and output in the industry.
(b) Illustrate the conditions that determine how much of a tax placed on suppliers can be passed on to consumers, explaining why a sales tax or value added tax (VAT) imposed on consumers through suppliers may not be fully passed on to the consumer

(c) Discuss the importance for policy makers to be cognizant of the factors which determine the incidence of a tax.

RECOMMENDED READING FOR CHAPTER 9

Kaldor, N. (1972) 'The Irrelevance of Equilibrium Economics', *Economic Journal*, 82(328): 1237–55.

McNulty, P. J. (1967) 'A Note on the History of Perfect Competition', *Journal of Political Economy*, 75(4 part 1): 395–99.

Stigler, J. C. (1987) 'Competition', *The New Palgrave: A Dictionary of Economics*, 1st Edn, 3: 531–46.

10 Monopoly

Equilibrium of the Firm, Industry in the Short-run and the Long-run; Multi-plant Monopoly; Price Discriminating Monopoly; Bi-lateral Monopoly; Government Regulation of Monopoly.

The model of monopoly is another of the traditional or 'marginalist' ($MC = MR$ for equilibrium) models of the firm. Typically, the smaller and more closed the economy, the more predominant is the monopoly form of market structure in certain industries. In theory, as an economy opens to global trade and investment, the importance of domestic monopolies should recede. Nevertheless, there are industries where, even in the most open economies, the market structure remains one of monopoly. This is particularly so in the case of domestic utility services and products such as electricity and water supply. This chapter examines how the monopolist market operates and considers monopoly in its many forms such as multi-plant, price discriminating and bi-lateral monopoly.

10.1 ASSUMPTIONS AND BEHAVIOURAL CONDITIONS

10.1.1 Basic assumptions of monopoly

- The firm is rational, that is, the goal of the firm is profit maximization.
- There is a single firm (i.e. there is a ***Single Seller***) in the industry. Consequently, the firm ***is*** the industry and there are no close substitutes, and hence no closely related industry.
- There is no entry of other firms to the industry. By definition a monopoly is an industry in which there can be no entry for various reasons, some of which are listed below.
- There is perfect knowledge of technology, demand and cost.
- All the required factors of production are available to the firm.

The factors which prevent entry and thereby permit monopolies to exist include:

- *Legal or Government Regulation* – a government might enact legislation to ensure that only one firm can operate in an industry. Government may have franchise or licensing laws that ensure the existence of the monopoly. In addition the existence of patents may prevent entry into an industry.

- *Raw Material Access* – a single firm may have sole access to a particular raw material(s) vital to the production of the output of the industry giving them total control over the industry (e.g. bauxite, iron ore).
- *Scale Barrier* – This is sometimes referred to as a 'natural' monopoly and may occur in an industry where the efficient size of plant is large relative to the size of the market (often seen in small economies). This may occur with respect to some utility companies and to extractive industries where the product or service is for the domestic market only (i.e. is not suitable for export).
- *Capital Barrier* – This is similar to and often linked with the scale barrier (above) and is the case where the amount of capital required to establish a firm is large relative to the market which the industry serves.

In the case of capital and scale barriers, even where, under global trading rules, a large foreign firm might have the capital required to enter the industry, the entrant firm has to consider that the domestic market may be too small to make sharing the market feasible.

This is particularly relevant in the case of a non-exportable good or service such as water or electricity distribution. In such cases the potential entrant has to plan a strategy for the take over or elimination of the existing domestic firm. In doing so the industry remains as a monopoly.

10.1.2 Demand and marginal revenue – Understanding the relationships

In studying the optimizing behaviour of the monopolist it is important to understand the relationship between the *MR* curve and the demand (*AR*) curve. It is important to recognize that the *MR* curve has twice the slope of the demand (*AR*) curve. This assists with graphing the model as well as the analysis.

For the monopolist, the typical demand curve is downward sloping. This is because of the absence of close substitutes. It is useful to examine some of the relationships to assist with understanding the diagrammatics of the industry and the process of equilibrium.

To understand the relationship between the demand or average revenue curve and the marginal revenue curve consider first the total Revenue (*R*) of Monopolist:

$$R = PQ$$

Then, writing the demand function as it is drawn with price as a function of quantity demanded (inverse of usual demand function):

$$P = a_0 - a_1 Q$$

The total revenue (*R*) may be written as:

$$R = PQ = a_0 Q - a_1 Q^2$$

Hence, the average revenue becomes:

$$AR = \frac{R}{Q} = a_0 - a_1 Q = P \quad \text{(i.e. same as the demand function)}$$

This confirms that the demand curve is indeed the *AR* curve.

Now, consider the marginal revenue (*MR*) curve. The *MR* is the first derivative of the total revenue (*R*). Hence, from above, where

$$R = PQ = a_0 Q - a_1 Q^2$$

then:

$$MR = \frac{dR}{dQ} \quad \text{or} \quad MR = a_0 - 2a_1 Q$$

If this is compared with the demand or *AR* curve ($P = a_0 - a_1 Q$), it can be seen that the MR curve has the ***same*** intercept as the demand (*AR*) curve (a_0) but has ***twice*** the gradient or slope ($2a_1 Q$ as opposed to $a_1 Q$) of the demand curve.

For this reason the marginal revenue curve is said to fall ***twice as fast*** as the demand curve. Diagrammatically, therefore, it falls ***half-way*** between the demand curve and the *Y*-axis, and therefore cuts the *X*-axis for the market in half. This is illustrated in Figure 10.1.

10.1.3 Costs

The cost curves used for the model of Monopoly are the same as those used for the model of perfect competition and for all of the traditional or marginalist models of the firm.

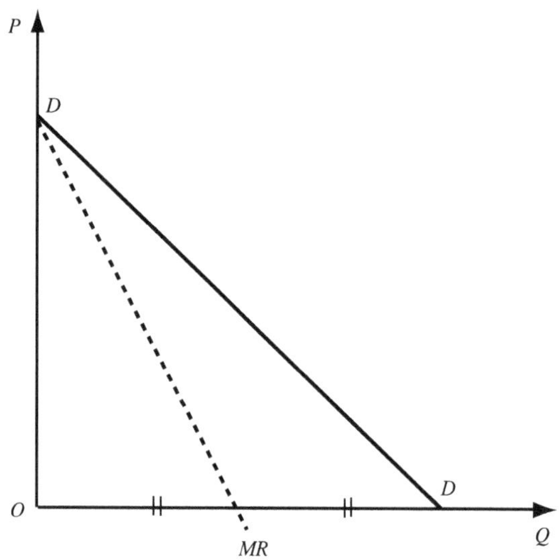

Figure 10.1
Demand and marginal revenue (*MR*) curves facing the monopolist

These are the traditional U-shaped short-run cost curves and the basin-shaped long-run cost curves.

It must be noted that the marginal cost (*MC*) curve cuts the average variable cost (*AVC*) curve where the *AVC* is at its minimum point. It is also important to note that, diagrammatically speaking, the marginal cost curve pulls the average cost downwards when it (the *MC*) is below the *AC* and pulls it upwards when it (the *MC*) is above the *AC*.

10.2 SHORT-RUN EQUILIBRIUM OF THE FIRM/INDUSTRY

With the monopolist, since the firm ***is*** the industry, the equilibrium of the firm is the equilibrium of the industry.

In considering the short-run equilibrium of the firm/industry there are a number of relationships that need to be clarified in order to enhance the practical usefulness of the model. These include:

- The reasons that lead to the second-order condition not being as important for a monopolist as for a firm in a perfectly competitive industry.
- Why the firm must always produce in the upper portion of the demand curve (above mid-point).
- The relationship between price elasticity of demand (η_P), marginal revenue, total revenue and profits showing how the effects of price changes on revenue and profits differ depending on whether $|\eta_P| > 1$ or $|\eta_P| < 1$.
- Following the formal derivation of the short-run equilibrium, these features are dealt with seriatim.

10.2.1 Deriving the equilibrium

As usual, noting that 'equilibrium' means profit maximization, it is best to start off with a mathematical derivation of equilibrium in order to set out more precisely the condition that must hold for this equilibrium to be achieved. This requires the derivation of the first-order or necessary condition and the second-order or sufficient condition for a maximum.

The aim of the firm is to maximize profits (Π), the difference between total revenue (R) and total cost (C). The first- and second-order conditions for profit maximization may therefore be set out as follows:

$$\text{Max}: \Pi = R - C$$

First-order condition

$$\frac{\partial \Pi}{\partial Q} = \frac{\partial R}{\partial Q} - \frac{\partial C}{\partial Q} = 0$$

$$\frac{\partial R}{\partial Q} = \frac{\partial C}{\partial Q} \quad \text{or} \quad MR = MC$$

In other words, the slopes of the total revenue (*MR*) and the total cost (*MC*) curves must be equal. ***It has already been pointed out that the geometry of curves is such that the two curves have their greatest distance from each other where their slopes are equal***.

Second-order condition

$$\frac{\partial^2 \Pi}{\partial Q^2} = \frac{\partial^2 R}{\partial Q^2} - \frac{\partial^2 C}{\partial Q^2} < 0$$

$$\frac{\partial^2 R}{\partial Q^2} < \frac{\partial^2 C}{\partial Q^2}$$

The second-order or sufficient condition requires that the slope of the *MC* curve be greater than the slope of the *MR* curve at the point of their intersection.

The monopolist must therefore equate *MC* with *MR* as illustrated in Figure 10.2. Both first- and second-order conditions are fulfilled at the intersection of the *MC* and *MR* curves. Here the slope of the *MC* curve is positive and so is greater than the slope of the *MR* curve which is negative. This determines the optimal quantity (Q^*). The price is then set at the corresponding point on the demand curve, giving P^* as the optimal price. These are the co-ordinates of the point Π on the demand curve which represents the point of profit maximization for the monopolist.

It may be observed that, whereas for the perfectly competitive firm price is equal to the marginal revenue, this is not so for the monopolist. In this case, price is always above the marginal revenue for any given level of output (*Q*).

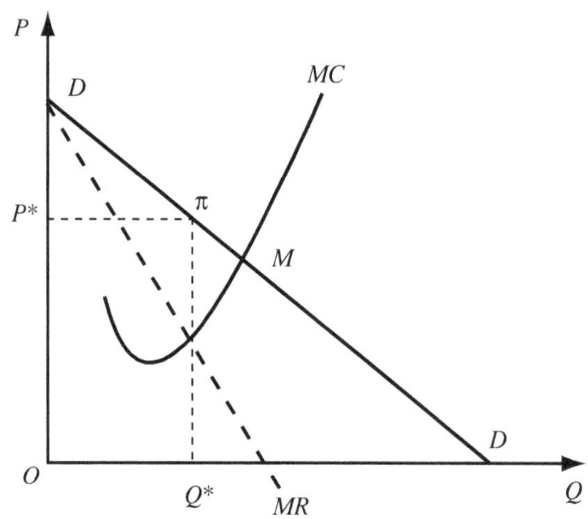

Figure 10.2
Short-run equilibrium for the monopolist

10.2.2 Limited importance of second-order condition

The second-order condition has been brought explicitly into the derivation of the equilibrium for the monopolist. However, although it is required for the profit maximization of the monopolist, its significance is of a somewhat lower order than it is for a perfectly competitive firm. The fulfilment of the second-order condition for the monopolist is not given, in practical applications, as much attention as it is for the perfectly competitive firm for three main reasons. These are:

1 With a negatively sloped *MR* curve, the second-order condition does not require that the *MC* curve be rising at its point of intersection with the *MR* curve as it does under perfect competition. It requires only that the slope of the *MC* curve be algebraically greater than (or, where both curves are negative, less steep than) the *MR* curve. Hence the second-order condition can still be fulfilled even when the *MC* curve cuts the *MR* curve when the *MC* curve is falling. This cannot happen with a perfectly competitive firm since the *MR* curve is horizontal (i.e. has a slope of zero) thereby requiring that the *MC* be rising (positively sloped) at its point of intersection with the *MR* curve.

2 Because the *MR* curve is so very steep in its downward slope (twice as steep as the demand curve which is already steep due to lack of goods that are close substitutes), it is highly unlikely that the *MC* curve will cut the *MR* curve twice (as at e_1 and e_2 in Figure 10.3). It is easy for this to occur under perfect competition where the *MR* curve is horizontal (slope of zero). For the second-order condition to be violated by a monopolist, therefore, the *MC* curve must be falling faster

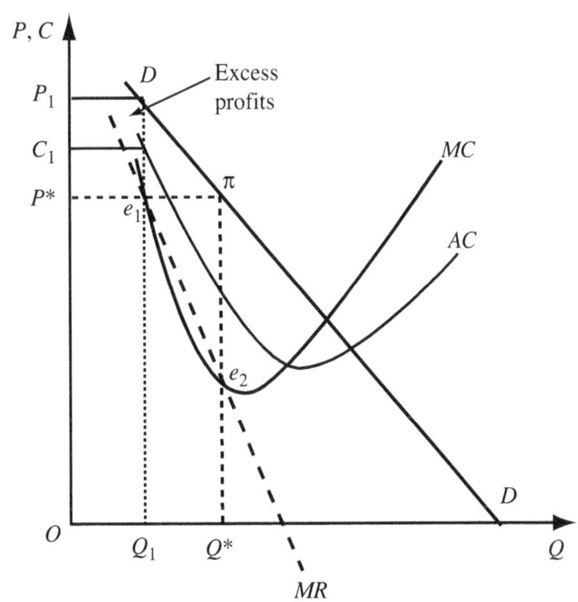

Figure 10.3
Monopolist profits without satisfying the second-order condition for profit maximization

(i.e. steeper negatively) than the already steep *MR* curve. This, though possible, as illustrated in the Figure 10.3, is an extreme case.

3 Furthermore, because for a monopolist, price is above *MR*, then, even where the second-order condition is violated (as e_1 in Figure 10.3), it is still possible for the monopolist to make profits and even excess profits at this point. This is the shaded area shown in Figure 10.3. Although *AC* is above *MC* when *MC* is falling, the fact that the price (*AR*) is above *MR* means that it is possible for the price (P_1) to be above the average cost (C_1) when selling the quantity Q_1. Consequently, the monopolist may make excess profits even when operating at e_1, where the second-order condition is not fulfilled and selling the quantity Q_1 at price P_1.

This is unlike the perfectly competitive firm where violation of the second-order condition means that the firm ***must*** makes a loss. Whether the monopolist makes a loss depends on the position of the demand curve relative to the average cost curve with respect to the e_1 position. In practice, therefore, checks for verification of the second-order condition are often omitted for the monopoly firm. It is important to note, however, that the monopolist ***will*** make greater profits by operating at e_2 (Q^*) where both the first- and the second-order condition are both satisfied and will ***maximize profits*** (or minimize losses) ***only*** at this point.

10.2.3 Why monopolist must sell above demand mid-point

It is important to note that the monopolist ***must always sell in the upper half of the demand curve*** if the firm is to maximize profits. From the equilibrium, as seen in Figures 10.2 and 10.3, it may be observed that the point of profit maximization must lie ***above the mid-point of the demand curve (M)***. This must always be so for two reasons:

1 Since profit maximization requires $MC = MR$, then, as long as *MC* is greater than zero, *MR* must be greater than zero for the two to be equal. *MR* is zero at the mid-point of the demand curve ($\eta_P = 1$) and positive everywhere above it.

2 Since *MC* is incremental or unit cost and relates only to variable (short-run) or operating costs then producing more units must be expected to incur additional incremental cost. *MC* can only be expected to be zero where there are zero operational or variable costs of production.

Consequently, the monopolist should produce only where $\eta_P > 1$ (i.e. $MR > 0$), that is, in the upper portion of the demand curve, if profits are to be maximized. This only occurs in the upper portion of the demand curve where price elasticity is greater than one.

10.2.4 Price changes, elasticity, revenue and profit

The relationship between price elasticity of demand, marginal revenue, total revenue and profit is one of the most significant for the monopolist for it determines how changes in price affect the income and the profitability of the firm. This is essential for informing decision making in areas vital to the survival of the firm.

10.2.4.1 MARGINAL REVENUE AND PRICE ELASTICITY

It is essential to understand the relationship between marginal revenue and price elasticity of demand (η_P).

The elasticity of demand may be written in an alternative format. The typical demand equation which expresses quantity demanded as function of price is used:

$$Q = b_0 - b_1 P$$

The slope or gradient of the demand function may be written as:

$$\frac{\mathrm{d}Q}{\mathrm{d}P} = -b_1$$

As set out previously, the elasticity of demand η_P may be written as:

$$\eta_P = \frac{\mathrm{d}Q/Q}{\mathrm{d}P/P} = \frac{\mathrm{d}Q}{\mathrm{d}P} \cdot \frac{P}{Q}$$

Then, it may be written as:

$$\eta_P = -b_1 \frac{P}{Q}$$

With the constant slope b_1, then elasticity varies as P/Q varies along the demand function.

Turning specifically to the relationship between MR and price elasticity (η_P), recall that MR is:

$$MR = \frac{\mathrm{d}R}{\mathrm{d}Q}$$

and:

$$R = PQ$$

Therefore MR can be written as:

$$MR = \frac{\mathrm{d}R}{\mathrm{d}Q} = P\frac{\mathrm{d}Q}{\mathrm{d}Q} + Q\frac{\mathrm{d}P}{\mathrm{d}Q}$$

Hence:

$$MR = P + Q\left(\frac{dP}{dQ}\right)$$

Recognizing that the slope of the demand function is negative, price elasticity of demand may be written as:

$$\eta_P = -\frac{dQ}{dP} \cdot \frac{P}{Q}$$

Consequently:

$$\frac{1}{\eta_P} = -\frac{dP}{dQ} \cdot \frac{Q}{P}$$

or:

$$\frac{dP}{dQ} = -\frac{1}{\eta_P} \cdot \frac{P}{Q}$$

Hence:

$$MR = P + Q\left(-\frac{1}{\eta_P} \cdot \frac{P}{Q}\right)$$

$$MR = P + \left(-\frac{P}{\eta_P}\right)$$

or:

$$MR = P\left(1 - \frac{1}{\eta_P}\right)$$

This relationship is important for the monopolist. It means that:

When $\eta_P = 1$,	$MR = 0$.	This occurs at the mid-point of the demand curve, where total revenue is at its maximum.
When $\eta_P > 1$,	$MR > 0$.	This occurs in the upper half of the demand curve.
When $\eta_P < 1$,	$MR < 0$.	This occurs in the lower half of the demand curve.

10.2.4.2 PRICE CHANGES, ELASTICITY AND REVENUE

The relationship between price elasticity of demand (η_P) and the marginal revenue of the firm is an extremely significant one, not only for a monopolist but for any imperfectly competitive firm. It is this relationship that determines the effects of price changes on the total revenue of the firm and on the profitability of the firm and should therefore be carefully studied.

The relationship:

$$MR = P\left(1 - \frac{1}{\eta_P}\right)$$

means that in the upper half (elastic portion) of the demand curve where $\eta_P > 1$ an increase in price reduces total revenue of the firm, while the reverse is true in the lower half (the inelastic portion) of the demand curve. Conversely, a reduction of price in the upper half (elastic portion) of the demand curve where $\eta_P > 1$ increases total revenue, while the reverse in true is the lower half (the inelastic portion) of the demand curve.

This comes about through the relationship between marginal and total revenue which has already been dealt with under the study of demand and elasticity in the analysis of consumer behaviour (Chapter 3). Moreover, the difference between maximum revenue (at the mid-point of the demand curve where $\eta_P = 1$) and maximum profit (somewhere in the upper half of the demand curve) is of further significance for the survival and profitability of the firm.

The diagrammatic representation is given in Figure 10.4. The lower portion of Figure 10.4 shows the demand and marginal revenue curves of the firm, whereas the respective total revenue curve is given in the upper portion of Figure 10.4.

Given that the mid-point of the demand curve is the point where price elasticity of demand is unity ($\eta_P = 1$), then by tracing the lines in Figure 10.4, it can be observed how price changes affect revenue. When price is increased in the upper or price-elastic portion of the demand curve ($\eta_P > 1$) from P_3 to P_4, the firm moves backwards down the total revenue curve TR_2 to TR_1 thereby lowering the total revenue of the firm. Hence, the increase in price lowers quantity and total revenue. Conversely, when the firm is operating in the lower or price-inelastic ($\eta_P < 1$) portion of the demand curve and it increases its price, say, from P_1 to P_2, the firm moves up the total revenue curve from TR_3 to TR_4 thereby lowering the total revenue of the firm. Here, while the price increase reduces quantity sold, it increases total revenue.

Furthermore, the situation is symmetric such that a lowering of price has the opposite effect. A lowering of price when the firm is operating in the upper (elastic) half of the demand curve brings an increase in total revenue to the firm, whereas a lowering of price when the firm is operating in the lower (inelastic) half causes the total revenue of the firm to fall.

The practical significance of marginal revenue and price elasticity is often lost on the less sophisticated firm. It has already been pointed out that firms should operate in the upper or elastic portion of the demand curve since it is only in this region that profits can be maximized. However, some firms operating in this elastic portion and seeking to increase revenue often expect to do so by way of a price increase. When a fall in revenue follows a price increase, the firm may seek a higher price increase, compounding the error. This could result in worsening a 'lose–lose' situation for both the firm and its consumers. Furthermore, in a globalized world, this situation could set up a domestic monopoly firm for takeover by a more sophisticated foreign firm.

But this is not the whole story for the firm which must consider not only total revenue but profit maximization. The aim of the firm is to maximize profit not total revenue; and

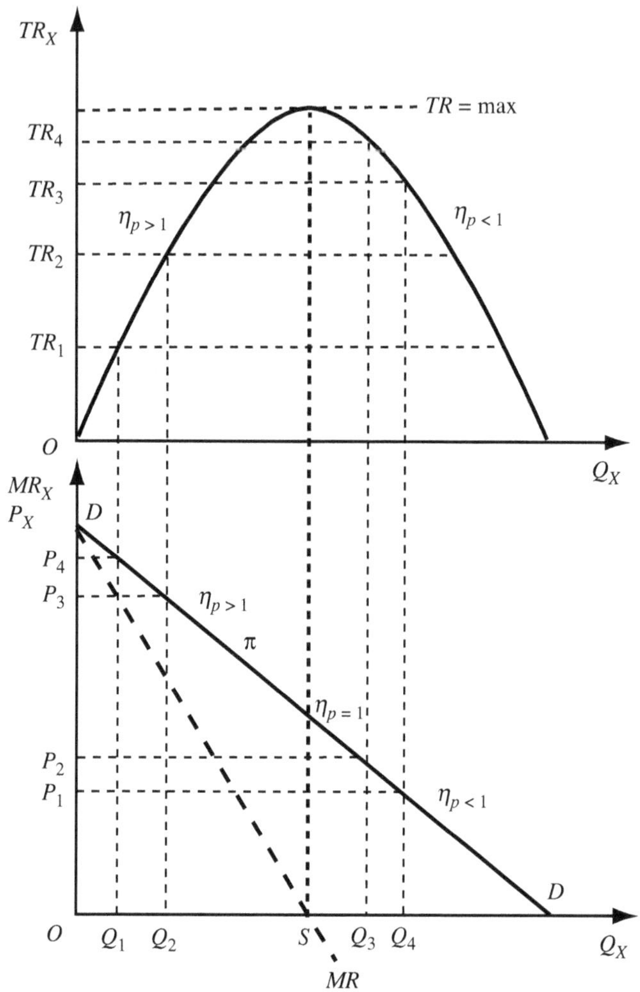

Figure 10.4
Effects of price changes on revenue as price elasticity of demand varies

the profit maximization and total revenue maximization positions do not coincide unless there is costless production.

10.2.4.3 TOTAL REVENUE VERSUS PROFIT MAXIMIZATION

This has two very significant implications for the monopolist. First, it means that the typical monopolist can almost always be expected to be in a position where an increase in price reduces total revenue. Second, and more importantly, it means that there is an area in the upper portion of the demand curve ***between the mid-point and the profit-maximization point (say π) on the demand curve*** where an increase in the price of the firm reduces the total revenue of the firm ***but increases the profit of the firm***. The converse also holds. If the firm is operating above this profit-maximization point (π) an increase in price causes a reduction in ***both*** total revenue ***and*** profit. Any monopolist, whether operating in a domestic market, a regional market or the global market must be cognizant of this feature.

10.2.5 Absence of supply curve

An interesting feature of the market structure of monopoly is the absence of a unique supply curve for the monopolist as there is for the perfectly competitive firm. This is so because:

- The *MC* curve does not describe unique equilibrium positions between price and quantity as it does for the perfectly competitive firm. This is because the price for the monopolist always lies above the *MR* curve as it is projected up to the demand curve. The height of the demand curve for the particular *MR* value will vary depending on the elasticity of demand (slope and position of the demand curve). The *MC* curve for a monopolist therefore cannot be described as a supply curve for the monopolist as it is for a firm under perfect competition.
- The same quantity may be offered at different prices to achieve profit maximization depending on the slope of the demand curve. This is seen at P_1 and P_2 in Figure 10.5 (the diagram on the left) where both prices may represent equilibrium with the same quantity $Q*$ as the demand curve is varied from D_1D_1 to D_2D_2.
- The same price may be asked for different quantities in order to achieve profit maximization. This is shown in Figure 10.5 where Q_1 and Q_2 represent equilibrium with the same P^* as the demand curve's slope is varied from D_1D_1 to D_2D_2.

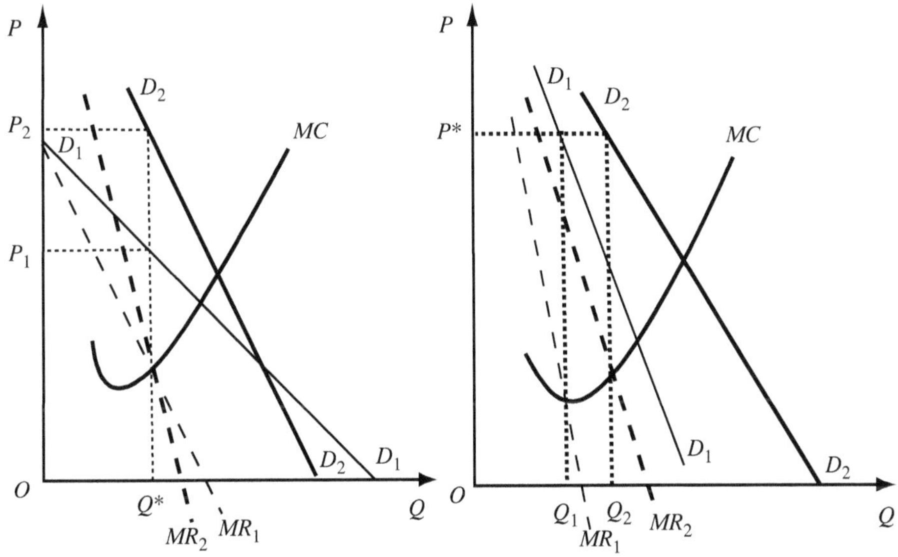

Figure 10.5
Non-unique price-quantity relationships under monopoly. Left: one quantity consistent with multiple prices. Right: one price consistent with multiple quantities

10.3 LONG-RUN EQUILIBRIUM

By definition, there is no entry in the long-run under this market structure. The monopolist may continue to earn super normal profits (entry barred) in the long-run but will not stay in business with losses.

10.3.1 Monopoly and economic efficiency in the long-run

10.3.1.1 ECONOMIC EFFICIENCY

Unlike the perfectly competitive industry, there is no market mechanism that forces the monopolist to achieve 'economic efficiency' in the long-run. In the market structure of perfect competition, 'economic efficiency' brings an optimal allocation of resources in the long-run manifested through the following features of the long run equilibrium:

- The firm operates at the optimal scale plant which means that output is produced at minimum feasible cost using the lowest cost plant (Min *LAC*).
- The optimal scale plant is used optimally at full or designed capacity (Min *SAC*).
- The consumer pays the minimum price possible. This is the price that just covers marginal cost (i.e. price = opportunity cost).
- The firm makes just normal profits (zero excess profits) since $P = ATC$.

10.3.1.2 MONOPOLY AND INEFFICIENCY

On the contrary, the monopolist is not likely to reach an optimal scale (min *LAC*) in the long-run. The monopolist may operate at a sub-optimal scale using the plant sub-optimally, or may operate at a super-optimal scale plant using that plant above its designed capacity. The monopolist may also operate at optimal scale with optimal use of the plant. The size of plant and degree of utilization depend on market size (position of the demand curve) only. Figure 10.6 shows a monopolist under-utilizing a sub-optimal scale plant.

The monopolist operates where the market demand dictates. This could be at the minimum point of the *LAC* curve, to the left or to the right of it. Thus the plant may be at sub-optimal scale with excess capacity or at greater than optimal scale with over-utilized capacity with consequent higher costs. Moreover, even if the monopolist operates at optimal scale plant with optimal utilization of plant capacity as shown at right, ***the price is still above average and marginal costs of production and there will still be excess profits*** (because *AR* is above *MR*). Figure 10.7 shows over-utilization of a larger-than-optimal scale plant by the monopolist.

Figure 10.8 illustrates the case of a monopolist producing at the minimum point of the *LAC* curve. Since price is determined at the demand curve rather than at the *MR* curve, the monopolist still makes excess profits shown by the shaded area. Since price is not the lowest possible (i.e. at min *LAC*) the firm still does not satisfy all the conditions for economic efficiency.

Hence the monopolist does not achieve the type of economic efficiency that occurs in perfect competition in theory.

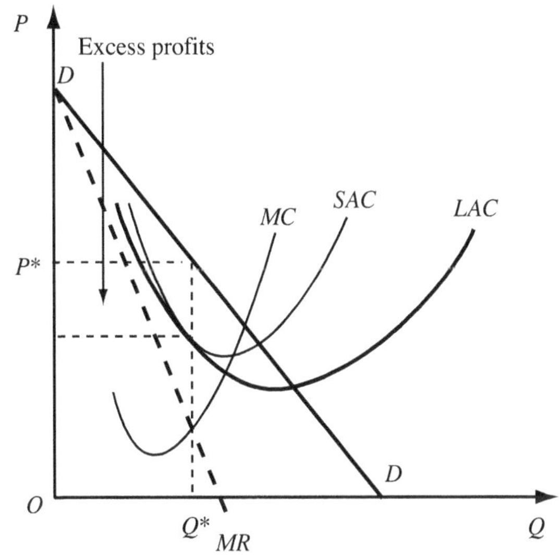

Figure 10.6
Monopolist operating with excess capacity in the long-run

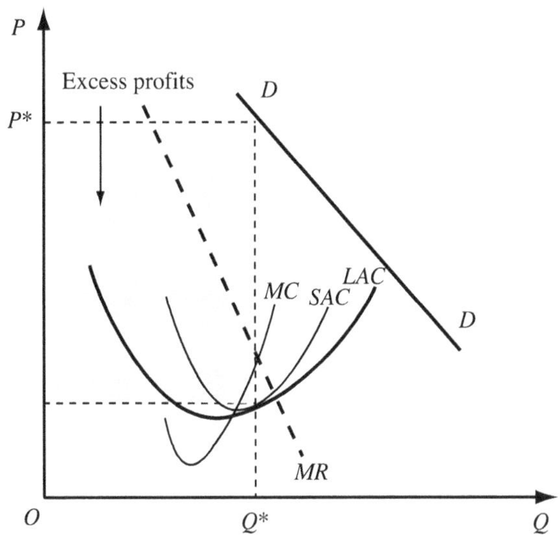

Figure 10.7
Monopolist operating with greater than optimal scale and over-utilization of capacity in the long-run

10.3.2 Economic efficiency and global competitiveness

It may be noted, however, that this concept of economic efficiency is a static one and does not consider economic growth or the need to become internationally competitive in the modern globalized trading environment. Typically domestic monopolies may need to use excess profits for expansion and for additional research and development (*R&D*)

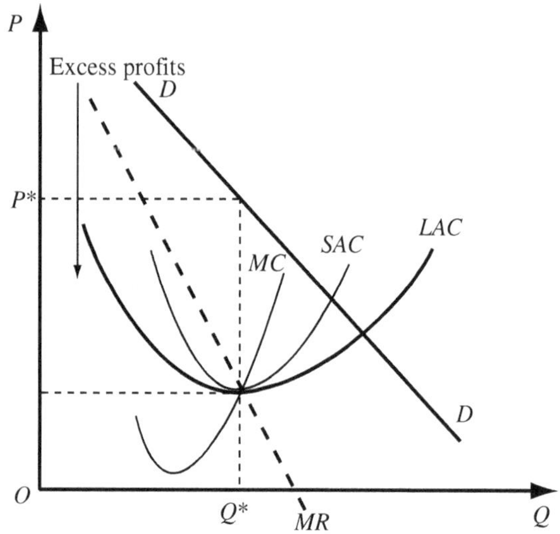

Figure 10.8
Monopolist operating at optimal scale and optimal capacity in the long-run but with excess profits

activities needed to bring new and innovative products on to the market and/or to improve technology and enhance their competitiveness in a dynamic global market.

10.4 PREDICTIONS – THE DYNAMICS OF THE MODEL

10.4.1 Changes in demand

Shift in demand

For a monopolist, if there is an increase in demand (i.e. an outward shift in the demand curve), then the quantity produced will be larger. For a parallel shift outwards, then the monopolist will sell more at a higher price. This is illustrated in Figure 10.9. As demand increases from D_1D_1 to D_2D_2 quantity increases from OQ_1 to OQ_2 and price increases from P_1 to P_2. In this case the firm can earn a higher level of profit. This is particularly so if the firm is on the falling part of the *LAC* experiencing increasing economies of scale.

This outward shift in demand may result from an increase in income, taste or preference for the good. For an increase in income to shift the demand curve outwards, the product or service must have an income elasticity of demand (η_Y) that is positive (i.e $\eta_Y > 0$). The higher the income elasticity of demand for the good or service, the greater is the outward shift of the demand curve for a given increase in income in the market supplied by the firm. It is therefore in the interest of the firm to engage in the sale of products with high income elasticities of demand. This result may also occur when a domestic monopoly enters the global market.

It is possible also to consider that the increase in demand may occur with a twist in the curve (i.e. its new price elasticity of demand at any given quantity). If the new demand

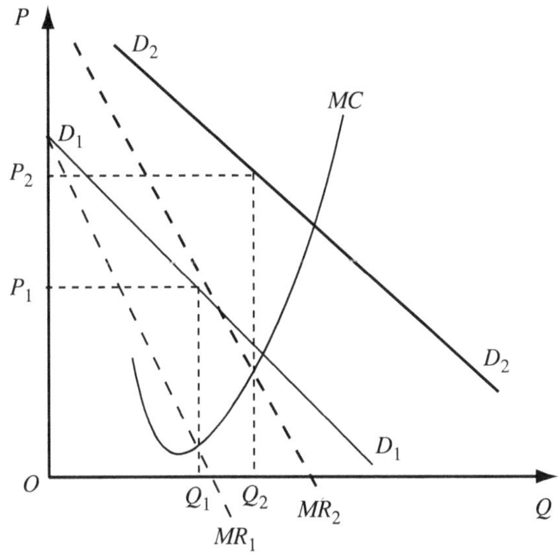

Figure 10.9
Effect of increase in demand for the product of the monopolist

curve is flatter (i.e. has a higher price elasticity) the monopolist may have to sell more at a lower price in order to achieve equilibrium.

10.4.2 Changes in costs and taxes

The effects are similar to those which obtain under perfect competition. However, in the long-run the monopolist is not restricted to the minimum point of the *LAC* as is the perfectly competitive firm.

Increase in fixed cost

With an increase in fixed cost the *MC* curve is not affected and hence the $MC = MR$ position does not change. This means there is no need for a change in the optimal output or price. If the cost increase puts the *LAC* above market demand, the monopolist will close down in long-run.

Increase in variable cost

For the monopolist, as with the perfectly competitive firm, an increase in variable cost shifts the *SMC* to the right. This leads to a decrease in output and an increase in price in the short-run and in the long-run. This is similar to that for perfect competition, only of a smaller magnitude due to the price (*AR*) being greater than *MR* under monopoly (but equal under perfect competition).

Lump-sum tax

The effect of the imposition of a lump-sum tax is the same as for an increase in fixed cost – $MC = MR$ is unaffected. The equilibrium price and quantity should remain the same. This is the best the firm can do. However, since it reduces the excess profits of a monopolist because it increases the fixed costs of the firm (in long-run as well as short-run), the firm may erroneously try to pass on the increased cost to the consumer in higher prices. This further worsens the profitability of the firm. The firm may eventually get back to the original $MC = MR$ position through a groping (tatônnement) process, but would have been better off if it had remained put. However, if the tax wipes out the excess profits and erodes the normal profits, the firm will close. Since the firm is the sole seller, the government may have to reduce the tax.

Profits tax

The effects of an increase in or imposition of a profits tax are the same as for the lump sum tax detailed above. Profits are reduced but equilibrium in the market is not affected. If profits tax exceeds the firm's normal profits, the firm will close down.

Sales tax

The imposition of a per unit sales tax will shift the *MC* curve upwards the same as for an increase in variable costs. Price increases and quantity decreases in the short-run and the long-run.

With taxes it is useful to note that:

- If *MC* has a positive slope some of the tax is passed on (as in perfect competition).
- If *MC* is horizontal, the monopolist will bear some part of the tax, unlike in perfect competition where all can be passed on if *MC* (supply curve) is flat.

Incidence of the tax

Government policy makers need to be aware that the extent to which a tax on a monopolist is borne by the firm depends on the relative elasticities of demand and supply. This has already been dealt with under the perfectly competitive market structure. However, in the case of monopoly, it is useful for policy makers to realize that, whereas a perfectly competitive industry can pass on the entire tax to the consumer (if demand is perfect inelastic or supply perfectly elastic), the monopolist can never pass on the entire tax. This is due to the downward sloping nature of the demand curve.

In Figure 10.10, the height of the tax is measured by the vertical distance between the two *MC* curves and shown as a solid black vertical line. The portion of the tax that is passed on to the consumer in higher prices is measured by the distance between the two prices P_1 and P_2. This distance is much less than the height of the tax. This is significant to policy makers who may be taxing consumers without realizing that the firm is paying the bulk of the tax. Conversely, the policy makers may be seeking to tax the firm without realizing that a portion is passed on to the consumer.

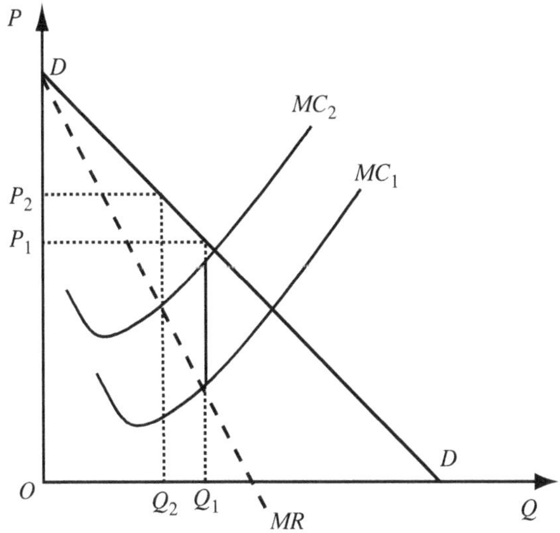

Figure 10.10
Incidence of a tax under monopoly

10.5 MULTI-PLANT MONOPOLY

Under multi-plant monopoly, the monopolist produces a homogeneous product in different plants for the same market.

10.5.1 Decisions of the monopolist

Consider the case of a single product being produced in two plants. The monopolist has to decide:

- How much to produce overall
- How much production to allocate to each plant.
- What price to sell at in order to maximize profits.

Assumptions

- Each plant has a different cost structure.
- The monopolist knows the cost structures in the different plants.
- The monopolist knows the market demand.

10.5.2 Equilibrium of the multi-plant monopolist

Using mathematics to lend precision to the determination of equilibrium, the monopolist's achievement of equilibrium with two plants (labelled 1 and 2) may be described by the following procedure.

10.5.2.1 MATHEMATICAL DERIVATION OF MULTI-PLANT EQUILIBRIUM

The derivation of equilibrium for the multi-plant (two-plant) monopolist proceeds as follows:

$$R = f(Q_1, Q_2)$$

where revenue depends on quantity, whether from plant 1 or plant 2:

$$C = f(Q_1) \quad \text{for plant 1}$$

and:

$$C = f(Q_2) \quad \text{for plant 2}$$

The aim of the firm is to maximize profits. Thus:

$$\text{Max: } \Pi = R - C_1 - C_2$$

where:

$$C_1 + C_2 = C_T$$

The first-order condition for each of the two plants becomes:

$$\frac{\partial \Pi}{\partial Q_1} = 0, \quad \frac{\partial \Pi}{\partial Q_2} = 0$$

Hence for plant 1, the condition becomes:

$$\frac{\partial \Pi}{\partial Q_1} = \frac{\partial R}{\partial Q_1} - \frac{\partial C_1}{\partial Q_1} = 0$$

This implies:

$$\frac{\partial R}{\partial Q_1} = \frac{\partial C_1}{\partial Q_1}$$

or:

$$MR_1 = MC_1$$

Similarly for plant 2:

$$MR_2 = MC_2$$

However, since each additional unit is sold at the same price irrespective of which plant it comes from, this gives the same marginal revenue for each unit sold, or:

$$MR_1 = MR_2 = MR$$

Since $MR_1 = MC_1$ and $MR_2 = MC_2$, then the equilibrium position is:

$$MC_1 = MC_2 = MC_T = MR$$

This indicates that each plant must have the same level of marginal cost which must be equal to the overall equilibrium level of marginal cost where: $MC_T = MR$.

10.5.2.2 EQUILIBRIUM DECISIONS

The achievement of profit maximization may therefore be described in the following way:

- The monopolist computes total *MC* (MC_T) by summing horizontally the *MC* curves of the individual plants. These two plants are represented by the first two diagrams from the left in Figure 10.10. Their *MC* curves are MC_1 and MC_2 respectively. Added together they give the total *MC* curve MC_T shown in Figure 10.11 (the diagram on the right).
- Since the monopolist knows the demand curve, the *MR* curve is also known. Thus the firm equates the total *MC* (MC_T) with *MR* as illustrated in Figure 10.11.
- The firm produces the optimum output Q^* and sells it at price P^*. This answers the first two decision questions as it tells the firm how much to produce overall and at what price.
- The firm then ensures that $MC_1 = MC_2 = MC_T$ at the level where $MC_T = MR$. Each plant then produces the quantity that corresponds to that equilibrium level of marginal cost. In plant 1, the corresponding quantity is Q_1, while in plant 2, that corresponding quantity is Q_2. It may be observed that $Q_1 + Q_2 = Q^*$.
- The firm makes varying levels of profits in each plant. The plant with the lower average cost makes the greater profit. The total profit is the sum of the profit derived from each plant.

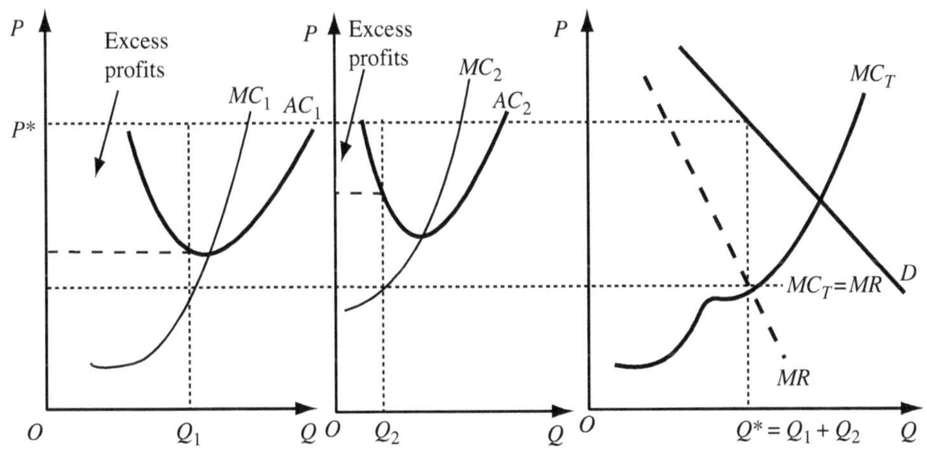

Figure 10.11
The multi-plant monopolist

- It should be observed that the plant with the highest cost gets the smaller allocation of output. This occurs because of the relationship between *MC* and *AC*. For a higher cost plant the *MC* curve moves upward to the left giving an equilibrium position that is closer to the *y*-axis.
- In a practical sense, therefore, a monopolist with several plants selling the product in a single market can only maximize profits if the firm allocates production to the various plants such that the plants all have the same marginal cost. In layman terms, the last unit of output should add the same amount to total cost in each plant and this should be equal to the overall optimal value when the marginal costs from each plant are summed to determine the overall optimal position of the firm. If one plant has a lower marginal cost than the other(s), then production should be shifted to that plant from others. This will cause the *MC* to rise in that plant and fall in the others from which production is shifted. This should continue until the same *MC* obtains in each plant.

10.6 PRICE DISCRIMINATION

Price discrimination refers to the case in which the same commodity is sold by the firm to different groups of consumers (i.e. different sub-markets) at different prices. These sub-markets may be in the same country, same regional grouping or across the global economy. An example of price discrimination is an electric power company selling electricity to two different sub-markets in an economy (e.g. domestic/households and commercial/industrial).

10.6.1 Rationale for price discrimination

The rationale for price discrimination is profit. Typically, a monopolist, by charging different prices to different market segments, is able to make a greater total profit than if all units of the product were sold at the same price. This is because the firm is able, through the exploitation of price elasticities, to extract more of the consumer surplus.

The conditions required to make price discrimination possible and profitable are:

- The firm must be selling the identical product to the different sub-markets.
- The production cost for the commodity must be the same no matter which market is receiving it.
- The sub-markets must be separable and distinguishable one from the other.
- There must be no possibility of reselling from one sub-market to the other. Thus those who receive the lower price cannot resell the product at an intermediate price to those who have to pay the higher price.
- The different sub-markets must have different price elasticities of demand. This allows different prices to be charged to the customers in the different sub-markets despite identical costs of production. It is this exploitation of different price elasticities that makes price discrimination profitable.
- The difference in price elasticity of demand is critical in determining the extent to which price discrimination is worthwhile. The differences may be due to variations

in buyers' preferences, income, location or ease with which substitutes are available. As a result, the firm is faced with demand curves with different price elasticities in the various market segments.

Although price discrimination is typically considered a practice of monopolists, it can be practiced in any imperfectly competitive market.

The charging of multiple prices is not considered price discrimination if the difference in prices is due to a difference in costs. Hence what often appears as price discrimination, especially across regional and international borders, may be due to a difference in supply costs in the different markets or sub-markets.

10.6.2 Equilibrium of the price discriminating monopolist

For the price discriminating monopolist, equilibrium is achieved through the application of the $MC = MR$ rule but this case is diametrically opposed to that of the multi-plant monopolist. Here, instead of two (or more) plants and a single market, there are two (or more) markets (or sub-markets) and a single plant. The price-discriminating monopolist must therefore make the following decisions:

- How much to produce overall in the plant.
- How much to sell in each sub-market (i.e. how to allocate sales to each sub-market).
- What price to sell at in each sub-market.

The following analysis considers that the monopolist firm is producing a product in a single plant and selling it in two sub-markets (1 and 2). Once again, a mathematical derivation of the equilibrium conditions is done to give more precise answers to the questions facing the price discrimination monopolist.

10.6.2.1 MATHEMATICAL DERIVATION

The derivation of equilibrium for the price discriminating monopolist proceeds by first establishing that the aim of the firm is to maximize profits. This may be written as:

$$\text{Max: } \Pi = R - C$$

The equilibrium position would normally be:

$$MC = MR$$

However, because of the two sub-markets:

$$R = R_1 + R_2 = R_T$$

This gives the equilibrium condition:

$$MC = MR_T$$

Hence, the objective function may be re-written as:

$$\text{Max: } \Pi = R_1 + R_2 - C$$

where:

$$R_1 = f(Q_1) \quad \text{for sub-market 1}$$
$$R_2 = f(Q_2) \quad \text{for sub-market 2}$$

and:

$$C = f(Q_1, Q_2)$$

where cost depends on quantity irrespective of whether from sub-market 1 or 2.

The first-order condition for each of the two sub-markets becomes:

$$\frac{\partial \Pi}{\partial Q_1} = 0, \quad \frac{\partial \Pi}{\partial Q_2} = 0$$

Hence for sub-market 1, the condition becomes:

$$\frac{\partial \Pi}{\partial Q_1} = \frac{\partial R}{\partial Q_1} - \frac{\partial C_1}{\partial Q_1} = 0$$

This implies:

$$\frac{\partial R}{\partial Q_1} = \frac{\partial C_1}{\partial Q_1}$$

This may be expressed as:

$$MR_1 = MC_1$$

Similarly for sub-market 2:

$$MR_2 = MC_2$$

However, since the cost of an additional unit does not depend on the sub-market in which it is sold this gives:

$$MR_1 = MR_2 = MC$$

Since:

$$MR_1 = MC_1 \quad \text{and} \quad MR_2 = MC_2$$

The equilibrium position becomes:

$$MR_1 = MR_2 = MR_T = MC$$

This says that each sub-market must have the same level of marginal revenue which must be equal to the overall equilibrium level of marginal revenue where $MR_T = MC$.

10.6.2.2 IDENTIFYING THE EQUILIBRIUM POSITION

Based on the equilibrium conditions set out above, the achievement of profit maximization and the making of decisions by the firm may therefore be described in the following way.

Overall production

The total quantity to be produced overall by the firm is determined by the intersection of the firm's MC and MR_T curves. In this case the firm's MR curve (MR_T) is the (horizontal) summation of the MR curves in each of the two sub-markets 1 and 2 ($MR_1 + MR_2 = MR_T$). The firm therefore achieves profit maximization at the equilibrium between MR_T and MC. This is illustrated in Figure 10.12. This equilibrium gives an optimal quantity overall for the firm of Q^* and suggests an optimal price of P^*. However, as explained further below, P^* is not the optimal price overall as the firm can improve its profit position by charging different prices in the different sub-markets in order to exploit the different elasticities in the sub-markets.

Allocation of sales to markets

For optimization across sub-markets, MR must be the same in each sub-market. If MR is higher in one sub-market than the other the firm will sell more in that sub-market

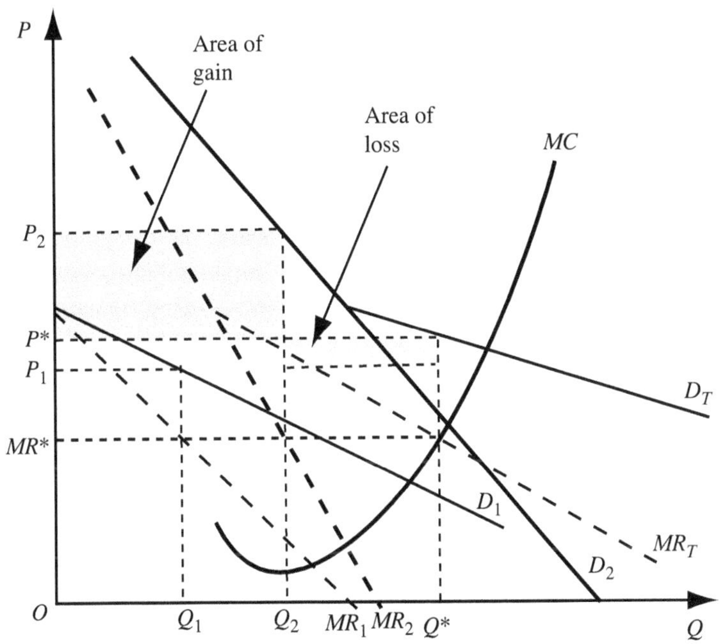

Figure 10.12
The price-discriminating monopolist

and less in the other. Maximum Π is obtained when MC is equal to the overall MR (MR_T) and this MR is the same in both sub-markets. Thus the firm uses the condition: $MC = MR_T = MR_1 = MR_2$. In each sub-market therefore, profit maximization of the firm overall is achieved by equating the marginal revenue in the sub-market with the equilibrium marginal cost ($- MR_T$) in the firm. It is at this intersection of equilibrium MC value in the firm with the MR in that sub-market that the optimal quantity to be sold in that market is found. These optimal quantities are shown in Figure 10.12 as Q_1 and Q_2 for sub-markets 1 and 2, respectively.

Determination of price in each sub-market

For the given (equilibrium) MR in both sub-markets, the firm is in a position to exploit the price elasticities of demand in order to achieve greater profits than if it charged a single price in both sub-markets. The difference in prices charged in each sub-market depends on the difference in price elasticity of demand. As established earlier, the relationship between marginal revenue, price and price elasticity of demand may be expressed as:

$$MR = P\left(1 - \frac{1}{n_p}\right)$$

Thus, since MR must be the same in each market for profit maximization, then, where price elasticity η_P is different, the price (P) must also be different. It can be seen from the equation that where price elasticity is lower, the price must be higher in order to have the same value for MR.

In Figure 10.12, the demand in market 1 and market 2 is represented by demand curves D_1 and D_2 respectively. Their respective MR curves are MR_1 and MR_2. D_T is the summed demand curves while MR_T is the summed MR curves for the two markets.

The overall equilibrium is given by the intersection of MR_T and MC. This gives Q^* as the optimal output to produce overall. The line MR^* gives the $MC = MR$ level that must obtain in all sub-markets.

The allocation of sales to each market is based on the MR^* line where it intersects with MR_1 and MR_2 in sub-markets 1 and 2 respectively. This gives the allocation of Q_1 to sub-market 1 and Q_2 to sub-market 2. It should be observed that Q_1 plus Q_2 is equal to the overall equilibrium quantity Q^* (through the horizontal summation of MR curves).

Diagrammatically, the determination of price for each sub-market is made by projecting from the equilibrium quantities vertically upwards to the respective demand curves. Using the relationship between marginal revenue, price and price elasticity:

$$\left(MR = P\left(1 - \frac{1}{n_p}\right)\right)$$

then with a constant MR, sub-market 1 with its higher price elasticity has the lower price ($P_1 < P_2$). The firm therefore is able to exploit the relative price elasticities of demand for its own benefit.

10.6.2.3 PROFITABILITY OF PRICE DISCRIMINATION

A monopolist practices price discrimination because, typically, the total revenue from price discrimination is greater for a given quantity of output sold than if a single price were used. This allows the firm to collect a larger amount of revenue for the same cost. This occurs because the firm is able to capture an extra portion of the consumer surplus and is achieved by the exploitation of the difference in price elasticity of demand between the two sub-markets.

Consider Figure 10.12. The monopolist equates MC with MR_T to maximize profits. The optimal quantity is Q^*. If this quantity is sold at the single plant single market price of P^*, the firm's total revenue would be: $OP^* \cdot OQ^*$. With price discrimination, the firm, keeping the same MR in each market ($MR_1 = MR_2 = MR_T = MC$) sells OQ_1 at OP_1 in sub-market 1 and OQ_2 at price P_2 in sub-market 2. Therefore, the total revenue from price discrimination is:

$$(OP_1 \cdot OQ_1) + (OP_2 \cdot OQ_2)$$

Now since $OQ_1 + OQ_2 = OQ^*$, the different revenues being compared ($OP^* \cdot OQ^*$ versus $(OP_1 \cdot OQ_1) + (OP_2 \cdot OQ_2)$) refer to the exact same quantity and hence the same total cost, a comparison of the difference in total revenue determines which option is the more profitable for the monopolist.

From Figure 10.12 it may be observed that $(OP_1 \cdot OQ_1) + (OP_2 \cdot OQ_2) > OP^* \cdot OQ^*$. This comparison is facilitated by removing $(OP_1 \cdot OQ_1)$ from inside of the $(OP_2 \cdot OQ_2)$ area and placing it to fill the space:

$$OP_1(OQ^* - OQ_2)$$

Since:

$$OQ^* = OQ_1 + OQ_2$$

Then:

$$OQ_1 = OQ^* - OQ_2$$

It is then possible to compare the space occupied by the two revenue rectangles for the sub-markets with that occupied by the single revenue rectangle obtained if one price were charged in both markets. The 'area of gain' shown in the diagram may then be compared with the 'area of loss'. It can be seen that the 'area of gain' is greater than the 'area of loss'. Hence by practicing price discrimination, the firm gains greater revenue for the same cost at the equilibrium quantity in the market. The firm therefore makes even more profit than if it followed the usual profit maximization formula and charged a single optimal price.

This type of price discrimination is described as ***third degree price discrimination***, a description attributed to the economist Pigou. It is the case where, because of the charging of two different prices, a part of consumers' surplus is taken away by the firm.

It is also possible to identify other degrees of price discrimination as follows.

Second-degree price discrimination

This is where the monopolist can sell at more than two prices higher than the normal equilibrium price. In this case the firm will receive an even greater portion of the consumers' surplus. This is typical in utility pricing where the price of units consumed may change in discrete steps as the quantity used by a consumer changes.

First-degree price discrimination

This is the limiting case in which a monopolist can negotiate individually with each buyer and sell each unit of the product at its corresponding price as determined from the demand curve. The firm is able to take away ***all*** of the consumer surplus. This is also known as 'take-it-or-leave-it' price discrimination.

10.6.2.4 CONSEQUENCES OF PRICE DISCRIMINATION

The consequences of the practice of price discrimination include:

- Consumers in the more elastic sub-market pay a lower price with price discrimination than would otherwise be the case. In the case of a utility company these consumers are usually the domestic households. Their lower price is not due to benevolence on the part of the monopolist firm but is part of an overall strategy for increasing revenue and profits.
- Consumers in the more inelastic sub-market pay a higher price. This is the market with consumers who have fewer (if any) substitutes and who have a greater desire and ability to pay than go without the product.
- In some cases output may increase if the firm can charge two different prices. In these cases a single price may eliminate the more elastic sub-market completely.
- The firm's total revenue will be higher still. The *MR* curve shifts until, in the limiting case of first degree price discrimination, it coincides with the demand curve. Here, the lower price at which an additional unit is sold is not the same for all previous units. The monopolist now extracts ***all*** of the consumer surplus from the market.

10.6.3 Exploitation of price elasticities of demand

The possibility and profitability of price discrimination for a firm depends critically on the existence not only on separable sub-markets but also on the presence of two different demand curves with ***different price elasticities of demand***. It was stated above that the market with the higher elasticity gets the lower price and vice-versa. This is explained further below.

The relationship between marginal revenue and price elasticity may again be set out as:

$$MR = P\left(1 - \frac{1}{\eta_P}\right)$$

In price discrimination there are two (or more) *MR* curves, one for each different sub-market. In equilibrium:

$$MR_1 = MR_2 = MR_T = MC$$

In market 1:

$$MR_1 = P_1\left(1 - \frac{1}{\eta_{P_1}}\right)$$

In market 2:

$$MR_2 = P_2\left(1 - \frac{1}{\eta_{P_2}}\right)$$

Now, since:

$$MR_1 = MR_2 (= MR_T)$$

then:

$$P_1\left(1 - \frac{1}{\eta_{P_1}}\right) = P_2\left(1 - \frac{1}{\eta_{P_2}}\right)$$

From this the following may be concluded:

$$\begin{aligned} &\text{if } \eta_{P_1} = \eta_{P_2} \quad \textit{then} \quad P_1 = P_2 \\ &\text{if } \eta_{P_1} > \eta_{P_2} \quad \textit{then} \quad P_1 < P_2 \\ &\text{if } \eta_{P_1} < \eta_{P_2} \quad \textit{then} \quad P_1 > P_2 \end{aligned}$$

This indicates that the sub-market with higher elasticity will have a lower price and vice versa.

10.6.4 Applications

Price discrimination does not only occur in monopoly. It may also characterize industries described by oligopoly.

Markets may be segmented in many ways. In some cases price discrimination may depend on time such as in cases where pre-purchasing of tickets for a performance may mean a lower price. This may vary between a lower price for earlier purchases to a lower price for last-minute purchases. The nature of near substitutes may also affect the ability of a firm to price-discriminate. Time dependent price-discrimination is also a major feature of the airline industry (oligopoly). The phenomenon of price discrimination in the airline industry has been examined fairly extensively in the literature. Some of this is captured in Stavins (1996) and in Gerardi and Shapiro (2007).

International price discrimination

With the globalization of markets, a firm that acts as a monopoly in a domestic economy may find an international demand curve that has a different price elasticity of demand than that in the domestic economy. This may be due to the difference in the preference structure for the product abroad and/or the difference in the availability of substitutes for the product. Where the product is a service (typical) and meets the requirements for possible and profitable price discrimination, the firm should price-differentiate. However, the firm must be careful to avoid the charge of dumping when the international price is lower than the domestic price.

10.7 BILATERAL MONOPOLY

Bilateral monopoly refers to the case of two firms in the market: a single seller (monopolist) and a single buyer (monopsonist). An example is that of a bauxite firm (a single seller) producing all the bauxite for a single buyer of bauxite to make the bauxite derivative, aluminium.

10.7.1 Monopoly vs. monopsony

In the case of monopoly vs. monopsony, the equilibrium position cannot be determined by regular tools of supply and demand in the market. It is possible to determine only the range in which price and output will settle but not the precise equilibrium level of price or output. The final position is resolved by exogenous factors such as financial strength and bargaining or negotiation strengths.

Figure 10.13 illustrates bilateral monopoly and the explanation is as follows:

- The sole buyer's (monopsonist) demand curve is D_B and is determined by the demand in the market for the buyer's output. It is therefore determined outside the buyers' control.
- Given the demand curve of the buyer firm, the MR curve facing the seller (monopolist) is MR_S.
- The seller firm has the marginal cost curve MC_S.
- The sole buyer considers the seller's MC curve as the seller's supply curve. Hence for the sole buyer, every incremental unit that the seller must supply can only be supplied at a higher cost not only for that unit but for all previous units as well. The higher price for each incremental unit becomes the going market price the buyer must pay for all units. Hence the buyer must use a Marginal Expenditure of Input (MEI_B) curve in lieu of the seller's 'supply' (MC) curve. This is explained in more detail below.

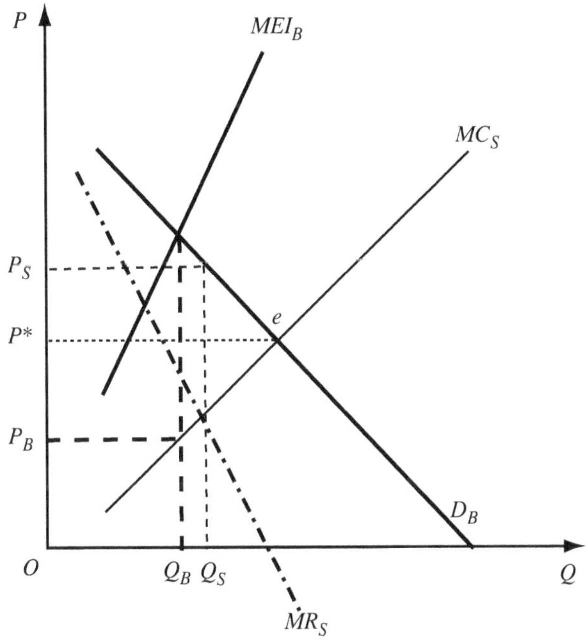

Figure 10.13
Bi-lateral monopoly

Based on the above, the two firms act differently to secure their own respective equilibrium positions. They act as follows:

- The seller wants to maximize profits by equating MC_S to MR_S. This would mean selling OQ_S at a price of OP_S.
- The buyer also seeks to maximize profits and this takes place where the buyer's marginal expenditure of input (MEI_B) intersects the buyer's demand curve (D_B). Hence the buyer wants to purchase OQ_B at a price of OP_B. The price OP_B is relevant here because the buyer sees it as the supply price (*MC* is seen as the supply curve) of the seller.

As a result, the sole buyer wants to buy OQ_B at a price of OP_B while the sole seller wants to sell OQ_S at a price of OP_S. There is therefore no existing equilibrium position for the market under bi-lateral monopoly. In this case the equilibrium price lies within the range between OP_B and OP_S and the equilibrium output between the OQ_B and OQ_S. Price and output are indeterminate.

10.7.2 The marginal expenditure of input curve

The marginal expenditure of input curve (*MEI*) is shown in Figure 10.13 based on a concept similar to that of the marginal revenue (i.e. marginal revenue turned upside-down). The principal difference is that whereas the marginal revenue is on the demand side, the marginal expenditure is on the supply side. Recall that marginal revenue lies below the demand curve because the sale of an additional unit of a good requires that a lower price be charged, not only for the extra unit, but for all (previous) units. Hence the total reduction in revenue from the lower price is greater than the reduction on the last unit sold alone.

Similarly for the marginal expenditure of input curve, but in reverse, the supplier, in order to supply an extra unit of a good, must charge a higher price (according to the supply curve) not only for that extra unit but for all (previous) units. As a result, the buyer, in order to obtain an extra unit of the good must pay the sole seller the higher supply price, not only for the extra unit demanded but for all units bought now the higher quantity is demanded. Consequently, the marginal expenditure curve of the buyer must lie above the supply (in this case *MC*) curve of the seller.

10.7.3 Conflict and vertical integration

As a result of this indeterminacy, there is likely to be a takeover of seller by the buyer (or vice-versa) who then attains vertical integration of that firm's production. The *MC* curve then becomes the marginal cost curve of the buyer. The former buyer firm thus equates demand and supply at point *e*. Output increases to Q^* and price settles at P^*. The result of the integration is therefore a higher output and possibly a lower price.

Recently, bi-lateral monopoly is being viewed as a game where it is shown that a Nash equilibrium (where one firm does its best given the position of the other firm) may work in a bi-lateral monopoly. Dubey and Sondermann (2005) show that smooth trading can be a substitute for conflict.

10.8 REGULATION OF MONOPOLY

There are some cases in which the government may wish to regulate a monopoly. Very often, in a small economy, a natural monopoly occurs where the economy cannot accommodate more than one firm or where other factors ensure a monopolistic industry. The government may wish to regulate such a monopoly.

10.8.1 Eliminating excess profits

Regulation of monopoly typically is effected through the setting of prices or determination of profit levels. Regulation tends to be focused on the reduction or elimination of the excess profits gained by the monopoly through its market power. Price regulation may take any of the forms set out below and illustrated in Figure 10.14. In the absence of government regulation, the monopolist produces at Q^* and charges price P^*. Under regulation, price may be set equal to *MC*. The firm is shifted from its profit maximization position. The effect is a lower price than P^* as price is set at P_M with a higher output than Q^* as output increases to Q_M. The firm now makes a lower profit but still earns excess profits as price (*AR*) is still above average cost at quantity Q_M.

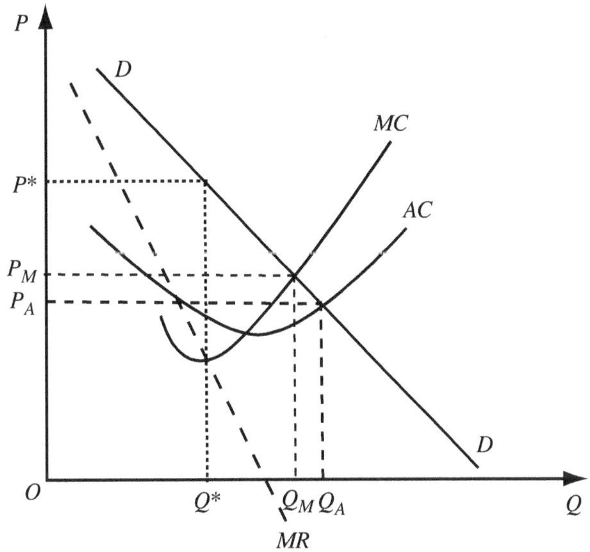

Figure 10.14
Government regulation of monopoly

Price may be set equal to *AC*. This gives an even lower price still at P_A and higher output at Q_A than with price set equal to *MC*. Here price (*AR*) just covers average total cost including a fair return on capital (included in cost curve) and there are zero excess profits as under perfect competition. This introduces the question of what is a 'fair' return and what should be the 'capital' on which the 'fair' return should apply.

Government may allow price discrimination. This would permit the monopolist to set a lower price in the more elastic market (usually households as opposed to commercial entities). Then questions of equity and fairness of treatment may have to be considered.

10.8.2 Monopoly profits and growth

The excess profits generated by monopoly, the ability to take away some of the consumer surplus through price discrimination and the failure of the firm to be forced by a market mechanism to operate at the bottom of the *LAC* and *SAC* are among those considered to be the undesirable features of monopoly. For this reason, monopolies are often viewed negatively in terms of contribution to economic efficiency and use of economic resources. Harberger (1954) examines the issue of monopoly and resource allocation.

It is important to recognize, however, that this is a static distributional inefficiency. It fails to take into account the dynamics of the use of the excess monopoly profits for research and development and to grow the capital and technological base of the industry and, by extension, the country in which the monopolist is willing to invest. One aspect of domestic policy with regard to monopolies should be to ensure that the excess profits are directed, as far as possible, into new productive activities to expand output and employment opportunities in the domestic economy.

10.8.3 Domestic monopolies and international markets

Under the 'new' globalization, domestic monopolies that may have long existed in the comfort of a relatively protected market could become vulnerable to take-over by more efficient foreign firms or could face more competition in the domestic market from the external supply of the good or service. In addition, domestic monopolies could be placed under pressure to venture into the international market with their products in order to earn foreign exchange and assist in balancing the country's external account (the Balance of Payments).

The upshot of all this is that the monopolist is forced to become more competitive. An understanding of the 'rules of the game' facilitates the development of a greater competitive edge. The monopolist must therefore be aware of the conditions for equilibrium: the significance of price elasticity for the effects of price change on revenue and profitability; the conditions under which the firm should price discriminate; the impact of positive price elasticity on the demand curve; the need to retain price and quantity in the face of a rise in fixed costs and other behavioural rules that are non-intuitive. These have all been dealt with in this chapter.

Governments as well as consumers also need to understand monopolies and how they work in order to successfully garner the greatest economic benefits from domestic monopolies, to deal more effectively with foreign firms that may enter as domestic monopolies and to assist domestic firms in their expansion into the international market. The analytical foundations provided here are essential to facilitate the achievement of these objectives.

REVIEW QUESTIONS FOR CHAPTER 10

1 Longtalk Inc is a company providing cellular telephone services operating as a monopoly. Carefully explain:

(a) Why the second-order condition for profit maximization may be of limited importance to Longtalk Inc as a monopolist compared to if they were a perfectly competitive firm.
(b) Why Longtalk Inc is not considered to have a supply curve.
(c) How and why Longtalk Inc will not produce with economic efficiency in the long-run.

2 Consider the hypothetical case of a firm, Metropolitan Power Inc (MPI), which is a monopoly supplier of electrical power in a market and is operating on its demand curve at a price where the price elasticity of demand (η_P) is such that $\eta_P > 1$. Explain:

(a) Why MPI should seek to continue operating only in the portion of its demand curve where $\eta_P > 1$.
(b) Why MPI is raising its price to increase revenue but finding its revenue decreasing instead.

(c) Why MPI might lower its price and, as a result, find its revenue increasing but its profits decreasing.

3 PowerGenCo is an electricity monopoly supplier. Explain how and why PowerGenCo can maximize profits while operating from two plants and selling in a single market.
4 SunIsle Telecom is a hypothetical monopoly supplier of landline telephone services in a domestic market. Explain:

(a) How it is possible for SunIsle Telecom to sell its telephone services at a higher price to commercial customers than to households.
(b) How and why SunIsle Telecom can benefit financially from this practice of price discrimination.
(c) How SunIsle Telecom can be said to be exploiting price elasticities of demand.

5 Consider a firm, Red Earth Inc, which has a natural monopoly in the production and sale of bauxite. This firm sells its entire output to Alumco, a sole buyer of the product. Illustrate and explain:

(a) How Red Earth Inc would seek to maximize profits from its sales to Alumco.
(b) Why and how Alumco creates a Marginal Expenditure of Input (*MEI*) curve.
(c) How and why the two firms end up with different equilibrium prices and quantities for their individual firms.
(d) What is likely to happen, over time, if the two firms cannot resolve their conflicting positions.

6 Illustrate why and how a government may regulate monopoly.
7 Discuss the likely effects of trade liberalization on a firm that is a monopoly in a small domestic market.

RECOMMENDED READING FOR CHAPTER 10

Dubey, P. and Sondermann, D. (2005) 'Perfect Competition in a Bilateral Monopoly (in Honor of Martin Shubik)', Yale University: Cowles Foundation Discussion Papers No. 1543. Online Posting. Available at: http://cowles.econ.yale.edu/P/cd/d1534.pdf

Gerardi, K. and Shapiro, A. (2007) 'Does Competition Reduce Price Discrimination? New Evidence from the Airline Industry', Federal Reserve Bank of Boston. Online Posting. Available at: http://www.bos.frb.org/economic/wp/index.htm

Harberger, A. C. (1954) 'Monopoly and Resource Allocation', *American Economic Review*, 44(2): 77–87.

Stavins, J. (1996) 'Price Discrimination in the Airline Market: The Effect of Market Concentration', *Review of Economics and Statistics*, 83(1): 200–2.

11 Monopolistic Competition

The Chamberlin Model: Short and Long-run equilibrium; Critique of the Model.

The market structure of monopolistic competition is situated between those of perfect competition and monopoly. This market structure gains increasing relevance as national markets become more integrated into the global market. Many firms that previously operated as monopolies in their individual domestic markets experience a greater level of competition when lowered trade barriers expose them to the global market. Moreover, the increasing relevance of this model of market structure may be gauged from the efforts made to incorporate increasing returns to scale and differentiated products (central features of monopolistic competition) into modern International Trade theory.

Until around the 1930s, perfect competition and monopoly were the principal market structures considered in Microeconomic theory. Around that time, a number of economists including Edward Chamberlin (1933), Joan Robinson (1933), and Piero Sraffa (1926), were raising questions about the general applicability of the older models based mainly on empirical grounds and were proposing new models of market structure which lie between the two polar extremes of perfect competition and monopoly. These new approaches, sometimes dubbed the imperfect competition (or monopolistic competition) revolution in microeconomic theory, saw the emergence of the model of monopolistic competition, a model largely attributed to Chamberlin (1933), and of models of oligopoly. Although oligopoly (duopoly) models date back to the nineteenth century (1830s), it was not until around the 1930s that they began to attract more widespread attention and became more popular as newer models were developed.

Monopolistic competition received more attention in the mid-1970s with the Dixit–Stiglitz (1977) reformulation that is sometimes referred to as the second monopolistic competition revolution. This work has served to revive flagging interest in the much criticized model. This was buttressed by its further application to issues of increasing returns and intra-industry trade in the area of international economics, associated primarily with the work of Krugman (1979, 1981). Neary (2002) examines the interaction of monopolistic competition and international trade theory.

11.1 BASIC FEATURES AND ASSUMPTIONS OF THE MONOPOLISTIC COMPETITION MODEL

11.1.1 Scenario and rationale for the model

The model was introduced against the background of concerns about inadequacies in the traditional models. The major issues raised against having only the two extreme models of Perfect Competition and Monopoly were primarily of an empirical nature and were based on the observations that:

- Firms tend to sell products that are heterogeneous rather than homogeneous as is assumed under the model of perfect competition.
- Many firms tend to use product differentiation as a sales tool (i.e. use product differences for competitive purposes) rather than price competition. Hence the product itself was becoming a policy variable. Chamberlin is credited with having introduced the term 'product differentiation'.
- Advertising was being increasingly used to create brand allegiance for products that are close substitutes but not identical (e.g. brands of toothpaste, chocolates) and so create some monopoly power in their industry even though they are not monopolies.
- Firms were found to operating with increasing returns to scale (i.e. on the downward portion of their long-run average cost curve (*LAC*)).

This led to certain developments in the modelling of the market structure. These include:

- The re-definition of the industry. There was the introduction of the concept of the 'product-group'. This group would include all items that may be substituted for what is essentially the same purpose. Hence the term 'product group' was introduced to replace that of the industry although the term was not always clear (e.g. if soy beans may be made into a meat substitute then should soy beans and meat be included in the same product group?).
- The introduction of the product as a policy variable through 'product differentiation', a term coined by Chamberlin (1933). The product is varied to distinguish it from others and is packaged or branded differently. These differences may be fancied (e.g. wrappers on chocolates, fragrances in soaps) or real (e.g. addition of bleach to detergents or additives to petrol).
- The introduction of advertising, selling and/or promotional expenses to the theory of the firm. These are the costs of branding or establishing the nature of the product differentiation in the minds of the consumer.

These issues are all addressed in the model of monopolistic competition that emerged. Although there were various strands of the model, monopolistic competition is being treated here as a single model based primarily on the work of Chamberlin.

11.1.2 Assumptions of the model

The principal assumptions of the model are:

- The aim of the firm is profit maximization.
- There are many firms in the product group, so many that each firm expects that its actions will go unnoticed by the others. The firm therefore tends to act automistically (a monopoly element). This is a major characteristic of this model since it suggests that firms do not consider or act upon their interdependence.
- Firms produce ***similar but differentiated*** products. The differentiation may be real or fancied. The differentiated products give the firm some semblance of monopoly power in the market, thereby allowing the firm to act on its own 'perceived' demand curve. This leads to the replacement of the industry by the concept of the 'product group' in the analysis of this market structure.
- There is free entry and exit. This is similar to the perfect competition model. However, the need for the firm under monopolistic competition to differentiate products, suggests that entry is not quite 'free' since brand loyalty could be seen as a barrier to entry.
- There is perfect knowledge of demand and costs and the technology used by the firms is given. The cost curve of the firm includes selling costs for the product. Firms, however, do not have sufficient knowledge to be aware of their market-share demand curve.
- Factors are freely available to the firm at given prices.
- Demand and cost curves are virtually identical for all firms. This is considered an heroic assumption given that the products are differentiated. Moreover, it suggests that the differentiated nature of the product does not signify a difference in technology. Nevertheless, it permits the construction of a 'representative' firm.

11.2 DEMAND AND COSTS

11.2.1 Demand

The model has the distinction of using ***two demand curves*** simultaneously. The two are the 'perceived demand curve and the market-share demand curve'.

The 'perceived' demand curve

The 'perceived' demand curve is a gently downward sloping demand curve which shows how much the firm will sell if it varies its price ***while other firms maintain their existing price***. This curve, labelled '*dd*' in Figure 11.1, is quite elastic. However, it is not perfectly elastic because the differentiated product gives the firm some market power due to brand loyalty and advertising.

This curve is theorized to exist because of product differentiation. The firm brands its product, hence, if the firm should raise its price, brand loyalty or the designed differences that distinguish the product would ensure that all its customers do not switch to another similar good.

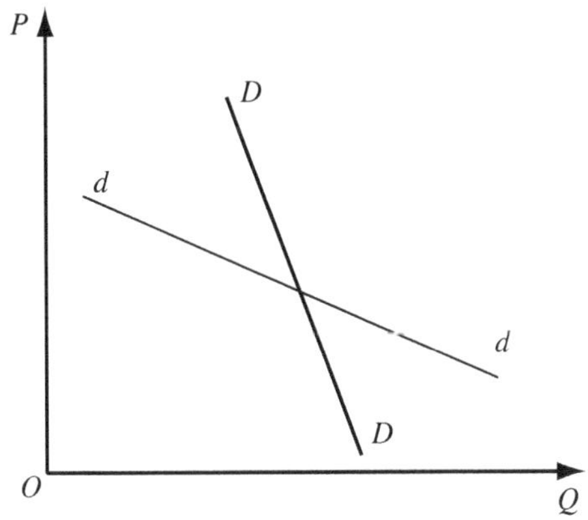

Figure 11.1
The 'perceived' (*dd*) and market-share (*DD*) demand curves

The firm sees only this curve and seeks to optimize with respect to this curve alone. This pattern of behaviour allows the firm to be described as myopic or naïve.

The market-share demand curve

The market-share demand curve is a steeply downward-sloping demand curve which would be the true demand curve for the firm if all firms were to raise or lower prices simultaneously. This is the share of the industry (or product group) demand that belongs to each individual firm. The curve, labelled *DD* in Figure 11.1, is less elastic (steeper) than the 'perceived' demand curve. The firm never becomes aware of this curve although it affects its optimizing behaviour. The myopic firm, although its behaviour is affected by this curve, consistently fails to recognize it and persists with its naïve pattern of behaviour.

The element of market power means that, unlike perfect competition, the firm's perceived demand curve (*dd*) is not horizontal (perfectly elastic), but has a moderate slope. It is however, not as steep a slope as would be expected to obtain under monopoly.

11.2.2 Costs

The model uses the traditional U-shaped short-run and basin-shaped long-run cost curves for production costs. The model introduces selling or product promotion costs which are associated with product differentiation. The selling, advertising, branding or promotion cost curves are also similarly shaped. This means that, as with production costs, there are scale economies and diseconomies of advertising or product differentiation costs. Selling costs plus production costs equal total costs. The selling costs, promotion or product differentiation costs are incorporated into the traditional cost curve.

11.3 EQUILIBRIUM IN THE SHORT-RUN

11.3.1 The use of two demand curves

The aim of the firm is to maximize profits. Because of the assumed naïve behaviour and myopia, each firm acts as though it possesses monopoly power and ignores the reactions of other firms operating solely with regard to its own (perceived) demand curve (*dd*). Firms decide on product characteristics they need to distinguish their brand and the desired selling expenses.

For profit maximization, the myopic firm uses its perceived demand curve (*dd*) and the *MR* curve relevant to it. Consequently, the firm operates where $MC = MR$ and attempts to sell quantity Q_0 at price P_0. This is illustrated in Figure 11.2.

However, given that this is the short-run, the market-share demand curve (*DD*) is fixed and, in this case, serves to constrain the firm in its efforts to maximize profits using its perceived demand curve. The position of this curve has to be fixed in the short-run since it is determined by the number of firms in the industry/product group and can only be affected in the long-run when entry or exit can take place.

In the scenario depicted in Figure 11.2, the firm, charging price P_0, cannot sell the quantity Q_0 that it expects to sell at that price because the firm is constrained by its market-share demand curve *DD* (which it does not see) and so is trying to sell more than its share of the market. It is constrained to operate on this market-share curve because all firms in the industry are sharing the market similarly. Consequently, the firm finds that, at that price P_0, it can sell only Q_0'. This shortfall may be measured by the distance *ab* represented by the solid line in Figure 11.2.

11.3.2 The short-run adjustment mechanism

As a result of not being able to sell what it expects to sell, the firm makes the assumption that it is not operating on its true perceived demand (*dd*) curve and concludes that the

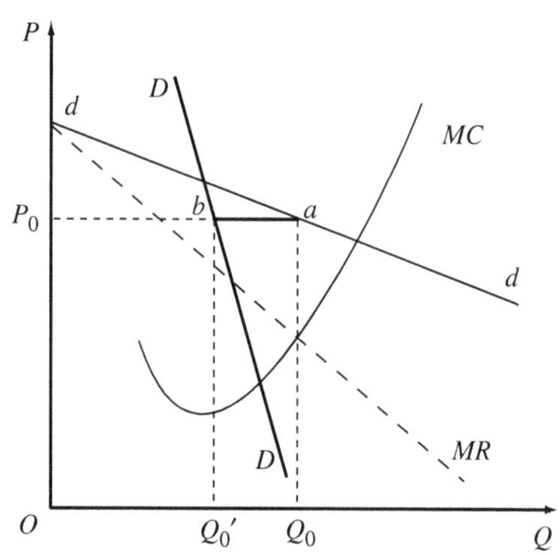

Figure 11.2
An initial perceived equilibrium position of the firm

true *dd* curve must pass through the point *b* with co-ordinates P_0Q_0' (the position at which it is being forced to operate). The firm therefore revises its perceived demand curve (*dd*) inwards (downward) to pass through the co-ordinates P_0Q_0' represented by the point *b* on the *DD* curve. The perceived demand curve now becomes (d_1d_1). As a consequence, the *MR* curve also moves inwards (visually downwards) to MR_1. The firm equates marginal cost to marginal revenue ($MC = MR$) again, now using the revised *MR* (MR_1) and charges the new equilibrium price P_1 expecting to sell quantity Q_1. This is shown in Figure 11.3.

The firm is now expecting to maximize profits at the point *s*. However, once again, the firm is unable to sell the quantity expected at the price chosen (Q_1 at P_1). This is so because the firm is still being constrained by the market-share curve *DD* (which the myopic firm still does not see) as all the firms in the industry are taking the same action simultaneously causing them to each retain their market share. Therefore, at price P_1 the firm can only sell Q_1' and operate at the point *t* on the *DD* curve. A revised perceived demand curve must now be made to pass through the point *t*.

The firm continues to act in this way. However, as this process continues, the difference between the quantity the firm expects to sell and the quantity the firm can actually sell diminishes. Hence, from Figure 11.3 the new distance *st* is less than the original *ab*. As the firm continues to revise its *dd* curve, this gap continues to narrow and tends to zero.

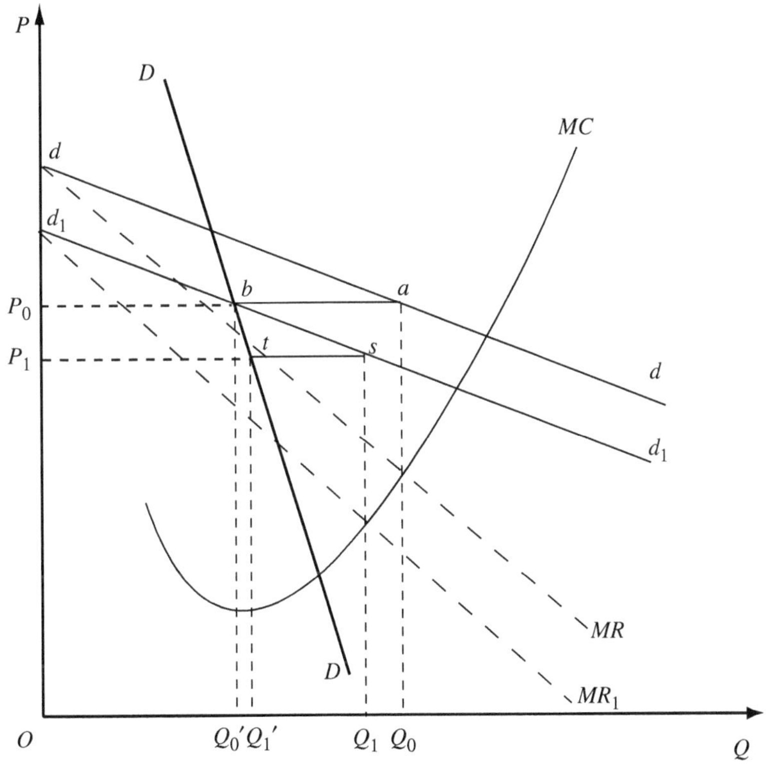

Figure 11.3
The short-run adjustment process

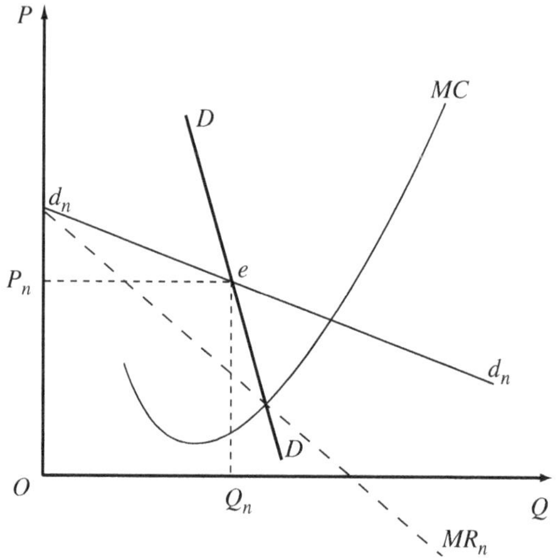

Figure 11.4
Final short-run equilibrium position under monopolistic competition

Finally, as the representative firm (and, by extension, every other firm) keeps adjusting the *dd* curve inwards, short-run equilibrium is achieved where $MC = MR$ (note that MR related to *dd* and not to *DD*) directly below the point where the perceived demand curve d_nd_n is intersected by the market-share demand curve *DD* (i.e. where the gap between what the firm expects to sell and what it can actually sell is zero). The firm can now sell Q_n at its perceived equilibrium price, P_n. This is illustrated in Figure 11.4.

There is symmetry in the short-run adjustment mechanism. This means that if the *DD* curve should lie to the right of the point *e*, the firm would revise its perceived demand curve outwards from the origin (visually upwards) until a new short-run equilibrium is reached.

In the final short-run equilibrium, now labelled P^*Q^*, and shown in Figure 11.5, the firm may be making excess profits. Inserting the relevant short-run average-cost and marginal-cost curves, the excess profits are shown as the shaded area P^*ebc.

It is also possible that, after the short-run process is complete, the firm may be making a loss. This would depend only on the position of the short-run average cost curve (*SAC*). So long as the firm covers its short-run average variable cost, it can be expected to remain in business in the short-run.

11.4 EQUILIBRIUM IN THE LONG-RUN

11.4.1 The long-run adjustment mechanism

In the long-run, the equilibrium is affected by the entry or exit of firms. So long as there are excess profits in the product group (industry), firms enter. If there are losses, firms exit. The effect of entry or exit is to shift the market-share demand curve (*DD*) for each firm. The curve shifts to the left as firms enter, causing each firm to have a smaller market

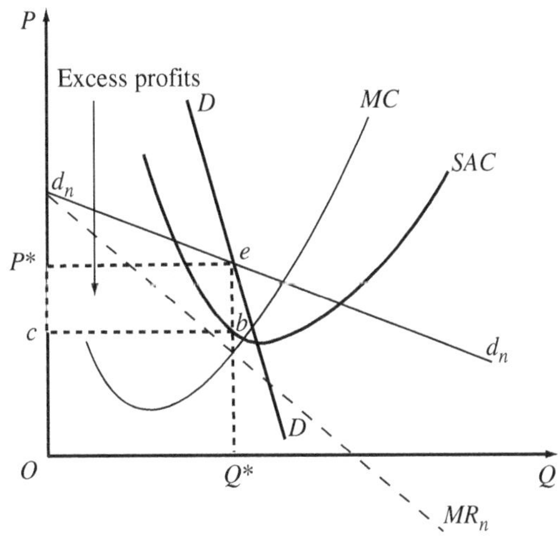

Figure 11.5
Short-run equilibrium with excess profits

share. Conversely, it shifts to the right as firms exit, allowing each remaining firm to have a larger share of the market.

Once entry or exit takes place, the market-share demand curve (*DD*) shifts and the short-run adjustment process takes over. These firms continue their naïve (myopic) behaviour, trying to optimize with respect to their *dd* curve and blissfully unaware of the way in which their market share is being affected by entry or exit. Equilibrium is reached only when what the firm expects to sell coincides with what they actually sell. This is where the *dd* curve cuts the *DD* curve.

The long-run adjustment mechanism therefore involves shifts in both demand curves, one deliberately by the firm (*dd*) in an effort to find its 'true' perceived demand curve and the other (*DD*) through entry and exit of firms. Figure 11.6 shows how the process takes place.

Entry causes the market-share demand curve (*DD*) to shift to the left as each firm gets a smaller share of the market. This is illustrated in Figure 11.6. Once the *DD* curve shifts to the left, firms find that they cannot sell what they expect to sell at the existing price. This means they can no longer sell at the short-run equilibrium combination of Q^* and P^*. At P^* the firm can now only sell Q_s.

Consequently, the short-run price adjustment mechanism through the inward (downward) shifts in the *dd* curve takes over. As long as excess profits remain, firms continue to enter and *DD* continues to shift to the left causing firms to respond by shifting the *dd* curve inwards. This inward shifting of both the *DD* and *dd* curves proceeds until all excess profits are exhausted. This occurs where the perceived demand curve *dd* is tangent to the *LAC* curve where the market-share curve *DD* passes through that point of tangency. The equilibrium at this point is stable as there is no further incentive for firms to enter (or exit) and each firm is selling what it expects to sell.

The movement to long-run equilibrium may be demonstrated using Figure 11.7. In the diagram, the point *e* is the initial equilibrium (short-run) position where $MC = MR$

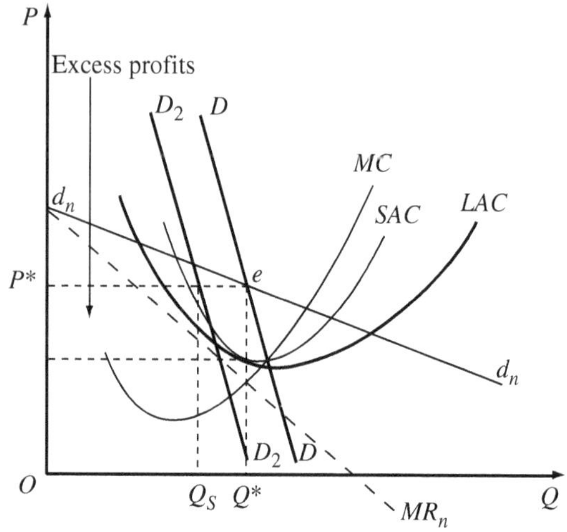

Figure 11.6
Effect of entry on market-share demand curve (*DD*) and on equilibrium

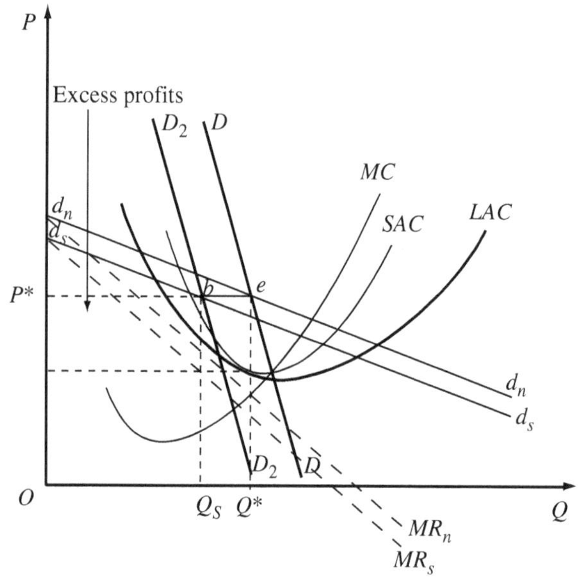

Figure 11.7
The adjustment process toward long-run equilibrium

at a quantity Q^* such that *DD* cuts *dd* and each firm is selling what it expects to sell at the price P^*. Each firm, however, is making excess profits (Π) indicated by the shaded area. As a consequence, firms enter the industry. This causes the share of market for each firm to fall to D_2D_2. With price P^* output Q^*, firms find that they cannot sell the Q^* they expect to sell at P^*. They can only sell Q_s at that price. Hence the short-run

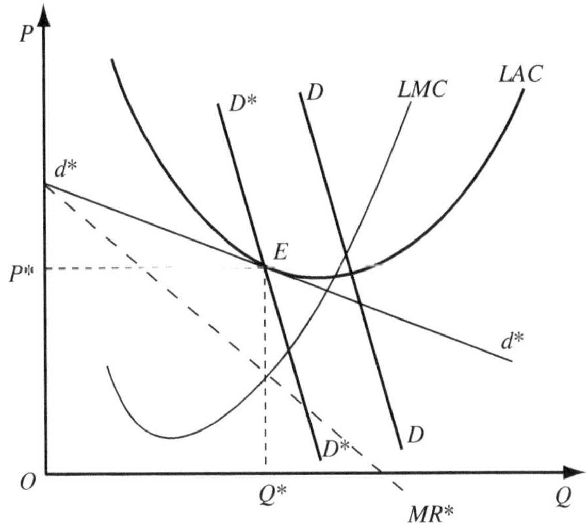

Figure 11.8
The long-run equilibrium position under monopolistic competition

adjustment mechanism takes over. Each firm revises downwards its *dd* curve to pass through the point consistent with P^*Q_s (point *b*) and tries to sell at a lower price where $MC = MR_s$. But since all firms are doing the same, all firms are again restricted to their market-share demand curve and so at the new lower price each firm cannot sell as much as it expects to sell.

However, the firms do not learn as they continue to engage in this myopic behaviour. As long as there are still excess profits to be made by each firm, there continues to be entry of new firms into the industry. Each time entry occurs, *DD* continues to shift to the left, thereby causing the short-run downward shifts in *dd* in an effort to restore equilibrium to where the firm can sell what it expects to sell in accordance with the profit maximization ($MC = MR$) price-quantity combination. In the final analysis, the *dd* is tangent to the *LAC* curve, signifying zero excess profits for each firm.

11.4.2 The long-run equilibrium position

The long-run equilibrium is stable at point *E* as shown in Figure 11.8. *MC* is equal to the MR^* relevant to the d^*d^* curve and the firm can sell the quantity they expect to sell (Q^*) at price P^*. At this point, the market-share curve, *DD*, intersects their *dd* curve. Furthermore *DD* has settled at D^*D^* because *dd* is tangent to the *LAC* and there are no more excess profits to encourage entry and shift *DD* any further to the left. At this position there are also no losses that would cause firms to exit and shift *DD* to the right, reversing the process and causing an upward shift in *dd*. The point E_1 therefore represents a stable long-run equilibrium position.

The significance of this position is that for the long-run equilibrium position to be achieved, *dd* ***must*** be tangent to the *LAC* on the left of the minimum point of the *LAC*.

This occurs because *dd* is downward sloping rather than horizontal and has implications for economic efficiency.

11.5 MONOPOLISTIC COMPETITION AND EXCESS CAPACITY

11.5.1 Economic efficiency

The final long-run equilibrium position under monopolistic competition does not allow the firm to achieve 'economic efficiency'. As stated in Chapter 9, 'economic efficiency' in this context refers to:

- Operating with the optimal scale plant (plant at min. *LAC*)
- Using the plant at its optimal (designed) capacity (min. *SAC*)
- Charging the lowest possible price (price at min. *LAC*)
- Having zero excess profits (price equal to average cost).

In this model, since the final long-run equilibrium places the firm on the left-hand side of the minimum point of the *LAC*, the firm does not operate with the optimal scale plant in the long-run.

The firm therefore reaches its long-run equilibrium with excess capacity. This excess capacity is measured as the difference between the ideal output (min. *LAC*) and the actual output at the long-run equilibrium point on the left-hand side of the minimum point of the *LAC*. The firm in this position is not just using a less-than-optimal scale plant but is also using its short-run plant sub-optimally (i.e. at less than its designed capacity), for when the long-run average cost curve is falling, the short-run average cost curve (*SAC*) is tangent to the *LAC* on the ***left***-hand side of the *SAC* curve. Therefore, in the long-run equilibrium, since the perceived demand curve, *dd*, has a negative slope, the equilibrium point ***must*** occur on left side of the minimum point of the *LAC*. Consequently, the firm under monopolistic competition must operate in the long-run by under-utilizing its plant capacity while using a less-than-optimal-scale plant.

The excess capacity occurs on two levels:

- *Short-run excess capacity*. This is identified on the short-run average cost curve before its lowest point (left of the minimum point), and
- *Long-run excess capacity*. This is found on the long-run average cost curve before its lowest point (left of the minimum point).

As a result, price is higher than the lowest possible price and quantity lower than the optimal quantity. However, the tangency of *dd* to the average cost curve means that there are zero excess profits (price equal to average cost) in the firm and industry and saves one degree of economic efficiency. Output is less than ideal output. In the long run, each firm builds a sub-optimal scale plant and uses it sub-optimally. For this reason there is some overcrowding in the industry, often considered to exist in product groups such as chocolate and detergent.

11.5.2 Non-price competition and waste

Whereas the firms' naïve behaviour in optimizing with regard to *dd* is considered to be responsible for a waste of resources, it is felt that if firms were less naïve the extent of waste in the long-run equilibrium would be much greater. If firms were less focused on their *dd* curve and recognized their market-share curve *DD*, then new firms would enter until *DD′* is tangent to the *LAC* (left side). This leads to a higher prices and greater ***waste*** because of the monopoly element.

Excess capacity or excess cost

Interestingly, although firms are not taking into account actions of competitors, the model still assumes they are concerned with product differentiation. It has been argued that what is seen as excess capacity under Monopolistic Competition is a reflection of consumers' desire for variety. Product differentiation reflects the desires of consumers who are willing to pay a higher price to have wider choice among differentiated products. Thus the higher cost is socially acceptable. The contention is that this difference is not a measure of excess capacity but a measure of excess cost.

Figure 11.9 illustrates the difference between firms competing by lowering price and shifting downward their *dd* curve and firms recognizing their monopoly element and optimizing with respect to their market share (*DD*) curve. If firms were to recognize other firms in the industry there would be greater excess capacity and higher prices. Here, the

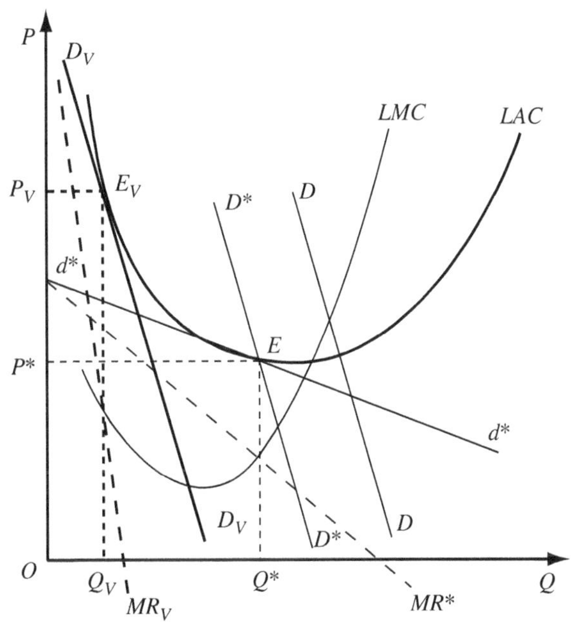

Figure 11.9
Excess capacity when using market-share demand curve for equilibrium

firm no longer relates to its *dd* curve as it can now see its share of the market-share curve (*DD*). Thus long run-equilibrium is reached when *DD* is tangent to *LAC* leading to much greater excess capacity in the long-run.

True excess capacity may be seen, then, as the difference between equilibrium output when *DD* is the relevant demand curve and the output when *dd* is the relevant demand curve. In Figure 11.9, if all firms see their market-share curve *DD* and optimize with respect to it, then, in the long-run firms would enter the industry or product group until all profits are eliminated. This would occur where the market-share curve that is now within their vision (DD_V) is tangent to the *LAC*. Using the relevant *MR* curve (MR_V) the firm would choose to operate at the lower quantity, Q_V, and charge a much higher price, P_V. This puts the firm much further from the optimal resource use position (min. *LAC*) than if the firm uses *dd*. The extent to which $Q_V P_V$ is away from $Q^* P^*$ can be considered to be the extent of the true excess capacity (distance between E and E_V).

11.5.3 Comparison with perfect competition and monopoly

Offered as an alternative to the models of perfect competition and monopoly, one of the criticisms of the monopolistic competition model related to its contribution and whether it was sufficiently distinguishable, particularly from perfect competition. Some comparisons may be made.

Under Monopolistic Competition, price is higher and output smaller compared to Perfect Competition. The difference depends on how close the slope of the *dd* curve is to infinite elasticity. Thus social optimum is not reached as it is under perfect competition even though the firm makes zero excess profits.

Compared with Monopoly, firms under Monopolistic Competition are likely to have lower profits and lower prices than under Monopoly. Unlike monopoly, where the firm can retain its short-run excess profits into the long-run, the firm under monopolistic competition is affected by entry. This entry and the subsequent adjustment of the firm prevent the firm from having any excess profits in the long-run as is possible under the model of pure monopoly.

In addition, whereas under monopoly the firm in its long-run equilibrium position may operate at sub-optimal, optimal or greater than optimal scale, the firm under monopolistic competition must, in the long-run, operate at a sub-optimal scale. Hence, whereas the monopolist's plant may be under-utilized, over-utilized or used at its designed capacity, the firm under Monopolistic Competition will always under-utilize its short-run plant and operate with excess capacity.

11.5.4 Product differentiation and waste

Despite the discussion on what constitutes 'true' excess capacity, much attention is still focused on the fact that the long-run equilibrium is to the left of the minimum point of the *LAC* and *SAC* curves. Some real world questions are still being asked. These include:

- ***What is the extent of product differentiation in the real world?*** The empirical question relates to the extent to which product differences allow firms with similar products to have a downward sloping *dd* curve. It is the slope of this *dd* curve that determines how high up the left side of the *LAC* the long-run equilibrium occurs. This has some relevance to how the model is applied to international trade theory.

- ***Does product differentiation help consumers get better quality products?*** At issue is whether product differentiation causes firms to try to maintain or improve quality in order to distinguish their product. This constant product improvement could compensate consumers for the higher price due to excess capacity.
- ***Do firms use advertising to cover up inferior product quality?*** Producers burdened with constant attempts to differentiate their products could try to use selling tactics to cover up or distract consumers as they seek to economize on quality. For example, a firm might put a smaller portion of food (e.g. roti or burrito) into a fancier wrapper as a distraction.

11.6 REFLECTIONS ON THE MODEL

11.6.1 Contribution to theory of the firm

The model is acknowledged to have made several notable contributions to the theory of the firm. These include:

- The introduction of the product (product differentiation) as a policy variable. This is a more modern approach as it allows for product branding and incorporates the effects of branding through the *dd* curve. It is product branding that allows the firm some degree of monopoly power and allows the firm to act as though it does not have to take into account the action of competitors. It is because of this branding that firms in this model tend to deny the existence of competition and so ignore the market-share demand curve. Recent extensions of the model into the area of international trade analysis use product differentiation to help explain the phenomenon of intra-industry trade (Krugman, 1981). The finding that customers have preferences for different varieties or brands of the same product (e.g. types of furniture, brands of electronic goods), is used to explain why a sizeable portion of international trade involves countries buying similar goods from each other.
- The provision of an explanation for the operation of firms on the falling portion of the average cost curve. The empirical observation of firms operating with excess capacity (i.e. operating with increasing returns to scale) has long been noted. More recently, the increasing returns to scale phenomenon have been studied in relation to international trade (Neary, 2002; Krugman, 1979).
- The introduction of two demand curves, namely the perceived demand curve (*dd*) and the market-share demand curve (*DD*). This concept appears in the kinked demand curve model in oligopoly.
- The introduction of advertising costs into the cost curve of the firm.

11.6.2 Major criticisms

The model has faced many criticisms. These include:

- The concept of the product group where products are similar yet differentiated. This concept was criticized by many, including George Stigler (1947). Where each firm produces a product that is similar, though not identical to that of the other firms, then the addition of these products together to form an industry posed a difficulty. Where products are not homogeneous then they must be heterogeneous and it is not clear how they may be added. Although the term product group was used, it was still treated as an industry (use of market-share demand curve and all firms having the same cost curves).
- The long-run equilibrium occurring at a point on the downward slope of the *LAC*. This excess capacity result received much criticism. It was believed that in the long-run demand is more elastic and so a flatter demand curve should be used. This would bring the equilibrium position closer to the minimum point of the *LAC* curve.
- The myopic behaviour of firms. It was felt that firms over time would get to know of other firms' reactions. Firms would therefore come to realize the existence of the share-of-the-market curve and would use it in their calculations. It would then be better to use the models of Perfect competition, Monopoly or Oligopoly depending on the conditions of entry.
- The incompatibility of product differentiation and myopic behaviour. There was the view that it is difficult to conceive of firms not being able to see that they have a share-of-the-market because of the many sellers of similar products yet at the same time be seeking to differentiate their products from those of their competitors. Many saw some incongruity here.
- The incompatibility of product differentiation and free entry. There was the view that free entry could not realistically co-exist with product differentiation particularly where the entrant is a new firm. Product differentiation requires advertising and the development of brand loyalty in order to permit the existence of some monopoly power by the firm. This could lead to the preference and advertising cost barriers preventing the free entry of firms.
- Strong preferences relate only to final consumer goods. The sticky preferences manifested by the *dd* curve are not expected to belong to intermediate goods, only to final consumer goods. This limits the relevance of the model to final goods product groups (industries) only.
- Adds little to the model of Perfect Competition. Several economists criticized the model on methodological grounds. In particular, Stigler (1949) considered that the theory had serious modelling limitations and that it was not so significantly different from the model of Perfect Competition to merit consideration as a separate market structure.

However, as mentioned earlier, despite the criticisms, the model received a revival of interest, beginning with the seminal work of Dixit and Stiglitz (1977) in what has been dubbed the second Monopolistic Competition revolution. Further interest in the model in relation to international trade, involving economists such as Krugman (1979, 1981), has brought the model back into the mainstream of economic analysis particularly with regard to issues of increasing returns and intra-industry trade.

REVIEW QUESTIONS FOR CHAPTER 11

1 With reference to the Chamberlin model of monopolistic competition:

(a) Set out and critically analyze the basic assumptions of the model.
(b) Discuss the major novel contributions introduced into the theory of the firm by this model.

2 Explain carefully with regard to the Monopolistic Competition model:

(a) The meaning of the 'perceived' demand curve in the model.
(b) The difference between the 'perceived' demand curve and the 'market-share' demand curve.
(c) The mechanics of the way in which the two demand curves are used to arrive at the firm's short-run equilibrium position.
(d) Why the firm's short-run profit maximizing behaviour may be described as 'myopic'.

3 Using the Chamberlin model of monopolistic competition show clearly:

(a) How entry and the short-run adjustment mechanisms combine to move the firm and industry to its long-run equilibrium position.
(b) How and why the long-run equilibrium position must be at a position of excess capacity for the firm.

4 Explain with regard to the Monopolistic Competition model:

(a) Why the firm, in its long-run equilibrium, cannot achieve 'economic efficiency'.
(b) Why excess capacity might be greater in the absence of the firm's myopic behaviour.

5 With regard to the Chamberlin model of monopolistic competition:

(a) Briefly summarize the major contributions and the criticisms of this theory of market structure.
(b) Comment on the more recent attempts to revive the model and to apply it to the arena of international trade theory.

RECOMMENDED READING FOR CHAPTER 11

Chamberlin, E. (1933) *The Theory of Monopolistic Competition*, Cambridge: Harvard University Press (8th ed, 1962).

Dixit, A. K. and Stiglitz, J. E. (1977) 'Monopolistic Competition and Optimum Product Diversity', *American Economic Review*, 67(3): 297–308.
Koutsoyiannis, A. (1979) *Modern Microeconomics*, (2nd Edn.) London: MacMillan
Krugman, P. R. (1979) 'Increasing Returns, Monopolistic Competition and International Trade', *Journal of International Economics*, 9(4): 469–79.
Krugman, P. R. (1981) 'Intra-Industry Specialization and the Gains from Trade', *Journal of Political Economy*, 89(5): 959–73.
Neary, J. P. (2002) 'Monopolistic Competition and International Trade Theory', in Brackman, S. and Heijdra, B. J. (eds.) *The Monopolistic Competition Revolution in Retrospect*, Cambridge: Cambridge University Press.
Roberts, J. and Sonnenschein, H. (1977) 'On the Foundations of the Theory of Monopolistic Competition', *Econometrica*, 45(1): 101–13.
Robinson, J. (1933) *The Economics of Imperfect Competition*, London: MacMillan (2nd ed. 1969).
Sraffa, P. (1926) 'The Laws of Returns under Competitive Conditions', *Economic Journal*, 36: 535–50.
Stigler, G. J. (1949) 'Monopolistic Competition in Retrospect', *Five Lectures on Economic Problems*, London: Longmans, Green & Co: 12–24.

12 Oligopoly

Non-Collusive Models: Cournot, Bertrand, Chamberlin, Kinked-Demand, Stackleberg; Collusive Models: Price-Leadership, Cartels; Game Theory.

The market structure of oligopoly, similar to that of monopolistic competition, is situated somewhere on the continuum between the models of perfect competition and monopoly. Unlike the three previous market structures, each of which can be dealt with as a single model, there are a plethora of models of oligopoly. A single thread running through this group of models is that the industry is composed of a ***few*** sellers, a small enough number that they are aware of each other. However, the way in which they acknowledge or act upon their interdependence with each other differs from one model to the other.

Firms that were previously monopolies in their own domestic markets may become oligopolies as a result of regional integration or from greater trade liberalization. It is useful to examine the myriad models, non-collusive and collusive, and to observe their evolution as market conditions change over time.

In this chapter, several of the classical or traditional models and the standard models of oligopoly, including the Game Theory are examined. The more recent developments in the theory of the firm pertaining mainly to the market structure of oligopoly are left to the next chapter.

12.1 ASSUMPTIONS, DEFINITIONS AND SUMMARY OF MODELS

12.1.1 Assumptions

There are a number of assumptions that are common to all models of oligopoly. These are:

- The industry consists of a small number of firms. This is understood to be fewer than under the market structure of Monopolistic Competition.
- The goal of the firm is to maximize profit.
- All factors are freely available to the firm at given prices.

- There is a great deal of interdependence (actual and/or perceived).
- The products in the industry may be homogeneous or differentiated.

Reasons for oligopoly

Typically, oligopoly exists because of:

- Economies of scale in production.
- Economies of scale in advertising or promotion of the product.
- Limited access to raw materials.
- Government controls on access to the market (e.g. permit requirements, etc.).
- Capital barriers to entry.
- Branding and preference barriers or other barriers to entry.

12.1.2 Definitions

Classical or traditional oligopoly

The term classical oligopoly is used to distinguish the traditional models from the modern or alternative models of the firm introduced since the 1950s. The non-collusive and collusive models listed above are all part of classical or traditional oligopoly.

Pure and differentiated oligopoly

Under pure oligopoly firms produce a homogenous product (e.g. flour, salt). Under differentiated oligopoly firms produce a differentiated product (e.g. automobiles, refrigerators). These products are usually differentiated by branding. As with Monopolistic Competition, the differences may be real or fancied. However, they must be such that the consumer perceives the products to be different.

12.1.3 Model summary

The various traditional or classical models of oligopoly may be grouped into the two major classes of non-collusive and collusive. The game theory approach to modelling oligopoly in terms of competitors in a game with strategies and counter-strategies may be included among the traditional models. The models may be summarized as follows.

Non-collusive models

- The Cournot duopoly model
- The Bertrand/Edgeworth duopoly model
- The Chamberlin duopoly model.
- The Sweezy Kinked Demand model.
- The Stackleberg Solution model of 'the sophisticated Duopolist'

Collusive models

- Cartels
- Price leadership
- The low cost price leader
- The dominant firm price leader
- The barometric price leader

Game theory

The two-person, zero-sum, strictly determined game.

Game theory provides an alternative way to model oligopoly in terms of strategy and counter-strategy. The two-person, zero-sum, strictly determined game is one of the simplest forms of the game that allows a clear insight into how the model works.

These models are dealt with seriatim.

12.2 THE COURNOT MODEL

A study of the non-collusive models reveals that although the firms in the industry recognize their interdependence and this affects their behaviour, they do not resort to collusion. This, of course, tends to reduce firm and industry profits, reduce price and increase output.

The Cournot model is one of the earliest oligopoly models and, in its original form, is a duopoly model (two sellers). It is associated with the economist A. Cournot (1801–1877), who first presented the model in 1838, writing later in 1897. It is a costless production model related to sale of water from mineral springs.

12.2.1 Assumptions of the Cournot model

1. The model is closed. There are two sellers of mineral water – each owns a mineral spring and no further entry takes place.
2. Both firms aim to maximize profit.
3. The firms have zero operating costs (hence $TC = AC = MC = 0$). Thus production is costless.
4. Firms sell in a market with a straight-line, negatively sloped demand curve.
5. Each firm acts on the assumption that other firms will not change the quantity of their output. This is central to the model and is known as ***the Cournot assumption***.

12.2.2 Behavioural process and equilibrium

The behavioural process is characterized by the naïve behaviour of the firms using ***the Cournot assumption***. The process may be described with respect to two firms (duopoly) described as firm A and firm B.

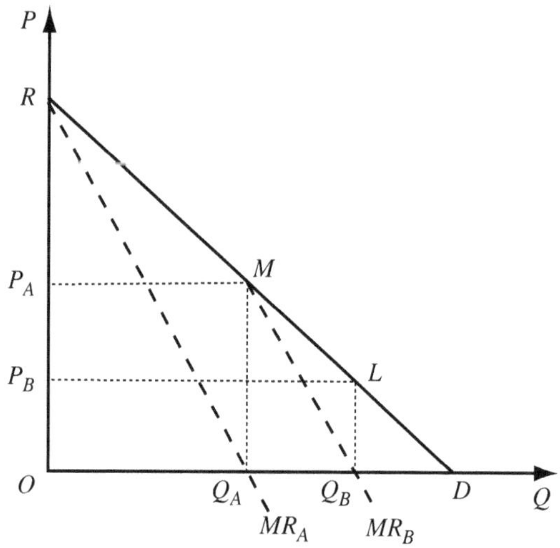

Figure 12.1
The Cournot duopoly model

Firm A starts to produce. The firm, a profit maximizer, produces at the point where $MR = 0$. This is because there are no production costs and as a result, $MC = 0$. Hence, in equilibrium, $MC = MR = 0$. This is illustrated in Figure 12.1.

This equilibrium of the firm takes place at the mid-point (M) of the demand curve. This is because $MR = 0$ where total revenue (TR) is a maximum and total revenue is a maximum at the mid-point of the demand curve. Since the MR curve lies halfway between the Y-axis and the demand curve, then at $MR = 0$, the MR curve bisects the quantity axis (i.e. cuts it in half between the origin (O) and the point D where the demand curve reaches the quantity axis (X-axis).

Where MR is equal to zero, total revenue is at its maximum. This occurs at the mid point of the demand curve. Hence in a market with zero costs, ***the maximization of profits becomes the same as the maximization of revenue*** and they both take place at M, the mid-point of the demand curve.

As a result, firm A may be said to sell half of the market (i.e. half of the total quantity that would be sold in the market at zero price). Hence, the profit maximization position for firm A is the quantity OQ_A and price OP_A as shown in Figure 12.1.

According to the model, firm B then enters and makes the Cournot assumption, that is, firm B assumes that firm A will keep producing OQ_A. Hence, firm B considers its market to be the part of the market not supplied by firm A. Therefore, firm B sees as their market the segment Q_AD on the quantity axis with Q_A as its origin. This indicates that firm B sees its demand curve as MD. Consequently, with zero cost, firm B maximizes profits at the mid-point (L) of what it perceives as its own demand curve, MD. The point (L) is the revenue maximization point, which in the absence of costs, is also the profit maximization point for firm B.

Firm B, operating optimally, according to its perception, at the point L, produces the quantity Q_AQ_B of mineral water and sells it at its profit maximizing price, P_B. Thus firm B's output is Q_AQ_B $\left(= \frac{1}{2}\right)$ of the market left by firm after firm A has sold one-half of the market. This makes it firm B's profit maximizing sales equal to one-quarter of the total overall market OD $\left[\left(\frac{1}{2} \times \frac{1}{2}\right) = \frac{1}{4}\right]$.

The process continues in this way:

- Firm A assumes firm B will keep selling $\frac{1}{4}$ of the total market – so firm A decides to sell one half $\left(\frac{1}{2}\right)$ of what's left. What's left is $1 - \frac{1}{4} = \frac{3}{4}$. Hence firm A now sells $\frac{1}{2}$ of $\frac{3}{4} = \frac{3}{8}$ of the total market.
- Firm B assumes again that firm A will continue to sell $\frac{3}{8}$ of the market. Hence, firm B looks at what's left, i.e. $\left(1 - \frac{3}{8}\right) = \frac{5}{8}$ and sells $\frac{1}{2}$ of this, i.e. $\frac{5}{16}$ of the market.
- Then firm A sells $\frac{1}{2}\left(1 - \frac{5}{16}\right) = \frac{1}{2}\left(\frac{11}{16}\right) = \frac{11}{32}$ of the market.
- Then firm B sells $\frac{1}{2}\left(1 - \frac{11}{32}\right) = \frac{1}{2}\left(\frac{21}{32}\right) = \frac{21}{64}$ of the market.

Thus A's output declines gradually as in the following sequence:

$$\frac{1}{2}, \frac{3}{8}, \frac{11}{32}, \frac{43}{128} \ldots$$

Each firm continues to make the ***Cournot assumption*** that the other will keep on selling the same output as before and firms do not learn from experience. This is the naïve behaviour that is characteristic of the model. Each firm is myopic and fails to see that the other firm does not hold its quantity constant.

Formally, then, the sequence for firm A is as follows (using a partial sequence only):

$$\begin{aligned} \text{Firm } A \text{ sells } &= \tfrac{1}{2}; \quad \tfrac{1}{2}\left(1 - \tfrac{1}{4}\right); \quad \tfrac{1}{2}\left(1 - \tfrac{5}{16}\right); \quad \tfrac{1}{2}\left(1 - \tfrac{21}{64}\right) \\ &= \tfrac{1}{2}; \quad \tfrac{1}{2} - \tfrac{1}{8}; \quad \tfrac{1}{2} - \tfrac{5}{32}; \quad \tfrac{1}{2} - \tfrac{21}{128} \\ &= \tfrac{1}{2}; \quad \tfrac{1}{2} - \tfrac{1}{8}; \quad \tfrac{1}{2} - \tfrac{1}{8} - \tfrac{1}{32}; \quad \tfrac{1}{2} - \tfrac{1}{8} - \tfrac{1}{32} - \tfrac{1}{128} \end{aligned}$$

This generates a declining geometric series with ratio $r = \frac{1}{4}$:

$$= \frac{1}{2} - \left[\frac{1}{8} + \frac{1}{8}\left(\frac{1}{4}\right) + \frac{1}{8}\left(\frac{1}{4}\right)^2 + \frac{1}{8}\left(\frac{1}{4}\right)^3 + \cdots\right]$$

Applying the summation formula for convergence of an infinite geometric series:

$$\sum\left(\frac{a}{1-r}\right)$$

where:

$$a = \text{ first term in series } = \left(\tfrac{1}{8}\right)$$

and:

$$r = \text{ ratio } = \left(\tfrac{1}{4}\right)$$

In equilibrium A's share is:

$$\tfrac{1}{2}-\left(\frac{\frac{1}{8}}{1-\frac{1}{4}}\right)=\tfrac{1}{2}-\tfrac{1}{8}\left(\tfrac{4}{3}\right)=\tfrac{1}{2}-\tfrac{1}{6}$$

or:

$$\tfrac{3-1}{6}=\tfrac{2}{6}=\tfrac{1}{3}$$

Now consider firm B

$$\text{Firm } B \text{ sells} =\tfrac{1}{4};\quad \tfrac{1}{2}\left(1-\tfrac{3}{8}\right);\quad \tfrac{1}{2}\left(1-\tfrac{11}{32}\right);\quad \tfrac{1}{2}\left(1-\tfrac{43}{128}\right);\cdots$$
$$=\tfrac{1}{4};\quad \tfrac{1}{4}+\tfrac{1}{4}\left(\tfrac{1}{4}\right);\quad \tfrac{1}{4}+\tfrac{1}{4}\left(\tfrac{1}{4}\right)+\tfrac{1}{4}\left(\tfrac{1}{4}\right)^2;\quad \tfrac{1}{4}+\tfrac{1}{4}\left(\tfrac{1}{4}\right)+\left(\tfrac{1}{4}\right)\left(\tfrac{1}{4}\right)^2+\tfrac{1}{4}\left(\tfrac{1}{4}\right)^3;\cdots$$

This generates an increasing geometric series,

$$\tfrac{1}{4}+\tfrac{1}{4}\left(\tfrac{1}{4}\right)+\tfrac{1}{4}\left(\tfrac{1}{4}\right)^2+\tfrac{1}{4}\left(\tfrac{1}{4}\right)^3+\cdots$$

Using the formula for summing a series:

$$\sum\left(\frac{a}{1-r}\right)=\left(\frac{\frac{1}{4}}{1-\frac{1}{4}}\right)=\tfrac{1}{4}\left(\tfrac{4}{3}\right)=\tfrac{1}{3}$$

Hence, in equilibrium, firm B's share is also $\frac{1}{3}$.

Final equilibrium

The final equilibrium is therefore stable with firms A and B each selling $\frac{1}{3}$ of the market. Together they sell $\frac{2}{3}$ of the market. This quantity sold represents more than the $\frac{1}{2}$ of the market which would be the monopoly quantity OQ_A. Furthermore, it is sold at less than the monopoly price OP_A. Because of their naïveté, the firms in the industry operating under the Cournot assumption do not maximize industry profits as they sell a greater quantity at a lower price than is necessary for this to happen.

Generalization

If there are three firms, it can be shown that each will produce $\frac{1}{4}$ of the market and together will supply $\frac{3}{4}$ of the market.

Furthermore, if there are n firms each firm's share of industry output would be:

$$\left(\frac{1}{n+1}\right)$$

Consequently, total industry output would be:

$$n\left(\frac{1}{n+1}\right) \quad \text{or} \quad \left(\frac{n}{n+1}\right) \quad \text{of the market}$$

As a result, the larger the number of firms, the larger the industry output as a proportion of the total market and the lower the price. Output and price therefore approach the competitive output and price.

It is possible to conclude that, if firms entering the global market in a globally oligopolistic industry make the Cournot assumption and behave in a myopic manner, the result would be a greater output at a lower price than otherwise.

Criticisms of the Cournot model

The model is criticized on several grounds. These include:

- The behaviour pattern is naïve. Firms do not learn from their experience and each one continues to believe that the other firm will keep its output constant even though this repeatedly fails to happen. This is considered to be unrealistic and particularly so in the modern world with the greater availability of information.
- The model is closed. There is neither entry nor exit after the initial entry of firms.

12.3 THE BERTRAND/EDGEWORTH DUOPOLY MODEL

J. Bertrand and F. Edgeworth, writing in the 1880s and 1890s, respectively developed a model in response to a criticism of the Cournot model. They took issue with the Cournot assumption that each rival firm believes the other will hold its quantity constant. They contended that it was more realistic to assume that firms believe that their competitors will hold their ***price*** rather than quantity constant. Consequently, this model replaces the 'Cournot' assumption with the 'Bertrand/Edgeworth' assumption substituting price competition rather than quantity competition among firms. The model considers that each firm faces the same market demand, and aims at the maximization of its own profits based on the assumption that the price of its competitor will remain constant.

The Bertrand/Edgeworth model uses the same 'mineral springs' model with the same assumption of zero costs. Hence, profit maximization again takes place at the mid-point of the demand curve. As in the Cournot model, there are only two firms (duopoly) and there is neither entry nor exit.

Figure 12.2 illustrates the model. Firm A starts the process and achieves maximization of profits at the mid-point of the demand curve (M) by selling quantity Q_A at price P_A.

Using the 'Bertrand/Edgeworth' assumption, firm B sells at price just below P_A, say P_B, in order to capture the market expecting that firm A will keep its price constant at P_A. In response, firm A lowers its price below that of firm B based on the assumption firm B will hold its price constant at P_B. The price cutting process continues until price is at the lowest possible.

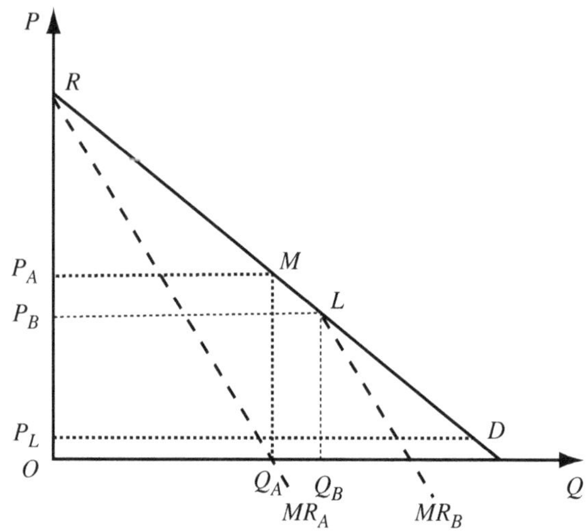

Figure 12.2
The Edgeworth/Bertrand duopoly model with price competition

The lowest price, P_L, is typically the perfectly competitive price or the price which just covers the average cost of production. In the case of costless production, as in this model, since AC is zero, P_L is expected to be at or near zero. In essence, then, the competition between the two firms should lead to the perfectly competitive price, which, without entry or exit should be the long-run price. The model would then be ultimately indistinguishable from that of Perfect Competition in the final analysis.

However, this is not entirely the case. When price falls too low at P_L, one firm, say firm A, realizes that it can increase its profits by raising its price back to P_A. At this point firm B sets its price just below P_A and the entire process is repeated. Thus price moves continually between P_A and P_L.

This is essentially a 'price war' model and, as naïve as the behaviour appears, it can be found in practice in some form or to some extent in some industries where prices keep fluctuating (e.g. computer memory).

Both the Cournot and the Bertrand/Edgeworth models have been roundly criticized for the assumed naïvety of the firms behaviour.

12.4 CHAMBERLIN AND STABILITY IN DUOPOLY

Although more well-known for the model of Monopolistic Competition, Chamberlin (1933) adds some flavour to the duopoly models as he summarizes and tries to bring stability to the Cournot and Bertrand/Edgeworth models.

Chamberlin's concern is with the continuance of the naïve behaviour by both firms in each of the two models. His contention is that, first of all, these two firms must be completely independent or else they would be a monopoly. Yet, because there are only two firms, the actions of each one must significantly affect the other in terms of price and quantity both directly and indirectly. This is because every action initiated by one competitor elicits a reaction from the other competitor that, in itself, has a further consequence for the initiator. He considers, therefore, that the two firms must recognize their mutual dependence.

According to Chamberlin, each seller, in seeking to maximize his profit, must reflect well and look at the total consequences of his move. The seller must therefore 'consider not merely what his competitor is doing now, but also what he will be forced to do in the light of the change which he himself is contemplating' (Chamberlin, 1933: 47).

The two firms, therefore, acting independently and ***without collusion***, would realize the repercussions of their actions and take appropriate steps to avoid making decisions that would be detrimental to their joint interests. The result would be actions taken for their mutual benefits bringing a stable equilibrium with the earning of monopoly profits for the two firms.

This stability outcome can be examined for the Cournot model. Using the same 'mineral springs' model with the assumptions of two sellers aiming to maximize profits and zero production costs, profit maximization takes place at the mid-point of the demand curve. The firm initially makes the Cournot assumption, but the naïve, myopic behaviour does not continue.

The Chamberlin version of the duopoly model is depicted in Figure 12.3. Firm A starts in the usual manner and sells $\frac{1}{2}$ of the market in order to maximize its profits. Price OP_A and quantity OQ_A are the initial equilibrium price and quantity for firm A. Then firm B enters and regards MD as its demand curve, as explained earlier with regard to the Cournot model. Thus firm B sells $\frac{1}{2}$ of $\left(1-\frac{1}{4}\right)=\frac{1}{2}$ of $\frac{1}{2}=\frac{1}{4}$ of the market. Price falls to P_B as the total output sold is now $OQ_B=\frac{3}{4}$ of the total market.

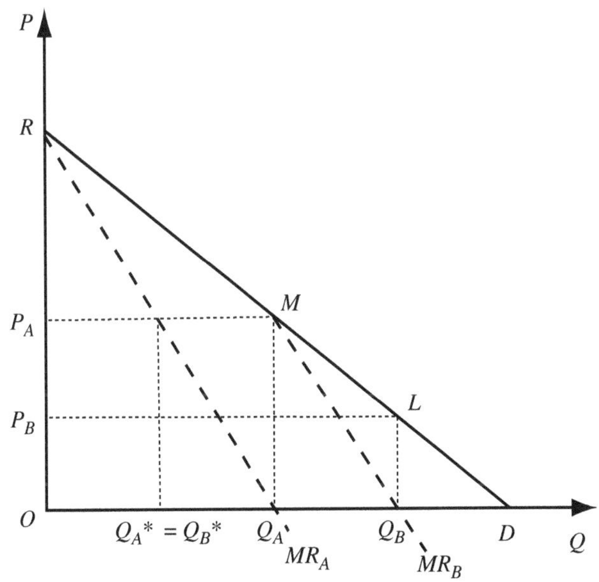

Figure 12.3
The Chamberlin duopoly model with market stability

However, instead of continuing this naïve behaviour, firm A realizes that it cannot continue to assume that firm B will maintain a constant output and considers that if they (firm A) change their output, then firm B will change their output also. So firm A realizes that the best they can do is to share the monopoly profits with firm B and each sell $\frac{1}{4}$ of the total market. Firm B also realizes that this is the best it can do and together they sell the monopoly quantity Q_A ($\frac{1}{2}$ the market) with each firm selling $\frac{1}{4}$ of the market at the monopoly price P_A. Each firm is therefore selling the same quantity $Q_A^* = Q_B^*$ where $Q_A^* + Q_B^* = Q_A$. Hence the equilibrium is stable and industry profits are maximized at the monopoly profits. There is no incentive for either firm to alter price or quantity.

While there is no collusion, only the recognition by firms of their interdependence, the effect is similar to that of a market sharing cartel. Price in the industry is higher and quantity is lower than under the Cournot equilibrium. The outcome is also no different from that of a multi-plant monopoly as the firms share the monopoly profits. Only the consumer comes out the loser due to the reduction in competitiveness in the market.

12.5 THE KINKED DEMAND MODEL

The 'kinked demand' model is considerably different from the previous three models. In this case there is a single representative firm which can be considered virtually identical to the others in the industry. Sweezy (1939) introduced this model to explain the 'stickiness' of price in oligopoly markets. This 'stickiness' is the tendency of prices to remain unchanged even in the face of changing costs. Sweezy asserted that if an oligopolistic firm cuts its price, it can be pretty sure that its rivals will meet the reduction; however, if it increases its price the others will not follow.

The model considers that there is a prevailing price P^* in the market as shown in Figure 10.4. It may be noted that the model does not explain how this price is set. However, it is assumed that above this price, the demand facing the oligopolist is highly elastic as the firm will lose most of his customers with a price increase. Below P^* the firm's demand is less elastic since all other firms will follow a price decrease by the firm.

The MR curve is disjointed because of the kink in the demand curve. This is illustrated in Figure 12.4. Up to the output Q^*, the relevant portion of the demand curve is DE. Beyond output Q^* the relevant portion is EG. This means that up to the quantity Q^* the relevant MR curve is the one related to the DE segment of the demand curve. Beyond Q^* the relevant MR curve is that related to the EG segment of the demand curve. Because the two portions of the demand curve have different slopes and because each MR curve has twice the slope of the relevant portion of the demand curve to which it refers, there is a vertical gap ($a\ b$) between the two segments of the MR curve. This gap occurs directly below the kink at the quantity Q^* where the change in demand slope takes place. The greater the difference between the slopes of the upper and lower portions of the kinked demand curve, the greater the vertical distance ($a\ b$) in the MR curve.

Because of the vertical gap in the marginal revenue (MR) curve, there is a range ($a\ b$) through which the marginal cost curve can shift without effecting a change in equilibrium price or quantity. Over this range, $MC = MR$ holds for several levels of marginal cost, curves ranging from MC_1 to MC_2, as shown in Figure 12.4. Thus price would tend to

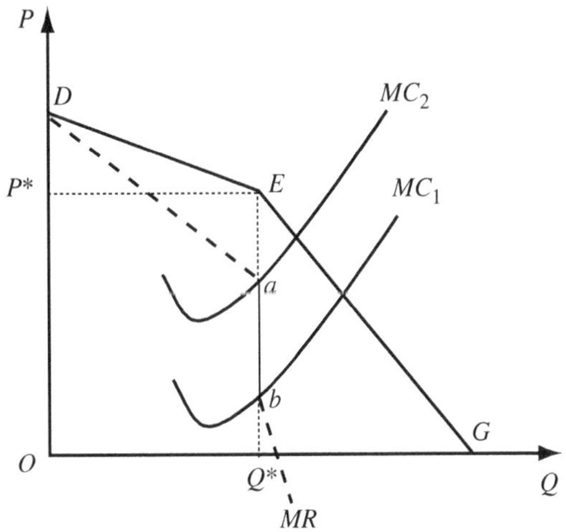

Figure 12.4
The kinked-demand model of oligopoly

remain stable despite changes in cost within this range. It would also remain stable with changes in demand as long as the kink remains at P^*.

It is useful to note that this is not a theory which explains how the equilibrium price (P^*) is set. It just explains why, once the price is set, it tends not to change. This phenomenon was observed during the depression years of the 1930s. However, it would also serve to explain cases where firms are so aware of their interdependence nationally, regionally or globally, that they are unwilling to either raise or lower their prices because of the different price elasticities in the upper and lower portions of the kinked demand curve.

One construction that can be put on the kinked demand curve is that the two parts of the kinked curve derive from the Monopolistic Competition model. In this case, the upper more elastic part would derive from the perceived demand curve (*dd*) while the lower more inelastic part would represent the market share demand curve (*DD*). The difference is that in this case, the firm is able to see both curves, unlike under the model of Monopolistic Competition.

12.6 THE STACKLEBERG SOPHISTICATED DUOPOLIST MODEL

The Stackleberg model of oligopoly (duopoly), appearing in the 1950s, is considered to represent an advance over the Cournot and Bertrand/Edgeworth models. The model follows those of Cournot and Bertrand/Edgeworth with two variants, one using the 'Cournot assumption' and the other using the 'Bertrand/Edgeworth assumption'. Stackleberg's work removes some of the concerns with the earlier models, principally the following:

- It obviates the need for the simplification of costless production in the older models by introducing iso-profit and reaction curves. This development is based on Stackleberg's contention that the previous models' assumption of costless production is unrealistic and could be relaxed without impairing the validity of the model.

- It introduces the 'sophisticated' firm which can anticipate its rivals reactions and incorporate them into their own profit function to replace the myopic and naïve behaviour of firms in the older models.

Stackleberg bases his model on a type of indifference curve analysis and focuses directly on profit as the difference between revenue and cost showing how profit varies as firms react to each other.

12.6.1 Iso-profit and reaction curves using the Cournot assumption

The reaction curves approach of Stackleberg is based on the use of the iso-profit curves and takes into account production costs by tracing the reaction to profits. The reaction process is therefore no longer based on revenue only as in the Cournot models.

The process consists of two steps:

1 Establish the shape of the iso-profit curves for substitute commodities.
2 From these iso-profit curves derive the reaction curves of the Cournot duopolists.

12.6.1.1 THE ISO-PROFIT CURVE

Stackleberg defines an ***iso-profit*** curve for a firm (firm A) as the locus of points defined by different levels of output of firm A and its rival firm B, which yield the same level of profit to A. These are shown below for the first variant of the model where the firms are assumed to make the 'Cournot' assumption. The iso-profit curve for a firm is drawn concave to the firm's quantity axis and so in this case the iso-profit curve for A is drawn concave to A's quantity axis (Q_A).

The quantities A_1, A_2, and beyond represent the quantities produced by firm A and the quantities B_1, B_2, and beyond are those produced by firm B and are measured along the X- and Y-axis respectively.

Using Figure 12.5, if firm B produces quantity B_1, then firm A must produce A_1 or A_5 to obtain the level of profit given by A's iso-profit curve. If firm B increases output to B_2 then firm A must move from A_5 (if started at A_5) to A_4 (or from A_1 to A_2) in order to maintain the same level of profits. If firm A remains at A_5 (or at A_1) it would move to a lower iso-profit curve (a curve farther away from firm A's quantity axis).

If firm A had started at A_1 instead, then, as B increases output A could also increase output, but if firm A starts at A_5 then A's output must be decreased as B's output increases. If firm B should increase output beyond B_3, firm A would not be able to maintain its level of profit. Firm A must therefore move on to a new iso-profit curve farther from its axis with consequently lower profits.

It may be noted that for any given output of B, there is a unique level of output for A which maximizes A's profit. This occurs at the peak of the iso-profit curve. If firm A is at the peak of an iso-profit curve and firm B increases its quantity, then the best that firm A can do is to move to the peak of the next best iso-profit curve for A. This would be a curve farther away from A's quantity axis thereby representing a lower profit for firm A.

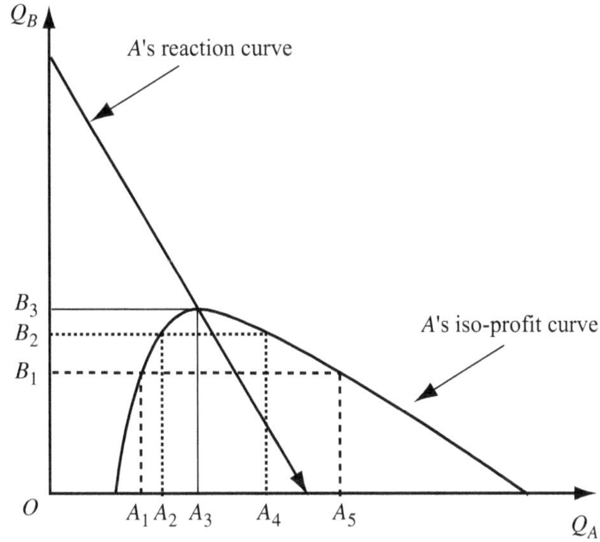

Figure 12.5
The Stackleberg duopolist model with iso-profit and reaction curves

12.6.1.2 THE REACTION CURVE

Firm *A* therefore reacts to increases in firm *B*'s output by moving from the peak of one iso-profit curve to the peak of the other farther from *A*'s axis. A line drawn through these peaks represents firm *A*'s ***reaction curve***. The reaction curve for firm *A* is drawn with an arrow pointing to *A*'s axis because this is the direction in which profit for firm *A* increases.

A similar analysis may be done for firm *B* and the arrow for firm *B*'s reaction curve points to the quantity axis for firm *B* where profit is higher for that firm. Firm *A*'s reaction curve is steeper than firm *B*'s.

12.6.1.3 THE COURNOT EQUILIBRIUM

In the Stackleberg model, the Cournot equilibrium occurs at the intersection of the two reaction curves. This is at point *E* in Figure 12.6 and is reached when firms react blindly to each other as in the Cournot model. At point *E*, each firm maximizes profit but industry profit is not maximized, that is the monopoly profit is not earned. Industry profit is maximized where *A*'s and *B*'s reaction curves are tangent to each other and occurs to the left of and below the point *E*, shown later in Figure 12.8 as the line *TU*.

12.6.2 The sophisticated duopolist and equilibrium

A central contribution of the Stackleberg model is the introduction of the concept of the 'sophisticated' duopolist. The sophisticated firm is the one that can anticipate its rival's reactions and learn to incorporate them into its profit function. Stackleberg assumes that

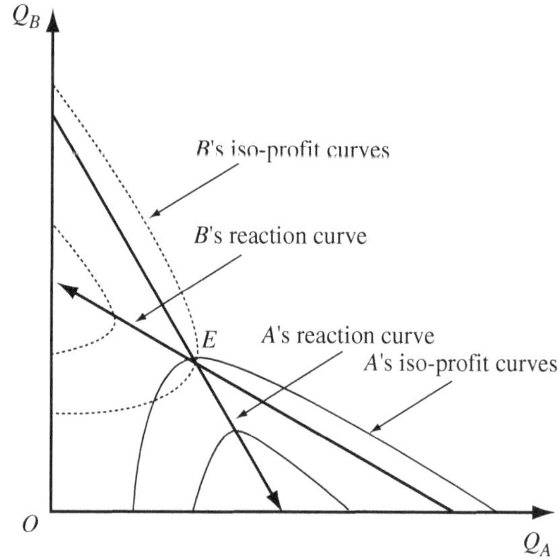

Figure 12.6
The Stackleberg model with Cournot equilibrium

at least one firm is 'sophisticated' and is therefore able to take advantage of the other naïve firm that just reacts along its 'reaction' curve. The sophisticated duopolist becomes the leader and the other firm the follower.

12.6.2.1 FIRM *A* IS THE 'SOPHISTICATED' DUOPOLIST

Where firm *A* is the sophisticated duopolist, firm *A* will choose the point *A* in Figure 12.7, where *A*'s iso-profit curve is tangent to *B*'s reaction curve. This puts firm *A* on an iso-profit curve representing a higher level of profit for firm *A* (i.e. an iso-profit curve closer to *A* quantity axis) than that for the Cournot equilibrium (*E*). Firm *A* has therefore learned to incorporate firm *B*'s reaction curve into firm *A*'s profit function and achieves a greater level of profit from this action. Meanwhile, firm *B*, the unsophisticated follower firm, is drawn on to an iso-profit curve further away from *B*'s axis, passing through the point *A* (dashed iso-profit line through the point *A*).

12.6.2.2 FIRM *B* IS THE 'SOPHISTICATED' DUOPOLIST

On the other hand, where firm *B* is the sophisticated duopolist and firm *A* is the unsophisticated follower, then *B* will move to an iso-profit curve tangent to *A*'s reaction curve and increase profits by moving from the Cournot equilibrium at *E* to the point *B*. This moves firm *B* to an iso-profit curve closer to *B*'s axis and therefore a higher level of profit for firm *B*. Firm *A*, by just reacting to firm *B*, is pulled on to an iso-profit curve much farther from firm *A*'s axis, passing through the point *B* and representing, therefore, a much lower profit for firm *A* (dashed line through point *B*).

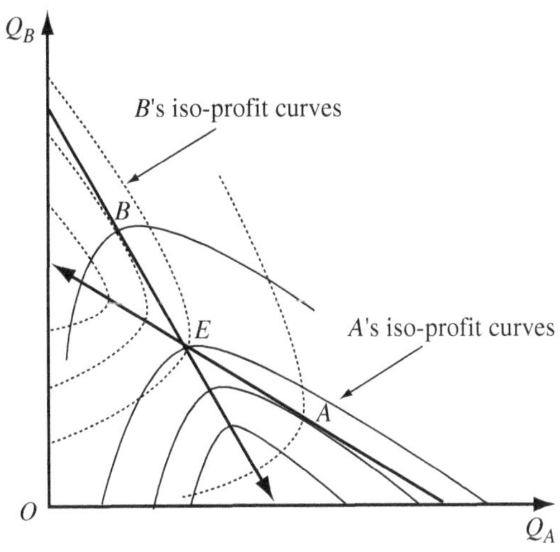

Figure 12.7
The Stackleberg 'sophisticated' duopolist

12.6.2.3 BOTH FIRMS ARE 'SOPHISTICATED'

Where both firms are sophisticated then the equilibrium position is indeterminate. Firm *A* wants to produce at the point *A* and firm *B* at the point *B*. Where they will settle is a matter of the relative strengths of the two firms in the market.

One outcome is that they will collude. If they decide to collude they will produce in the area where their iso-profit curves are tangent to each other and maximize industry profits. This area of tangency of iso-profit curves from the two firms is to the south-west of the Cournot equilibrium point and extends over a range such as that shown in Figure 12.8 by the wavy line *TU*.

Another outcome is that one firm will buy out the other, particularly where financial resource strengths vary widely from one firm to the other.

One message that may be derived from the model is that unsophisticated domestic firms entering a larger regional or global oligopoly market may find that they become the follower firms and, by just reacting on the Cournot assumption, can be forced into a position of achieving reduced profits at the expense of the more sophisticated firm even as they believe that they are maximizing profits.

12.6.3 The Stackleberg solution and the Bertrand assumption

The Stackleberg analysis can also be used to illustrate the Bertrand and Edgeworth models and provide an enhancement to the model. In this case, each firm is faced with the same market demand, and aims at the maximization of its own profit using the Bertrand and Edgeworth assumption that ***the price of its competitor will remain constant***. This analysis also employs iso-profit and reaction curves though sloped in the opposite direction.

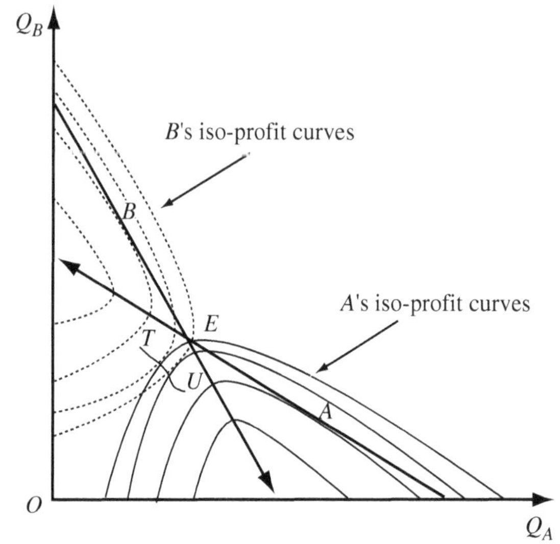

Figure 12.8
The Stackleberg model with collusion

12.6.3.1 ISO-PROFIT AND REACTION CURVE USING THE BERTRAND ASSUMPTION

In Figure 12.9, the price of firm A (P_A) and price of firm B (P_B) are on the X- and Y-axis respectively. In this case the axis for the respective firms must contain price rather than quantity values, since the firms react by making price changes rather than quantity changes, as in the Cournot version of this model.

The iso-profit curves are now convex (rather than concave) to the axes. An iso-profit curve for firm A shows the same level of profits which would accrue to A from various levels of prices charged by firm A and its competitor, firm B.

The isoprofit curve for A is convex to A's price axis to show that firm A must lower its price up to a certain level to meet the price cutting of its competitor in order to maintain the same level of profits. After that price is reached then if B continues to cut its price, A will be unable to maintain its level of profits and will have to go to a lower (closer to the firm's price axis) iso-profit curve. In this case, ***the further away from the firm's price axis is the iso-profit curve, the higher is the firm's profits***.

The analysis for firm B is similar to that of firm A except that firm B's curves are relevant to B's axis.

12.6.3.2 EQUILIBRIUM USING BERTRAND ASSUMPTION

Using Figure 12.9, the Bertrand/Edgeworth equilibrium is at E where the two reaction curves intersect. However, if firm A is the sophisticated duopolist then the equilibrium is at the point A where firm A's iso-profit curve is tangent to firm B's reaction curve. If firm B is the sophisticated duopolist then equilibrium is at point B where firm B's iso-profit curve is tangent to firm A's reaction curve. In each case the sophisticated firm

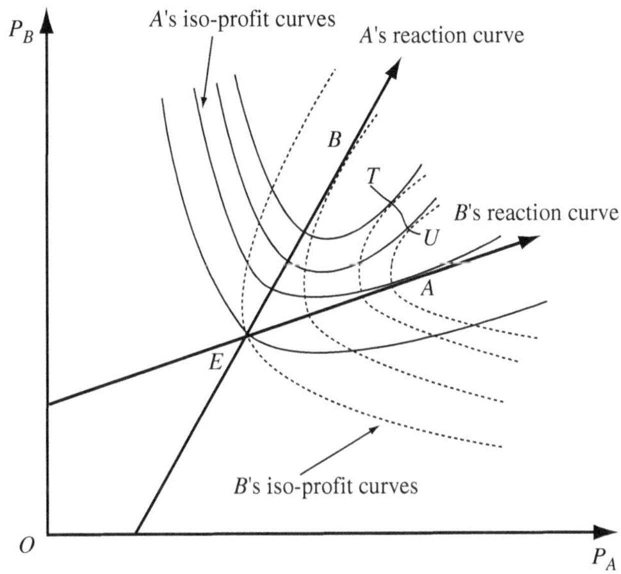

Figure 12.9
The Stackleberg reaction curves using the Edgeworth/Bertrand assumption

moves further away from its axis which, in this version, gives the firm a higher level of profit.

Once again firm *A*'s reaction curve must be steeper than firm *B*'s. This leads to a stable equilibrium. There is the same naïve behaviour as in the Bertrand/Edgeworth version of the model unless one firm is sophisticated.

Industry profit is not maximized. However, if firms were to learn from their past behaviour they could maximize industry profits by operating on one of the points in the short range where *A*'s and *B*'s iso-profit curves are tangent to each other. This is to the north-east of the point *E* and is represented in Figure 12.9 by the wavy line *TU*.

First mover advantage

The Stackleberg model has been extended to cover more than two firms. The model also considers firms entering the industry at different times where the leader acts first and the other firm(s) follows. This gives the leader the '***first mover***' advantage that allows that firm to be the 'sophisticated' duopolist.

Once again, the message from this type of analysis is that naïve or unsophisticated firms can be exploited by more sophisticated firms through an understanding of their reactions. This leads to lower profits for the less sophisticated firm and more for their competitor(s). If both are naïve, the result is more competitiveness in the market. This is better for the consumer but worse for the firm. Through collusion, the firms can achieve monopoly profits for the industry.

12.7 THE CARTEL

Most models of classical oligopoly (except Chamberlin's) are based upon the assumption that entrepreneurs act independently even though they recognize their interdependence, as seen in their making assumptions about their competitors' behaviour. In practice, however, there is much collusion, tacit or otherwise, through industry associations, trade groupings, professional bodies, membership in various types of organizations or formal collusive arrangements. One of the major types of formal collusive arrangements is the cartel.

12.7.1 Definition and characteristics of cartels

The cartel is a model where the recognition of firms' interdependence is raised to the level of open collusion. A cartel may be defined as a combination of firms whose object is to limit the scope of competitive forces within a market. It represents explicit collusion. Cartels are legal in Europe but are illegal in the USA under anti-trust laws. However, some cartels may be targeted under a country's competition policy which seeks to prevent excessive concentration of market power in a small number of firms in an industry. In October 2008, the European Union fined nine wax producers €676 million for being members of a paraffin wax cartel even though the leader of the cartel (SASOL) was a South African (foreign) firm. It is not clear why action cannot similarly be taken against an international cartel such as OPEC, one of the best known cartels. The issues of legality and jurisdiction with regard to cartels are not clear.

Trade associations and professional associations may perform functions similar to a cartel and many are legal (e.g. airline associations agreeing to fares, lawyers associations agreeing to common fees for legal services, etc.). Cartels also exist for illegal drugs goods such as the former Medellin cocaine cartel prominent in the 1970s and 1980s and the Cali cartel, both in Columbia.

Apart from OPEC, cartels have been formed for many goods and have even been supported by some international development associations, which view them as a way for developing countries to maintain acceptably high price levels in their major exports such as cocoa, coffee, tin and nickel. For many developing countries cartels may be seen as a way of preventing a fall in the price of their main exports (and hence the country's income) even if not as a way of seeking very high prices. They may be seeking to prevent wild fluctuations in price and provide stability of income. These have however not had major success for reasons that are discussed later as cartels tend to be short-lived for reasons discussed further below.

Small countries may have the potential to play a large role in a cartel where they supply a large part of a relatively small market for the product. One example is the small island of Grenada in the Caribbean which supplies over 95 per cent of the world's nutmeg. Ivory Coast in West Africa produces more than half of the world's cocoa.

There are open and closed cartels. Many cartels, like OPEC, are open cartels where the cartel does not control the complete supply of the good. Other cartels such as the DeBeers diamond cartel control virtually 100 per cent of the supply. Much of the analysis below relates to closed cartels.

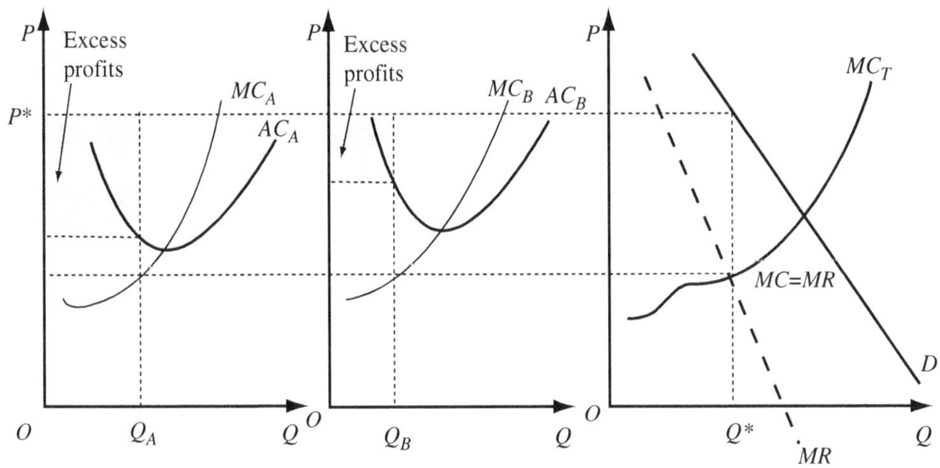

Figure 12.10
Taking monopoly profits in a closed cartel

At a fundamental level cartels have to determine:

- How to find the optimum price (price fixing)
- How to share the market among members (market sharing)

12.7.2 Price fixing

The price fixing cartel operates in theory similar to a multi-plant monopolist. Figure 12.10 illustrates equilibrium for a formal closed cartel. *DD* is the demand curve facing the total group (the industry) with marginal revenue curve *MR*. MC_T is the horizontal summation of the *MC* curves (MC_A and MC_B) of all the firms in the cartel. Allowance must be made for the possibility that *MC* might rise as more inputs are used. The cartel equates MC_T with *MR* giving the ideal quantity Q^* and price P^* that would maximize industry (or group) profits (i.e. the monopoly price and quantity for the industry).

12.7.3 Market sharing

Having decided on the optimal price and overall output in the industry, the decision on the allocation of the market share to individual members must be made. The ideal market sharing arrangement is to allocate sales to firms such that *MC* is equal in all firms. Firms with lower costs would have higher output allocation than those with higher costs. However allocation may be done by negotiation in the cartel.

Figure 12.10 shows the ideal allocation as each member produces where the optimal $MC = MR$ value cuts their individual *MC* curves. Thus firm *A* produces Q_A and firm *B* produces Q_B. The firm with lower cost (*A*) produces larger amounts of output and makes the greater amount of excess profits. This allocation is a factor that could make for instability in a cartel since higher cost firms may see it in their interest to declare lower costs in order to be allocated a larger output.

12.7.4 Formal derivation of equilibrium

For simplicity, assume the cartel is the entire industry (closed) consisting of two firms A and B. For two firms in a cartel, the formal derivation of equilibrium is similar to that of a multi-plant monopolist and may be set out as follows.

The aim of the cartel is to maximize profits:

$$\text{Max: } \Pi = R - C$$

Revenue depends on quantity irrespective of whether it comes from firm A or firm B since they are all selling in the same market.

$$R = f(Q_A, Q_B)$$

$$C_A = f(Q_A) \text{ for firm } A$$

$$C_B = f(Q_B) \text{ for firm } B$$

The aim of the firm is to maximize profits:

$$\text{Max: } \Pi = R - C_A - C_B$$

where:

$$C_A + C_B = C_T$$

First-order condition

The first-order condition respectively for each of the two firms becomes:

$$\frac{\partial \Pi}{\partial Q_A} = 0, \qquad \frac{\partial \Pi}{\partial Q_B} = 0$$

Hence for firm A the condition becomes:

$$\frac{\partial \Pi}{\partial Q_A} = \frac{\partial R}{\partial Q_B} - \frac{\partial C_A}{\partial Q_A} = 0$$

This implies:

$$\frac{\partial R}{\partial Q_A} = \frac{\partial C_A}{\partial Q_A}$$

or:

$$MR_A = MC_A$$

Similarly for firm B:

$$MR_B = MC_B$$

However, since each additional unit is sold at same price irrespective of which firm in the cartel it comes from, this gives the same marginal revenue for each unit sold, or:

$$MR_A = MR_B = MR$$

However, since:

$$MR_A = MC_A \qquad \text{and} \qquad MR_B = MC_B$$

then the overall equilibrium position is:

$$MC_A = MC_B = MC_T = MR$$

Consequently, if the closed cartel is to maximize industry profits (earn the monopoly profits), then each firm in the cartel must operate at the same level of marginal cost which must be equal to the overall equilibrium level of marginal cost where:

$$MC_T = MR$$

If one firm is producing at a higher marginal cost than the other, then production should be shifted out of this firm to the one with the lower marginal cost.

12.7.5 Problems with cartels

Cartels tend to be unstable as the organization may be plagued by many problems due to the nature of the arrangement. These include:

- Firms may deliberately quote lower costs to get greater output allocation. The temptation is always there to do this since the lower cost firm gets a higher allocation in the market and makes greater excess profits.
- The cartel may have difficulty estimating the demand curve and with the summation of cost curves.
- Some cartel members may try to cheat by lowering prices and making deals outside of the cartel for their own benefit.
- The high profits tend to attract entry to the industry. Firms may therefore want to prevent entry.
- Some members may keep the cartel price but enter into non-price competition to improve their competitiveness and gain further benefits for themselves. Firms may therefore vary the quality of packaging of the product and add extra services for the consumer in order to attract sales over its quota.

Hence cartels are prone to instability and often break up. Other than the organization of petroleum exporting countries (OPEC) and a few others, many cartels have had relatively short lives and have been largely unsuccessful. Other attempts at cartelization for products such as bauxite (Jamaica), timber and jute have also not had much success, mainly because sufficient supplies are available outside of the cartel or because there is monopolistic control on the buyer's side of the market (monopsony). The availability of substitutes can also derail a cartel. One successful long-term cartel is the diamond cartel (DeBeers).

The lure of the higher monopoly profits provides a strong motivation for the formation of a cartel. Many cartels operate clandestinely because of their illegal status in many countries. More recently, much research has been done to uncover these cartels which engage in price fixing and market sharing in order to earn monopoly profits. Connor (2008) examines the nature of the collusion in the markets for lysine, vitamins and citric acid used by the food, feed and pharmaceutical manufacturers and examines the effect of this conclusion, not only on the suppliers but on their consumers as well. A concise yet insightful look at cartels is provided by Perloff (2006).

With an open cartel high prices may be counter productive as they often stimulate additional supply from countries or suppliers outside of the cartel. Like many cartels, the Organization of Petroleum Exporting Countries (OPEC) is not a closed industry cartel in the sense that it does not control the total supply of the oil producing and exporting countries. It therefore more closely resembles the Price Leadership model in which the cartel becomes the price leader. Once the petroleum (oil) price is set by OPEC, the non-OPEC producers use that as a benchmark price for their sales. Hence, it is important that, in setting the price, some attention is paid to the supply schedules of these followers in order for there to be some stability. Setting too high a price could evoke such a strong supply response from non-OPEC members that oil prices would be forced downward leading to instability. The value to the price leader of anticipating the actions of the followers is examined in the section below on the dominant firm price leadership model.

12.8 THE PRICE LEADERSHIP MODEL

The price leadership model is a collusive model. It is based on the assumption that one of the firms in the industry is a price leader. The leader sets the price and the others follow. This is sometimes found in industries such as distribution and communications (e.g. supermarkets, telephone services).

Three forms of price leadership are usually identified:

- The low-cost price leader.
- The dominant-firm price leader.
- The barometric-firm price leader.

12.8.1 The low-cost price leader model

In this price-leadership model there are at least two firms, one a high- and the other a low-cost firm. The low-cost firm becomes the leader. For simplicity of the analysis, the industry is considered to be composed of two firms only.

The low-cost price-leadership model generally assumes:

- There is a cost difference among firms such that one firm has lower costs than the other(s).

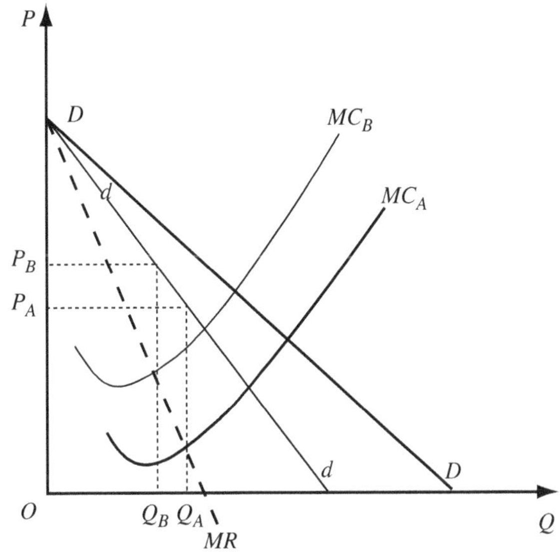

Figure 12.11
The low-cost price leader

- Firms in the industry have equal market shares.
- The low-cost price leader operates where $MC = MR$ and maximizes profits.
- The other firms follow but may not maximize their profits.

Figure 12.11 illustrates the low-cost price-leader model. In the diagram, *DD* is the market demand curve. Firm *A* has lower costs than firm *B* and is therefore the low-cost leader firm. The firms are assumed to have equal market shares and so *dd* is the demand curve (market-share curve) facing each firm. Consequently, the *MR* curve is the same for each firm ($MR = MR_A = MR_B$). Firm *A* maximizes profits by equating MC_A to *MR*. This gives the optimal quantity Q_A for firm *A* with P_A as the equilibrium price for that firm. Firm *B*, the higher cost firm, in order to maximize profits, would operate where $MC_B = MR_B$ and would wish to sell the lower quantity Q_B at the higher price P_B. However, because firm *B* would not be able to enter into serious competition with the lower cost firm *A*, firm *B* assumes the role of price follower. Firm *B* follows firm *A*, sacrifices some of its profits, and also sells Q_A at price P_A.

Firm *B* tries to avoid a price war with firm *A*, a war which it would not be in a favourable position to win because of its higher costs. Since firm *B* accepts smaller profits, the two firms must agree to share the market. If firm *B* chooses to use the leader's price but restricts quantity then the leader could be forced to a non-profit-maximizing position. As a result, the model must include collusion between the firms in the industry.

The model has implications for a higher cost (i.e. less efficient) domestic firm entering a regional or global market dominated by a lower cost firm. This could force the higher cost firm into a non-profit maximizing position taking on the role of follower. It may, however, be in the higher cost firm's interest to accept the role of follower than to attempt to compete with the low cost leader firm.

12.8.2 The dominant firm price leadership model

In the dominant firm price leadership model, the industry is comprised of a very large, low cost firm which is the dominant firm in the industry, co-existing with a large number of small, higher cost firms.

12.8.2.1 PRINCIPAL FEATURES

The main features of the model may be summarized as follows:

- The dominant firm has a large share of the market, while the other firms have smaller shares.
- The dominant firm knows *MC* curves of the smaller firms.
- The dominant firm can sum horizontally the *MC* curves of the small firms to give the total *MC* curve for the industry (ΣMC_S).
- The dominant firm sets price and quantity to maximize its profits.
- The smaller firms act as firms under perfect competition and so are price takers. They take the price set by the dominant firm which becomes their *MR* and sell up to their *MC* curve ($MC = MR$). Hence, their *MC* curve becomes their supply curve.
- The demand curve for the dominant firm is what's left of the market after the small firms have supplied all they can given the price. It is a ***residual*** demand curve.

12.8.2.2 EQUILIBRIUM

The residual demand curve

Special attention needs to be paid to the derivation of the demand curve of the dominant firm. This demand curve may be described as a residual demand curve and is illustrated in Figure 12.12.

- *DD* is the market demand curve for the industry.
- ΣMC_S is the horizontal summation of the small firms supply (*MC*) curves.

The kinked demand curve *ddD* is the demand curve facing the dominant firm price leader. It is a ***residual*** demand or what's left of the market after the small firms have supplied up to their marginal cost curves. The *ddD* curve represents the horizontal difference between the market demand curve *DD* and the collective supply curve of the small firms (ΣMC_S). The *ddD* curve is measured from the *Y*-axis and represents the horizontal distance $DD - \Sigma MC_S$.

The *ddD* curve starts on the *Y*-axis horizontally across from the point where ΣMC_S intersects the *DD* curve. The horizontal distance between the *Y*-axis and the *dd* portion of the curve is equal to the distance between *DD* and ΣMC_S. The point where *dd* joins the *DD* curve is directly horizontally across from the point where ΣMC_S reaches the *Y*-axis (i.e. where the small firms can now only supply zero quantity). This is the price

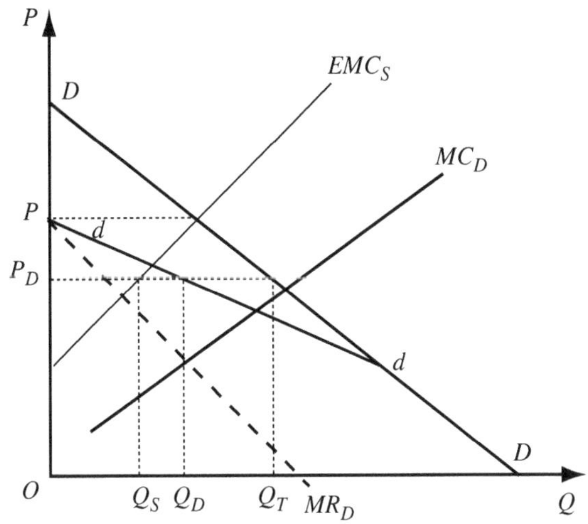

Figure 12.12
The dominant-firm price leader

at which (and below which) the dominant firm now has the total market demand for itself.

MR_D is the MR curve pertaining to the demand curve of the dominant firm (ddD). MC_D is the marginal cost curve of the dominant firm which is expected to be lower than the summed marginal cost curve of the smaller firms.

Industry equilibrium

In order to achieve equilibrium, the dominant firm sets $MC = MR$ with respect to its own demand curve:

$$MR_D = MC_D$$

This gives the profit maximizing quantity for the dominant firm of Q_D with optimal price P_D.

Once the dominant firm sets the price the other small firms act as perfectly competitive firms (price takers) and, using P_D, sell up to their individual MC curves. For all the small firms combined this takes output at P_D up to the ΣMC_S curve. Hence the small firms supply their equilibrium quantity, OQ_S.

The total supply in the industry at the dominant firm's equilibrium price, P_D, is the sum of the dominant firm supply, Q_D and the small firms' supply, Q_S. This gives $Q_D + Q_S = Q_T$ as the total industry supply at that price. This equation holds because $Q_S = Q_T - Q_D$ by definition. To explain further Q_S is the portion of the market the small firms can supply at price P_D and is therefore the amount subtracted from the entire market curve DD to give the demand curve facing the dominant firm, ddD. This is a stable equilibrium.

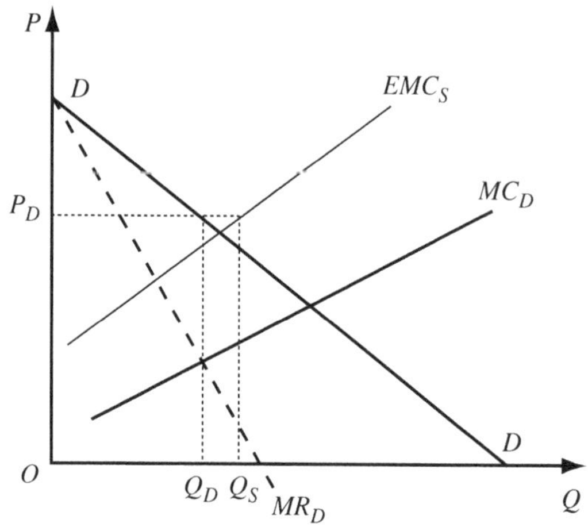

Figure 12.13
The dominant firm ignoring the small firms

12.8.2.3 IGNORING THE SMALL FIRMS

If the large firm decides to ignore the small firms and acts as if they do not exist or do not matter, this introduces serious instability into the market. It explains why the dominant firm must take the smaller firms into account and is illustrated in Figure 12.13.

In this case the large dominant firm considers the market (industry) demand curve DD to be its own demand curve thereby ***ignoring the small firms***. The dominant firm therefore perceives its equilibrium to be where $MR_D = MC_D$. It therefore attempts to supply the perceived equilibrium quantity Q_D at price P_D. However, once the price P_D is set by the dominant firm, the small firms take this price and try to sell all they can at the leader's price. This means the small firms try to sell up to the ΣMC_S curve, an amount equal to the distance OQ_S. Hence the total amount of the good being supplied to the market at price P_D is now $Q_D + Q_S$ whereas the market can only absorb a total amount of Q_D.

This cannot lead to a stable equilibrium. The supply is now in excess of the demand for the product at that price. This must force the price down thereby affecting both the dominant firm and the small firms with the players groping for equilibrium in the market and neither party being able to maximize profits. For stability, ***the only solution is for the dominant firm to acknowledge the presence of and accommodate the small firms***.

The need for the large dominant firm to accommodate the smaller follower firms has many practical implications. Because it is counter-intuitive, it may tend to be violated frequently in practice without the dominant firm realizing that it is the cause of the unstable market. This could also apply in the case of an open cartel and is a cause of the well noted cartel instability. The leader has set the price too high which attracts the additional supply for the follower firms (or those outside the cartel). The price set by the leader therefore cannot hold in the market as there is excess supply at that price. This has application to any industry where a large player, sometimes a multinational firm in the global economy, ignores the plethora of small follower firms, leading to greater volatility in the industry than is warranted.

12.9 GAME THEORY AND OLIGOPOLY

Game theory is a technique which facilitates the handling of what is considered a basic feature of oligopoly – firms using strategies and counter strategies in their competitive interaction with each other. This competitive interaction takes on the form of a game and can be played according to certain rules. Much of application in economics of Game theory is associated with the work of Jon Von Neümann and Oskar Morgenstern (1944). The understanding of oligopoly as a game with strategies and counter-strategies is invaluable to firms' ability to compete, whether domestically, regionally or globally.

A game is characterized by:

- The players (participating firms).
- The rules of the game.
- The payoffs of the game (gains and/or losses for the players).
- The conditions during play.
- The strategies available to each player.

An example of a two-person, zero-sum, strictly-determined game is considered here in order to illustrate the application of the technique of Game theory.

12.9.1 A two person, zero-sum, strictly determined game

In a zero sum-game, the amount one player wins is exactly that amount which the other player loses. Where a game is strictly determined, there is only one solution and the outcome is the same no matter which player initiates the game. For simplicity, a game with only two players will be used as an example of the application of game theory.

The following is an example of a two-person, zero-sum, strictly determined game using the data provided in Table 12.1.

Consider two firms starting an advertising campaign and having choice of strategies. Firm I has two strategies *A* and *B*. Firm II has three strategies 1, 2, 3. If firm I chooses strategy *A* and, as a counter to this, firm II chooses strategy 3, then firm I gains $4m

Table 12.1 A payoff matrix for a strictly determined, two-person, zero-sum game

The Payoff matrix – A strictly determined game				
	Possible strategies for firm II			
Possible strategies for firm I	1	2	3	Row minimum
(Profits for firm I, or losses for firm II)				
A	$3m	**$2m**	$4m	**$2m**
B	$1m	$1.5m	$3m	$1m
Column maximum	$3m	**$2m**	$4m	

and firm *A* loses \$4m. Thus if firm I chooses strategy *A* firm II will choose strategy 2 to minimize its losses. If firm I chooses strategy *B* firm II chooses strategy 1. Thus the game is strictly determined because there is a definite optimal choice for each firm.

Note that if firm I is the first one to choose a strategy and this firm knows that firm II will always use a counter strategy to minimize its (firm II)'s loss (and consequently firm I's profits) firm I will choose the strategy that has the highest minimum for firm II's counter strategy.

12.9.2 Maximin and Minimax strategies

Firm I, always the gainer from the game, focuses on the row minimum and takes the highest row minimum. That is, this firm adopts a ***Maximin*** policy. This means that it chooses the maximum of the minimum values expressed here as the row minima (seeking the maximum of the minimum profit values the firm can gain). This assumes that firm II will always seek to minimize its loss.

Firm II, always the loser, focuses on the column maximum, that is, the maximum profit firm I is trying to get (which would mean equal loss for firm II). Firm II looks at this and seeks the lowest of the maxima to correspond with firm I's strategy. Thus firm II would choose a ***Minimax*** policy (seeking the minimum of the maximum losses possible). This assumes that firm I would always seek to maximize its gain which are firm II's losses.

Thus, from the table, the optimum choice is strategy *A* for firm I and strategy 2 for firm II and the game is strictly determined with firm I gaining \$2m and firm II losing \$2m.

12.9.3 Limitations

There are some limitations to this approach to oligopolistic competition among firms. In particular, the following must be noted:

- The mimimax/maximin principle is overly conservative. It is unnecessarily pessimistic for each firm to assume that its competitor will adopt the strategy that is most damaging to its rival and best for itself. If one firm makes this assumption and the rival firm does take that approach then the firm has foregone much extra profit or is realizing a greater loss than necessary. This fits the case known as the Prisoner's Dilemma.
- The benefits and gains may not easily be quantified, particularly where unsophisticated firms enter into new markets or face new competition due to trade liberalization. Existing or sophisticated firms may have adequate knowledge of the strategies of newcomers while newcomers may be unable to devise appropriate counter strategies because of limited knowledge or experience.
- Most problems are not of the zero sum variety. The games can become very complicated.
- Typically, one firm may not always be the gainer and the other the loser.
- Firms can often increase their total profits by collusion, as one need not be gaining at the other's expense.
- Not all games are strictly determined. In some cases mixed strategies have to be used.

Many of the new developments in the theory of the firm are attempts at revision to the oligopoly market structure. These new models and approaches have proliferated since the 1930s. Some of these attempts at new models are examined in the following chapter.

REVIEW QUESTIONS FOR CHAPTER 12

1 With regards to the Cournot duopoly model:

(a) Explain what is meant by the 'Cournot'.
(b) Carefully explain how two firms reach a stable equilibrium under the Cournot model.

2 Explain the differences between the Cournot duopoly model and the Bertrand model with regards to:

(a) Their assumptions about the behaviour of competing firms.
(b) The nature of the stability of their equilibrium.
(c) The type of stability proposed by Chamberlin and how it alters the behaviour of the firms in the Cournot model.

3 Set out the Sweezy kinked-demand model showing:

(a) How the kink affects the marginal revenue curve.
(b) The significance for explaining 'sticky' prices under oligopoly.

4 With regard to the Stackleberg model:

(a) Explain why it was considered to be an improvement over the Cournot and Bertrand models.
(b) Illustrate how iso-profit and reaction curves are drawn based on the Cournot assumption.
(c) Using the iso-profit and reaction curves distinguish between the Cournot equilibrium position and the positions where either firm *A* or firm *B* is the 'sophisticated' duopolist.
(d) Identify the point of joint profit maximization where both firms are 'sophisticated'.

5 With respect to the Cartel model:

(a) Define a cartel and identify some of the products that are in industries characterized by open or closed cartels.
(b) Illustrate the theoretical profit maximizing solution to price fixing and market sharing in a closed cartel.
(c) Discuss why cartels tend to be unstable.

Table 12.2 Payoff matrix #2 for a strictly determined, two-person, zero-sum game

The payoff matrix – A strictly determined game				
	Possible strategies for firm II			
Possible strategies for firm I	1	2	3	Row minimum
(Profits for firm I, or losses for firm II)				
A	\$4m	\$8m	\$3m	\$3m
B	\$5m	\$7m	\$9m	\$5m
Column maximum	\$5m	\$8m	\$9m	

6 Consider the Dominant-firm Price Leadership model illustrating:

(a) How the dominant firm residual demand curve may be derived.
(b) How the industry reaches a stable equilibrium price and quantity with regard to the dominant firm and the small follower firms.
(c) Why it is important for the dominant firm to accommodate the smaller follower firms.

7 Using the payoff matrix given as Table 12.2:

(a) Discuss the use of Minimax and Maximin policies in a two-person, zero-sum, strictly determined game.
(b) Examine the details of the game in Table 12.2 and identify the single solution.

RECOMMENDED READING FOR CHAPTER 12

Chamberlin, E. (1933) *The Theory of Monopolistic Competition*, Cambridge: Harvard University Press (8th edn, 1962).
Connor, J. M. (2008) *Global Price Fixing* (2nd Edn), Springer.
Henderson, J. M. and Quandt, R. E. (1984) *Microeconomic Theory: A Mathematical Approach*, New York: McGraw-Hill.
Neumann, V. and Morgenstern, O. (1944) *Theory of Games and Economic Behaviour*, New York: Princeton University Press.
Perloff, J. M. (2006) 'Cartels', *Journal of Industrial Organization Education*, 1 (1: 6). Available online. http://www.bepress.com/jioe/vol1/iss1/6.
Sweezy, P. (1939) 'Demand under Conditions of Oligopoly', *The Journal of Political Economy*, 4: 568–73.

13 Alternative Theories of the Firm

The Marginalist Controversy: Managerial Models – Baumol's Model; Pricing Models – Mark-up Pricing Model; Behavioural Models; Entrepreneurial Models - Transaction and Information Costs; Economics of Information.

Several issues have been raised concerning the neo-classical models of the firm. These traditional models, namely, perfect competition, monopoly, monopolistic competition and oligopoly, are all subsumed under the label of marginalist models of the firm. This label derives from the way in which equilibrium (profit maximization) is achieved in all the models through the equating of the firm's marginal cost with marginal revenue. From around the 1950s, these traditional theories have been seriously challenged and alternatives offered. In the same way that the traditional models were developed and modified to meet the changes in the business and productive sectors, newer models have emerged to take into account largely empirical changes observed in the market. Many of the newer alternatives tend to tread a thin line between economics and management.

Of the many and varied alternatives proposed, this chapter examines a sample of the more popular offerings and makes some comparisons with the traditional marginalist models. This sample includes Baumol's version of the managerial models, a representation of the Average-cost or Mark-up pricing model, an outline of the Behavioural model and a brief examination of multiple models related to entrepreneurship, transaction costs and information economics.

13.1 MAJOR ISSUES AND ALTERNATIVES

Many objections have been raised against the traditional models of the firm. Those who support the traditional marginal models are referred to as 'marginalists' whereas the proponents and supporters of the various alternative theories are usually referred to as the 'anti-marginalists'.

13.1.1 Concern with the traditional theories

Some of the issues raised against the continued use and relevance of the traditional theory and in favour of the adoption of new modern theories include:

- The traditional theories have been variously described as static, marginalistic and automistic. This is because these theories are based on profit maximization which was modelled to occur in every time period and to be done in an automatic way. That is, the firm would equate its marginal revenue to marginal cost automatically with every variation of cost and/or revenue. This was viewed as unrealistic and largely impractical.
- The traditional theories assume that the firm has a monolithic structure in that the firm's owners and managers are one and the same. Consequently, the owner-manager could act with what has been described as 'global rationality' and allows a central focus on meeting the goal of profit maximization. This was considered to no longer be the case particularly with the advent of the large divisionalized firms and the separation of ownership and management.
- The traditional firm has a single goal, that of profit maximization. The firm's rationality is defined in terms of its aim to maximize profits. It was now being felt that the modern divisionalized firms with separate owners and managers would have multiple goals.
- The traditional firm was assumed to have perfect knowledge of costs (technology), demand and prices. The cost of acquiring the necessary information was not considered. Time and uncertainty were ignored. Moreover, there was no role in the traditional theory for the entrepreneur, whose interest is not in a static profit-maximizing exercise but in a dynamic role of organizing production in new ways and seeking to minimize transactions and information costs.
- There was an absence of conflict in the traditional model of the firm. The owner/managers paid the factors according to the value of their marginal product or their marginal revenue product (considered fair or equitable). Hence there was no conflict.

Reasons given for the alternative models

Based on the issues raised, a number of reasons have been given to justify the need for alternative models of the firm and to suggest the new features that should be included. These include:

- New or additional goals for the firm. The owner manager dichotomy means that the firm may no longer have a single goal of profit maximization. New models must take into account that, whereas the owners (shareholders) may want to have an acceptable level of profits, the managers may have other goals (managerial models).
- Rationality must be defined not only in terms of profit maximization. The divisionalized firm acts with bounded rather than global rationality and theory must take into account the internal workings of the firm (behavioural models).

- Uncertainty must be considered. New models must focus on long term goals rather than a firm acting automistically, equating marginal cost to marginal revenue in every time period as costs and demand are changing (average-cost pricing models).
- Information and transaction costs must be considered, particularly for multi-product firms where it would be difficult for them to determine costs and demand for each product to the extent required for equating marginal cost (*MC*) with marginal revenue (*MR*) in each time period.
- The goal of long-run survival should replace short-run profit maximization. Firms may therefore be willing to sacrifice profits in the short-run in order to gain market share, by forcing rivals out of the industry or to discourage entry by new firms (entry prevention models).
- The idea that the firm may not want to maximize anything but to 'satisfice' should be taken into account. Firms may be 'satisficers', a term attributed to Simon (1947, 1962). The implication is that some firms may just want a satisfactory level of achievement with regard to multiple goals.

It is useful to note that some proponents of the new theories contend that the importance of the shareholders in forcing managers to seek profits is limited. They contend that, while it is true that shareholders appoint the board of directors, the shareholders are widely distributed but do not bother to vote. Managers send notices out and the shareholders give authority to managers to vote by proxy, which means that managers can manipulate votes. The anti-marginalists therefore conclude that the argument that shareholders are powerful is not valid. Managers therefore have much leeway in pursuing their own goals.

13.1.2 Major alternatives to marginalism

Several alternatives to the traditional marginalist theories have therefore been proposed as noted above. To elaborate further, the more popular ones may be summarized under the following headings:

Managerial theories

Managerial theories are based on the dichotomy that exists in the structure of the modern firm between managers and owners of firms. These theories consider that the shareholders as owners of the firm have somewhat different goals from the managers who actually run the firm. Moreover, they consider that the shareholders are somewhat remote from the day to day activities of the firms and, hence, the managers have some leeway in pursuing their own goals and maximizing their own utility functions.

As a consequence of this separation of ownership and management of the firm, the managerial theories assume multiple goals of the firm. These include owners' goals (mainly related to profit) and managers' goals. The firm is not a single monolithic entity focused on equating marginal cost with marginal revenue for profit maximization.

There are many managerial models with the major ones being those of the Sales Revenue Maximization model attributed to Baumol (1959, 1971), the Balanced Growth Maximization model of Marris (1963) and the Managerial Utility Maximizing model of Williamson (1966). The managerial models led to the more recent principal-agent analysis in which the shareholder is considered to the principal and the manager the agent. This analysis focuses on how difficult and costly it is for the principal to find out or predict how the agent will behave when information is asymmetric.

Baumol's model will be considered further in this chapter as an example of the managerial models.

Pricing theories

The alternative pricing theories are based on the rejection of the automistic pricing in the marginalist models equating marginal revenue to marginal cost in order to determine equilibrium quantity and price in each time period. They are based variously on the views that the firm does not have sufficient information particularly about demand (and hence, marginal revenue) to act in the deterministic way required by the marginalist theories, or that the firm is more interested in survival in the long-run thereby sacrificing short-run profits for long-run growth in market share.

Included in the alternative pricing models are those of Mark-up pricing and Entry-prevention pricing. The Mark-up pricing models, also known variously as Average-Cost pricing, Cost-plus pricing, Administrative pricing and Rule-of-Thumb pricing, replace the marginal principal with a price setting mechanism based on the average cost of production and the application of a percentage mark-up in order to arrive at a selling price. They discard the demand and marginal revenue curves so central to the marginal analysis. The suggestion is that equating marginal revenue and marginal cost is irrelevant. This approach is typically associated with the model of Hall and Hitch (1939).

The Entry Prevention or Limit Pricing models are based on the view that the firm has a long-term survival goal and so may sacrifice immediate profits in the interest of preventing new entrants into their industry. These models are largely associated with Bain (1956) although there are several variants.

In the model, the price set by the firm is in response to the threat of entry. Where the threat of entry is high the price set is low to dissuade entrants from joining the industry. Conversely, when the threat of entry is low or non-existent, the firm sets a higher price up to the monopoly price. Getting rid of competition in the short-run is done in an effort to gain more profits and have a better survival rate in the long-run. In reality many firms are seen to use a low-price strategy, which makes it difficult for rivals to enter or remain in the industry and, over time, the aggressive firm gains market share (e.g. Dell computers).

A model of mark-up pricing will be used as an example of the alternative pricing models drawing on that of Hall and Hitch (1939).

Behavioural theories

The behavioural theories are associated primarily with Cyert and March (1963), Monsen and Downes (1965), Cyert and Kamien (1967) and Williamson (1979). The genesis of these models may be considered to lie in the path-breaking work of Simon (1947, 1962) for which he received a Nobel Prize in Economics (1978).

Behavioural theories consider internal workings of the large divisionalized firm. The firm is seen as having multiple goals because of the varied and different objectives of the heads of the various divisions. This is why the firm is incapable of acting with the 'global rationality' required to consistently equate marginal revenue to marginal cost by having a single focus on the goal of profit maximization. The firm is therefore modelled as an organization in which different parts act with 'bounded rationality', a term attributed to Simon.

Moreover, the firm is a 'satisficer' rather than a maximizer, determining their satisfactory levels by a process of adaptive expectations. That is, if targets are easily attained in one time period, then they may be revised upwards in the next, whereas if the targets prove unattainable in one time period, they may be lowered in the next time period.

The behavioural approach is examined in greater depth later in this chapter.

Entrepreneurship, transaction and information cost theories

Theories on entrepreneurship, transaction costs, information costs and other aspects of a creative and non-equilibrium-focused firm abound. Much of this work resolves around the reasons for the existence of firm as an entity, and how and why the firm maintains itself in the market. These reasons relate to the cost of transactions that can be minimized by an entrepreneur through combining activities into a single firm. The traditional marginalist models do not include a role for an entrepreneur seeking to find new ways in which to organize production and to compress many transactions which require negotiations with other agents into fewer such transactions within a firm, in order to reduce the costs of producing for the market. The marginalist model also does not consider the economics of information and information costs.

These approaches are generally considered to have begun with the pioneering work of Ronald Coase (1937) who was concerned with the reasons for the coming into existence of the firm. He saw the relationships in the firm as dependent on the way in which the entrepreneur directs the resources available. The firm grows larger or smaller depending on whether the entrepreneur directs more or fewer transactions.

There is a general presumption that an entrepreneur, by nature, thrives in disequilibrium rather than in equilibrium and is therefore out of place in the traditional marginalist model. New profit opportunities often arise out of disequilibrium and the desire by the entrepreneur for innovation and new ways of organizing production must result in movements away from any equilibrium.

This focus on the entrepreneur and the reasons for the existence of the firm has been extended into models that consider factors such as 'asset specificity' (Williamson, 1986), 'team production' (Alchian and Demsetz, 1972), reciprocity (Akerlof, 1982) and 'efficiency wage' (Shapiro and Stiglitz, 1984). These are all attempts to show how and why firms exist and how this existence depends on the way in which the firm achieves greater efficiency and hence lower costs than the market. The emphasis is completely shifted from that of the marginalist models.

In the case of 'asset specificity' firms exist because they reduce bargaining costs by bringing together the assets specific into their operations rather than continuously bargaining for them from various other suppliers. 'Team production' relates to the efficiencies that may be gained in a firm from group behaviour where the behaviour of any one in the group in influenced by others in the group. This allows the individuals to be more productive and cost effective in a group (firm) than as separate individuals out in the market. Reciprocity involves the employers paying high wages to workers in a firm who then reciprocate by giving greater effort, making it cost effective for the firm to do so. The firm exists until it is no longer worthwhile to do so. The 'efficiency wage' refers to payments in lieu of supervision to get workers to be more productive. If workers shirk, the penalty is being fired. The efficiency wage dissuades workers from shirking since being unemployed has a higher cost in wages forgone. These are all costs that are worthwhile so long as they lead to such efficiencies when concentrated in the firm, that it is better to incur them than to rely on the market. The benefits of having a firm ends when these costs rise to such a level that the market itself rather than the firm would be able to provide these functions at a lower cost. Hence there would be no need for the firm.

Further, by 2006 the whole issue of the distinction in Microeconomics between firms and markets is questioned (Benkler, 2006) and attention shifts to the more recent issue of open source goods (e.g. computer freeware (software), Linux operating system). Referred to as Common-based-peer-production, the view is that shared information leads to greater economic efficiency overall in the market.

13.1.3 The marginalists' response to the alternatives

Supporters of the traditional marginalist theories have made their responses to the concerns raised against the traditional theories. In general there has been much scepticism among marginalists about the ability of the newer models to be considered as true alternatives to the marginal models particularly since the newer models tend to be less rigorous and to be less definitive about an equilibrium position.

The Marginalists' view of the alternative models

The views of the Marginalists on the alternative managerial, pricing and behavioural models may be summarized as follows:

- Managers may indeed have different goals from owners but are unlikely to have the discretion to pursue them.
- Whatever goals the managers may have, they are best achieved through the maximization of profits. Managers must still consider the constraints of the commercial banks and the capital market.
- Managers are hired by the shareholders. Shareholders require the highest profits they believe they can get. Managers are therefore forced to deliver the maximum profits to the shareholders if they are to keep their positions.
- In order to remain competitive in the market, managers are driven to greater efficiency and consequently to higher profitability.
- The idea of a firm engaging in ***satisficing*** behaviour with adaptive expectations is a tautology. There is nothing definitive as any level of profit can be called satisfactory.

- Pricing to limit entry is compatible with profit maximization ($MC = MR$). Lowering prices is no guarantee that potential entrants would stay away. The entrant may be an existing firm seeking to diversify.
- Long-run survival goals are compatible with marginalist profit maximization. In the long-run the fittest survive. The fittest are the profit maximizers.
- Behavioural theories consider the inner workings of the large divisionalized firm but do not replace the marginalist theories. The large divisionalized firm maintains itself best when profits are being maximized.
- Alternative theories are lax and cannot replace the marginal theories. They are often not formalized in a way that allows for predictions to be derived from them (e.g. satisficing and how to determine what is satisfactory). While they help to show the empirics of the firm in terms of how they are structured and operate in the real world, they do not invalidate the marginal theories.

A more overarching type of defence of the traditional marginalist theories was made by Machlup (1967) which is along the lines of the methodological controversy discussed in Chapter 1.

13.1.4 The fallacy of misplaced concreteness

One of the staunchest defenders of the marginalist theories, Machlup (1967) made a passionate case for the traditional marginalist theories of the firm. An ardent defender of validity of the application of the $MC = MR$ rule and the profit maximizing firm, he set out to show that researchers bringing new alternative models were committing what he termed the 'fallacy of misplaced concreteness'.

The gist of the defence is that theory and reality are two different creatures. This is similar to the issues raised in the Methodological Controversy (see Chapter 1) in which differing views were found on the need for realism in assumptions versus the need for accuracy in predictions. The realization then that a theory, by nature, must be an abstraction from reality and cannot describe all of reality is applicable in this case. Moreover, there is the contention that the representation of that reality may not appear to exist in that reality, yet is fully representative of it. Refer to Chapter 1, where it was pointed out that a representative statistic such as the mean (average) can represent a reality and yet not be contained in it, since, for example, the numbers 2, 4, 8, 10 may be represented by the number 6 which is the mean of the set of numbers but is not contained in that set. The point is that showing that the reality is different in the letter from the representation does not invalidate the representation of that reality.

In making his point, Machlup contended that business persons do not consciously apply the marginalistic ($MC = MR$) rule. However, they apply it subconsciously. This implies that, if businessmen were to be asked whether they were applying the marginalistic rule, the answer is not likely to be in the affirmative since they were not conscious of doing so. Yet this is what they are doing but in the way in which they understand, through experience, how to make the most profits (profit maximization). However, they can only obtain maximum profits when they equate the marginal revenue to the marginal cost. Not knowing this, they grope around (tatônnement process) until they reach this point or find other methods (e.g. variations in the mark-up) to make the most profits.

With regard to the managerial theories, Machlup (1967) contended that there are three different views regarding the relative independence of corporate management. These are:

- Owners seek maximum money profits but managers have several supplementary goals.
- Owners allow non-profit considerations to enter into their decision making. Managers have a sense of dedication and identification with the business that makes them more single-minded seekers of profits.
- Managers are trained professionals who are able to make better profits than owners could ever hope to make running their own show.

One suggestion made is to merge ***Marginalism*** with ***Managerialism*** by integrating money-profits with other managerial goals within one formula of 'maximizing behaviour'. To do this it would be necessary to select a couple of the main managerial objectives that are amenable to a quantitative formulation and combine them in a single manageable objective function.

In essence, then, a theory requires only a small number of assumptions, and should be able to predict for a wide range of firms. The aim is not specifically to predict the actual reactions of any one particular firm. Moreover, the model of the firm in the marginalist theory is not designed to explain and predict the behaviour of real firms, but to predict changes in observed prices as effects of particular changes in conditions (wages, interest rates, duties, etc.).

The 'firm' is only a theoretical construct, helping to explain how one gets from the cause to the effect. Hence, according to Machlup, the ***explanans*** are being confused with the ***explanandum***. To confuse these two ideas, according to him, is to commit the '***fallacy of misplaced concreteness***'.

13.2 BAUMOL'S SALES REVENUE MAXIMIZATION MODEL

Managerial models of the firm are often considered to have originated with the work of Berle and Means (1933). The most popular of the managerial models of the firm are those by Baumol (1962), Marris (1963) and Williamson (1963). They present alternative goals of the firm that result from the influence of managers who try to maximize their own utility function. They present the following alternative goals of the firm:

- Sales Revenue Maximization (Baumol)
- Balanced Growth Maximization (Marris)
- Managerial Utility Maximization (Williamson)

The managerial models were made to correct the traditional theory's goals of the firm (i.e. the maximization of profit) in large firms where the owners (shareholders) did not actively participate in the day-to-day management of the enterprise. Baumol's model is examined in detail here as an example of a managerial model.

In Baumol's model the managers control the running of the organization and have their own utility function and have the leeway to pursue this within the parameters set by the shareholders (owners). Baumol contends that firms run by managers are not focused on maximizing profit but on maximizing sales revenue. The reason for this alternative goal is that managers find the award of perquisites and other benefits to management more likely to be given when they can report high and growing sales revenue to the Board of Directors in the financial statements. These benefits are in the nature of luxury vehicles, executive jets, hotel suites, salary increases, prestige, easier handling of staff problems and better relations with banks, among others. Consequently, managers remain focused on sales revenue maximization.

The model is based on real world observation and is understood to derive from Baumol's experience as a consultant to large firms where he found that managers were more preoccupied with maximization of sales rather than profits.

The model used as an example here is Baumol's single period, static model without advertising.

13.2.1 Assumptions

The principal assumptions of the model are as follows:

1 The aim of the manager-controlled firm is to maximize sales revenue within a given time period.
2 The shareholders set a minimum acceptable level of profits based on the demands of the financial market. This level is therefore determined exogenously. Once managers meet this level they are free to maximize their own utility function.
3 There is a single time period under consideration (long-run and short-run are not distinguished).
4 The demand curve is downward sloping.
5 Costs curves are U-shaped.

13.2.2 Workings of the model

Figure 13.1 shows the standard total cost (*TC*) and total revenue (*TR*) curves with a profits curve (π). The points to note are as follows:

- The profit maximizer operates where the difference between the *TR* and *TC* is greatest. That is where *MC* is equal to *MR* meaning that the tangents to both the *TR* and *TC* curves are parallel to each other. This occurs at point *M* on the *TR* curve. Consequently, the profit maximizing firm sells quantity Q_π and earns the maximum profit of π_π. The price is the *tangent* (opposite/adjacent $= AR = P$) of a ray from the origin to the point *M* on the total revenue (*TR*) curve.
- The sales revenue maximizer wishes to operate at the highest point of the total revenue (*TR*) curve. This is at point *S* on the total revenue (*TR*) curve. Hence the sales revenue maximizer wants to sell the quantity Q_S. This would earn them a profit of π_S. The price would be measured by the *tangent* of the angle made by a ray from the origin to the point *S* on the *TR* curve. Note that this angle is smaller than that made by a ray to the point *M* on the *TR* curve meaning

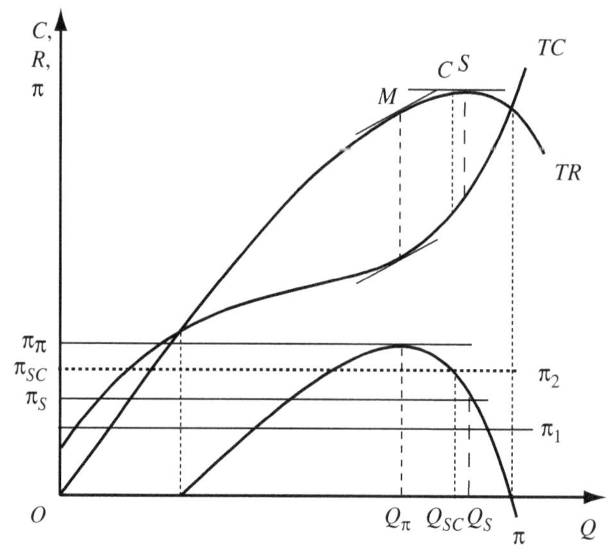

Figure 13.1
Sales revenue maximization

that the price for the sales revenue maximizer is lower than that for the price maximizer.

- However, for the sales revenue maximizing firm, the shareholders would impose a minimum profit constraint on the managers. The outcome could be as follows:
  - If the minimum profit constraint imposed by the shareholders is π_1 (i.e. below π_S), then it is said to be non-operative. The suggestion is that the managers can go ahead and maximize sales revenue by operating at the quantity Q_S which would earn them a profit π_S, already higher then the profit π_1 demanded by the shareholders. The shareholders' minimum profit requirement therefore does not constrain the managers in their effort to maximize sales revenue.
  - If the minimum profit constraint imposed by the shareholders is π_2 (i.e. above π_S) then it is said to be operative. It operates to constrain the manager from achieving the maximum sales revenue. In order to achieve the profit level of π_2, the sales maximizer must cut back output from the desired Q_S to the sales-constrained output of Q_{sC} which gives the lower total revenue at C on the TR curve. Along with this lower output goes a higher price since a ray from the origin to the point C makes a larger angle than the ray to the point S. The larger angle (i.e. the steeper gradient of the ray) gives a larger *tangent* of the angle and hence a larger average revenue or price.

Generalizing, the profit maximizer operates where $MC = MR$. Since MC is positive then MR must also be positive in order to be equal. Where MR is positive, TR is still increasing. The sales revenue maximizer operates where *TR* is a maximum (i.e. where $MR = 0$). Consequently, the achievement of maximum sales revenue is with the sacrifice of profits. The firm therefore sells a quantity greater that that at which profits are maximized.

Consequently, the output of the sales maximizer will be greater and price and profits will be lower than those of the profit maximizer. For comparison, using the subscript *S* for the sales revenue maximizer and the subscript π for the profit maximizer, the following are the differences in output (Q), price (P) and profits (π) between the two types of firms:

$$Q_S > Q_\pi$$

$$P_S < P_\pi$$

$$\pi_S < \pi_\pi$$

Relating the respective equilibrium positions to the demand curve, the sales revenue maximizer with a non-operative profit constraint will be operating at the mid-point of the demand curve where total revenue is maximized. This is also where price elasticity is unity or:

$$\eta_P = 1$$

The profit maximizer will be operating in the upper portion of the demand curve where $MC = MR$ obtains.

The equilibrium positions for both the profit and sales revenue maximizing firms will be the same only where the minimum profit constraint set by the shareholders is identical to the maximum profit. It is not clear from the model why the shareholders are not aware of the true maximum profit level available from the firm.

13.2.3 Predictions of the model

The alternative theories of the firm were claiming to be more realistic. It is important, therefore, to examine the predictions of the theory. In this regard, the following dynamics will be considered:

- Shifts in costs
  - Fixed costs
  - Variable costs
- Effects of taxation
  - Lump sum tax
  - Profits tax
  - Specific sales tax
- Shifts in Market Demand

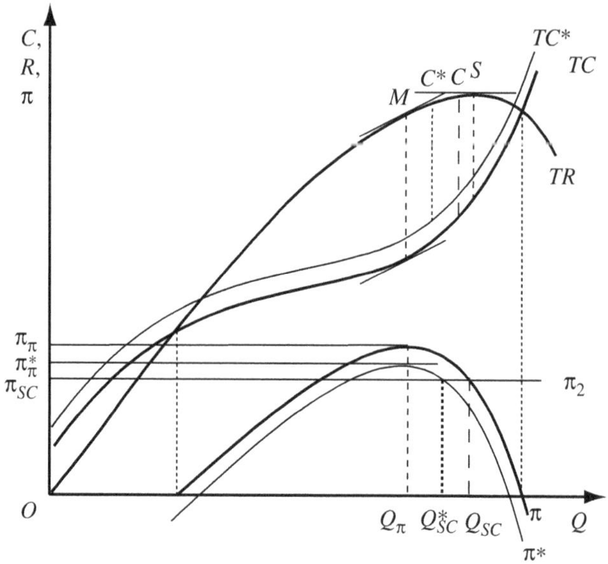

Figure 13.2
Sales revenue maximization: effect of changes in fixed costs

The effects will be examined from the point of view of the shifts representing increases. It may be considered that the response to increases and decreases are symmetric.

13.2.3.1 INCREASE IN FIXED COSTS

Consider that the sales maximizer is operating with a profit constraint of π_2 as shown in Figure 13.2. Before the increase in fixed cost, production is at the profit-constrained output of Q_{SC} which is less than the sales revenue maximizing output given in Figure 13.1 as Q_S, price is given by the *tangent* (opposite/adjacent) of the angle made by a ray from the origin to point C on the total revenue (*TR*) curve and the firm earns a profit of π_{SC}. In addition, before the increase in fixed cost, the profit maximizer is at the position given previously in Figure 13.1 with the maximum profit of π_π, output of Q_π and price given by the *tangent* of the angle made by a ray from the origin to the point M on the total revenue curve.

The increase in fixed cost shifts the total cost (*TC*) curve upwards in parallel fashion to TC*. With total revenue remaining unchanged, this cost increase reduces profit and thereby shifts the profit curve (π) downwards in parallel fashion to (π^*). A change in fixed cost does not affect the marginal cost as marginal cost relates only to variable cost and so the profit maximizing position ($MC = MR$) is not affected. Hence, for the profit maximizing firm, equilibrium price and quantity remain the same in the short-run for an increase in fixed cost but the level of profit is reduced to the lower peak π_π^* of the new profit curve (π^*).

However, the sales revenue maximizing firm, operating under the profit constraint π_2, will be forced to reduce output and increase price in order to meet the profit constraint imposed by the shareholders. The firm is constrained to achieve a profit of at least π_{SC}.

Hence, in order to maintain this level of profit, the sales revenue maximizing firm must reduce output from Q_{SC} to Q^*_{SC}. In doing this, price is increased as given by the wider angle which would be made by the ray from the origin to the new point C^* relative to Q^*_{SC} on the total revenue (*TR*) curve. C^* is to the left of the original point C and the wider angle of the ray (steeper ray) gives a larger *tangent* and hence a higher price (average revenue).

Comparison with prediction of marginalist model

Consequently, the Baumol model predicts that, for a given increase in fixed cost, the managerial controlled firm will pass on the increase right away in the form of a higher price and a reduced quantity of output in order to retain the same level of profits stipulated by the shareholders. This is considered to be more realistic than the profit maximization (marginalist) model where, since MC (and so, $MC = MR$) is not affected, price and quantity remains the same and there is no attempt to pass on the increased fixed cost in the short-run. The profit maximization model with free entry and exit will show firms exiting in the long-run because of losses made due to the increase in fixed cost. This would lead to an increase in price only in the long-run.

Rationalization

Empirically, firms are usually observed to attempt to pass on all cost increases right away. It is however possible to rationalize this behaviour by noting that many firms do not know of the marginalist condition for profit maximization, or, if so, find it difficult to compute in each time period. Hence, through a groping, trial and error, roundabout process, the firm gradually reaches equilibrium.

13.2.3.2 INCREASE IN VARIABLE COSTS

An increase in variable cost affects the marginal cost of the firm. The marginal cost curve shifts up and to the left. This affects the total cost curve pulling it increasingly further away to the left from the original curve as output increases. This pulling effect on the total cost curve is shown in the movement from TC to TC^* in Figure 13.3. This causes the profit curve to shift downwards, not in parallel fashion as with the fixed cost above but in a skewed manner as well.

As a result of this movement in the TC curve, the following is predicted to happen for the different models.

The profit maximizer

Since the shift in variable cost affects the marginal cost (MC) curve, the profit maximizing firm must move to a new equilibrium position in the short-run. The profit maximizer will cut back output from Q_π to Q^*_π at the peak of the new profit curve. As a result, price will be increased when measured by the change in the steepness of the ray from the origin to the new profit maximizing point on the TR curve at M^* (i.e. steeper

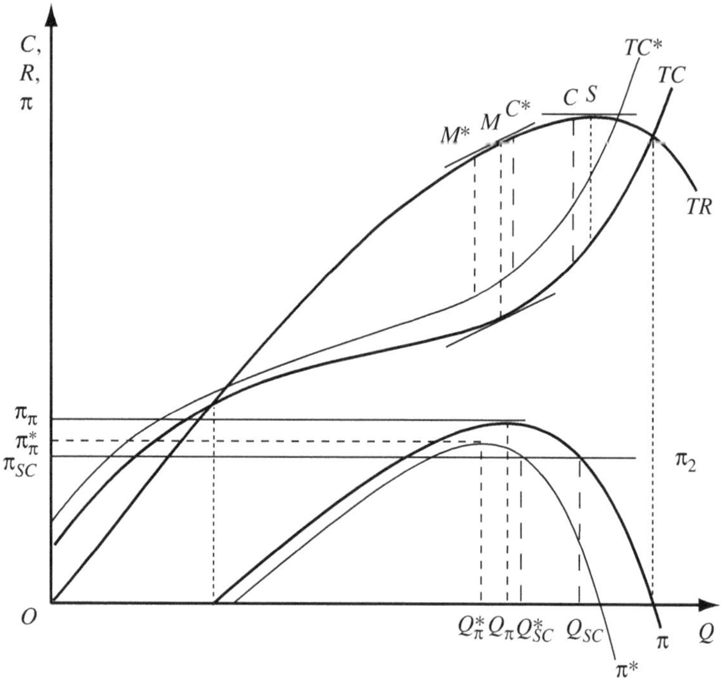

Figure 13.3
Sales revenue maximization: effect of changes in variable costs

than at M). The profit is also reduced from the level π_π obtained at the peak of the original profit curve to π_π^* which occurs at the peak of the new profit curve (π^*).

The sales revenue maximizer

In order to continue to meet the minimum profit constraint of the shareholders, π_{SC}, the sales revenue maximizer cuts back output from Q_{SC} to Q_{SC}^*. This engenders a price increase noted by the greater slope of the ray from the origin to the point C^*, corresponding to the reduced output Q_{SC}^*, than that to the original point C.

Comparison of sales revenue maximizer with profit maximizer

1. *Quantity* – An increase in variable cost results in a reduction in quantity for both the profit maximizer and the sales revenue maximizer. However, because of the pull to the left of the TC^* curve, the reduction in quantity is greater for the sales revenue maximizer than for the profit maximizer.
2. *Price* – As a result of the increase in variable cost both types of firm increase their price. However, the increase in price is greater for the sales revenue maximizer than for the profit maximizer.

3 *Profit* – The profit-constrained sales revenue maximizer should have the same profit as before the increase in variable cost, whereas the profit is reduced for the profit maximizer.

Hence the movement in price and quantity is in the same direction for both types of firms but the magnitude is greater for the sales revenue maximizer. This is said by Baumol to accord more accurately with what happens in the real world.

Changes in taxes

The effect of changes in taxes can be easily dealt with under fixed and variable costs (above).

1 *Lump-sum taxes* – Lump-sum taxes represent a fixed cost to the firm as they are independent of output. Consequently, they may be treated as fixed costs. Accordingly, the Baumol model predicts that firms will move to pass these taxes on to the consumer right away (in the short-run) unlike the profit maximization model where they are not passed on in the short-run (see above).
2 *Profits taxes* – Taxes on profits are also treated as a fixed cost.
3 *Sales or per-unit taxes* – Taxes that vary with the quantity of output are treated as variable costs. Hence, in the Baumol model, a greater portion of a sales tax is passed on to the consumer than in the profit maximization model. This is considered to be more realistic.

13.2.3.3 INCREASE IN DEMAND

An increase in demand is represented by an outward shift in the demand curve and hence the marginal revenue curve. The increased demand pulls the total revenue (*TR*) curve up. Assuming that costs do not change as demand expands, or that it is a constant-cost industry (see Chapter 9), then the profit maximizing firm should experience an increase in output, price and profits in the short-run. Under the model of Perfect Competition, entry would reduce profits to just normal profits in the long-run.

The sales revenue maximizing firm with an operative profit constraint would be able to move closer to or attain full sales revenue maximization while meeting the profit constraint. This would be achieved through an increase in output and in price. It is even possible that, with an increase in demand, an operative profit constraint may become inoperative.

13.2.4 A replacement for the marginalist model?

An interesting question is whether the Sales Revenue Maximizing model can be considered a replacement for the marginalist model of the firm or has Baumol committed the Fallacy of Misplaced Concreteness?

One possible explanation is that, in many cases, managers of firms may tend to focus on sales revenue in the belief that the greater the sales revenue, the greater the profits. Moreover, since the owners (shareholders) are often not directly involved in the running of the business, they also believe that increased revenue is tantamount to increased profits. In training economists, it is often very difficult to convince them, even with illustrations or with mathematics, that the point of maximum revenue is not the point of maximum profits.

Another plausible explanation is that the managers, in their training, are more exposed to the straight line total revenue and total cost curves and to break-even analysis. Consequently, they believe that, once they reach the break-even point, all sales beyond that point represent an increase in profit. Managers, because of their training, or because of the cost of information gathering and analysis, may be unable to fully identify the shape of revenue and cost curves. As a result they may inadvertently by-pass the profit maximization point as they push sales in an effort to garner more profits for the firm.

Figure 13.4 illustrates the break-even analysis. The firm may consider that the current price for its product is the price at which it can sell all of its output within the current range of the plant. The firm would essentially be a price taker and face a straight-line total revenue (*TR*) curve. Similarly, the firm could consider that, within the current output range, the unit costs remain unchanged, giving a straight line total cost (*TC*) curve as a good approximation. This gives a break-even point of *B* in Figure 13.4. Beyond the break-even point, an increase in sales brings an increase in profit within the current purview of the firm. The profit curve (π) is open ended. If the shareholders consider π_{SC} to be a reasonable profit (the profit constraint), then the managers can satisfy the shareholders by operating at or beyond point *C* on the total revenue curve. This is achieved with an output at or above Q_{SC}.

In such cases, the model describes the way firms operate in the real world but does not invalidate the marginal rule ($MC = MR$) as the way in which profits are maximized. Neither the managers nor the shareholders may be aware of this rule yet they are all groping towards a position of maximum profits using methods they understand. The managers are pushing sales in order to please the shareholders and receive more perquisites from the shareholders. This signifies that the shareholders also believe that

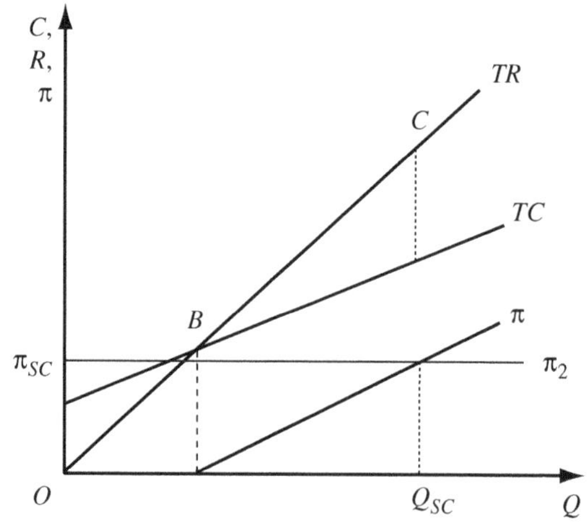

Figure 13.4
Sales revenue and profit maximization using the break-even model

the increased sales mean more profits. Moreover, the setting of a minimum profit constraint by the shareholders which is not the maximum profit available suggests that the shareholders themselves are unable to identify the maximum profit available from the enterprise. In reality, then, both sides are simply groping around in an effort to maximize profits.

The exogenous determination of the profit constraint tends to also weaken the managerial model's claim to be a replacement for the marginalist model. It is simply the level that is acceptable to the shareholders, the basis for which is not clearly set out.

Hence, although the firm as a theoretical construct may not exist in concrete form in the real world, knowledge of the marginalist rule and the ability to identify the true revenue and cost curves at any point in time would allow the firm to proceed directly to the maximization of profits.

13.3 THE MARK-UP PRICING MODEL OF THE FIRM

Various pricing models of the firm were offered as alternatives to the profit maximizing model. Like the managerial model discussed above, the alternative was the result of empirical findings that suggested firms did not apply the marginalist principle of $MC = MR$. Among the pricing models, the ones with the greatest acclaim are the Limit Entry Pricing models and the Mark-up or Average Cost Pricing model. The latter is examined in some detail here drawing heavily on the version by Hall and Hitch (1939).

13.3.1 Assumptions and basis for the model

The empirical study by Hall and Hitch (1939) covered 38 firms. They chose firms from what were described as 'efficiently managed enterprises'. The study found that firms did not attempt to maximize their profits, did not use $MC = MR$ in order to determine price and quantity and that, in the business world, oligopoly was the main market structure.

The model has similarities with a number of other market structure models as may be seen below. The empirical basis for the model and the assumptions on which it rests may be summarized as follows:

- The goal of the firm is long-run rather than short-run profit maximization.
- Firms want a fair level of profit in the short-run.
- There is no demand curve so the firm cannot set MC to MR for equilibrium.
- Even if the firm could determine its MR, it would not want to set $MC = MR$ in each time period as this does not lead to profit maximization in the long-run because the individual time periods are not independent.
- The firm operates in the short-run because of uncertainty.
- Firms sell a near homogeneous product but there are some differences in branding, etc. (i.e. differentiated products). This is similar to the market of monopolistic competition and to that of differentiated oligopoly.

- Firms set a price based on their average cost and price tends to remain at this point (i.e. price is sticky). This is similar to the kinked-demand model of oligopoly.
- Firms are aware of each other's reactions. This is similar to the traditional oligopoly market in general.
- Where firms have varying costs there tends to be price wars. This often leads to the emergence of a price leader. This is similar to the Price Leadership model in oligopoly.
- With a high threat of entry a firm may use the perfectly competitive price to dissuade entrants.
- Firms have little or no knowledge of their demand curve. ***Hence the demand curve is abandoned in this model.***
- Many firms are multi-product firms so their marginal cost (MC) curves are generally unknown.

Demand and cost schedules

1 ***Demand***
The demand curve as a tool of analysis is rejected by this model. The absence of the demand curve means that half of the apparatus of the traditional theory of the firm has been abandoned. This is because of uncertainty due to the continuous change in tastes in the market, such that extrapolation of past demand does not give sufficient information on the present or future demand. As a result of the absence of a demand curve, there is no marginal revenue curve. Hence, there can be no application of the marginalist principle ($MC = MR$).

2 ***Costs***

- The firm uses the modern short-run cost curve which has flat stretch representing 'reserve capacity' and allows for flexibility (see Chapter 6).
- The firm makes decisions based on its short-run average costs. The long-run cost curve is not considered because of uncertainty due to rapid technological change and variations in factor prices which make it difficult to estimate long-run costs.

Based on the above, the firm decides on quantity and sets its price.

13.3.2 Price setting rules

According to the Hall and Hitch (1939) model, firms aim at long run profit maximization and set their price based on the average cost principle. In the absence of a demand curve and its related marginal revenue curve, the optimal price quantity combination is not determined endogenously in this model. Output and price are determined separately.

Output determination – the budgeted output

In the model, output is determined exogenously. The firm decides on a suitable level of output (Q^*). This is referred to as the 'planned', 'budgeted' or 'normal' level of output and is the level which the firm expects to produce and sell with normal utilization of its plant. It is therefore somewhat arbitrary and does not allow an equilibrium position to be determined within the model.

Since the model uses the modern short-run cost curve where the average variable cost curve has a flat stretch representing reserve capacity, it is considered that the firm's planned or budget output Q^* lies somewhere in this range of optimal capacity.

Price determination – the mark-up rule

The firm bases its price on the average cost of production. Price determination is viewed as being done in two stages:

1 Having identified the budget output, the firm determines the price (P) that would cover its average total costs when its plant is operated at the budgeted output and earns a 'reasonable' profit. What is a reasonable level of profit is therefore subjectively determined and is somewhat arbitrary.
2 The firm tries to assess the threat of entry into the industry by other firms in order to determine the price level needed to prevent or deter entry by these firms. It compares this entry-prevention price with the estimated price for a reasonable profit and raises or lowers it as necessary depending on the potential or actual threat of entry. Essentially then, price is set to ***deter entry***.

In the first stage of setting a price for a 'reasonable' profit, the firm identifies a price to cover the average variable cost (AVC) and a gross profit margin (GPM). This price setting formula may be expressed as:

$$P = AVC + GPM$$

The gross profit margin (GPM) desired by the firm is to cover the average fixed cost (AFC) and a net profit margin (NPM) (say, 10 per cent). Hence:

$$GPM = AFC + NPM$$

Consequently, the pricing rule may be expressed as:

$$P = AVC + AFC + NPM$$

The firm is considered to know its average variable cost (AVC) with certainty. This is a short-run curve and, because it has flexibility as given by the flat stretch of reserve capacity, the firm expects that costs will remain constant as it expands. Thus the short-run average cost ($SRAC$) is taken as a good approximation of the long-run average cost ($LRAC$).

The net profit margin

The firm may be able to determine, with some accuracy, the average variable cost curve and the average fixed cost curve. However, it is not clear how the net profit margin (NPM) may be objectively determined. According to the model the net profit margin

(*NPM*) is known 'as a matter of experience'. It should be enough to give a 'fair' return on investment, and cover all risks peculiar to the product. The *NPM* is therefore subjective in nature.

Other factors in price setting

The firm must not only decide what level of mark-up is 'fair' but must assess the potential competition and the economic conditions as follows.

- Under economic boom conditions will charge a higher gross profit margin (*GPM*) and the converse would occur in times of depression
- Where there is a high capital or natural barrier to new entrants the firm will charge a higher *GPM*
- When there is a great threat of entry, the leading firm will drop its price even as far as the perfectly competitive price to make just normal profits (zero excess profits).
- If a new entrant charges a lower price on entry, the existing firm responds by adjusting the *GPM* downwards.

Price setting procedure

Figure 13.5 shows the typical cost curve used by the firm in this model. The average variable cost curve has a flat stretch representing an area of reserve capacity. The budgeted output of the firm is Q^*. There is no demand curve. Having determined its output, the firm, in this model, can also determine its price. This is a significant departure from an understanding of how the firm can act in a market. Typically, the firm can set only price (and the market will determine how much will be bought at that price) or only quantity (and the market will determine the price that will clear that quantity) but not both simultaneously. Presumably, by ditching the demand curve, consumer choice is eliminated and consumers can be forced to buy a given quantity at any price set by the firm. This is shown in Figure 13.5.

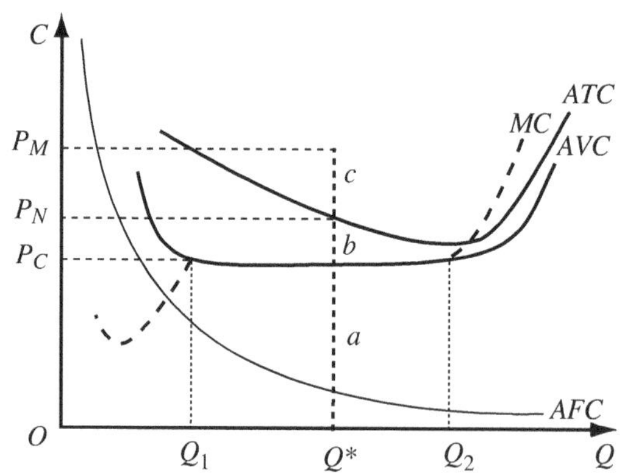

Figure 13.5
Average cost or cost-plus pricing model

According to the model, the firm can sell the quantity Q^* at any of the following prices, depending on the reasons given which relate only to supply and not to demand:

$$P_C = AVC$$
$$P_N = AVC + AFC = ATC$$
$$P_M = AVC + AFC + NPM$$

The firm will sell the budgeted quantity, Q^*, at P_C when the threat of potential entry is great, so great that the firm is just covering its average variable cost or is at the closing down point. P_C may be referred to as the closing down price. This is done in order to dissuade potential entrants from coming into the industry. This covers the distance a, and can only be done for a short period of time and by a firm with sufficient financial resources that they can continue to absorb the loss since they are not covering their fixed cost.

When the threat of potential entry is present but is not as great as above, the firm will sell the budgeted quantity, Q^*, at P_N. This is where price is set to cover the average total cost (ATC) which is the sum of the average variable cost and the average fixed cost (ATC $= AVC + AFC$). This covers the vertical distances a and b in Figure 13.5. This is the perfectly competitive price at which the firm earns only normal profit.

When the threat of entry is remote or virtually non-existent, the firm may charge a price of P_M. This could be viewed as the monopoly price. P_M is the average variable cost plus a gross profit margin or the average total cost plus a net profit margin. This incorporates all of the three vertical distances in Figure 13.5 of a, b and c.

Relationship between firm and industry

In this model the relationship between firm and industry is not clear. Although there is no collusion between firms, firms, acting autonomously, come to much the same position on price. This is similar to the Chamberlin non-collusive oligopoly model (see Chapter 12). In general:

- All firms arrive at the same price by following the same procedure without any form of collusion.
- Firms do not collude to raise price because of fear of the ***potential threat of entry*** as outside firms are attracted to the industry.
- Firms are of the view that frequent price changes do not find favour with consumers and so, in any case, would not wish to apply $MC = MR$ in each time period.

Comparison with perfect competition

Price under mark-up pricing will generally be higher than under perfect competition under the marginalist model as long as the threat of entry into the industry by other firms is not too severe. With a strong threat of potential entry price could fall to a perfectly competitive level where the firm earns just normal profit (P_N) as included in its average total cost (ATC) curve. Then price, output and profit would be identical with perfect competition.

In the absence of demand and marginal revenue curves, it is difficult to make meaningful comparison with price under monopoly. It may be assumed that the highest price (say P_M) is the monopoly price. It would have to coincide with the (absent) demand curve.

13.3.3 Predictions of the model

In general, the predictions of the model are not precise due to the nature of the model. The following outcomes are expected.

Change in costs

1. Small change in cost – likely to be absorbed by a firm as mark-up pricing firms tend to resist varying prices (price is sticky). Firm would possibly vary quality or quantity of product.
2. Substantial rise in cost – price would rise.
3. Fall in costs of inputs – firms will tend to lower price in order to avoid attracting other firms for excess profits.

Change in demand

1. When demand increases firms may be cautious in increasing price for fear of entry.
2. Where increase in demand seems to be of a permanent nature firms will tend to expand along the flat portion (reserve capacity) of the average cost curve rather than raise price.

Imposition of a tax

1. A lump-sum or profits tax, since it affects all firms similarly, would tend to cause a rise in price as the tax is shifted to consumers.
2. A sales tax per unit tax shifts the AVC upwards and, with the same GPM, the entire tax could be passed on in the price increase.

13.3.4 Marginalism in theory and in practice

The mark-up pricing model associated with Hall and Hitch (1939) was opposed by the marginalists and others on empirical and theoretical grounds.

Compatibility with marginalism

A study by Earley (1965) contradicted the empirical findings of the Hall and Hitch study. Early studied 110 'excellently managed' firms in the USA and found that they applied the marginalist principle, $MC = MR$, and had enough information to do so. The contention was that firms may not want to reveal to the public or to the government that their goal is to maximize profits. Rather, firms are likely to say they are aiming for a fair profit or for long-term survival or something that sounds less greedy.

On a theoretical level, others, including Machlup, opposed mark-up pricing as a new theory of the firm and contended that the mark-up pricing model is compatible with profit maximization. This again relates to the 'fallacy of misplaced concreteness' discussed earlier in this chapter. The question is whether firms understand economic terminology such as marginal revenue, marginal cost and elasticity, concepts with which businessmen are not familiar. Since many of them do not, they act in ways usually based on experience that allow them to grope towards a profit maximization position in a more roundabout way than equating marginal revenue to marginal cost. If they were familiar with the marginalist principle and were able to obtain the data required to make it operational, they would use it.

The marginalist contention is that the pricing routines used by so-called mark-up pricing firms have actually originated from marginalistic rules.

The marginalists' contention

The abandonment of the demand curve and the dispensing with the marginalist principle make the average-cost or mark-up model appear to be a significant departure from the profit maximization model. However, the marginalists contend that this is another example of how firms act in reality to achieve the same outcome as the application of the marginalist principle in the firm as a theoretical construct.

The marginalists argue that the setting of price on basis of the average-cost principle involves implicitly the (subjective) estimation of the price elasticity of demand. According to this contention, when firms use $P = AVC = GPM$, they guess the value of the price elasticity of demand which they can do provided that the AVC is constant over the relevant range of output.

Consider the following explanation:

1 Profit maximization requires that $MC = MR$

2 The relationship between price (P), price elasticity (η_P) and marginal revenue (MR) has already been shown to be:

$$MR = P\left(1 - \frac{1}{\eta_P}\right)$$

3 Given that, for profit maximization MR must be positive (since MC is positive), then profit maximization requires that $|\eta_P| > 1$. As shown previously:

$$\text{If } |\eta_P| = 1, \quad MR = 0$$

$$\text{If } |\eta_P| < 1, \quad MR < 0$$

$$\text{If } |\eta_P| > 1, \quad MR > 0$$

4 Now the firm produces in the flat stretch of the AVC in which $AVC = MC$ (see Figure 13.5). This is where $AVC = MC = MR$. Thus, for profit maximization, $AVC = MR$ can be used instead of $MC = MR$.
5 This substitution can then be used in the elasticity relationship to give:

$$AVC = P\left(1 - \frac{1}{\eta_P}\right)$$

The above may be manipulated in order to make price (P) the subject:

$$AVC = P\left(\frac{\eta_P - 1}{\eta_P}\right)$$

Therefore:

$$P = AVC\left(\frac{\eta_P}{\eta_P - 1}\right)$$

6 Since the firm must operate where $|\eta_P| > 1$, then the following must hold:

$$\left(\frac{\eta_P}{\eta_P - 1}\right) > 1$$

7 Hence:

$$\left(\frac{\eta_P}{\eta_P - 1}\right) = 1 + k$$

where $k > 0$ and represents the gross profit margin (GPM).
8 Consequently, the result:

$$P = AVC\left(\frac{\eta_P}{\eta_P - 1}\right)$$

may be re-written as:

$$P = AVC(1 + k)$$

or:

$$P = AVC + k(AVC)$$

9 Hence if a firm sets 20 per cent of its AVC as the profit margin, this gives:

$$P = AVC + 0.20(AVC)$$

Example

Box 13.1 provides an example of the relationship between price elasticity of demand (η_P) and the mark-up.

Thus the marginalists contend that setting the *GPM* (k) is tantamount to estimating the price elasticity of demand as a substitute for applying the marginal rule. Thus, although the firm may not be aware of the concept of elasticity, they would be aware from experience of the responsiveness of the quantity demanded to variation in prices of these commodities. Commodities with many substitutes (e.g. soaps, plastic kitchen ware) and with inelastic demand (e.g. car parts for specific models) tend to carry higher mark-ups.

BOX 13.1 EXAMPLE – RELATIONSHIP BETWEEN MARK-UP AND PRICE ELASTICITY OF DEMAND

Consider a product with a price elasticity (η_P) such that: $\eta_P = 3$. Then the mark-up (*GPM*) is found by:

$$\left(\frac{\eta_P}{\eta_P - 1}\right) = \left(\frac{3}{3-1}\right) = \frac{3}{2} = 1\frac{1}{2} = 1 + 0.5$$

This means that the $k = 0.5$ or the mark-up is 50 per cent.

Consider further, a price elasticity (η_P) such that $\eta_P = 4$. Then the mark-up (*GPM*) is:

$$\left(\frac{\eta_P}{\eta_P - 1}\right) = \left(\frac{4}{4-1}\right) = \frac{4}{3} = 1\frac{1}{3} = 1 + 0.33$$

This means that the $k = 0.33$ or the mark-up is $33\frac{1}{3}$ per cent.

This indicates that the higher the price elasticity, the lower the mark-up. A schedule can be drawn up to show how the profit-maximizing mark-up falls as the price elasticity (η_P) rises.

Relationship of mark-up to price elasticity of demand

Price elasticity of demand (η_P)	Profit-maximizing mark-up
1.5	200%
2.0	100%
2.5	67%
3.0	50%
5.0	25%
10.0	11%
20	5%

13.4 THE BEHAVIOURAL THEORIES

The behavioural theories are associated with the work of Cyert and March (1963) and Monsen and Downes (1965) among others. These theories consider the inner workings of the large divisionalized firm. Divisions exist between owners and managers and between managers and the labour force. According to Cyert and March, the owners have no power. The managers have all the power and are ***satisficers*** rather than maximizers and act with bounded rationality rather than global rationality. Moreover, these theories contend that firms face uncertainty about the future and must incur information costs in acquiring the data needed to function as marginalists. The behavioural theories draw on the work of the 1978 Nobel Laureate in Economics, Herbert Simon (1947), who coined the terms ***bounded rationality*** and ***satisficing***.

Drawing on the work of these authors, the elements of the theories are presented in summary.

13.4.1 The goals of the firm – satisficing

The firm has a multiplicity of goals, all of which are for ***satisfactory*** (not maximum) levels of achievement. These goals come from different departments or divisions of the firm. The primary ones are:

1. Production or output goals from the production department.
2. Sales targets as goals from the sales or distribution department.
3. Share-of-the-market goals from the marketing department.
4. Inventory level goals to manage product availability and minimize waste.
5. Profit goals that envisage a satisfactory level of profit.

Monsen and Downes consider that the goal of the owners is profit maximization but, because of the structure of the organization, the owners are coerced into accepting the goals set by the managers. The managers are concerned with their own utility which focuses on salaries, rank and job security, among others.

Bounded rationality

In the model '***bounded rationality***' is contrasted with ***global rationality***. The concept is used to refer to the way in which the divisionalized firm is not infused with all the knowledge and singularity of purpose to act as a cohesive whole. Consequently, it cannot pursue a single objective such as profit maximization.

The main features of bounded rationality are:

- The dynamic adaptation of goals to the environment. Goal setting is based on adaptive expectations. There are aspiration levels and the target levels considered satisfactory in any time period depend on the levels achieved in the previous time period. Once goals are not achieved, then the expectation is revised for the next time period.
- The translation of goals into rules-of-thumb. The aspiration levels are translated into administrative or behavioural rules, the adoption of which depends on the revision

of aspiration levels. These are mechanical rules such as the level of the mark-up, or the timing of new investment in response to increases in sales.
- The reliance on planned, programmed, decision making. The administrative rules help to simplify decision making, for example, price equals cost plus 10 per cent.
- Sequential attention to problems. This bounded rationality means that they do not look at all problems within the organization as a whole but they deal with problems sequentially. Issues arising from within different departments are screened and prioritized, then handled in some order.

The role of conflict

In the monolithic firm of the traditional theory, conflict between owners and managers or between managers and supervisors or workers did not exist. Conflict was disregarded. Workers unions were absent. In the behavioural theories, the goals of the firm are set by the owners but these goals often conflict with those of the managers and those of the managers conflict with the rest of the firm. Conflict therefore plays a central role in the behavioural theories. The divisionalized firm must therefore find ways to deal with conflict.

In the model internal conflict is resolved by resorting to the use of:

- Direct payments.
- Side payments.
- Slack payments.
- Delegating authority.
- Sequential attention to the demands of various departments or individuals within the firm.

Functions of top management

The firm is layered with levels of management such as top management, middle management, supervisors and others, each with different responsibilities and goals. At the highest level, the top management team have various decision-making functions which include:

- Approval of the firm's budget.
- Approval of major projects.
- Allocation of the budget among departments.

Within the firm, the department heads have a goal of trying to attract a larger share of the budget for their department. The allocation is based on the past performance of the department and on the bargaining power of the department.

Relationship between firm and industry

Firms are aware of the others in the industry. There is no collusion but there is a quick response by firms to the actions of the others. As firms learn from past mistakes and from past reactions of others, the response to competitive action becomes increasingly quicker. This appears similar to collusion but results from quick reactions.

There is ongoing movement as firms enter, exit or merge. In a new industry (say a firm produces solar energy), new firms enter when the outlook is improving. Should conditions deteriorate, some go out of business while others merge to face the new environment.

Compatibility with profit maximization

The behavioural theory alleges that firms are only interested in achieving a satisfactory level of profits. They do, however, set a profit goal among other goals and this is revised based on adaptive expectations and adaptive behaviour. If the goal is not reached, firms cut costs and/or revise demand and set new targets. ***The model does not determine what is a satisfactory level of profit***.

It could be argued however, that with this satisficing and adaptive behaviour, if managers set targets for profit and continually raise the target whenever it is attained , they will eventually come to profit maximization.

It is said that this model was not conceived of as a theory of the firm but as a model of the allocation of resources. The behavioural theory is one of allocation inside the firm. ***Thus the behavioural theory and the profit maximization theory are not competitive but complementary***.

13.5 THE ECONOMICS OF INFORMATION

In the new globalization, information plays a critical role in decision making at the level of the individual firm, the individual consumer and the market, the principal units of microeconomics. While there is no clearly accepted definition of Information Economics or the Economics of Information, it may be simply described as the study of how information affects economic decision making. It is, however, much wider and more complicated than this. While most of economic theory assumes the existence of perfect knowledge, a part of the economics of information is concerned with imperfect knowledge or uncertainty. More recently, the study of the economics of information has been extended into the study of the economics of information technology (IT) and the role of the internet and search engines in changing the information available to consumers and producers. This emphasis on the study of information is among the new approaches to the study of the firm.

The market for lemons

The genesis of the study of the economics of information is considered to lie in the path breaking work of 2001 Nobel laureate in Economics George Akerlof (1970) titled 'The Market for Lemons' referring to the asymmetric nature of information in the used car industry. After initially being rejected by journals, Akerlof's article, once accepted, brought a whole new dimension to the study of microeconomics. The area of study gained further popularity through the work of a small group of economists who became joint 2001 Nobel laureates with Akerlof (Akerlof, Spence and Stiglitz). However, earlier work by Stigler (1961), a 1982 Nobel laureate in economics, and by Arrow (Nobel laureate of 1972) are also considered major contributions to the study of information economics.

Economics of information must be distinguished from what was previously known as information theory.

Asymmetric information

Asymmetric information is the case where, for some reason(s), some persons in the market have more or better information than others. All consumers and producers then do not have perfect information as is assumed in the traditional theory of markets. Those with better information are in a position to make more appropriate choices.

Certain classes of persons, such as used car sales persons, mortgage brokers or insurance salesmen tend to have more information than the clients they serve. Lack of the necessary information can lead to unfavourable outcomes, usually subsumed under labels such as moral hazard and adverse selection. Because these persons are in a position to dupe (or 'spoof') the consumer and because consumers are somewhat wary of them, the market demand for the commodities they are peddling tends to be reduced. Adverse selection can be moderated with recourse to signalling and screening.

1 ***Signalling***. This relates to the way in which an action may give a signal that provides some desired information or knowledge.
2 ***Screening***. This is concerned with the way in which it is possible to get another party to reveal their information. This is the method of giving the other party a set of choices such that, by making a choice, they reveal the desired information.

Information goods and services – characteristics

The study of the economics of information has been extended into areas of information goods and services. Information, however defined, can be viewed as an economic product (good or service). As such, it can have a value, can be demanded and supplied. The more recent extension into the area of Information Technology (IT) has taken it to what is sometimes referred to as the 'next' economy, a title used by DeLong and Froomkin (1998).

Information goods and services are viewed as having their own special characteristics among which are the following:

1 They are non-rivalrous (i.e the consumption by one does not preclude the consumption by another of the same information). This tends to give information a marginal cost of zero.
2 They are typically non-excludable. It is usually difficult to exclude people from information available to others. A fee may be charged or persons may be required to log-in, but once they do, the information becomes available to them and to whomever they wish to share or distribute it.
3 Transparency is typically absent with information goods and services. The payment made for, say, a suite of software, may be payment for a bundle of present and future

goods and services. Moreover, the consumer may be paying for a relationship which may involve future upgrades and additions.

The development and use of what may be termed shop bots (shopping search engines) has been seen by DeLong and Froomkin (1998) as bringing more information to the public and possibly leading to greater efficiency and reduced prices in the market. The subsequent growth of ***Google*** as a search engine and more (Google Earth, etc.) shows the demand for information as a modern day commodity.

There are myriad new approaches to the theory of the firm and they extend in many directions. Many of them have been criticized for lacking rigour and for being unable to serve the purpose of predicting firm behaviour. For this reason, the alternatives are generally considered as adjuncts to the standard traditional theories that help give more insights into the workings of the firm rather than replacements for these theories.

REVIEW QUESTIONS FOR CHAPTER 13

1 Enumerate the objections raised against the traditional (marginalist) models of the firm, taking care to explain the 'fallacy of misplaced concreteness' .
2 Explain and illustrate Baumol's Managerial model and consider whether there is any way of reconciling the empirical observation with the application of the marginalist principal.
3 Illustrate the Mark-up pricing model and examine the view that this pricing practice is tantamount to marginalist pricing for profit maximization.
4 Give the gist of the behavioural model of Cyert and March and assess the view that this model is not an alternative to the marginalist model.
5 Briefly discuss the new theories of the firm with regard to the role of transaction costs and costs of information.

RECOMMENDED READING FOR CHAPTER 13

Alchian, A. and Demsetz, H. (1972) 'Production, information costs, and economic organization', *American Economic Review*, 62: 777–95.

Akerlof, G. A. (1970) 'The Market for "Lemons": Quality, Uncertainty and the Market Mechanism', *Quarterly Journal of Economics*, 84(3): 488–500.

Akerlof, G. A. (1982) 'Labour Contracts as Partial Gift Exchange,' *Quarterly Journal of Economics*, 97(4): 543–69.

Bain, J. S. (1956) *Barriers to New Competition*, New Haven: Harvard University Press.

Baumol, W. J. (1959) *Business Behaviour, Value and Growth*, New York: Macmillan.

Baumol, W. J. (1962) 'On the Theory of the Expansion of the Firm', *The American Economic Review*, 52: 1078–87.

Baumol, W. J. and Stewart, M. (1971) 'On the Behavioural Theory of the Firm', in R. Marris and A. Wood, *The Corporate Economy*, London: Macmillan.

Benkler, Y. (2006) *The Wealth of Networks: How Social Production Transforms Markets and Freedom*, New Haven: Yale University Press.

Berle, A. and Means, G. (1933) *The Modern Corporation and Private Property*, New York: The Macmillan Company.
Boudreaux, D. J. and Holcombe, R. G. (1989) 'The Coasian and Knightian Theories of the Firm', *Managerial and Decision Economics*, 10(2): 61–9.
Coase, R. H. (1937) 'The Nature of the Firm', *Economica*, 4: 386–405.
Cyert, R. and March, J. G. (1963) *Behavioral Theory of the Firm*, Oxford: Blackwell.
DeLong, J. and Froomkin, A. M. (1998) 'The Next Economy?', in Deborah Hurley, Brian Kahin, and Hal Varian (eds), *Internet Publishing and Beyond: The Economics of Digital Information and Intellectual Property*, Cambridge, MA: MIT Press.
Earley, J. S. (1965) 'Marginal Policies of "Excellently Managed" Companies', *American Economic Review*, 46(1): 44–70.
Hall, R. and Hitch, C. (1939) 'Price Theory and Business Behaviour', London: *Oxford Economic Papers*, 2: 12–44.
Machlup, F. (1967) 'Theories of the Firm: Marginalist, Behavioural, Managerial', *American Economic Review*, 57: 1–33.
Marris, R. (1963) 'A Model of the Managerial Enterprise', *Quarterly Journal of Economics*, 77: 1852-902.
Monsen, R. J. and Downs, A. (1965) 'A Theory of Large Managerial Firms', *Journal of Political Economy*, 73: 221–36.
Roberts, J. (2004) *The Modern Firm: Organizational Design for Performance and Growth*, Oxford University Press.
Shapiro, C. and Stiglitz, J. E. (1984) Equilibrium Unemployment as a Worker Discipline Device', *American Economic Review*, 74: 433–44.
Simon, H. (1947) *Administrative Behavior: A Study of Decision-Making Processes in Administrative Organizations* (4th edn in 1997), New York: The Free Press.
Simon, H. (1962) 'New Developments in the Theory of the Firm', *American Economic Review*, 52: 1–15.
Stigler, G. J. (1961) 'The Economics of Information', *Journal of Political Economy*, 69(3): 213–225.
Williamson, J. (1966) 'Profit, Growth and Sales Maximization', *Economica*, 33: 1–16.
Williamson, O. E. (1963) 'Managerial Discretion and Business Behaviour', *American Economic Review*, 53(5): 1032–57.
Williamson, O. E. (1979) 'Transaction Cost Economics: The Governance of Contractual Relations', *Journal of Law and Economics*, 22: 233–61.
Williamson, O. E. (1986) *Economic Organization: Firms, Markets, and Policy Control*, New York: University Press.

14 The Factor Market

The Factor Market; Factor Demand under The Marginal Productivity Theory of Distribution; Factor Supply under The Marginal Productivity Theory of Distribution; Monopolistic and Monopsonistic Exploitation; Labour Unions and Unemployment Product Exhaustion theorems.

14.1 INTRODUCTION TO DISTRIBUTION THEORY

The earlier chapters dealt with the theory of value or price theory as it pertains to the product market. The emphasis was on the analysis of consumer demand for a good or service and producer supply of goods and services. In essence, it was the study of the way in which equilibrium was achieved in the product market based on supply and demand analysis. This equilibrium gave the optimum price (or market value) of the product and the optimal quantities.

The focus now moves from the product market to the factor market. These factor inputs into the production process are typically identified as labour, capital, land and entrepreneurship, among others. The interest centres on how the value of the product is distributed among the factor inputs that generate output in what is referred to as Distribution Theory. It is still, in a sense, a theory of value and price – the valuing and pricing of inputs into the production process.

14.1.1 Derived demand

Factor market theory considers the demand for and supply of the factors of production and the way in which the value of output is created by and shared among these factor inputs. In this case, the major difference between the theory of value and the theory of distribution is that, whereas goods and services are considered to be desired for their intrinsic quality (utility), factor inputs are considered to be desired only for their contribution to output. Hence the demand for factors is seen as a ***derived demand***.

Studying the nature of the demand for and supply of factors of production is important at all levels of production and consumption from a small domestic protected market to the large global market. This is particularly so for the increasingly mobile factors in a globalized world, factors such as international capital and entrepreneurship. The study of the factor market provides an understanding of how the structure of the market affects the demand for factors and, particularly in the case of labour, how income and preferences for leisure/work affect factor supply.

14.1.2 Classical vs. modern distribution theory

In the nineteenth century, it was customary for economists to classify productive inputs into three basic categories, namely land, labour and capital. The theory of input pricing for the classicists was therefore a theory of the distribution of income among land owners, wage earners and the owners of capital (capitalists), three economic ***and*** social factor supplying classes. Rent, wages and profit were the returns to the three factors respectively. A fourth factor, entrepreneurship, was later introduced.

The marginal productivity theory

The modern theory is more general. It takes into account all types of factor inputs and how they receive their remuneration. This is the counterpart to the modern theory of value which was the focus of the earlier chapters. The modern theory is mainly marginalist in nature. Consequently, the modern distribution theory has been given the title of the ***Marginal Productivity theory***. John Bates Clark, writing at the turn of the twentieth century, is considered to be responsible for the marginal productive theory.

The Marginal Productivity theory is therefore based on supply and demand analysis in similar manner to that of the pricing of products except that the demand for factors is a derived demand, derived, as is evident later, from the marginal productivity of the factor and the value of the product it produces at the margin. This chapter deals with the Marginal Productivity theory.

14.2 SHORT-RUN FACTOR DEMAND UNDER MARGINAL PRODUCTIVITY THEORY

The demand for a factor of production in the short-run is done under certain assumptions. These include:

- There is a single variable factor input. This is usually considered to be labour. All other factors are assumed to be fixed and can therefore be subsumed under capital (K).
- There is Perfect Competition in the factor market. In the short-run analysis of the demand for a factor of production, it is assumed that the price of the factor is fixed. That is, the firm can hire all the supply of the factor it wants at the going price. This is generally referred to as having Perfect Competition in the factor market.
- The supply of the variable factor is unlimited at the fixed price. Therefore, the firm can have the quantity of the factor it wants at the going factor price (e.g. wage rate of labour).

- Technology is given and known.
- The prices of other factors are given.
- The demand depends on whether the product market is characterized by perfect competition or imperfect competition.

14.2.1 Short-run demand for labour with perfect competition in the product market

In the short-run labour is typically the single variable factor. In this analysis of the short-run demand for labour, the following should be noted:

- The short-run demand for labour may be restyled as: the demand for labour when labour is the single variable factor input.
- Perfect competition in the factor market means that the wage rate (w) is given.
- The demand for labour is a derived demand, and so labour is demanded only for its contribution to the output and profit of a profit maximizing firm and not for any intrinsic value in itself.
- The analysis is done at the level of the individual firm.
- The firm is selling the product in a perfectly competitive product market.

The issue resolves into that of how much of an input would a firm demand in order to maximize its profits given the state of technology, the fixed nature of the other inputs and the fixed market price of the output produced.

The demand for labour by the firm therefore comes out of the firm's optimization (profit maximization) process as follows.

Consider the short-run production function where quantity (Q) is a function of labour (L) for all other factors (K) being fixed:

$$Q_x = f(L)_{\overline{K}}$$

The producer (firm) aims to maximize profits (Π) as the difference between total revenue (R) and total cost (C). The objective may be stated formally as:

$$\text{Max: } \Pi = R - C$$

where revenue is:

$$R = \overline{P}_x Q_x$$

and total cost (C), for capital (K) fixed is:

$$C = \overline{w}L + r\overline{K}$$

This may be re-written as:

$$C = \overline{w}L + \overline{F}$$

The objective function may therefore be expressed as:

$$\text{Max: } \Pi = \overline{P}_x Q_x - (\overline{w}L + \overline{F})$$

Differentiating with respect to labour only (since all other factors are fixed) gives:

$$\frac{\partial \Pi}{\partial L} = \overline{P}_x \frac{\mathrm{d}Q_x}{\mathrm{d}L} - \overline{w} = 0.$$

where:

$$\frac{\mathrm{d}Q_x}{\mathrm{d}L} = MP_L$$

However, in dealing with the factor market, the Marginal Product (*MP*) is re-styled the Marginal Physical Product (*MPP*) in order to clearly distinguish between physical quantities and values. Hence, MP_L becomes MPP_L. Consequently, the result now shows that profit maximization is achieved where:

$$\overline{P}_x MPP_L - \overline{w} = 0$$

or:

$$\overline{P}_x MPP_L = \overline{w}$$

Now, $\overline{P}_x MPP_L$ is the marginal physical product of labour multiplied by the price of that product. In other words, it is the output produced by the last unit of labour hired, multiplied by the price of that output. This is called the Value of the Marginal Product of Labour (VMP_L). Hence:

$$\overline{P}_x MPP_L = VMP_L$$

Consequently, the equilibrium condition can be re-stated as:

$$VMP_L = \overline{w}$$

It means that the incremental contribution to the value of the firm's output by an extra unit of labour must be equal to the cost of that extra unit of labour for the firm to maximize profits in the short-run, the period when labour is the only variable factor (all other factors are fixed).

Generally then, the firm's demand curve for labour is the value of marginal product curve and the equilibrium quantity of labour would depend on the wage rate. Hence as the (given) wage rate rises or falls, the quantity of labour demanded will move left or right respectively along the VMP_L curve. The VMP_Lcurve slopes downwards to the right because it is proportional to the curve showing the input's marginal productivity. This is illustrated in Figure 14.1.

In Chapter 5, it was shown that a firm, operating in the short-run, maximizes profit in what is described as Stage II of the production function. This is where the marginal

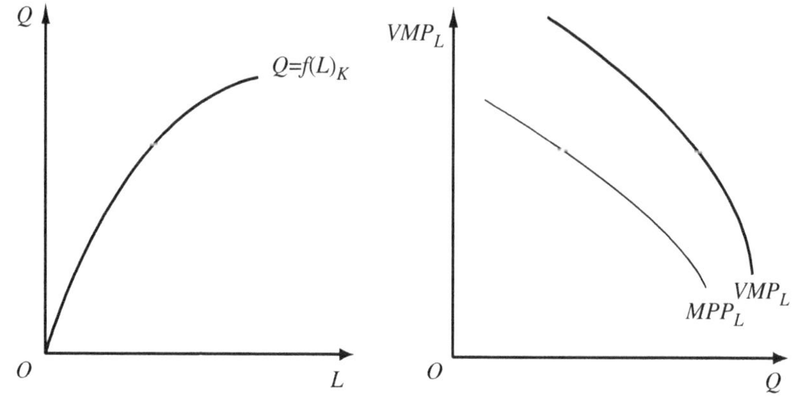

Figure 14.1
Derivation of MPP_L and VMP_L curves from the production function

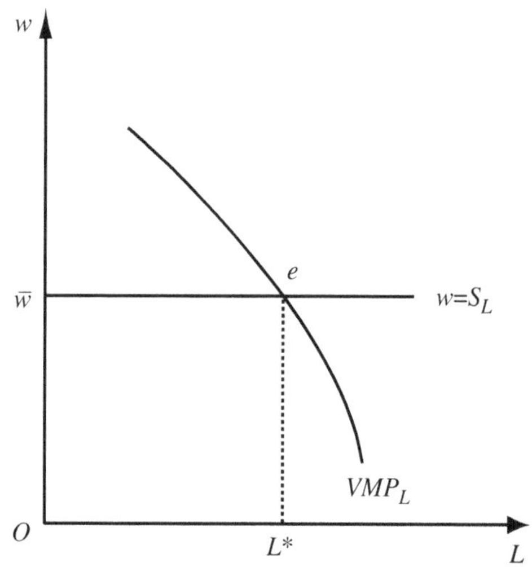

Figure 14.2
Short-run equilibrium demand for labour by producer in a perfectly competitive product market

product of labour is decreasing and is below the average product, but still is greater than zero.

In Figure 14.1 the drawing on the left shows the production function $Q_x = f(L)_{\overline{K}}$. The drawing on the right shows the resulting MPP_L curve and the VMP_L curve from this function.

At any given wage rate (w), the supply of labour S_L is infinitely elastic (i.e. the firm can have all the labour it wants at the going wage rate ($\overline{w}$)). Figure 14.2 shows the equilibrium (profit maximizing) quantity of labour (L^*) that the firm should choose based on the given wage rate ($\overline{w}$).

From Figure 14.2, the following may be observed:

- To the left of the equilibrium point e, $VMP_L > \overline{w}$. This signifies that the producer is getting more value (revenue) from the output of the last person (unit of labour) hired than the producer has to pay that last unit. As a result, each additional unit of labour hired is augmenting the profit of the firm. Consequently, the advice in such a case is for the producer to continue expanding production by hiring more labour.
- To the right of the equilibrium point e, $VMP_L < \overline{w}$. As a result, the producer is now receiving less value (revenue) from the output of the last unit of labour hired than the producer has to pay that last unit. Hence, each additional unit of labour hired is reducing from the profit of the firm. Consequently, the advice in such a case is for the producer to reduce the amount of labour used. As the amount of labour hired is reduced the marginal productivity of labour rises.
- It is only at the equilibrium point e, where $VMP_L = \overline{w}$, that the firm's profits are neither increasing nor decreasing. This is a stationary point. Here profits which have been increasing with the use of additional labour are maximized with the employment of L^* units of labour. After this, the additional cost of hiring labour exceeds the additional revenues generated by that labour, thus reducing profits.

It is critical therefore, for a producer to be aware of, and to be able to identify, this point in the employment of labour.

The total revenue–total cost approach

An alternative method is to use the Total Revenue–Total Cost approach. This is done as follows:

- Consider that profit maximization occurs when the difference between Total Revenue and Total Cost ($TR - TC$) is at the greatest.
- When $TR - TC$ is at its maximum, the slope of TR (MR) is equal to the slope of TC (MC). (Recall from Chapter 1 that the greatest distance between two curves is where their slopes are equal.)
- Since MR is the value of marginal output (VMP) and marginal output comes only from labour in the short-run, then marginal revenue is the change in revenue resulting from a change in the quantity of labour used. This may be expressed as:

$$MR = \frac{\partial R}{\partial L} = \frac{\partial\left(\overline{P_x} Q_x\right)}{\partial L}$$

- Since price is a constant, the above equation becomes:

$$MR = \overline{P_x}\frac{\partial Q_x}{\partial L}$$

or:

$$VMP_L = \overline{P_x} MPP_L$$

This is the same result as derived earlier.

14.2.2 Short-run demand for labour with monopoly in the product market

For imperfectly competitive product markets, the analytical principles for analyzing the short-run demand for labour are the same as in perfectly competitive product markets. The major features are:

- In the short-run, labour is the single variable factor.
- The wage rate is given (factor supply is perfectly elastic to the firm).
- Marginal productivity considerations are the fundamental determinants of demand.

The main difference lies in the fact that the price of the output differs from the marginal revenue. Consequently, the value of the marginal product (*VMP*) of a factor is not the relevant guide. Rather, it is the Marginal Revenue Product (*MRP*).

The analysis for monopoly in the product market also includes oligopoly and monopolistic competition in the product market. However, the assumption of Perfect Competition in the factor market remains. This gives a horizontal labour supply curve.

14.2.2.1 SHORT-RUN EQUILIBRIUM DEMAND FOR LABOUR OF THE MONOPOLIST

Once again, as with the case of perfect competition in the product market, the short-run production function is used. This is expressed as follows:

$$Q_x = f(L)_{\overline{K}}$$

Similarly, the goal of the producer is to maximize profits, expressed as:

$$\text{Max: } \Pi = R - C$$

There is a difference, however, with how revenue (R) is expressed. This is because the price to the monopolist or imperfectly competitive firm is not given. Hence revenue is expressed as:

$$R = P_x Q_x \quad (\text{instead of: } R = \overline{P}_x Q_x)$$

where:

$$Q_x = f(L)$$

Total cost (C), for capital (K) fixed is expressed as before:

$$C = \overline{w}L + \overline{F}$$

The objective function becomes:

$$\text{Max: } \Pi = P_x Q_x - (\overline{w}L + \overline{F})$$

14.2.2.2 THE MARGINAL REVENUE PRODUCT OF LABOUR

In this case, since price (P_x) is not fixed, the process of differentiating with respect to labour is different. With revenue (R) being a product of both price and quantity and both being variable, the product rule of differentiation must apply. However, differentiation is respect to labour (L) and, whereas output is a function of labour ($Q_x = f(L)$), price is not a function of labour. Price is a function of quantity and quantity is a function of labour, which makes price a function of a function and the appropriate rule of differentiation must apply. This gives the condition:

$$\frac{\partial \Pi}{\partial L} = P_x \frac{\mathrm{d}Q_x}{\mathrm{d}L} + Q_x \left[\frac{\mathrm{d}P_x}{\mathrm{d}Q_x} \cdot \frac{\mathrm{d}Q_x}{\mathrm{d}L} \right] - \overline{w} = 0$$

This somewhat convoluted expression may be simplified by factoring out $\mathrm{d}Q_x/\mathrm{d}L$ to give the equilibrium condition:

$$\frac{\mathrm{d}Q_x}{\mathrm{d}L} \left(P_x + Q_x \left[\frac{\mathrm{d}P_x}{\mathrm{d}Q_x} \right] \right) = \overline{w}$$

From before, it is known that:

$$\frac{\mathrm{d}Q_x}{\mathrm{d}L} = MPP_L$$

Consequently, the equilibrium condition becomes:

$$MPP_L \left(P_x + Q_x \left[\frac{\mathrm{d}P_x}{\mathrm{d}Q_x} \right] \right) = \overline{w}$$

It may be observed that the expression:

$$\left(P_x + Q_x \left[\frac{\mathrm{d}P_x}{\mathrm{d}Q_x} \right] \right)$$

is the Marginal Revenue.

This gives the result for the equilibrium condition as:

$$MPP_L \cdot MR = \overline{w}$$

In terms of nomenclature, the following is used:

$$MPP_L \cdot MR = MRP_L$$

MRP_L stands for the Marginal Revenue Product of Labour.

Hence, for an imperfectly competitive firm to maximize profits, the following condition must hold:

$$MRP_L = \overline{w}$$

Since the marginal product of labour changes as additional units of labour are used, so does the MRP_L. Hence as the given wage rate ($\overline{w}$) changes, a new quantity of labour must be used in order to preserve the equilibrium between the two. The MRP_L curve therefore describes the demand curve for labour under an imperfectly competitive factor market.

The expression:

$$\left(P_x + Q_x\left[\frac{\mathrm{d}P_x}{\mathrm{d}Q_x}\right]\right)$$

is the Marginal Revenue because it is derived from the total revenue ($R = P_xQ_x$). From this, the following result is obtained:

$$TR = P_xQ_x = [f(Q_x)]Q_x$$

Hence:

$$MR = \frac{\mathrm{d}(PQ_x)}{\mathrm{d}Q_x} = P_x\frac{\mathrm{d}Q_x}{\mathrm{d}Q_x} + Q_x\frac{\mathrm{d}P_x}{\mathrm{d}Q_x}$$

Thus:

$$MR = P_x + Q_x\frac{\mathrm{d}P_x}{\mathrm{d}Q_x}$$

Once again, the equilibrium condition means that the incremental contribution to the value to a firm of the output generated by an extra unit of labour must be equal to the cost of that extra unit of labour. The difference is that, under imperfect competition or monopoly, it is the marginal revenue that is combined with the marginal product. Under perfect competition, marginal revenue is equal to price and therefore price is what is combined with the marginal product. Hence, for Perfect Competition, the monopoly result:

$$MPP_L \cdot MR = \overline{w}$$

becomes:

$$MPP_L \cdot P_x = \overline{w}$$

Consider further that, for a monopolist, total revenue is not increased by the value of the marginal product, because, in order to sell an additional unit, the price on all other units must be decreased. But total output expands by the marginal product. Thus the marginal product (in units of output) must be multiplied by the marginal revenue (i.e. change in revenue per unit of output). The MRP_L is the change in total revenue from selling the increased output from one additional unit of labour (e.g. labour hours). Hence MRP_L is the net addition to the total revenue of the producer attributable to the addition of one unit of the variable productive factor.

Like the Value of Marginal Product curve, the Marginal Revenue Product curve is downward sloping since it relates to the Marginal Physical Product (MPP_L) curve.

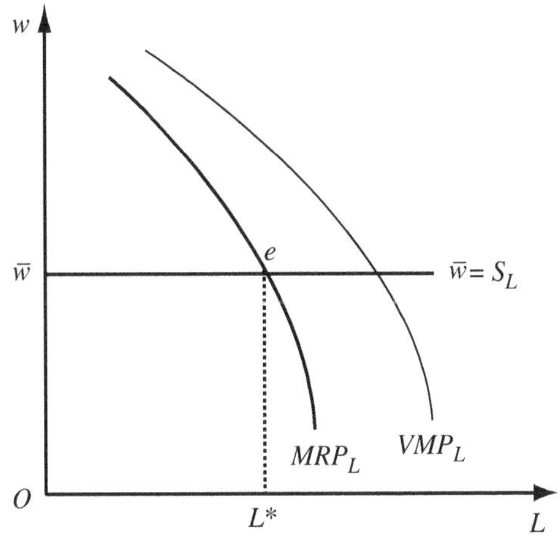

Figure 14.3
Short-run demand for labour under monopoly in the product market

This indicates that MRP_L declines as employment of the variable factor increases. This is shown in Figure 14.3.

The quantity of labour that allows the monopolist to maximize profits is L^*. The monopolist will purchase the input until the Marginal Revenue Product is equal to the price of the input. This is similar to the equilibrium of the producer in a perfectly competitive market except that the equilibrium is now along the MRP_L curve rather than the VMP_L curve. It must be noted that the value of the marginal product lies above the marginal revenue product or:

$$MPP_L \cdot MR < MPP_L \cdot P_x$$

This is because marginal revenue lies below price as:

$$P_x > MR$$

For evidence, consider Figure 14.4. With the fall of price from P_1 to P_2, output expands from Q_1 to Q_2. But MR is not equal to the total revenue from selling an additional unit of output. Thus, MR is not equal to $Q_1LP_2'Q_2$, the area of additional revenue. Instead, MR (the change in total revenue) is the additional revenue area minus the loss from selling all the other units at the lower price. Thus the Marginal Revenue area is:

$$MR = Q_1LP_2'Q_2 - P_1P_2LP_1'$$

Hence, while $Q_1LP_2'Q_2$ represents the gain in additional revenue, $P_1P_2LP_1'$ represents the loss from total revenue and must be subtracted from it.

In this example, it can be seen that the area of gain is less than the area of loss. This implies that marginal revenue is negative, even while price, which is the average revenue, is positive. This confirms that, under imperfect competition, $P_x > MR$.

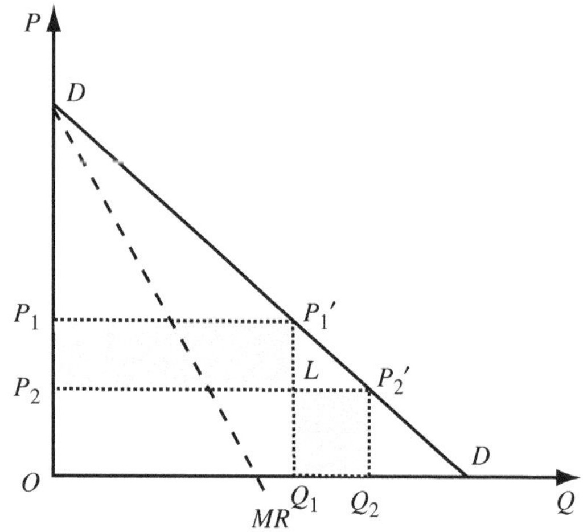

Figure 14.4
Relationship between marginal revenue and price

Consequently, for profit maximization under monopoly or imperfect competition, the producer's demand for labour curve lies below that of a producer in a perfectly competitive market ($MRP_L < VMP_L$).

The significance of this to a producer, whether in a small domestic market or a larger regional or global market, is that, in a short-run situation, the variable factor (labour) with a given factor price (wage) should continue to be added and production expanded until the addition to total revenue (whether *MR* or *P*) is equal to the factor price. Added to that, it should be noted by the producer that the marginal productivity of the factor in question should be ***declining*** as each additional unit is brought into production.

This is not likely to be intuitive to the way the producer rationalizes operations. Indeed, much of economics is counter-intuitive. However, with an understanding of the process and the application of the rule, the producer has a better chance of becoming or remaining competitive in the market.

14.3 LONG-RUN FACTOR DEMAND UNDER MARGINAL PRODUCTIVITY THEORY

Under Marginal Productivity theory, the long-run demand for a factor of production may be re-styled as: ***the demand for a factor when there are several variable factors***.

In the long-run all factors are variable. In this regard, the firm's demand curve is no longer the Value of Marginal Product curve. This is because a change in price of an input such as labour (*L*) will result in a change in the quantities of other inputs used, and a change in the quantity of other inputs used will affect the productivity of labour and hence, the quantity of labour used.

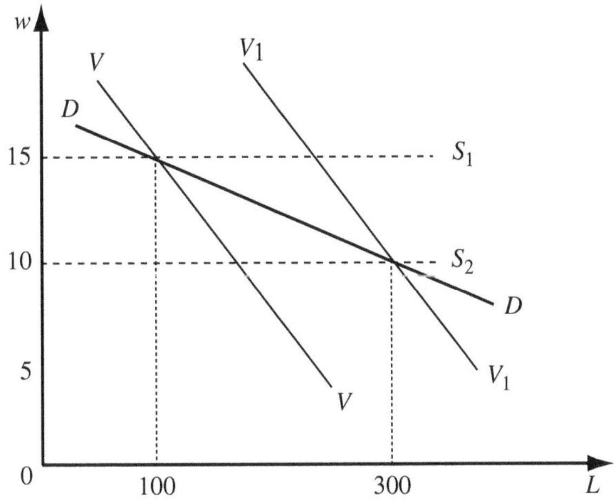

Figure 14.5
Long-run demand for labour (several variable factors) under perfect competition in the product market

As a result, when there is a change in the price of any one factor, there is a shift in the demand curve for that factor. The shift occurs because the demand for a factor is a ***derived demand***, derived from the marginal productivity of the factor and the price (or marginal revenue) of the product the factor is producing. In the case of several variable factors (long-run), the impact on the demand curve derives from the effect of a price change in the factor on the marginal productivity of the factor, through the relative changes in the usage of the factors.

14.3.1 Long-run demand for labour with perfect competition

The relationship between the short-run and the long-run demand for labour is illustrated in Figure 14.5. In this figure, *VV* is the demand curve of labour (VMP_L) if labour is the only variable input. The movement to the long-run may be described as follows:

- Assume initially the price of *L* is $15.00 and 100 units of *L* are demanded.
- Suppose the price of *L* falls to $10.00. When the price of labour falls the VMP_L will exceed its price of $15.00. Consequently, the firm is paying its last unit of labour $10.00 but that unit of labour is contributing $15.00 to the revenue of the firm (thereby adding $5.00 in profit to the producing firm).
- The producing firm should logically seek to expand the quantity of labour hired as each additional unit is adding more to revenue than to cost, thereby increasing profit. This does not affect the price of labour as there is perfect competition in the factor market and an infinite elasticity of supply of labour.
- With the expansion in the use of labour, the *VMP* curves of other inputs will shift.

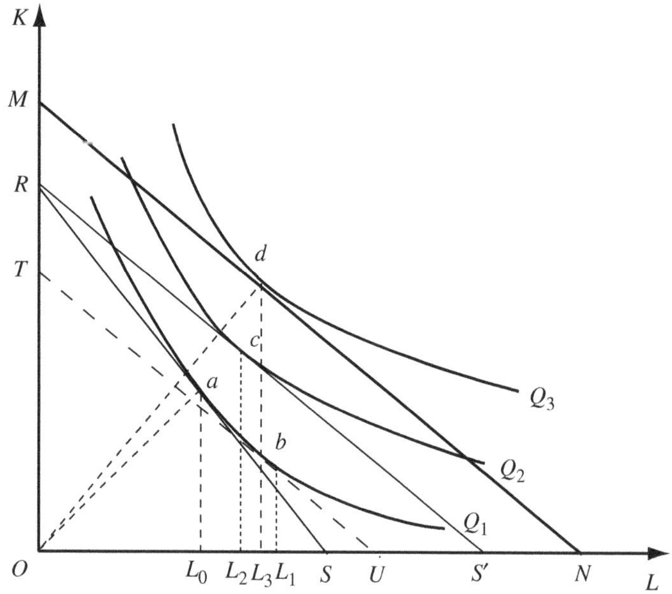

Figure 14.6
Substitution, output and profit maximization effects of a fall in the price of labour

How and why will they shift?

The way in which the VMP_L curves (VV) will shift depends on three effects. These three effects are identified as: the Substitution effect, the Output effect, and the Profit Maximization effect. This is illustrated in Figure 14.6.

In Figure 14.6, the initial equilibrium is at point *a*. The price of labour relative to the price of capital (*K*) is given by the slope of the isocost line *RS*. Three effects are noted. These are identified as: the substitution effect, the output effect and the profit maximization effect.

The substitution effect

The fall in the price of labour (wage rate) is shown by a pivoting of the line RS to *RS*′. There is a compensating variation as the new isocost line (*RS*′) is shifted back to *TU* on the original isoquant Q_1. The movement from point *a* to point *b* is the substitution effect similar to that found for the consumer in constructing the demand curve. This effect is always negative, that is, as the price of labour falls, more labour is used to remain along the same isoquant. Labour employed increases from L_0 to L_1 and there is a consequent reduction in the quantity of capital (*K*) employed.

The ***substitution effect*** means more of the cheaper factor (labour) is used and there is less of the co-operating factor with which to work. This causes a fall in the productivity of labour. Thus labour's marginal product curve tends to shift to the left. This is because the marginal product of a factor decreases as relatively more is used in relation to other factors. Since the demand curve for labour is a derived demand, as the marginal productivity of labour declines so to does the value of marginal product curve. The outcome is a leftward (inward) shift in the VMP_L curve (VV in Figure 14.5).

The output effect

The output effect, however, tends to compensate for the fall in the marginal product of labour. The reduction in the price of labour means that the producer has some saving in expenditure. The implication is that the producer can expand output by producing on the new isocost line RS'. The output effect for a normal factor should be positive. That is, the increased output should lead to an increase in the use of the factor (over and above the increase caused by the substitution effect).

However, in many cases, labour tends to be an inferior factor whereby an increase in output, although leading to an increase in the absolute use of the factor generally means a ***relative*** decline in its use. Put differently, the capital–labour ratio (K/L) in production tends to increase as output increases. This in shown in Figure 14.6 where the output effect, in the movement to point c, subtracts from the substitution effect, taking the quantity of labour from L_1 back to L_2. The capital–labour ratio (K/L) may be drawn as a ray from the origin to the points on the isoquant and it can be envisaged from Figure 14.6 that the slope of the ray from the origin (O) to c would be greater than to the point b.

The ***output effect*** increases the use of both inputs but tends to shift labour's VMP curve to the right (from where it is after the substitution effect) because labour's productivity (MP_L) is improved as there is more of the cooperating factor for labour to work with.

The profit-maximization effect

The profit-maximizing effect further reinforces the output effect. When the price of labour falls, the marginal cost of production is reduced for every level of output since labour is the variable factor. The marginal cost (MC) curve shifts to the right and the profit maximizing output increases. This leads to an increase in the use of both factors of production as output expands. The expansion of output tends to increase the capital labour ratio (K/L) in production (as labour tends to become an inferior factor as output increases). The relatively more capital intensive method of production means an increase in the productivity of labour (MP_L).

The effect then is to shift the marginal physical product of labour curve to the right and, by extension, the value of marginal product curve (since the price of the product does not change). The movement from c to d in Figure 14.6 is profit maximization effect. Labour use is shown to decrease from L_1 to L_3. This reinforces the inferior status of labour as a factor of production as the plant expands but could also be shown as a positive movement in the use of labour over the output effect. Nevertheless, labour use is still greater than it was originally (before the fall in the price of labour) and the marginal physical productivity of labour (MP_L) is now higher than it was before the fall in the price of labour.

Thus with the fall in price of labour, there have been changes in:

- The quantity of labour used.
- The level of output.
- The use of other inputs.

Nevertheless, the final overall effect is to increase the productivity of labour as it now has more of the co-operating factors to work with. The substitution effect causes a leftward shift in MPP_L (and hence VMP_L). The output and the profit maximizing effect cause rightward shifts in the MPP_L (and hence VMP_L). As a result, the VMP_L is expected to shift overall ***outwards to the right***. Consequently, as the price of labour falls, the expansion in the use of labour does not take place along the original demand for labour (VV) curve, but shifts to a new VMP_L curve (V_1V_1) as previously shown in Figure 14.5.

It may be noted that the curve may shift outwards, inwards or twist depending on the nature of the effect the use of the other co-operating factors has on the productivity of the factor in question. In this example of the factor labour, the process becomes relatively more capital intensive, thereby increasing the productivity of labour. However, the process could become less capital intensive or the capital intensity could vary depending on the level of output reached.

In the example above, the long-run demand for the factor labour (DD) is more elastic in the long-run than the individual short-run curves. However, it may be noted that, where the process becomes less capital intensive with a reduction in the price of labour (inward shift in VV), the long-run demand curve for labour becomes less elastic (steeper) than the short-run demand curve. Where the curve twists, the final outcome is unclear.

14.3.2 Long-run demand for labour with monopoly in the product market

The long-run demand for a factor, namely, the demand for a single input when several variable inputs are used, has a similar method of analysis under monopoly in the product market as under perfect competition in the product market. The MRP_L curve is no longer the true demand curve for similar reasons as before. With a fall in the price of the input, the expansion in its use is affected by the same substitution, output and profit maximizing effects as explained under perfect competition in the product market. Consequently, the MRP_L curve (MM in Figure 14.7) may shift outwards, shift inwards or twist.

The major difference between the case of Perfect Competition in the product market and Monopoly in the product market is that the Marginal Product of Labour (MRP_L) curve is used instead of the VMP_L curve. If MRP_L shifts outwards then the long-run demand curve (DD) becomes less steep. If it shifts inwards it becomes steeper. If it twists it may leave a meandering demand curve for a single input under consideration where several inputs are variable.

14.3.3 Long-run demand for multiple factors

For profit maximization, the firm must pick a combination of inputs where the ratio of each input's marginal physical product to its price is equal to the similar ratios for all the others. Consider three factors: labour (L), capital (K) and land (D). Then equilibrium (profit maximization) requires:

$$\frac{MPP_L}{P_L} = \frac{MPP_K}{P_K} = \frac{MPP_D}{P_D}$$

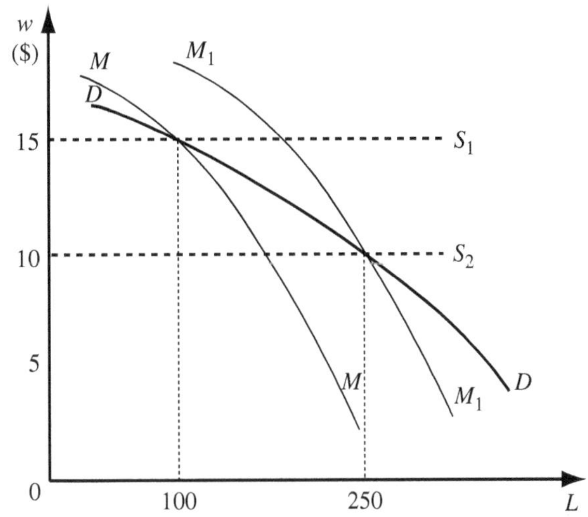

Figure 14.7
Long-run demand for labour under monopoly in the product market

An alternative method of reaching this conclusion is as follows:

$$1L \text{ (input)} = MPP_L \text{ (extra output)}$$

Then:

$$MPP_L \text{ (output)} = 1L \text{ (input)}$$

Consequently, one (1) extra unit of output is:

$$1 = \frac{1L}{MPP_L} = \frac{1}{MPP_L}(L)$$

Now:

$$\frac{1}{MPP_L} \text{ units of input labour } (L) \text{ will cost } \frac{1}{MPP_L}(P_L)$$

Therefore:

$$\frac{P_L}{MPP_L} \text{ is the marginal cost of labour}$$

Thus:

$$\frac{P_L}{MPP_L} = \frac{P_K}{MPP_K} = \frac{P_D}{MPP_D} = MC$$

Noting that for a firm to ***maximize profits*** it must operate at a point where $MC = MR$, then the following condition must hold:

$$\frac{P_L}{MPP_L} = \frac{P_K}{MPP_K} = \frac{P_D}{MPP_D} = MR$$

Thus, since:

$$\frac{P_L}{MPP_L} = MR$$

Then, using r for rental rate of capital, w for the wage rate and t for the cost of land services, the equilibrium conditions may be written as:

$$P_L = w = MPP_L \cdot MR$$

and:

$$P_K = r = MPP_K \cdot MR$$

and:

$$P_D = t = MPP_D \cdot MR$$

This says that the wage rate must equal the marginal revenue product (marginal revenue times the marginal physical product) of labour, and similarly, for the other factors of production.

Where there is perfect competition in the product market, marginal revenue is equal to price, as set out below:

$$MR = \overline{P}_x$$

This gives the conditions, from above, that:

$$P_L = w = MPP_L \cdot \overline{P}_x$$

and:

$$P_K = r = MPP_K \cdot \overline{P}_x$$

and:

$$P_D = t = MPP_D \cdot \overline{P}_x$$

The conclusion is that the profit-maximizing producer must employ each input in an amount such that the input's marginal physical product, multiplied by the firm's marginal revenue (or price if it is a perfectly competitive firm), equals the input's price.

This provides the basis for the firm's demand curve for an input under any market structure in the product market. Where there are several variable inputs, the ratio of the marginal physical product (incremental output) from an extra unit of input to the price of the input must be the same for all factor inputs.

Using this knowledge, a producer, with adequate knowledge of the production function (technology) and the market (price or marginal revenue information) knows how to achieve profit maximization. This could mean the difference between survival in a market or extinction, or between great success in a market or marginal survival. Knowledge of the rules of the games gives a greater chance of success so vital to producers facing greater global competition.

14.4 MARKET DEMAND FOR A SINGLE INPUT

14.4.1 The market demand curve for labour under perfect competition

From the single producer to the market

In making the transition from the factor demand of the single producer/firm to the factor demand of the market, the major consideration is that: ***The factor demand curves for the individual producers (firms) cannot be summed to find market demand for a factor of production.***

This is the primary difference between the construction of the market demand for a good and that for a factor of production. This difference derives from the nature of the demand for a factor input where that demand is described as a ***derived demand***. It has previously been shown that the demand for a factor of production is derived from the marginal physical productivity of that factor and the price (or marginal revenue) of the product it produces (VMP_L or MRP_L).

In moving from the short-run (single variable factor) to the long-run (several variable factors) factor demand, there are shifts in demand due to the effect on the marginal physical productivity of the factor. In moving from the individual producer to the market, there are also shifts in the demand curve for a factor, this time because of the effect on the ***price*** (or marginal revenue) of the product produced by the factor.

The shift in the factor's demand curve occurs because, in the total market, ***the changes in the factor input's price affect the use of the factor, the level of output and hence, the price of the product***. The individual producer's demand curve is based on the supposition that the producer's decisions cannot affect the price of the output. But consider what happens when all producers together respond to a fall in the price of an input at the same time.

To illustrate this, consider a fall in the price of the input labour (L). All producers will utilize more labour and all will increase output. The combined increase in output causes a fall in the price (and marginal revenue) of the output. This fall in price of output (good x) causes the VMP_L (i.e. $MPP_L \cdot \overline{P}_x$) curve to shift leftwards (inwards). This is illustrated in Figure 14.8.

Using Figure 14.8, when the wage rate (w) is \$15.00, the demand by all producers of good x for the factor input labour (L) is OL_1 on VV. The horizontal summation across all

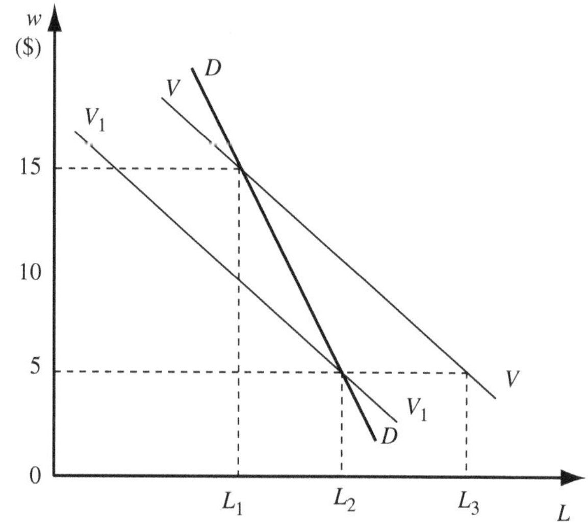

Figure 14.8
Market demand for labour

producers gives the market demand for labour at this price. With the fall in the price of labour to \$5.00, the summed demand for labour by all producers should expand to OL_3. However, the expanded output of good x by all the individual producers leads to a fall in the price (marginal revenue) of good x. The fall in the price of good x shifts the VMP_L (i.e. $MPP_L \cdot \overline{P}_x$) curve inwards to V_1V_1 for each producer, thereby resulting in a lower demand for labour in the market. The MPP_L is now being multiplied by a lower price. Thus, instead of moving from demanding to OL_1 to demanding OL_3, the market now demands only OL_2 after the adjustments are made. Consequently, the curve that describes the market demand for labour is the *DD* curve, as shown in Figure 14.8, rather than the curve representing the sum of the individual VMP_L curves (*VV*). This renders the market demand curve for a factor more inelastic (steeper) than the simple summation of the individual producer's (firm's) original demand curves would suggest. *DD* is the market demand curve for labour.

An example of the application of shifting curves on the demand for a factor is given in Box 14.1.

This is important for producers, firms, unions and public sector policy makers to note, since the fall in the price of labour does not result in the anticipated increase in the demand for that factor when based on the demands of the individual firms before the fall in the price of labour takes place. This would occur with any other domestic resource under the same circumstances.

14.4.2 The market demand curve under monopoly (imperfect competition)

The monopolist is the industry, hence, by purchasing a factor in a perfectly competitive factor market, the monopolist's demand curve for a factor ***is*** the market demand curve.

BOX 14.1 DEVALUATION AND EMPLOYMENT IN A LABOUR SURPLUS ECONOMY – A MICRO LEVEL ANALYSIS

Consider this hypothetical scenario:

Country A is a major international supplier of a product that is highly labour intensive in its production (e.g. a unique spice or condiment). The country may be described as a labour-surplus economy and is seeking to expand employment in this major export industry with its high labour intensity. The product is sold in the international market in a hard currency (US$). Since labour is the principal domestic resource in the production of this export good, the country considers that a devaluation of the local currency would be reflected in a reduced international price of its labour and lead to an expansion in the demand for labour since labour is paid in the (now devalued) local currency. It is anticipated that, after the devaluation, the product will continue to be sold at its existing international hard currency price.

The country has computed the increased demand for labour based on the individual demands for labour by the producers involved in the export trade as it relates to current international prices. Consequent upon the devaluation, the country finds the expansion in the demand for labour is much less than it anticipated. Recourse to Figure 14.8 in the text illustrates why this occurs.

As Country A's producers of the export product expand their production with the cheaper labour, trying to sell the product at the same international price, the country, being a major international supplier, finds that the global market can only accept more of the product if it is offered at a lower price (in US$). The reduction in the price of the product shifts the sum of the individual producers demand for labour curve (VV) inwards to V_1V_1. This occurs because the demand for labour is a derived demand – derived from the marginal productivity of labour and the price of the product (VMP_L). Holding the marginal productivity of labour constant, the (VMP_L) curve will shift outwards or inwards as the price of the product increases or decreases. Consequently, in this case, the expansion of labour employment with the lower wage due to the devaluation is less than was anticipated.

There are no external effects of expanded output on price. The effect of expansion is internal to each monopolist (change in marginal revenue with change in output from increased use of input).

In the case of monopolistic competition or oligopoly however, when all sellers in the group expand output, market price diminishes along the producer's market-share demand (DD) curve similar to that of the perfectly competitive industry. Thus, to obtain the market demand from individual demand curves it is necessary to allow for the decrease in market price and in marginal revenue.

Derivation is the same as under perfect competition in the product market except that the individual factor demand curves are based upon marginal revenue product MRP_L ($MPP_L \cdot MR$) curves rather than on the value of the marginal product VMP_L ($MPP_L \cdot \overline{P}_x$) curves for the labour factor and similar curves for any other resource factor.

14.5 THE SUPPLY CURVE OF LABOUR

Under perfect competition in the factor market, the supply of an input to an individual firm is infinitely elastic. But the market supply is not likely to be perfectly elastic. It is likely to be highly inelastic for certain types of inputs (e.g. land of a particular type). Some inputs such as labour and land are primary inputs while others, such as coal and oil for electricity production, are more in the nature of intermediate inputs. The elasticity of supply of these inputs would vary from one to the other depending on their accessibility or availability relative to the size of the market.

It should be taken into account that, for most resource inputs, the market supply schedule usually slopes upwards. But for some fixed inputs such as land that are limited in supply, it may be vertical (perfectly inelastic). In the case, for example, of a labour surplus economy, the supply of labour curve can be taken as completely horizontal (infinitely elastic) in the relevant range of production for that economy.

As a special case, the supply of labour curve may be considered to be backward bending. This may be understood by considering the supply of labour by an individual.

14.5.1 Supply of labour by an individual

The analysis of the supply of labour by an individual is based of the choice of an individual between hours of leisure (H) and hours of work (L). Labour is a unique resource in that individuals can choose to give their time to an employer or can use if for themselves in leisure.

The price of leisure is the wage rate (per time period) or, in terms or opportunity cost, it may be measured as the amount of money a worker gives up in order to enjoy a time period of leisure.

A change in real income (real wage) may be analyzed in terms of income and substitution effects. The real income would refer to the individual's command over real goods and services due to having the income. Consider the substitution and income effects.

Substitution effect

A rise in the real wage would have a substitution effect. The rise in the real wage makes leisure more expensive (i.e. in income lost). The individual worker is therefore expected to want to work more and take less leisure time with a rise in real income.

Income effect

As real income increases the individual may want to increase the hours of work as the opportunity cost of leisure in terms of income foregone increases. However, beyond a certain (undefined) level of real income, as the individual worker becomes more affluent, the worker may want more leisure (less work). The worker can now afford the cost of leisure (loss in real income from not working). Thus, at some level of real income, the income effect begins to offset the substitution effect. Consequently, an increase in

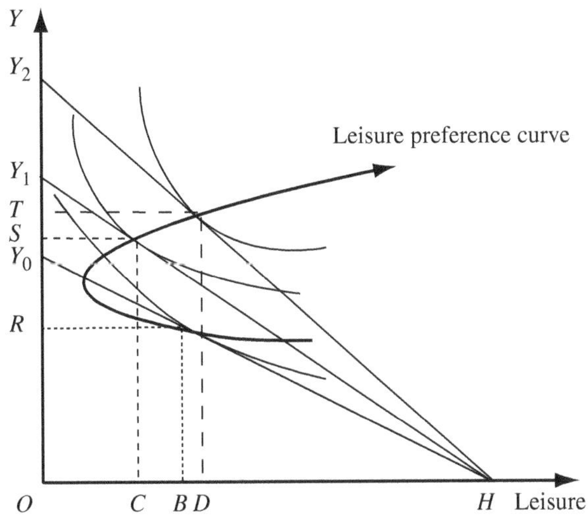

Figure 14.9
The individual's preference for work/leisure

the real wage rate (at certain wage levels) may, instead of increasing the supply of labour, actually reduce the supply of labour forthcoming for employment. This leads to a backward bending supply of labour curve and is illustrated in Figure 14.9.

Using Figure 14.9, H represents hours of leisure and Y represents real income (the real wage). There is a maximum of OH number of hours for leisure in a day. The slope of a line from H to any point on the real income axis (Y) represents the wage/hr. With income available at Y_0, an individual can earn Y_0 by taking zero hours of leisure. Income received falls as a person takes more hours of leisure. The wage rate is OY_0/OH. The higher the hourly rate the steeper the line. Indifference curves represent the individual's preference between income and leisure.

Referring to Figure 14.9, it may be observed that at wage rate:

$$\frac{OY_0}{OH}$$

the worker chooses to have OB hours of leisure (BH hours of work) and earn an income of OR.

Consider, now, an increase in the real wage rate to:

$$\frac{OY_1}{OH}$$

The individual now chooses to take absolutely fewer hours of leisure at OC, thereby working a longer time as in CH hours of work and earning a higher real income, OS. Thus, initially, as the real wage rate increases, hours of leisure decrease (hours of work increase) and the worker receives a higher real income.

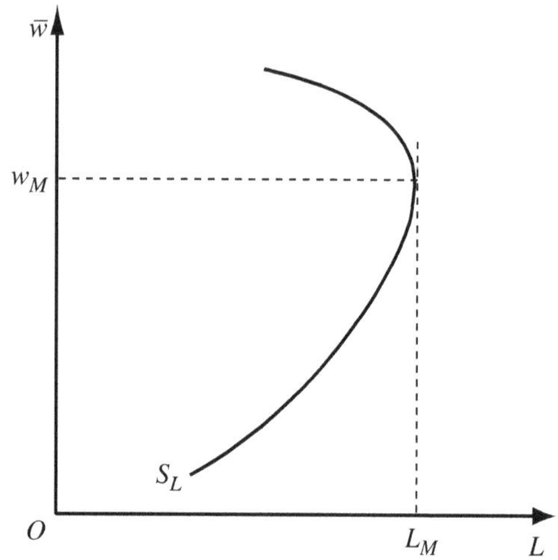

Figure 14.10
The backward bending supply of labour curve

However, at some higher real income, workers begin to choose more hours of leisure at the expense or more real income. At real wage rate:

$$\frac{OY_2}{OH}$$

the worker increases hours of leisure from OC to OD thereby reducing the hours of work from CH to DH. The worker achieves an increase in real income from OS to OT, but could have had a higher real income if the choice had been made to have the same or fewer hours of leisure.

14.5.2 The market supply curve of labour

Translating this leisure curve into real wage space the supply of labour curve may be described as backward bending. This is illustrated in Figure 14.10. Assuming that the supply of labour by one individual does not affect the supply by the other individual, the individual supply of labour curve may be summed for all individuals in the market to give the market supply curve of labour.

Based on Figure 14.10, an increase in the real wage initially draws a larger supply of labour into the work force. This impact slows until a turning point is reached at real wage $\overline{w}_M$ beyond which a higher real wage fails to draw in more labour units than L_M. Instead an increase in the real wage above that level actually leads to a reduction in the supply of labour as workers substitute leisure for hours of work.

The extent to which increases in real wages draw out more labour units may be used to measure the level of development of an economy. In the early stages of development, increases in real wages draw greater supplies of labour. When this process slows or reverses, this is taken as an indication of a country reaching a level of affluence that marks it as a developed society or one that may be described as an affluent society.

This supply analysis is supposed to hold in theory whether the supply of labour is for a perfectly competitive or imperfectly competitive market.

In reality, some countries may show a secular deterioration in real wages over time but it may be difficult to draw the reverse conclusion (i.e. that the country is becoming less affluent). There are multiple factors that could affect the trends in real wages. Teal (1995) found a substantial decline in real wages in Ghana over the previous twenty years and noted there was insufficient investment to raise labour demand faster than supply and there was a fall in productivity. Nevertheless, he found it possible that output was rising.

14.6 FACTOR MARKET EQUILIBRIUM UNDER THE MARGINAL PRODUCTIVITY THEORY

Determination of price and employment of an input

Regular supply and demand analysis is used in the market. Equilibrium is found the same way as in the product market by using demand and supply analysis. The equation of demand and supply determines the equilibrium price for the factor and the equilibrium quantity of the factor employed. This occurs at the intersection of the market demand and supply curves. This supply and demand analysis is similar to that of the product market with the exception that the demand for a factor is a ***derived demand***. As shown before, this demand is derived from the marginal physical product of the factor input and the output price or marginal revenue depending on the market structure.

Under perfect competition in the product market, the equilibrium will take place at the intersection of the VMP_L (D_{LC}) and the supply curve (S_L) as illustrated in Figure 14.11. This gives the equilibrium wage rate of (w_C) and the equilibrium quantity of labour demanded of (L_C). In equilibrium the value of the marginal product of an input will be

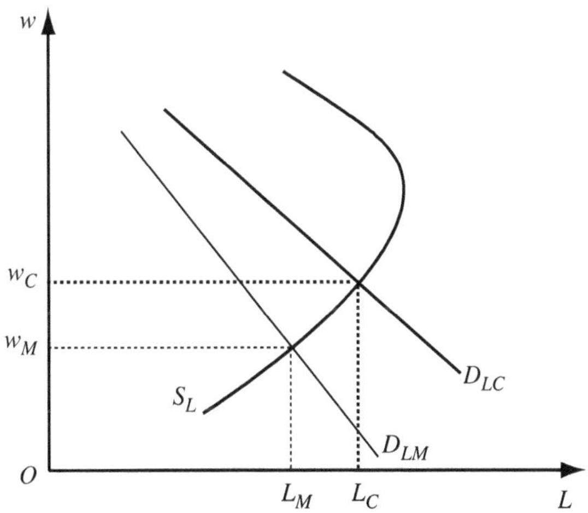

Figure 14.11
Equilibrium wage and labour demand in the market

equal in each and every place where the input is used. For every factor input, the value of its marginal product must equal the price of the input and the price of the input will be the same to all firms where the market displays the features of perfect competition.

This theory suggests that there is an element of fairness or equity in that payment to a factor by the value of its marginal product, required for profit maximization for the perfectly competitive firm, means that the factor gets paid according to its contribution to the firm, leaving no surplus to be appropriated by any factor that has not contributed.

Under imperfect competition or monopoly, the major difference is that the D_{LC} curve (value of marginal product curve) is replaced by the D_{LM} (marginal revenue product) curve. This brings equilibrium at a lower wage w_M and a lower quantity of labour L_M. This occurs because the marginal revenue lies below the price.

The is also considered to be fair (equitable) since the factor has been paid in accordance with the marginal revenue product, which is the incremental revenue generated by that factor.

14.7 MONOPSONY IN THE FACTOR MARKET

In some cases, a monopolist or sole seller in the product market may also be a monopsonist or sole buyer in the factor market. This monopolist producer then has influence in both markets. This gives rise to a new set of conditions determining the equilibrium wage and employment of the factor. These new conditions result in what is emotively called monopolistic and monopsonistic exploitation.

14.7.1 Monopolistic and monopsonistic exploitation

Having the demand for labour curve under monopoly based on the marginal revenue product rather than the value of the marginal product gives rise to what is sometimes called monopolistic exploitation. This is because the factor is paid its *MRP* which is less than the *VMP*.

The definition of monopolistic exploitation is that associated with economist Joan Robinson. The general definition is that where a productive service is employed at a price that is less than the value of its marginal product then it is exploited. This does not indicate, however, that there is some surplus that falls to other factors that have not contributed or that it is inequitable. It however indicates that, under the market structure of monopoly, the marginal revenue is below the price hence the equilibrium demand must take place at a lower factor price than under the market structure of perfect competition. In this case the term 'exploitation' is more of a definition than the emotive term it appears to be.

The justification for the use of the term exploitation is based on the argument that since, under monopoly, $MR < P$, and as a consequence, the marginal revenue product (*MRP*) is less than the value of the marginal product (*VMP*) then, the market price of a productive service is less than the value of its marginal product. Hence, if the market price of a good reflects the good's social value, then the productive service receives less than its contribution to social value. However, any attempt to raise the price of the factor input would see a reduction in the level of employment to the point where the *MRP* is equal to the higher factor input price.

In this context, imperfectly competitive producers do not use as much of a resource as is socially desirable and do not attain the corresponding desirable level of output.

14.7.2 Monopoly with monopsony

Where a monopolist in the product market, as the sole seller of a good, is also a monopsonist or sole buyer of a factor input in the factor market there is a further complication. Here, in equilibrium, the factor is paid less than its Marginal Revenue Product. Again, as a definition, this is given the label of monopsonistic exploitation.

Consider the case of monopoly in the product market with monopsony in the factor (input) market. This is the case where the monopolist is the sole seller of the good ***and*** the sole buyer of the input (labour).

In order to determine the equilibrium demand for a factor (labour) a new tool of analysis is introduced into the study of the factor market. This is the Marginal Expenditure of Input (*MEI*) curve. This is similar to the curve used before under the case of bi-lateral monopoly.

The monopsonist, as the sole buyer of the productive service, who is also a monopolist in the product market, faces a positively sloped supply curve. That is, the monopolist faces the whole market supply. The result is that, as the monopolist varies the quantity demanded of the input, it affects the supply price of the input. In order to get a greater quantity of the factor input, the monopolist must pay a higher price for all units of the factor.

Consequently, the monopolist, as a monopsonist, must consider the ***marginal expense*** of purchasing an additional unit of a variable productive factor. The marginal expense is the change in total cost of inputs to the monopolist producer when an additional unit of the input is employed. Obtaining an additional unit of the factor increases total cost by more than the price of that additional unit because all the other units must be purchased at the new, higher price. This is similar to the marginal revenue concept, only in reverse.

Thus as the producer (monopolist) expands the purchase of an input, the marginal expense of the input (*MEI*) rises. Hence the *MEI* curve is upward sloping but rises faster than the supply curve (*S*) of the input since, for any given quantity of a factor input, the marginal expense is higher than the supply price for that unit of the productive factor. Consequently, the Marginal Expenditure of Input curve is steeper than the supply curve. Proof of this is provided in an ***Appendix*** to this chapter. The two curves are illustrated in Figure 14.12 for the factor labour.

14.7.3 Equilibrium under monopsony

14.7.3.1 THE CASE OF ONE VARIABLE INPUT – SHORT-RUN

The demand curve for labour under consideration is the demand curve of the monopolist who is also the single buyer of labour in the market (monopsonist). As a monopolist, the demand for labour curve by the monopsonist is the Marginal Revenue Product (MRP_L) curve.

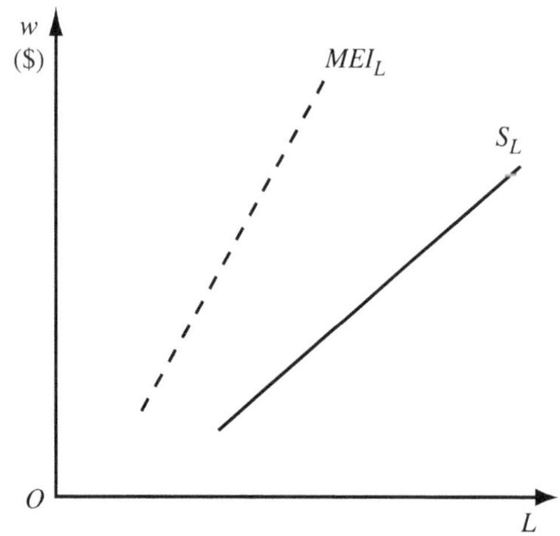

Figure 14.12
The marginal expenditure of input curve for a monopsonist

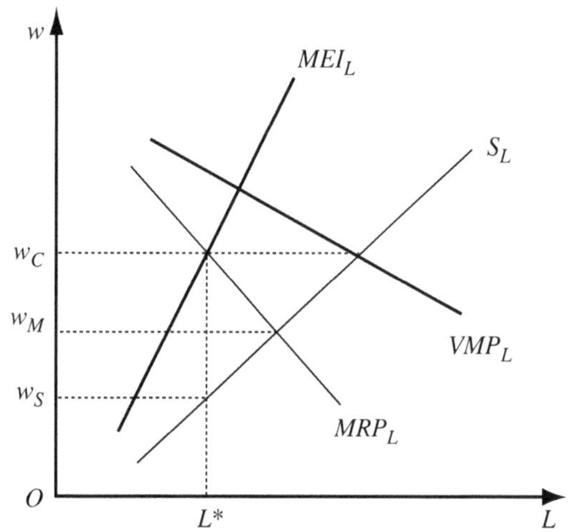

Figure 14.13
Equilibrium of the monopolist as monopsonist

Confronting the monopolist as monoposonist is S_L, the positively sloped supply curve of the factor input (labour). The monopsonist also faces the higher marginal expenditure of input curve (MEI_L). Figure 14.13 shows the equilibrium demand for labour of the monopolist who is a monopsonist.

The profit maximizing monopolist as monopsonist will employ a variable productive factor until the point is reached at which the marginal expenditure of that input (addition to total cost) is equal to its marginal revenue product (addition to total revenue). This is the same principle as before, except that the addition to expenditure is not the supply price of the factor but the higher marginal expense. The intersection of the MRP_L and the MEI_L curves gives the equilibrium quantity of labour for the monopolist as monopsonist to employ. The price of the factor input (w) to be paid by the monopsonist is determined by the corresponding point, not on the MEI_L curve but on the factor supply curve S_L. This gives an equilibrium wage of w_S.

Thus the factor paid at price lower than its MRP_L equilibrium price w_M (which already is lower than its VMP_L equilibrium price of w_S). Monopsonistic exploitation therefore now is added to Monopolistic Exploitation to lower the equilibrium wage rate.

As a result, it is possible to identify the two types of exploitation using Figure 14.13 as follows:

- Monopolistic exploitation is equal to the distance $w_C - w_M$.
- Monosonistic exploitation is equal to the distance $w_M - w_S$.

The distance $w_C - w_M$ is the part due to the monopolistic power of the firm in the product market and $w_M - w_S$ is the part due to the monopsonistic power of the same firm in the factor (input) market.

14.7.3.2 THE CASE WITH SEVERAL VARIABLE INPUTS – LONG-RUN

In the long-run (with several variable inputs), the monopsonist should adjust the input composition until the ratio of marginal product or the marginal rate of technical substitution ($MRTS$) to marginal expense (or price) of input is the same for all variable inputs used. The least cost combination is accordingly obtained when the $MRTS$ is equal to the Marginal Expense of Input ratio.

14.7.4 Monopolistic vs. monopsonistic exploitation

Figure 14.14 provides a further comparison of monopolistic and monopsonistic exploitation along with the perfectly competitive equilibrium. The figure shows, for comparison, the separate cases of a perfectly competitive firm, a monopolist and a monopolist who is a monopsonist. The supply curve of labour in the market is the S_L curve.

For the perfectly competitive firm the demand curve for labour by the firm is the VMP_L curve. Equilibrium is with the supply of labour curve S_L at C and labour is paid the value of its marginal product w_C. The quantity of labour hired by the perfectly competitive firm is L_C.

For the monopolist, the demand curve by the firm is the Marginal Revenue Product of Labour (MRP_L) curve. This is equated with the supply of labour curve (S_L) at M. The monopolist hires L_M units of labour and pays a wage equal to the Marginal Revenue Product of Labour at w_M.

Because the firm is a monopolist rather than a perfectly competitive firm in the product market, the employment of labour is less at L_M compared to L_C ***and*** the wage is lower at w_M compared to w_C. The difference between wage rates corresponding to points C and M, or the distance $Ow_C - Ow_M$, is called ***Monopolistic Exploitation***. Nevertheless labour receives a wage equal to what its employment adds to total receipts of the firm.

Where the monopolist in the product market is a monopsonist in the factor market, the equilbirum is between the MRP_L and the MEI_L rather than the S_L curve. This places

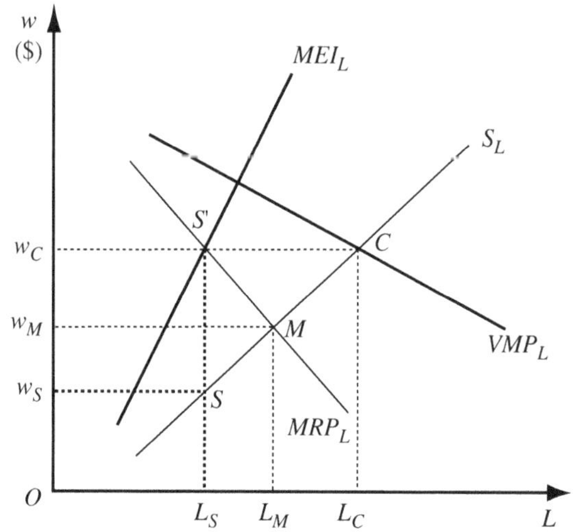

Figure 14.14
Monopolistic and monopsonistic exploitation

the actual equilibrium point at S' but since this is not on the supply of labour curve the wage rate has to be at the corresponding point S on the S_L curve. This gives the wage rate of w_S.

The monopolist who is a monopsonist in the factor market therefore employs the lowest quantity of labour of the three cases, L_S, compared to L_M for the monopolist who is not a monopsonist and compared to L_C for the perfectly competitive firm. Moreover, this firm also pays the lowest of the three wage rates. The distance $Ow_M - Ow_S$ is a measure of ***monopsonistic exploitation***.

However, there are counter measures to monopolistic and monopsonistic exploitation that a union may take within limits. These are dealt with below.

14.8 THE LABOUR UNIONS, EXPLOITATION AND UNEMPLOYMENT

A workers' union can effectively make the supply curve of labour a horizontal line at a particular price until it reaches the existing supply curve. This union has to be of the '***closed shop***' type union. Hence, the monopoly producer must be forced to purchase all units of labour services through the union. The union would also need to have the legislative authority to set and hold the wage and prevent workers who are not members of the union from encroaching on the employment in the industry. It would also need to prevent some members from bidding down the wage in order to get employment ahead of others.

Once the union sets the wage, the monopolist becomes a price taker and can have all the workers available at the same wage rate. The supply of labour therefore becomes a horizontal straight line at the given wage. Over the horizontal stretch, the Marginal Expenditure of Input becomes equal to the supply price. This is because every additional unit of the factor (labour) can be obtained at the same price as the one before. The incremental expenditure on another unit of the input is the same as the price of the input. The factor price (w) is the same as the marginal expenditure in the same way that the marginal revenue becomes the same as the price when the demand curve is horizontal.

14.8.1 Employment and the labour union in a perfectly competitive product market

Figure 14.15 shows the effect of unions in a perfectly competitive product market. The equilibrium wage rate (w^*) occurs at the intersection of the labour demand and supply curves (D_L and S_L). The equilibrium amount of labour employed is L^*. This represents full employment where all those seeking employment at the going wage w^* are employed. The union may now set a higher wage rate such as w_u. The producer can obtain all the labour needed for production at this fixed wage up to where the horizontal wage line reaches the supply of labour (S_L) curve.

At the union set wage rate of w_u only L_u of the labour is now employed. This creates unemployment measured by the horizontal distance between the D_L and S_L curves at w_u. This unemployment is due to two factors:

1. At the higher wage rate, the demand for labour falls off from L^* to L_u. This represents labour that was previously employed at the lower wage that can no longer find employment now that the new higher wage is in effect.
2. At the higher wage rate, the supply of labour increases from L^* to L_n. This represents new entrants into the labour market attracted by the higher wage rate who are seeking employment opportunities that do not exist at that wage.

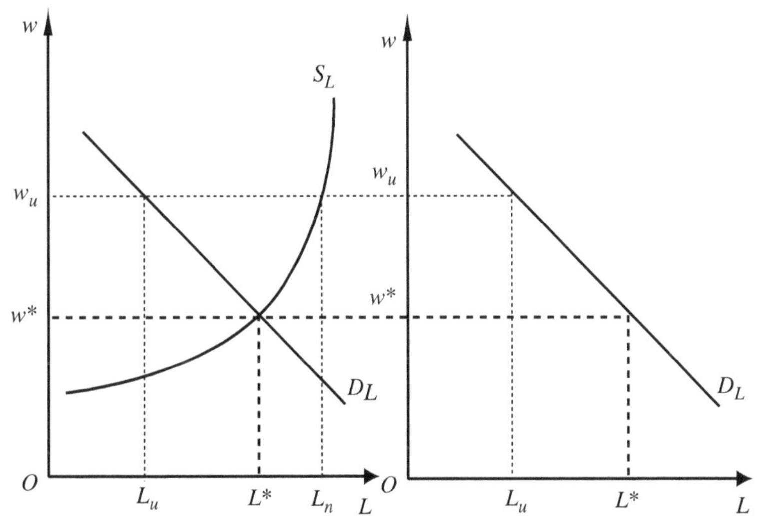

Figure 14.15
Effect on unemployment of higher-than-equilibrium wage imposed by a labour union under perfect competition

Hence, the higher wage creates unemployment between L_u to L_n, although, the actual jobs lost are only between L^* and L_u. The wage increase, *ceteris paribus*, has the double effect of reducing previously employed labour to the status of unemployed and leaving new employment seekers who have come forward now that the wage is higher, frustrated at not finding employment. The effect is similar to that of a rise in the minimum wage through legislation in industries to which the minimum wage applies. There is some controversy on the actual impact of higher minimum wages on employment in reality as some economists have found effects contrary to the theory. Card and Kreuger (1994) found an increase in the number of fast food workers employed after an increase in minimum wages. However, Neumark and Wascher (1995) found that the increase in the number of persons employed after the increase in the minimum wage was accompanied by a reduction in hours worked. The controversy rages on and may be due in part to the difficulty of holding everything else constant (*ceteris paribus*) in the analysis.

Typically, the labour force is considered to comprise only those persons 'actively seeking employment' rather than all 'able bodied' adult persons in the community. It is these 'able bodied' persons who now come forward and actively seek employment with the new higher wage that add to the unemployment figures. A definition of the labour force as 'all persons capable of working, whether they wish to or not', would give a perfectly inelastic supply curve of labour (vertical line).

An interesting footnote to this analysis is the case in which the union raises the wage where the supply of labour curve is in the backward bending region. The higher wage could cause a fall in the supply of labour (reduction in the labour force) to mitigate the effects of the reduced demand for labour.

14.8.2 Employment and the labour union under monopoly and monopsony

Figure 14.16 illustrates the effect of a union in the case of with monopoly in the product market coupled with monopsony (or oligopsony) in the factor market. Without unionization, equilibrium is at *c* (where $MRP_L = MEI_L$), the corresponding wage is at w^* (on S_L) , and employment is at L^*.

Removal of monopsonistic exploitation by the labour union

Consider that the union seeks a higher wage and establishes a new fixed wage at w_M. The supply curve for labour now becomes horizontal at w_M up to the S_L curve (at point *a*). The horizontal supply curve also becomes the Marginal Expenditure of Input curve up to the point *a* before rejoining MEI_L curve at the point *b*, giving an MEI_L curve described by the points $w_M ab$. Consequently, at the point *a*, $MRP_L = MEI_L$.

As a result of the labour union's intervention, OL_M of labour is now employed at wage Ow_M instead of OL^* at w^*. The union intervention has brought ***both a wage increase and an increase in employment***. Moreover, each unit of labour now receives its marginal revenue product and, hence, the exploitation uniquely attributable to ***monopsony*** has been eliminated.

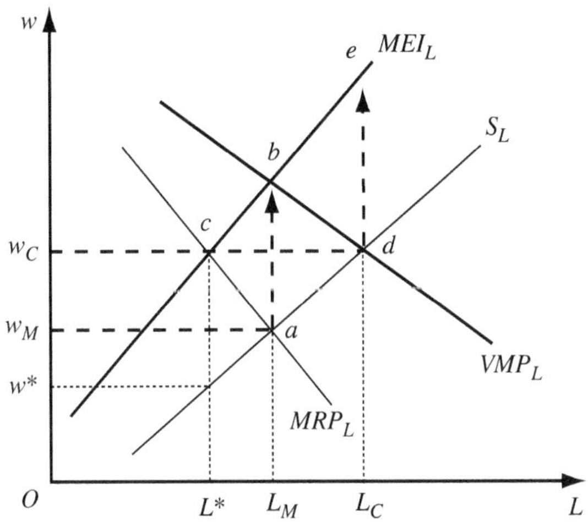

Figure 14.16
The labour unions: Eliminating monopolistic and monopsonistic exploitation

Further to this, the union may choose a wage equal to w_C. In this case, and by the same token, the Marginal Expenditure of Input labour (MEI_L) curve now becomes $w_C de$, where e is the point reached on the MEI_L curve directly above the point d. Equilibrium is where MEI_L is equal to MRP_L. This occurs at point c. Hence OL^* of labour is now employed at wage w_C. This is the same employment level as when the wage rate was at w^* but at a higher wage. The union has now succeeded in eliminating both ***monopsonistic and monopolistic exploitation***.

It must be noted however, that in the elimination of monopolistic exploitation, the level of employment of labour fell from L_M to L^*. It must be noted further, that, although this is the same level of employment as initially when there was monopsonistic and monopolistic exploitation, there is now considerable unemployment of labour. This unemployment may be measured as the distance between L_C and L^*. The unemployment is due to the higher wage drawing out a larger supply of labour and since the monopolist employs only up the MRP_L curve (at L^*), the supply of labour now exceeds the demand for labour.

As a result, the elimination of monopolistic exploitation can be frustrating to the new entrants into the workforce and reflect negatively in the unemployment figures for a country, even though the same amount of persons are employed as existed prior to the union's intervention.

If the labour union sets a higher wage level than w_C then employment falls below L^* ($MEI_L = MEI_L$) which would mean a further loss of jobs for those who were employed initially.

In summary then, the 'closed shop' labour union can eliminate monopsonistic exploitation thereby raising the wage rate and increasing employment. However, if the union attempts to eliminate monopolistic exploitation, it can achieve a higher wage by losing the employment gains from the elimination of monopsonistic exploitation plus create further unemployment as supply expands at the new higher wage. Any further increase in wages leads to greater unemployment and the loss of jobs by some of those employed initially before the union's intervention.

14.9 PRODUCT EXHAUSTION THEOREMS AND DISTRIBUTION

Product exhaustion theorems raise the issue of deservingness of the respective factor inputs in relation to the rewards from the production and sale of commodities. At issue is how or whether the payments to factor inputs into the production process account for (exhaust) the full value of the product. The concerns relate to whether there is a surplus in value created by the factor inputs that do not go to these inputs and whether the factors are rewarded according to their contribution to the value of output. The concern is with equity or fairness in the distribution to inputs of the value of the output created by them rather than with equality per se.

The principal product exhaustion theorem is the Eüler's theorem and this is examined in some detail below. A more general theorem is the Clark–Wicksteed product exhaustion theorem.

14.9.1 Eüler's product exhaustion theorem

Eüler's product exhaustion theorem says that if a production function is characterized by constant returns to scale and each factor is paid the value of its marginal product (i.e. under perfect competition in the product market), the total value of the product is exhausted in the payments to the factors (i.e. there is no residual or surplus).

Product exhaustion requires that the factor payments equal the total value of the product. This may be expressed as:

$$P_x Q_x = wL + rK$$

or:

$$[\text{Value of total product}] = [\text{cost of labour}] + [\text{cost of capital}]$$

Since $VMP_L = w$ and $VMP_L = k$, the product exhaustion equation may be re-written as:

$$P_x Q_x = VMP_L \cdot L + VMP_K \cdot K$$

Alternatively, it may be expressed as:

$$P_x Q_x = P_x(MPP_L)L + P_x(MPP_K)K$$

The above expressions are in value terms. In order for them to hold, the physical or real relationship must hold as follows:

$$Q_x = (MPP_L)L + (MPP_K)K$$

And this holds so long as the production function exhibits ***constant Returns to scale***. This requires a Cobb–Douglas production function that is homogeneous of degree one (refer to Chapter 6).

The Eüler's theorem may be demonstrated as follows:

- Take a production function such that:

$$Q = f(K, L)$$

- A production function is homogenous of degree one (i.e. exhibits constant returns to scale) if:

$$Q(\lambda K, \lambda L) = \lambda^{V} f(K, L) \text{ where } v = 1$$

where λ is the factor by which L, K are increased.
- Differentiating with respect to λ gives:

$$K\frac{dQ}{dK} + L\frac{dQ}{dL} = v\lambda^{v-1} f(K, L)$$

- Since $v = 1$, and:

$$\frac{dQ}{dK} = MPP_L \qquad \text{and} \qquad \frac{dQ}{dL} = MPP_L$$

- It follows that:

$$K \cdot MPP_K + L \cdot MPP_L = 1\lambda^0 f(K, L)$$

- Further, since $\lambda^0 = 1$, then:

$$K \cdot MPP_K + L \cdot MPP_L = Q$$

This equation establishes the result.

The outcome is that, under a Cobb–Douglas production function, the total real physical product is equal to the total real physical contribution of the factors. Consequently, payment of factors according to the value of the marginal product would exhaust the value of the physical product. That is:

$$P(MPP_K)K + P(MPP_L)L = PQ$$

or:

$$(VMP_K)K + (VMP_L)L = PQ$$

Since it is the perfectly competitive product market that pays factors according to the value of their marginal product, then this theorem says essentially, that for equity in the distribution of the value of the product, the product market must be characterized by perfect competition and the production function must be of the Cobb–Douglas, constant returns to scale type.

Once both these conditions do not hold, nothing can be concluded about the fairness of the distribution of the value of the product among the factors that contribute to the creation of the product. The existence of these conditions may be desirable but are highly unlikely to be found except in special cases.

14.9.2 Clark-Wicksteed product exhaustion theorem

The Clark–Wicksteed theorem makes a simpler case for product exhaustion. It is not as restricted as the Eüler's theorem as it does not require a Cobb–Douglas production function. Instead, it simply requires that firms be at their long-run perfectly competitive equilibrium position. Consequently, firms should be operating at the minimum point of their long-run average cost curve.

The minimum point of the long-run average cost curve is the point where the production function exhibits constant returns to scale. In this regard, then, it may be said that, whereas the Eüler's theorem requires a full Cobb–Douglas constant-returns-to-scale production function, the Clark–Wicksteed approach requires only that producers be at the Cobb–Douglas (constant-returns-to-scale) point on their long-run average-cost curve.

This position is achieved in the long-run equilibrium of the firm in a perfectly competitive industry where all firms in the industry produce at the minimum point of the long-run average cost (*LAC*) curve.

The implications are in order to ensure distributional equity, production must take place under perfect competition with a Cobb–Douglas constant-returns-to-scale production function or with production taking place at the minimum point of the long-run average cost curve. This, however desirable, is purely a static concept and does not involve any consideration of growth and development.

REVIEW QUESTIONS FOR CHAPTER 14

1 Explain with regard to the Marginal Productivity theory of distribution why the demand for factors of production is described as a 'derived' demand.

2 ABC Inc. is a firm in a perfectly competitive product market buying labour in a perfectly competitive factor market. With reference to the Marginal Productivity theory of distribution, explain:

   (a) How ABC Inc. may derive the demand function for labour in the short-run and determine its equilibrium amount of labour in production.
   (b) How this demand curve and equilibrium demand for labour would change if ABC Inc. were a monopolist in the product market.

3 With reference to ABC Inc. above explain and illustrate:

   (a) How and why the demand-for-labour curve might be expected to change from the short-run to the long-run.
   (b) Why the market demand curve for a factor is less elastic than the demand curve at the firm level.

4 With regard to the supply of labour:

   (a) Explain how leisure preference analysis is used to establish the relationship between real income and supply of labour.

(b) Discuss the significance of the backward bending supply curve of labour for economic analysis.

5 Consider the hypothetical case of *CompactZoom*, an automobile manufacturing firm that is a monopolist in a small country. The firm is also the sole buyer of the services of automobile mechanics in the market (monopsonist).

(a) Show how, as a monopolist, *CompactZoom* can be said to be responsible for monopolistic exploitation.
(b) Explain the origin of the marginal expenditure of input curve and how it relates to the supply of labour curve.
(c) Distinguish between monopolistic and monopsonistic exploitation in *CompactZoom*'s equilibrium position.

6 Explain how a 'closed shop' labour union may be able to eliminate monopsonistic and monopolistic exploitation and the significance for unemployment.
7 Examine the significance of the Eüler and Clark–Wicksteed theorems for the concern with distributional equity in the factor market.

RECOMMENDED READING FOR CHAPTER 14

Blundell, R. and MaCurdy, T. (2008) 'Labour Supply', *The New Palgrave: A Dictionary of Economics* (2nd Edn.).

Card, D. and Kreuger, A. (1994) 'Minimum Wages and Employment: A Case Study of the Fast-Food Industry in New Jersey and Pennsylvania', *American Economic Review*, 84 (4): 772–93.

Karier, T. (1985) 'Unions and Monopoly Profits', *Review of Economics and Statistics*, 67: 34–42.

Neumark, D. and Wascher, W. (1995) 'Minimum-Wage Effects on School and Work Transitions of Teenagers', *American Economic Review*, 85(2): 244–9.

Teal, F. (1995) 'Real Wages and the Demand for Labour in Ghana's Manufacturing Sector', University of Oxford: *Centre for the Study of African Economies*, WPS/95-7. Available online: http://www.csae.ox.ac.uk/workingpapers/pdfs/9507text.pdf

APPENDIX – THE MARGINAL EXPENDITURE OF INPUT CURVE

Proof that the marginal expenditure of input curve is steeper than the input supply curve

Consider that the supply curve of labour has the slope:

$$\frac{\mathrm{d}w}{\mathrm{d}L}$$

Total expenditure on a factor (TE) is:

$$TE = wL$$

The Marginal Expenditure of Input curve (*MEI*) is:

$$ME = \frac{\mathrm{d}(TE)}{\mathrm{d}L} = w\frac{\mathrm{d}L}{\mathrm{d}L} + L\frac{\mathrm{d}w}{\mathrm{d}L}$$

$$ME = w + L\frac{\mathrm{d}w}{\mathrm{d}L}$$

Thus $MEI > w$ for any value of L (since $w > 0$, $L > 0$ and $\mathrm{d}w/\mathrm{d}L > 0$).

To expand, find the slope of the marginal expenditure curve as follows:

$$w = f(L)$$

then, the slope of the *MEI* curve is found by:

$$\frac{\mathrm{d}(MEI)}{\mathrm{d}L} = \frac{\mathrm{d}w}{\mathrm{d}L} + \left[L\frac{\mathrm{d}^2w}{\mathrm{d}L^2} + \frac{\mathrm{d}w}{\mathrm{d}L}\cdot\frac{\partial L}{\partial L}\right]$$

$$= \frac{\mathrm{d}w}{\mathrm{d}L} + \frac{\mathrm{d}w}{\mathrm{d}L} + L\frac{\mathrm{d}^2w}{\mathrm{d}L^2}$$

Hence, the slope of the MEI_L curve is:

$$= 2\frac{\mathrm{d}w}{\mathrm{d}L} + L\frac{\mathrm{d}^2w}{\mathrm{d}L^2}$$

Consequently, the slope of the Marginal Expenditure of Input (MEI_L) curve is steeper compared to the slope of the supply curve:

$$\frac{\mathrm{d}w}{\mathrm{d}L}$$

Under monopsonistic conditions, an additional unit of labour adds its marginal product to output but it does not add wages to cost, instead it adds its (higher) marginal expense *MEI* (or MEI_L, MEI_K). Thus it is possible to substitute MEI_L and MEI_k for w and r.

As a result, the equilibrium condition for several variable factors becomes:

$$\frac{MP_K}{MEI_K} = \frac{MP_L}{MEI_L}$$

This may be re-written as:

$$\frac{MP_K}{MP_L} = \frac{MEI_K}{MEI_L}$$

15 General Equilibrium and Welfare Maximization

Nature and Existence; Pareto Optimality; The Edgeworth Box; Equilibrium of exchange, production, product mix; Perfect competition and general equilibrium; The social welfare function; Compensation criteria; Arrow possibility theorem; Theory of the second best.

The existence of a general equilibrium in an economy is, in theory, a necessary condition for the achievement of a welfare maximum. It is a static concept. A general equilibrium is intended to represent the greatest efficiency in the use of given (scarce) economic resources and the achievement of an overall harmony in the economy between production and consumption. It is, therefore, concerned only with the product (commodity) market and the factor market. The money market is not included. The exclusion of the money market means that prices can be determined only up to a ratio and not absolutely.

Once the most efficient combinations have been identified, the social welfare function is added to provide the sufficient condition for a welfare maximum. Welfare theory is concerned with distributional equity.

15.1 THE NATURE AND TOOLS OF GENERAL EQUILIBRIUM

General equilibrium takes the analysis beyond that of partial equilibrium analysis which relates only to a single isolated market. In an isolated market supply and demand curves are drawn on the assumption that all other prices are given. General equilibrium analysis considers repercussions in other markets and the feedbacks to the original market under consideration.

15.1.1 Existence of general equilibrium

Considering only the commodity and factor markets, general equilibrium analysis seeks to establish whether it is possible for equilibrium to occur simultaneously in all markets and, if so, what conditions would be required for this to happen. This would mean producers are maximizing profits and consumers are maximizing utility in consonance with each other.

Perfect competition

In the absence of the money market to give absolute prices, the major question becomes whether a set of price ratios can exist at which all commodity and factor markets can simultaneously be in equilibrium.

Since all producers and consumers must face the same price ratios, these price ratios must be taken as given by all parties. This requires the existence of perfect competition everywhere. Another question therefore is whether it is possible to have perfect competition established everywhere.

It can be shown that it is possible to have a set of prices under which a general equilibrium can be achieved in an economy. Moreover, it can be established that this general equilibrium can be achieved under a perfectly competitive economy. Much of the findings in the area of general equilibrium and welfare economics can be attributed to economist Arrow (1950, 1951, 1969). This is explained in greater detail as the topic is developed. Additional sources on the topic include Moore (2007) and Scarf (2008).

The optimal allocation of resources

With regard to resource allocation, the general equilibrium obtains when the following conditions hold:

- Every consumer chooses his/her preferred market basket subject to his/her given income (budget line).
- Every factor of production supplies its chosen quantity of inputs given the prevailing input and product prices.
- Every commodity producer maximizes profits subject to the constraints imposed by the available technology (production function), prices and supply of factor inputs.
- The quantity demanded is equal to the quantity supplied at the prevailing prices in all commodity and factor markets.

It therefore represents an ideal state in the production and consumption of goods and services where there is the 'best' or most efficient use of given resources.

15.1.2 Concepts and tools of general equilibrium

For simplicity, the model used to illustrate the achievement of a general equilibrium may be described as the '2 × 2 × 2' model. This is a two-consumer (A, B), two-factor (K, L), two-commodity (x, y) model. The simplicity of this model is that it allows two-dimensional diagrams to be used for illustration.

15.1.2.1 THE PARETO-OPTIMALITY CRITERION

At the centre of general equilibrium analysis is the concept of Pareto optimality or Pareto efficiency. This is a criterion that refers to economic efficiency which can be objectively measured. It is called the Pareto criterion after the famous Italian economist Vilfredo Pareto (1848–1923).

According to this criterion, any change that increases any one value without reducing any other value is a Pareto improvement. From a production viewpoint, if a change increases the output of one commodity without reducing the output of any others, then this change has brought a Pareto improvement and represents an increase in efficiency. With regard to consumption, a change that gives more to one consumer without reducing what the other consumer gets is a Pareto improvement. The converse is also true.

Following from this, a situation in which it is impossible to increase the output of one commodity without reducing the output of another, is said to be Pareto optimal or Pareto efficient. The same is true for the case in which it is impossible to give one consumer more without giving another less. Pareto optimality or Pareto efficiency could therefore be described as being on the frontier of production or consumption as there is no further increase in efficiency possible. Now, any gain in one area must be met by a loss in another.

15.1.2.2 THE EDGEWORTH BOX DIAGRAM AND THE CONTRACT CURVE

The Edgeworth box diagram is a technique used, in this case, to identify the locus of Pareto efficiency points where factor inputs or commodities to be allocated are in fixed supply. In the $2 \times 2 \times 2$ model, the Edgeworth box of production is formed by taking the isoquant map for the two goods under consideration, rotating one isoquant map through 180° and placing it on the other to form a box. For consumption, the indifference curves replace the isoquants. The dimensions of the box represent the absolute and relative quantities of the factors, in the case of the production box and commodities, in the case of the consumption box.

15.1.2.3 THE CONTRACT CURVE

In the Edgeworth box, with isoquants (production) or the indifference curves (consumption) coming from opposite ends, the points of tangency of these curves can be identified. The locus of points of tangency of isoquants or of indifference curves in such a box is called the contract curve. It is this contract curve that represents Pareto efficiency of optimality. Conversely, points off the curve are Pareto inefficient. Therefore, a movement from off the curve to the curve brings a Pareto improvement.

The production or utility possibility frontier

The locus of points that make up the contract curve in an Edgeworth Box of production can be translated into production space to form the Production Possibility Frontier (*PPF*) or the Product Transformation Curve. Points of the contract curve (or efficiency locus) lie on the frontier while points off the contract curve lie inside the frontier. A Pareto improvement takes place by moving from inside the frontier to the frontier. Pareto optimality or Pareto efficiency exists all along the frontier.

For consumption, a Utility Possibility Frontier may similarly be derived from the Edgeworth box of exchange.

The production frontier is typically considered to be concave (to the origin) representing increasing opportunity costs in transferring resources from the production of one commodity into the production of the other. This derives from the differences in the factor intensities of the two goods, the greater the differences, the greater the concavity. The concavity of the utility (consumption) frontier is less pronounced and the curve may be wavy as individual preferences are not expected to be mechanical.

The three marginal conditions for a general equilibrium

The three marginal conditions which must be satisfied for a general equilibrium to exist are based on the following Pareto based efficiencies:

1 Efficiency of distribution of commodities among consumers (efficiency in exchange or consumption).
2 Efficiency of the allocation of factors among commodities (efficiency in production).
3 Joint efficiency in the allocation of factors among commodities and of commodities among consumers (efficiency in the product – mix in the composition of output and composition of consumption).

15.2 GENERAL EQUILIBRIUM OF EXCHANGE OR CONSUMPTION – EFFICIENCY IN DISTRIBUTION OF THE PRODUCT

Using the $2 \times 2 \times 2$ model consider the achievement of Pareto optimality in the distribution of the product among consumers. This is called the efficiency of exchange or of consumption. This is done to identify the first marginal condition for a general equilibrium.

In this simple economy, there are only two consumers A and B and two commodities x and y. It is assumed that there is no production. There is only the problem of allocation. This is illustrated in Figure 15.1.

The indifference curve map for consumer B is rotated 180° and placed on top of that for consumer A to form the Edgeworth box of consumption (exchange). This is done in order to identify the Pareto efficiency locus (contract curve) for the distribution of the goods x and y among consumers A and B.

In Figure 15.1 the total quantities of commodities in the Edgeworth box are:

- Total quantity of good x available is O_Ax as measured on the X-axis.
- Total quantity of good y available is O_Ay as measured on the Y-axis.

Initially there are some amounts of goods x and y bought by each consumer and then they begin to trade. Initially consumer A has Ox_1 of good x and Oy_1 of good y. Consumer B has the remainder.

The contract curve joins the points O_A and O_B. Along this curve consumer A's indifference curves are tangent to consumer B's.

Initially, at the point Z, consumer A is on indifference level A_2 and consumer B is on indifference level B_2. At this point the marginal rate of substitution in consumption for the two consumers (MRS_{xy}) is different (A's is higher than B's). This is shown by the difference in the slopes of the tangents to their respective indifference curves which cross at the point Z. All consumers are not in equilibrium and, as a result, consumption

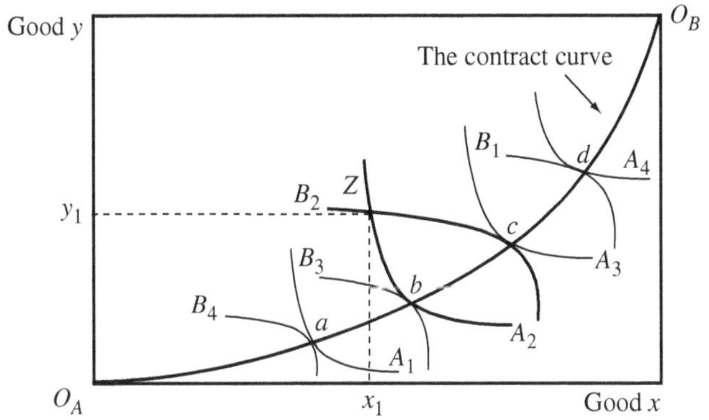

Figure 15.1
The equilibrium of exchange with two goods (*x* and *y*) and two consumers (*A* and *B*)

in this two person economy is off the efficiency locus. Full consumption potential is not reached for consumers. There can be a Pareto improvement in consumption.

15.2.1 Pareto improvement

Trading or exchange now takes place. If they move from the point Z to the point b on the contract curve, then, while consumer A remains on indifference level A_2, consumer B moves to the higher indifference level B_3. If the movement from Z is to point c on the contract curve, then, while consumer B remains on indifference level B_2, consumer A moves higher to indifference level A_3. Hence, in each of these cases one consumer has been able to improve while the other has remained constant.

Thus, by moving on to the contract curve there has been a ***Pareto improvement.***

15.2.2 Pareto optimality in consumption (exchange)

It is important to note that in moving from the point Z to any point between points b and c on the contract curve, both consumer A and consumer B are on higher indifference curves. However, in moving along the contract curve, say, from point b to point c (also a to b or c to d, etc.), it is only possible for one consumer's consumption level to be increased if the other's level is reduced. At point b, the consumption levels, consumers A and B respectively, are A_2 and B_3. Moving from point b to point c, the respective consumption levels become A_3 and B_2 thereby giving an increase to consumer A and a reduction to consumer B. Hence, once the contract curve has been reached, no increase in efficiency can be achieved as one consumer can be made better off only by making the other worse off.

Therefore, it can be seen that the positions along the contract curve represent ***Pareto optimality***.

Where the indifference curves are tangent to each other the MRS_{xy} is equal for consumers A and B. However, where the curves intersect, meaning that the MRS_{xy} is not equal for both consumers, one consumer can always be better off without making the other worse off by moving to a position of equality of MRS_{xy} for both consumers.

As a whole, therefore, the community has attained exchange equilibrium (efficiency in consumption) if and only if, there is no reorganization that will benefit some of the members without harming at least one. Any re-organization which leads to a point where, from there, any change that will make someone better off will also make someone else worse off, then this organization is Pareto-optimal. Consequently, the contract curve of exchange is ***a locus of Pareto-optimality***.

This gives the first of the three necessary conditions of general equilibrium:

$$MRS_{x,y}^{A} = MRS_{x,y}^{B} = \frac{P_x}{P_y}$$

Perfect competition

Perfect competition is required for this to occur. Under Perfect competition both consumers are price takers and are faced with the same price ratios.

15.3 GENERAL EQUILIBRIUM OF PRODUCTION – EFFICIENCY IN THE ALLOCATION OF FACTORS

Continuing with the 2 × 2 × 2 model consider the achievement of Pareto optimality in the allocation of factors among goods. This is called the efficiency of production. It allows the identification of the second marginal condition for a general equilibrium.

It is assumed that the only problem is that of the allocation of factor inputs into the production process. Consider the following:

- Only two goods are being produced, goods x and y.
- Only two factor inputs are used, capital (K) and labour (L).
- These factor inputs are in fixed amounts.

15.3.1 The Edgeworth box of production

Figure 15.2 illustrates the Edgeworth box of production. The isoquant map for product y is rotated 180° and placed on the isoquant map for product x to form the box. The dimensions of the box are the fixed amounts of the two factor inputs, capital (K) and labour (L).

Pareto optimality in production

The isoquants for good x and good y are tangent along the contract curve. This is the Pareto efficiency locus. Using Figure 15.2, consider the initial production point is at Z. At this point the marginal rate of technical substitution ($MRTS_{LK}$) for good x is higher than for good y as shown by the slopes of the tangents to the isoquants that cross at Z. This signifies that inputs are not being allocated efficiently.

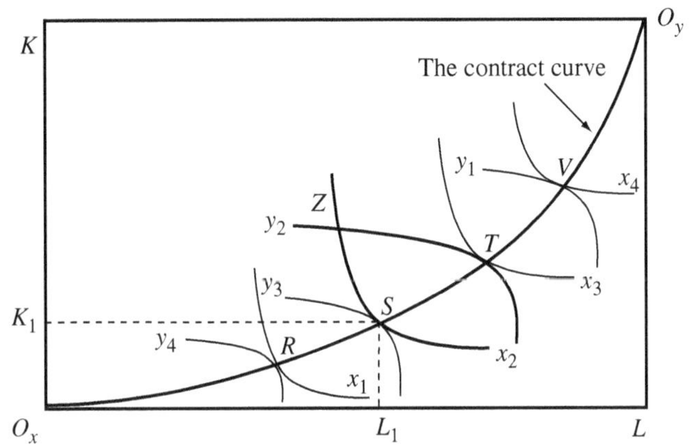

Figure 15.2
The equilibrium of production with two factors (*K* and *L*) and two goods (*x* and *y*)

Within the Edgeworth box all the factor inputs are being used and it can be shown that, by moving on to the contract curve, the output of one good can be increased without reducing the output of the other while using the same total amount of inputs. There is simply a re-allocation of inputs to the production of goods x and y.

In Figure 15.2 the movement from Z to S increases the production of good y from y_2 to y_3 while the production of good x remains at x_2. If the movement is from Z to T then the production of good x increases from x_2 to x_3 while the production of good y remains at y_2. Hence, the reallocation in input resources, consequent upon the move from off the contract curve to a point on the contract curve, has led to a Pareto improvement.

Along the contract curve efficiency in the allocation of resources is optimal, hence moving, for example, from point R to point S can only increase the production of good x (e.g. from x_1 to x_2) by reducing the production of good y (from y_4 to y_3) and similarly, along the rest of the contract curve. When the maximum efficiency is attained, an increase in the production of one commodity can only be accomplished by a reduction in the production of the other.

Since the optimal allocation of factor input resources takes along the contract curve it means that it takes place where the isoquant slopes are equal for the two goods x and y. Hence, this is where the marginal rate of technical substitution in the production of good x ($MRTS^x_{L,K}$) is equal to the marginal rate of technical substitution in the production of good y ($MRTS^y_{L,K}$) written as:

$$MRTS^x_{L,K} = MRTS^y_{L,K}$$

15.3.2 Perfect competition

This Pareto efficiency condition can be assured only where the producer of each good faces the same factor price ratio w/r. This would be so under perfect competition. Consequently, each would then equate the slope of the isoquant with the same price ratio to give:

$$MRTS^x_{L,K} = MRTS^y_{L,K} = \frac{w}{r}$$

This is the second marginal condition for a general equilibrium.

15.4 EFFICIENCY OF THE PRODUCT MIX – JOINT EFFICIENCY IN PRODUCTION AND CONSUMPTION

Continuing with the $2 \times 2 \times 2$ model, the next step is to find the condition for the simultaneous optimal efficiency condition for both production and consumption. This provides the third marginal condition for a general equilibrium.

Given:

- Two consumers (A, B) seeking to maximize utility with their utility functions and using the same price ratio:

$$MRS^A_{x,y} = MRS^B_{x,y} = \frac{P_x}{P_y}$$

- Two producers of goods (x, y) seeking to maximize profits using the same factor-price ratio:

$$MRTS^x_{L,K} = MRTS^y_{L,K} = \frac{w}{r}$$

- A given factor input resource base in the economy.

The question becomes that of how these inputs should be allocated between industries and how the output of goods should be allocated between consumers to achieve an overall harmony in efficiency between production and consumption.

To do this, the technique of the product transformation curve is applied.

15.4.1 The product transformation curve

From the contract curve in the Edgeworth box the Production Possibility Frontier (PPF) or Product Transformation Curve is derived. The Product Transformation Curve is illustrated in Figure 15.3. This *PPF* represents the information taken from the Edgeworth box of production and mapped into product space. The products x and y are on the x and y axes respectively.

15.4.1.1 CONSTRUCTION OF THE PRODUCT TRANSFORMATION CURVE

- Each point on the contract curve corresponds to a particular of output of good x and good y.

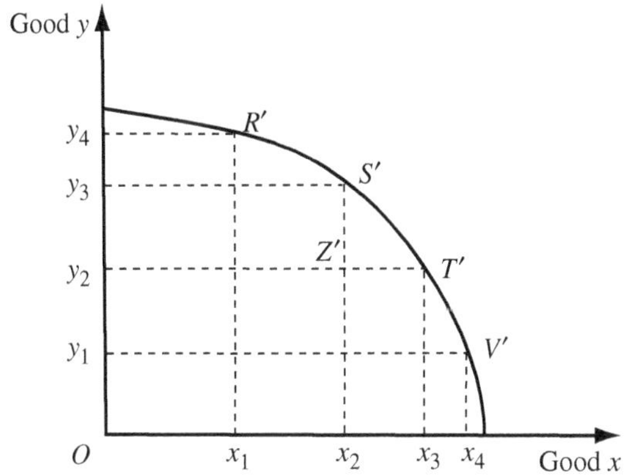

Figure 15.3
The product transformation curve for two goods (x and y)

- This information is placed on a diagram with quantities of x and y on the axes as shown in the diagram at right.
- The locus of points showing combinations of goods x and y from the contract curve make the Production Possibility Frontier (PPF) on the transformation curve.

Pareto efficiency in production must occur along the transformation curve since it is derived from the contract curve. Consider the point R on the contract curve of production which is in factor space. This point represents y_4 of good y and x_1 of good x. On the product transformation curve, in product space, the point R becomes the point R' where the respective quantities y_4 of good y and x_1 of good x can be read off the axis. Similarly, points S, T and V, on the contract curve, are translated into the corresponding points S', T' *and* V' on the product transformation curve.

By the same token, the point Z, which is off the contract curve, is now represented in product space by its quantities y_2 of good y and x_2 of good x and is shown to be situated at point Z' inside of the production possibility frontier. This shows that production off the contract curve is sub-optimal. It holds the economy inside, rather than on, its production frontier. At point Z, therefore, the economy cannot realize its full production possibilities.

15.4.1.2 THE SHAPE OF THE PRODUCT TRANSFORMATION CURVE

The slope of the product transformation curve represents the rate at which one product has to be given up to get an additional unit of the other good. This is called the Marginal Rate of Product Transformation ($MRPT$).

The concave (to the origin) shape of the product transformation curve derives from the shape of the contract curve as it is bowed out from the diagonal in the Edgeworth box. The more the contract curve is bowed out from the diagonal, the greater is the concavity of the product transformation curve. This shape reflects the ***increasing marginal rate of product transformation***.

Representing the locus of Pareto efficiency points, an increase in one good must come as a result of a decrease in the other good. However, the shape says that in order to keep increasing good y by the same incremental amount, an increasingly greater amount of good x must be given up and *vice versa*. This reflects the ***increasing opportunity cost*** of one good in terms of the other.

This increasing opportunity cost is due to the differences in relative factor intensities of the two goods. Typically, good x is considered to be the relatively labour-intensive good and good y the relatively capital-intensive good. This is shown in the way the contract curve bows off the diagonal of the Edgeworth box of production. As the curve moves from the origin for good x (O_x), it bends towards the x-axis reflecting the high labour-intensity of good x. From the other end (O_y), the contract curve first bends towards the y-axis because of the high capital intensity of good y. The greater the difference in factor intensity, the more bowed is the contract curve from the diagonal and consequently, the greater is the concavity of the product transformation curve.

Because of the difference in factor intensities, it becomes increasingly difficult to transform production from one good to the other. Consider good x is using two units of labour to one unit of capital when good y is using two units of capital to one unit of labour. When an attempt is made to give up units of good x in order to get an additional unit of good y, the extra unit of good y requires two units of capital and one unit of labour. However, releasing a unit of good x gives only one unit of capital but two units of labour. Hence, in order to get the two units of capital required by good y, two units of good x must be released (one unit of capital each). However, in doing so, four units of labour from good x are released as well and only one of these is required by good y. This is a cost. It forces the production of good y to become more labour-intensive than is desirable.

A similar situation occurs where the transformation is in the other direction and good y is being given up so that the production of good x could be increased. The substitution becomes increasingly difficult and, hence, the opportunity cost increases as substitution of one good for the other continues along the product transformation curve.

15.4.1.3 THE MARGINAL RATE OF PRODUCT TRANSFORMATION

The slope of this product transformation curve therefore gives the Marginal Rate of Product Transformation (*MRPT*). It measures how much of one good must be given up in order to get an extra unit of the other good, or the opportunity cost of substituting one good for the other.

The marginal rate of product transformation of good x into good y ($MRPT_{x,y}$) may be written as:

$$MRPT_{x,y} = -\frac{dy}{dx}$$

This slope of the transformation curve is equal to the ratio of the marginal costs of goods x and y and may be written as:

$$MRPT_{x,y} = -\frac{dy}{dx} = \frac{MC_x}{MC_y}$$

Proof of this is given in the Appendix.

15.4.2 Joint equilibrium of production and consumption

Having established that Pareto optimality (efficiency) exists all along the production possibilities frontier (*PPF*), any point along this frontier fulfils the equilibrium of production known as the second marginal condition for a general equilibrium. It has been noted that the slope of this *PPF* is the marginal rate of product transformation. The information on the various combinations of goods x and y that may be derived from the given inputs are known. This has been translated from the contract curve to the *PPF*.

15.4.2.1 PRODUCTION AND CONSUMPTION

In order to find the third marginal condition for a general equilibrium, it is necessary, at this stage, to identify a point (any point) on the *PPF*. Once this is done, the result can be shown to apply to any other point on the *PPF*. In this case, the point T' may be chosen arbitrarily to identify the actual combination of goods x and y that will be produced. It was established earlier that the point T' on the *PPF* represents the point T on the contract curve in the Edgeworth Box of production.

Once the point T' has been selected, an Edgeworth Box of consumption (exchange) can be inserted inside the transformation curve from the point T', representing the total available amounts of each good (x and y) produced efficiently in the economy at this point. These amounts are x_3 of good x and y_2 of good y and they are now to be distributed efficiently between the two consumers A and B. This is illustrated in Figure 15.4.

The Edgeworth box of exchange generated at the point T' has the standard characteristics as described earlier. Within the box the contract curve identifies the locus of points where Pareto optimality (efficiency) is achieved. This is the locus of points where:

$$MRS^{A}_{x,y} = MRS^{B}_{x,y}$$

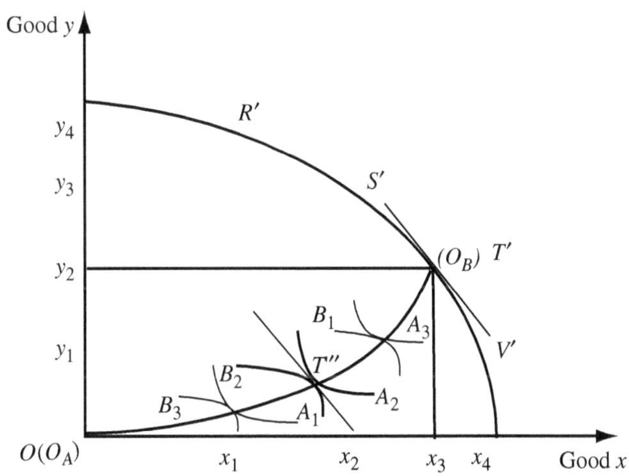

Figure 15.4
The equilibrium of the product mix with two goods (x and y) and two consumers (A and B)

15.4.2.2 SIMULTANEOUS EQUILIBRIUM

For the economy's output to be allocated so that consumer and producer optimization is achieved simultaneously, the slope of the transformation curve or the marginal rate of product transformation for the two goods $MRPT_{x,y}$ must be equal to the marginal rate of substitution in consumption of the two goods for the two consumers. This may be expressed as:

$$MRPT_{x,y} = MRS^{A}_{x,y} = MRS^{B}_{x,y}$$

Hence, the economy is at its greatest efficiency in the production of goods, given its input resources of labour and capital and the consumers are maximizing their utility.

More than that, however, the rate of which it is necessary to give up the production of one good to get an extra unit of the other ($MRPT_{x,y}$) is the same as the rate at which consumers are willing to give up the consumption of one good to gain an extra unit of the other ($MRS^{A}_{x,y}$, $MRS^{B}_{x,y}$). This is what brings the harmony along with the efficiency within the economy.

In order for this harmonious equilibrium to be achieved, consumers must be at a point on the contract curve of exchange at which the common slope of their indifference curves ($MRS^{A}_{x,y} = MRS^{B}_{x,y}$) equals the slope of the product transformation curve ($MRPT_{x,y}$) at T'. This takes place inside the Edgeworth box of exchange at the point T'' in Figure 15.4. For this to happen, the slopes of the tangents at T' and at T'' must be the same. For this to happen, the tangent lines must be parallel.

Consumer A gets Ox_2 of good x and Oy_4 of good y, while consumer B gets $Ox_3 - Ox_2$ of good x and $Oy_3 - Oy_4$ of good y.

15.4.2.3 PERFECT COMPETITION

It has already been established that the slope of the product transformation curve is the ratio of the marginal costs of the goods x and y. This has been expressed as:

$$MRPT_{x,y} = -\frac{dy}{dx} = \frac{MC_x}{MC_y}$$

Now, under perfect competition, in equilibrium, the marginal cost is equal to the marginal revenue and the marginal revenue is equal to the price. This gives:

$$MC_x = P_x \quad and \quad MC_y = P_y$$

Therefore, under perfect competition, the ratio of the marginal costs of production (the slope of the product transformation curve) is equal to the ratio of the prices of the products. This may be expressed as:

$$MRPT_{x,y} = -\frac{dy}{dx} = \frac{MC_x}{MC_y} = \frac{P_x}{P_y}$$

It has already been demonstrated that, in the Edgeworth box of exchange (consumption), perfect competition ensures that both consumers can be in joint equilibrium as they both optimize with respect to the same price ratio. This gives:

$$MRS^A_{x,y} = MRS^B_{x,y} = \frac{P_x}{P_y}$$

This price ratio is the slope of the tangent inside the Edgeworth box of exchange. Hence, in order to achieve an overall harmony of production and consumption, the price ratio on the product transformation curve and that within the box of exchange, derived from that point on the transformation curve, must be the same. Perfect competition ensures this by ensuring they face the same price ratio:

$$MRPT_{x,y} = \frac{P_x}{P_y} = MRS^A_{x,y} = MRS^B_{x,y}$$

15.4.2.4 GENERAL EQUILIBRIUM OF PRODUCTION AND CONSUMPTION (PRODUCT MIX) – THIRD MARGINAL CONDITION

Where the point on the contract curve in the Edgeworth box of exchange has the same price ratio as the point on the transformation curve from which the box was created, this final general equilibrium is achieved. Hence,

$$MRPT_{x,y} = MRS^A_{x,y} = MRS^B_{x,y}$$

This is the third marginal condition for a general equilibrium.

15.5 FEATURES OF THE EQUILIBRIUM POSITION

15.5.1 Finding the optimal allocations – the trace

Having derived an overall general equilibrium at T' and at T'' the optimal allocations must be identified and their characteristics understood. In order to do this it is necessary to trace back through the process from the final equilibrium position.

Starting with the point T' on the production possibilities curve (PP) in Figure 15.4, the optimal combination of goods x and y at that point can be identified as x_3 of good x and y_2 of good y.

The information from Figures 15.2 and 15.4 are captured in summary form in Figure 15.5. The optimal amount of labour and capital that is needed to produce these quantities of the commodities is found by tracing back to the Edgeworth box of production that generated the production possibility (transformation) curve. This traces back to the point T. Taking perpendiculars from the point T to the x-axis and the y-axis, it can be found that the optimal allocation of the factor labour (L) and the factor capital (K) to the production of good x is O_xL_x and O_xL_x respectively. The remainder of these two factors are allocated to the production of good y.

The line in the Edgeworth box of production at T represents the tangency of the isoquants for goods x and y at that point. Hence, it identifies the optimal wage/rental

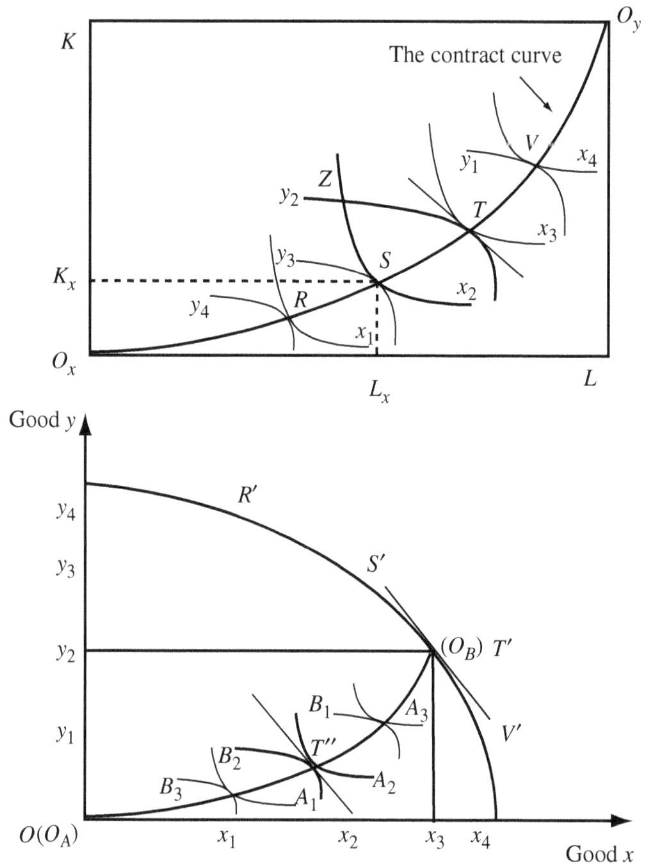

Figure 15.5
The general equilibrium trace

ratio (w/r) with regard to an overall general equilibrium with production at the point T'.

Tracing from the point T' to the point T'' the allocation of goods to consumers A and B can be identified by using perpendiculars from the point T'' to the x-axis and the y-axis. However, the gains to consumers can also be measured by their respective utility levels through the indifference curves that are tangent to each other at the point T''. From Figure 15.4, these utility levels have been identified as A_2 and B_2 respectively.

In addition, the optimal price ratio for the goods x and y is known to be that at the points T' and T''.

The trace therefore identifies the allocation of factors among goods, the allocation of goods among consumers, the levels of satisfaction of the consumers, the commodity price ratios facing the consumers and the factor price ratios facing the producers.

It must be noted that the amount (or combination) of the two goods to be produced is taken as given at the point T'. However, the same may be done for any other point along the product transformation curve that is used to illustrate a general equilibrium.

Later the model is completed showing how to decide which combination on the product transformation should be produce in order to have a welfare maximum.

15.5.2 Multiple equilibria

In describing the achievement of a general equilibrium at point T' on the production possibility frontier (transformation curve), it was noted that the point T was chosen arbitrarily. Pareto optimality in production exists at every point along the production possibility frontier. Therefore, there are an infinite number of points along the frontier that can be chosen for the derivation of a general equilibrium. Each of these points represents a different combination of goods x and y in product space and has its own slope defined as the marginal rate of product transformation (*MRPT*) and equivalent price ratio. All that is required is that, at each point, the relevant Edgeworth box of consumption (exchange) be constructed and the point along its contract curve be found such that:

$$MRPT_{x,y} = MRS^{A}_{x,y} = MRS^{B}_{x,y}$$

This would identify the point on the contract curve of consumption (exchange) where the marginal rate of substitution of the two consumers is tangent to the same commodity price ratio as that of the marginal rate of product transformation on the production possibility frontier from which that Edgeworth box of consumption was constructed.

Figure 15.6 shows multiple general equilibrium positions. For simplicity, only two points on the production possibility frontier are identified – R' and T'. Based on these points, the relevant Edgeworth boxes of consumption (exchange) are constructed. Using the respective contract curves in these boxes, the points are identified where the final

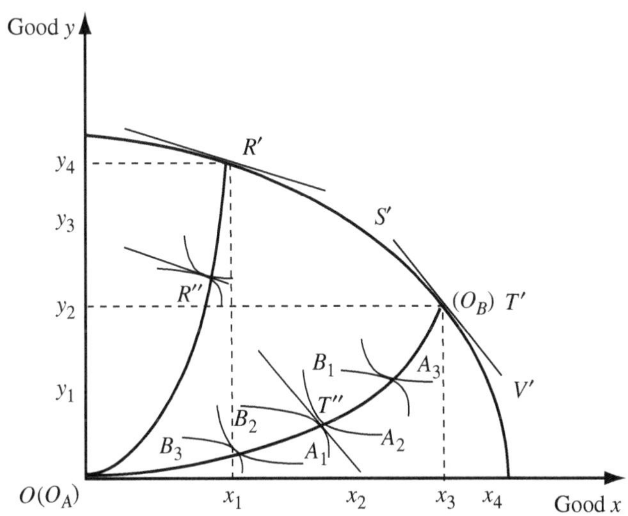

Figure 15.6
Multiple general equilibrium positions: R' with R'' and T' with T''

equilibrium condition is met:

$$MRPT_{x,y} = MRS^{A}_{x,y} = MRS^{B}_{x,y}$$

A general equilibrium therefore can be identified for the combinations R' with R'' as well as T' with T''. Moreover, similar combinations that cause a general equilibrium, may be identified for every point along the *PPF*. These combinations all satisfy the Pareto optimality (efficiency) conditions.

A major challenge, therefore, is to discover which one of these points is the best for the society. This is done in the next section (15.6).

15.5.3 Uniqueness and stability of general equilbrium

The question is whether a general equilibrium can be unique in the sense that it can only exist for one set of prices and quantities. This is explored a bit further below.

Uniqueness

In the simple $2 \times 2 \times 2$ model, there are four prices to be determined P_x, P_y, w (i.e. P_L) and r (i.e. P_K). In order to do this, four independent relations are needed. However, there are only three.

Having established that, for the factor market, the marginal product is written as the marginal physical product (*MPP*), the following relations can be derived.

For the producer:

$$MRTS^{x}_{LK} = MRTS^{y}_{LK} \tag{1}$$

For labour, the wage rate is equal to the value of the marginal physical product of labour. This gives:

$$w = (MPP_{L,x})P_x = \left(MPP_{L,y}\right)P_y \tag{2}$$

Similarly for capital:

$$r = (MP_{K,x})P_x = \left(MP_{K,y}\right)P_y \tag{3}$$

For the consumer, for a given price ratio:

$$MRS^{A}_{x,y} = \frac{P_x}{P_y} = MRS^{B}_{x,y} \tag{4}$$

This suggests that there are four relations. However one is not independent. To find out why this is so, divide Equation (2) by Equation (3) to get the wage–rental ratio. This gives:

$$\frac{w}{r} = \frac{MPP_{L,x}}{MPP_{K,x}} = MRTS^{x}_{L,K}$$

Hence the absolute values of w, r, P_x, P_y cannot be determined uniquely even though the solution to the general equilibrium is unique. Consequently, it is said that the general equilibrium is unique up to a price ratio or scale factor.

The numèraire

In order to obtain a solution, any three prices may be expressed in terms of the fourth, which is chosen arbitrarily as ***numèraire*** or unit of account.

Consider the case where P_x is chosen as numèraire, other prices are expressed in terms of P_x.

For w and r: since

$$\frac{w}{r} = MRTS_{LK}$$

then:

$$w = r(MRTS_{LK})$$

and:

$$r = (MPP_{K,x})P_x$$

Substituting:

$$w = (MRTS_{LK})(MPP_{K,x})P_x$$

Now, for P_y:

$$\frac{Px}{Py} = MRS_{xy}$$

Therefore:

$$P_y = \frac{P_x}{MRS_{x,y}}$$

or:

$$\frac{P_y}{P_x} = MRS_{y,x}$$

Consequently:

$$P_y = \left(MRS_{y,x}\right)P_x$$

It may be noted that a change of numèraire will leave relative prices unaffected.

In order for the general equilibrium model to be uniquely determined there must be the introduction of money into the system. Money, used for transactions or as a store of wealth, provides the numèraire and brings absolute uniqueness.

Stability of equilibrium

Stability of equilibrium relates to whether the equilibrium, once disturbed, returns to equilibrium of its own accord. Whether a general equilibrium is stable, in this sense, is a complex issue. Economist Walras contended that the general equilibrium is stable. The system, if in disequilibrium, would reach equilibrium by a process of iteration or groping (tatônnement) through the operation of the market mechanism.

15.6 WELFARE MAXIMIZATION

Having identified the conditions under which an economy reaches its efficiency frontier and achieves equilibrium between production and consumption (the necessary conditions), the attention now turns to the question of distribution and welfare maximization (the sufficient condition). This sufficient condition is provided by a social welfare function, a concept largely attributed to economist Abram Bergson (1938) which was further popularized by economist Paul Samuelson (1947, 1983). It is sometimes referred to as the Bergson–Samuelson social welfare function.

15.6.1 From general equilibrium to welfare

For a general equilibrium, the principal concern is with optimal resource use. Pareto efficiency or optimality is concerned only with delivering the most from given resources but has no concern with how the product is distributed. This is why it is said to provide only the necessary conditions for a welfare maximum.

Using the two-commodity, two-consumer, two-input case, the aim of welfare economics is to determine the 'best' distribution of income given that full economic efficiency (Pareto optimality) has been achieved.

There is, however, no scientifically meaningful way to compare the utility levels of various individuals. It cannot be determined scientifically how much more or less satisfaction a piece of cheese cake will bring to one person than it will bring to another. There is no scale on which pleasure or pain can be measured so that interpersonal comparisons can validly be made. This makes it difficult to determine whether one distribution of income is better than another. Consequently, economists typically tend to view income distributions that are less unequal as the more desirable.

While the three marginal conditions for a general equilibrium provide the necessary conditions for a welfare maximum in a society, the social welfare function provides the sufficient condition.

The necessary conditions

Recapping, the three marginal conditions for optimal resource allocation derived under general equilibrium analysis and which provide the three necessary conditions for a welfare maximum, may be summarized as follows:

1 Optimal allocation of commodities among consumers. The marginal Rate of Substitution between any two commodities must be the same for any two consumers.

This is expressed as:

$$MRS^A_{x,y} = MRS^B_{x,y}$$

2 The marginal rate of technical substitution between any two inputs must be the same for any pair of producers. This is expressed as:

$$MRTS^x_{LK} = MRTS^y_{LK}$$

3 The marginal rate of substitution between any two commodities must be the same as the marginal rate of transformation between these two commodities. This is expressed as:

$$MRPT_{x,y} = MRS^A_{x,y} = MRS^B_{x,y}$$

In order to use the social welfare function as the sufficient condition for a welfare maximum, it is necessary to develop the utility possibility frontier.

15.6.2 The utility possibility frontier

The exchange equilibrium locus can be transformed from commodity space to utility space to give the utility possibility frontier. This is done in the same way the contract curve of production was translated into the production possibility curve.

Take points R'' and T'' in Figure 15.7 and consider the points R', S', T' and V' on the respective contract curve of consumption (exchange) that satisfies the condition for the fulfilment of a general equilibrium. These points are R'', S'', T'' and V'' and, for each one, Pareto optimality is achieved. However, each one represents different levels of satisfaction for the two consumers A and B.

In order to understand how the distributions change as production points are changed, it is necessary to introduce the Utility Possibility Frontier (*UPF*). The utility possibility frontier in the two-consumer model is the locus of the maximum level of satisfaction attainable by one consumer for every given level of satisfaction attained by the other. Figure 15.7 illustrates how this is derived. Consider the point R' on the *PPF*. Since the contract curve of exchange is the locus of points where the marginal rate of substitution is the same for the two consumers, the contract curve represents the points of tangency between the indifference curves for the two consumers A and B. These indifference curves have been omitted from the diagram to avoid clutter.

Any movement up (from left to right) along the contract curve gives more utility to consumer A and less to consumer B. The point R'' on the contract curve of the exchange box at R' reflects the consumption point that gives the general equilibrium between production and consumption.

The contract curve in the Edgeworth box of consumption (exchange) at R' becomes the utility possibility frontier U_1U_1 in utility space for consumers A and B. The point R'' is mapped into utility space as R''' on the utility possibility frontier U_1U_1.

Similarly, the contract curve of exchange in the Edgeworth box at the point S' becomes the utility possibility frontier U_2U_2, and the general equilibrium matching point S''

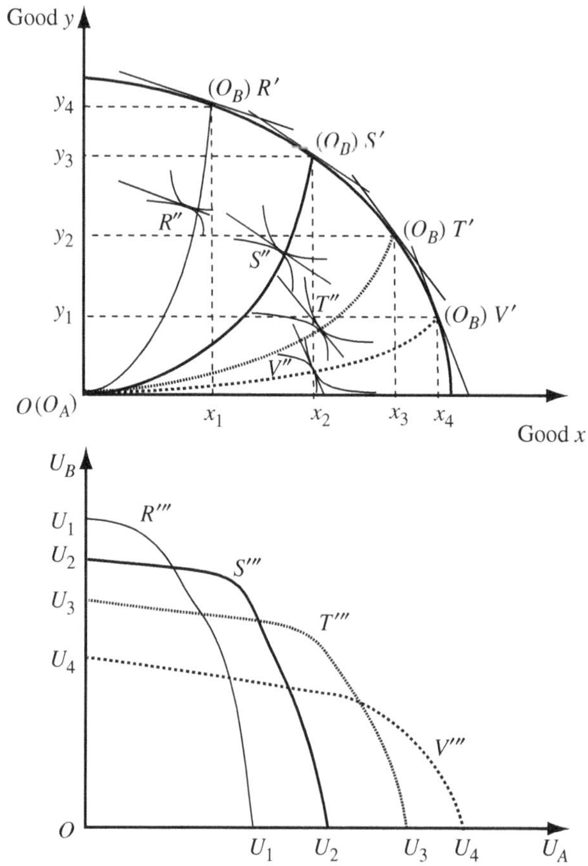

Figure 15.7
Utility possibility frontiers derived from contract curves of exchange at R', S', T' and V'

becomes the point S''' on that utility possibility frontier. The corresponding positions at T''' and V''' on utility possibility frontiers U_3U_3 and U_4U_4 have been similarly derived.

It may be noted that there are an infinite number of points such as R''', S'', T''' and V''', each on its relevant utility possibility frontier. It may also be noted that the utility possibility curve does not have the smooth concavity (to the origin) that the production possibility curve has. This is because individual preferences are not expected to be as well ordered as for output for a production process.

15.6.3 The Grand Utility Possibility Frontier (*GUPF*)

The Grand Utility Possibility Frontier (GUPF) is illustrated below in Figure 15.8. ***U*U**** is the locus of the points R''', S''', T''' and V''' along with all the other such points that exist. The *GUPF* shows the various possible pairs of utility levels for *A* and *B* given that the three marginal conditions for a general equilibrium are met (i.e. when the economy is operating at maximum efficiency). Along the *GUPF*, the greater is consumer *A*'s

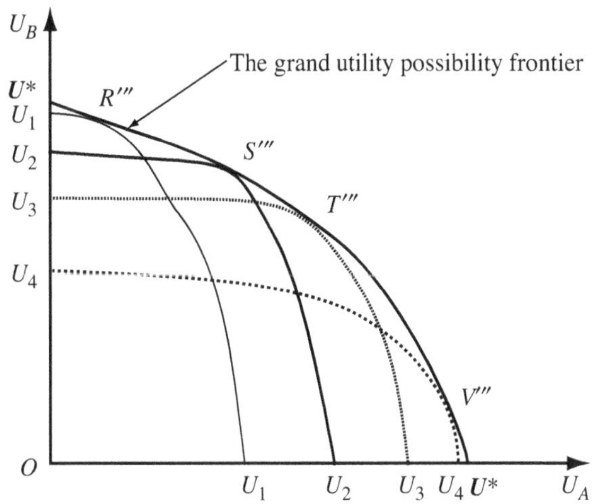

Figure 15.8
The grand utility possibility frontier (***U*U****)

satisfaction (utility), the less is consumer B's satisfaction (utility). Society must choose some point on ***U*U****.

The determination of an optimal point for social welfare depends on the existence of a ***social welfare function***. This function gives an aggregate measure of national or social well-being. It takes into account the 'deservingness' of A and B as seen by society as a whole. In a democracy such a function is developed by voting.

15.6.4 The social welfare function and the point of bliss

Based on the Bergson–Samuelson welfare function concept, a social welfare function is assumed to exist. This may be represented by the social indifference curves W_1 and W_2 shown in Figure 15.9. These curves represent the collective preferences of the society. Each social indifference curve is a locus of points at which social welfare expressed by the community is the same. The function is assumed to be real-valued and differentiable.

A social welfare function is an ordinal index of society's welfare and is a function of the utility levels of all individuals. It depends upon the value judgements of the persons for whom it is a desirable welfare function. In the two-consumer model, the social welfare function may be written as:

$$W = f(U_A, U_B)$$

where U_A is the level of the utility index of individual A in the community. The goal of the society is to maximize welfare subject to the constraint given by the production function. In this case, each point on the PPF generates a new utility possibility frontier for the community and gives a unique point on each that fulfils the condition for efficiency in the product mix in the Paretian sense (Pareto optimality).

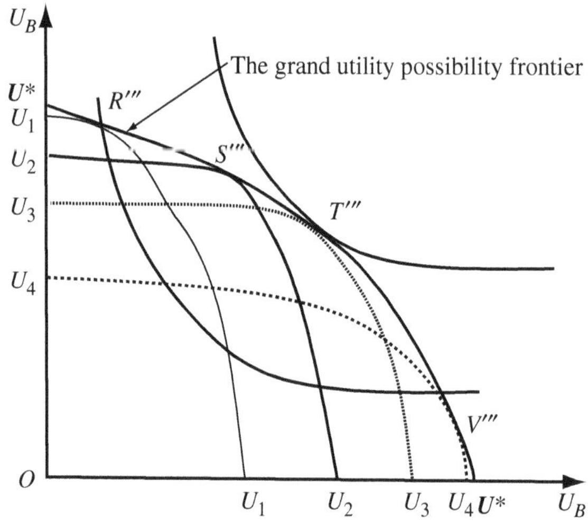

Figure 15.9
The point of welfare maximum (T''') – The Point of Bliss

The social welfare curves are analogous to indifference curves for the individual consumer and possess essentially the same characteristics. These include:

- The curves do not cross.
- The further from the origin they are, the higher the welfare.
- They are negatively sloped.
- They are convex to the origin.

Maintaining the analogy with the consumer analysis, while the society's welfare curves are similar to the indifference curves for the individual, the Grand Utility Possibility Frontier (*GUPF*) may be considered similar to the consumer's budget line. Consequently, the society tries to reach the highest social welfare indifference curve given the *GUPF*.

The Point of Bliss

The optimal point (sufficient condition) for the society to achieve maximum welfare is at T''' where a ***social welfare curve*** is tangent to the ***Grand Utility Possibility Frontier***. This is known euphemistically as the ***Point of Bliss***. It is the highest social welfare (sufficient condition) attainable by the society given the most efficient production possibilities (necessary conditions).

The social welfare function then, takes into account the deservingness of individuals as they make up a society. Its existence depends on the ability of a society, as a community, to be able to express its preferences in an ordered manner. It must be recognized that, along any one of the *UU* curves in Figure 15.9, the relative levels of utility (satisfaction) of the two consumers varies. At the upper left points on the curve W_1W_1 Individual *B*'s utility is relatively higher and individual *A*'s utility is relatively lower than they are at the lower right points on the curve.

The issue then, is whether it is possible for a society as a community of individuals, to have these social rankings that allow them to express an indifference of preference between positions that make them as individuals either relatively better or worse off.

This issue is taken up by the economist Kenneth Arrow (1950) and is usually referred to as the Arrow 'Possibility' (or 'Impossibility') theorem and is dealt with in the following section (Section 15.7).

15.7 FACTORS AFFECTING A WELFARE MAXIMUM

15.7.1 The Arrow possibility theorem

Arrow investigated the formulation of social preferences. He describes individual and social preferences in terms of ranking of alternatives states formed by the relation 'is at least as well liked as'. He was concerned with how social preferences can be formed from individual preferences, whether they must be determined by dictator, by a majority vote of individual members, or some other way. The Arrow theory rests on five (5) axioms which he believes that social preference structures must satisfy to be minimally acceptable as representative of the individual preferences of that society (community). They are:

Axiom 1 – Complete ordering

Preferences must be completely ordered by the relation 'is at least as well liked socially as' and therefore must satisfy the conditions of completeness, reflexivity and transitivity. Consider three outcomes a, b and c. Then if $a > b$; $b < a$ and if $a > b$; $b > c$; *then* $a > c$.

Axiom 2 – Responsiveness to individual preferences

If a is socially preferred to b for a given set of individual preferences and individual rankings change so that one individual raises a to higher rank and no one lowers a in rank, a must remain socially preferred to b. The implication is that there must be no social inequality where some individuals can raise a to a higher rank yet the social (community) desirability of that alternative is reduced.

Axiom 3 – Non-discrimination

Social preferences must not be imposed independently of individual preferences. If no individual prefers b to a and at least one individual prefers a to b, then society must prefer a to b.

Axiom 4 – Non-dictatorship

Social preferences must not totally reflect the preferences of any ***single individual***. Society must not prefer a to b only if some particular individual (the dictator) prefers a to b and the community must accept this individual's preference as theirs.

Axiom 5 – Independence of irrelevant alternatives

The most preferred state in a set of alternatives must be independent of the existence of other alternatives. That is, if a, b and c are available and $a > b > c$, then if c is no longer available then $a > b$ still holds. Hence, c is one alternative, the others must be independent of c and not change their ranking depending on whether c is available or not.

Arrow's impossibility

In general, Arrow's theorem states that it is impossible to construct social preferences that satisfy all five axioms.

A way around Arrow's dilemma is to limit individual preferences so that social preferences that satisfy all five axioms can always be constructed. One possibility is to assume that all individuals always assign the same ranking to each alternative.

15.7.2 Perfect competition and welfare maximization

Perfect competition requirements

It has been shown that, in order for the three conditions for the achievement of a general equilibrium, perfect competition must exist in all markets. Since these general equilibrium conditions are the necessary conditions for a welfare maximum, the same must apply. It should be recognized that Pareto conditions will be achieved under perfect competitions if:

- Second-order conditions are satisfied for each consumer and producer. If the first-order condition is fulfilled but the second-order condition is not fulfilled under perfect competition then the optimum becomes a pessimum as the perfectly competitive firm goes from maximizing profits to maximizing losses.
- No consumer is satiated.
- Consumers' utilities are not interdependent. This requires that there are no external effects on consumption.
- There are no external effects on production.

Perfect competition, therefore, allows the existence of welfare maximum since it is necessary to fulfil the requirements of Pareto optimality unless one (or more) of the above conditions is not fulfilled.

Pareto optimality accepts the prevailing factor endowment and makes no value judgements. How the gains from the achievement of Pareto efficiency are distributed (the value judgements involved) are the preserve of welfare theory.

Increasing returns to scale

Perfect competition implies that, in the long-run firms will be at the minimum point of their long-run average cost curve. This indicates that there are constant returns to scale even if there is not a constant-returns-to-scale (*CRTS*) production function.

This *CRTS* function is essential for the general equilibrium and hence for the welfare maximum.

Where there are increasing returns to scale in production, the shape of the *PPF* or product transformation curve may change. This could give rise to the existence of multiple equilibria such that the price system with all the three conditions fulfilled would give faulty signals to producers as well as consumers. It would be difficult to identify the point of welfare maximum.

Factor ownership and distribution

Despite the conditions of Perfect Competition and constant returns to scale being met, the general equilibrium and welfare maximum is not clear on factor ownership and the resulting income distribution.

Consumers' income depends on the distribution of factor ownership (quantities of factors which they own) and on factor prices. But under general equilibrium and welfare, prices determined only up to a ratio.

As a result, the equilibrium position does not give absolute values for the distribution of ownership of the factors and money incomes between individuals *A* and *B*. This indeterminacy can be resolved only partly if by arbitrarily fixing the value of one of the four prices, and then allocating the remaining three so as to make the individual incomes of *A* and *B* such that they will lead them to the consumption pattern implied by the appropriate point on the product transformation curve.

15.7.3 Externalities, taxes and compensation

15.7.3.1 EXTERNAL EFFECTS ON CONSUMPTION AND PRODUCTION

Pareto optimality under perfect competition requires that there are no external effects in consuming. The implication is that the utility level of a consumer must not depend upon the consumption level of others. The partial derivatives of the utility functions are functions of all variables because the optimum position of each consumer depends upon the consumption level of the other.

For production, the total production cost of an entrepreneur must not depend upon the output levels of others. If so, Pareto optimality may not be realized.

Public goods

A different type of externality is the case of a public good. With a public good, no one consumer's satisfaction is diminished by the satisfaction gained by another. No one can appropriate a public good to his own personal use. The conditions for Pareto optimality are not valid for public goods.

For ordinary goods, the $MRS_{x,y}$ for every consumer must equal the $MRPT_{x,y}$ for the goods produced. In the case of public goods, it is the sum of the $MRS_{x,y}$ for the consumers that must equal the $MRPT_{x,y}$ for the two goods in production. It is not necessary that the $MRS_{x,y}$ of individual consumers be equal.

With public goods, the conditions for Pareto optimality are obtained by maximizing Consumer A's utility assuming that Consumer B's utility is at some predetermined level and that the production function is satisfied.

External economics and diseconomics

It has been shown that $P = MC$ is necessary for Pareto optimality when relating it to the *PPF*. This allows the $MRPT_{x,y}$ to be equal to the price ratio of the goods x and y and so equal to the marginal rate of substitution in consumption. It has already been established that the slope of the *PPF* represents the (increasing) opportunity cost of substituting one good for the other. This refers to the private opportunity cost (internal) and is considered to also represent the cost to the society. However, private and social opportunity costs are identical only in the absence of external economies and diseconomies.

With external economies and diseconomies, the welfare associated with production must now be measured to show the difference between the social benefit received and the social costs incurred.

To attain Pareto optimality it is the producers' joint profits that must be maximized rather than that of the individual producer. Now, for Pareto optimality to be achieved, social costs must replace private costs. Hence social equilibrium requires that price must equal social marginal cost, instead of private marginal cost, and that social marginal cost be increasing. Then consumers' $MRS_{x,y}$ will equal not the private producers' $MRPT_{x,y}$ but society's $MRPT_{x,y}$.

The opportunity costs measured along the *PPF* would represent the society's alternatives forgone by producing an additional unit of a commodity. Hence, for welfare maximization, the producer causing external diseconomies (e.g. pollution) should produce at a lower level than for private maximization and the producer causing external economies should produce more. In order to achieve this, government would need to apply the appropriate taxes and subsidies.

Taxes and subsidies

Where market and social values diverge, then for the maximization of social welfare, economies can be led to Pareto optimality through the imposition of appropriate taxes and subsidies.

Per unit taxes have their impact on marginal costs. These may be imposed to decrease levels of consumption and production by increasing their marginal costs. Per unit subsidies may be imposed to have the opposite effect.

Lump-sum taxes and subsidies are in the nature of fixed costs. These taxes and subsidies do not affect marginal costs and hence do not affect the equilibrium position for the producer. Consequently, they may be used to socially re-distribute the gains from moving to a Pareto-optimal allocation. These gains may be re-distributed to either producer or consumer in order to achieve redress of the external economy or diseconomy.

15.7.3.2 COMPENSATION CRITERIA

The nature of the Pareto conditions would suggest that any change leads to an efficiency or welfare improvement if, by that change, no one's utility is decreased when at least one person's utility is increased. Moreover, where there is Pareto efficiency, a change that results in the increase in one person's utility must result in the decrease in another's.

In order to determine if a change that makes one worse off while making another better off is beneficial for society some criteria must be used to determine how the reduction in utility must be compensated for. For this, compensation criteria are employed. The main compensation criteria are:

1 ***The Kaldor criterion***
Allocation X is socially preferable to allocation Y if those who gain from the change to allocation X could compensate the losers (i.e. bribe the losers to accept X) and still be better off than at Y.
2 ***The Hicks criterion***
Allocation X is socially preferable to allocation Y if those who would lose from the change to allocation X could not profitably bribe the gainers into not making the change from allocation Y to X.
3 ***The Scitovsky criterion***
Allocation X is socially preferable to allocation Y if the gainers could bribe the losers into accepting the change and simultaneously the losers could not bribe the gainers into not making the change. This represents a combination of the two other criteria.

It is useful to note that the compensation criteria do not require that compensation actually be paid. Hence they refer to potential rather than actual welfare. In a movement from allocation X to allocation Y, some are better off and some worse off. Even if all three criteria above are met, there is no guarantee that the compensation will take place.

15.7.4 The theory of the second best

The achievement of a welfare maximum depends on the achievement of Pareto optimality, which in turn depends on certain institutional features including the existence of perfect competition everywhere.

Questions of the theory of the second best

Where institutional restrictions (e.g. monopoly) prevent an economy from achieving overall Pareto optimality, the question is whether it is possible or desirable to identify a second-best position on which welfare maximization can be based. The theory of the second best says this is not so. It says that if any one or more of the necessary conditions for Pareto optimality cannot be satisfied, in general it is neither necessary nor desirable to satisfy the remaining conditions.

More specifically, the theory of the second best asks if one or more of the Pareto conditions cannot be satisfied because of institutional restrictions, whether it is useful to satisfy the remaining Pareto conditions to achieve the next best outcome for welfare. The theory of the second best denies this possibility.

Characteristics of the theory

The essence of the theory of the second best may be set out in summary as follows.

Take a utility function for a single consumer:

$$U = f(Q_x, Q_y)$$

Add an aggregate production function:

$$Q_x = f(K, L)$$

In general equilibrium consumer is maximizing utility subject to the production function. Hence, the composite function is formed using the Lagrangian method for constrained optimization. This gives the composite function:

$$\Phi = f(Q_x, Q_y) + \lambda[f(K, L) - Q_x]$$

The partial derivatives are set to zero. It is then assumed that institutional conditions prevent the attainment of one of the conditions. The failure to meet this condition can be expressed in various ways. In this case the conditions for a second best welfare optimum can be obtained by maximizing utility subject to the aggregate production function and the distorted relationship. As a result, there are two constraints. Hence, the relevant Lagrangian function is formed where there are two λ and μ undetermined multipliers (λ and μ) and partial derivatives are set equal to zero.

The upshot of this is that there are cross partial derivatives, the sign of which are not known a priori and which therefore cannot be used to provide a second best solution. Without knowledge of these signs, it is not possible to even attempt to measure the direction or magnitude of the effect of a change in one variable on the next. Therefore, in general, it is not possible to determine how and which of the usual Pareto conditions may be required for the attainment of a second best optimum.

Consequently, the theory of the second best is used to question the usefulness of policies which attempt to attain the Pareto conditions for a welfare maximum on a piece-meal basis for markets considered in isolation. One question that is asked is whether, in a case where there is not perfect competition everywhere, attempts should be made to force it to obtain in any one industry or market. The theory of the second best says it is an exercise in futility.

The theory of the second best can be summarized as saying that, when the Paretian requirements are not fulfilled everywhere to provide the conditions for a welfare maximum, there is no way to identify a second best position. The theory of the second best, therefore, says there is no second best.

As a counter to the theory of the second best, there is the argument that piece-meal policies, though not valid in general, may be valid for specific cases. In particular, they are valid if production and utility functions are both separable. This is the case where, for example, the activity in one industry or market is completely unrelated to that in another. The issue of cross partial derivatives would not arise and it is possible to try to have the Pareto optimality conditions apply in one single industry or market.

15.8 POSTSCRIPT

It should be recognized that general equilibrium and welfare theory is static. General equilibrium is concerned with the achievement of efficiency in production and distribution given the existing technology, availability of resources for production, tastes and preferences of the consumer.

The achievement of the Point of Bliss depends on the assumption of the existence of a social welfare function which requires individuals to be indifferent between options more favourable to them and those less favourable to them. Arrow (1950) shows the difficulty with this concept.

Additionally, the achievement of the general equilibrium relies on some unrealistic foundations: perfect competition everywhere in the market and constant returns to scale in production. The theory of the second best points to the futility of finding a second best position if perfect competition does not exist in every single market.

The major concerns with this approach are:

- The likelihood of the existence of such a state of efficiency in production and equity in the distribution of the benefits of production in an economy being realized is remote.
- That it neither generates nor accommodates any further growth and development raises the fundamental question of the desirability of such a state.

Nevertheless the theory provides some useful tools, many of which have been used in the theory of international trade to determine the pattern of trade and the nature of international equilibrium. Trade theory, using the Edgeworth box and Production Possibility Frontier tools, has been able to develop some comparative static (changes in technology and in the quantity of factors of production).

In addition, the use of Computable General Equilibrium models has been extended to many areas of economic research.

REVIEW QUESTIONS FOR CHAPTER 15

1 With regard to the standard model of General Equilibrium and Welfare explain:

(a) The concepts of Pareto improvement and Pareto optimality.
(b) The use of the Edgeworth box and the meaning of the Contract curve.
(c) The first marginal condition for a general equilibrium and why it may be called the equilibrium of exchange.

2 Illustrate and explain:

(a) How the equilibrium of production takes place within the Edgeworth box.
(b) The derivation of the Production Possibility Frontier from the Edgeworth box.
(c) How the second marginal condition for a general equilibrium may be set out.

3 Using the Product Transformation Curve show:

(a) How this curve is used in conjunction with the Edgeworth box of consumption to identify the third marginal condition for a general equilibrium.
(b) Why there are multiple points where this third marginal condition is fulfilled.
(c) The role of Perfect Competition in ensuring that all three marginal conditions for a general equilibrium are fulfilled.

4 With regard to Welfare theory:

(a) Show how the third marginal condition for a general equilibrium is used to derive the utility possibility curves.
(b) Explain and illustrate the construction of the Grand Utility Possibility Frontier.
(c) Examine the use of the Social Welfare Function to provide the sufficient condition for a welfare maximum and identify the theoretical Point of Bliss for a society.

5 With regard to General Equilibrium and Welfare theory:

(a) Set out the five axioms of the Arrow 'possibility' theory and consider why it is also called the 'impossibility' theory.
(b) Briefly summarize the point made by the Theory of the Second Best.

RECOMMENDED READING FOR CHAPTER 15

Arrow, K. J. (1950) 'A Difficulty in the Concept of Social Welfare', *Journal of Political Economy*, 58(4): 328–46, also in Mansfield, E. (ed.) (1975) *Microeconomics: Selected Readings*, NY: Norton, pp. 466–82.

Arrow, K. J. (1951) *Social Choice and Individual Values,* NY: Wiley (2nd Edn 1963).

Arrow, K. J. (1969) 'The Organization of Economics Activity: Issues Pertinent to the choice of Market Versus Non-Market Allocation', in *The Analysis and Evaluation of Public Expenditures: The PPB System*, (ed.) Joint Economic Committee, Washington, DC: Government Printing Office.

Bergson, A. (1938) 'A Reformulation of Certain Aspects of Welfare Economics', *Quarterly Journal of Economics*, 52(2): 310–34.

Moore, J. C. (2007) *General Equilibrium and Welfare Economics: An Introduction*, Berlin: Springer.

Samuelson, P. (1947) *Foundations of Economic Analysis* (1983 edn), Cambridge, Mass: Harvard Economic Studies (Ch. 8 – Welfare Economics).

Scarf, H. (2008) 'Computation of General Equilibria', *The New Palgrave Dictionary of Economics* (2nd Edn), Palgrave MacMillan.

APPENDIX – MRPT AND MARGINAL COSTS

Proof that the Marginal Rate of Product Transformation (MRPT) is the ratio of the marginal cost of good x to good y

The Marginal Rate of Product Transformation is written as:

$$MRPT_{x,y} = -\frac{\mathrm{d}y}{\mathrm{d}x} = \frac{MC_X}{MC_Y}$$

This may be proven mathematically as follows.

Proof

By definition:

$$MC_x = \frac{\mathrm{d}\,(TC_x)}{\mathrm{d}x}$$

and:

$$MC_y = \frac{\mathrm{d}\left(TC_y\right)}{\mathrm{d}y} \tag{1}$$

Thus:

$$\frac{MC_x}{MC_y} = \frac{\mathrm{d}\,(TC_x)}{\mathrm{d}\left(TC_y\right)}\frac{\mathrm{d}y}{\mathrm{d}x} \tag{2}$$

Now the aim is to show that:

$$\frac{\mathrm{d}\left(TC_y\right)}{\mathrm{d}\,(TC_x)} = -1$$

But:

$$TC_x = w\,(L_x) + r\,(K_x)$$

So:

$$\mathrm{d}\,(TC_x) = w\,(\mathrm{d}L_x) + r\,(\mathrm{d}K_x)$$

and:

$$\mathrm{d}\left(TC_y\right) = w\left(\mathrm{d}L_y\right) + r\left(\mathrm{d}K_y\right).$$

Hence:

$$\frac{\mathrm{d}\,(TC_x)}{\mathrm{d}\left(TC_y\right)} = \frac{w\,(\mathrm{d}L_x) + r\,(\mathrm{d}k_x)}{w\left(\mathrm{d}L_y\right) + r\left(\mathrm{d}k_y\right)} \tag{3}$$

In order to remain on the production possibilities curve, the factors released from the decrease in commodity y must be equal to the factors absorbed by the increase in the production of commodity x.

$$\mathrm{d}L_x = \mathrm{d}L_y$$

and:

$$\mathrm{d}K_x = \mathrm{d}K_y \tag{4}$$

This means that:

$$\frac{\mathrm{d}\left(TC_x\right)}{\mathrm{d}\left(TC_y\right)} = \frac{w\left(-\mathrm{d}L_y\right) + r\left(-\mathrm{d}K_y\right)}{w\left(\mathrm{d}L_y\right) + r\left(\mathrm{d}K_y\right)} = -1 \tag{5}$$

Substituting Equation (5) in Equation (2) gives:

$$\frac{MC_x}{MC_y} = -1\,\frac{\mathrm{d}y}{\mathrm{d}x} = -\frac{\mathrm{d}y}{\mathrm{d}x} = \text{ slope of } PPF = MRPT_{x,y}$$

16 Investment Criteria

Investment Decision Making; Cash Flow Analysis; Net Present Value, Internal Rate of Return, Benefit–Cost Ratio/Profitability Index, Payback Period

A firm or an individual, as producer or supplier of goods or services, is often confronted with a multiplicity of decisions that have implications for a successful implementation or for the continued financial success of an enterprise. These decisions are of significance to firms or individual investors regardless of the scale of the operation, whether in rural areas or in urban commercial agglomerations. Investment decisions take on even greater significance where investing units seek to make the transition from a protected domestic market to a regional or global market or where there is need for new investment following a recession or economic crisis.

At the heart of the decisions are those related to the selection and ranking of investment projects. This is a part of Project Analysis or Project Evaluation which is typically included under the heading of Capital Budgeting. There are tools of Project Analysis that assist in this type of decision making by the firm. These tools involve the use of Cash Flow analysis, specifically Discounted Cash Flow (*DCF*) analysis and the employment of investment criteria, including the Net Present Value (*NPV*) criterion, the Internal Rate of Return (*IRR*) criterion, the Benefit–Cost Ratio (*BCR*) or Profitability Index (*PI*) criterion and the Payback Period (*PP*) criterion.

Moreover, in the standard production theory, producers are assumed to have perfect knowledge of their product and the market. The firm knows the available technology, the full specification of the production function, the full extent of the demand for its product and the price of the required factor inputs. There are occasions where the firm seeks to expand through new investment and, in going into the world of the unknown, the firm must first gather information and then apply certain techniques to assist in decision making.

This chapter provides an introduction to the use of investment decision-making criteria as part of the discipline of Project Analysis.

INVESTMENT CRITERIA

16.1 DEFINITION OF A PROJECT

For the purpose of project analysis, a project may be defined as: Any scheme or part of a scheme for investing resources which can reasonably be analysed and evaluated as an independent unit. It is a definition that is somewhat vague or arbitrary. Essentially, a project is any item of investment which can be evaluated separately. Project sizes run the gamut from ultra large-scale government or international organization projects to minuscule projects that can be analyzed on the back of an envelope. For purposes of analysis, it is possible to break a large project into smaller projects for separate consideration or to consolidate several small projects into a large one. What is important, however, is that each project should be capable of being evaluated separately and should not be so inextricably linked to another project that one cannot be completed without the other.

As the size of a project varies, the depth of analysis also varies. The depth of project analysis ranges from the most cursory to the more highly elaborate studies involving high-level computer programs with scientific data and volumes of analytical data and reports. Based on the results of the analyses, the decisions on projects are made at all levels. Some decisions are of the nature of accept/reject. Other decisions involve the ranking of all acceptable projects to determine the order of selection. As a result of this ranking, a single project or multiple projects may be selected depending on the extent of the investment funds accessible.

All those involved in appraising a project must use the same methods and principles for the evaluation. Hence, a project found acceptable by, say, a junior engineer, must also be found acceptable by the most senior project officer. It is important that an acceptable project must not fail to reach the higher-level decision makers because it was rejected at a lower level within the organization. Planning harmony of this type must be readily achievable since the goal of the firm is that of profit or, in this context, present value maximization.

16.2 CASH FLOW ANALYSIS

Decision making on new projects is concerned primarily with:

- Whether the project is acceptable (i.e. will increase the profitability/wealth of the firm or investor).
- How the project ranks in acceptability with other projects in order to determine which project is the most acceptable or, depending on available funds, how many projects may be accepted.

One of the best methods of making this determination is that known as cash flow analysis.

16.2.1 Cash flow accounting

Investment decisions rely on cash flow analysis. These decisions are based on cash flow accounting which is different from normal accounting. In normal accounting income and expenditure represent the values of goods and services delivered and received. In cash flow accounting income (benefits) and expenditures (costs) represent the cash received and paid out for goods and services.

Interest payments – The payment of interest is included as a financial liability in normal accounting but these are not included in cash flow accounting.

Taxes – The payment of taxes is included in normal accounting but not in cash flow accounting. For a private project, payment of a tax is just considered a use of resources. In a social project, payments of direct taxes are not included.

Borrowing and Lending – These are not normally included in cash flow accounting. It is assumed that capital funds and current account receipts need not be treated differently as they are both just money. This is acceptable where the investor can borrow or lend without restriction at a fixed interest rate which is identical to the discount rate to be used in discounting the cash flow.

Private vs. social cash flow accounting

Cash flow accounting needs to distinguish between private and social projects. Typically, social costs and benefits may be substantially different from private costs and benefits. For a private project, market prices and values are generally used to measure costs and benefits and determine profitability. For social projects, the costs and benefits often need to be measured through a process of revaluing goods and services on which the prices are placed. The resulting social values become known as 'shadow prices'. The difference between private or market values and social values is a function of externalities. These externalities occur where market failure causes the costs or benefits to society to differ from the costs or benefits to the private investor/firm. This may occur for a number of reasons. These include:

- *Distortions due to government interference in the market with instruments such as taxes, subsidies or price controls (ceilings and floors).* For example, projects using inputs that are subsidized would have costs that do not reflect the full cost to the society since other groups would have provided the funds (taxes) used to enable the subsidy.
- *The environmental costs or benefits of the project that are not reflected in the market prices of the inputs or outputs.* A project may cause environmental damage through pollution or environmental degradation and this cost may not be reflected in the private market price of the product. In this case, the social cost must be re-valued upwards in determining the shadow price for the social project. On the contrary, where a project generates a positive environmental benefit (e.g. it make use of a waste product), then the social benefit value would tend to be higher than the private benefit to the individual investor/firm.
- *Poor income distribution.* Social projects may seek to assist the more disadvantaged groups and, because of this, may have benefits that are not reflected by the market price of the output. For example, a project to extend public transportation services into remote areas of the countryside may have the benefits of bringing marginalized rural producers and consumers more fully into the economy to increase economic growth and development. The benefits to the economy as a whole may far exceed the

individual benefits to the members of these groups and their willingness or capacity to pay. Many social projects that seek to effect the re-distribution of income and to initiate or accelerate the process of development have externalities that extend beyond the capacity to pay off the main recipients (social benefits exceed private benefits). These are found predominantly in areas such as:

- Education
- Health
- Transport
- National Security (police, fire service, etc.)

Clearly, shadow prices contain some measure of arbitrariness and so, more recently, many developed countries have tended to eschew the use of shadow prices. However, in developing countries, where it is considered that there is a greater degree of market failure, their use seems more appropriate. Nevertheless, some international organizations or multi-lateral lending institutions have been favouring the use of international prices to give the requisite values for social projects in developing countries considered to be afflicted by serious market failure.

16.2.2 Data needed for cash flow analysis

In order to determine the benefits (cash inflows) and costs (cash outflows) over the life of a project, the analyst must first specify and quantify all the goods and services that are to be used as inputs into the project and all those that will be generated as outputs from the project from its inception to its demise (including salvage material at the end of the life of the project). These real inputs and outputs must then be converted to cash values by attaching the appropriate prices to the individual inputs and outputs. This gives the anticipated cash inflows (receipts) from goods and services sold and cash outflows (expenditures) from goods and services purchased from the beginning to the end of the project.

These anticipated future costs and benefits, even when inputs and outputs are valued at market prices, are often little more than guesstimates. Moreover, the quality or usefulness of these estimates depends on a variety of factors which together contribute to determine the integrity of the data. These factors may be classified as technical/environmental, managerial/human and economic and include the following.

Technical factors (physical considerations)

- Whether the production function is properly specified.
- Whether the most appropriate technology is being chosen for the project.
- Whether future technological changes may alter the relationships between inputs during the life of the project.
- Whether the appropriate Environmental Impact Assessment is being done so that environmental costs and benefits may be taken into account at the costing or valuing stage.

Human/managerial

- Whether the human capital required will be available at start-up and throughout the life of the project.
- Whether management skill will be of the quality required to handle a project of that size or sophistication.
- Whether project managers can ensure that the project is completed as scheduled.
- Whether the specified production function (relating inputs to outputs) is appropriate in that particular socio-cultural-economic environment. This relates to worker productivity, effective use of physical capital and the attitudes and effectiveness of management.
- Whether management can source the required raw materials to maintain the desired capacity and can market sufficiently well to maintain the anticipated level of demand for the output.

Economic

- Whether the costing of inputs is realistic. This relates to whether domestic market values are being used or whether shadow prices or international prices are considered more appropriate.
- Whether external costs are considered (i.e. whether the project is in a decreasing, increasing or constant cost industry). This could mean that, when the project comes on stream, it could have an effect on the cost of inputs into the industry. This is particularly likely where the project is sufficiently large relative to the size of the economy.
- Whether proper economic forecasting has been done particularly with regard to future demand for the output.
- Whether there are local environmental factors that may cause delays (e.g. construction delays) and increase the initial outlay (investment cost) of the project.

Despite the drawbacks, the cash flow method remains popular and the resulting estimates may be used to determine:

- Whether the project is acceptable (i.e. will increase the profitability/wealth of the firm or investor) and/or
- How the project ranks in acceptability with other projects.

The best method of analyzing the cash flow data for this purpose is that known as 'discounted cash flow' (*DCF*).

16.3 DISCOUNTED CASH FLOW ANALYSIS

The cash flows generated by the project are done over the life of the project. Since this may go far into the future, it is imperative that the future benefits/costs are made to relate to the current investments made in the project. To evaluate future costs and benefits in relation to a current investment (outflow or cost) of funds, it is necessary to value these future sums in comparative terms to the present investment. To achieve this, the method of Discounted Cash Flow (*DCF*) analysis is used. It is on this foundation of discounted cash flow that the investment criteria used to select and rank projects are based.

DCF analysis is based on the principle that money has a time value. $100 received a year from now is worth less than $100 received now. This is because $100.00 received now can be used to earn a return in the interim between now and next year.

Consider that $100.00 can be invested now at a rate of 10 per cent per annum. In one year's time this $100.00 would be worth $110.00. After two years at the same interest rate, it would be worth $121. Thus $121 received in two years can be said to have been equivalent to $100.00 now. By the same token, using the 10 per cent interest rate, $100.00 in one year's time is worth only $90.91 now, since $90.91 earning 10 per cent per annum becomes $100.00 in one year's time. Consequently, the $100.00 in the future has been 'discounted' at the rate of 10 per cent per annum, done as follows:

$$\frac{100}{(1+0.1)} = 90.91$$

The discounting process may be viewed as compound interest worked backwards.

16.3.1 The discounted cash flow method

Assuming that the project life can be measured in years, where a time period consists of one year, the cash flow method may be set out as follows:

- Record individually for each year of the projected life of the project all anticipated payments for good and services (expenditures) to be used as inputs for the project (including capital expenditures). These are the costs (C).
- Record individually for each year of the projected life of the project all anticipated receipts for goods and services produced as outputs from the project. These are the benefits (B).
- For each year of the projected life of the project, subtract costs from benefits. This gives the net benefit ($B - C = \beta$), where β can be negative or positive for any given year.
- Find the ***Present Value (PV)*** of the future net benefits by discounting all the anticipated future net benefits (β) to the present. This has to be done for each year of the projected life of the project. For this purpose, a ***discount rate*** must be found.

16.3.2 Finding the Present Value (*PV*)

The Present Value is an important measure of profitability. The aim of finding the Present Value is to revalue all receipts and expenditures that occur throughout the life of the project to make them comparable to expenditures and receipts in the present time period (i.e. at the start of the project).

The process is carried out in the following sequence.

1 Determine the future net benefit (β_t) for each year (time period) of the life of the project. This gives a stream on net benefits (whether positive, negative or zero) for the n years of the project life of:

$$\beta_1, \beta_2, \ldots, \beta_n$$

2 Discount each future net benefit to the present (β) by multiplying the future net benefit for each time period by $1/(1+r)^t$ where t is the number of time periods in the future and r is the discount rate. This gives the Present Value of the net benefits for each individual time period (t). Hence, for each future time period, the following formula is applied:

$$\beta_t \frac{1}{(1+r)^t} \quad \text{or} \quad \frac{\beta_t}{(1+r)^t}$$

3 Sum the present values of all the individual time periods of the project in order to determine the discounted net value (or Present Value) for the entire life of the project. If there are n time periods for the life of the project, then the present values for all the time periods can be summed as follows to give the Present Value (PV) of the project:

$$PV = \frac{\beta_1}{(1+r)^1} + \frac{\beta_2}{(1+r)^2} + \cdots + \frac{\beta_n}{(1+r)^n}$$

This can also be written as:

$$PV = \sum_{t=1}^{n} \frac{\beta_t}{(1+r)^t}$$

It may be noted that this does not include the initial period at the start of the project when, typically, there is the original investment made into the project. This initial time period may be included when attempting to use the Net Present Value (NPV) criterion (see below) and usually carries the sub-script 0 ($t = 0$).

Where the discount rate is anticipated to vary from one time period to the other then the future net benefits must be discounted using a different rate for each on the n time periods. The formula to be used then becomes:

$$PV = \frac{\beta_1}{(1+r_1)^1} + \frac{\beta_2}{(1+r_2)^2} + \cdots + \frac{\beta_n}{(1+r_n)^n}$$

16.3.3 The rate of discount

A critical part of the discounting process is the determination of the appropriate rate of discount (r). This rate may be considered as the opportunity cost of placing the funds into the project. As such, it would reflect the rate of interest that could be earned by the investing firm or individual in the highest valued alternative earning activity over the life of the project. It could also be considered to be the rate of return a financially savvy investor deems it necessary to earn. This may be no different from the interest rate available for such funds in the banking system. In more sophisticated analyses, however, two other measures of determining the appropriate discount rate may be used. These are the Weighted Average of the Cost of Capital (*WACC*) and the Capital Asset Pricing Model (*CAPM*).

The WACC and the CAPM

The *WACC* and the *CAPM* are two different approaches to determining the cost of capital. It is this cost that is generally used to identify an appropriate discount rate to be used in discounted cash flow analysis. It is generally considered that the nature of the proposed investment determines which of these measures should be used.

The *WACC* is considered to be appropriate in the case where the new project is in the same business as the investing firm/individual. It is used in the case where the proposed investment is not expected to alter the financial structure or leverage of the business. That means that the investor is expected to have the same level of business risk with this project as already exists. The firm can retain the same debt/equity ratio (i.e. have the same leverage). It is therefore a weighted value of the cost of debt (e.g. through the banking system) and the cost of equity (e.g. through finance raised by issuing shares in the company). Equity financing typically carries a risk premium and has a higher cost to the firm. These two forms of capital sources with differences in costs are averaged out to give the *WACC*. This becomes the rate of discount (r) used in cash flow analysis.

The *CAPM*, on the other hand, is generally considered to be appropriate for projects that are not in the same business as the investing firm/individual. This is because it relates to costs that are market driven (i.e. outside the investing firm). The *CAPM* therefore adds a risk premium to the expected return on the equity of the investing firm/individual that raises the cost above the risk free rate for the cost of capital.

The *WACC* tends to be the more popular of the two. However, in many developing countries or newly emerging market economies, or in less sophisticated capital markets, the rate of discount tends to be determined by the rate of interest which the investor may be able to obtain from the banking system.

For a social project, the market interest rate may not be considered appropriate since it may be considered that there is the existence of market failure. In this case, the chosen 'shadow' interest rate may be described as that which measures society's rate of time preference. A society's rate of time preference is said to be 10 per cent per annum if the society is considered to be indifferent between $1,000 now and $1,100 next year. This social rate of discount is therefore, to some extent, arbitrary and subjective. Nevertheless, in the presence of market failure, some divergence between the private and social rates of discount can be expected and a shadow rate must be found.

Once the rate of discount is selected, the cash flow technique can be applied to the problem of selecting and ranking investment projects through the use of several investment criteria. The criteria are used principally to answer two questions required to facilitate investment decision making:

- Is the project suitable for selection? That is, will it contribute to the profitability of the firm (or benefit the society, in the case of a social project)?
- Which project(s), from among a number of alternative projects that could be undertaken, is the most suitable for selection (i.e. will give the greatest benefits)?

The investor may employ one or more of the available investment criteria to assist in making this determination.

16.4 INVESTMENT CRITERIA CHOICES

There are several investment criteria available to potential investors. The most popular of these criteria, the Net Present Value (*NPV*), the Internal Rate of Return (*IRR*), the Benefit–Cost Ratio (*CBR*)/Profitability Index (*PI*) and the Payback Period (*PP*) are considered in more detail.

16.4.1 Criterion 1 – the Net Present Value (*NPV*)

The Net Present Value (*NPV*) is a highly popular investment criterion for private and public sector decision making on new projects. The *NPV* may be identified as the sum of the net benefits (β_t), suitably discounted to the present, minus the initial investment of the project. In this case the formula includes the initial time period ($t = 0$) when the investment outlay (β_0) is made. At this initial time period, the net benefit should be negative, that is, it should represent only an outflow of funds (costs) as the investment is made.

The stream of net benefits (β) is now represented as:

$$\beta_0, \beta_1, \beta_2, \ldots, \beta_n$$

Thus the formula for finding the Net Present Value becomes:

$$NPV = \frac{\beta_0}{(1+r)^0} + \frac{\beta_1}{(1+r)^1} + \frac{\beta_2}{(1+r)^2} + \cdots + \frac{\beta_n}{(1+r)^n}$$

or:

$$NPV = \sum_{t=0}^{n} \frac{\beta_t}{(1+r)^t}$$

Since any number raised to the power 0 is equal to 1, then:

$$\frac{\beta_0}{(1+r)^0} = \frac{\beta_0}{1} = \beta_0.$$

It is therefore possible to re-write the *NPV* formula for practical purposes as:

$$NPV = \beta_0 + \frac{\beta_1}{(1+r)^1} + \frac{\beta_2}{(1+r)^2} + \cdots + \frac{\beta_n}{(1+r)^n}$$

16.4.1.1 APPLICATION OF THE *NPV* CRITERION – SINGLE PROJECT

For a single project, the application of the criterion is as follows:

- Where the *NPV* is positive (> 0), the project is acceptable.
- Otherwise, the project should be rejected.

An *NPV* that is greater than zero means that, in today's values, the cash inflows (benefits) over the life of the project exceed the initial cash outflow (costs) and any other cash outflows over the life of the project ***for a given discount rate***. A positive *NPV* therefore means that the investment increases the wealth of the investing firm or individual when compared to the next highest valued alternative (opportunity cost) such as placing the cash in a bank where it will earn a rate of interest equal to the chosen discount rate.

As a corollary, the finding of an *NPV* of zero ($NPV = 0$) means that there is no difference between choice of the project under consideration and using the funds in the next best alternative. Further, the finding of a negative *NPV* ($NPV < 0$) means that the investor would be better off not undertaking the proposed project as the opportunity cost is greater than the benefits. It should be realized that this all depends critically on the accuracy of the data used and the guesstimates made about future receipts and costs as well on the appropriate choice of a discount rate.

16.4.1.2 APPLICATION OF THE *NPV* CRITERION – MULTIPLE PROJECTS

In selecting from among alternative or competing projects, the *NPV* may be used to rank all projects with *NPV* greater than zero (i.e. all acceptable projects). The higher the *NPV*, the higher the rank of the project, irrespective of the initial investment outlay on that project. Projects are selected from the highest ranked and the number of projects selected depends on the quantum of funds available for investment outlay.

Consider five proposed projects, *A*, *B*, *C*, *D* and *E* with computed *NPV*s as set out in Table 16.1.

Projects *A*, *B* and *C* all have positive *NPV*s and are therefore ranked. Projects *D* and *E* with zero and negative *NPV* respectively are not to be considered, are therefore not ranked and should not be undertaken by the investor under the circumstances.

Project *B* has the highest *NPV* ($50.00) and therefore, according to the use of the criterion, it is the most valuable project to be chosen by the investing firm or individual. Hence it is ranked #1, which is the highest rank and is given the highest priority for selection. That this project requires the highest cash outlay of all the projects is not strictly relevant under *NPV*. This only comes into consideration when applying the benefit/cost ratio criterion (see below). What is important here is that undertaking the project increases the wealth of the investor by the greatest absolute amount. Project *A*,

BOX 16.1 COMPUTATION OF NET PRESENT VALUE – AN EXAMPLE

A young investor needs to make a decision on whether to accept or reject a proposal for a project to rake the neighbours' gardens during the autumn (fall) each year. The proposed project has a life of two time periods (years) beyond the original investment period. The original investment is $200.00. This gives $(\beta_0) = -\$200$ and has a negative value since the initial investment represents an outflow of funds (cost). The net benefits (β_t) over the two years $(t = 1, 2)$ may be set out as follows:

	Year 1	*Year 2*
Net benefit stream	$50.00 $(= \beta_1)$	$200.00 $(= \beta_2)$

The investing firm has determined that the appropriate discount rate is ten percent $(r = 0.1)$.

Applying the *NPV* formula for the initial investment time period $(t = 0)$ plus two additional time periods $(t = 1, 2)$, the *NPV* is computed as:

$$NPV = \sum_{t=0}^{2} \frac{\beta_t}{(1+r)^t}$$

or:

$$NPV = \frac{\beta_0}{(1+r)^0} + \frac{\beta_1}{(1+r)^1} + \frac{\beta_2}{(1+r)^2}$$

This becomes:

$$NPV = \frac{-\$200}{(1+0.1)^0} + \frac{\$50}{(1+0.1)^1} + \frac{\$200}{(1+0.1)^2}$$

This gives:

$$NPV = \frac{-200}{1} + \frac{50}{1.1} + \frac{200}{1.21}$$

Thus, for this project the *NPV* is:

$$NPV = 10.74$$

Since the $NPV > 0$, the project is acceptable. This means that the $200.00 invested in this project today brings in a cash flow over the next two years equivalent to $210.74 in today's values. This is $10.74 ($210.74 – $200.00) more than the investor could earn in the next best alternative for use of the funds. The investor is therefore wealthier by $10.74 in today's values.

Table 16.1 Project ranking by net present value

Project	Original outlay	*NPV* value	Rank
Project *A*	\$500	\$30	#2
Project *B*	\$1000	\$50	#1
Project *C*	\$750	\$20	#3
Project *D*	\$300	\$0	—
Project *E*	\$200	−\$10	—

with an *NPV* of \$30.00 and project *C* with an *NPV* of \$20.00, are consequently ranked lower at #2 and #3 respectively.

Based on this ranking, the number of projects chosen by the investing firm/individual depends on the cash available for investment in these projects. If, for example, there were only \$1,200.00 available for investment, then Project *B* alone would be the appropriate choice. However, if the amount should extend to \$1,500.00, then the investor ought to undertake both Project *B* and Project *A*. With at least \$2,250 available, then all three ranked projects could be undertaken and the rank order would be irrelevant.

16.4.1.3 PROBLEMS OR CAUTIONS WITH THE USE OF THE *NPV*

The *NPV* criterion is highly popular and valuable as a tool for investment decision-making. However, there are some problems and cautions associated with its use.

One concern is that the *NPV* criterion assumes that there is no constraint to the availability of capital. Once the *NPV* is positive, the project is acceptable regardless of the quantum of investment funds required.

Principally among the other concerns are issues relating to the selection of the discount rate and the effect of the pattern of net benefit streams over the life of the project on the ranking of projects. These concerns are as follows:

- *Single project* – The acceptability of any project depends critically on the discount rate chosen.
- *Multiple projects* – The ranking of projects with different patterns in their net benefit streams may change depending on the discount rate chosen.

Single project

With regard to the decision on a single project, it can be shown that the *NPV* value of a project with a given investment stream depends on the discount rate chosen. This is more pronounced where the net benefits fluctuate greatly from one time period to the next.

Consider, for example, a project with an original outlay (β_0) and a net benefit stream as set out in Table 16.2.

Then, a discount rate of 5 per cent gives:

$$NPV = \frac{-\$200}{(1+0.05)^0} + \frac{\$0}{(1+0.05)^1} + \frac{\$350}{(1+0.05)^2}$$

Table 16.2 *NPV* project data for single project

	$t = 0$	$t = 1$	$t = 2$
Project net-benefit stream	$(\beta_0) = -\$200.00$	$(\beta_1) = \$0.00$	$(\beta_2) = \$350.00$

or:

$$NPV = -\$200 + 0 + \$317.46$$

This gives a value of:

$$NPV = \$117.46$$

Hence at the discount rate of 5 per cent, the project with this stream is acceptable.

Consider, now, a discount rate of 40 per cent. The *NPV* becomes:

$$NPV = \frac{-\$200}{(1+0.40)^0} + \frac{\$0}{(1+0.40)^1} + \frac{\$350}{(1+0.40)^2}$$

or:

$$NPV = -\$200 + 0 + \$178.57$$

This gives a value of:

$$NPV = -\$21.43$$

This indicated that at a discount rate of 40 per cent, the same project that was acceptable at a rate of 5 per cent is now unacceptable. A major caution therefore is with the selection of the appropriate discount rate.

Multiple projects

In the case of multiple projects, the choice of discount rate can seriously affect not only whether a project is acceptable or not, but how the projects are ranked for selection. The following should be noted.

Where the projects under consideration have only one time period beyond the original outlay period (i.e. $t = 0$, $t = 1$), any rate of discount will rank the projects by *NPV* in the same order even with a change in the acceptability of some projects.

Where the projects under consideration have two or more time periods beyond the initial time period, the ranking of projects by *NPV* could change as the rate of discount is changed.

Where multiple-period projects have net benefit profiles that are very different in terms of how the values fluctuate (i.e. the pattern in the changes in net benefits from one time period to the next in terms of high/low or positive/negative values) then the ranking may be altered dramatically as the discount rate is changed.

Table 16.3 *NPV* project data for multiple projects

	$t=0$	$t=1$	$t=2$
Project *A* net-benefit stream	$(\beta_0) = -\$200.00$	$(\beta_1) = \$0.00$	$(\beta_2) = \$350.00$
Project *B* net-benefit stream	$(\beta_0) = -\$200.00$	$(\beta_1) = \$320.00$	$(\beta_2) = \$0.00$

This may be illustrated for two projects (*A* and *B*) with net benefit (β) streams as set out in Table 16.3.

For these two projects, the net-benefit streams have very different profiles. Project *A* reaps all the net benefits in time period 2 and nothing in time period 1, whereas Project *B* reaps all the net benefits in time period 1 and nothing in time period 2.

Consider, then, the difference in the ranking of these two projects at discount rates of 5 per cent and 20 per cent.

At a discount rate of 5 per cent, the *NPV*s for projects *A* and *B* (NPV_A and NPV_B) are computed as follows:

$$NPV_A = \frac{-\$200}{(1+0.05)^0} + \frac{\$0}{(1+0.05)^1} + \frac{\$350}{(1+0.05)^2} = -\$200 + \$317.46 = \$117.46$$

and:

$$NPV_B = \frac{-\$200}{(1+0.05)^0} + \frac{\$320}{(1+0.05)^1} + \frac{\$0}{(1+0.05)^2} = -\$200 + \$304.76 = \$104.76$$

Thus at the 5 per cent rate of discount, Project *A* ranks above Project *B*.

Now consider a discount rate of 20 per cent. The respective *NPV*s for the two projects become:

$$NPV_A = \frac{-\$200}{(1+0.2)^0} + \frac{\$0}{(1+0.2)^1} + \frac{\$350}{(1+0.2)^2} = -\$200 + \$243.06 = \$43.06$$

and:

$$NPV_B = \frac{-\$200}{(1+0.2)^0} + \frac{\$320}{(1+0.2)^1} + \frac{\$0}{(1+0.2)^2} = -\$200 + \$266.67 = \$66.67$$

This shows that at a discount rate of 20 per cent, Project *B* now ranks above Project *A*.

Further to this, as explained previously, a change in discount rate can move a project from its acceptable status to unacceptable. Hence, not only would the ranking change but one or more of the projects being ranked could be taken out of the ranking altogether. This confirms that great care must be taken in choosing a discount rate.

The differences in the net-benefit stream profiles in the above projects are somewhat extreme, but the variations in rankings occur where, for each project, there is great variation in net-benefits from one year to the other and even more so if the net-benefits alternate in sign over the years of the life of the project.

As a corollary, attention should be paid to the fact that the greater the similarity of the net-benefit stream profile for different projects, the more unlikely it is for the ranking to change at the discount rate changes.

Further to this, it may be noted that there exists a particular discount rate lying between 5 per cent and 20 per cent for which the two projects net-benefit streams will be the same Net Present Value. The value of this discount rate (r) can be derived mathematically as:

$$-200 + \frac{350}{(1+r)^2} = -200 + \frac{320}{(1+r)^1}$$

$$r = 9.38\%$$

Consequently, at a discount rate of 9.38 per cent both Project A and Project B would have the same *NPV*. If this were the chosen discount rate, then these two projects would have the same rank and, with limited funds, the investing firm or individual would have to find another means of selecting one of the two projects.

What is happening is that Project A, with its gains extending further into the future than Project B ($t = 2$ as opposed to $t = 1$), is more heavily discounted as r is increased. This causes Project A's *NPV* to fall faster than Project B's *NPV* as r increases. Hence, whereas at a low value of r the *NPV* of Project A will exceed that of Project B, this reverses at a higher value of r. It follows then, that at some value of r (r^*), the *NPV* of both projects will be the same. This is illustrated in Figure 16.1 where r^* is the equilibrating discount rate which gives the common *NPV* for the two projects.

16.4.2 Investment Criterion 2 – the Internal Rate of Return (IRR)

The Internal Rate of Return (*IRR*) is another measure of profitability. It refers to the 'yield' of the project.

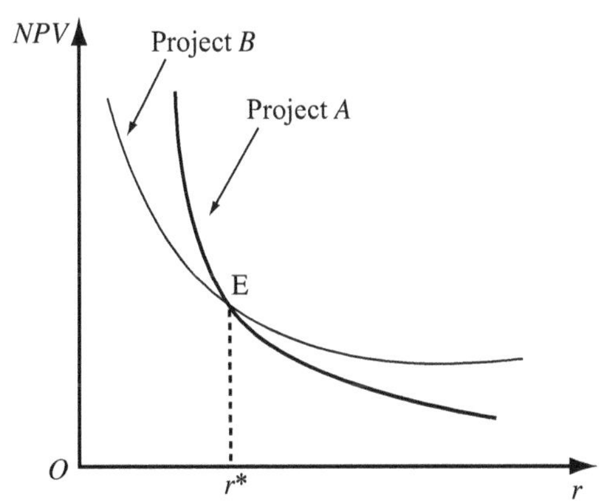

Figure 16.1
Equilibrating discount rate for two income streams with different payback profiles

The concept of yield may be explained with reference to an instrument of investment such as a security or bond. Where a bond is issued and pays a dividend or interest of 10 per cent per annum in perpetuity, it is said that the yield on that bond is 10 per cent. Considering the bond as an investment project, the 10 per cent yield is, in essence, the Internal Rate of Return (*IRR*) of the project.

16.4.2.1 DEFINITION

The Internal Rate of Return or yield of a project may be defined as that rate of discount which makes the present value (*PV*) of the benefits over the life of a project exactly equal to the present value of costs. Alternatively, it may be defined as the rate of discount (r) which makes the *NPV* of the project exactly equal to zero.

Consider the example of a bond paying an annual rate (yield) of 10 per cent. If the bond costs \$100.00, it will pay \$10.00 every year *ad infinitum*. Hence, after the initial outflow of \$100.00, the cash inflow, or net benefit, in every time period from $t = 1$ to $t = \infty$ is \$10.00. This \$10.00 discounted *ad infinitum* at 10 per cent gives \$100.00, which is equivalent to the original outlay on the bond of \$100.00 thereby making the *NPV* of the bond project equal to zero.

Formally, it may be said that for an investment with a stream of net benefits (β) represented as:

$$\beta_0, \beta_1, \beta_2, \ldots, \beta_n$$

Thus finding the *IRR* becomes finding the value of r which gives:

$$NPV = \frac{\beta_0}{(1+r)^0} + \frac{\beta_1}{(1+r)^1} + \frac{\beta_2}{(1+r)^2} + \cdots + \frac{\beta_n}{(1+r)^n} = 0$$

or where:

$$NPV = \sum_{t=0}^{n} \frac{\beta_t}{(1+r)^t} = 0$$

The objective, then, is to solve the equation(s) above to find the value of r that gives $NPV = 0$.

16.4.2.2 THE 'HURDLE' RATE OF DISCOUNT

However, while it may be difficult to understand why an investigator would wish to invest in a project if the *NPV* is zero, it must be recognized that, using the example given above, the *NPV* goes to zero when the rate of interest (i.e. rate of discount) or yield on the bond is 10 per cent. What this means is that the *NPV* would be greater than zero if the discount rate were less than 10 per cent. The investing firm/individual must therefore decide on a target rate of discount that represents the opportunity cost of investing in the project, just as would have to be done when using the *NPV*. Once the appropriate target rate is determined, it becomes the 'hurdle' rate for purposes of the *IRR*. This means the project would have to jump over or exceed this rate in order to be acceptable.

The 'hurdle' rate may therefore be described as the private (or social) opportunity cost of capital. It is important to the use of this criterion in that it becomes the standard by which the yield of the project is judged.

16.4.2.3 APPLICATION OF THE *IRR* CRITERION – SINGLE PROJECT

For a single project, the *IRR* decision tool is applied in a manner similar to that of the *NPV*. This gives an answer to whether a proposed project is acceptable or not acceptable. In this case, however, the rate of discount (r) is now referred to as the yield of the project and the solution is to find this rate rather than to have it pre-determined. Once r is found, it does not by itself indicate whether the proposed project is acceptable or not and has little or no meaning without a 'hurdle' rate for comparison. Once this hurdle rate has been determined, then the computed r must be compared with the 'hurdle' rate.

The decision condition for acceptance becomes:

- If $r >$ hurdle rate, the project is acceptable.
- Otherwise, the project is not acceptable.

An r greater than the hurdle rate means that, at the hurdle rate, the project would have a positive *NPV* (i.e. it would increase the wealth of the investor compared to placing the funds in the next best alternative). Moreover, with regard to the *IRR*, the r being greater than the hurdle rate means that the proposed project gives the investor a greater yield on the investment than it could earn in the next highest valued alternative (e.g. say, in a bank interest bearing account).

16.4.2.4 APPLICATION OF THE *IRR* CRITERION – PROJECT SELECTION AND RANKING FOR MULTIPLE PROJECTS

For multiple projects, all projects with *IRR* higher than the hurdle rate are ranked for selection. The criteria for selection would be as follows:

- Assign the highest rank (highest priority for selection) to the project with the highest *IRR* above the hurdle rate.
- Set out the original cash investment outlay for each project on the list of acceptable projects.
- Select, from the highest ranked downwards on the priority list, as many projects in the rank order such that the total cash available for investment in the projects is not exceeded.

16.4.2.5 PROBLEMS OR CAUTIONS WITH THE USE OF THE *IRR*

There are some problems which afflict the *IRR* and tend to moderate its use as an investment decision tool. These include the following.

BOX 16.2 COMPUTATION OF INTERNAL RATE OF RETURN – AN EXAMPLE

Consider a proposed project that has a life of two time periods (years) beyond the original investment period. The original investment is \$100.00. This gives (β_0) = −\$100 and has a negative value since the initial investment represents an outflow of funds (cost). The net benefits (β_t) over the two years ($t = 1, 2$) may be set out as follows:

	Year 1	***Year 2***
Net benefit stream	\$0.00 ($= \beta_1$)	\$115.00 ($= \beta_2$)

The investing firm/individual has determined that the appropriate hurdle rate is 5 per cent ($r = 0.05$).

Applying the IRR formula for the initial investment time period ($t = 0$) plus two additional time periods ($t = 1, 2$), the *IRR* is computed as:

$$\sum_{t=0}^{2} \frac{\beta_t}{(1+r)^t} = 0$$

or:

$$\frac{\beta_0}{(1+r)^0} + \frac{\beta_1}{(1+r)^1} + \frac{\beta_2}{(1+r)^2} = 0$$

This becomes:

$$\frac{-\$100}{(1+r)^0} + \frac{\$0}{(1+r)^1} + \frac{\$115}{(1+r)^2} = 0.$$

Thus, for this project the *IRR* is:

$$IRR = 7.23\%$$

With a hurdle rate of 5 per cent, the computed *IRR* of 7.23 per cent means that the project is acceptable. This means that the \$100.00 invested in this project today brings in a return to the investor of 7.23 per cent per annum over the life of the project which is greater than the investor could obtain from the next highest yielding alternative (5 per cent). Moreover, it indirectly says that, at the discount rate of 5 per cent, the *NPV* would be greater than zero. This means that the cash flow over the two years of the life of the project, when discounted at 5 per cent, would be greater than the \$100.00 invested today (\$104.31).

Single projects

The *IRR* tends to be computationally complex. It requires the solution to a difficult algebraic equation and, in all but the simplest formulations, requires solution by computer or advanced calculator. It does not easily lend itself to mental calculations or to 'back of the envelope' computations. Its solution requires a polynomial equation. In general, it cannot be solved analytically but only iteratively.

The choice of a target or hurdle rate is critical. The criterion is useless without a target rate for comparison.

The *IRR* is an average yield so complications arise where the stream of net benefits of a project alternate in sign (i.e. some time periods have net inflows of cash while others have net outflows). During periods of net outflows, a lower, rather than a higher *IRR* is more desirable since money needs to be borrowed during such times, hence a lower interest rate (r) is preferable. Overall, then, it is not clear whether a higher or lower *IRR* is the best for such a project.

There may be multiple *IRRs* for the same project (i.e. for a single stream of net benefits). This occurs when the cost outlays are not all done at the beginning of the project and some of the net benefits during the later part of the life of the project carry a negative value (i.e. represent a net cash outflow).

Figure 16.2 illustrates the case.

In Figure 16.2, as the discount rate (r) is increased the *NPV* of the project moves from a negative value to zero. This occurs at the discount rate r_1 and gives the *IRR* for the project. Beyond this rate, the *NPV* becomes positive and, as the discount rate continues to be increased, the *NPV* reaches a peak and then begins to fall. As the *NPV* falls it again reaches a value of zero at rate r_2. This gives the second *IRR* for the project. Using the definition of *IRR* as the rate of discount that makes the *NPV* equal to zero, both rates r_1 and r_2 are equally valid as the *IRR* for the project. This can be a serious complication and, since it occurs when there are net cash outflows in the later part of the life of a project, tends to make the usefulness of the *IRR* criterion limited to projects where the net outflows are incurred in the early part of the life of the project with the net inflows later on.

It may be noted that there is some contention that only the second point r_2 should be considered the correct rate. This is where the $NPV = 0$ and the *NPV* is declining. It can,

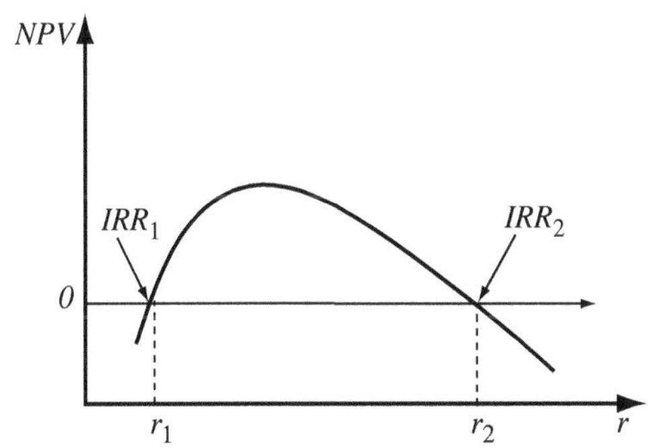

Figure 16.2
Multiple *IRR*s for a single income stream

however, be shown that for certain net benefit streams, there may exist more than one point where both these conditions hold.

Multiple projects

In dealing with multiple projects, the *IRR* presents additional complications. These include:

- The *IRR* does not tell which project is more valuable in today's values as the *NPV* does. It tells which rate of discount makes the *NPV* go to zero thereby giving the yield of the project. It means that lower values of the discount rate would give a positive *NPV* but does not set out these values. Hence, it is not clear how the different projects would increase the wealth of the investor.
- The way in which the *IRR* varies, depending on the pattern and sign of inflows and outflows of a project, makes it of limited use when comparing mutually exclusive projects where these projects have very different patterns of inflows and outflows.
- Two different projects with very different net benefit streams may have the same *IRR* since the *IRR* reflects only the average yield over the life of the project. For example, in one project there may be net benefits reaped each year of the life of the project, whereas, in another project, there may be no net benefits until the last year of the project. This could give the same *IRR*. Once they both have the same *IRR*, they would be considered equivalent. This makes it difficult to establish meaningful equivalences across projects that are to be ranked.
- Risk is often not taken into account in comparing multiple projects. One project may have a higher yield but much greater risk.
- The *IRR* does not consider how the cash generated during the life of the project is reinvested. A newer method, the Modified *IRR* (*MIRR*) is often applied to correct for this. The *MIRR* assumes that the cash generated is reinvested at the cost of capital. This is usually the Weighted Average Cost of Capital (*WACC*) as discussed earlier.

16.4.3 Investment Criterion 3 – the Benefit–Cost Ratio (*BCR*) or Profitability Index (*PI*)

The Benefit–Cost Ratio (*BCR*) and the Profitability Index (*PI*) usually refer to the same criterion. In addition, terms such as Profit Investment Ratio and Value Investment Ratio are sometimes used.

This criterion, although usually considered as a separate method for evaluating a proposed investment, may, in effect, be more aptly described as a modification of the Net Present Value (*NPV*) criterion. In essence, it serves to standardize *NPV* and may be considered to be an improvement on the *NPV*.

16.4.3.1 DEFINITION OF *BCR/PI*

In its more popular formulation the Benefit–Cost Ratio or Profitability Index may be defined as the present value (*PV*) of future cash flows divided by the value of the initial investment outlay (*I*).

Recall that the formula for the NPV is:

$$NPV = \sum_{t=0}^{n} \frac{\beta_t}{(1+r)^t}$$

or:

$$NPV = \frac{\beta_0}{(1+r)^0} + \frac{\beta_1}{(1+r)^1} + \frac{\beta_2}{(1+r)^2} + \cdots + \frac{\beta_n}{(1+r)^n}$$

The *BCR/PI* requires only the discounted future values in its numerator for comparison with the initial outlay and therefore eliminates the first term which represents the initial outlay on the project in time period $t = 0$:

$$\frac{\beta_0}{(1+r)^0}$$

Hence the PV rather than the NPV is used. This is:

$$PV = \frac{\beta_1}{(1+r)^1} + \frac{\beta_2}{(1+r)^2} + \cdots + \frac{\beta_n}{(1+r)^n}$$

Alternatively, the NPV may be used with the original outlay, represented as (β_0), added back to it. In this formulation, however, whereas β_0 is entered into the NPV formula as a negative value (cash outflow), it retains a positive value when used to represent the initial investment in the *BCR* formulation. Hence:

$$I = (-1)\beta_0$$

Using *BCR* and *PI* interchangeably, they may therefore be written as either:

$$BCR = \frac{PV}{I}$$

or:

$$BCR = \frac{NPV + I}{I}$$

The *BCR* or Profitability Index may, under some circumstances, be considered an improvement on the NPV because it standardizes the wealth gain from the proposed investment project by measuring the size of the gain against the size of the initial investment that generates that gain. It therefore measures the value for money of a proposed project and is particularly useful where the investor is facing a capital constraint and where alternative projects are being compared.

It is useful to note that there is less popular alternative formulation of the Benefit–Cost Ratio in which it is specified simply as the Net Present Value (NPV) divided by the initial investment outlay (I). This formulation serves much the same purpose as the one above and gives much the same information as the more popular formulations above, particularly with regard to the ranking of projects.

16.4.3.2 APPLICATION OF THE *BCR/PI* CRITERION – SINGLE PROJECT

Using the standard formulation given above, the condition for acceptance of a single proposed project is:

$$BCR > 1$$

The requirement for this condition to hold is $PV > I$ which means that the future discounted net benefits of the proposed project are greater than the initial outlay on the project. This means that when the initial outlay is subtracted in the *NPV* formulation, the result becomes:

$$NPV > 0$$

Hence, both the *NPV* and the *BCR/PI* give the same answer for the acceptability of a single project.

As an example, consider a project with a net-benefit stream, as given in Table 16.4, with the time period $t = 0$ representing the initial outlay.

Then, with a chosen discount rate of 10 per cent, the *NPV* is:

$$NPV = -\$1000 + \$1,302.78 = \$302.78$$

Since $NPV > 0$, the conclusion is that the project is acceptable.

By the same token, the *BCR/PI* gives:

$$BCR = \frac{1302.78}{1000} = 1.30$$

Hence, since $BCR > 1$, the conclusion is the same (i.e. that the project is acceptable). The major difference is that, whereas the *NPV* says that the investor would be \$302.78 wealthier by making the investment in the proposed project, the *BCR* shows directly that the gain (profitability) of the investment is in the order of 30 per cent based on today's values.

16.4.3.3 APPLICATION OF THE *BCR/PI* CRITERION – MULTIPLE PROJECTS

It is in the area of ranking multiple projects that the difference between the *NPV* and the *BCR/PI* is more pronounced.

Table 16.4 Data stream for comparison between *NPV* and *BCR/PI*

	$t=0$	$t=1$	$t=2$	$t=3$
Net-benefit stream	$(\beta_0) = -\$1000.00$	$(\beta_1) = \$400.00$	$(\beta_2) = \$500.00$	$(\beta_3) = \$700.00$

It was noted earlier that, with the ranking of projects by *NPV*, the higher the absolute value of the *NPV*, the higher the project is ranked regardless of the initial outlay it requires. The *BCR/PI* criterion standardizes the gains by relating the Present Value of the benefits for each project to its initial outlay. This can completely rearrange the ranking of projects. This criterion tells not simply which project will increase the investor's wealth the most but which would use the available funds most efficiently and is particularly useful in a situation where there is a capital constraint by the investor.

The *BCR/PI* can completely change the ranking of projects from that given by the *NPV*. Using the information set out in Table 16.1, Project *A* has an original outlay of \$500.00 and a *NPV* of \$30.00, whereas Project *B* has an original outlay of \$1000 and a *NPV* of \$50.00. Based on this information, the ranking by *NPV* gives Project *B* the higher ranking because of the higher *NPV*. Thus:

$$NPV_B > NPV_A$$

However, when ranking is done by *BCR/PI*, the ranking is reversed. This is because for Project *A* and for Project *B* the BCR_A and BCR_B respectively are:

$$BCR_A = \frac{530}{500} = 1.06$$

and:

$$BCR_B = \frac{1050}{1000} = 1.05$$

This gives:

$$BCR_A > BCR_B$$

Consequently, where an investing firm/individual is operating without a capital constraint, the higher *NPV* given by project *B* means that the firm can increase its wealth more by undertaking project *B*. On the other hand, the higher *BCR* for project *A* allows an investor with a capital constraint to realize that Project *A* brings greater profitability as there is a greater proportionate increase in wealth relative to the outlay on the project.

16.4.4 Investment Criterion 4 – the Payback Period (*PP*)

The payback period measures the length of time (number of time periods) in which it takes to recoup an investment outlay. It is sometimes described as the length of time it takes for the benefits from a project to be exactly equal to costs.

The payback rule is to simply calculate the time (t) that it takes to recoup the initial investment (β_0). This rule typically does not involve the discounting of the future net benefits but is a simple computation of the number of time periods into the future until the initial outlay is recouped.

A more sophisticated version of the *PP* criterion uses discounting of the future net benefits. In that formulation the payback period may be described as the length of time it takes for the *NPV* of the project to be equal to zero.

16.4.4.1 APPLICATION OF THE PAYBACK PERIOD CRITERION – SINGLE PROJECT

For a single project the payback rule is applied as follows:

- Compute the number of time periods in the future ($t = ?$) that it takes to make the future cash flows equal to the initial cash outlay on the project.
- Determine the maximum length of time the investor is willing to wait for the initial cash outflow to be recouped (t^*).
- If $t < t^*$, accept project.
- Otherwise, reject.

The critical determinant here is the acceptable number of time periods on which acceptability is to be based. Furthermore, no attention to the cash flows beyond the time period at which the original investment is recouped. Hence, consider a project with a stream of net benefits as set out in Table 16.5.

The project has an economic life of five years. However, the initial investment of $1,000.00 is recouped by the end of the third year ($400 + 400 + 600 > 1000$). The remaining cash flows for the fourth and fifth time periods of the life of the project are ignored. If the target number of time periods for the recouping of the initial outlay is greater than three, then the project is considered to be acceptable (e.g. if $t^* = 4$).

However, an assumption can be made to the effect that the time periods are individually divisible. This would allow the individual time periods to be broken down to identify the exact period at which the payback occurs. In this case, only a $200.00 amount is required in time period three ($t = 3$). This is one-third of the net benefits for that time period. Thus, the payback period could be expressed as:

$$t = 2\tfrac{1}{3}$$

Measuring it in this way makes the project acceptable even if $t^* = 3$ is the desired payback period.

Where discounted future values are used, the process is the same except that the future (discounted) values will be smaller and hence the payback period will be longer. Projects found acceptable without discounting may no longer be acceptable when discounting is used unless the desired payback period is adjusted.

Table 16.5 Data stream for application of payback period criterion

	$t = 0$ (β_0)	$t = 1$ (β_1)	$t = 2$ (β_2)	$t = 3$ (β_3)	$t = 4$ (β_4)	$t = 5$ (β_5)
Net-benefit stream	–$1000.00	$400.00	$400.00	$600.00	$700.00	$700.00

16.4.4.2 APPLICATION OF THE PAYBACK PERIOD CRITERION – MULTIPLE PROJECTS

For multiple projects the procedure for the application of the payback period is as follows:

- Compute the payback period for each project.
- Rank projects by payback period such that projects with the shortest payback period are given the highest rank.
- Determine the maximum payback period acceptable (t^*).
- Mark as acceptable all projects with a payback period less than the desired payback period limit.
- In the case where there is no capital constraint, accept all projects which meet the criterion.
- In the case where there is a capital constraint, give priority to the projects with the shortest payback period until the capital availability is exhausted.

This approach tends to ignore the differences in original outlays for the individual projects and focuses on the recovery time. It should be expected that projects with a larger initial cash outlay should have a longer payback period. The *PP* criterion therefore, is more appropriate to the comparison of alternative projects which have a similar initial cash outlay.

16.4.4.3 PROBLEMS OR CAUTIONS WITH THE USE OF THE PAYBACK PERIOD

The following are the major drawbacks identified with the use of the payback period criterion:

- In its typical formulation, there is no adjustment to take into account the time value of money. The length of time to receive the payback does not discount the future cash flows from the project.
- Once the payback is achieved, the remaining cash flows for the rest of the period during which the payback is reached are ignored. Hence all the incremental cash flows are ignored.
- The time chosen for the payback is done arbitrarily. This is subjective and determined by the investor without reference to any objective benchmark or one that is objective or economically justifiable.
- In comparing mutually exclusive projects, the failure to discount future cash flows presents some inconsistency in comparing values and ensuring value maximization.

Discounted payback period (DPP)

This may be considered a sub-criterion of the Payback Period criterion. It seeks to remedy one of the more blatant deficiencies of the standard Payback Period method. In this approach, the net cash flows are discounted using the standard rate of discount (or a rate that represents the Weighted Average Cost of Capital (*WACC*).

This method (the *DPP*), although representing an improvement on the standard *PP* method, still suffers from the failure to use all incremental cash flows during the period in which the payback occurs and the failure to use an economically justifiable benchmark for determining the acceptable length of the payback period.

16.5 CHOICE OF INVESTMENT CRITERIA

There are advantages and disadvantages to the use of each of the four criteria discussed above. The Net Present Value criterion and the Internal Rate of Return criterion tend to be the most popular. However, they all answer slightly different questions and so the choice of criterion depends on the information required by the investing firm in order for a decision to be made.

In summary, the Net Present Value (*NPV*) criterion reveals the extent to which the project is expected to increase the wealth of the investor in today's values. The Internal Rate of Return (*IRR*), on the other hand, gives information on the anticipated yield of the project over its life. The Benefit–Cost Ratio (*BCR*) or Profitability Index (*PI*) shows how the future wealth increase from the proposed project is related to the initial investment outlay and the Payback Period (*PP*) shows how soon the initial outlay on the project will be recovered.

Except for the *NPV* and the *BCR/PI*, the answer to the question of whether to accept or reject the proposed project will not necessarily be the same for different criteria. Hence, it is critical to determine the most appropriate criterion in the circumstances.

With regard to ranking, the criteria can all give different ranking of proposed projects. It is useful to note that *NPV* and *IRR* will give the same ranking where the projects under consideration have only two time periods ($t = 0$ *and* $t = 1$) or, more specifically, where there is just one time period into the future. Beyond that, the one-to-one correspondence between *NPV* and *IRR* breaks down. Hence, for projects with more than two time periods, great care must be taken with the choice of criterion.

Investors may use multiple criteria. Table 16.6 sets out the difference in the ranking and the information provided for analysis.

The application of the criteria to determine rank and acceptance of each of five projects, all with different investment outlays and having four time periods ($t = 0, 1, 2, 3$), may be done using Table 16.6. The table shows that according to the *NPV*, using a discount rate of 10 per cent, project *A* has the highest rank, followed by projects *B* and *C* (*NPV* = $60.00, $50.00 and $35.00 respectively). Projects *D* and *E* do not have positive *NPV*s and so are ranked since they are not acceptable. Based on this ranking, an investor for whom there is no meaningful capital constraint within the specific context would be advised to pursue all three of projects *A*, *B* and *C*. If the investor has only, say, $1500.00 available, then only project *A* should be adopted while projects *B* and *C* should be excluded.

Table 16.6 Project ranking by alternative criteria

Project	(β_0) $	(β_1) $	(β_2) $	(β_3) $	*PV* ($r = 0.1$) $	*NPV* ($r = 0.1$) $	*NPV Rank*	*IRR %*	*BCR/PI* (*PV/I*) ($r = 0.1$)	*PP* (*Years*)
A	−1000	30	350	990	1060	60	#1	12%	1.06	2.63
B	−750	500	400	20	800	50	#2	15%	1.12	1.63
C	−500	100	165	410	535	35	#3	13%	1.07	2.57
D	−300	100	130	135	300	0	—	10%	1.00	2.52
E	−200	75	70	85	−190	−10	—	7%	0.95	2.65

Ranking by *IRR* changes the priority listing of the projects. The highest-ranking project is now project *B*, while projects *C* and *A* follow in that order. They have yields of 15 per cent, 13 per cent and 12 per cent respectively (*B*, *C*, *A*). Consider that the 'hurdle' rate for the *IRR* is the same as the discount rate for the *NPV* (10 per cent), then these three projects are also the acceptable projects but in a different order. In this case, project *A*, which was the most preferred under the *NPV*, is now ranked in third place under the *IRR*. Moreover, an investor with a capital budget of $1500.00 as before is now given the information that the two top projects (*B* and *C*) can both be pursued ($750.00 + $500.00 = $1,250.00 < $1,500.00).

The Benefit–Cost Ratio or Profitability Index, a standardized version of the *NPV*, tells a different story from the *NPV*. Here, instead of a ranking of *A*, *B*, *C*, it gives a ranking of *B*, *C*, *A* and, by definition, the same projects must be found to be acceptable. That the *BCR's* ranking is the same as that of the *IRR* is purely co-incidental. The *BCR/PI* shows that, although project *A* gives the absolutely greatest increase in wealth, it is project *B* that gives the greatest proportionate increase relative to the initial cash outlay required. This suggests that project *B* is a more efficient user of the invested cash. This is important for an investor with limited cash for investment. As with the *IRR*, projects *B* and *C* would be the projects of choice when there is a $1,500.00 limit on cash for investment.

Where the investor wants to get the initial outlay back in the shortest possible time, then the Payback Period criterion gives project *B* as the best choice. Here the original investment is recovered in less than two years. Where the investor's aim is to recover the investment outlay in less than three years, all the projects are acceptable. Moreover, assuming that the cash flow comes in at equal intervals throughout the year, then project *D* is the next acceptable (2.52 years). This is a project that has been found unacceptable by every other criterion. It is useful to note that this criterion relegates project *A* to second last place in the priority ranking. This, however, is the project that creates the most wealth and is ranked number one by the *NPV* criterion. This occurs because the *PP* criterion ignores all the cash flows after the payback is reached.

In the example in Table 16.6, project *B* ranks first on three of the four criteria. This may be used as sufficient evidence to determine its acceptability in a capital constraint situation. However, it omits the fact that project *A* increases the investor's wealth the most, given its first place on the *NPV* ranking. Typically, in considering alternative investments, the projects are evaluated on as many criteria as is feasible. Where a project ranks first on all criteria, a clear choice emerges in a capital constraint situation. However, where the rankings change according to criteria, the investor has to determine the principal aim of the investment, in order to make the appropriate decision. In any case, it all rests on the quality of the data used to measure the cash flows over the life of the project.

REVIEW QUESTIONS FOR CHAPTER 16

1 With regard to the techniques of project analysis:

(a) Discuss the concept of cash flow analysis.
(b) Explain how cash flow accounting differs from 'normal' accounting.

(c) Indicate the type of information required for a cash flow analysis.
(d) Set out the differences between private and social cost/benefit analysis.

2 Show and illustrate how the Net Present Value (*NPV*) criterion may be used to:

(a) Assist in the decision on whether a project is acceptable for investment.
(b) Assist in the ranking of projects to be selected for investment.

3 With regard to the Internal Rate of Return (*IRR*):

(a) Attempt a definition of (*IRR*) and show how it may be related to *NPV*.
(b) Show how *IRR* may be used for determining whether a project is acceptable as an investment project.
(c) Identify the major drawbacks to the use of *IRR*.

4 Define the Benefit–Cost Ratio or Profitability Index criterion and discuss how it relates to the *NPV* criterion and whether it should be considered as an improvement over the *NPV*.

5 Examine:

(a) The use of the payback period as an investment criterion pointing out any advantages or drawbacks to its use compared to other criteria.
(b) The differences in the ranking of projects by different criteria and the factors that should influence criteria choice for an individual investor.

RECOMMENDED READING FOR CHAPTER 16

Boardman, A., Greenberg, D., Vining, A. and Weimer, D. (2006) *Cost Benefit Analysis: Concepts and Practice*, 3rd edn, New York: Prentice-Hall.
Jenkins, G. P. (1997) 'Project Analysis and the World Bank', *American Economic Review*, 87(2): 38–42.
McKean, R. N. (1970) 'The Nature of Cost–Benefit Analysis', in Mansfield, E. (ed.) (1985) *Microeconomics – Selected Readings,* New York: Norton, 530–9.
Mishan, E. J and Quah, E. (2007) *Cost-Benefit Analysis* (5th Edn.), London: Routledge.
Prest, A. R. and Turvey, R. (1965) 'Cost–Benefit Analysis: A Survey', *Economic Journal*, 75(300): 683–735.

INDEX

eBooks – at www.eBookstore.tandf.co.uk

A library at your fingertips!

eBooks are electronic versions of printed books. You can store them on your PC/laptop or browse them online.

They have advantages for anyone needing rapid access to a wide variety of published, copyright information.

eBooks can help your research by enabling you to bookmark chapters, annotate text and use instant searches to find specific words or phrases. Several eBook files would fit on even a small laptop or PDA.

NEW: Save money by eSubscribing: cheap, online access to any eBook for as long as you need it.

Annual subscription packages

We now offer special low-cost bulk subscriptions to packages of eBooks in certain subject areas. These are available to libraries or to individuals.

For more information please contact webmaster.ebooks@tandf.co.uk

We're continually developing the eBook concept, so keep up to date by visiting the website.

www.eBookstore.tandf.co.uk

For Product Safety Concerns and Information please contact our EU representative GPSR@taylorandfrancis.com
Taylor & Francis Verlag GmbH, Kaufingerstraße 24, 80331 München, Germany

www.ingramcontent.com/pod-product-compliance
Ingram Content Group UK Ltd.
Pitfield, Milton Keynes, MK11 3LW, UK
UKHW052214190926
475702UK00006B/1014
9780415454520